International Conference on ICT, Society, and Human Beings 2016, International Conference on Web-Based Communities and Social Media 2016, International Conference on Big Data Analytics, Data Mining and Computational Intelligence 2016 and Theory and Practice in Modern Computing 2016

Held at the Multi-Conference on Computer Science and Information Systems (MCCSIS 2016)

Madeira, Portugal
1 – 4 July 2016

Editors:

Piet Kommers
Ajith P. Abraham
Jorg Roth

Piet Kommers
Pedro Isaias
Luis Rodrigues

ISBN: 978-1-5108-6526-6

Printed from e-media with permission by:

Curran Associates, Inc.
57 Morehouse Lane
Red Hook, NY 12571

Some format issues inherent in the e-media version may also appear in this print version.

Printed by Curran Associates, Inc. (2018)

International Association for Development of the Information Society (IADIS)
Rua Sao Sebastiao Da Pedreira
No. 100, 30, 1050-209
Lisbon, Portugal

Phone: 351 21 3151373
Fax: 351 21 3151244

secretariat@iadis.org

Additional copies of this publication are available from:

Curran Associates, Inc.
57 Morehouse Lane
Red Hook, NY 12571 USA
Phone: 845-758-0400
Fax: 845-758-2633
Email: curran@proceedings.com
Web: www.proceedings.com

INTERNATIONAL CONFERENCES ON

ICT, SOCIETY, AND HUMAN BEINGS 2016

WEB BASED COMMUNITIES AND SOCIAL MEDIA 2016

BIG DATA ANALYTICS, DATA MINING AND COMPUTATIONAL INTELLIGENCE 2016

and

THEORY AND PRACTICE IN MODERN COMPUTING 2016

part of the

MULTI CONFERENCE ON COMPUTER SCIENCE AND

INFORMATION SYSTEMS 2016

PROCEEDINGS OF THE INTERNATIONAL CONFERENCES ON

ICT, SOCIETY, AND HUMAN BEINGS 2016

WEB BASED COMMUNITIES AND SOCIAL MEDIA 2016

BIG DATA ANALYTICS, DATA MINING AND COMPUTATIONAL INTELLIGENCE 2016

and

THEORY AND PRACTICE IN MODERN COMPUTING 2016

Madeira, Portugal
JULY 1 - 4, 2016

Organised by
IADIS
International Association for Development of the Information Society

Sponsored by

TURISMO DE PORTUGAL madeira islands

Official Carrier

TAP PORTUGAL
with arms wide open
A STAR ALLIANCE MEMBER

Volume Editors:
Piet Kommers
Ajith P. Abraham
Jörg Roth

Computer Science and Information Systems Series Editors:
Piet Kommers and Pedro Isaías

Associate Editor: Luís Rodrigues

TABLE OF CONTENTS

SHORT PAPERS

ICT, SOCIETY, AND HUMAN BEINGS

WEB BASED COMMUNITIES AND SOCIAL MEDIA

BIG DATA ANALYTICS, DATA MINING AND COMPUTATIONAL INTELLIGENCE

THEORY AND PRACTICE IN MODERN COMPUTING

REFLECTION PAPER

POSTERS

FOREWORD

These proceedings contain the papers of the International Conferences on ICT, Society, and Human Beings 2016, Web Based Communities and Social Media 2016, Big Data Analytics, Data Mining and Computational Intelligence 2016 and Theory and Practice in Modern Computing 2016, which were organised by the International Association for Development of the Information Society, from 2 - 4 July, 2016. These conferences are part of the Multi Conference on Computer Science and Information Systems 2016, 1 - 4 July, which had a total of 606 submissions.

The Network period in the evolution of computer technology is very much based on the convergence and integration of three main technologies; computer technology, tele technology and media technology. Telecommunication technology is playing a more and more dominant role in this convergence, especially internet and web technology. Embedded (ubiquitous) computer technology is making the process invisible, and media technologies converge within itself (multimedia and cross media). The convergence process is enforced all the time by smaller, cheaper, and more powerful components.

ICT and its applications are interacting with environments, roles, and processes which can also be modelled by converging circles. The process of social and psychosocial change and ICT from a global perspective is described graphically in the convergence model in figure 1 (Bradley 2006 Routledge) with concepts and their interrelations. Both "convergence" and "interactions" are important features in the model. Read from the left hand side in the model for the titles of some main tracks of the conference:

- Globalisation and ICT: When technology, economy, norms/values and labour market are converging on a global level, what are the hard questions? When the geographical space in the future will be both global and beyond – including virtual reality (VR) what is the state of art in research? (see the list of key words under ´globalisation´)
- Information and Communication Technology (ICT), next cluster of circles to the left in the figure, what applications contribute to desirable goals in the society?
- When Work Environment, Home Environment, and Public Environment are converging and the work and public issues tend to merge into the private sphere of our homes – what main changes in peoples Life Environment occur?.
- If the Professional Role (Work Life), Private Role (Private Life) and Citizen's Role (Public Life) converge forming a Life Role, what are the main social-psychologial changes?
- Four circles representing Virtual Reality (VR) are marked with dotted lines and are surrounding the set of converging circles. These circles reflect our participation in cyberspace on various levels. To the left part in figure we could talk about Virtual Worlds on the global level. Within the concept of ICT, the steps taken by applied Embedded and ubiquitous technology make technology more hidden to the individual and society as a whole.

  Virtual Environments are already a common concept. Finally we could talk about Virtual Human Roles, which could in more extreme forms be another personality that you play e g avatars. The converging circles are forming a Life Role and new life styles are being shaped.

• Effects on humans become more multi faceted and complex. Research focusing upon the individual is crucial i. e. research on how the use of ICT interacts with and impacts identity, social competence, creativity, integrity, trust, dependency etc. A compass rose (card) for "Effects on Humans" (to the right) is used as a metaphor reminding us of the importance to keep the direction towards desirable human and societal goals and qualities at the development and use of ICT.

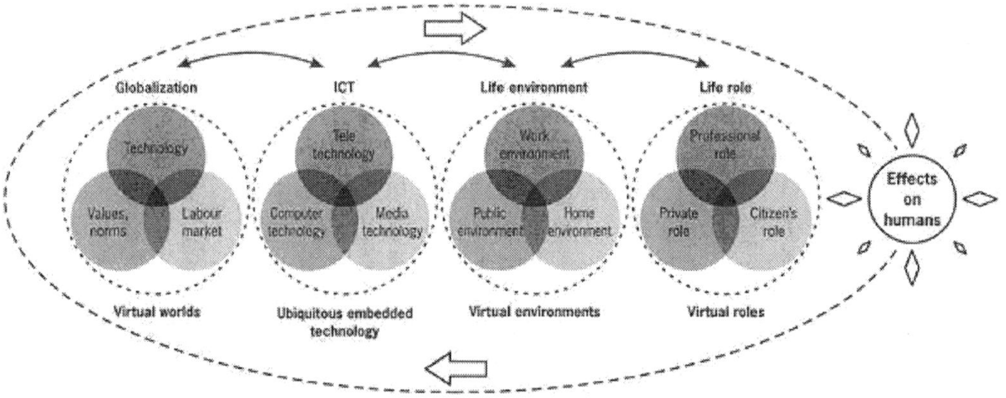

Figure 1. Convergence Model on ICT and Psychosocial Life Environment (Source: Bradley, 2005, 2006)

ICT can provide tools for promoting sustainability (environmental, economic, and social sustainability) but can also be a threat for sustainability. Sustainability as a guiding principle involves system perspective, holism, human aspects, bottom up approach, common good, and equality. A change in focus regarding research and development is taking place. Analysis and design increasingly address both the work process and management connected to the sphere of production life and people's life environment. Analysis and design of ICT and societal systems both at local level and globally become important. What research in the field exists or is needed?

Community research in a broad sense comes to the fore – both physical and virtual communities. There is also a requirement to involve new and additional actors at the deeper and broader integration of ICT in the society (children, elderly, and consumer organisations). Educational programs on Community Informatics and Social Informatics are appearing in many academic institutions. Can a new infrastructure of the society be identified?

The effects of ICT on human beings as well as the interaction between ICT, individuals, and society are all within the focus of this conference. Both analyses of interactions and effects are important. Changes in behaviour, perspectives, values, competencies, human and psychological aspects and feelings are all of interest. Reflections on past, present, and future challenges – especially planning for handling the latter – are encouraged.

Today, computer science and ICT-related disciplines are working more and more together with various behavioural and social sciences including child psychology and developmental psychology. For this reason, the conference pays attention to societal changes, global and more local organisational and institutional changes, changes in values and in lifestyles, as well as individual cognitive effects and changes, motivational and emotional changes. It also appeals to solution-building in terms of desirable goals and actions for reaching a Good Information Society.

In general all types of research strategies are encouraged, and especially cross-disciplinary and multi-disciplinary studies. Case studies, broader empirical field studies, theoretical analyses, cross-cultural studies, scenarios, ethnographic studies, epistemological analyses may all be presented.

The ICT, Society and Human Beings (ICT) conference addresses in detail seven main aspects:
- Globalization and ICT
- Life environment and ICT
- Life role and ICT
- ICT and effects on humans
- Perspectives on ICT
- Desirable goals and ICT
- Actions for reaching the Good Information Society

The World Wide Web has migrated from information space into opportunities for social communication. Social Media are growing rapidly and play an increasingly important role in the development of Online Communities. They are all about identity, reputation, presence and relationships. Web based communities announce themselves both in your professional and private life through several new media such as LinkedIn, Twitter, Plaxo, etc. In order to keep you up to date with the pace of these new technological developments this Conference offers a dedicated overview and informative discussion on today's most relevant issues in new media for social life on the web.

Social Media are growing rapidly and play an increasingly important role in the development of Online Communities. Social Network Sites and Web-based communities announce themselves both in your professional and private life through new media such as Facebook, LinkedIn, Twitter, Plaxo, etc. Social media allow more dynamic roles in participation, virtual presence and online communities. These new ways to communicate via online social media have great societal effects and are motivating the creation of best practices to help individuals, corporations and authorities to make the best of it. It raises the awareness of the growing impact of social media and the influence of web based communities in today's users / consumers behavior; many organizations spend an increasing share of their budget in online social marketing strategies.

The mission of the Web Based Communities and Social Media (WBC) conference is to publish and integrate scientific results and act catalytically to the fast developing culture of web communities, while helping to disseminate and understand the latest developments social media and their impact.

Submissions were accepted under the following 6 main topics:
- The History, Architecture and Future of Virtual Communities
- Cyborgs, Teleworking, Telemedicine, Art Games and Learning Communities
- Virtual Communities for People with Special Needs
- Group Processes and Self-Organization
- Expanding Markets through Virtual Communities
- Collaborative Technologies
- Social Media

The growth of data both structured and unstructured will present challenges as well as opportunities for industries and academia over the next few years. With the explosive growth of data volumes, it is essential that real-time information that is of use to the business can be extracted to deliver better insights to decision-makers, understand complex patterns etc. Computational Intelligence tools offer adaptive mechanisms that enable the understanding of data in complex and changing environments. The main building blocks of computational intelligence involve computational modelling of biological and natural intelligent systems, multi-agent systems, hybrid intelligent systems etc. The conference is expected to provide an opportunity for the researchers to meet and discuss the latest solutions, scientific results and methods in solving intriguing problems in the fields of Big Data Analytics, Intelligent Agents and Computational Intelligence. The conference programme will include workshops, special sessions and tutorials, along with prominent keynote speakers and regular paper presentations in parallel tracks.

The aim of BigDaCI'16 is to serve as a forum to present current and future work as well as to exchange research ideas in this field.

BigDaCI'16 invites authors to submit their original and unpublished work that demonstrate current research using big data analytics, computational intelligence and other intelligent computing techniques and their applications in science, technology, business and commerce.
Submissions were accepted under the following areas and topics:
- Big Data Algorithms and Architectures
- Computational Intelligent Frameworks for Big Data Processing
- Data Mining Topics and Applications
- Big Data Applications
- Multi-Agent Systems: Models, Architectures and Applications

The International Conference on Theory and Practice in Modern Computing (TPMC 2016) provides a forum for research and developments in the field of computing foundations and technology. Modern computing comes not only with efficient concepts and their application, but also it often addresses networking and mobility topics. Hence, the view in TPMC ranges from fundamentals like new or improved algorithms to very recent and modern applications like ubiquitous scenarios or even everyday computing.

Complementary to these technically-oriented contents, TPMC also shall serve as discussion platform about ethics and social impact of those technologies. In its main focus, this scientific conference aims to attract research reports on efficient application and realization of simple algorithmic methods, new architectures in design and data structures, new and improved communication protocols, and synthesis of known computing concepts and approaches.

Submissions were accepted under the following main areas and topics:
- Design Foundations
- Realization Aspects
- Mobility Communication and Services
- Networking and Grid Approaches

These conferences received 169 submissions from more than 32 countries. Each submission has been anonymously reviewed by an average of five independent reviewers, to ensure that accepted submissions were of a high standard. Consequently only 25 full papers were approved which means an acceptance rate of 15%. A few more papers were accepted as short papers, reflection paper and posters. An extended version of the best papers may be published in the IADIS International Journal on Computer Science and Information Systems (ISSN: 1646-3692) and/or in the IADIS International Journal on WWW/Internet (ISSN: 1645-7641) and also in other selected journals, including journals from Inderscience.

Besides the presentation of full papers, short papers, reflection paper and posters, the conferences also included two keynote presentations from internationally distinguished researchers. We would therefore like to express our gratitude to Professor Emerita Gunilla Bradley (Informatics, School of ICT, Royal Institute of Technology (KTH), Stockholm, Sweden) and Professor Alfred Inselberg (Senior Fellow San Diego Supercomputing Center & Computer Science and Applied Mathematics Departments, Tel Aviv University, Israel) for accepting our invitation as keynote speakers.

This volume has taken shape as a result of the contributions from a number of individuals. We are grateful to all authors who have submitted their papers to enrich the conference proceedings. We wish to thank all members of the organizing committee, delegates, invitees and guests whose contribution and involvement are crucial for the success of the conference.

Last but not the least, we hope that everybody has a good time in Madeira, and we invite all participants for the next edition of these conferences.

Piet Kommers, University of Twente, The Netherlands
ICT, Society and Human Beings 2016 Program Chair
Web Based Communities and Social Media 2016 Program Chair

Ajith P. Abraham, Machine Intelligence Research Labs (MIR Labs), USA
Big Data Analytics, Data Mining and Computational Intelligence 2016 Program Chair

Jörg Roth, University of Applied Sciences Nuremberg, Germany
Theory and Practice in Modern Computing 2016 Program Chair

Piet Kommers, University of Twente, The Netherlands
Pedro Isaías, Universidade Aberta (Portuguese Open University), Portugal
MCCSIS 2016 General Conference Co-Chairs

Madeira, Portugal
July 2016

PROGRAM COMMITTEE

ICT, SOCIETY AND HUMAN BEINGS

WEB BASED COMMUNITIES AND SOCIAL MEDIA

PROGRAM CHAIR

Piet Kommers, University of Twente, The Netherlands

BIG DATA ANALYTICS, DATA MINING AND COMPUTATIONAL INTELLIGENCE

PROGRAM CHAIR

Ajith P. Abraham, Machine Intelligence Research Labs (MIR Labs), USA

THEORY AND PRACTICE IN MODERN COMPUTING

Jörg Roth, University of Applied Sciences Nuremberg, Germany

MCCSIS GENERAL CONFERENCE CO-CHAIRS

Piet Kommers, University of Twente, The Netherlands
Pedro Isaías, Universidade Aberta (Portuguese Open University), Portugal

ICT, SOCIETY AND HUMAN BEINGS

COMMITTEE MEMBERS

Adriana Burlea Schiopoiu, University of Craiova, Romania
Alena Buchalcevova, University of Economics, Czech Republic
Alice Robbin, Indiana University Bloomington, USA
Ana Isabel Paraguay, Officio e Ambiente Ltda, Brazil
Andreas Gadatsch, Bonn-Rhein-Sieg University of Applied Sciences, Germany
Anita Mirijamdotter, Linnaeus University, Sweden
Antonio Marturano, University of Rome Tor Vergata, Italy
Asma Sellami, Université de Sfax, Tunisia
Carlos Rodriguez Dominguez, University of Granada, Spain
Cecile K. M. Crutzen, Open University of The Netherlands, The Netherlands
Daniyal Alghazzawi, King Abdulaziz University, Saudi Arabia
David J. Gunkel, Northern Illinois University, USA
Denise Oram, Glyndwr University, UK
Dimitri Schuurman, Iminds, Belgium
Dimitris Dranidis, CITY College, The University of Sheffield International Faculty, Greece
Eila Jarvenpaa, Aalto University, Finland
Eleni Berki, University of Tampere, Finland
Elsa Negre, University Paris – Dauphine, France
Elspeth Mckay, Rmit University , Australia
Elvis Mazzoni, University of Bologna, Italy
Hugo Rehesaar, Griffith University, Australia

WEB BASED COMMUNITIES AND SOCIAL MEDIA

COMMITTEE MEMBERS

Abdulrahman Alothaim, University of Nebraska at Omaha, USA
Andrea Lapa, Federal University of Santa Catarina, Brazil
Andrei Semeniuta, Belarus Trade Economics University, Belarus
Anirban Kundu, Kuang-Chi Institute of Advanced Technology, Shenzh, China
Antonio Moreira, University of Aveiro, Portugal
Apostolos Gkamas, University Ecclesiastical Academy of Vella of Ioan, Greece
Arianna D'ulizia, National Research Council – IRPPS, Italy
Atsuo Hazeyama, Tokyo Gakugei University, Japan
Boyan Bontchev, Sofia University St. Kl. Ohridski, Bulgaria
Carmen Celina Torres Arcadia, Tecnológico de Monterrey, Mexico
Chien-sing Lee, Universiti Tunku Abdul Rahman, Malaysia
Christos Bouras, University of Patras, Greece
Christos Karageorgopoulos, KETHEA, Greece
Cigdem Turhan, Atilim University, Turkey
Claudia Raibulet, University of Milano-Bicocca, Italy
Cuong Nguyen, University of Nebraska At Omaha, USA
Daniela Godoy, Isistan – Conicet – Instituto de Sistemas Tandil, Argentina
Edison Spina, University of Sao Paulo, Brazil
El Hassan Abdelwahed, University Cadi Ayyad, Morocco
Elaheh Pourabbas, National Research Council, Italy
Elisaveta Gurova, Sofia University, Bulgaria
Eliza Stefanova, St. Kl. Ohridski University of Sofia, Bulgaria
Emmanouil Stiakakis, University of Macedonia, Greece
Eugenia Kovatcheva, University of Library Studies and Information Technology, Bulgaria
Eugenio Martínez Cámara , University of Jaén, Spain
Fabio Nascimbeni, Menon Network, Belgium
Fernando Albuquerque Costa, University of Lisbon, Portugal
Flavio Correa Da Silva, University of Sao Paulo, Brazil
Francesca Pozzi , Istituto Tecnologie Didattiche – CNR, Italy
Gabriela Moise, PG University of Ploiesti, Romania
Gayle Davidson Shivers, University of South Alabama, USA
Gert-Jan de Vreede, University of South Florida, USA
Giuliana Dettori, Istituto Per Le Tecnologie Didattiche, Italy
Grigore Albeanu, Spiru Haret University, Romania
Grigorios Beligiannis, University of Patras, Greece
Guillermo Jimenez, Instituto Tecnologico de Monterrey (ITESM), Mexico
Ilias Karasavvidis, University of Thessaly, Greece
Jan Frick, University of Stavanger, Norway
Jesus Arias Fisteus, Universidad Carlos III de Madrid, Spain
Joop Van Schie, Onderwijskundig Adviesbureau Cocon, The Netherlands
Jozef Hvorecky, City University, Slovakia
Julio Villena-Román , University Carlos III of Madrid / s|ngular Meaning, Spain
Karl Steffens, University of Cologne, Germany
Konstantinos Giotopoulos, University of Patras, Greece
Ljuan Marko Gashi, University of Novi Sad, Serbia
Lorna Uden, Staffordshire University, UK

Manolis Tzagarakis, Computer Technology Institute, Greece
Manuel Caeiro Rodriguez, University of Vigo, Spain
Marcello Sarini, University of Milan-Bicocca, Italy
Marcelo Armentano, Isistan – Instituto de Sistemas Tandil, Argentina
Martin Llamas-Nistal, Etsi Telecomunicación, Spain
Michael Filsecker, University Duisburg-Essen, Germany
Michael Vassilakopoulos, University of Thessaly, Greece
Michail Kalogiannakis, University of Crete, Greece
Michał Grega, AGH University of Science and Technology, Poland
Nikos Karacapilidis, University of Patras, Greece
Oriol Miralbell, Open University of Catalonia, Spain
Panayotis Fouliras, University of Macedonia, Greece
Peter Mikulecky, University of Hradec Kralove, Czech Republic
Peter Sloep, The Netherlands Open University, The Netherlands
Radojica Petrovic, Technical Faculty of Cacak, Serbia
Raquel Trillo Lado, University of Zaragoza, Spain
Raul Ramirez Velarde, Tecnologico de Monterrey, Mexico
Sandra Lovrencic, University of Zagreb, Croatia
Sergio Ilarri, University of Zaragoza, Spain
Silvia Schiaffino, Universidad Nacional del Centro de la Provincia de Buenos Aires, Argentina
Slavi Stoyanov, The Netherlands Open University, The Netherlands
Spiros Sirmakessis, TEI of Western Greece, Greece
Spyros Polykalas, Digital Media and Communication TEI of Ionian Island, Greece
Stylianos Hatzipanagos, King's College London, UK
Tatyana Pashnyak, Bainbridge College, USA
Ulrich Thiel, Fraunhofer, Germany
Vanessa Dennen, Florida State University, USA
Vassilis Kollias, University of Thessaly, Greece
Violeta Vidacek-Hains, University of Zagreb, Croatia
Vladimir Bures, University of Hradec Kralove, Czech Republic
Witold Abramowicz, Poznan University of Economics, Poland
Zinayida Petrushyna, RWTH Aachen University, Germany

BIG DATA ANALYTICS, DATA MINING AND COMPUTATIONAL INTELLIGENCE

COMMITTEE MEMBERS

Abdel-Badeeh Salem, Ain Shams University, Egypt
Abderrafiaa Koukam, Université de Technologie de Belfort-Montbeliard, France
Albertas Caplinskas, Vilnius University, Lithuania
Alessandro Giuliani, University of Cagliari, Italy
Alexander Gelbukh, Instituto Politécnico Nacional, Mexico
Alla Anohina-Naumeca, Riga Technical University, Latvia
Alvaro Luis Bustamante, Universidad Carlos III de Madrid, Spain
Ambra Molesini, Università di Bologna, Italy
Andrei Mogos, University Politehnica of Bucharest, Romania
Andrew Kusiak, University of Iowa, USA
Anirban Kundu, West Bengal University of Technology, India

THEORY AND PRACTICE IN MODERN COMPUTING

COMMITTEE MEMBERS

Cyril Onwubiko, Research Series, UK
Djamal Benslimane, Lyon 1 University, France
Dongkyun Kim, Korea Institute of Science and Technology Information, South Korea
Edgar Weippl, Sba Research , Austria
Elad Michael Schiller, Chalmers University of Technology, Sweden
Eleni Vlahogianni, National Technical University of Athens, Greece
Emilio Serrano, Universidad Politécnica de Madrid, Spain
Fausto Fasano, Università degli Studi del Molise, Italy
Felix Strohmeier, Salzburg Research, Austria
Felix J. Garcia, University of Murcia, Spain
Felix J. Garcia Clemente, University of Murcia, Spain
Fernando Pereñiguez García, University of Murcia, Spain
Fernando Zacarias Flores, Benemerita Universidad Autonoma de Puebla, Mexico
Francesca Lonetti, CNR, Italy
Francesca Martelli, Institute of Informatics and Telematics of CNR, Italy
Francesco Maiorana, University of Catania, Italy
Francois Siewe, de Montfort University, UK
George Gravvanis, Democritus University of Thrace, Greece
Giuseppe Mangioni, DIEEI – University of Catania, Italy
Grammati Pantziou, Technological Educational Institute of Athens, Greece
Guu-Chang Yang, National Chung Hsing University, Taiwan
Gyu Myoung Lee, Liverpool John Moores University, UK
Hakima Chaouchi, Telecom Sud Paris, France
Humberto Razente, Universidade Federal de Uberlandia, Brazil
Ion Tutanescu, University of Pitesti, Romania
Isabel Muench, BSI, Germany
J. Paul Gibson, Télécom Sud Paris, France
Jaime Delgado, Universitat Politècnica de Catalunya, Spain
Janos Mohacsi, NIIF/Hungarnet, Hungary
Jean-louis Boulanger, CERTIFER, France
Jitender Grover, Maharishi Markandeshwar University, India
Jorge Barbosa, University of Vale do Rio dos Sinos (UNISINOS), Brazil
José Guimarães, Universidade Federal de São Carlos (UFSCAR), Brazil
Jose Maria Alcaraz Calero, University of the West of Scotland, UK
Kiran Patil, GM Global R&D, General Motors India, India
Laura Carnevali, DSI, Italy
Lina Yao, University of Adelaide, Australia
Ljiljana Trajkovic, Simon Fraser University, Canada
Manuel Gil Pérez, University of Murcia, Spain
Marcelo Zanchetta do Nascimento, Federal University of Uberlândia, Brazil
Marek Stanuszek, Cracow University of Technology, Poland
Marek Woda, Wroclaw University of Technology, Poland
María Antonia Martínez, University of Murcia, Spain
Mary Grammatikou, Ntua Netmode, Greece
Michal Choras, Institute of Telecommunications and Computer Science, Poland
Nadine Akkari, Telecom Paristech, France
Nicholas Race, Lancaster University, UK
Olaf Maennel, Tallinn University of Technology, Estonia
Ouri Wolfson, University of Illinois at Chicago, USA
Panos Kudumakis, Queen Mary University of London, UK

KEYNOTE LECTURES

SOCIAL AND PSYCHOLOGICAL CHANGES IN THE ICT SOCIETY – ABOUT VISIONS AND WISDOM

Gunilla Bradley, Professor Emerita, Royal Institute of Technology (KTH) Stockholm

ABSTRACT

What is Quality of Life in the ICT society? Important contributing and hindering factors. Convergence and acceleration are main processes at the interplay between technology, societal structure, organizational design, and human roles in the society. Risks and opportunities in the 21st Century ICT society. What is the Good ICT society? Where are the "energy centers" that can activate and create changes towards "The Good Information Community" and "The Good Information Society"? How can wisdom be extracted – wisdom on various levels of analysis? Actions towards a good and sustainable society? Who are strategic stakeholders – active, passive, silent?

Keywords

Convergence Theory, ICT, Quality of Life, Human Beings, Identity, Stress, Power, Wisdom, Actions.

TED-talk on YouTube http://tedxtalks.ted.com/video/Understanding-the-Change-of-Hab
(Bradley, G. 2015)

VISUALIZATION AND DATA MINING FOR HIGH DIMENSIONAL DATA

Professor Alfred Inselberg, Senior Fellow San Diego Supercomputing Center & Computer Science and Applied Mathematics Departments, Tel Aviv University, Israel

ABSTRACT

A dataset with M items has 2M subsets anyone of which may be the one satisfying our objectives. With a good data display and interactivity our fantastic pattern-recognition can cut great swaths searching through this combinatorial explosion unlocking surprising insights. That is the core reason for data visualization. With parallel coordinates the search for relations in multivariate data is transformed into a 2-D pattern recognition problem. The knowledge discovery process is illustrated on several real multidimensional datasets. There is also a geometric classification algorithm with low computational complexity providing the classification rule explicitly and visually. The minimal set of variables required to state the rule, features, is found and ordered by their predictive value. A complex system is modeled as a hypersurface enabling interactive exploration of its functions, sensitivities, trade-offs, impact of constraints and more. An overview of the methodology provides foundational understanding; learning the patterns corresponding to various multivariate relations. These patterns are robust in the presence of errors and that is good news for the applications. The parallel coordinates methodology has been applied to collision avoidance and conflict resolution algorithms for air traffic control (3 USA patents), computer vision (USA patent), data mining (USA patent) and elsewhere.

Full Papers

STUDYING THE VIRTUAL USER COMMUNITY IN AN INTERNATIONAL INNOVATION PROJECT: THE ATTITUDES AND THE CULTURAL BACKGROUND

Borka Jerman Blažič-Džonova[1] and Andrej Jerman Blažič[2]
[1]*Institut Jožef Stefan, Ljubljana, Slovenia*
[2]*International Postgraduate School Jožef Stefan, Ljubljana, Slovenia*

ABSTRACT

The aim of the research work presented in this paper is to explore a virtual-user community's influence on the design of a new, multimedia-based service within EU funded innovation project. The virtual communities considered here are the researchers and associated administrative staff, who are working on, or managing, collaboration projects or common tasks in distant laboratories all over the world. The acceptance and the attitudes of the community were studied and applied in the design of a new service offered by the Virtual Conference Centre Portal (VCCP) – Global Plaza. During the study reflection of the cultural backgrounds of the user community on their attitudes towards the VCCP were seek out and the findings are discussed and presented. The studies were carried out with communities coming from three continents: Africa, South America and Europe. The paper gives a brief presentation of the service platform facilities and an analysis of the results of the performed studies.

KEYWORDS

Virtual community, Service design and acceptance, Virtual video-conferencing center, Collaborative environment,

1. INTRODUCTION

In recent years, services offered by Google, Flickr, YouTube, LinkedIn, Facebook, MySpace, Skype and many more have become extremely successful. This has triggered the growth of large, virtual communities, which are frequently referred to as social networks. One of the factors in this success was the user-friendly interfaces used by these services, together with the services' ease of use. As these communities are accustomed to use simple user interfaces, the service providers, when launching new services or new facilities, generally try to aggregate their collected knowledge without conducting any serious study about the real needs of users, needs that are sometimes reflected in their cultural backgrounds. Services such as video-conferencing and the associated collaboration tools have become increasingly popular in the past decade due to the availability of sufficient network bandwidth, even in less-developed parts of the world. The most frequently used tool for video-communication is Skype, which offers simple video-conferencing services, although these are usually restricted to a small group of virtual community members. Other, more sophisticated, video-conferencing tools do not usually inter-work among them or with other services in most cases and are mainly used for relatively simple tasks, like working meetings, substituting for popular audio-call conferences, connecting remote speakers at co-located conferences or meetings, etc. Recent research in this area showed no publications or studies that have looked at this phenomenon, especially in terms of user acceptance and user attitudes to high-tech systems for organizing large, distributed events at a distance. A usability and user-friendliness study of these systems is expected to be applied during the lifecycle development of the service, especially when integration is being envisaged with some popular Web 2.0 tools (GLOBAL, 2011), but usually this is not the case.

Members of virtual teams from the scientific community usually collaborate on a particular project by performing various actions during a project's lifetime and discussing and working on events such as conferences, workshops, symposia, etc. The significant increase in the number of scientific publications within a number of scientific collaborations between distant teams that span fields, institutions, sectors, and countries is a clear indication of increased levels of collaboration in the scientific community working at a distance. For example, the percentage of published papers that involve international collaborations increased from 9% in 1983 to 33% in 2007 (Walsh & Maloney, 2007). This increase in team science has been driven by a variety of factors, including a growing interest in scientific problems that span disciplines (e.g., mapping the human genome or studying global climate change), but most probably due to advances in communication technologies, e.g., web-based services and the Internet, which make remote collaborations easier to sustain. Factor that sometimes influence the working process flow has origin in the diversified cultures, languages, and worldviews of the team members. The design of new, more advanced collaborative tool is always faced with the problem of the user's satisfaction with the tool and its acceptance. The user's satisfaction is usually measured in terms of the usability and the friendliness of the tool, and this is defined as the extent to which people can use the product quickly and easily in order to accomplish their tasks (Hvannberg et al., 2007), with the ultimate goal being accepted by the users.

The study of postcolonial computing inspired by the MIT project "One laptop per child project" (Kavita et al., 2012) has reflected the problems of the acceptance of information-communication technology (ICT) and its use related to the level of development and the cultural background of the studied user environments. Unexpectedly, the results of the study showed that no specific ICT design that reflects the cultural background is required for techno-science in most parts of the world. These findings motivated a team of researchers working on the development of a new, Internet-based service known as Global Plaza (Cortes and Barra, 2009), designed within the project GLOBAL from the EU's 6th Framework Program to examine users' attitudes and the reflection of the cultural background to them by involvement of the virtual community that emerged around the Virtual Conference Centre Portal (VCCP).

The VCCP was designed as a multifunctional portal for organizing large, distributed events, but also for building a virtual academic community around the world that collaborates most frequently at a distance. As the portal was intended to be a service for the global scientific community working on joint projects, it was necessary during the portal's design and later during its operation to be evaluated in terms of usability, user acceptance, user satisfaction that also reflects the cultural differences of the participating regions. The user community that participated in the evaluation of these values came from three different continents. The advancement in the network infrastructure has solved a number of the limitations associated with the use of distance ICT technologies for collaboration as the European Union has set a very powerful backbone with high-speed technology known as GEANT (GEANT, 2013) for the scientific community. This network has enabled connectivity to other continents by the associations of academic networks in Africa, South America, the USA and the countries of the Pacific Rim. New projects from the EU research program were launched to enable more intense scientific collaboration between different parts of the world. One such project was the Global Plaza project, which had as partners the association of the academic networks of South America (CLARA) and a similar association from Africa, i.e., the UbuntuNet Association.

The study presented in this paper is focused on issues dealing with user acceptance of the new, on-line communication service, and the study of the user attitudes (The Virtual Conference Centre, 2013). The influence of the users' culture on their attitudes was sought out as well. The project Global Plaza provided an excellent research platform to study all these issues on a larger scale and in different parts of the world, with the objective being to develop a service that will be usable and will meet the needs of the scientific community for collaboration at a distance.

2. THE INNOVATION PLATFORM DESIGN AND THE VIRTUAL COMMUNITY STUDY

2.1 The Platform

The Global Plaza service was designed and re-designed within the EU-funded FP6 project Global and was named the Virtual Conference Centre Portal (VCCP). It was designed in accordance with the methodology known as User View-Controller Model (Fowler, 2003). The portal provides the following facilities by default:

- collaboration in announcing the distributed events,
- setting up working spaces,
- preparing the event program,
- inviting speakers,
- setting up auditoriums with different capacities and communication channels,
- connecting the distant auditoriums,
- organizing panels and inviting panelists,
- preparing event scenarios,
- setting up a working space for a particular part of the virtual collaborative community,
- recording and archiving the events
- indexing and searching the recorded events and other material in the portal depository.

The underlying infrastructure of the Global Plaza service was composed of the following components: (1) a Virtual Auditorium based on the Isabel (Isabel Plaza, 2011) video-conferencing collaboration tool developed by the Technical University of Madrid (http://www.upm.es); (2) an Event Repository, allowing the distribution and dissemination of the content presented during the distributed events and other collaboration outcomes (joint papers, documents, project deliverables and the event documentation); (3) a Virtual Corridor, representing a user-centric site that encourages participation and collaboration among the event participants, the members of the virtual community, by offering different access technologies and (4) an Event Manager.

The collaborating communities on the VCCP act within a grouped Space facility set up by the community members. The Space(s) facility is used to announce the event and to invite any interested members or new users to join. A Space is organized as a set of different sections represented by tablets. They provide information about the latest posts, events, or users who have joined. The portal was designed to offer a single, unified point of access to the virtual users with respect to the auditorium's features and access to the different functionalities through facilities represented with tags such as Home, Events, Posts, People, and Spaces. Specific buttons were set up to enable direct access to a particular collaborating project, containing a description of the project partners, and the possibility to join with a Login and a User Registration button. With a valid registration the user can access publicly available spaces, documents, event announcements, etc. Each user gets a user profile, enabling him/her to update the information stored, e.g., password, address, email contact, project interests, etc. The profile is intended to facilitate collaboration and partnership-building. In addition a People tag displays the registered members for a quick search of specific contacts. Each Space has its own repository with public and private documentation and events. The Space's public area is customized to be the public face of a running project.

The Events tag in the Space points to the page dealing with the event scheduler and the central part of the VCCP. It allows registered members to create events and organize distributed events and post documentation (e.g., conference material, papers, and documents). More technical details can be found in the Global Plaza deliverables (Arh et al., 2010). The core of the VCCP is the Isabel video-conferencing tool that provides the Virtual Auditorium service and the communication face-to-face corridor. This tool provides advanced broadband and, at the same time, narrowband access methods through several types of gateways, such as the Session Initiation Protocol (SIP) (Johnston, 2004), enabling access to SIP-compliant devices (e.g., IP-based phones), the H232 protocol gateway and compliant devices, the Skype protocol (Skype protocol, 2004) with an access gateway, and the web gateway with Flash protocol (GLOBAL, 2011), which are inbuilt in the system. The VCCP screen from a distributed event is presented in Figure 1. On the left part of the screen a bar with the participating auditoriums is presented, enabling the user to enter the screen by clicking on the user name site (the relevant auditorium). The event and the collaboration are recorded and stored in the depository, which is managed with a content-management tool that allows the flexible management of each Space, enabling any item, document, picture or recorded session, to be uploaded to the repository with a new number assignment. The tags are used for a filtered search, using filters such as: author, type of item, title, speaker, name tags, etc.

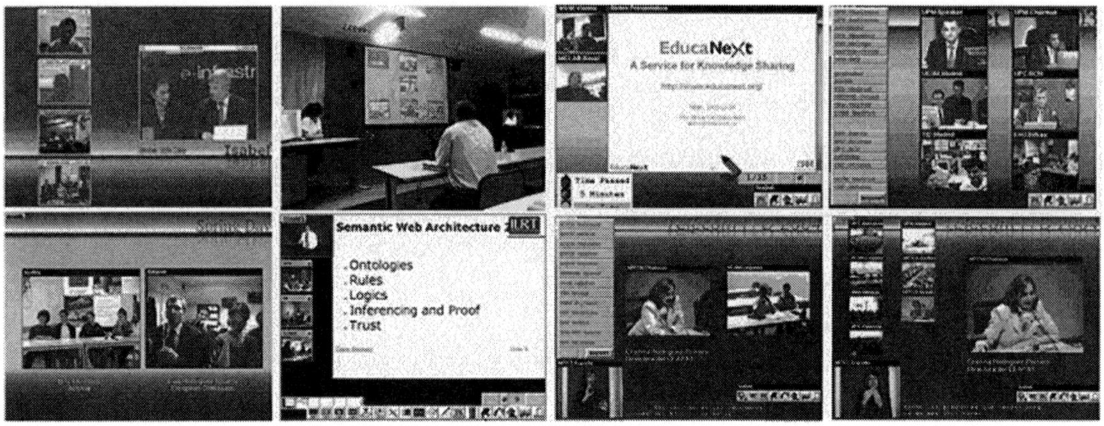

Figure 1. Events organized through the Global Plaza platform

2.2 Methods and Participants Demography

The design process for the VCCP consisted of several consecutive steps, starting with the development phase, the testing phase in a real environment, the evaluation of the users' acceptance and a re-design based on the identified drawbacks. The service was evaluated in face-to-face collaborative meetings and large, distributed events between 30 collaborating sites that have set up virtual auditoriums (Cortes & Barra, 2009). The user community and the audience that took part in the evaluation process consisted mainly of researchers involved in research or development projects, some administrative staff of the research institutes or centers involved, teachers and staff from higher-education institutions, research-funding bodies, e.g., the staff from the EU Commission, including directors, professors, lecturers, tutors, and researchers, with a certain level of experience and knowledge of using ICT tools. In addition, students, scholars and members of professional societies or standardization bodies were considered as a part of the user community, albeit with a somewhat lower level of experience. These user communities participated in 21 distributed events over a period of three years.

The usual number of remote auditoria was between 6 and 30, depending on the event. The size of the collaborating membership from different countries was between 3 and 28, but the number of people that followed a particular event varied a lot, depending on the nature of the event and on the invited audience. The most popular event recorded in the service depository was followed by 350 people.

In addition to the collaboration-intensity indicators, an additional evaluation of the user satisfaction and service acceptance was made with the help of the community that attended the events. After each event a 7-item questionnaire was posted on the VCCP page, and if the event had a main central event on some of the sites then the questionnaires were also delivered by the local organizers to the local participants. Collected answers were classified according to the origin and the location of particular participants. The information later was used in the analysis of the differences in the user attitudes toward the VCCP service. The questionnaire contained questions about the users viewing the new service and the users' satisfaction in following mixed presentations from a distance and locally, and with the discussions between all the participants that followed after each presentation. Round-table discussions with participants from different continents were also frequently part of these events. The questionnaire started with questions about the way the user participated in the event; it continued with questions regarding the use of different technological corridors for communication, e.g., the type of communication tool enabled by the web gateway of the VCCP. Then a question followed about the functionality of the system, the ease of use, the quality of the audio and the video data, the quality of the system regarding direct participation and the preparatory information for the event, the need for support from more skilled user(s) and, finally, questions regarding the assessment of the motivation for using the VCCP as a collaborative tool, which was also expected to influence the acceptance of the service.

The study took place in several different environments located in one of the three continents: Africa, Europe and South America. The English-language version of the VCCP was used, so enabling harmonization of the results, despite the fact that the VCCP services were also available in other languages (e.g., Spanish for the Latin America community). In summary, the acceptance of the VCCP study was performed at six different sites on three different continents. In Africa, the evaluation environment was provided by the UbuntuNet (UBU) association in Malawi. In Europe, several sites were involved in different countries where the national language was not English: the Zentrum für Soziale Innovation in Austria (ZSI) with German, the Jožef Stefan Institute (JSI) in Slovenia, with Slovene, the University of Politécnica de Madrid (UPM), Spain, in Spanish, and University College London (UCL), United Kingdom, in English. In South America the evaluation environment was provided by the CLARA Association at their location in Peru. The total number of community members involved in the experiment was 89 (40 female and 49 male). The participants in this study were recruited from the consortium teams of the participating projects at the distance events. In the first phase of the portal's development, 29 users were involved, and in the second phase, with an improved version of the portal, the number of participating users was 60. All of them had an educational level comparable to a first university degree. Demographic data (gender, age, job title, experiences (competency) and the nationality/location/origin) were provided before the evaluation, together with a user agreement for the participation...In addition to the demographic data, information about the average level of competence in ICT use for a particular user was also collected. The average value of the users' competence was 3.80 ($M = 3.80$ on a scale from 1 to 5, where a higher value indicated more competence), while the average level of competence in the use of video-conferencing systems was 3.09 ($M = 3.09$, again on a scale from 1 to 5). None of the participants had interacted previously with the service offered by the VCCP, so the system was unknown to them. In assessing the level of ICT competence, the following information was collected from the participating users: experience in the use of software applications, the level of knowledge of ICT and video-conferencing systems, and proficiency in English (at least a good level of reading, comprehension and talking). The local experts that performed the evaluation tests within the defined scenarios and tasks were also carefully selected. Several criteria were applied in the selection process, as they guaranteed that the local evaluator performed his/her role correctly. The local expert was required to be experienced in conducting experiments with human participants, to have knowledge of Human Computer Interaction (HCI), to be fluent in the native language of the cultural environment/background he/she was acting in and in English, to have some motivation in doing research, to be good at observation, to be able to manage several tasks at one time. As part of the applied methodology it was demanded that the same local evaluator conduct all of the evaluation sessions with the users in phases, the initial assessment and the one that followed after the improved portal in each of the cultural environments. This approach provided a guarantee that the consistency of the data and the interpretation of the information that were passed from the users to the evaluators could be correctly recorded. A set of ten tasks to be completed was developed and employed:

Task 1: Obtaining a user account for the VCCP, -
Task 2: Creating a new space in the VCCP and joining an existing one,
Task 3: Creating a new event, -
Task 4: Modifying an event in the event manager,
Task 5: Sending a private message,
Task 6: Using the Search Function,
Task 7: Using the Repository,
Task 8: Managing large events,
Task 9: Managing a community,
Task 10: Organizing a Virtual Meeting.

The tasks were translated into task scenarios to render the evaluation more realistic and problem oriented (e.g., you are organizing a workshop or other distributed event in your virtual collaborating community like a face-to-face site meeting. Therefore, you need to create an event in the space you created in task 2. Log yourself into the VCCP and create a new event. The event must be marked as a distributed event that uses the video-conferencing tool. For each of the task scenarios, quantitative usability parameters that were measured in terms of the task-completion time and the number of errors were set. This information was also benchmarked by an experienced user of the VCCP.

The collected data were analyzed with standard parameters that were classified into two groups: objective and subjective measures enabling an assessment of the effectiveness, efficiency and satisfaction (i.e., the three usability metrics from ISO/IEC FCD 25010). The effectiveness of the VCCP was assessed as the completion rate (percentage of participants who completed each task correctly), the errors (number of errors in the menu choice, number of errors in selecting an item from a list, the number of other errors), the assistance (number of times a tester asked for a help). The efficiency of the VCCP was assessed as the task time (mean time to complete each of the tasks – for correctly completed tasks), the range and standard deviation of the times across the participant`s timing and the completion rate efficiency (completion rate/mean task time – for unassisted tasks only). The user satisfaction was assessed with data obtained from the ratings found in the answers of the Feedback Questionnaire (FQ) (Brooke, 1996) and System Usability Scale (Lewis, 1995). The Subjective measures were extracted from the testing participant's self-reporting, providing an insight into the user's perceptions, opinions and attitudes.

2.3 The Study Results

The first feedback about the users' experience with the VCCP was obtained from the answers of the questionnaire collected after each of the distributed events. The majority of the collected answers showed a positive user attitude towards the VCCP. The most important question dealing with the replacement of the face-to-face presence for a meeting requiring travel with the possibility to attend a virtual event that does not require travel received the majority of positive answers. The numbers of collected user responses for the five events were 256, with 56% of them participating in the events remotely. Most of them (84%) used the web gateways as a virtual corridor to the video-conferencing service. This is considered as evidence of the users' familiarity with web-based services and the ease of use of the service. A total of 63% of them found the web communication gateways for the VCCP's virtual corridor to be very useful, 60% of them declared that the quality of the video streaming was very good, but 35% of them declared that to use the VCCP service they needed some technical support (most of them from Africa). The questions formulated as "Would you participate remotely again next time if you had the choice between travel and remote access from your office/home? was answered positively by the majority of users. A total of 72% of the virtual community members expressed very positive or positive attitudes (92%) regarding the use of the service as a collaborative platform for their projects and other types of research collaboration. Here, no noticeable differences between the communities from the three continents and cultural environment were observed, especially regarding the service acceptance.

Based on the data collected from the 29 participants that took part in the evaluation of the initial service design, the average time for the completed 10 tasks per task was found to be 31.72 minutes (SD = 4.05), with or without assistance from the local evaluator. Altogether, 345 tasks were performed and all of them were successfully completed. As shown in Table 2, among the ten tasks, Task 8 (Managing large events) was found to be most problematic, as its average time-on-task was 10.40 minutes, exceeding the benchmarked upper bound (i.e., 5.00 minutes) by 113.33%. The range of the time-on-task for Task 8 was large, ranging from 4.00 min (JSI-P2) to 29.00 min (UBU-P1). Eleven of the participants performing Tasks 4 and 9 needed help from the local evaluator when they were navigating to a wrong menu item after clicking on some misleading links. The effectiveness of the service was measured as a task-completion time without any assistance from the local evaluator; the efficiency was calculated by dividing this time by the mean time for completing an unassisted time for a task.

Table 1. The VCCP effectiveness & efficiencies per task

Task	*Total Completion (with or without assist)* Rate (%)	Mean Time	*Effectiveness (%) (tasks without assist)* Rate (%)	Mean Time	*Efficiency (%/min)*	*Total no. Assists*
1	100	4.72	100.00	4.72	21.19	0
2	100	4.79	100.00	4.79	20.88	0
3	100	6.21	96.55	6.14	15.72	1
4	100	9.48	62.07	10.22	6.07	11
5	100	5.44	100.00	5.45	18.35	0
6	100	6.35	100.00	6.35	15.75	0
7	100	5.45	100.00	5.45	18.35	0
8	100	10.40	80.00	7.75	10.32	1
9	100	7.25	70.00	6.21	11.27	11
10	100	3.35	100.00	3.35	29.85	0

Legend. Effectiveness = Unassisted Completion Rate; Efficiency = Unassisted Completion Rate/ Mean time-on-task.

Table 1 presents, for a comparison, both the assisted and unassisted completion rates, together with their corresponding mean times-on-task. All the participants were able to complete all the given tasks, either with or without assistance from the local evaluator. The average effectiveness was found to be 90.86% and the average efficiency was calculated to be 16.77%/minute, ranging from 6.07%/min (Task 4) to 29.85 %/min (Task 10). Subjective quantitative measures collected from answers to the Feedback Questionnaire (FQ) provided a deeper insight into the users' satisfaction with the service: ease of task completion and the adequacy of support information from the service (online help, messages, and documentation). Each answer was rated on a 7-point Likert scale, with 1 being "Strongly disagree" and 7 "Strongly agree". The items are phrased in a positive manner. Hence, the higher the score, the more the user is satisfied with the system. Table 2 shows the results of the FQ for the ten tasks. Q1.1 addresses the ease of task completion for Task 1, as perceived by a user. Q1.2 addresses the degree to which the user is satisfied with the time to complete Task 1. Q1.3 addresses the adequacy of the support information for Task 1, as perceived by a user. The same scheme applies for the other tasks.

The best-evaluated task (satisfaction with the performance) was Task 2 (Creation of a new space in the VCCP): the ease of use was rated as 5.90, the degree of satisfaction with the completion time was 5.90, and the adequacy of the support information was 5.59. These ratings imply that the users were satisfied with the system use. The worst-assessed task was Task 4 (Modifying an event in the event manager). The level of ease-of-use for this functionality was ranked as 4.38 (range 1-7), the degree of satisfaction with the completion time was 4.48, and the adequacy of the support information was 3.76. The numbers pointed to the need for an improvement in this functionality of the service, as the time to learn and become familiar with the event management was longer than expected by the designers. This request was followed in the service re-design.

The results obtained from the first service release pointed to some usability problems (UPs). There were 21 such UPs identified. Some of the UPs have a single frequency, but the highest observed frequency was 12 for the usability problem numbered 13 (Task 4: Modify the event in the event manager). Users found difficulties in inviting people to the event during the run time of the event as well as in the option to invite people during the event's creation. These problems required the repair of the portal, and this was realized in the next phase of the service development. The second version of the portal enabled users to create an event more easily, as this function was simplified and the setting up of a distributed auditorium needed only two steps, compared to the four needed before the applied change, the setting up and the running of the user community within the allocated space(s) was much more friendly, enabling easy evidence of the created space and the member's identity. The exchange of messages was designed to be as user friendly as possible and the information space about on-going events was much easier to survey. The use of the repository was also made friendlier, as most of the actions were performed by clicking on the selected items and the search algorithms for specific items were improved as well. The identified and reported usability problems in the second evaluation after the redesign were of a minor (and one of a moderate) nature and the latter involved breaking the audio signal, as happens with other audio systems. The cause of this problem may lay in the particular session signal transmission problems. The total number of reported problems in the second evaluation was only 5, compared to 21 in the first evaluation process.

2.4 Attitudes and Cultural Differences

The basic objective of the performed studies was to examine the acceptance of the service offered by the VCCP and to highlight if possible differences in the attitudes when embracing the new ICT service among the studied communities have origin in the different cultural background. It should be noted here, that interpretation of what "culture" addresses in general terms is very difficult, as this term has many different meanings and interpretations depending on the field of the application. In our study we mainly considered the attitudes regarding the working and communicating of a person, who followed from the definition of the term "individual culture" present in a particular region. Individual culture is understood as a common property of the values that the members of a particular cultural background broadly share (Santrock, 2007). The value clarification in that context consists of actions like, for example, »help people clarify what their lives are for and what is worth working for and how they accomplish this". The cultural context in our study was understood to be similar to the understanding of "culture" in the Kappas and Kramer study from the book "Face-to-face communication over the Internet", where they examined the age, gender and the language (Kappas and Kramer, 2011) and the user attitudes to on-line communication that reflect these characteristics in addition to the "individual" culture. In our case we tried to reveal the community members' attitudes towards working in a virtual environment, that were displayed during the evaluation of the VCC tool and working in the aligned distance sessions. Our intention was to found whether these attitudes and capabilities differ due to the individual cultural values among the participants from the three regions. Important research question was in the study was if these potential differences were noticeable during the evaluation of the VCCP.

We were aware that the three different groups of users do not come from the same environment and that individuals among them follow some of the individual cultural values that they share and are typical for the large regions: Africa, Latin America and Europe. In general, we found no evidence for any profound differences. In the African team from Malawi we had participants that differed in age, gender and origin (very young people, from 25-30 years old, mainly men and then an elderly lady (over 55 years) of European origin), but the attitudes and values towards the new technology adoption displayed by this team do not much differ from the others. Despite the problems they had with network connectivity at the beginning of the project all of them were very active and eager to learn and adapt to the new way of working. Later, the usability results showed that the African users still had some difficulties that were not experienced by the other two communities, e.g., in accomplishing some of the tasks. Most of their negative comments addressed the ease of use and the functionality. The language (English was used) seemed not to be a cultural barrier, as the participants that were recruited for the evaluation had an education in ICT, and this is taught in English

The Latin American team that was in charge of organizing several large events showed some negligence regarding the timing and their presence at the project-team meetings. They were also failing to answer project mails regarding meetings or work organization regularly. They either missed the meeting or were late. This could be explained by the time difference between the European and the Latin American countries despite the fact that the timing was always set up to accommodate the overlapping of both regions working hours. However, in virtual team collaboration this is a disturbing attitude. Most of Latin America positive comments were allocated to the interactivity property of the VCCP and the negative comments to the user interface. This could be explained by the property dealing with communication attitudes in the region and maybe to the changed design of the interface during the translation into Spanish. On the other hand, there were no particular differences between the Latin America users and the Europeans participating in the large distance events. This fact can be explained by the availability of the service in Spanish (the language was considered as a part of the cultural environment) for the Latin America users and the good knowledge of English within the European user community. Some not very good results were obtained with the Slovenian users when performing Task 3. This can also be explained by the lack of a local language presentation of the VCCP's services. On the other hand, many more preferences for using the tool were expressed by most of the European users, compared to the users in Latin America and Africa. The European user community expressed greater enthusiasm for not travelling to an event in the case that the service allowed a replacement for the required collaboration. The same findings applied to the satisfaction with the service. This can be explained by the availability of better equipment and the faster connectivity available in Europe, which caused, as a consequence, fewer technical difficulties with the service settings. On the other hand, business trips are considered as very tiring and time-consuming among the European researchers. Participation in EU research programs usually involves travelling to many meetings and events. Avoiding some trips for them is considered as beneficial. We concluded that this property is more typical for the European researchers.

Besides the differences presented in the above section, a detailed inspection of the results of the conducted study led us to the conclusion that most of the differences found among the three communities were mainly due to the lack of proper equipment as well as a lack of knowledge and experience. The African community required more technical support than the other two, but the willingness to learn and use the service was the highest among this group. A large percentage of the community members (72%) expressed very positive or positive attitudes (92%) regarding the use of the service as a collaborative platform for their projects and other types of collaboration, including the members of the African community. In this context no noticeable differences between the communities of the three continents were observed. This finding also confirms some of the previous results found in the studies of Kappas and Krämer (Kappas & Krämer, 2011), where they claim that "the current global connectivity deletes the cultural differences between communities with similar interest and value". This can be considered as a relevant finding, especially if the younger generation that has grown together with the Internet and mobile networks is considered. Compared to the other cultural values regarding attitudes to work, if the technology is available and used, then the cultural background becomes a minor problem, especially when younger generation is considered.

3. CONCLUSION

The products of the research communities and the educational practices that span the globe are always transnational and with tools such as VCCP they will continue to be even more transnational and international. Such services contribute to the removal of the differences in the communities, such as those studied in this paper. The EU-based support in connecting these communities in the use of the European research networking infrastructure that foster collaboration is the right approach for the promotion and further cooperation within joint research projects and collaborative work that brings innovation sometimes triggered by the cultural differences.

It should be noted that the presented study of the new service acceptance pointed to some problems that have no origin in the cultural differences but appeared because the differences in the quality of the equipment, the quality of the communication network and the lack of appropriate instructions to provide help to the users that are beginners. Here, the benefit introduced by the high-quality connectivity and the aligned bandwidth, enabling a good video-transmission quality between African, South America and the EU should be recognized. Other significant differences between the scientific communities from the three continents regarding their attitudes towards new technology for collaboration were not observed, which paves the way to the further joint research collaboration on distance. Our study has also proved that the scientific community is sufficiently collaborative and as such is open to acceptance of sophisticated technologies for cooperation and distance work. Collaborative technologies provide productive outcomes when motivated people use them to evolve social and organizational behavior that exploits a system designed for their own purposes.

ACKNOWLEDGEMENT

This work has been performed in the framework of the EU funded FP6 project GLOBAL.

REFERENCES

Arh, T. et al. (2010). Usability Tests on the Global Plaza, part 1 and 2. GLOBAL project internal report.

Brooke, J. (1996). SUS: a "quick and dirty" usability scale. In Jordan, P. W., Thomas, B., Weerdmeester,

B. A., McClelland, A. L. (Eds.), *Usability Evaluation in Industry.* London: Taylor and Francis (pp. 90- 123).

Cortes, M., & Barra, E. (2009, November 29). Virtual Auditorium Infrastructure /VCC v2 – Deliverable 1.2. Retrieved from https://webcache.zsi.at/global/.

GEANT (2013). Transforming the way researchers collaborate. http://www.geant.net/pages/home.aspx. Retrieved 25 Februar, 2013.

GLOBAL project. (n.d). Retrieved January 26, 2012, from http://www.global-project.eu.

Hvannberg, E., Lárusdóttir, M. & Law, E. L-C. (2007). Heuristic Evaluation: Comparing Ways of Finding and Reporting Usability Problems, *Interacting with Computers*, 19(2), 225-240.

Isabel Plaza. (n.d.). Retrieved January 26, 2012, from http://isabel.dit.upm.es.

ISO/IEC FCD 25010 (2010). Systems and software engineering – Software product Quality Requirements and Evaluation (SQuaRE) – *Software product quality and system quality in use models*.

Jerman-Blažič, B., Lai-Chong Law, E., & Arh, T. (2007). An assessment of the usability of an Internet-based education system in a cross-cultural environment: The case of the Interreg crossborder program in Central Europe. *Journal of the American Society for Information Science and Technology*, 58(1),66.

Kappas, A., & Krämer, N. C. (2011). *Face-to-face communication over the Internet. Emotions in a web of culture, language and technology*. Cambridge: Cambridge University Press.

Kavita, P., Irani, L., & Dourish, P. (2012). Post-colonial Computing: A Tactical Survey. *Science, Technology & Human Values, 37(1), 3-29.*

Lewis, L. R. (1995). IBM Computer Usability Satisfaction Questionnaires: Psychometric evaluation and instructions for use. *International Journal of Human-Computer Interaction*, 7(1), 57-78.

Santrock, J.W. (2007). Culture-fair tests: intelligence tests intended not to be culturally biased, in Topical Approach to Intelligence *The McGraw-Hill Companies, Inc*

Walsh, J. P. & Maloney, N. G. (2007). Collaboration structure, communication media, and problems in scientific work teams. *Journal of Computer-Mediated Communication*, 12(2), article 19. Retrieved January 15, 2012 from http://jcmc.indiana.edu/vol12/issue2/walsh.html.

STUDY OF THE VIABILITY OF USING TWITTER SENTIMENT ANALYSIS IN THE HOTEL INDUSTRY

Elisa Mena-Maldonado[1], Richard Sinnott[2] and Maritzol Tenemaza[1]
[1]*Escuela Politécnica Nacional, Ladrón de Guevara E11·253, Quito, Ecuador*
[2]*The University of Melbourne, Parkville VIC 3010, Melbourne, Australia*

ABSTRACT

Twitter is a form of microblogging that is a very popular way of communication nowadays. The authors of these messages usually share thoughts, emotions and different types of subjective and objective data. Hence, microblogging has become a great source for opinion mining. However, is there enough relevant data to the hotel industry in Twitter?
In this paper we focus on search and analyze sentiments from Twitter data. This analysis aims to know whether Twitter data is a useful source for generating hotel rankings or not. Our contribution is in regards the public opinion of the best hotels in the city of Melbourne, Australia. For this purpose, we did the experiment over 53 million tweets collected for 3 months.

KEYWORDS

Sentiment analysis, hotels rankings, machine learning, Twitter, Elasticsearch

1. INTRODUCTION

Sentiment analysis is related to sociology with focus on emotions and feelings; these emotions are often part of a person's decision making process or capture their personal experience (Kouloumpis et al., 2011). "Others' opinions can be crucial when it's time to make a decision or choose among multiple options" (Cambria et al., 2013).

The tourism industry has been capturing reviews from restaurants, hotels and holiday places and research has shown that people tend to trust on reviews posted by other consumers as superior to marketer information (Gretzel and Yoo, 2008). In fact, "80 per cent of users who have reviewed opinions on restaurants, hotels and other services state that these opinions significantly influenced their decisions" (Martínez-Cámara et al., 2014).

Twitter is a great source of public data for it has been widely used as a type of microblogging site since 2006 with around 340 million tweets per day(Oreskovic, 2015). It allows users to write messages (tweets) of 140 characters that correspond to thoughts, ideas and feelings about any topic such as politics, religion, economics, business and so on (Martínez-Cámara et al., 2014).

As such, Twitter data can potentially help to identify public opinion about hotels and to create a ranking based on the people's sentiment. Twitter has been widely used for sentiment analysis in applications for political opinion, stock picking and the most common application that is monitoring reputation of a brand.

In this paper we focus on search and analyze sentiments from Twitter data for the hotel industry. This analysis aims to know whether Twitter data is a useful source for generating hotel rankings or not. Our contribution has to do with the sentiment analysis from Twitter data regarding the best hotels in the city of Melbourne, Australia based on the top 10 ranked hotels in the same city by TripAdvisor. For this purpose, we did the experiment over 53 million tweets collected for 3 months.

In order to do sentiment analysis on the data gathered from Twitter, it was necessary to perform various steps that include collecting and preparing data, classifying the data and presenting it in a visual manner.

We faced challenges not only on the data source subject but on the data preparation and classification. Some sentiment analysis applications have been developed using hotel reviews collected from websites with crawlers (Kasper and Vela, 2011). While others used TripAdvisor's corpus to construct a domain-specific lexicon (Gräbner et al., 2012). The approaches of (Kasper and Vela, 2011) and (Gräbner et al., 2012) use linguistic information extraction that is applicable to data more structured than Twitter's.

In this document we present the steps followed to support sentiment analysis of Twitter data regarding hotel reviews. First we present a review of the related literature where we evaluate the approaches of different authors for handling Twitter data. In the third section we show the methodology and layout used to build the infrastructure required by the system. In the fourth section we present the experiments and results by evaluating the two training data sets and their accuracy, we also include the evaluation of the ranking of the best hotels in the city of Melbourne. Finally, in the fifth section we present the conclusions of this work as a whole.

2. LITERATURE REVIEW

Sentiment analysis is one of the hottest research areas in computer science; it has around 7000 articles (Feldman, 2013). There have been a number of projects related to social media data analysis in different topics like politics, movie ranking and marketing. The most popular approaches to do sentiment analysis consistent with (Kaur and Gupta, 2013) are: a subjective lexicon where a list of words labeled as positive, negative or neutral are given according to a score assigned to each word, the N-gram model is made by unigram, bigram or a combination in training data given for classification, and machine learning where classification is performed using a set of features extracted from the text. Some authors use and compare the three approaches for different types of data including Twitter and other data collected from the web.

The work of (Kasper and Vela, 2011) gathered data from different web sites using a crawler and compiled them into one system called BESAHOT, they processed data written only in the German language and used a statistical polarity classifier and linguistic information extraction. The polarity values were assigned to the text segments only. With this system, they achieved 72% accuracy in neutral content with the identified topic polarity and 75% with multi-topic content.

In (Kaur and Gupta, 2013), they used a corpus from TripAdvisor reviews and constructed a domain-specific lexicon using part of speech (POS) tags. This lexicon contained high frequency words such as "hotel" or "room". They evaluated the system by measuring precision and recall for two ratings: a 5-star rating and a 3-way rating (positive, negative and neutral). They demonstrated that the classification accuracy was significantly better when they used less numbers of labels for the data (3-way rating) with a larger training data set.

The approaches in (Kasper and Vela, 2011) and (Gräbner et al., 2012) process and analyze data gathered from the web specifically hotel reviews in travel web sites. Those approaches use linguistic information extraction or POS that is applicable to data that is more structured than Twitter data, which has a restriction of 140 characters. In this context, (Agarwal et al., 2011) explored the use of tree kernels in order to avoid the use of feature vectors. They also used a 3-way classification and a unigram model, a feature based model and a tree kernel based model. The unigram model was used as a baseline, for the feature-based model. They also included new features and a Twitter tree representation for the tree kernel model. They demonstrated that using a set of 100 features could perform similar accuracy as with a unigram model comprised of 10,000 features. The tree kernel approach dramatically impacts on the accuracy of the system. Moreover, they found out that feature-specific twitter data like hashtags and emoticons add slight values to the classifier. For their purpose, they used 5,000 manually labeled tweets.

In a 2011 study, published in (Kouloumpis et al., 2011), authors investigated the information and informal language used in microblogging for 3-way classification. They used supervised machine learning systems and included three different corpora for training data sets: emoticons, hashtags and manually labeled data. Since microblogging data is different from more verbose and well-structured data, the features and techniques used in other approaches may not be applicable to more concise Twitter data. They used POS and microblogging features including hashtags and emoticons. They found that POS features contributed to a decrease in the performance of their classifier. Moreover, including emoticons for data training improves the performance. Furthermore, the inclusion of microblogging features such as emoticons, intensifiers and abbreviations were identified as being beneficial.

Many authors use general Twitter data containing different topics. We instead used a Naïve Bayes classifier with two different types of corpora: the natural language toolkit (NLTK) movies reviews and a manually labeled hotel-related twitter data set.

3. METHODOLOGY

Sentiment analysis is a systematic analysis of online expressions. In order to do this type of analysis we followed the methodology proposed by (Rambocas and Gama, 2013), here is a short summary of the process: Data collection, text preparation, sentiment detection, sentiment classification and presentation.

The data collection process involves gathering data from one or more sources including blogs, social media, microblogs or web portals. The text preparation stage requires to clean pertinent data of non-textual content or content that is not relevant to the study i.e. slang or data from unrelated contexts. The third stage, sentiment detection involves detecting emotions and subjectivity of the text in order to classify new data based on the analysis of formerly data collected. For the next stage, sentiment classification, supervised machine learning techniques are used to classify the sentiments. Finally, in the presentation stage, the analysis of the data is presented in a meaningful and graphical way, so visual analytics can be performed.

In the data collection stage we collected tweets using the Twitter streaming API for the city of Melbourne and then we stored them in a Couchbase database instance. For the text preparation stage we filtered the data using Elasticsearch (Elastic, 2016a) to get only hotel-related tweets and then we cleaned those tweets of non-English characters. For sentiment detection we used two different training data sets for a Naïve Bayes classifier in order to perform sentiment analysis and classify tweets as positive, negative or neutral: the natural language toolkit (NLTK) movies reviews that has 2000 reviews (Bird et al., 2009) and a manually labeled data set that contains 400 hotel-related tweets. Then, we calculated the accuracy of the NLTK corpus and our manually classified data set and in both cases we got approximately an accuracy of 68%. Finally, for the presentation stage of the system we used the Kibana (Elastic, 2016b) web interface that provided us a flexible tool to analyze the data processes for the city of Melbourne.

3.1 Data Collection

According to the methodology explained in the previous section 3 . We collected data from the Twitter streaming API. The data gathered was stored in JavaScript Object Notation (JSON) format with a defined structure. For instance, each tweet is comprised of an id, user or text fields. Through use of a developer account it was possible to retrieve around 1% of all the tweets generated from a given area when using bounding boxes to get geotagged tweets (Morstatter et al., 2013). We also got tweets by setting other parameters such as the name of the city or the name of the neighborhood.

In order to find the hotel-related tweets, we used the Elasticsearch search engine that performed full-text search and retrieved only the tweets that had in their text field i.e. the word "hotel" (Figure 1).

_score ▼	truncated	text
2.7924678	false	@aleaguequizzes Hotel.
2.7382162	false	Hotel nostalgia
2.7382162	false	Hotel booked
2.7382162	false	Hotel Books
2.4104388	false	Revamped hotel. (@ Racecourse Hotel) https://t.co/F1jIY3UmEA
2.326543	false	@tinaunicorn station hotel!!
2.326543	false	Real great hotel
2.326543	false	Our hotel is amazing

Figure 1. Hotel-related tweets

We retrieved around 11 thousand tweets that contained the word "hotel" from the 53 million tweets database that had been harvesting tweets from May to November 2014.

3.2 Text Preparation

This stage involves preparing the data for analysis that includes, identifying and cleaning characters that were not part of the English alphabet from the dataset. Indeed, we used regular expressions to remove all non-alphanumeric characters such as links attached to the text, hashtags and emoticons, then, the text was transformed to lowercase. We did not considered methods such as part of speech identifiers since (Kouloumpis et al., 2011) demonstrated those features might not be useful for Twitter data. We also never used the emoticons corpus described in (Kouloumpis et al., 2011) because we found in the Twitter hotel data that people use Unicode  emoticons instead of text like :)

The results of this cleaning process are shown here:

Original text: I like it raw, #Melbourne #Australia #crowncasino #d600 @ Crown Casino Melbourne http://t.co/wUjGPUZKfT"

Clean text: i like it raw melbourne australia crowncasino crown casino melbourne

3.3 Sentiment Detection and Classification

The sentiment detection stage requires the use of natural language processing to evaluate and extract subjective content from the dataset.

In the sentiment classification stage, the subjective content was classified using the three-way classification: positive, negative and neutral.

Thus, in order to determine what sentiment a tweet had, we performed sentiment analysis using the TextBlob (Steven, 2016) library for Python that is built on top of the natural language toolkit (NLTK). The NLTK sentiment analyzer uses a corpus of movie reviews that contains 2000 reviews for polarity data set and for sentence polarity data set, it contains 5331 sentences (Pang, 2005).

The NLTK sentiment analyzer uses a Naïve Bayes classifier with the movie reviews corpus as a training dataset, and when the text is analyzed, it returns a number representing its polarity and its subjectivity.

We also used the TextBlob Naïve Bayes classifier with our manually classified data comprised of 400 manually classified tweets as a training dataset.

In both cases the classifier returned a polarity number, we used this number to classify the data as "positive" if the number was greater than zero, "negative" if the number was less than zero and "neutral" if the number was equal to zero.

Although, there are several techniques that have been used to support sentiment detection from text, it is also important to consider the objectivity of the text to be analyzed. Most tweets are written to share information that more often than not, does not contain emotions, i.e. they have neutral sentiment. For instance:

I'm at Crown Casino http://t.co/l8XcmmczEg

3.4 Presentation

In the last stage of the process we address that "the general purpose of the analysis is to convert unstructured fragmented text into meaningful information." (Rambocas and Gama, 2013)

Therefore, after having the data classified, we used Kibana for presenting it. Kibana allows handling data dynamically from Elasticsearch server and creating customizable dashboards. Since this tool was created using HTML and JavaScript, it was not necessary to use extra modules on a standard web server (Elastic, 2016a).

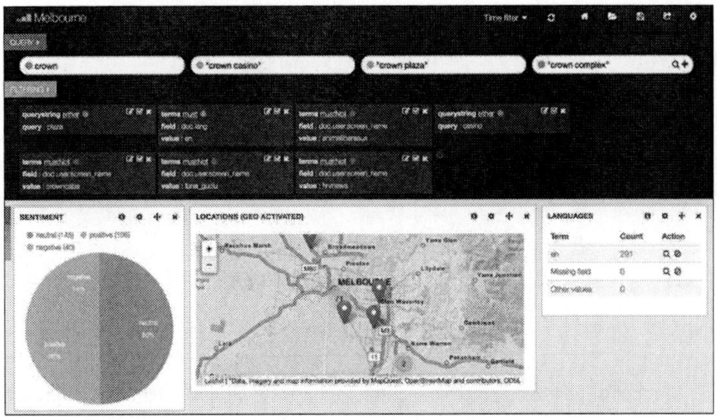

Figure 2. Kibana dashboard for Melbourne reviews in Twitter

The Figure 2 shows a pie chart on the left of the positive, negative and neutral tweets for the hotel Crown in Melbourne.

On top of the figure there are some filters that let us discard irrelevant data for the study when we queried the Elasticsearch server i.e. we picked the words "crown", "crown casino", "crown plaza", "crown complex" that refer to the hotel Crown that we analyzed. Thus, we retrieved 291 tweets that contained those words.

On the center, there is a map that shows 73 geotagged tweets out of 291.

Some other filters were also applied for the presentation i.e. the terms that may or not be important when querying Elasticsearch: "plaza" and "casino" are two examples. Additionally, the terms: "animaliberaaus", "hvnews", "tuna_guclu" must not be considered in the query since they are users that represent organizations or are part of the hotel staff according to their Twitter profiles.

4. EXPERIMENTS AND RESULTS

4.1 Sentiment Analysis

In order to determine whether or not the Twitter data is accurate to do sentiment analysis for the hotel industry we evaluated the accuracy of the two classifiers, as stated previously in this document.

To calculate NLTK accuracy, we classified 400 hotel-related tweets as positive, negative or neutral with the NLTK sentiment analyzer. We then classified the same 400 tweets manually, so we calculated the accuracy of the NLTK classifier respect to the 400 manually classified tweets by comparing each tweet classification with NLTK and the manual classification. To normalize the data, the number of true positive tweets was divided by the total number of tweets. Hence, the accuracy for NLTK was 68.35%.

To calculate the accuracy of the manually labeled 400 tweets, we trained a Naïve Bayes classifier with this dataset and then we used a test dataset of 50 new tweets. The accuracy calculated by TextBlob library in this case was 68.18%.

Even though we used a unique feature for classification in the manual process (the text of the tweet), the accuracy of the second classifier was similar to the NLTK classifier. In addition, it is important to point out that we labeled only 400 tweets compared to the 5000 sentences of the NLTK corpora.

Most of the data classified corresponds to the class "neutral" because most of these tweets are related to news or to factual information.

4.2 Hotel Reviews in Twitter

We gathered the top 10 best ranked hotels of the city of Melbourne in November 2014 by TripAdvisor; the top in the ranking was The Langham and the last in this list was the Marriott as shown in Figure 3. We performed analytics over the 53 million tweets and looked for data of each hotel using Kibana.

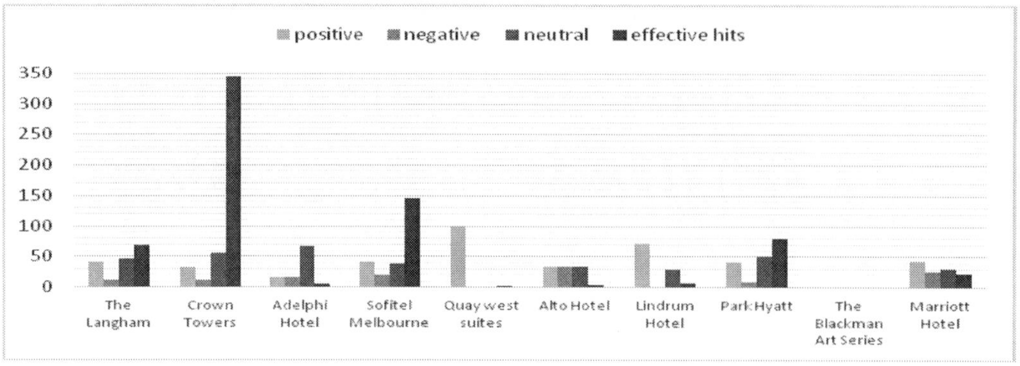

Figure 3. Number of positive, negative, neutral and effective tweets per hotel in the city of Melbourne

The number of all the tweets related to The Crown Towers was 345. However, these tweets were written in different languages. Despite we did not classify tweets in other languages but English, it helped us to know that The Crown Towers had been mentioned 345 times; this number is what we call "effective hits".

In the case of The Crown Towers, the number of positive tweets is 32, negative is 11 and neutral is 56, the other 246 could not be classified.

According to our findings, the Crown Complex is the hotel with most tweets (greater number of effective hits) in Melbourne, and the top 3 most tweeted hotels were:

- Crown Towers,
- Sofitel,
- The Langham

To include these three hotels in the top 3, we considered the number of total tweets and the neutral content of each one.

In general, we could see that the positive emotions are more than the negative, it might be due to our choice to evaluate the top 10 ranked hotels in Melbourne by TripAdvisor. However, the number of positive and negative tweets is predominantly less than the number of neutral tweets.

We could count the number of positive vs. the number of negative tweets and identify what are the best hotels, but the neutral sentiment is also important to consider for finding the motive to share this factual information instead of emotions or feelings.

Thus, considering this tweet: "*I'm at Crown Casino* ", the classification is *neutral*; however, the question remains: why did this person share that? Was s/he trying to make his followers jealous because Crown Casino offers a good social status? If that was the case, this situation may be considered as something positive instead of neutral for the Crown Complex.

The hotel with most negative sentiment was the Marriott; the reason for this was published on the 3rd of October 2014. According to this news, the Marriott hotel used a jamming system to prevent phones guests using mobile data hence forcing them to purchase Marriot Wi-Fi services (Fung, 2014). Several Australian guests and Twitter users were outraged, so shared the news even though this event was in Tennessee, US.

The hotel with the least number of tweets was The Blackman, although it was one of the top hotels in Melbourne, we could not find tweets that at least mention it; this may be because during the data collection stage of our work, there were no events that triggered people to share opinions of this hotel like they did with the Marriott.

5. CONCLUSIONS

In this paper we explored how Twitter data can be used and analyzed to identify general opinions (sentiment) on hotels and determine whether this can be useful or not for this industry.

Therefore, we used a methodology to do sentiment analysis that included gathering data, cleaning the data, sentiment detection and classification using supervised machine learning and finally we presented the data using Kibana dashboards. To determine how accurate was our system we evaluated a Naïve Bayes classifier with two different training data sets. The first one contained around 5000 movie reviews labeled sentences and the second one 400 hotel-related twitter data. Although the second data set contained significantly less data than the first one, the accuracy for both systems was similar: around 68%. Thus, the more relevant data we use for training the classifier, the better.

This classification was oriented to subjective (emotional) data, but the objective (neutral) data was also worthy of evaluation. In this sense, people tend not to share thoughts unless they have a motive: either positive or negative sentiment. In some cases, people share data that is objective, which may impact on other's opinions like the Marriott news. The neutral data can also reveal positive implied meanings where social standing can be gauged by the content of the tweet.

We used TripAdvisor's top 10 best hotels in Melbourne ranking to check whether the data we gathered from Twitter could rank those hotels in a similar way. The data of a tourism dedicated web site like TripAdvisor and the data of Twitter are completely different in terms of structure and meaning. TripAdvisor is a social medium where reviews about travel-related places are given, while Twitter is a microblogging web site that facilitates sharing of opinions and thoughts about any topic. Finding relevant data in Twitter is a complex process that requires a deep analysis of the language used, the type of user, the event and the topic that are being analyzed. We leveraged a database of about 53-million tweets, but when we analyzed the public opinion of a given hotel, the best result was 345 tweets.

To conclude, it is possible to use Twitter data to get relevant information of public opinion about hotels, for this purpose we used sentiment analysis techniques that let us setup an environment for analysis. However, after searching over a large database of tweets, the relevant data for our study was scarce.

REFERENCES

Agarwal A, et al, 2011. Sentiment analysis of twitter data. *Proceedings of the Workshop on Languages in Social Media.* Association for Computational Linguistics, pp. 30-38.

Bird S, et al, 2009. *Natural language processing with Python*, O'Reilly Media, Inc, Beijing, China.

Cambria E, et al, 2013. New avenues in opinion mining and sentiment analysis. *IEEE Intelligent Systems*, pp. 15-21.

Elastic, 2016a. *Elasticsearch | Search & Analyze Data in Real Time*. Available at: https://www.elastic.co/products/elasticsearch.

Elastic, 2016b. *Kibana | Explore & Visualize Your Data*. Available at: https://www.elastic.co/products/kibana.

Feldman R, 2013. Techniques and applications for sentiment analysis. *Communications of the ACM* 56, pp. 82-89.

Fung B, 2014. FCC to Marriott: No, you can't force your customers onto terrible hotel WiFi. The Washington Post.

Gräbner D, et al, 2012. Classification of customer reviews based on sentiment analysis. *Information and Communication Technologies in Tourism 2012,* pp. 460-470.

Gretzel U and Yoo KH, 2008. Use and impact of online travel reviews. *Information and communication technologies in tourism 2008*, pp. 35-46.

Kasper W. and Vela M., 2011. Sentiment analysis for hotel reviews. *Proceedings of the Computational Linguistics-Applications Conference (CLA-2011).* Jachranka, Poland, pp. 45-52.

Kaur A. and Gupta V., 2013. A Survey on Sentiment Analysis and Opinion Mining Techniques. *Journal of Emerging Technologies in Web Intelligence* 5, pp. 367-371.

Kouloumpis E, et al, 2011. Twitter sentiment analysis: The good the bad and the omg!. *ICWSM* 1. Barcelona, Spain, pp. 538-541.

Pang, B and Lee, L., 2005. Seeing stars: Exploiting class relationships for sentiment categorization with respect to rating scales. *Proceedings of the 43rd Annual Meeting on Association for Computational Linguistics*. Ann Arbor, U.S, pp. 115-124.

Martínez-Cámara E, et al, 2014. Sentiment analysis in Twitter. *Natural Language Engineering* 20, pp. 1-28.

Morstatter F, et al, 2013. Is the sample good enough? comparing data from twitter's streaming api with twitter's firehose. *arXiv preprint arXiv:1306.5204*.

Oreskovic A, 2015. *Here's another area where Twitter appears to have stalled: tweets per day*. Available at: http://www.businessinsider.com/twitter-tweets-per-day-appears-to-have-stalled-2015-6.

Rambocas M and Gama J, 2013. Marketing Research: The Role of Sentiment Analysis. Universidade do Porto, Faculdade de Economia do Porto.

Steven L, 2016. *TextBlob: simplified Text Processing*. Available at: http://textblob.readthedocs.org/en/dev/.

A THEORETICAL FRAMEWORK TO EXPLAIN THE EFFECTS OF INTERNET-MEDIATED COMMUNICATION ON GERMAN AND CHINESE TEMPORAL UNDERSTANDING

Maria Faust M.A.
University of Leipzig, Institute for Communication & Media Studies, Dpt. for Empirical Communication & Media Research, Burgstrasse 21, D-04109 Leipzig, Germany

ABSTRACT

This paper explains changes in Chinese and German temporal understanding as a cultural construct due to internet-mediated communication as one oft the key mediating factors aside others. It integrates the anthropological construct of polychronicity, pace of life and temporal horizon into a broader framework, which goes beyond Western biased constructs through the theory driven incorporation of Confucian notions. A central question is whether and how many of the sub dimensions of temporal understanding could be changed through internet-mediated communication. Current media theoretical assumptions are evaluated. Mediatization and recent acceleration theory are taken into consideration. Prospective research is advized to take a closer look at this issue through an interdisciplinary transnational approach.

KEYWORDS

Time, Germany, China, Internet, Mediatization, Intercultural Communication

1. INTRODUCTION

In recent years, the scholarly debate on the issue of time in society has been closely linked to

i. its changing nature in modernity,
ii. acceleration phenomena,
iii. globalization processes,
iv. and finally the way it is influenced by technologies in a broad, or media in a narrow, sense.

All four issues are discussed in public controversially. Debate is represented by *exhibitions* (Pace Beijing, 2014; National Museum of American History, 2016; Museum for Communication Berlin, 2013) and *documentaries* (Opitz, 2013). Semi-institutionalized formats, such as *open lectures* (University of Leipzig, 2011) or *nongovernmental organizations* (German Society for Time Politics e.V., 2014; The International Society for the Study of Time, 2005) have also analyzed these concepts. Yet on a more informal level society shapes its feedback to these issues in the form of *handbooks* and *guides* (Long and Schweppe, 2010) suggesting a meaningful and reflective way to deal with time. Likewise, through means such as *weekend seminars*, *workshops* and *trainings* people seek ways to achieve a more balanced lifestyle and the feeling of being rushed less. (Somweber, 2013). So, if technology, or media in general, is presumed to be one of the core drivers of these processes of temporal change in society, how would we know about it? And if these four issues are debated side by side, empirical research has to relate to all of them, and raise the question:

Which influence does internet-mediated communication have on temporal understanding?

Temporal understanding is determined by culture and at a time of globalization and mediatization subject to change. However, in order to strengthen the argument, it is logical to contrast two cultural contexts to underpin it with theoretical and empirical evidence. There is evidence that German and Chinese cultural contexts are different. (Hofstede, 2001; Triandis, 1995) Thus, there seems to be plausible evidence to contrast the two cultural contexts following the idea of a 'Most Different Systems Design' (Anckar, 2008, pp. 389–390). An Anglo-Saxon country, e.g. the UK, might be more interesting due to a greater variety of

English internet-mediated communication; however, it would lack an emic perspective and not follow the Anckar's idea as much as the German cultural context does. This circumstance gives rise to the question:

Which influence does internet-mediated communication have on temporal understanding when comparing German and Chinese cultural context?

The results may benefit science and societal understanding. First, research desiderata on time (State Ministry for Education and Research, 2010) and questionable conceptions of cultural time, e.g. Hofstede's Long-Term Orientation support the solid conceptualization of cultural time. Furthermore, theories of temporal change in a broader sense (eg. Castells, 2010; Eriksen, 2001; Rosa, 2005; Neverla, 2010b etc.) will be enriched from an empirical and particularly quantitative empirical fundaments. (Lee and Liebenau, 2000a, p. 184) Finally, investigating Chinese internet usage, which is a clear research desiderate in Europe (Herold, 2013), and its effects overcomes Western research biases. Second, this research aims to address permanent availability, connectivity and flexibility. If such values become generally binding and are represented in day-by-day activities and action plans, downtime and time-outs (Nowotny, 1989, p. 42; Rinderspacher, 2011, p. 23) might be recognized as essential in order to ensure physic and mental health and well-being. Political lobbyism would eventually have to guarantee such basic liberties.

2. TEMPORAL UNDERSTANDING AS A DIMENSION OF CULTURE

The study of time has been truly interdisciplinary and closely linked to both epistemological and ontological problems. (Kant and Timmermann, 1998) However, discussion of these issues goes beyond the scope of this paper. Therefore, the main focus here is on time as a dimension of culture which relates it to the social sphere (Elias and Schröter, 2005) and has to be understood as a human concept, although it cannot be reduced to coming into one's consciousness through perception only.

2.1 Time as a Dimension of Culture

Anthropologists, social scientists and economists have conceptualized the notion of time in culture for several decades. (Geertz, 1991; Levine, 1996, 1998a; Gesteland, 2005) Some scholars have treated it is one cultural dimension beside others (Kluckhohn and Strodtbeck, 1961; Hall, 1984), implying it might be one of the essential issues each social group has to face and pursue differently. Yet, attempts to capture time as a dimension of culture quantitatively only really began in 1991 when Hofstede introduced his fifth dimension long-term-orientation (LTO). (Hofstede, 1991, pp. 159–174) However, since its publication this dimension has not been widely received in the scientific community. (Fang, 1998, 2003, p. 350) Hence reasonable arguments against LTO-scores on both theoretical (Fang, 2003, p. 355) and methodological (Fang, 2003, pp. 350–351; Newman and Nollen, 1996, p. 776; Redpath and O. Nielsen, 1997, pp. 329–330; Yeh and Lawrence, 1995, pp. 657–665) reasons were given, research on cultural concepts of time proceeded in different directions researching time in cultures. Hofstede's student Trompenaars and Hampden-Turner approached the issue using Cottle's circle test, yet still lacking a precise theoretical terminology and definition of which level of time one should examine. (Trompenaars and Hampden-Turner, 2000) The GLOBE Study conceptualized time in cultures already twofold: as cultural practice ("as is") and cultural values ("should be") and related future orientation to gratification delay, planning activities and investment in the future. (House, 2004) As became evident, research at this very general level of time in cultures often sufficed conceptual problems as it tends to ignore and relate different levels of time. It was not until Helfrich-Hölter's scholarly work that such a systematic, level-centered overview of time across cultures was provided. (Helfrich, 1996; Helfrich and Quitterer, 1999; Helfrich-Hölter, 2011) She differentiates four levels of time:

i. image of time,
ii. time horizon or time perspective,
iii. dealing with time,
iv. and time perception.

Each dimension allows for further differentiation into sub dimensions. (Helfrich and Quitterer, 1999, pp. 104–105) Her fourfold differentiation puts recent research into a better perspective and benefits the development of my own model of temporal understanding. Since my own model is intended for quantitative operationalization, such measures are particularly in focus. First, there is a considerable lack of quantitative research in terms of image of time, mainly due to its demanding measurement. The theoretical differentiation between cyclical and linear, concrete and abstract, however, can be found across various reference sources (Hägerstrand, 1988, p. 36; Bodde, 1991; Jones, 1988; Quitterer, 2000, p. 158) and is often, but not necessarily, related to modernity. Second, much progress has been made on researching temporal horizon or temporal perspective, which describes the way people relate to the concepts of past, present and future. (for an overview and different conceptualizations see Klapproth, 2011) However, quite often research has not explicitly focused on cultural differences. (e.g. (Zimbardo and Boyd, 1999; Strathman *et al.*, 1994) On the contrary, Usunier and Valette-Florence provide a more comprehensive framework of time which includes internal and external facettes. (Usunier and Valette-Florence, 2007, p. 338) They distinguish general past and general future; yet, present falls into different sub categories. Third, various efforts have been made to capture polychronicity as one way of dealing with time in the present (Goonetilleke and Luximon, 2010; Lindquist and Kaufman-Scarborough, 2007; Bluedorn *et al.*, 1999; Palmer and Schoorman, 1999; Lee, 1999). Fourth, time perception has a broad research tradition, particularly in psychology. However, less often it is related to cross cultural issues since it is assumed that it falls into a universally valid cognition process.

Before developing my own model based on Helfrich-Hölter's schematic, the abstract term "culture" has to be defined. The multidimensionality of the construct culture has been discussed thoroughly in literature. (Reckwitz, 2000, pp. 64–90) However, a clear definition is particularly important. Following Thomas, this implies, that

> "[c]ulture is a universally spread, for a nation, society, organisation, group, thus for every *social formation*, that humans feel a sense of belonging towards, very specific, typical and identity giving orientation system. This orientation system is manifested in *specific symbols* (e.g. *language, norms, behavioral rules, behavioral scripts*) and is traditionalised in every social formation through the process of socialisation and enculturation. The culture specific orientation system *influences cognition, thinking, evaluating, judging, emotional and motivational processes* and action of all members of any social formation. It thus defines the belonging of the members (function of constituting identity). According to the culture definition of Boesch (see (1980, p. 17)) culture structures a specific field of action for the individuals feeling the sense of belonging towards a social group. This field spans out from created and used objects to institutions, ideas and values. It thus lays the foundation for developing individual forms of *dealing with the environment.*" (Thomas, 2011, 100, italics added)

This definition offers a variety of advantages over other definitions of culture and can incorporate the notion of time as will be shown. Thomas' culture definition is based on the psychological need for orientation and implies that sense-making processes are based on both individual perception processes and collective, socially binding values, norms and rules (Thomas, 2005, p. 41) and incorporates both material and non-material aspects and relates them to one another. Furthermore, it includes the notion of Yin Yang (Fang, 2012) beyond a culture which is implicitly solely reduced to values. This type of perspective points towards dynamics, paradox and holism and enriches it. It stands out in contrast to other definitions which narrows down culture to norms and values only. Finally, as Hepp points out, culture is not a single entity in the empirical world but rather cultures in a pluralistic sense. (Hepp, 2013) Thus, in this paper, we follow the term cultural contexts rather than culture to differentiate between the different contexts.

2.2 Time in German and Chinese Cultural Contexts and Model of Temporal Understanding

Based on the above, why contextualize on a national level in the first place? There are mainly three reasons:

i. because national culture has been extremely under-researched (Leung *et al.*, 2005),
ii. since internet-mediated communication is largely focused on language based communication patterns and can be narrowed down to political legitimacy (Chevrier, 2009) going hand in hand with censorship in China (Becker, 2011),
iii. finally, former research has placed German and Chinese cultural contexts on different ends, for example in terms of individualism and collectivism and recognized national culture as such (Hofstede, 2001, p. 10).

As discussed earlier, not only Hofstede's work suggests differences between the two cultural contexts. (Triandis, 1995) The 'Most Different Systems Design' (Anckar, 2008, pp. 389–390) explicates this cultural comparison and is intended to show greater effects due to increase in variance.

Former theoretical and empirical research on time in Chinese and German cultural context *does not* paint a *clear and straightforward* picture of how it is conceptualized. This results mainly from the fact, that time in China and Germany is approached from different perspectives e.g. analysis of linguistic structures (e.g. Mittag, 1997, p. 256), individual action in everyday life (e.g. Plocher *et al.*, 2013), management efforts on a meso level (e.g. Faure and Fang, 2008; Chen, 2002), etc. Helfrich-Hölter's four level model serves as framework of explication. (Helfrich-Hölter, 2011)

The Chinese image of time still tends be approached from a creation myth perspective (Mittag, 1997, p. 261) and viewed as cyclical (Bodde, 1991, p. 133; Chen, 2002, p. 186) as opposed to Western, thus including German, linear time. (Hägerstrand, 1988, p. 36; Helfrich-Hölter, 2011, p. 126) Yet, Quitterer and Helfrich-Hölter argue that Confucian time, central to Chinese notions of time, is linear yet two-directional thus pointing towards past and future. (Quitterer, 2000, p. 158; Helfrich-Hölter, 2011)

The second level is considered time horizon and relates to the cultural process (Zimbardo and Boyd, 2008; Kluckhohn and Strodtbeck, 1961, p. 12) of dividing time into sub-categories, mostly divided into past, present and future with only some indigenous cultures following a different model. This level includes long- and short-term orientation which relates present to future in terms of planning or achieving certain goals. Hofstede considers Chinese cultural context to be long-term oriented. It scores 118 points on his scale with 100 being usually the highest. (Hofstede, 2001, p. 356) However, from an integrative Yin Yang perspective, long- and short-term orientation coexist in Chinese cultural context. (Faure and Fang, 2008, p. 204) For example, management is thus a matter of wei-ji: "acting when the time is right – responding quickly but with a holistic, long-term view." (Chen, 2002, p. 186) Germany is usually considered a medium long-term oriented country, with people and organizations less investing in future goals and planning ahead. (Hofstede, 2001, p. 356)

In this sense, time horizon is automatically related to dealing with time. On this level, distinctions are usually made between polychronicity and monochronicity which were later classified as two different ways to organize activities. Thus, Bluedorn defines it as "the extent to which people in a culture *prefer* to be engaged in two or more tasks or events simultaneously and *believe their preference* is the best way to do things." (Bluedorn *et al.*, 1999, 205; italics added) However, earlier literature highlights human-orientation, interruption for communication for polychronicity vs. task-orientation, straightforward work for monochronicity. (compare e.g. (Quitterer, 2000, p. 159; Hall and Hall, 1990, pp. 14–15) for more detailed explanations} Efforts have been made to locate Chinese cultural context on the polychronic side, mainly in management literature. In Hall's original work, only Japan was classified (Hall, 1984), as being monochronic in working environments and polychronic in family life. Hall, who first introduced the concept, classified Germans as monochronic (Hall and Hall, 1990), whereas later research provided a different picture. Furthermore, pace of life is also part of dealing with time. (Levine, 1998b) Levine hypothesized, that "[i]ndividualistic cultures are faster than those emphasizing collectivism" implying that pace of life should be faster in German than in Chinese cultural context. (Levine and Norenzayan, 1999, p. 182) His findings show a country pace rank with third place for Germany. China scores 23rd out of 31 countries, implying a much slower pace of life. (Levine and Norenzayan, 1999, pp. 182–183)

As far as time perception is concerned, Helfrich-Hölter only found differences in temporal discrimination of minute, seconds and millisecond intervals when language comes into play. Her results are only partially applicable for this research since she compared Germans with Japanese. However, she found evidence that perception as such is widely invariant across cultures. (Helfrich-Hölter, 2011, pp. 133–134)

In order to develop a model considering both specifics of Chinese and German time and serving empirical investigation, we thus focus on time horizon and dealing with time. Image of time is not considered as it is hard to verbalize and thus complex to investigate (Möhring and Schlütz, 2010) and if any change takes place on this level due to internet-mediated communication, it would probably be a process of several decades rather than years. Time perception is unaccounted for because perception processes are highly invariant across cultures and furthermore, its methodological setup would require an experimental design which is not feasible here. However, as the term time has been used in multidisciplinary contexts and social time and dealing with time fall into one in some scholarly debate, we introduce the term temporal understanding, focusing on both individual and social sense making processes relating to time. The following model (see table 1) thus consists of three levels which are related to one another (past, present and future). Temporal understanding should be defined as

> "a human category of time which is individually undertaken but socially constituted. It encompasses the act of standardising two or more events of which at least one must be progressing and is used as reference system in order to relate the other event(s) to it. This relation constitutes the interdependent time horizon and dealing with time." (my own definition, based on (Elias and Schröter, 2005; Helfrich-Hölter, 2011)

Resulting from the definition of culture, the model incorporates preferences as in the sense of normative prescriptions which are closely linked to behavioral scripts. Furthermore, beyond the distinction between past, present and future, which is by no means universal but holds true for both Chinese and German cultural context, it incorporates the notions of monochronicity and polychronicity, fatalism, pace of life as well as future as planned expectation and future as trust-based interacting expectation and result of present positive behavior. It seeks to include both emic and etic aspects of either cultural context.

Table 1. Temporal understanding theoretically

<table>
<tr><th colspan="5">Dimensions of Temporal Understanding (1 to 7)</th></tr>
<tr><td colspan="5">(1) PAST as GENERAL PAST = Classifying events as former and relation towards these events</td></tr>
<tr><td>PRESENT (2, 3, 4, 5) = Classifying personal and social events ongoing and dealing with these ongoing experiences to help to give order, coherence and meaning those events</td><td>(2) INSTRUMENTAL EXPERIENCE (MONOCHRONICITY) is based on classification acts and implies the extent to which people in a culture prefer to do one task at time and believe their preference is the best way to do things (my own definition, based on Hall 1984)</td><td rowspan="2">(3) FATALISM is based on the classification act but lacks active engagement in tasks or events as future is predestined and not influenced by individual action and has thus be accepted</td><td>(4) POLYCHRONICITY is based on classification acts and implies the extent to which people in a culture prefer to be engaged in two or more tasks or events simultaneously; and believe their preference is the best way to do things (my own definition, based on Bluedorn et al. 1998)</td><td rowspan="2">(5) PACE OF LÌFE is based on classification acts and implies the extent to which people prefer tasks or events to be close together i.e. immediate follow up events</td></tr>
<tr><td>FUTURE as GENERAL FUTURE (6, 3, 7, 5) = Classifying personal and social events prospective and relating these to the current situation through different means to help to give order, coherence and meaning to these events</td><td>(6) FUTURE AS PLANNED EXPECTATION & RESULT OF PROXIMAL GOALS is based on classification acts and implies an either transactional relationship between present ideas and envisioned long-term tasks and events or a focus on proximal goals in the believe they add up to long-term goals</td><td>(7) FUTURE AS TRUST-BASED INTERACTING EXPECTATION & RESULT OF PRESENT POSITIVE BEHAVIOR is based on classification acts and implies positive outcomes of tasks and events due to balanced interaction in the present (based on values 3 容忍 (tolerance of others), 4 随和 (Harmony with others), 8礼尚往来 (Reciprocation of greetings, favours, and gifts), 26报恩与报仇 (Repayment of both the good or evil that another person has caused to you), 30信用, 33安分守己 (Contentedness with one's position in life), 35要面子 (Protecting your "face") of the (Chinese Culture Connection, 1987)</td></tr>
</table>

3. THE INFLUENCE OF INTERNET-MEDIATED COMMUNICATION ON TEMPORAL UNDERSTANDING

Literature on time and information communication technologies has been manifold. (e.g. Bukow *et al.*, 2012; Wurm, 2012; Nowzad, 2011; Westerbarkey, 2010; Neuberger, 2010; Neverla, 2010a, 2010b; Hauser, 2008;

Felsmann, 2008; Rantanen, 2005; Funken and Löw, 2003; Ellrich, 2003; Faulstich and Steininger, 2002; Eriksen, 2001; Geißler and Schneider, 1999) However, two main issues characterize literature in the field: first, literature is on a rather abstract theoretical level (e.g. Castells notion of 'timeless time' Castells, 2010). Second, medium range theories are rarely discussed or even developed, with few exceptions e.g. Lee and Sawyer (Lee and Sawyer, 2010, p. 296). Consequently, studies seldom apply empirical perspectives to this issue (few exceptions (Dimmick *et al.*, 2011; Faust, 2010; Flaherty, 2005; Lee and Liebenau, 2000b) If these abstract theories are focused on a macro level (Lee and Sawyer, 2010, p. 294) why would they hardly specify how exactly cultural change in temporal understanding takes place? Furthermore, why does this not go beyond a descriptive approach using metaphors to capture time and internet technology (Leong *et al.*, 2010)? Theory building in communication and media studies has to seek empirical answers to the problems addressed. Here we follow a twofold strategy to conceptualize and explain the change in temporal understanding due to internet-mediated communication. First, we seek to develop a general model of cultural change due to internet-mediated communication and thereafter, we try to break down the aforementioned abstract theories in order to specify the change in temporal understanding.

3.1 A Model of Change of Temporal Understanding through Internet-mediated Communication

We deal with a cultural construct; hence the process has to be both individual and collective. But how can internet-mediated communication be compared in such different cultural contexts? It is proposed that situations and internet usage is similar and thus functionally equivalent even though the Chinese internet is profoundly censored and Western sites rarely appear (for discussion see Becker, 2011; Dong, 2012).

1. "Similiar" means that internet use situations occur on a regular basis, under the same circumstances and that internet-mediated communicates are comparable (e.g. checking work emails after getting up in the morning) in both cultural contexts.
2. "Functionally equivalent" means that situations and internet use i.e. selection and reception processes are comparable (e.g. using WhatsApp is comparable to WeChat/微信) in both German and Chinese cultural context.

In spite of the "Golden Shield" (jindung gongcheng, 金盾工程), I argue that processes are not the same (!), but comparable in both German and Chinese cultural context. Furthermore, there is evidence, that people prefer culturally proximate content on the internet (Harsh and Xiao Wu, 2013) with language being a key factor for reception. Thus, the general influence of the firewall of China may be less than it i soften considered to be. Both German and Chinese internet are largely isolated, the German one even more so than the Chinese possibly due to the huge Chinese diaspora accessing it from abroad. (Harsh and Xiao Wu, 2013) The issue of internet "separation" has been discussed controversially throughout research on Chinese Internet usage mainly emphasizing the differences of both "Internets". (Herold, 2013, p. 2) However, scholars have made an increasing effort to look at differences between Western and Chinese internet-mediated communicates more thoroughly. (Bolsover, 2013; Yang, 2012; Tang, 2011; Lan, 2004) From a mere technological perspective, there are differences concerning Western and Chinese internet services. Image and video sharing on Sina Weibo as well as more complex retweeting functions are just one example of distinct Chinese qualities. (Yang, 2012, p. 50) Even internet-mediated imagery varies across cultural contexts. Through content analysis of university websites, Tang found that whereas "Chinese universities focused on featuring a university's buildings and landscapes in their institutional promotions, (…) US universities portrayed their institution as a place where students and faculty were learning and enjoying the environment". (Tang, 2011, p. 426) At the same time, Chinese users show different usage patterns – such as communicating more thoroughly over both political incidents as well as entertainment issues reflected in dissemination spread. (Bolsover, 2013, p. 16) Comparative research has to look at *both* similarities *and* differences. The concept of functional equivalence is crucial to comparative research – both conceptually and methodologically (Rippl and Seipel, 2008; Harkness *et al.*, 2003). Simultaneously, the specific cultural context may serve as a background to interpret and explain cultural differences in internet-mediated communication. Usually, Hofstede's cultural dimensions have been applied (Tang, 2011) – with collectivism as a rather prominent explanatory factor for phenomena such as more thorough and intense communicative processes. (Bolsover, 2013, p. 5) However, research may benefit from more emic perspectives such as Thomas' culture standard model.

Internet-mediated communication, as every type of communication, is based on individual reception of communicates, which may be of interpersonal or mass mediated nature. If communication now takes place in increasingly similar situations, it allows for the development of habits. Habits are defined as knowledge structures, which are learned through regular repetition and trigger a certain behavior (and the mental processes connected to it) when indicative cues appear. (Koch, 2010, p. 44) Koch explicates the four aspects of the definition as follows (Koch, 2010, pp. 33–41): First, habits are learned through regular repetition. They are more likely to be developed if the action undertaken has a positive outcome and if situations, under which these actions occur, are similar to one another. Second, habits are knowledge structures and do not refer to the actual behavior. According to Koch, knowledge structures can be conceptualized differently – either as neuronal associated response patterns, decision heuristics or behavioral scripts. Third, habits trigger behavior automatically. It remains debatable whether habitualized behavior is automated or just the triggering process is. However, since automation is relevant regardless of its degree, Koch follows the Weberian differentiation and subsumes habits under behavior rather than social action. Finally, triggering is caused by certain indicative cues such as external circumstances, times, mood or prior respectively ongoing behavior.

Concluding from this, how would we generally be able to explain cultural change? Collective reception should not be misunderstood in terms of reception of internet-mediated mass communication, but draws on the ideas of institutionalization, objectification and legitimating as proposed by Berger and Luckmann. (Berger and Luckmann, 2010) Institutionalization refers to the process of developing habits and with it types of behavior. (Knorr-Cetina, 1989, p. 87) This reciprocal typecasting of habitual behavior on base of stable societal situation is eventually reflected in social roles and completes institutionalization when social roles are passed on to future generations that reach beyond the individual behavior of two actors. (Berger and Luckmann, 2010, p. 63) Roles deploy knowledge threefold: cognitive, affective, as well as norms and values. (Berger and Luckmann, 2010, p. 83) The institutional world comes into play through objectification and externalization. (Berger and Luckmann, 2010, p. 66) So when generations change, legitimating as 'secondary' objectification comes into thought. (Berger and Luckmann, 2010, p. 98) Such processes of legitimation explain and justify such institutional processes towards those, who have not been part of such production processes. (Knorr-Cetina, 1989, p. 87) They therefore allow for sense- making: actors make sense of their different roles, but also throughout their lifetime. (Berger and Luckmann, 2010, p. 99)

Concluding from the explicated processes, both individual and collective reception lead to a *qualitative* and *quantitative* change of temporal understanding. (see figure one).

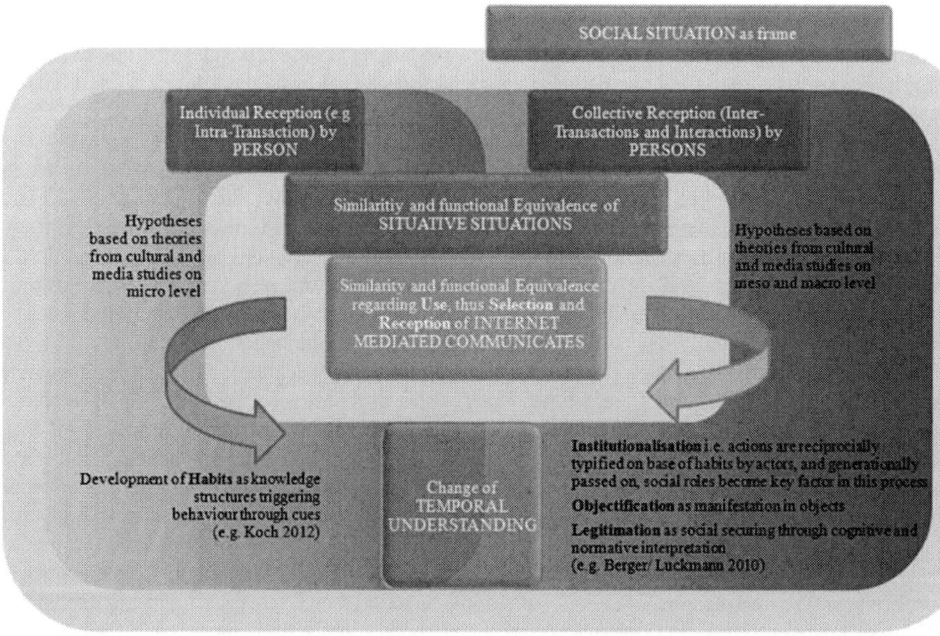

Figure 1. General model of change of temporal understanding

3.2 Cultural and Media Theories to explain change in Temporal Understanding

Assuming that there is an equivalence of temporal understanding in both cultural contexts on the abstract levels of time horizon and dealing with time (Helfrich-Hölter 2011: 128), we now examine at the sub-dimension of temporal understanding and the way it would be changed in more detail. Both mediatization concept (Krotz, 2012b, 2001) and acceleration theory (Rosa, 2005) serve as framework but cannot be fully verified or falsified:

Krotz defines mediatization as a current, long-term (meta) change process of culture and society on different levels that roots in the changing media. (Krotz, 2012b, p. 26) This processual change takes place on different levels. People and their everyday life media communication (micro level), organizations and institutions (meso level) and culture and society as a whole (macro level) are included. (Krotz, 2012a, p. 37)

> "Mediatization thus should be defined as a historical, ongoing, long-term process in which more and more media emerge and are institutionalized. Mediatization describes the process whereby communication refers to media and uses media so that media in the long run increasingly become relevant for the social construction of everyday life, society, and culture as a whole."

So how can mediatization theory help to develop hypothesis? As Krotz regards media as agents of cultural homogenization, it may be assumed that convergence tendencies occur. (Krotz, 2001, p. 204) First, media as used means change temporal understanding quantitatively and qualitatively. Temporally, media offering content evince an increasing availability at all times and are used more often. Furthermore, each individual medium is available more often for a longer period of time. And finally, the internet as an integration medium allows simultaneous communication vertically. Vertical integration means the simultaneous usage of standardized communication (i.e. mass communication), interpersonal communication and interactive communication. (Krotz, 2007, pp. 91–114)

> *H1: Internet-mediated interpersonal communication as well as vertical communication lead towards an orientation of polychronicity in both German and Chinese cultural context.*
> *H1.1: Chinese cultural context remains on the side of polychronicity.*
> *H1.2: German cultural context shifts from the side of instrumental experience (monochronicity) towards polychronicity.*

This goes conjointly with another dimension, pace of life. According to Rosa (Rosa, 2005, pp. 113–114), acceleration phenomena are threefold. They become visible through technical acceleration of processes, through increasing social rates of change and through shortening/increasing of social action episodes. Practices such as multitasking shorten, compress or overlap interaction periods. As we concluded earlier, as a general increase in mediated interpersonal communication means that we have to deal with decreasing response latency in internet-mediated interpersonal communication.

> *H2: Internet-mediated communication leads towards a faster pace of life.*
> *H2.1: Chinese cultural context shifts from a slower pace of life to a faster pace of life.*
> *H2.2: German cultural context remains on the side of faster pace of life.*

4. CONCLUSION

Further research should address the following issues:

i. operationalize the construct temporal understanding,
ii. specify more hypotheses in the sense of a differentiated change of temporal understanding,
iii. and investigate potential outcomes thoroughly.

In order to address the first problem, a comprehensive literature review has to be done, considering quantitative measures with high reliability and validity in both target languages Chinese and German. Concerning the second issue, further theories have to be incorporated. For example, future as planned behavior may decline, which would point towards fatalism and could be postulated on Castells idea of 'timeless time'. (Castells, 2010) Scholars who also dealt with time and technology such as Neverla (Neverla, 2010b, 2010a), Eriksen (Eriksen, 2001), Hassan (Hassan, 2003) or Nowotny (Nowotny, 1995) may also be taken into consideration. Third and finally, the molar context (Früh, 2001) which consists of person, medium and situation should be investigated and sub-hypothesis specified. Potential outcomes should finally be interpreted in the light of Yin Yang (Fang, 2012) and specific culture standards (Thomas, 2011).

REFERENCES

Anckar, C. (2008), "On the Applicability of the Most Similar Systems Design and the Most Different Systems Design in Comparative Research", *International Journal of Social Research Methodology*, Vol. 11 No. 5, pp. 389–401.

Becker, K.-B. (2011), *Internetzensur in China: Aufbau und Grenzen des chinesischen Kontrollsystems*, VS Verlag für Sozialwissenschaften / Springer Fachmedien Wiesbaden GmbH, Wiesbaden, Wiesbaden.

Berger, P.L. and Luckmann, T. (2010), *Die gesellschaftliche Konstruktion der Wirklichkeit: Eine Theorie der Wissenssoziologie,* 23rd ed., Fischer Taschenbuch-Verlag, Frankfurt am Main.

Bluedorn, A.C., Kalliath, T.J., Strube, M.J. and Martin, G.D. (1999), "Polychronicity and the Inventory of Polychronic Values (IPV). The development of an instrument to measure a fundamental dimension of organizational culture", *Journal of Managerial Psychology*, Vol. 14 No. 3/4, pp. 205–230.

Bodde, D. (1991), "Cyclical and linear time", in Bodde, D. (Ed.), *Chinese thought, society, and science: The intellectual and social background of science and technology in pre-modern China*, University of Hawaii Press, Honolulu, pp. 122–133.

Boesch, E.E. (1980), *Kultur und Handlung: Einführung in die Kulturpsychologie*, H. Huber, Bern.

Bolsover, G. (2013), *News in China's new information environment: Dissemination patterns, opinion leaders and news commentary on Weibo, Chinese Internet Research Conference*, Oxford.

Bukow, G.C., Fromme, J. and Jörissen, B. (Eds.) (2012), *Mediale Transformationen unseres Verhältnisses zu Raum und Zeit*, VS Verlag für Sozialwissenschaften, Wiesbaden.

Castells, M. (2010), *The rise of the network society,* 2nd ed., Wiley-Blackwell, Chichester, West Sussex, Malden, MA.

Chen, M.-J. (2002), "Transcending Paradox: The Chinese “Middle Way” Perspective", *Asia Pacific Journal of Management*, Vol. 19, pp. 179–199.

Chevrier, S. (2009), "Is National Culture Still Relevant to Management in a Global Context?: The Case of Switzerland", *International Journal of Cross Cultural Management*, Vol. 9 No. 2, pp. 169–183.

Chinese Culture Connection (1987), "Chinese Values and the Search for Culture-Free Dimensions of Culture", *Journal of Cross-Cultural Psychology*, Vol. 18 No. 2, pp. 143–164.

Dimmick, J., Feaster, J.C. and Hoplamazian, G.J. (2011), "News in the interstices: The niches of mobile media in space and time", *New Media & Society*, Vol. 13 No. 1, pp. 23–39.

Dong, F. (2012), "Controlling the internet in China: The real story", *Convergence: The International Journal of Research into New Media Technologies*, Vol. 18 No. 4, pp. 403–425.

Elias, N. and Schröter, M. (2005), *Über die Zeit.: Arbeiten zur Wissenssoziologie.*, Suhrkamp, Frankfurt am Main.

Ellrich, L. (2003), "Cyber-Zeit. Bemerkungen zur Veränderung des Zeitbegriffs durch die Computertechnik", in Funken, C. and Löw, M. (Eds.), *Raum, Zeit, Medialität: Interdisziplinäre Studien zu neuen Kommunikationstechnologien*, Leske + Budrich, Opladen, pp. 39–69.

Eriksen, T.H. (2001), *Tyranny of the moment: Fast and slow time in the information age*, Pluto Press, London, Sterling, Va.

Fang, T. (1998), *Reflection on Hofstede's fifth dimension: A critique of "Confucian dynamism"., Annual Meeting*, San Diego, CA.

Fang, T. (2003), "A Critique of Hofstede's Fifth National Culture Dimension", *International Journal of Cross Cultural Management*, Vol. 3 No. 3, pp. 347–368.

Fang, T. (2012), "Yin Yang: A New Perspective on Culture", *Management and Organization Review*, Vol. 8 No. 1, pp. 25–50.

Faulstich, W. and Steininger, C. (Eds.) (2002), *Zeit in den Medien, Medien in der Zeit*, W. Fink, München.

Faure, G.O. and Fang, T. (2008), "Changing Chinese values: Keeping up with paradoxes", *International Business Review*, Vol. 17 No. 2, pp. 194–207.

Faust, M. (2010), "Zeitliche Nutzungsmuster des Internet im Tagesablauf. Eine empirische Untersuchung zu den Einflüssen zeitlicher Nutzungsmotive, der zeitlichen Flexibilität der Tätigkeit und der Zeitgebundenheit der Kommunikationsformen", Institut für Kommunikations- und Medienwissenschaft, Universität Leipzig, Leipzig, 14 January.

Felsmann, K.-D. (Ed.) (2008), *Der Rezipient im Spannungsfeld von Zeit und Medien: Erweiterte Dokumentation zu den 11. Buckower Mediengesprächen 2007*, kopaed, München.

Flaherty, M.G. (2005), "Sociotemporal Rhythms in E-mail: A case study", *Time & Society*, Vol. 14 No. 1, pp. 39–49.

Früh, W. (2001), "Der dynamisch-transaktionale Ansatz. Ein integratives Paradigma für Medienrezeption und Medienwirkungen", in Rössler, P., Hasebrink, U. and Jäckel, M. (Eds.), *Theoretische Perspektiven der Rezeptionsforschung*, Fischer, München, pp. 11–34.

Funken, C. and Löw, M. (Eds.) (2003), *Raum, Zeit, Medialität: Interdisziplinäre Studien zu neuen Kommunikationstechnologien*, Leske + Budrich, Opladen.

Geertz, C. (1991), *Dichte Beschreibung: Beiträge zum Verstehen kultureller Systeme,* 2nd ed., Suhrkamp, Frankfurt am Main, Germany.

Geißler, K.A. and Schneider, M. (Eds.) (1999), *Flimmernde Zeiten: Vom Tempo der Medien*, Hirzel, Stuttgart.

German Society for Time Politics e.V. (2014), "Die Deutsche Gesellschaft für Zeitpolitik e.V. stellt sich vor. Wer wir sind und was wir wollen", available at: http://www.zeitpolitik.de/gesellschaft.html (accessed 16 February 2014).

Gesteland, R.R. (2005), *Cross-cultural business behavior: Negotiating, selling, sourcing and managing across cultures,* 4th ed., Copenhagen Business School Press, Copenhagen.

Goonetilleke, R.S. and Luximon, Y. (2010), "The relationship between monochronicity, polychronicity and individual characteristics", *Behaviour & Information Technology*, Vol. 29 No. 2, pp. 187–198.

Hägerstrand, T. (1988), "Time and culture", in Kirsch, G., Nijkamp, P. and Zimmermann, K. (Eds.), *The Formulation of time preferences in a multidisciplinary perspective: Their consequences for individual behaviour and collective decision-making*, Avebury, Aldershot, Hants, England, Brookfield, Vt., USA, pp. 33–42.

Hall, E.T. (1984), *The dance of life: The other dimension of time*, Anchor Press, New York.

Hall, E.T. and Hall, M.R. (1990), *Understanding cultural differences,* 7th ed., Intercultural Press, Yarmouth.

Harkness, J.A., Vijver, Fons J. R. van de and Mohler, P.P. (2003), *Cross-cultural survey methods, Wiley series in survey methodology*, J. Wiley, Hoboken, N.J.

Harsh, T. and Xiao Wu, A. (2013), *How Does the Great Firewall of China Affect User Behaviour?: Isolated 'Internets' as Culturally Defined Markets on the WWW., 11th Chinese Internet Research Conference*, Oxford.

Hassan, R. (2003), *The chronoscopic society: Globalization, time and knowledge in the network economy*, P.Lang, New York.

Hauser, R. (2008), *The Information Society*, Polity Press, Cambridge.

Helfrich, H. (1996), "Psychology of time from a cross-cultural perspective", in Helfrich, H. (Ed.), *Time and mind*, Hogrefe & Huber, Seattle, pp. 103–118.

Helfrich, H. and Quitterer, B. (1999), "Kulturell geprägte Zeitvorstellungen und Unternehmenspraxis in Japan und Deutschland", in German-Japanese Society for Social Sciences (Ed.), *Social and Psychological change of Japan and Germany the last decade of the 20th century: Proceedings of the 5th meeting of the German-Japanese Society for Social Sciences, Waseda University, Tokyo, September 13 - 17, 1998*, Waseda University Press, Tokyo.

Helfrich-Hölter, H. (2011), "Zeit und Kultur", in Dreyer, W. and Hößler, U. (Eds.), *Perspektiven interkultureller Kompetenz*, Vandenhoeck & Ruprecht, Göttingen, pp. 125–136.

Hepp, A. (2013), *Medienkultur: Die Kultur Mediatisierter Welten, Medien - Kultur - Kommunikation*, Springer, Dordrecht.

Herold, D.K. (2013), "Through the Looking Glass. Twenty years of research into the Chinese Internet", available at: http://ssrn.com/abstract=2259045 or http://dx.doi.org/10.2139/ssrn.2259045 (accessed 25 February 2014).

Hofstede, G. (1991), *Cultures and organizations: Software of the mind*, McGraw-Hill, New York.

Hofstede, G.H. (2001), *Culture's consequences: Comparing values, behaviors, institutions, and organizations across nations,* 2nd ed., Sage, Thousand Oaks, Calif.

House, R.J. (Ed.) (2004), *Culture, leadership, and organizations: The GLOBE study of 62 societies*, Sage Publications, Thousand Oaks, Calif.

Jones, J. (1988), "Cultural differences in temporal perspectives: Instrumental and expressive behaviours in time", in McGrath, J.E. (Ed.), *The Social psychology of time: New perspectives*, Sage, Newbury Park, Calif, pp. 21–38.

Kant, I. and Timmermann, J. (1998), *Kritik der reinen Vernunft*, F. Meiner, Hamburg.

Klapproth, F. (2011), "Stable and Variable Characteristics of the Time Perspective in Humans 1", *KronoScope*, Vol. 11 No. 1-2, pp. 41–59.

Kluckhohn, F.R. and Strodtbeck, F.L. (1961), *Variations in Value Orientations*, Row, Peterson, Evanston.

Knorr-Cetina, K. (1989), "Spielarten des Konstruktivismus. Einige Notizen und Anmerkungen", *Soziale Welt*, Vol. 40 No. 1/2, pp. 86–96.

Koch, T. (2010), *Macht der Gewohnheit?: Der Einfluss der Habitualisierung auf die Fernsehnutzung*, VS Verlag für Sozialwissenschaften, Wiesbaden.

Krotz, F. (2001), *Die Mediatisierung kommunikativen Handelns: Der Wandel von Alltag und sozialen Beziehungen, Kultur und Gesellschaft durch die Medien*, Westdeutscher Verlag, Wiesbaden.

Krotz, F. (2007), *Mediatisierung: Fallstudien zum Wandel von Kommunikation*, VS Verlag für Sozialwissenschaften.

Krotz, F. (2012a), "Von der Entdeckung der Zentralperspektive zur Augmented Reality. Wie Mediatisierung funktioniert", in Krotz, F. and Hepp, A. (Eds.), *Mediatisierte Welten: Beschreibungsansatze Und Forschungsfelder*, VS Verlag fur Sozialwissenschaften, pp. 27–55.

Krotz, F. (2012b), "Zeit der Mediatisierung - Mediatisierung der Zeit. Aktuelle Beobachtungen und ihre historischen Bezüge", *Medien & Zeit*, No. 2, pp. 25–34.

Lan, P. (2004), "Is the "Wolf" Coming? An Empirical Study on Cultural Information Spread on Chinese Websites.", in Zhang, J. and Woesler, M. (Eds.), *China's Digital Dream: The Impact of the Internet on Chinese Society*, European University Press, Berlin, pp. 208–225.

Lee, H. (1999), "Time and information technology: monochronicity, polychronicity and temporal symmetry", *European Journal of Information Systems*, Vol. 8 No. 1, pp. 16–26.

Lee, H. and Liebenau, J. (2000a), "Temporal effects of information systems on business processes: focusing on the dimensions of temporality", *Accounting Management and Information Technologies*, Vol. 10, pp. 157–185.

Lee, H. and Liebenau, J. (2000b), "Time and the Internet at the Turn of the Millenium", *Time & Society*, Vol. 9 No. 1, pp. 43–56.

Lee, H. and Sawyer, S. (2010), "Conceptualizing time, space and computing for work and organizing", *Time & Society*, Vol. 19 No. 3, pp. 293–317.

Leong, S., Mitew, T., Celletti, M. and Pearson, E. (2010), "The question concerning (internet) time", *New Media & Society*, Vol. 11 No. 8, pp. 1267–1285.

Leung, K., Bhagat, R.S., Buchan, N.R., Erez, M. and Gibson, C.B. (2005), "Culture and international business: recent advances and their implications for future research", available at: http://iew3.technion.ac.il/~merez/papers/jibs_culture_Intern_B.pdf (accessed 10 July 2012).

Levine, R.V. (1996), "Cultural differences in the pace of life", in Helfrich, H. (Ed.), *Time and mind*, Hogrefe & Huber, Seattle, pp. 119–140.

Levine, R.V. (1998a), *A geography of time: On tempo, culture, and the pace of life*, Basic Books, New York.

Levine, R.V. (1998b), *Eine Landkarte der Zeit: Wie Kulturen mit der Zeit umgehen*, Piper, München, Zürich.

Levine, R.V. and Norenzayan, A. (1999), "The Pace of Life in 31 Countries", *Journal of Cross-Cultural Psychology*, Vol. 30 No. 2, pp. 178–205.

Lindquist, J.D. and Kaufman-Scarborough, C. (2007), "The Polychronic Monochronic Tendency Model: PMTS scale development and validation", *Time & Society*, Vol. 16 No. 2/3, pp. 253–285.

Long, A. and Schweppe, R.P. (2010), *Die 7 Geheimnisse der Schildkröte: Den Alltag entschleunigen, das Leben entdecken, Heyne*, Vol. 70148, Taschenbucherstausg, Heyne, München.

Mittag, A. (1997), "Zeitkonzepte in China", in Rüsen, J. and Müller, K.E. (Eds.), *Historische Sinnbildung: Problemstellungen, Zeitkonzepte, Wahrnehmungshorizonte, Darstellungsstrategien*, Rowohlt, Reinbek bei Hamburg, pp. 251–276.

Möhring, W. and Schlütz, D. (2010), *Die Befragung in der Medien- und Kommunikationswissenschaft: Eine praxisorientierte Einführung,* 2nd ed., VS Verlag für Sozialwissenschaften, Wiesbaden.

Museum for Communication Berlin (2013), "Tempo, Tempo! Im Wettlauf mit der Zeit", available at: http://www.mfk-berlin.de/tempo-tempo-im-wettlauf-mit-der-zeit/ (accessed 10 February 2014).

National Museum of American History (2016), "On Time. How America Has Learned to Live by the Clock", available at: http://americanhistory.si.edu/ontime/ (accessed 15 April 2016).

Neuberger, C. (2010), ""Jetzt" ist Trumpf. Beschleunigungstendenzen im Internetjournalismus", in Westerbarkey, J. (Ed.), *End-Zeit-Kommunikation: Diskurse der Temporalität*, Lit, Berlin, Münster.

Neverla, I. (2010a), "Medien als soziale Zeitgeber im Alltag. Ein Beitrag zur kultursoziologischen Wirkungsforschung", in Hepp, A. and Hartmann, M. (Eds.), *Die Mediatisierung der Alltagswelt*, 1st ed., VS Verlag für Sozialwissenschaften, Wiesbaden, pp. 183–194.

Neverla, I. (2010b), "Zeit als Schlüsselkategorie der Medienkultur und ihrer Wandlungsprozesse", in Hepp, A. (Ed.), *Medienkultur im Wandel*, 1st ed., UVK, Konstanz, pp. 135–147.

Newman, K.L. and Nollen, S.D. (1996), "Culture and Congruence: The Fit between Management Practices and National Culture", *Journal of International Business Studies*, Vol. 27 No. 4, pp. 753–779.

Nowotny, H. (1989), *Eigenzeit: Entstehung und Strukturierung eines Zeitgefühls*, Suhrkamp, Frankfurt am Main.

Nowotny, H. (1995), *Eigenzeit: Entstehung und Strukturierung eines Zeitgefühls,* 2nd ed., Suhrkamp, Frankfurt am Main.

Nowzad, R.M. (2011), *Zeit der Medien Medien der Zeit,* 1st ed., Lit, Münster, Westf.

Opitz, F. (2013), *Speed - Auf der Suche nach der verlorenen Zeit.*

Pace Beijing (2014), *Bejing Voice: Exhibition Poster*, 798 Art District, No. 2 Jiuxianqiao Road Beijing, p. 1.

Palmer, D.K. and Schoorman, F.D. (1999), "Unpackaging the multiple aspects of time in polychronicity", *Journal of Managerial Psychology*, Vol. 14 No. 3/4, pp. 323–345.

Plocher, T., Gonnetilleke, R.S., Yan, Z. and Liang, S.-F.M. (2013), "Time Orientaton Across Cultures", available at: http://www-ieem.ust.hk/dfaculty/ravi/papers/iwips.pdf (accessed 6 June 2013).

Quitterer, B. (2000), "Die Esskultur als Spiegelbild japanischer Lebensrhythmen", in Liscutin, N. and Haak, R. (Eds.), *Japanstudien: Jahrbuch des Deutschen Instituts für Japanstudien der Philipp Franz von Siebold Stiftung*, Judicium, München, pp. 157–182.

Rantanen, T. (2005), *The media and globalization*, Sage, London.

Reckwitz, A. (2000), *Die Transformation der Kulturtheorien: Zur Entwicklung eines Theorieprogramms,* 1st ed., Velbrück Wissenschaft, Weilerswist.

Redpath, L. and O. Nielsen, M. (1997), "A Comparison of Native Culture, Non-Native Culture and New Management Ideology", *Canadian Journal of Administrative Sciences*, Vol. 14 No. 3, pp. 327–339.

Rinderspacher, J. (2011), "Rezension. Nils Weichert: Zeitpolitik - Legitimation und Reichweite eines neuen Politikfeldes.", *Zeitpolitisches Magazin*, Vol. 8 No. 18, pp. 22–23.

Rippl, S. and Seipel, C. (2008), *Methoden kulturvergleichender Sozialforschung: Eine Einführung*, VS Verlag für Sozialwissenschaften, Wiesbaden.

Rosa, H. (2005), *Beschleunigung: Die Veränderung der Zeitstrukturen in der Moderne,* 1st ed., Suhrkamp, Frankfurt am Main.

Somweber, M. (2013), "erschöpft. Zum Umgang mit Zeit, Leistung und Sinn", available at: http://www.virgil.at/fileadmin/user_upload/downloads/Folder_erschoepft-2013_e3.pdf (accessed 16 February 2014).

State Ministry for Education and Research (2010), "BMBF-Foresight-Prozess", available at: http://www.bmbf.de/de/12673.php (accessed 3 August 2011).

Strathman, A., Gleicher, F., Boninger, D.S. and Edwards, C.S. (1994), "The consideration of future consequences: Weighing immediate and distant outcomes of behavior", *Journal of Personality and Social Psychology*, Vol. 66 No. 4, pp. 742–752.

Tang, T. (2011), "Marketing higher education across borders: a cross-cultural analysis of university websites in the US and China", *Chinese Journal of Communication*, Vol. 4 No. 4, pp. 417–429.

The International Society for the Study of Time (2005), "ISST Home Page", available at: http://www.studyoftime.org/ (accessed 16 May 2011).

Thomas, A. (2005), *Grundlagen der interkulturellen Psychologie, Interkulturelle Bibliothek*, Vol. 55, Bautz, Nordhausen.

Thomas, A. (2011), "Das Kulturstandardkonzept", in Dreyer, W. and Hößler, U. (Eds.), *Perspektiven interkultureller Kompetenz*, Vandenhoeck & Ruprecht, Göttingen, pp. 97–124.

Triandis, H.C. (1995), *Individualism & collectivism, New directions in social psychology*, Westview Press, Boulder.

Trompenaars, F. and Hampden-Turner, C. (2000), *Riding the waves of culture: Understanding cultural diversity in business,* 2nd ed., Brealey, London.

University of Leipzig (2011), "Studium universale zum Thema Zeit startet am 12. Oktober", available at: http://www.zv.uni-leipzig.de/service/presse/pressemeldungen.html?ifab_modus=detail&ifab_id=4264 (accessed 10 October 2011).

Usunier, J.-C. and Valette-Florence, P. (2007), "The Time Styles Scale: A review of developments and replications over 15 years", *Time & Society*, Vol. 16 No. 2/3, pp. 333–366.

Westerbarkey, J. (Ed.) (2010), *End-Zeit-Kommunikation: Diskurse der Temporalität*, Lit, Berlin, Münster.

Wurm, K.-G. (2012), "Phänomen Zeit – Medien als Zeittreiber Medieninduzierte Moralvorstellungen und Erwartungshaltungen im Bezug auf die Zeit", in Bukow, G.C., Fromme, J. and Jörissen, B. (Eds.), *Mediale Transformationen unseres Verhältnisses zu Raum und Zeit*, VS Verlag für Sozialwissenschaften, Wiesbaden, pp. 101–116.

Yang, G. (2012), "A Chinese Internet? History, practice, and globalization", *Chinese Journal of Communication*, Vol. 5 No. 1, pp. 49–54.

Yeh, R.-S. and Lawrence, J.J. (1995), "Individualism and Confucian Dynamism: A Note on Hofstede's Cultural Root to Economic Growth", *Journal of International Business Studies*, Vol. 26 No. 3, pp. 655–669.

Zimbardo, P.G. and Boyd, J. (1999), "Putting Time in Perspective. A Valid, Reliable Individual-Differences Metric", *Journal of Personality & Social Psychology*, Vol. 77 No. 6, pp. 1271–1288.

Zimbardo, P.G. and Boyd, J. (2008), *The time paradox: The new psychology of time that will change your life*, Free Press, New York.

THE ROLE OF ARCHITECTURAL DESIGN IN VIRTUAL WORLDS FOR EDUCATIONAL PURPOSES

Noha Saleeb, Georgios Dafoulas and Martin Loomes
Computer Science Department, School of Science & Technology
Middlesex University

ABSTRACT

This paper discusses the investigation of how architectural digital design elements of virtual worlds affect learning experiences. In particular, the research study focused on 3D virtual educational facilities and their impact on learning experience in comparison to real life in-class experiences. Emphasis is given on how a range of learning objectives affect design efforts in virtual worlds intended for supporting learning activities. Examples of how virtual worlds may transform learning experiences include information retention, participation and enjoyment. The paper considers design elements that have a causal effect to such learning objectives and considers what design recommendations could be used to enhance the student's overall learning experience in 3D VLEs.

KEYWORDS

Virtual Worlds, Second Life, 3D Virtual Learning Environments, architectural design

1. INTRODUCTION

This paper revisits previous work in an effort to provide a research method for collecting and analyzing data on virtual worlds used for educational purposes. The paper's scope is twofold (i) to provide a set of guidelines for a multi-stage research approach in investigating how 3D worlds' educational features can be used for enhancing e-learning activities and (ii) to discuss the findings relating to the impact of various architectural features in the effectiveness of 3D virtual learning environments.

The work presented in this paper provides a concise summary of data collection practices over several years in multi-disciplinary area. The authors focused on various aspects from three areas of work, namely education (in particular e-learning practices), architecture (emphasis on specific elements of learning spaces) and Information & Communication technologies (ICT) and their role in supporting learning activities. Second Life was the platform of choice at the beginning of this study and is currently used as there is a significant infrastructure that supports learning activities.

Initially this work was concerned with the ways virtual world environments affected student satisfaction, and in particular the role of architecture in 3D education (Saleeb and Dafoulas, 2011). The research followed a more detailed investigation in the way 3D learning spaces enhance e-learning experiences and how certain design measures can help improving learning experiences (Saleeb and Dafoulas, 2012). An interesting twist of previous work involved considerations in how Artificial Intelligence (AI) could be used for supporting e-learning pedagogies with the use of 3D Virtual Learning Environments (VLE) (Saleeb and Dafoulas, 2013). Most recent work focuses on ubiquitous learning and personalization of 3D learning spaces for improving learning experiences (Saleeb et al, 2015).

2. RESEARCH METHODOLOGY

As mentioned in the introductory section, the research study was based on collecting information about the impact certain 3D virtual world architectural features would have in the learning process. It was imperative to follow an approach that would be based on different techniques in order to ensure the accuracy of the investigation results. Within the research discussed in this paper, data collection is divided into four (4) phases, each with a definite objective, conducted using different methods, to feed its results into the next phase and help design it.

2.1 Sequential Research Phases

The **first phase** of the data collection involved survey questionnaires consisting of a number of closed-ended questions which were distributed, after pilot trials involving students, in order to record participants' opinions about different architectural design characteristics in different existing 3D virtual learning spaces that the students are subjected to in Second Life. Furthermore open-ended survey questions were used to capture students' propositions and requirements from the design of 3D educational facilities. Interviews and focus groups with students and staff were then used for validating the previous results. This phase was designed in a way to derive how learners experienced the different architectural features of the learning space within the virtual world. Statistical conclusions derived from these quantitative methods would preliminarily verify the presence of an effect for 3D architectural design elements of learning spaces on students (proving the deductive hypothesis within this research), and also highlight some of the more appreciated or depreciated features of design to be taken into consideration in the next phase of data collection. It is obvious that this first stage is feasible for most research studies, as far as the researchers are able to follow a questionnaire design process and have the skills to analyse responses, as well as triangulate data collection with the use of additional techniques (e.g. focus groups and observations).

The **second phase**, was based on controlled quantitative experiments conducted after pilot trials inside Second Life, as a representative of 3D VLEs, where only one independent variable per experiment is changed e.g. colour, texture, shape of space, dimensions. This approach provides an opportunity to engage in observations through pilot studies with end users. This technique provides an alternative way to determine those architectural features that have a significant impact on the learning process. The focus is on a selection of variables that should be tested which are determined based on (i) most appreciated 3D virtual design elements recorded during the first phase, and (ii) the element to test must be previously researched for its effect on learning in the physical world. During this phase, students were placed inside this controlled environment, and after taking an e-learning session inside it while changing the attributes of this controlled variable several times, quantitative survey questionnaires were collected to depict students' opinions and feelings throughout the session towards different variations of the variable (e.g. different shapes, different colours). Qualitative video and audio recordings were also taken of the sessions to be analysed for validation of findings and for further extraction of student satisfaction or dissatisfaction evidences towards different design elements. Findings from this phase should determine best and worst variations, of each 3D architectural design element, to be used in the final phase (phase 4) to test their measured effects on the e-learning process.

The **third phase**, is concerned with the triangulation and validation of findings from students' data in phase 2, which is done through performing individual interviews with experts in the field (educational staff and 3D architectural designers and architects). The phase aims to derive what practical guidelines they utilise for designing 3D virtual educational facilities and what feedback they know from experience with students about their requirements from architectural design of their 3D learning spaces. This is a critical stage as it aligns primary data representing findings from pilot studies and surveys with end users to the views of experts. The techniques used offer a reality check as it can be used to compare own research findings with the views of experts and other practitioners.

The **fourth phase**, of data collection provides a qualitative approach as it involves conducting controlled qualitative experiments involving students who receive an e-learning session inside a learning space, that is a predesigned prototype in which only one variation of one architectural feature is applied per experiment (independent variable). This experiment is repeated for two variations of each architectural element identified and chosen during phases 2 & 3. This technique is very important in order to obtain an understanding of the impact specific architectural features have for specific learning experiences. These experiments are then repeated with different groups of students. This is also necessary to establish a good understanding of how each feature impacts learning with the involvement of a significant number of subjects. It is also necessary to reflect on whether the effects of architectural features are the same across different learning groups. The two chosen variations of each tested element are what phase 2 results initially show as being the best and worst preferred by students for that design element. This is done to capture the change or effect these variations have on the e-learning process itself, by measuring students' retention (understanding), participation and enjoyment during each experiment. One of the key contributions of this research study has been the proof of impact towards these three concepts associated with learning experiences of students.

In terms of applying the proposed method, it is important to clarify that when one experiment is completed with all groups of students, the next experiment with another design element variation is performed with the same groups of students. This means that each experiment goes through a sequence of element testing with the same cohort. Besides measuring experiment outcomes, sessions inside Second Life are recorded audio visually to be transcribed and examined. The authors found that having a detailed archive of recordings from all experiments allowed them to put their quantitative results in perspective by observing the behavior of avatars during each learning session.

During the final data analysis phase, from all surveys, controlled quantitative and qualitative experiments, and interviews the authors determined which architectural design elements have an effect on a student's e-learning experience, and what the extent of that effect is with specific variations of that design element. This helped initiating a framework of guidelines, for 3D architectural design of educational buildings, inside 3D virtual learning environments.

2.2 List of Proposed Research steps and Corresponding Outputs

The sequential research process described above provides a structured approach towards the collection of primary data for the impact of architectural features in e-learning experiences using virtual worlds. This research study was based on using a series of pilot studies and various data collection techniques involving learners, instructors and experts. The authors have presented their findings widely and applied them in different learning settings such as undergraduate and postgraduate cohorts, distance and blended learning modes, higher and further education programmes, educational programmes and continuous professional development short courses, university classes and training sessions. The aim of the proposed series of data collection steps was to establish a set of guidelines for good practice that could be used by practitioners and researchers in various fields. The approach could be used in the same field that is the experimentation with virtual world environments, related areas such as e-learning, mentoring, teaching and instruction-centred design, but also in the wider research context of data collection through application, observation and surveying.

A summary of the approach is illustrated in the figure below that clarifies how each phase consists of a number of steps and their associated outputs. Each output has a specific objective that must be mapped to specific research objectives, while the identified steps compose the overall research process of the study.

As shown in figure 1, the four data collection phases can be identified as follows:

I. Verifying the impact and specific effects of 3D architectural elements on e-learning.
II. Identifying variations of design elements for testing with respect to different effects on e-learning.
III. Obtaining expert views on 3D architectural design.
IV. Findings the effect of best and worst variations from design elements on e-learning components.

Many participants within the experiments, in this phase of data collection, took part earlier in phase 1 surveys and phase 2 quantitative experiments. The total number of students who consented to participate was 77, from the School of Engineering at Middlesex University, distributed almost evenly among 6 groups (classes) from different year levels – foundation and final year.

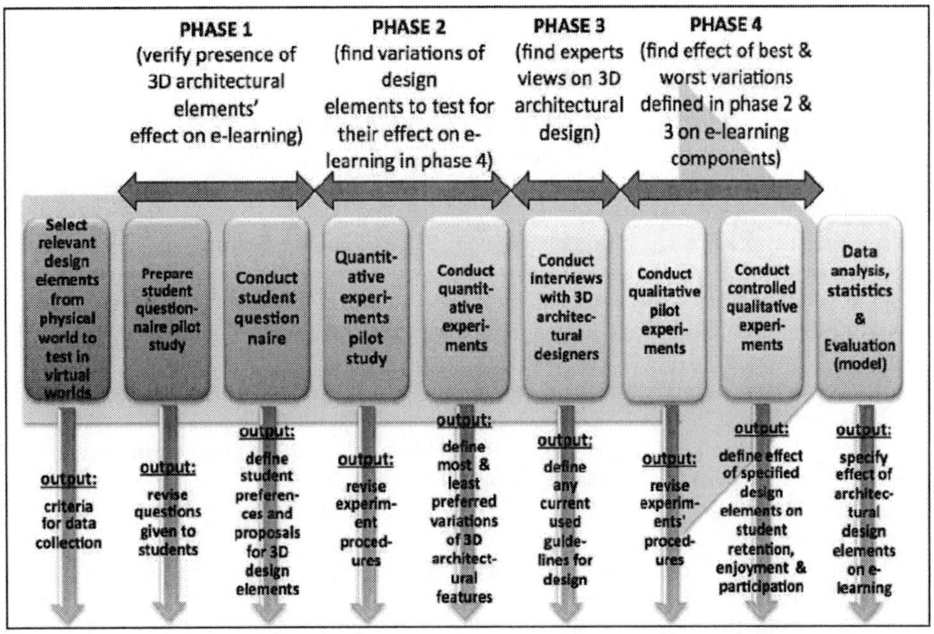

Figure 1. Sequential research stages to prepare a working list of 3D architectural design elements for 3D virtual educational facilities to enhance the e-learning process

The steps associated with each phase are as follows:

I. Architectural element impact
  a. Collection of design elements, focusing on selecting relevant design elements from physical world to test in virtual worlds (associated output: criteria for data collection).
  b. Design of primary data collection tools focusing on preparing student questionnaires for pilot studies (associated output: revised questions for student participants)
  c. Conduct data collection focusing on conducting student surveys (associated output: definition of student preferences and proposals for 3D design elements)

II. Design element variations
  a. Design pilot study for quantitative data collection focusing on designing quantitative experiments pilot study (associated output: revised experiment procedures)
  b. Conduct quantitative experiments focusing on experiment stages and data collection (associated output: definition of the most and least preferred variations of 3D architectural features)

III. Expert views
  a. Design interview-based data collection focusing on conducting interviews with 3D architectural designers (associated output: definition of currently used design guidelines for 3D spaces)
  b. Conduct semi-structured interviews focusing on obtaining expert views (associated output: collection of architectural features used in 3D spaces)

IV. Effect of element variations
  a. Design pilot study for quantitative data collection focusing on preparing the necessary data collection tools (associated output: experiment guidelines and pilot scenarios)
  b. Conduct qualitative experiments focusing on (associated output: revised experiment procedures)
  c. Perform statistical data analysis focusing on (associated output: definitions of the effects from each design element on student retention, enjoyment and participation)
  d. Evaluate proposed conceptual model focusing on reflecting on aspects of each architectural feature and its impact on e-learning (associated output: revised conceptual model and framework for good practices)

3. PROPOSING BEST DESIGN PRACTICES FOR 3D VIRTUAL LEARNING SPACES

The results of the data collection process in this research study are summarized in a series of three tables. Due to the page limitations only one of these tables is included in this paper. The data collection results were analysed using inferential statistics tests ANOVA and CHI^2 to prove their representation of the whole population of higher education students in 3D VLEs. Included in the tables is also a set of guidelines to help initialize a framework for architectural design of 3D educational facilities in 3DVLEs analogous to that existing in the physical world. For each row in the table representing an architectural design element, the findings are divided up into 5 sections denoting the 5 columns in the tables as follows.

- Best design recommendations for that architectural element used in real-life to build physical learning spaces – derived from literature review.
- 3D virtual design elements favoured by students (under-graduate, post-graduate and adult learners) for an e-learning space in 3D VLEs – derived from phase 1 questionnaires.
- Specific variations of the design element that are best preferred by students (males and females) for their 3D virtual learning space – derived from phase 2 experiments.
- Best design guidelines provided by designers for each architectural element – derived from phase 3 interviews.
- The variation of each design element inducing most retention, participation and enjoyment from students – derived from phase 4 experiments.

The findings of the 5th column in the tables are the only ones, which can be included in an initial framework of guidelines for designing educational spaces in 3D VLEs. This is because their specific effects on retention, participation and enjoyment of students during e-learning have been tested, measured and validated, unlike other recommendations in the other columns which have not all been tested and thus can only be considered tentatively for designing in 3D VLEs until further tested in future work.

The colour codes used in the table are representing the following:

- Green denotes all design recommendations for virtual buildings (from phases 1-4 / columns 2-5) that are **similar** to design guidelines for real-life buildings (column 1).
- Red denotes all design recommendations for virtual buildings (from phases 1-4 / columns 2-5) that are **different** from design guidelines for real-life buildings (column 1).
- Yellow denotes all design recommendations for virtual buildings (from phases 1-4 / columns 2-5) that are **contradicting** with all other columns including contradictions inside the same column.

As evident from the table, the only architectural element where the best design recommendations for building 3D virtual learning spaces were the same as those for building physical learning spaces was colour. All other 3D virtual design recommendations for all other architectural elements, whether tested in phase 4 or just preferences of students, were different from those used in real-life. This provides evidence for the research argument, mentioned in chapter 1, that best design specifications for building 3D virtual educational facilities might be different from those in the physical world due to the disparity in nature between both environments. This therefore emphasizes the significance of this research to derive the new design specifications best suited for students' e-learning in 3D VLEs. Furthermore this fact highlights the ad-hoc practices of current virtual designers who either use real life design guidelines based on their experience to build in 3D VLEs, or other untested virtual design guidelines based on their personal tastes not on students'.

Table 1. General Results and an initial framework of architectural design recommendations for Building in 3D VLEs

Architectural Design Guidelines Recommended for Building Educational Facilities in Real Life, and 3D VLEs					
	Most recommended in Real Life Design of Educational Facilities (Literature)	Virtual Design Elements in 3D VLEs from the 4 Phases of Data Collection & Analysis			
		Most preferred by students **(Phase 1)**	Most preferred by students **(Phase 2)**	Most recommended by designers **(Phase3)**	Most enhancing Retention, Participation, Enjoyment **(Phase 4)**
Space Shape	**L-shaped, Rectangle width:length = 1:2**	under graduate: **circle** post graduate: **rectangle** adult learner: **circle**	males: **circle** females: **circle**	**- rectangle / cube shape** **- circular or octagon shape**	**Circle**
Size Dimensions & Height	**Area ~ 30m sq. length : width = 2:1 minimum width 4m**	under graduate: **large, width:height = 4:1** post graduate: **large, width:length:height = 1:2:1** adult learner: **large, width:height = 4:1**	males: **large width, height, length than real-life** females: **large width, height, length than real-life**	**- size 200% > real-life** **- size 150% > real-life** **- size 25% > real-life** **- maximum length 40m** **- maximum length 20m** **- minimum length 15m** **- minimum length 10m** **- no minimum length** **- minimum height 5m**	**Area (~ 250m sq. = 8 times size of class in real-life) Height - 7m**
Interior Lighting & Open Walls %	**20% open walls for windows**	under graduate: **50% open walls/roof, strong internal lighting** post graduate: **60% open walls/roof** adult learner: **50% open walls/roof**	not tested	**- 50% open space** **- 100% open space** **- define completely open spaces with borders e.g. trees, pillars** **- phantom (walk-through) walls** **- walls transparent on approach**	**60% open walls and ceiling**
Colours	**Light colours e.g. white, green, blue**	under graduate: **light bright colors, paneling above windows** post graduate: **light bright colors, paneling above windows** adult learner: **light bright colors**	males: **green, grey, white, light blue** females: **white, green, pink, light blue**	**- no overcolouring** **- soft cool neutral pastel colours** **- colours not too bright or warm (except for children)** **- no solid black or white**	**Light blue**
Textures / Floor, Wall & Ceiling Design	**Tiles, wood for floors. Stucco for walls. Stucco, artificial panels for false ceiling**	under graduate: **mixed color wood , dark smooth carpeting** post graduate: **smooth carpet flooring, rough outdoor tiles, retractable glass roof** adult learner: **light wood, open roof, no dark textures**	males: **light wood, metallic, carpet / stained glass & glass / decorative, arabian, coloured panels** females: **light wood, vinyl carpet / stained glass & glass / arabian**	**- no over texturing or patterns** **- plain textures e.g. stone wood concrete stucco marble tiles** **- no glow or interlacing** **- no carpet , brick, plywood (SL default)** **- use high quality texture** **- use sky, nature texture** **- grey industrial feel** **- corroded faded effect** **- glass walls** **- dome roof, semi-open or open**	**Light wood, glass & stained glass, coloured panels**

Shape

Regarding the shape of the learning space, best recommended in real-life is the rectangular shape or L-shape. According to Rensselaer (2010), this is because a rectangle with width more than half and less than two-thirds the length is much more pleasing than a shape with no comparative dimensions - the shape would be obvious at once, nothing is left to the imagination. Also the L-shape is multi functional and provides less variation of decay rate of sound than the rectangle (Sato and Koyasu, 1959). However table 2 demonstrates that preferences of students (from phases 1 and 2), and tests (from phase 4) reveal that the circular shape induces higher retention, participation and enjoyment during e-learning in 3D VLEs than the rectangular shape of the same size (but similar to a rectangle with double the size of the circle). This could be because as Batson (2010) claims, rooms should be rounded since sight lines and visual perception of space is relatively easy with equal dimension shapes. Also the circle gives a sense of connection, community, wholeness, safety, perfection, and comfort (which students agreed on in phase 2 experiments), while rectangles are associated with order, logic, and containment. While rectangles also suggest mass and volume in real-life because of their rigid points, the perception is possibly different in 3D VLEs, since as told by students during phase 2 and 4 experiments in Second Life, the circle room was perceived as bigger even though it was the same area as the rectangle room also tested. Interviews with designers showed contradictory opinions between commending rectangular, circular and octagonal shapes, proving the ad-hoc, currently undefined process of 3D virtual design, which is not based on students' needs. Conclusively, usage of circular shapes for e-learning spaces in 3D VLEs can be added to the framework of design guidelines for 3D virtual educational buildings.

Size

The association between class size and student achievement has been investigated in the past (Ehrenberg et al, 2001) According to Hall (2001) the optimum number of students in a physical classroom is 15 to give maximum benefit for learning achievement. Hence all physical and virtual learning space sizes considered in this thesis are for 15 students. In real-life, a common classroom size for such a number is 30m2 with ceiling height 3-4m, although Eberhard (2008) recommends a minimum area of 60m2, and an optimum area of 80m2 to allow adequate movement between students. In Second Life, during phase 4 experiments, this area was found to be too small for students' comfort and preference. As demonstrated in table 2, the area of a 3D virtual class or seminar room encouraging highest retention, participation and enjoyment in 3D VLEs was 240m2 with a ceiling height of 7m for a 15-student group. This is 8 times the size of a normal physical classroom, and 3 times the size of an optimum physical area. This contradicting finding to real-life was encouraged by students' preferences from phase 1 and 2, and tested in phase 4. A much larger 3D virtual size of 500m2 also induced high enjoyment but with a decrease in retention and participation. Similar to the previous design element, designers' opinions from interviews of phase 3 were contradictory with each other regarding minimum and maximum lengths, widths and heights, as shown in table 2. This provides further evidence to the indeterminate current process of 3D virtual design. Conclusively, recommending usage of 240m2 area and 7m height for e-learning spaces in 3D VLEs can be added to the framework of design guidelines for 3D virtual educational buildings.

Colours

Fink (2002) suggested soft colours in classrooms were associated with better attendance and positive attitudes in real-life. Also while warm colours can visually reduce space scale and size, cool colours visually enlarge a space making it less confining (Daggett et al., 2008). Specifically, lighter shades of green and blue, like nature, induce positive relaxation and comfort emotions, helping create a calm learning atmosphere, filter negativity and reduce disciplinary problems (Sasson, 2007). Also no more than 6 colours should be used in a learning environment as this could strain the mind's cognitive abilities, cause eyestrain, glare and distraction. As shown in table 2 there was an agreement regarding best favoured colours to use inside a learning environment in both physical and virtual class rooms. For while white, blue and green (cool colours) are most prominently used in real-life, light blue was found in phase 4 experiments to induce higher retention, participation and enjoyment for students than the other tested colour (yellow). Furthermore blue received highest regard by students in phase 1 and 2, and also by designers in phase 3 interviews, along with recommendation for soft colours and no over colouring of the virtual environment. Thus using light blue colour can be recommended for the framework of design specifications for 3D virtual educational buildings.

Textures

According to Interrante & Kim (2001), highly anisotropic textures in real-life can hinder perception of shape, i.e. if they consist of elements that are elongated in a specific direction. Commonly used textures in real-life are tiles and wood for floors, stucco and tiles for walls, stucco and artificial panels for ceilings. These are contrary to findings for the optimum textures to be used in 3D virtual spaces, as derived from phase 4 experiments and approved by students in phase 1 and 2. The 3D textures inducing highest retention, participation and enjoyment for floors, walls and ceilings were lightwood, glass and stained glass, and coloured panels. The only agreement with real-life textures was that all should be plain as indicated by Interrante & Kim (2001). Designers suggested completely contradicting textures between grey, rough, brick and others, which are completely different from students' needs and desires. Thus using lightwood, glass and coloured panel textures can be recommended for the framework of design specifications for 3D virtual educational buildings.

4. CONTRIBUTION TO KNOWLEDGE

The main contribution to knowledge within this research is providing evidence that 3D virtual architecture affects e-learning in 3D VLEs. However, this research study offers the following four (4) contribution outcomes to the body of knowledge. Each contribution complements all three (3) major fields addressed in this study, namely (i) education, (ii) architecture, and (iii) information and communication technology (ICT) as follows:

- By synthesising and defining advantageous and disadvantageous themes of using 3D Virtual Learning Environments. This contribution allows future researchers to determine how 3D VLEs can be used for enhancing learning and support learners in various activities.
- By producing evaluation and assessment reports of the effects of 3D virtual educational architecture on student satisfaction from e-learning in 3D Virtual Learning Environments to fill in the gap of research in this area. This was attained through analysis of the data results collected from the questionnaires of phase 1 and experiments of phase 2 during the process of this research.
- By deriving 3D virtual design elements of learning spaces best suited to enhance students' e-learning experiences, namely retention, participation and enjoyment. This was attained through analysis of the data results collected from phase 4 experiments during the process of this research. This contribution is essential for organizing the otherwise ad-hoc current 3D user specifications used for building educational facilities in 3D Virtual Learning Environments unveiled by designers in phase 3 interviews.
- By creating an initial framework of design guidelines or specifications for modelling successful learning spaces in 3D Virtual Learning Environments, which is currently non-present, to be comparable to its counterpart used for building in the physical world. This was achieved through analysis of the data results collected from phase 4 experiments

The first contribution is theoretically beneficial for educators considering incorporating 3D virtual Learning environments in their programs and weighing the advantages against disadvantages of utilising them for teaching students. The second, third and fourth contributions are practically beneficial for practitioners in the field, namely designers and experts building inside 3D VLEs, to utilize the issued tested recommendations and findings in this thesis to create future 3D virtual educational buildings and campuses inside 3D VLEs for best enhancement of the e-learning experience. This is because in agreement with Smelik et al. (2010), one of the main challenges ahead is to enhance the level of control provided to designers, who will often wish to manually edit and fine-tune built entities on a more detailed level than just terrain features in a virtual world, to more precisely fit their requirements. The work done in this research helps customisation and enhancement of the 3D learning space by (i) providing definite preferences and dislikes towards certain variations of architectural design elements, and proposed suggestions offered by students for improvement of their learning space design and (ii) providing specific variations of 3D architectural elements to enhance measured retention, participation and enjoyment of students.

5. CONCLUSION

This paper presented a multi-stage method for primary data collection in virtual worlds, with emphasis on the 3D VLE elements and their impact on e-learning. The paper emphasized on the importance of each stage for collecting user perceptions and monitoring user behavior in learning scenarios. The method also covers primary data collection tasks associated with the collection of expert views, as well as offering data collection triangulation and validation. The proposed method provides a good practice framework for similar studies but also any scenario-based research pilots involving 3D VLEs or virtual worlds in general. The paper also provides a summary of findings for key architectural elements with proven impact on learning processes supported with 3D VLEs.

REFERENCES

Batson, T. (2010). The Imagined Space of The Web 2.0 Classroom. Campus Technology. Retrieved June 15, 2016, from http://campustechnology.com/Articles/2010/01/20/The-Imagined-Space-of-The-Web-2-Classroom.aspx?Page=1

Daggett, W. R., Cobble, J. E., & Gertel, S. J. (2008). Color in an Optimum Learning Environment. International Center for Leadership in Education, Rexford, NY.

Eberhard, J. P. (2008). 'A Place to Learn: How Architecture Affects Hearing and Learning', The ASHA Leader, vol.13, no. 14, pp.26-27,29

Ehrenberg, R.G., Brewer, D.J., Gamoran, A. Willms, J.D. (2001) Class Size and Student Achievement. Psychological Science in the Public Interest. Vol. 2. No. 1.

Fink, I. (2002). Classroom Use and Utilization. Facilities Manager - APPA, May/June.

Hall, L. D. (2001). Effect of School Architecture on its students (Environmental psychology). Retrieved June 15, 2016, from Design Community Architecture Discussion: http://www.designcommunity.com/discussion/26903.html

Interrante, V. L. & Kim, S. (2001). 'Investigating the Effect of Texture Orientation on the Perception of 3D Shape', in Human Vision and Electronic Imaging VI, vol. 4299, SPIE, pp. 330–339

Rensselaer, M. (2010). A Manual of Homemaking. Retrieved June 15, 2016, from http://chestofbooks.com/food/household/A-Manual-Of-Home-Making/Room-Shape-And-Proportion.html

Saleeb, N. & Dafoulas, G. (2011). 'Effects of Virtual World Environments in Student Satisfaction: An Investigation of Role of Architecture in 3D Education', International Journal of Knowledge Society Research (IJKSR), vol. 2, no.1, pp.28-48.

Saleeb, N. & Dafoulas, G. (2012). 'Architectural Evolution of e-Learning Virtual Worlds: Proposed Design Measures to Enhance the e-Learning Experience within 3D Learning Spaces', in Wankel C. & Hinrichs R. (2012) Engaging the Avatar: New Frontiers in Immersive Education, Emerald Publishing, Bingley, UK, pp. 49-81.

Saleeb, N. & Dafoulas, G. (2013). 'Artificial Intelligence in 3D Virtual Environments as Technological Support for Pedagogy', Proceedings of the 2nd Conference on Future Intelligent Educational Environments (WOFIEE'13), 16-17 July 2013 Athens, Greece.

Saleeb, N., Dafoulas, G. & Loomes, M. (2015). 'Personalisation of 3D Virtual Spaces for Enhanced Ubiquitous Learning' in Neto, F. et al. (2015) Handbook of Research on 3-D Virtual Environments and Hypermedia for Ubiquitous Learning, IGI-Global

Sato, K. & Koyasu, M. (1959). 'The Effect of the Room Shape on the Sound Field in Rooms (Studies on the Measurement of Absorption Coefficient by the Reverberation Chamber Method I)', Journal of the Physical Society of Japan, vol. 14, issue 3, pp. 365

Smelik RM,Tutenel T, de Kraker KJ, Bidarra R. (2010). Integrating procedural generation and manual editing of virtual worlds. In: PCGames '10: proceedings of the 2010 workshop on procedural content generation in games. New York, NY, USA: ACM; 2010. p. 1–8.

UNLOCKING THE POTENTIAL OF INFORMATION AND COMMUNICATION TECHNOLOGY FOR BUSINESS SUSTAINABILITY BY SMALL, MICRO AND MEDIUM ENTERPRISES IN VHEMBE DISTRICT, SOUTH AFRICA

Manzira Mungofa Francis and Munyoka Willard
Department of Business Information Systems, University of Venda, Thohoyandou, Limpopo-South Africa

ABSTRACT

Small, Micro and Medium Scale Enterprises (SMMEs) are slow to adopt Information and Communication Technologies (ICT) to assist in day to day business operations. In South Africa, this is a major concern for business operating in rural areas because of great influence SMMEs have in the growth of economy and greater contribution to overall gross domestic product (GDP). This research focused on unlocking the potential of Information and Communication Technologies on (SMMEs) towards improving their operations and survival in today's dynamic modern business environment. In addition, the impact on growth and success of SMMEs through implementation of ICT was another area of concern. 138 SMMES were surveyed in the rural municipal area of Thulamela in Vhembe District, Limpopo. Data was collected from the SMMEs in Sibasa, Thohoyandou, Shayandima and Tshififi towns. Results show that SMMEs' major setbacks include lack of infrastructure, inadequate resources and limited access to finance for funding the implementation and maintenance of information systems in their operations. Inadequate technological infrastructure, transport and the basic electricity which SMMEs deemed to be important for the implementation of sound ICT utilization were identified as challenges. Despite the challenges, most SMMEs indicated that they do make use of ICT tools in their day to day operations and have a greater role in the long term operations of a business against the changing technological environment.

KEYWORDS

Rural, Small, Micro and Medium Scale Enterprises, Information and Communication Technologies, Vhembe.

1. INTRODUCTION

Small, micro and medium enterprises, hereafter referred to SMMEs, have become a priority in many economies worldwide. This has resulted in an increased focus by developing countries to embark on SMME policies for economic growth and poverty alleviation (Cakmak and Tas 2012). Consoli (2012) highlighted that there is growing recognition of the important role small, micro and medium enterprises play in economic development. SMMEs are described as efficient and prolific job creators and the fuel of national economic engines. The author further argues that even in the developed industrial economies, it is the SMME sector rather than the multinationals that are the largest employer of workforce.

The adoption of Information and Communication Technologies (ICTs) by SMMEs is pivotal for improved business operational efficiency. ICT is defined as "diverse set of technological tools and resources used to communicate, and to create, disseminate, store, and manage information" (Seyal, et al 2000:5). Kiveu (2013a) indicated that the value of investing in ICT is fundamental and returns on investment are remunerative towards overall business success. Said (2014:3) stated that: "*The current wave of Information Technology calls for the attention by SMMEs Entrepreneurial*", the author further suggested that for small, micro and medium businesses to avoid becoming dysfunctional, improved communication channels through effective electronic mail (e-mail), video conferencing and social applications are essential. Stansfield & Grant (2003) identified the effects of ICT usage with reference to its global utilization by business professionals. He suggested that the widespread application of ICT has provided new innovative ways to perform business activities which are simpler and more organized while adhering to international standards organization (ISO) principles. The adoption of environmental friendly business activities provides international recognition and attracts more business opportunities. This practice is evident from suggestions made by Manuere, et al (2012), argued that by making use of information technology business organizations are contributing to the reduction of waste pollution, environment preservations and sustainability. They further portray that IT is the modern platform to conduct business activities that are efficient, fast, collaborative and consistent. As all these authors describe the importance of SMMEs to economic growth and the beneficial practices that are offered by ICT utilization, it is evident that these two have an impeccable relationship, it is therefore essential to identify the impact of ICT to ensure better business sustainability in SMMEs.

2. OBJECTIVES OF THE STUDY

The central theme in this research was to ascertain the impact of ICT adoption by SMMEs and the influence it has on their overall business sustainability. This study seeks to:

i. Investigate the ICTs adopted by rural based SMMEs.
ii. Determine the benefits of utilizing ICTs for business sustainability.
iii. Examine whether SMMEs possess the resources to utilize modern ICTs.

3. LITERATURE REVIEW

SMMEs have been failing to adopt and implement ICT that can contribute towards long term sustainability of business operations thereby increasing failure rate within SMMEs in the first ten years of establishment. In United States of America, Jenkin et. al (2011), states that 50% of SMMEs venturing into the market fail to sustain continuation of business after 2 years and for the ones that exceed past 2 years become obsolete in year 10. In South Africa the situation is not excluded, according to Adeniran and Johnston (2011), it is estimated that the failure rate of SMMEs in South Africa is between 70% and 80% initially the first 25 months. Statistics revealed by Adcorp (2012), indicated that around 440,000 small businesses have closed in the last five years in South Africa. Bazhenova, et al (2011), the evolution of technology influences significantly the business by changing the industry infrastructure and business operations and also creating the premises for the emergence of competitive advantages for those organizations that are adopting ICT in their business processes. Fatoki and Odeyemi (2010); Monks (2010) argues that SMMEs risk failure due to lack of adequate usage of modern technology damages the economy to some extent and stunts development because SMMEs are a source of dynamism, innovation and flexibility. One of the daring contributions of failure rates in South Africa, Reza, et al (2011:8) evoked that surveys of small business failure maintain that entrepreneurs often have good ideas and are competent but they do not keep up with the technology pace which helps in better competitive advantage.

3.1 Small, Micro and Medium Enterprises

Smit and Watkins (2012) argued that there is no common definition for SMME because the classification of business organizations into large, medium and small is based on a variety of judgments and regions. The issue of what constitutes a small or medium enterprise is a major concern in the literature. Different authors have usually given different definitions to this category of business. Stansfield and Grant (2003) discussed what constitutes small to medium enterprises and they identified the following:

- Capital assets
- Turnover
- Number of employees

According to Matarirano (2007) defines small, micro to medium enterprises as businesses that employ fifty people or fewer and are not a subsidiary of a public limited company. Brynard and Hanekom (2006) states that the definition of SMMES differ by industrial sector and also region or location and must not be confined to a particular dimension. He further justifies his argument by mentioning that the African

Development Bank classifies SMMES as having less than 50 employees. The South African economy in its own right has legislative parameters governing the grouping of business firms into large, medium, micro and small scale enterprises. The National Small Business Act 102 of 1996 as amended by Act 29 of 2004 categorize small organizations into micro enterprises, very small enterprises, small enterprises and medium enterprises, (Government Gazette of the Republic of South Africa, 2003). The Act defines an SMME on the basis of the number of employees, total turnover and total asset value. Berry, et al (2002) defines SMMES as businesses having relatively small market share, businesses which are managed by owners or part owners and also that they are independent in terms of forming into a larger enterprise.

3.2 The Importance of Small, Micro to Medium Enterprises

Four important drivers which make SMMES one of the most crucial aspects in any economy are:

i. SMMES are the engine of an economies growth
ii. SMMES are essential for a competitive and efficient market
iii. SMMES are critical for poverty reduction
iv. SMMES play particularly important role in developing countries

Sevrani and Bahiti (2008) explained that the only way to reduce poverty in a sustainable way is to promote economic growth, through wealth and employment creation. In developing countries, SMMES are the major source of income, a breeding ground for entrepreneurs and a provider of employment. This was also seconded by Kiveu (2013b) who emphasized that SMMES cut across all sectors of a country's economy, providing a prolific source of employment, income, government revenue and poverty reduction. Monks (2013) argued that in most developed economies, SMMES are the engine that drives economic progress by employing more than half of those in the private sector and generating between 60 and 80 percent of all new jobs. In the European Union SMMEs, as far as 2012 was concerned, they contributed 67% to total employment and 58% to gross value added (GVA), (Easterby-Smith, et al 2013). According to Kiveu (2013b), SMMES are contributing more than 68% to all Chinese exports and employ 78% of the employable population in China. Thus SMMES have a contribution towards the gross domestic product (GDP) of many economies. In India SMMES add more than 35% to GDP, in China 60% and more than 57% in most African emerging economies including Egypt, Ghana, Nigeria and Malawi. The role that SMMES are playing in many economies is very significant as supported by the statistics provided.

3.3 SMMES Contribution to Employment Creation

Statistics South Africa (2013) revealed the unemployment rate for the first quarter of 2013 as having amounted to 25.2%, indicating that about 4.6 million South Africans were unemployed. This increase of unemployed was propelled by the economic recession that took place during 2008-2009 and most businesses have not been able to bounce back to their normal operations and some are still reducing their labor force. However, statistics show that there is an increase in the number of SMMES that opened during the period between 2010 and 2012. This is so because many retrenched experienced personnel went on to open their own small businesses. It is therefore safe to point out that SMMES absorb labor starting with those who are skilled and are between jobs. The other reason why SMMES create more employment opportunities than large firms is that large firms have more preference for capital to labor. Large firms strive to be competitive by acquiring more capital stock than they do labor and ultimately just employ few highly skilled personnel. SMMES on the other hand have the capacity to absorb more labor because they are not very much capital intensive and therefore employ even the lowly skilled labor force. This is because the jobs created by SMMES usually do not require very high qualifications. Gabriel (2005) highlighted that SMMES play an intermediate role and have the potential to generate sustainable jobs for the majority poor population. According to Subrata and Komal (2012), SMMES create better paying jobs than those created by the larger sector because SMMES have a high productivity. In addition, SMMES create more jobs than large firms because they do so using a smaller share of the capital stock.

3.4 ICT in Business Organizations

Technology adoption and use in offices is increasing rapidly with the changes happening in business environment. Application software is being utilized for activities as processing business documents, reports and analyzing financial information, databases for managing and storing personnel data, presentation software for presentations using projectors in meetings and desktop publishers for producing newsletters are examples of the use of ICT in offices. ICT further provides communication platforms as stated by Adebayo, et al (2013), that IT can be described as tools that facilitates communication, process and transmit information and share knowledge through electronic means. According to Bazhenova (2011), the evolution of technology influences significantly the business by changing the industry infrastructure and business operations and also creating the premises for the emergence of competitive advantages for those organizations that are adopting ICT in their business processes. Making reference to Cakmak and Tas (2012), ICT impacts significantly on diverse industries.

3.5 ICT in Small, Micro to Medium Enterprises

As postulated by Stansfield & Grant (2003), the successful operation of companies in most industries is becoming increasingly dependent on their ability to adopt and utilize ICT systems. The authors further outline that the rapid growth of ICT has changed the dynamics of business operations which has become effective and efficient. Consoli (2012), outlines that in today's dynamic business environment, use of ICT is crucial especially in SMMES, which forms a large percentage of companies in most economies. He also points out that the use of ICT can bring benefits in terms of efficiency, effectiveness, innovation, growth and competitive advantages.

In Zanzibar, ICT use has become unavoidable in different aspects of human life; the development of business depends largely on the utilization of new technology. However, SMMEs in Zanzibar are yet to fully utilize the opportunity of ICT (Said, 2014). In Tanzania, according to Ndekwa (2014), the market is currently global, operating environment of businesses is continuously becoming complex and competition is a cut-throat, most businesses strive for competitive advantage over their competitors. Coping with these complex and dynamic business environments, both small and large enterprises requires continuous adoption and innovation in deployment of emerging technologies and management concepts.

Reza, et al (2011) argued that, SMMEs are seen not only as a strong engine of economic growth and productivity, but also, as a means of distributing income amongst its employees and their affiliates in South Africa. The authors' further outline that information technology has shifted from being a resource barely employed in businesses to one of extreme importance, which businesses invest in to gain competitive advantage. According to Plomp, et al (2011), inter-organizational ICT has become critical for the performance of both small and large organizations. SMMEs however, traditionally lag behind in adoption and implementation of these systems. In many countries, various policies are initiated to improve ICT uptake by SMMEs and support them in digital linking throughout their value chain. As reflected from the literature ICT plays a significant role in well establishment of SMMEs and their success especially now in a competitive business environment. Exploration of new markets remaining competitive will be an important factor in achieving future economic stability and success for SMMES, this depends on their ability to harness Internet related technology, (Stansfield and Grant, 2003).

4. MATERIAL AND METHODS

The study followed a number of stages which involves the use of quantitative data collection techniques and approaches. The main emphasis in this paper is on the quantitative aspects, regarding adoption and integration of ICT. The questionnaire was designed and piloted with a sample of 20 businesses. There was peer evaluation undertaken to fine tune the final questionnaire design. Survey area, which is the geographic place under study and where respondents will be extracted from Cooper and Schindler (2006), in this case was Thulamela rural municipal area of Vhembe District in Limpopo. Data was collected from the SMMEs in Sibasa, Thohoyandou, Shayandima and Tshififi. In addition, there were several SMMEs in these towns which are also in the different industries/sector of the economy.

Survey population described by Burns and Burns (2008), as the total number of entities that are of interest to the researcher was used for drawing a sample for data collection. Thus it is believed to share the same characteristics and therefore can be represented by a subset in collecting data especially when the population is large (McDaniel and Gates, 2001). The study comprised of all registered SMMEs in Vhembe District basing on an interview conducted with a representative of SEDA (Small Enterprises Development Agency) in Thohoyandou. According to the interview, there are about 292 registered SMMEs. A total population of 292 SMMEs was selected from Vhembe District using simple random sampling to draw up the sample population of the study. It was regardless of any specific industry which the SMMEs operated in yielding a sample size of 138 with a confidence level of 95%, a margin of error of 6.08% and a response distribution of 50%. Questionnaires were distributed to the respondents who formed the sample population. The respondents for the study were SMME owners, managers and senior employees that have relevant information because they possess the understanding on the Information Technology structure of their businesses. The respondents in the research study were all at managerial levels mainly middle and lower management with hands on experience as the average working period for all the 102 respondents were five years. They had knowledge of their business environment they were working in, hence could provide reliable information on the viability of the ICT adoption in SMMEs.

Out of 138 questionnaires distributed only 111 were returned and qualified to be used for data analysis. The response rate was affected by the busy schedule of the respondents and failure of response from some SMMEs. This yielded a response rate of 80% although 6% of the returned questionnaires were spoiled leaving in 74% being used for data analysis. The below formula was used to calculate a sample size using the specified absolute precision. This formula assumes that the investigator desires to have a 95% confidence interval (the 1.96 value in the formula). The formula also incorporates the finite population correction.

Sample size formula for simple random sampling (SRS) with the finite population correction factor (fpc).

$$n_{srs} = \frac{N\hat{p}_{srs}\hat{q}_{srs}}{\frac{d^2}{1.96^2}(N-1) + \hat{p}_{srs}\hat{q}_{srs}}$$

$where: n_{srs} = \text{sample size}, N = \text{population size}, \hat{p}_{srs} = \text{the estimated proportion}, \hat{q}_{srs} = 1 - \hat{p}_{srs},$

$d = \text{desired absolute precision}$

5. RESULTS

5.1 Type of Business

The type of organisational structure was also considered and it yielded results outlined in summary as follows: 69.37% of the SMMEs are operating as sole traders whilst 18.92% are in partnerships and 11.71% private companies. A perspective can arise that the existence of the majority of SMMEs as sole trading businesses might be contributing to the fewer number of employees in these SMMEs. It is most likely that in a sole trading business the owner might be the manager as well. Partnerships and private companies have a possibility of having other people than the owner managing, however, this does not overrule the concept that sole proprietors can hire people to be managers.

The statistics which SMMEs have been in business were compiled and had the following results reflected that 80% of businesses had 5 or fewer years old with 41% being between start-up and 2 years of age. Only 23 businesses out of 102 are above 5 years of age. This is consistent with previous literature stated by (Fatoki, 2010), many SMMEs are not able to reach 5 years of business operation. Another reason of failures can be attached to unsound business practices and inadequate financial resources.

5.2 Industry of the SMMEs

This study was not focused on a particular industry/sector but rather on the SMMEs in general. This question was included in the data collection instrument so that there would be inclusion of SMMEs in the various sectors of the economy. The summary of results is as follows: Most SMMEs (66.67%) are in retailing, there is a fair representation of other industries; 12.61% in construction, 14.41% in wholesaling and 6.31% in the service industry. The findings are consistent with the literature that says that most SMMEs are into retailing where they do not need large capital intensive investment but rather use their own, borrow from friends and make some few bank overdrafts (Agyei-Mensah and Phenya, 2011).

5.3 Positions of Respondents in Business

Positions of respondents in business were articulated to remove doubt on the respondents' qualification so as to provide relevant information for the study. Mainly the business owners, managers and senior employees have access to firm's private technology infrastructure, financial and policy information. From population surveyed 61% of the hold a managerial position in their SMMEs whilst 20%, 26% and 4% of the respondents are owners, owner-managers and senior employees, respectively.

5.4 ICT Usage in Business Operations

Statistics shows that 79.5% of the respondents from SMMEs use ICT tools in their day to day business operations. It implies that most of the business people are aware about ICT and understand its importance and therefore use ICT tools in their day to day business operations. However, 20.5% of the total respondents did not use any kind of ICT tools. From the respondents using these tools, highest preference was in Marketing and Sales with 95.0%, maximum usage of ICT tools is done for promoting sales and marketing activities by different companies (SMMEs). This is mainly because of the easy communication channels provided by ICT tools for example e-mail services, e-commerce, internet, etc Finance and Market research functions had 67%, followed by Human resources having 44 % and last Supply chain function had the lowest percentage of 26%. This is attributed to the fact that manufacturing is very minimal within the region where most of the businesses relies on couriers and logistic companies for the delivery of their stock. Another possible reason is the lack of awareness amongst the entrepreneurs about different enterprise wide information systems software such as ERP SAP, Pastel, Sage, Bar code scanning systems. which can integrate their supply chain activities and make the process of inventory management very effective, majority of the companies use the basic ICT tools like internet, emails, B2B portals, tally etc. Another contributory factor is of SMMEs failing to identify the need to implement sophisticated software/ICT tools like ERP, Bar Code system (BCS) etc.

In terms of website technology integration, the respondents were requested to indicate whether they have an operational website which they are making use of as part of their business operations. The findings on this question indicated that quite a considerable number of SMMEs in Thulamela municipal area does not make use of Website technologies. 73.5% of the responses showed that they do not have a website meaning perhaps they use traditional ways of marketing, advertising and image build up. 26.5% of the responses were positive resembling the presence and usage of a website. This indicates that although the percentage of SMMEs with websites is low the perspective of the people understanding the importance of such ICT tools to improve their presence in the market and amongst the potential customers.

5.5 Business Performance through use of ICT

In this question the 79.5% from Section 5.4 of the respondents who indicated that they make use of ICT tools were also requested to indicate how their businesses benefited from the use of ICT. The results obtained are summarized as follows: Out of the SMMEs who use ICT tools in their day to day business operations, maximum respondents (90%) find them beneficial in one or the other way except only about 9% respondents who that there has been no noticeable effect/result in their business after the usage of ICT tools.

90% of the respondents that maximum effect has been in time saving this is use of ICT tools has considerably reduced time of business operations across business verticals (sales & marketing, finance, market research etc. 81% of respondents said they enjoy improvements in the business partner and customer relationship after use of ICT tools like internet, B2B portals, social media like Facebook, twitter etc. The rating on the improvement in inventory control side has been very low (29%). The reason for this is very less or no use of ICT tools in the business operations. In terms of increase in business productivity, 835 responded positively whilst a notable higher percentage was on Improvement in business partner/ Customer Relationship (81%) and Increase in sales and revenue (78%).

6. CONCLUSION

Results positively shows that SMMEs in the rural areas consider high importance of technology in various activities within their business. Most SMMEs make use of ICT tools in their day to day operations. Rural businesses have the potential to boost their revenues through cost reductions that are enabled with technology considering the fact that very few manufacturing industries operates within these geographic areas leading to much reliance on effective transport network to procure and distribute their stock. This study confirmed that ICT use in SMMEs add value to operations and business performance, with highest rated value added being: Time savings, Cost reduction, Improvement in business partner/ Customer Relationship, Increase in revenue, profit and overall business productivity.

SMMEs major setbacks towards inclusion of ICTs in their operations included inadequate human resources, infrastructure and limited access to finance. Such barriers have a negative effect towards adoption, use and value that could be gained from adopting of technology to enhance sustainability in operations. It is worth noting that technology integration in business operations is now a necessity to drive performance. In addition, SMMEs seemed not aware or not making use of such services as Information Technology Agency, Institute of Information Technology South Africa, and Business Partners. SMMEs in this study reported to be in shortfall of resources which are necessary for them to have an environment of business and effective management which is driven by ICT. Buildings and space is one of the troubling challenges, such that some SMMEs have to pay high rentals for the use of buildings in strategic places which do not belong to them. The other inadequate resources include technological infrastructure, transport and the basic electricity which SMMEs feel are important for the implementation of sound ICT utilization, as such it leads to the idea of viewing ICT as an expense to their operations compared to its added value. This concurs with findings from previous research by MacGregor et al. (2002) who identified barriers that to ICT adoption are unique to SMMEs. These include: low level of existing hardware technology, the need to see immediate returns on investment (ROI), preference for traditional technologies such as telephone system or face to face interaction, lack of IT skills and technical knowledge amongst employees, time constraints to pay attention to system demands, lack of awareness about ICTs. To address these challenges, the Government has set some institutions as remedy action to train and help SMMEs in their infancy stages and those already operating. E-commerce/ICT is considered a long term investment with no immediate realizable benefits, resistance to change. As South Africa is striving towards establishing itself as a knowledge-based economy, SMMEs are more likely to benefit from ICT through economies of scale because of their ability to develop, participate in networks and benefit from networks that can be created through which are formed to serve their interests in business activities. Despite the challenges faced and encountered, SMMEs owners are believe that ICT adds value and is likely to contribute towards long business operations as the most people prefer to make use of internet when doing business.

REFERENCES

Adcorp (2012), New Business Start-ups Slump to all-time Low. Available at: www.adcorp.co.za/NEws/ P a g e s / New business start - ups slump to all - timelow.aspx, Accessed 28 January 2016.

Adeniran T. V., and Johnston, K.A.2011. Investigating the Levels of Internet Capabilities in South African Small and Medium Enterprises in Changing Environments. *13th Annual Conference on WWW Applications*. Johannesburg, South Africa.

Agyei-Mensah, B.K. 2011. Financial management practices of small firms in Ghana: An Empirical study. *African journal of Business Management.* Vol. 5, No.10, pp. 3781-3793.

Bazhenova, E., Taratukhin, V and Becker, J. (2011). Impact of information and communication technologies on business process management on small and medium enterprises in the emerging countries. *Journal of economics*. Vol.2, No.10, pp. 26-40.

Berry, A., von Botnets, M., Cassin, R., Keeper, A., Rajaratnam, B. and Seventer, D.E. 2002. The economics of smmes in South Africa. Online available at http://www.tips.org.za/506.pdf. Accessed: 23 January 2016.

Brynard, P.A. and Hanekom, S.X. 2006. *Introduction to Research in Management related fields*. 2nd ed. Pretoria: Van Schaik Publishers.

Burns, R.B. and Burns, R.A. 2008. *Business Research Methods and Statistics Using SPSS*. Sage Publications.

Cakmak, P. I., & Tas, E. 2012. The Use of Information Technology on Gaining Competitive Advantage in Turkish Contractor Firms. *World Applied Sciences Journal*, Vol.18, No.3,pp 274-285.

Consoli, D. 2012. Literature analysis on determinant factors and the impact of ICT in SMEs. *Procedia-Social and Behavioral Sciences*,Vol.62, pp. 93-97.

Cooper, D.R. and Schindler, P.S. 2006. *Business Research Methods*. New York: McGraw-Hill.

Easterby-Smith, M.V.P., Thorpe, R. and Jackson, P. 2013. *Management Research*. 3rd ed. London: Sage Publications.

Fatoki, O. 2010. An Investigation into the Financial Management Practices of New Micro-enterprises in South Africa. *Journal of Social Science*, Vol. 33, No.32, pp. 179-188.

Fatoki, O. and Odeyemi, A. 2010. Which New Small and Medium Enterprises in South Africa Have Access to Bank Credit? *International Journal of Business and Management*. Vol. 5, No.10,pp. 128-136.

Government Gazette of the Republic of South Africa. (2003), National Small Business Amendment Act. Available at:
http://www.info.gov.za/gazette/acts/2003/a26-03.pdf, Accessed 29 January 2016.

Jenkin, T, Webster, J, Mcshane, L. 2011. An agenda for Green information technology and systems research: Boston District. *Journal of Information and Organization*. Vol.21, pp 17-40.

Kiveu, M. 2013. (a) Determinants of ICT adoption and use by small and medium enterprises: the case of SMMEs in Thika municipality, Kenya, *International Journal of Advanced Research*, Vol. 1, No.7, pp. 717-726.

Kiveu, M. 2013. (b) Enhancing market access in Kenyan SMME"s using ICT. *Global Business and Economics Research Journal*, Vol. 2, No.9, pp. 29-46.

Manuere, F., Gwangawa, E. & Gutu, K. 2012. Barriers to the Adoption of ICT by SMMES in Zimbabwe: an Exploratory Study in Chinhoyi District. *Interdisciplinary Journal of Contemporary Research in Business*. Vol. 4, No.6, pp. 1142-1156.

Matarirano, O. 2007. An Investigation into the Impact of Debt Financing on the Profitability of Small Manufacturing Firms in Bulawayo, Zimbabwe. Research paper. http://www.rbi-ssa.org/resources/data/SMME-Dev-p6-OMatarirano.pdf, Accessed 10 January 2016.

McDaniel, C., & Gates, R. (2001). Marketing Research. Burr Ridge, IL.

Monks P. G. S. 2013. Sustainable Growth of SMMEs.
http://dspace.nmmu.ac.za:8080/jspui/bitstream/10948/1488/1/Sustainable%20Growth%, Accessed 19 January 2106.

Ndekwa, A, G, (2014). Factors Influencing Adoption of Information and Communication Technology (ICT) among Small and Medium Enterprises (SMMEs) in Tanzania, *International Journal of Research in Management & Technology*. Vol. 4, No.5, pp. 65-85.

Plomp, M. G., Batenburg, R. S., & Den Hertog, P. 2011. Does ICT policy improve interorganisational ICT for SMEs? A Dutch policy evaluation study. *Proceedings of the 24th Bled eConference" eFuture: Creating Solutions for the Individual, Organisations and Society"*, pp. 558-571.

Ismail, R., Jeffery, R., & Van Belle, J. P. (2011). Using ICT as a value adding tool in South African SMEs. *Journal of African Research in Business & Technology*, pp. 1-11.

Said, H, 2014. Untapped Opportunities: ICT use by Zanzibar SMMEs. *Journal of Information Engineering and Applications*. Vol.4, No. 8, pp. 30-55.

Sevrani, K. Bahiti, R. 2008. ICT in small and medium enterprises: Case of Albania. *Journal of Economics*. Vol.20, No.2. pp. 30-50.

Seyal, A. H., Rahim, M. M., & Rahman, M. N. A. 2000. An empirical investigation of use of information technology among small and medium business organizations: A Bruneian scenario. EJISDC: *The Electronic Journal on Information Systems in Developing Countries*, Vol.2, No.7, pp.1-17.

Smit, Y and Watkins, J.A. 2012. A Literature Review of Small and Medium Enterprises (SMME) Risk Management Practices in South Africa, *African Journal of Business Management* Vol. 6, No.21, pp. 6324-6330.

Stansfield, M., & Grant, K. (2003). An Investigation into Issues Influencing the Use of the Internet and Electronic Commerce among Small-Medium Sized Enterprises. *Journal of Electronic Commerce Research*, Vol. 4, No.1, pp. 15-33.

Statistics South Africa. 2013. Stats online: unemployment. Available at: http://www.statssa.gov.za. Accessed: 21 January 2016.

Subrata, D and Komal, D. 2012. Factors influencing the information Technology adoption of micro, small and medium enterprises (MSME): An Empirical Study. Vol.2, No.3, pp. 2493-2498.

PLAYFUL E-PARTICIPATION WITH MINECRAFT AS DEVELOPMENT TOOL FOR URBAN REDESIGN: A CASE STUDY

Artan Rexhepi, Sonja Filiposka and Vladimir Trajkovik
Faculty of Computer Science and Engineering, "Ss. Cyril and Methodius" University in Skopje, Skopje, Macedonia

ABSTRACT

Accessing ICTs among citizens, especially youth, is gaining momentum as it is assumed to contribute to increased participation and general improvement in citizens' present and future welfare. The move to create opportunities for engagement of youth in processes of urban planning represents one common vision for empowering local communities with ICT platforms, with which they can face existing concerns on existing public spaces and actively contribute in revitalizing planning processes through civic engagement. This paper is based on a local government case study, an initiative for using Minecraft as a citizen participation tool for urban redesign in local development. The aim is to examine how this initiative has approached the common vision of access, utilization, participation, and engagement of citizens in the community. By presenting this vision of access to ICT promotion for civic engagement among citizens and youths, this paper aims to provide a practical illustration of how serious games may be used in urban planning and to explore the potential by applying the application in the context of local governments. We draw interesting lessons from this case and implications for e-Participation.

KEYWORDS

e-government, e-participation, e-municipality, playful public participation, citizen participation

1. INTRODUCTION AND BACKGROUND

The involvement of citizens in influencing public decisions is an element of democratic decision-making processes. Rowe and Frewer (Rowe & Frewer, 2004) have defined public participation as the practice of consulting and involving members of the public in the agenda-setting, decision-making and policy forming activities of organizations or institutions responsible for policy development. While the public participation has positive implications for good governance, there is a general concern about the tradeoff between inclusiveness and the required knowledge level of participating citizens (Hong, 2015). Fortunately, the issue of participation is finding its way onto national and international agendas and it is now accepted that citizen participation in local development is crucial for equality, inclusiveness, and sustainability of development (Meldon, Kenny, & Walsh, 2002).

There are different e-Government benchmarking models that reflect how public authorities, citizens and other stakeholders can interact with each other (Jayashree & Marthandan, 2010). Depending on its level of development, e-government is generally categorized in the following stages (Budinoski & Trajkovik, 2012). e-Participation and citizen engagement is encouraged by stage 6 of digital governance and citizen inclusion (See Figure 1). Through community involvement, the governments ensure that citizens have a direct voice in public discussions and decisions. Political willingness, an adequate technological infrastructure, and an overall client-oriented development strategy remain the most critical factors for a successful e-government project implementation (Rexhepi, Rexha, & Dika, 2012). e-Participation, as a hybrid of various technologies, social, and political measures, is the use of ICTs to support information provision and "top-down" engagement, i.e., government-led initiatives, or "ground-up" efforts to empower citizens, civil society organizations, and other democratically constituted groups to gain the support of their elected representatives (Macintosh & Whyte, 2008).

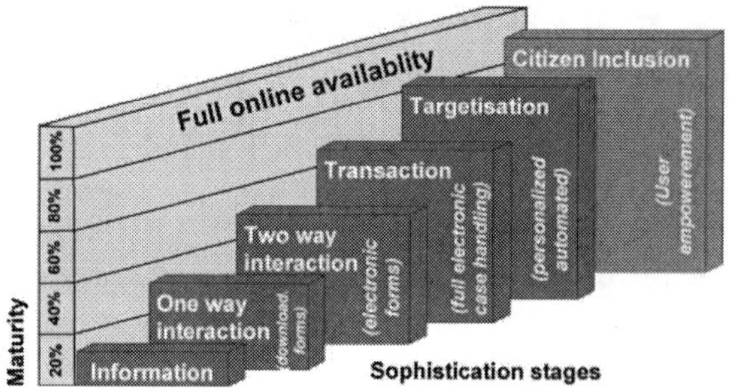

Figure 1. Sophistication stages of a six stage maturity model

The provision of tools, which could help to manage the twin threats of political disengagement and technological stagnatio, remain an important factor for utilisation of e-Participation by local governments. Such set of tools could grasp the key opportunities embedded within the modernization agenda, feeding directly into a powerful rationale for taking participation more seriously in an environment, in which the participation levels are declining steadily while the internet and usage rates are moving constantly upward (Kearns, Bend, & Stern, 2002).

The goal of this paper is to describe and analyze the different aspects of utilization of the Minecraft game as a tool to encourage citizen participation for urban redesign in local development. The focus is on the Minecraft game which brings playfulness and pleasure to non-professionals and ordinary citizens in the process of drafting urban plans. Minecraft contains elements of game play, collaboration, competition, reward, and other motivating factors that could attract mainly young people to effectively take part in and contribute in urban planning processes. Under the assumption that games can potentially attract more people to participate in and learn about urban planning situations, this study intends to provide a new insight into Minecraft utilization for redesign of public spaces as a valuable input for local government, towards its efforts for improved public participation in planning of public projects.

2. E-PARTICIPATION AND THE KOSOVO LOCAL GOVERNMENT CONTEXT

It is evident that an increased number of governments worldwide have understood the importance of e-Participation to more actively engage citizens in democratic processes.

The continuing challenge remains about how to promote public participation and involvement in democratic decision processes. Various Government-Citizen interactive models are employed and developed as virtual community models with special debate structures. They include social opportunities for citizens to engage as individuals responsible for community decisions, starting with initiating the process; creating a virtual community of citizens; registering and posting demands; conducting a consultative debate; clustering demands, voting, and deliberating. There are various prototypes to integrate virtual community models that have been developed and used by citizens. The analysis of these environments sheds further light on understanding of and improving areas for better e-Participation for decision making processes in government. Chun highlights that in order for government to be transparent, government information should be easily accessible, searchable, and integrated. (Chun, Shulman, Sandoval, & Hovy, 2010)

A large array of tools is available today to form the basis for e-participation applications. It is well accepted that technical, social and political factors need to be considered when e-participation applications are developed, while the use of any type of ICT to enhance democracy remains a challenging task (Macintosh & Whyte, 2008). The development of systems that are used for e-participation purposes is mainly based on the exploitation of already existing tools that allow users to interact with each other in various ways. Even if these tools cannot be directly characterized as e-participation tools, however, due to the fact that they concentrate a large number of users within their operation, they can be easily called Tools for Enhancement of e-Participation (Ergazakis, Metaxiotis, & Tsitsanis, 2011). Wimmer noted a scope of existing e-participation tools, components, software applications and products, from weblogs to more sophisticated consultation platforms, which cover both core e-participation tools (extensively used in e-Participation) and tools that are used in but are not specific to e-Participation. (Wimmer, 2007) .

Local government institutions nowadays face new challenges as well as new expectations if compared to earlier institutions. A 2013 survey on the state of use and penetration of internet in Kosovo showed that internet users constitute 76% of total Kosovo population above 10 years old (Fazliu, 2013). This analysis provides some relevant facts about ICT tools at hand within administration and converging views that key officials are having an increased understanding of the importance and utilization of the ICT tools with special focus on social media. The fact that approximately 71% of all local government institutions are present on social networks, is encouraging. And in view of current general usage statisticsof social media networks in Kosovo (Fazliu, 2013; "Internet World Statistics," 2013), indicate an estimated internet penetration of 76% among the 1.85 million population. There is, as such, a large potential for a rapid substantial strengthening of an e-participation component of eGovernment, which would not only cover the public consultations processes but, moreover, it could strengthen the cooperation with citizens at the local level as well as significantly increase the institutional transparency towards citizens; thus building on the trust of citizens towards governmental institutions. The data gathered so far show that the Kosovo government institutions are in the initial stage of utilization of social networks for interaction with citizens. The results show that one-third of local governments are still not using any social media, which requires further consideration. In comparison, a 2010 study found that 54% of U.S. small and medium sized local governments with a similar population size have adopted social networking tools to enable participation by citizens and external stakeholder groups (Feeney, Welch, & Haller, 2011). Among various ICT tools that support achievement of e-participation objectives, such as social media, online surveys, etc., games can also be considered for facilitating the interaction between the local government and citizens and could offer an stimulating instrument for experimenting and participation.

3. YOUTH AND E-PARTICIPATION

A 2014 United Nations report highlights that half of the current global population is under the age of 25. The majority lives in cities, with cities of the developing world accounting for over 90% of urban growth worldwide. An estimated 60% of all urban dwellers will be under 18 by 2030 ("The Role of Youth in the Urban Future ", 2012). Similar to other social groups, the young people have a legitimate voice and important role in society, but that voice is regularly not heard adequately and their contribution to the society is not always universally recognized. Young people are a group that is traditionally constructed and perceived as being incapable of making decisions on their own. This has led to a situation of underrepresentation of youth in decision-making processes which today can be viewed as a real threat to the future of participatory democracy. Young people face real obstacles to fully exercising their rights (Lugarić, 2009).

It is assumed that the increased usage of ICT by young people will contribute to democratic and distributive justice, increased participation, and general improvement in citizens' present and future welfare. The move to create spaces for young people in an era of increasing apathy represents a common vision and provides an opportunity by empowering local communities with communicative platforms and sources of information with which they can face mainstream discourses that overlook concerns on the one hand and revitalize the collapsing levels of interest in political and civic engagement on the other hand (Dralega, Due, & Skogerbø, 2010).

Youth participation involves youth in responsible, challenging actions that meet genuine needs and that gives them an opportunity to participate in planning and decision-making. Lugaric (2009) has emphasized the particular importance of their participation in decision-making, because it leads to better decisions, actions and outcomes since young people have, as social actors, experiences unique to their situation. It further promotes the well-being of young people and development of their skills, strengthens the commitment to and understanding of human rights and democracy and empowers and protects young people. ICT has therefore become a very important factor today which influence the political, economic and social spheres and creates many opportunities and challenges to the fuller involvement of young people in society. Through the Internet and other technologies, young people today have an opportunity to be engaged in various public activities, using increasingly accessible information and thereby becoming better acquainted with current local, national and global issues while being empowered to provide user generated information to policy makers.

What young people need is an enabling environment that provides opportunities for them to be seen and heard (DESA, 2007). Giving youth greater visibility and a role in the development process strengthens their resolve to contribute to the advancement of a world in which they are equal stakeholders – a world for which they will be responsible for many decades to come. Local governments are increasingly becoming dependent on communicating with citizens. Therefore, it is required that existing ICT communication channels be permanently evaluated and that new ICT platforms are investigated and considered for proper utilization. In this regard, special attention should be given to popular ICT applications and games, which could support reducing the distance between citizens and youth.

4. GAMES AS TOOLS FOR E-PARTICIPATION

Besides other "pure" forms of e-participation platforms, use of online games in the field of urban planning is more familiar and enjoyable when used by citizens, especially by youth and, therefore, is an innovative, effective and attractive public participation tool for citizen engagement in consultation processes that relate to their environment. Although GIS and other map-based planning applications were considered too complex for the majority of potential users (Steinmann, Krek, & Blaschke, 2004), Krek (2005) observed that many citizens are rationally ignorant, especially about public participation in urban planning, because participation would require a high investment of time and effort to learn the current planning situation. He asked what it would take to overcome these significant barriers to public participation and encourage citizens to participate.

For this purpose, new alternative forms of collaboration and technical tools such as games should be considered that can be used by non-experts and lay users to expand the work in public participatory GIS and include a much wider and distributed participation (Poplin, 2012). Users can interact through such games both with intervention areas and with each other through graphic animation environments. Various entertainment simulation games were developed with the concept of urban planning such as UrbanPlan, SimCity, CitiesXL, Skylines, SuperCity and others. They have the potential for deployment in discussions about spatial planning through playful public participation. Poplin noted that with its inbuilt elements of collaboration, competition, reward and fun, game play adds additional motivational factors to people to participate in urban planning processes and provides conventional factors, such as incentives, self-interest and altruism with its play elements.

In 2009 a new sandbox construction game, Minecraft, was created by Mojang founder Markus Persson. It immediately gained incredible popularity and has become the best selling PC game in history and one of the best-selling games of all times with over 70 million copies between various platforms in 2015 (Prince, 2015). The gameplay of Minecraft is perhaps best imagined as a complex "digital Lego" with mechanical similarity between the blocks. The creative and building aspects of Minecraft allow players to build structures out of textured cubes in a three-dimensional generated world. Players playing in creative mode can easily create buildings and structures similar to those produced by complex 3D modeling software, with the additional benefit of being able to construct things together through the multiplayer setting. As a result, the building process is more similar to real-life construction projects with lots of workers carrying out different roles simultaneously compared to traditional digital 3D model-making with only one designer.

Minecraft also has several basic benefits: starting from a technical perspective, where the game is free from restrictions imposed by Digital Rights Management and is therefore easily distributable, to its minimum hardware requirements, which makes it easy to play and set up Minecraft and maintain multiplayer servers with built in monitoring in the form of server logs (Marklund, 2011).

5. USING MINECRAFT AS E-PARTICIPATION TOOL

The basis for this study is the implementation of a pilot project in Kosovo in 2015, based on using the UN-Habitat and Minecraft Block-by-Block (Block, 2015) project as a community participation tool. The main reasons for selecting Kosovo for field-testing the use of Minecraft as an e-governance tool for community participation in public space projects are its demographic structure, where 50% of the population is under 25 years old, its cultural diversity and political complexity, poverty/deprivation and access to public space, and ICT penetration in Kosovo society, where ICT users in Kosovo constitute 76% of total Kosovo population older than 10 years. While Minecraft is very popular among schoolchildren in Kosovo, reliable data makes it difficult to estimate the total number of Minecraft users in Kosovo. Additionally, consideration is also given to available local expertise, experience, and interest in the revival of public spaces.

The specific study case of the implementation of this game relates to a selected site in the municipality of Prishtina, namely the "Former Market Place" in Bregu i Diellit/Sunny Hill neighborhood as shown in figure 2. The site was selected based on various criteria, such as location in an area that is currently used or could potentially be used by a large variety of social groups; a location where reinforcing the engagement of youth is particularly needed; an intervention would improve the quality of life of all urban residents; a demonstration of support and commitment from relevant political authorities at the local level and access to ICT facilities. The project site covers about 1,836 m2 of land under municipal ownership. The population in the project site is diverse in terms of income, gender and age (reflecting the national situation, 38% under 20 years). In addition, the advantage of the selected site lies in the connectivity, position, visibility, accessibility, and mixed social groups. Based on images, plans, google maps locations, and other relevant data, UN-Habitat through the Block-By-Block initiative has modeled the site in Minecraft environment.

Figure 2. Location of the selected intervention location through Minecraft

Once the Minecraft model images of the project site were prepared, they were shared and cross-checked with the Municipality of Prishtina (M-Pr) staff. The strategies for communication and documentation of the entire process were managed by the Municipal Press Office, that informed and invited all local and national media for the community presentation, arranged interviews for digital and written media, documented the community presentations and the charrette, and managed a Facebook page www.facebook.com/BllokpasBlloku to follow key project activities throughout the development cycle, during the preparations, community presentation, the charrette, and until the implementation and impact assessment for further information dissemination. The communication channels used for community groups involved printed and audio-visual media, social media, invitation letters, and posters.

Thirty-nine participants were identified and selected representing different social and age classes. The basic criteria for the participants selection were: young male/female age 7-16, women, senior citizen age more than 60, middle aged group 40-50, university/college students (20-30), disabled people, low income group, participants from city corporations/municipalities (partnering agencies), and representatives from NGOs or civil society. The participants were identified through a community information meeting held prior to the charrette and through recommendations from various local NGOs operating in the neighborhood. The table below provide a description of the gender, residency, and profile of selected 'Minecrafters'.

Table 1. Structure/Location/Profile of residency of local 'Minecrafters' charrette participants

Participants	No. of participants	%
Female	18	46 %
Male	21	54 %
Total	**39**	**100 %**
"Bregu i Diellit" neighborhood residents	19	49 %
Residents from other parts of the city	20	51 %
Total	**39**	**100 %**
Children (elementary / secondary school)	16	41 %
University/ College students	17	43 %
Urban planners/ Architects (professionals)	6	16 %
Total	**39**	**100 %**

The primary aim of the charrette was to develop draft design solutions in a Minecraft environment to revitalize the former market place in "Bregu i Diellit" neighborhood through inclusive participation, community discussion and consultation on the eventual future of the selected site and suggestions for public space design and computer gaming. In the design and building sessions each group modified the existing model and reflected on their preferred changes and additions to the site. Each team made a real time presentation (using Minecraft software) and provided necessary justifications for the introduced amenities and solutions.

The final model was created based on directions derived from the team discussions and 17 developed Minecraft model solutions.

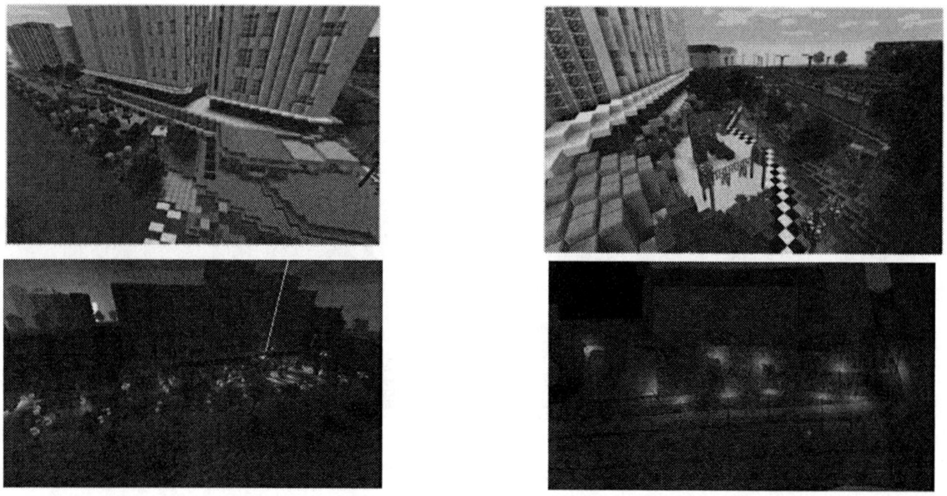

Figure 3. Selected Minecraft solutions developed from the charrette participants: upper left: Minecraft licence no.: 63, upper right: Minecraft license no.:64, bottom left: Final consolidated and agreed Minecraft model, bottom right: rendered project design for the intervention in the selected site based on final selected Minecraft model

The most creative ideas as well as the final model, shown in figure 3, were presented to a wider audience, including the Mayor of Prishtina. In a nutshell, the amenities included in the final Minecraft model were comprised of speed bumps for speed reduction and a clear roundabout, climbing wall and wall art/ decorations, tables and benches, and recreational facilities.

An empirical study has been conducted for measuring the success of this project implementation. The research utilized a structured questionnaire that was adjusted to adapt to the conditions of this pilot case. The questionnaire included 18 questions designed to measure participants' perception of the priority and performance of selected factors, important for the success of such citizen collaboration projects. The questionnaire also contained additional questions typical to demographics. Questions on success factors required respondents to assess the priority of every factor on a scale from 1 (not important) to 4 (most important). A total of 39 questionnaires were distributed to all charrette participants, of which 38 questionnaires were validated and used for this empirical study. The data collected through this survey were digitalized, coded, and analyzed using statistical analysis software. The direct output is a set of recommended measures for improvement of such initiatives in the future.

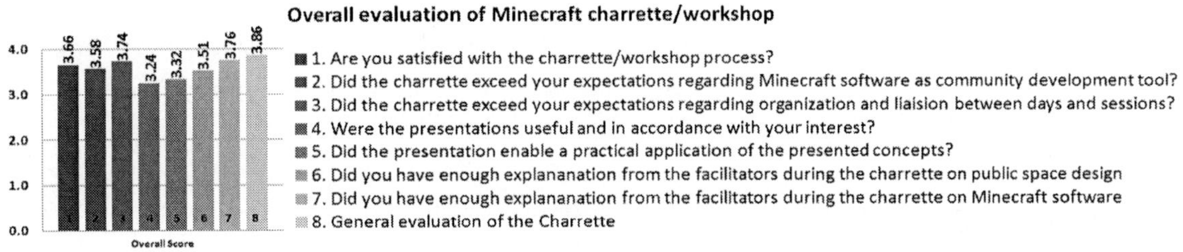

Figure 4. Structure of general evaluated factors assessed by the Minecraft charrette participants

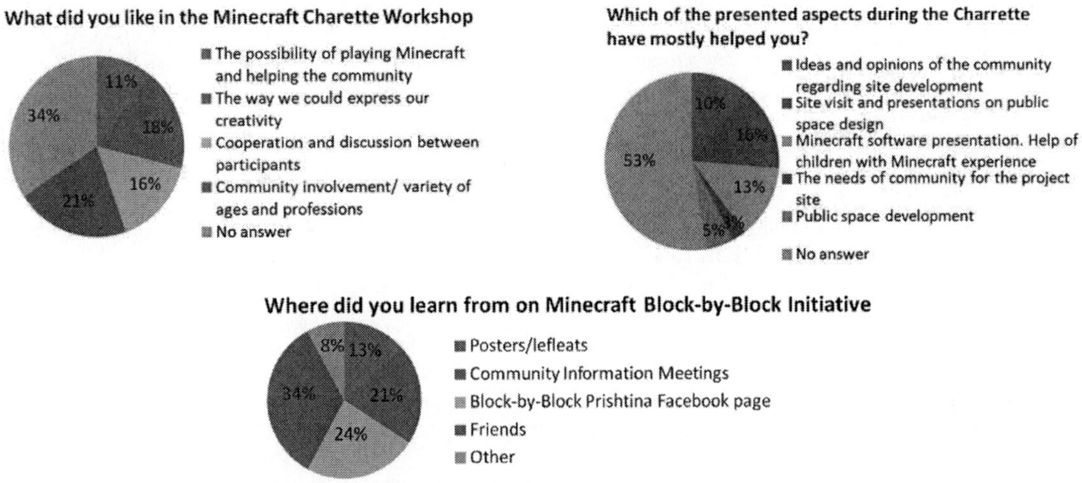

Figure 5. The perception of participants from the Minecraft charrette *(upper left and upper right diagrams) and the source of information for this event (bottom center)*

The results of the conducted survey (figures 4 and 5) show that participants appreciated the initiative at all levels, including concept, organization, creativity, and community engagement. The participants had a clear understanding regarding the requirements for the project site through the presentations, site visit, community consultation. and own ideas and suggestions. Minecraft gave them the opportunity for a simple and unique way of expressing their ideas and transforming them into virtual elements, through a consolidated team work.

6. CONCLUSION

This paper aims to provide a practical illustration of how Minecraft game can be used in urban planning and to explore the potential by applying the application of this approach in the context of a particular local government in Kosovo. The Minecraft Initiative proved to be a successful way of mobilizing and engaging the community, especially the youth, in the bottom-up process of design and decision-making versus public space improvement. Also, an important success factor was the opportunity for raising awareness about public space design and management issues. The promising results of the survey demonstrate that using of Minecraft, is favorably viewed when used by citizens, especially by youth, and confirmed the strong innovative, effective and attractive aspect of this playful public participation tool for the engagement of citizens in consultation processes related to their living environment.

REFERENCES

Block, B. B. (2015). UN-Habitat and Mojang using Minecraft to involve citizens in public space design. 2015, from http://blockbyblock.org

Budinoski, K., & Trajkovik, V. (2012). Incorporating Social Network Services in eGovernment Solutions: A Case Study. *European Journal of ePractice, 16*, 58-70.

Chun, S. A., Shulman, S., Sandoval, R., & Hovy, E. (2010). Government 2.0: Making connections between citizens, data and government. *Info. Pol., 15*(1,2), 1-9.

DESA, U. (2007). *World Youth Report: Young People's Transition to Adulthood: Progress and Challenges* (U. Nations Ed.): Department of Economic and Social Affairs.

Dralega, C. A., Due, B., & Skogerbø, E. (2010). Community Engagement of Youth: eParticipation Realities in Uganda and Norway (Vol. 6, pp. 94-108): Annenberg School for Communication & Journalism.

Ergazakis, K., Metaxiotis, K., & Tsitsanis, T. (2011). A State-of-The-Art Review of Applied Forms and Areas, Tools and Technologies for e-Participation. *International Journal of Electronic Government Research, 7*(1), 1-19.

Fazliu, A. (2013). Internet Penetration and Usage in Kosovo (pp. 18-24). Prishtina: Kosovo Association of Information and Communication Technology.

Feeney, M., Welch, E., & Haller, M. (2011). Transparency, Civic Engagement, and Technology Use in Local Government Agencies: Findings from a National Survey. Chicago: Institute for Policy and Civic Engagement at University of Illinois at Chicago.

Hong, S. (2015). Citizen Participation in Budgeting: A Trade-Off between Knowledge and Inclusiveness? *Public Administration Review, 75*(4), 572-582. doi: 10.1111/puar.12377

Internet World Statistics. (2013, 02.09.2014). Retrieved 15.09.2014, 2014, from http://www.internetworldstats.com/europa2.htm#kv

Jayashree, S., & Marthandan, G. (2010). Government to E-government to E-society. *Journal of Applied Sciences, 10*, 2205-2210. doi: 10.3923/jas.2010.2205.2210

Kearns, I., Bend, J., & Stern, B. (2002). *e-participation in local government*. (ISBN 1860301894). London.

Lugarić, M. (2009). Youth Participation in the Democtratic Processes (Vol. A/121/3(c)-R.1). Geneva: Inter-Parliamentary Union.

Macintosh, A., & Whyte, A. (2008). Towards an evaluation framework for eParticipation. *Transforming Government: People, Process and Policy, 2*(1), 16-30. doi: doi:10.1108/17506160810862928

Marklund, B. B. (2011). *Peer collaboration and learning in user driven environments.* (Master Degree Project), University of Skövde. Retrieved from http://playmakers.instituteofplay.org/wp-content/files_mf/fulltext01.pdf

Meldon, J., Kenny, M., & Walsh, J. (2002). *Local Government, local development and citizen participation*: Universite Libre de Bruxelles.

Poplin, A. (2012). Playful public participation in urban planning: A case study for online serious games. *Computers, Environment and Urban Systems, 36*(3), 195-206. doi: http://dx.doi.org/10.1016/j.compenvurbsys.2011.10.003

Prince, N. (2015). Discovering Minecraft in 2015 Retrieved 10.01.2016, 2016, from http://www.ign.com/articles/2015/11/27/discovering-minecraft-in-2015

Rexhepi, A., Rexha, B., & Dika, A. (2012). *Assessment of success factors of e-government project implementation: challenges for the Kosovo e-government perspective.* Paper presented at the ICEGOV '12 - 6th International Conference on Theory and Practice of Electronic Governance, Albany, New York.

The Role of Youth in the Urban Future (2012) *Concept Note for the World Urban Youth Assembly, WUF6.* Nairobi: UN-Habitat.

Rowe, G., & Frewer, L. J. (2004). Evaluating PublicParticipation Exercises: A Research Agenda. *Science, Technology and Human Values, 29*(4), 512-557. doi: 10.1177/0162243903259197

Steinmann, R., Krek, A., & Blaschke, T. (2004). *Can online map-based applications improve citizen participation?* Paper presented at the TED conference on e-government, Bozen, Italy.

Wimmer, M. A. (2007). *Ontology for an e-participation virtual resource centre.* Paper presented at the Proceedings of the 1st international conference on Theory and practice of electronic governance, Macao, China.

DIGITAL KNOWLEDGE ECOSYSTEMS: EMPOWERING USERS THROUGH CONTEXT SPECIFIC ACTIONABLE INFORMATION

Athula Ginige
Western Sydney University, Australia

ABSTRACT

Today we have to solve many global development problems often termed as Grand Challenges aiming at enhancing livelihood processes for achieving better economic, social and environmental outcomes. Increasing take-up of Smartphones and the resulting digitally connected society has opened up new possibilities to address these challenges. To better understand how this connectivity can be effectively used to enhance outcomes a project was initiated to develop a Mobile Based Information System (MBIS) for farmers in Sri Lanka. The aim was to provide farmers and other stakeholders in the agriculture domain with context specific actionable information to make optimal decisions. The term actionable information refers to such information that will enable a stakeholder to act with least amount of further processing. The research challenge was to discover a way to generate context specific actionable information to support decision making throughout all stages of a farming cycle in a way to empower users. To initiate the information flow published knowledge relevant to the domain activities were disaggregated and reorganised into an ontological knowledgebase to provide context specific actionable information. A system was devised for users to act on this information generating transaction data which in turn was aggregated or disaggregated to provide new actionable information. This mechanism will keep the information flowing in the system similar to biological ecosystems. Thus MBIS evolved into a Digital Knowledge Ecosystem. Since its deployment we observed many new major stakeholder groups joining the system confirming the correctness of the ecosystem design. It was found the evolved Digital Knowledge Ecosystem architecture and the approach to develop the system is very generic and can be applied to other domains such as healthcare and business to enhance information flow among key stakeholders, thus empowering the users.

KEYWORDS

Digital Knowledge Ecosystem, Actionable Information, User Empowerment, Design for Evolution, Mobile Based Information System for Agriculture, ICT for Sustainability.

1. INTRODUCTION

Today we have to solve many global development problems often termed as Grand Challenges aiming at enhancing livelihood processes for achieving better economic, social and environmental outcomes. Solution to some of these challenges depends on being able to create better coordinated approaches to increase efficiency and reduce waste. This requires enhancing the flow of information among stakeholders in a domain which will enable each individual to make informed decisions optimal to them. This creates a win-win situation. The advances in Information and Communication technologies and very high take up of mobile phones have created a highly connected society laying the foundation to exchanging information digitally. This has enabled us to explore innovative solutions to some of the global development Grand Challenges.

By September 2015, 3.56 Billion people, that is 51% of global population were part of this connected society (Kemp 2015). This has given rise to a new computing paradigm; Social Computing (Ginige and Fernando 2015). Facebook is an online social networking application launched in 2004. Within ten years it became the most popular social computing application used by 1 Billion users, and by 2015 it has reached 1.5 Billion users worldwide (Statista 2015). Attempts to develop such applications for the wider society raise a fundamental question; what will motivate the people to use the developed system. A closer analysis of an application such as Facebook reveals some of its functionality such as "status updates" and "likes" give rise to a feeling of belongingness and self-esteem, identified as level 3 and 4 needs respectively in the Maslow Hierarchy of human needs (Ginige and Fernando 2015). Most of livelihood processes that needs to be enhanced related to global development Grand Challenges can be mapped to level 2 of Maslow Hierarchy. This level identifies different types of security needs such as food security, economic security, health and wellbeing, etc. (Maslow 1943) that can be achieved through better coordinated processes, reducing waste to achieve sustainability, reducing exploitation by enhancing access to information through which choices can be provided. This insight enables us to explore innovative solutions to some of the global development Grand Challenges making use of the unprecedented connectivity now available to share information digitally.

Thus to better understand how this connectivity can be effectively used to enhance livelihood processes to achieve economic security a project was initiated to develop a Mobile Based Information System (MBIS) for farmers in Sri Lanka. In Sri Lanka there has been a significant growth in mobile phone usage in the past few years. According to Telecommunications Regulatory Commission of Sri Lanka, the number of Cellular Mobile Subscribers at the end of December 2010 was around 80.95% of the total population which has increased to around 116.7% of the total population by December 2015 (TRC 2015). Even the farmers in rural areas, irrespective of their native language, tend to carry a mobile phone to the farm, and use it in their day to day activities. Further Sri Lanka's population has a literacy rate of 92%, one of the highest literacy rates in Asia (Wikipedia 2016).

The system that was developed over a period of 4 years has evolved into a Digital Knowledge Ecosystem (Ginige et al. 2014a). This paper describes the insights that were gained when developing the mobile based information system for farmers in Sri Lanka, reconceptualising it as a Digital Knowledge Ecosystem, identification of specific functionality that can stimulate the growth of the ecosystem and how the Digital Knowledge Ecosystems concept has started to propagate to other application domains.

2. MOBILE BASED INFORMATION SYSTEM FOR AGRICULTURE

In Sri Lanka overproduction of vegetables due to many farmers growing the same crop without having an awareness of what others are growing is a major problem (Hettiarachchi 2011; Hettiarachchi 2012). As there is a very high mobile penetration in the country, in August 2011 an international collaborative research team consisting of researchers from 4 continents embarked on a project to explore a possible mobile based solution (Ginige 2011). The aim was to explore ways to share production information through this system to reduce the overproduction. The research team found over production is only a symptom of a much deeper problem; which is farmers not being able to find necessary information at the right time to make informed decisions at various stages of the crop life cycle (L. De Silva et al. 2012). In order to develop a system that can provide right information at the right time to farmers the team had to first investigate following research questions.

(i) What information farmers need, when and what is an effective format?
(ii) How we can source or generate this information?
(iii) What will motivate farmers to use this system?

2.1 Farmer Information Needs

Using scenario analysis and transformation techniques the team identified the information needs of farmers relating to various stages of the crop lifecycle (De Silva et al. 2013a; Giovanni et al. 2012b; L. De Silva et al. 2012). The information needs of farmers can be divided into two broad categories; Quasi Static and Dynamic. Quasi Static information includes crop varieties, how to grow different varieties, types of fertilizer to be used, how to manage pests, diseases etc. These types of information evolve slowly with time; thus the term quasi static. Farmers also wanted information about local weather, market prices, current production of various crops, current demand, closest location from where they can purchase seeds, fertilizer and corresponding price information etc. which changes rapidly, thus the term Dynamic information (De Silva et al. 2013b; L. De Silva et al. 2012).

Most of Quasi Static information is available from various Government agencies in the form of booklets, TV programs, seminar programs etc. But this information was not reaching the farmers in a manner that they can act on it. Various Government publications have information on how to grow various crops. For a farmer to find out what crops will grow in his farm based on available information they need to perform considerable amount of cognitive processing. This led us to formulate the concept of "actionable information", information at a level of granularity that a person can act with least amount of further processing. This information needs to be provided in context. In the case of a farmer asking what crops will grow in my farm, we need to model the farm context in terms of rainfall, temperature, elevation, soil condition etc. and provide a list of crops that will grow under these conditions. Further if we know a farmer has specific preferences such as cash crops, vegetables etc. the list can be further narrowed down based on farmer preference. After obtaining the information this will minimise further processing a farmer needs to perform prior to being able to make a decision.

Thus we identified the need to provide context specific actionable information to farmers. This led us to investigate two other issues. What is a suitable context model and how to obtain parameter values for variables in the model that are specific to a user.

For example a typical question farmers will ask is "What crops will grow in my farm?" The MBIS made use of the fact that this question is asked using a Smartphone. The system captures the geo-coordinates and maps the location of the farm onto an agro ecological zone map. From this the MBIS can find the agro ecological zone relevant to the farm. Each agro ecological zone has specific climatic and weather conditions. These values specify the farm context that can be used to find the crops that will grow in that farm (Mathai and Ginige 2013; Mathai and Ginige 2014). Agriculture ontology for Sri Lanka farming domain was developed and the information in the booklets were organised into an Ontological Knowledgebase that can be queried based on context parameters (Walisadeera et al. 2015). The response to this query is a list of crops that grows in that farm. Thus by reorganising the published information into an Ontological knowledgebase (disaggregation of information) coupled with specific parameter values of the corresponding context model instance the MBIS was able to generate the context specific actionable information (Walisadeera et al. 2014; Walisadeera et al. 2013). The deployed system can also provide context specific actionable information relating to crop varieties, fertilizer, crop diseases and their control methods (Walisadeera et al. 2015). The user interfaces of the deployed system for selecting crops to grow based on farm location and environmental parameters are shown in figure 1.

2.2 Sourcing Dynamic Information

Dynamic information needs to be generated from information captured in real-time. If users share information then using some aggregation or predictive algorithm the required information can be generated. Capturing information from users on an ongoing basis is a challenge. To overcome this challenge the team found an innovative approach. As MBIS is providing actionable information, if the system also provides functions for users to act on this information then the system can capture transaction data. From these transaction data MBIS can generate some of the required dynamic information.

The way this was implemented in the MBIS is farmers can ask what crops will grow in my farm. As described above the application will give a list of crops that will grow in his farm. The team found next bit of information that farmers need is how much it will cost them to grow a selected crop. To assist the farmers MBIS provides an expense calculator. For the selected crop when farmers provide the extent in land area or number of plants that they plan to grow MBIS generates a query to the Ontological Knowledgebase to find fertilizer and chemical requirements for the specified extent and computes an approximate cost (Ginige et al. 2014b). Now using a predictive algorithm based on the planted extent provided by farmers to calculate the approximate cost, the MBIS can predict in real time the types of crops and extent of land area being planned for different regions as well as the country as a whole.

This dynamically generated information is provided to farmers who are asking the question "What crops will grow in my farm". Together with the list of crops that can be grown in the farm, the aggregated planned production quantity for each of the crops is also provided. This helps farmers to make an informed decision when selecting crops for the coming season to avoid an over or under supply situation. The team found this aggregated planned production information is also very valuable for some of the Government agencies; especially those involved in maintaining food security for the country. By knowing if a particular food item is going to be in short supply at least few months ahead, gives them time to issue import licences to traders or reduce the import tax for that item, promoting traders to import such items to reach the market at the right time to maintain food security.

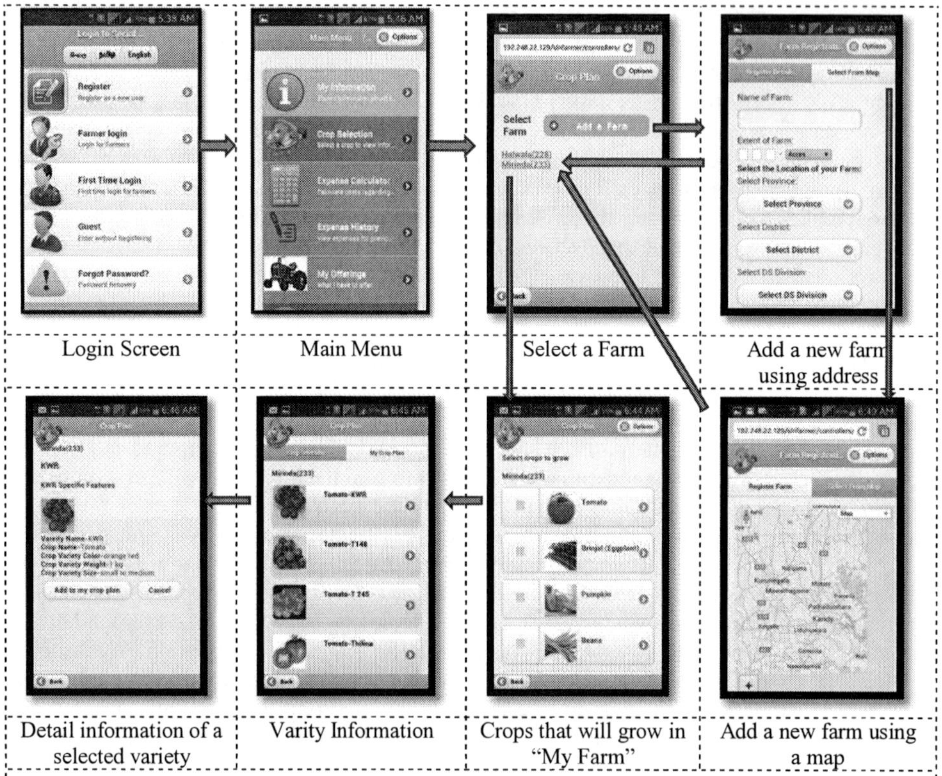

Figure 1. User Interfaces for Crop Selection – "What will grow in my farm?"

This dynamically generated information is provided to farmers who are asking the question "What crops will grow in my farm". Together with the list of crops that can be grown in the farm, the aggregated planned production quantity for each of the crops is also provided. This helps farmers to make an informed decision when selecting crops for the coming season to avoid an over or under supply situation. The team found this aggregated planned production information is also very valuable for some of the Government agencies; especially those involved in maintaining food security for the country. By knowing if a particular food item is going to be in short supply at least few months ahead, gives them time to issue import licences to traders or reduce the import tax for that item, promoting traders to import such items to reach the market at the right time to maintain food security.

To calculate the approximate cost of production farmers had to select fertilizer, pesticides and other chemicals they are planning to use and the quantities based on the recommendations provided by the Ontological Knowledgebase. The team found based on this information it is now possible to predict the demand for fertilizer and pesticides in various parts of the country for coming months. The agro chemical companies found that this information is very useful for them to plan their supply chains and wanted access to this information. In return the team requested them to supply list of items that they sell and the prices, with the aim i) to display these to the farmers via the MBIS and ii) to increase the accuracy of cost of production calculation provided by the MBIS. This led to the suggestion that MBIS should include functionality to support online ordering of these items and at this stage some banks expressed interest to provide micro finance to support farmers who have cash flow issues.

The team found that by using information produced by some groups of stakeholders in the Agriculture Domain, actionable information for another group of stakeholders can be generated. Often to generate this actionable information we need to use information disaggregation or aggregation operations. For example the information about how to grow crops produced by the Department of Agriculture had to be disaggregated and reorganised into an Ontological Knowledgebase to produce actionable information for farmers to assist with crop selection, applying fertilizer and pesticides etc. Information obtained from farmers on crops that they have planned to grow, selected fertilizer etc. had to be aggregated to derive actionable information for farmers themselves on current planned production levels and for people dealing with food security. Aggregated planned fertilizer and chemical usage produced actionable information required for supply chain planning to Agro Chemical companies. Thus using aggregation and disaggregation operations a comprehensive information flow model was developed for the Agriculture Domain (De Silva et al. 2014).

2.3 Motivating Stakeholders to use the System

Next challenge was to discover a method to achieve a sustained flow of information within MBIS. This was essential to keep actionable information derived from dynamic data current. Unlike in enterprise information systems farmers will use MBIS voluntarily. Today Social Networks have been adopted by billions of users. Thus we looked into Social Computing domain to identify ways to motivate farmers to use the system. The literature reveals popular social computing applications support symmetric two way communication enabling a user to be both an information consumer and producer. This two way communication has been exploited to generate aggregated knowledge and social interaction. This in turn empowers users and motivates them to repeatedly use the system (Fernando et al. 2016; Ginige and Fernando 2015).

Empowerment is the process of increasing the capacity of individuals or groups to make choices and to transform those choices into desired actions and outcomes (WorldBank 2016). MBIS was designed to provide choices, for example "what crops will grow in my farm". From the list of crops being presented farmers can take further action to explore the cost of production using the inbuilt expense calculator and types of fertilizer and pesticides needed. Thus through empowerment the system motivates farmers to use the system (Ginige and Richards 2013; Ginige et al. 2014b)

3. DIGITAL KNOWLEDGE ECOSYSTEMS (DKES)

The initial aim of developing the MBIS was to minimise the overproduction problem by providing necessary information to make informed decisions. As a result of using a user centred design concept the system evolved into providing information to assist many other activities in a crop life-cycle (Giovanni et al. 2012a; Giovanni et al. 2012b; Silva et al. 2014). When attempting to find an efficient way to source the required information a complex information flow model for the agriculture domain evolved connecting all major stakeholders (De Silva et al. 2014; L. De Silva et al. 2012). At this stage the information flow model of the MBIS started to resemble energy and nutrient flow model of biological ecosystems.

The concept of biological ecosystem was first proposed by A.G Tansely in the 1930s (Tansley 1935) and has been studied by many since then. From these studies some important aspects relating to biological ecosystems has evolved. A biological ecosystem is a community of living organisms (plants, animals and microbes) in conjunction with the nonliving components of their environment (things like air, water and mineral soil), interacting as a system linked together through nutrient cycles and energy flow (Chapin III et al. 2011).

Similarly the MBIS that evolved for Sri Lankan farmers consisted of major stakeholders of the agriculture domain which formed the community, linked together through information flow with the help of various ICT technologies. In Biological ecosystems energy gets aggregated when animals feed on plants and one another. Decomposers such as worms and microbes decompose the dead animals and biomass releasing this energy and converting matter to a form that can again be absorbed mainly by plants creating a continuous flow pattern (Chapin III et al. 2011). Similarly to create an information flow pattern among main agriculture domain stakeholders we had to introduce information aggregation and disaggregation modules into our system. Like decomposers convert matter to a form that can again be absorbed, MBIS breaks down large chunks of information to actionable information. For this a domain ontology that can be queried in context was developed and based on the ontology an ontological knowledgebase was created. Thus the architecture that evolved for MBIS can be considered as a form of an ecosystem (Ginige et al. 2014a).

When performing the comparison between ecosystems and MBIS the energy flow got mapped to information flow. Aggregation of information produced by one group of stakeholders or a community such as farmers (current production levels, demand for fertilizer etc) becomes a valuable resource for other stakeholders such as Government agencies and agro-chemical companies. Similarly information produced by agro-chemical companies such as price list, how to apply fertilizer when reorganised as crop specific actionable information through disaggregation becomes valuable information to farmers.

4. GROWTH OF DKES FOR AGRICULTURE

Ecosystems start small and then grow. Evolutionary behaviour is a specific characteristic of an ecosystem that helps to grow the population as well as to attract new communities (example – Stakeholder groups such as farmers, agriculture extension officers, agro chemical companies etc). In a Marine ecosystem when weeds start to grow in a waterway it attracts small fish. Then some big fish migrate to that area to eat the small fish. These big fish become food for even bigger fish, other marine animals and birds. When fish, animals and plants die microbes decompose the biomass so that it again becomes nutrients for small plants and fish. These energy and nutrients flow cycles stimulate the growth of communities and the population of the ecosystem.

The overall information flow and its growth of the evolved Digital Knowledge Ecosystem can be mapped as follows. Initially among farmers there is an information need which needs to be satisfied by providing context specific actionable information as shown in figure 2. The quasi static part of this information can be sourced from published knowledge in the domain. This can be reorganised (in MBIS agriculture ontology was developed for this) and provided to farmers as actionable information as shown in figure 3. MBIS provides functions for farmers to act based on this information. Farmers are provided a list of crops that grow in their farm and an expense calculator to find out how much it will cost to grow the planned extent. For this farmers need to input the planned extent and select fertilizer and pesticides recommended by the system based on published literature. The input data provided by farmers are aggregated to derive current level of crop production and demand for fertilizer and pesticides in various parts of the country in the coming months. Now some of the actionable information that needs to be derived based on user inputs is also becoming available. This starts to attract more farmers and other stakeholders growing the population and communities in the ecosystem. This is shown in figure 4. Over time some of the Dynamic information derived previously from user inputs start to become prior knowledge such as production levels in the previous years and the trends, whether the trend indicates effectiveness of a policy being implemented etc. providing actionable information to some other communities such as economic planners and policy makers linked to agriculture domain. This in turn increase the communities and hence the population. This is shown in figure 5.

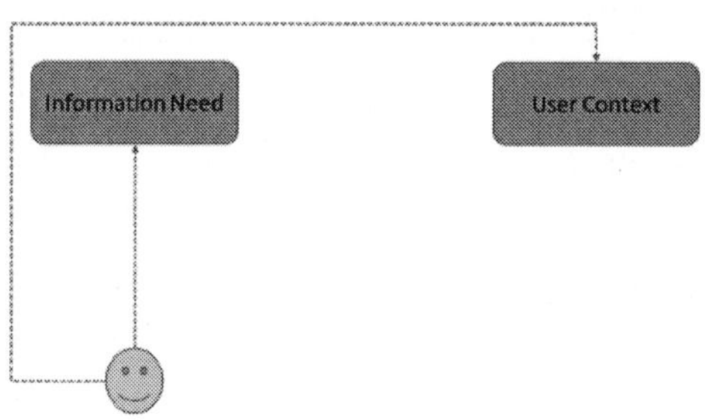

Figure 2. Context specific Information Need

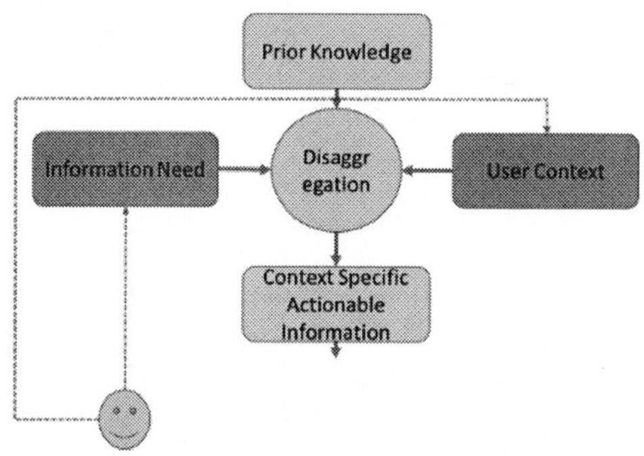

Figure 3. Providing Actionable Information derived from published knowledge

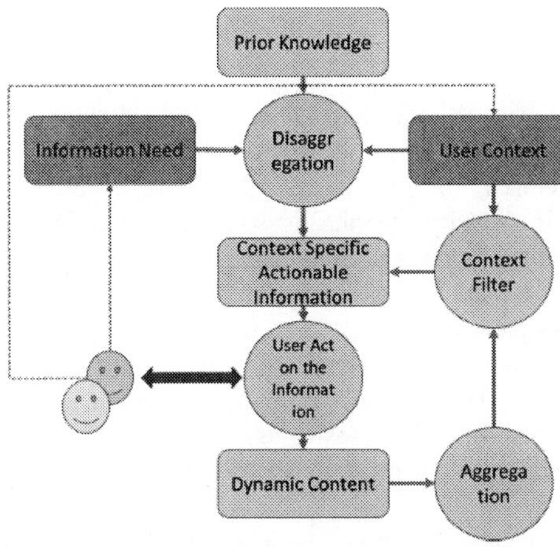

Figure 4. User input data is aggregated to generate Dynamic content which attracts few more farmers, government agencies and agro chemical companies

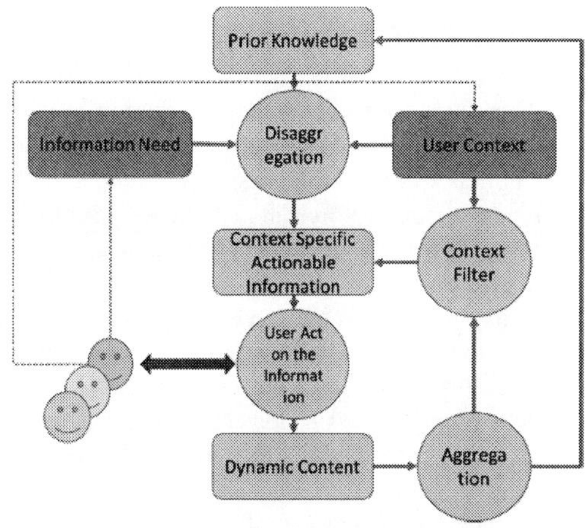

Figure 5. Previously generated Dynamic Information now becomes prior knowledge to derive actionable information to economic planners and policy makers

Since the launch of MBIS in April 2015 we started to observe such growth pattern as shown in figure 6. The initial growth is coming from different communities joining the ecosystem. Initial launch was fully functional research prototype. It did not have the infrastructure capacity to support tens of thousands of users. So initially we restrict the growth of farmer population until new infrastructure is developed.

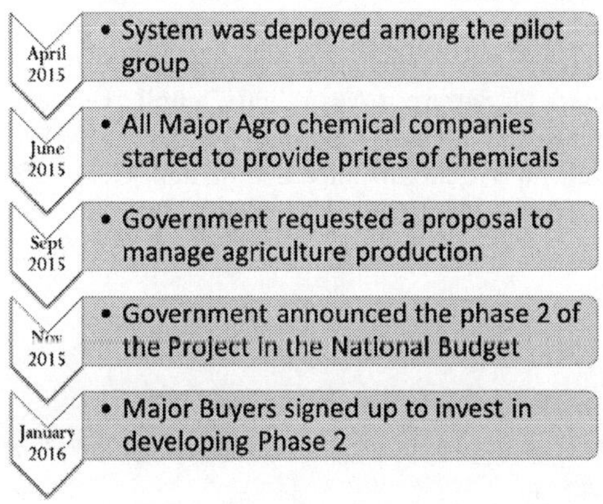

Figure 6. Growth of MBIS Communities since its launch in April 2015

At present few major projects are underway in Sri Lanka, Australia and India to develop Digital Knowledge Ecosystems based on this approach. In Sri Lanka the current Digital Knowledge Ecosystem for farmers is getting enhanced by major agro chemical companies and Super Market chains wanting to provide value added services. In Australia we are exploring the possibility of using Digital Knowledge Ecosystem for chronic Disease management. In India based on Digital Knowledge Ecosystem architecture a Rural Participatory Sensing based Adaptive Agriculture Ontology has been planned to enhance the current mKrishi system developed by Tata Consulting Services to scale up its capacity from current 100,000 farmers to 10 million farmers by 2020.

5. CONCLUSION

As shown above using unprecedented levels of mobile connectivity now available to exchange information digitally, Digital Knowledge Ecosystems can be developed to address a class of global development Grand Challenges that can be mapped to level 2 of Maslow hierarchy of human needs. This level identifies different types of security needs such as food security, economic security, health and wellbeing, etc. Well-designed Digital Knowledge Ecosystems can generate and sustain information flow among all stakeholders through providing context specific actionable information enabling them to make informed decisions optimal to them. It also provides functionality for users to act on the selected choice. Providing choices and enabling them to act empowers and motivate them to continuously use the system. As shown above in a given domain there is a strong dependency among stakeholders in relation to meeting their information needs. This is not a dependency based on direct information sharing but by using techniques to aggregate and disaggregate, an effective information flow model can be developed. Such a flow model creates a win-win situation to all stakeholders.

The key to success of these systems is the ability to provide context specific actionable information in a way to empower users. This motivates users to regularly use the system which in turn keep the information flowing in the system. Using this flow of information it becomes possible to generate actionable information for other stakeholders in the domain which will result in more users joining the Digital Knowledge Ecosystem facilitating its growth both in terms of knowledge and users.

ACKNOWLEDGEMENT

I would like to acknowledge the International Collaborative Research team that developed the Mobile based application for Sri Lankan farmers. This project provided the insights that were reconceptualised in this paper. The team is Lasanthi De Silva, Jeevani Goonetillake, and Gihan Wikramanayake from University of Colombo, Sri Lanka, Tamara Ginige from Australian Catholic University, Australia, Anusha I. Walisadeera from University of Ruhuna, Sri Lanka, Maneesh Mathai from Western Sydney University, Australia, Pasquale Di Giovanni, Giuliana Vitiello, Monica Sebillo and Genoveffa Tortora from University of Salerno, Italy, Deborah Richards from Macquarie University, Australia and Ramesh Jain from University of California Irvine, USA.

REFERENCES

Chapin III, F. S., Matson, P. A., and Vitousek, P. 2011. *Principles of Terrestrial Ecosystem Ecology*. Springer Science & Business Media.

De Silva, L., Goonetillake, J., Wikramanayake, G., and Ginige, A. 2014. "Towards an Agriculture Information Ecosystem," *25th Australasian Conference on Information Systems,*: ACIS.

De Silva, L. N. C., Goonethilaka, J., Wikramanayake, G. N., and Ginige, A. 2013a. "Farmer Response Towards the Initial Agriculture Information Dissemination Mobile Prototype," in: *1st International Workshop on Agricultural and Environmental Information and Decision Support Systems -AEIDSS 2013*. Ho Chi Minh City, Vietnam.

De Silva, L. N. C., Goonetillake, J. S., Wikramanayake, G. N., and Ginige, A. 2013b. "Farmer Response Towards the Initial Agriculture Information Dissemination Mobile Prototype," in *Computational Science and Its Applications – Iccsa 2013,* B. Murgante, S. Misra, M. Carlini, C. Torre, H.-Q. Nguyen, D. Taniar, B. Apduhan and O. Gervasi (eds.). Springer Berlin Heidelberg, pp. 264-278.

Fernando, M. D., Ginige, A., and Hol, A. 2016. "Impact of Social Computing on Business Outcomes," in: *13th International Conference on Web Based Communities and Social Media*. Funchal, Madeira, Portugal.

Ginige, A. 2011. "Social Life Networks for the Middle of the Pyramid." Retrieved 25/03/2012, 2012, from http://www.sln4mop.org//index.php/sln/articles/index/1/3

Ginige, A., and Fernando, M. D. 2015. "Towards a Generic Model for Social Computing and Emergent Characteristics," in: *2nd Asia-Pacific World Congress on Computer Science & Engineering (APWC on CSE 2015)*. Shangri-La Fijian Resort, Fiji.

Ginige, A., Silva, L. D., Ginige, T., Giovanni, P. D., Walisadeera, A. I., Mathai, M., Goonetillake, J., Wikramanayake, G., Vitiello, G., Sebillo, M., Tortora, G., Richards, D., and Jain, R. 2014a. "Towards an Agriculture Knowledge Ecosystem: A Social Life Network for Farmers in Sri Lanka," *9th Conference of the Asian Federation for Information Technology in Agriculture - 2014,* L. Armstrong and A. Neuhaus (eds.), Perth, Australia: Australian Society of Information and Communication Technologies in Agriculture Inc., pp. 170 -179.

Ginige, T., and Richards, D. 2013. "Development of Mobile-Based Empowerment Processes for Sri Lankan Farmers," in: *24th Australasian Conference on Information Systems* Melbourne.

Ginige, T., Richards, D., and Hitchens, M. 2014b. "Cultivation Planning Application to Enhance Decision Making among Sri Lankan Farmers," in *Knowledge Management and Acquisition for Smart Systems and Services,* Y. Kim, B. Kang and D. Richards (eds.). Springer International Publishing, pp. 180-194.

Giovanni, P. D., Romano, M., Sebillo, M., Tortora, G., Vitiello, G., Silva, L. D., Goonethilaka, J., Wikramanayake, G., Ginige, T., and Ginige, A. 2012a. "Building Social Life Networks through Mobile Interfaces– the Case Study of Sri Lanka Farmers " in: *IX Conference of the Italian Chapter of AIS (ITAIS 2012)*. Rome, Italy.

Giovanni, P. D., Romano, M., Sebillo, M., Tortora, G., Vitiello, G., Silva, L. D., Goonethilaka, J., Wikramanayake, G., Ginige, T., and Ginige, A. 2012b. "User Centered Scenario Based Approach for Developing Mobile Interfaces for Social Life Networks," in: *34th International Conference on Software Engineering (ICSE 2012) - UsARE Workshops*. Zurich, Switzerland.

Hettiarachchi, S. 2011. "Leeks Cultivators Desperate as Price Drops to Record Low," in: *Sunday Times*. Sri Lanka.

Hettiarachchi, S. 2012. "N'eliya Carrot Farmers in the Dumps: Bumper Harvest, but Prices Low," in: *The Sunday Times* Sri Lanka.

Kemp, S. 2015. "We Are Social." *We are Social's Compendium of Global Digital Statistics* Retrieved 1 October, 2015, from http://www.slideshare.net/wearesocialsg/digital-social-mobile-in-2015

L. De Silva, J. S. Goonethilake, G.N. Wickramanayake, and A. Ginige. 2012. "Towards Using Ict to Enhance Flow of Information to Aid Farmer Sustainability in Sri Lanka," in: *Australasian Conference on Information Systems (ACIS)*. Geelong Australia: p. 10.

Maslow, A. H. 1943. "A Theory of Human Motivation," *Psychological Review* (50), pp. 370-396.

Mathai, M., and Ginige, A. 2013. "Context Based Contenet Aggregation for Social Life Networks," in: *8th International Conference on Software Paradigm Trends (ICSOFT-PT 2013)*. Reykjavik, Iceland: SCITEPRESS.

Mathai, M., and Ginige, A. 2014. "Task Oriented Context Models for Social Life Networks," in *Software Technologies*. Springer Berlin Heidelberg, pp. 306-321.

Silva, L. D., Goonetillake, J., Wikramanayake, G., Ginige, A., Ginige, T., Giovanni, P. D., Walisadeera, A. I., Mathai, M., Vitiello, G., Sebillo, M., and Tortora, G. 2014. "Design Science Research Based Blended Approach for Usability Driven Requirements Gathering and Application Development," *Second International Workshop on Usability and Accessibility focused Requirements Engineering*, Karlskrona, Sweden: IEEE Xplore, pp. 17 - 24.

Statista. 2015. "The Statistics Portal." Retrieved 5th August 2015, from http://www.statista.com/statistics/264810/number-of-monthly-active-facebook-users-worldwide/

Tansley, A. G. 1935. "The Use and Abuse of Vegetational Concepts and Terms," *Ecology* (16:3), pp. 284-307.

TRC. 2015. "Telecommunications Regulatory Commission of Sri Lanka - Statistics." from http://www.trc.gov.lk/2014-05-13-03-56-46/statistics.html

Walisadeera, A. I., Ginige, A., and Wikramanayake, G. N. 2014. "Conceptualizing Crop Life Cycle Events to Create a User Centered Ontology for Farmers," *International Conference on Computational Science and its Applications (ICCSA 2014),* B.e.a. Murgante (ed.), Poroto, Portugal: Springer International Publishing, Switzerland, pp. 791–806.

Walisadeera, A. I., Ginige, A., and Wikramanayake, G. N. 2015. "User Centered Ontology for Sri Lankan Farmers," *Ecological Informatics* (26, Part 2:0), pp. 140-150.

Walisadeera, A. I., Wikramanayake, G. N., and Ginige, A. 2013. "An Ontological Approach to Meet Information Needs of Farmers in Sri Lanka," in: *1st International Workshop on Agricultural and Environmental Information and Decision Support Systems (AEIDSS 2013).* Ho Chi Minh City, Vietnam.: Springer.

Wikipedia. 2016. "Education in Sri Lanka." *Wikipedia*, from https://en.wikipedia.org/wiki/Education_in_Sri_Lanka

WorldBank. 2016. "Empowerment." Retrieved 12 May 2016, 2016, from http://go.worldbank.org/V45HD4P100

AFTER-SALES AND CRM: THEIR ROLE AS A DIFFERENTIATION STRATEGY FOR CLIENTS

Carlos Santos[1] and Pedro Isaias[2]
[1]*ISEG - Universidade Aberta (Portuguese Open University), Portugal*
[2]*Universidade Aberta (Portuguese Open University), Portugal & ADVANCE Research Center, ISEG – University of Lisbon, Portugal*

ABSTRACT

Longevity, in the relationship with customers, is becoming increasingly more important in sustainable enterprises. Their continuity on the market depends on these relationships; hence, the strategic focus in differentiating factors for competitive advantage achievement is increasingly common. All aspects of the relationship with the client are extremely important; however some have been less explored, such as after-sales service and CRM, which can be the strategic basis for differentiation. This paper aims to demonstrate that after-sales service and CRM can be used by companies as instruments to measure customer satisfaction, to gather their opinions, to share experiences, to motivate client loyalty and to attract new customers. This research used the motor vehicle repair industry as an example, and conducted a questionnaire using a sample of 269 clients to assess their satisfaction.

KEYWORDS

After-sales; CRM; Differentiation Strategy; Client Loyalty

1. INTRODUCTION

There is an increasing tendency for companies to create their marketing budgets with a focus on the achievement of sales and new customers. They allocate large amounts of funding for marketing and advertising campaigns that are often aggressive, but in most companies, the relationship with the customer ends after the sale as been completed. Usually, there is no follow-up with the client, which results in a complete negligence of the wealth of information contained in clients' databases. The investment in after-sale segment is beneficial not only for the customers but also for the companies, which could collect valuable data about their clients' purchasing behaviour, their experience and about their critiques and suggestions.

The after-sales service is another important way to show the customer that his/her satisfaction is a priority. It serves as an important support after the purchase and it is fundamental in the understanding of the company's responsibility in dealing with unhappy customers or problems arising from the purchase. These problems lead, most of the time, to the end of the relationship.

Thus, rather than investing on aggressive marketing policies, on messaging and promotion emails in an uncoordinated manner stating the existence of promotions and new products that dissatisfied customers choose to ignore, companies should invest in CRM (customer Relationship Management) and after-sales service. These two elements of the customer relationship are important factors to consider in defining a strategy of differentiation. They demonstrate support and provide the client with a follow-up, enabling the company to ensure that the customers' satisfaction remains a priority even after the sale has been completed and that the company is concerned with addressing their expectations.

2. BACKGROUND

The market is increasingly volatile and it is constantly changing. There are increasingly more differentiating factors that play a key role in the consumer choice. Quality, timeliness and good service have become basic requirements and they are no longer considered differentiators. In order for companies to obtain a competitive advantage, long-term sustainability and to keep a central place in the market they have to, necessarily, set new differentiation strategies that can distinguish them from their competitors.

The investment in CRM and after-sales service can no doubt be a great advantage as the elements of loyalty assume a greater importance. However in most companies these services are undervalued. Poor after-sales service and millionaire marketing campaigns are sometimes counterproductive, because the client feels deceived and unsupported after the purchase. Understanding that after the sale the customer relationship does not end brings long-term benefits to the connection that companies can establish with their clients. The customers can be surveyed as to their satisfaction with the repair, they can be offered a clarification in terms of the need to replace parts and they can be given the opportunity to pose questions or place a complaint. It is important for customers to feel that their satisfaction is more important that the sale.

Although the CRM concept has already been very exploited, its alliance with the after-sales service is under researched. It is important to view customer relationship as an outcome of the management of the entire relationship with the customer after the sale. This management should be done through a constant survey of the consumers' satisfaction and in situations where there is discontent or a poor service, the after-sales should work not only as a mere complaints' desk, but as a full department that can address all dissatisfaction and minimize the disruption caused to the client in the shortest possible time.

2.1 Customer Satisfaction

The term client is common in all businesses regardless of their sector or country and has evolved through time and the more traditional definition that characterizes the client as a mere individual who acquired goods or services produced by a company, has been replaced by a more empowering concept of customers that places them in the spotlight, as stated by Kotler and Armstrong (2008). The company only reaches its full quality when their products and services meet or exceed the customer expectations. This basic principle is behind the popular sentence "the customer is always right". Companies that focus their efforts on customer satisfaction, make decisions, monitor and manage their business according to the clients, their needs, their expectations, their tastes and their opinion. The customer becomes the ultimate goal of business, because it has became clear that it is the customer that ensures the survival of the company. The competition among companies in the market has grown more aggressive and satisfied customers are central, since they can not only return and continue to buy, but they can also work as a recommender and he/she will bring in new customers.

It is now indisputable that the customers are key factors in the success of any business, it is crucial that companies become aware that their tastes, needs and expectations are constantly evolving and changing. The increase of competitiveness has led companies to invest in innovative methods of addressing the needs and tastes of their clients and focus on their satisfaction (Simon & Honore Petnji Yaya, 2012).

According to ORACLE (2012) around 86% of the customers will choose to use a competitor as the result of a bad customer experience. Also, 79% of the clients that decide to share, online, their negative views about a company, do so because their initial protests were ignored.

Kotler and Keller (2006) argue that companies that are focused on customer satisfaction and define their market strategies based on the principle that the customer is unique and the key element in their long-term sustainability, achieve greater commercial success. The same authors also advocate the idea that customers are more informed and fully integrated into the global market. In light of the fierce competition and supply that exists, they now evaluate beyond the product and the provision of service. Additional services, such as after-sale care, take a distinctive role that can be decisive. This depends on the quality of the service offered, i.e., the budget and the time that the company spends on this type of service and the information and support that are given to the customer.

Despite the fact that Kotler (2000) highlights the importance of attracting new customers in order to obtain growth and results that allows a companies' expansion, he also states that if a company wishes to maintain its profits and sustained growth, it has to retain the customers it attracts. The priority in this case, is to pay special attention to their wants and needs, to be aware that customers often evaluate the offers that are available to them and that they always choose those that represent more value to them. The loyalty of consumers can be achieved if the offers that companies have available meet their needs and expectations. The key to customer retention is the delivery of a high level of satisfaction and value. Although companies are increasingly more aware of the importance of retaining their customers, the larger part of marketing budgets focuses on attracting new clients (Kotler, 2000).

Kotler (2000) also notes that acquiring new customers costs up to five times more than the costs involved in assuring customer satisfaction and retention and that companies lose an average of 10 % of its customers every year.

As mentioned by Frederick and Sasser (1990) if there is a 5% increase in the customer loyalty indicator, the overall profit of the business can reach 100%. Satisfied customers buy more frequently and in greater quantities. Moreover, they are less sensitive to prices' variation, since they are willing to pay more for products that they have tested and that match their expectations and needs.

2.2 After-sales Service

After-sales refers to the customer service that takes place after the client's purchase. It encompasses all the required activities to ensure the proper functionality of the product or to ensure an effective quality service provision (Vitasek, 2005). The after-sales service can be viewed through two perspectives: the services can be considered as one of the several additional services provided (Oliva & Kallenberg, 2003); and they can also be viewed as an operational stage of the distribution chain (Gaiardelli, Saccani, & Songini, 2007). Gaiardelli et al. (2007) highlighted the strategic importance of after-sales service, by stating that none of the actors of the whole supply chain should discontinue their relationship with the customer after purchase. It is precisely at this stage that a more committed effort should be made to ensure a stable and long-lasting relationship with the consumer.

Along with the evolution of the customers' focus and their constant concern with meeting their needs, the strategic importance of after-sales service has evolved over time. It is no longer seen as a mere and expensive extension of the main service. It acquired an important strategic role, with a great weight in the results of companies. After-sales service allows the collection of important strategic information, maximising the continual improvement of the company and it concentrates on customer satisfaction. According to Kotler and Keller (2006) it is strategically important, from the viewpoint of sustainability and continuity of long-term business, that top managers and those responsible for marketing firms, realize and understand the whole process of buying and their respective steps since the stage of capture of the customers' attention, through their evaluation of other alternatives on the market, to after-sales services. The after-sales service is of great importance for both the customer and the company.

Around 70 % of the customers who make a complaint return to the service provider again, if the issue is resolved, while 95% of them return if the issue is resolved in the shortest time possible. Thus, the service providers who make a close follow-up and care about the satisfaction of its customers, working on the basis of rich and updated information about their costumers, will help to improve the quality of costumer care and their consequent satisfaction (Kotler & Keller, 2006).

In a study they conducted, Gaiardelli et al. (2007) concluded that service provision, particularly after-sales, will necessarily imply a constant monitoring and continuous evaluation of all stages of the service delivery process. The authors identified four types of strategic after-sales profiles within companies: support the product, make money, generate business and promote the brand. These profiles range from the mere requirement to have an extension after the sale, which helps the client in case of damage or doubt about the functionality after the acquisition; the companies that follow strategic guidelines based on meeting customer needs; and looking to the after-sale service not as an obligation but as an opportunity (Gaiardelli et al., 2007).

2.3 Customer Relationship Management

The existing definition of CRM have one aspect in common, they all refer to customer focus and loyalty. As mentioned by Kotler and Keller (2006), CRM is not more than the detailed management information about each customer and all aspects related to this. The main goal of CRM is to create and improve relationships with the clients, across their life cycle and not just at the moment of the sale.

With the information available through CRM, it is possible to enhance and adapt the offers to the customers' needs in order to secure their loyalty. For this to happen, it is essential that companies clearly identify the attributes of products and services that add value to the customer and that are capable of generating loyalty.

For Feinberg and Kadam (2002), CRM had a greater impetus, with the evolution of Web 1.0 to Web 2.0. The authors define the concept as a:

> *discipline associated with the business and technology that uses information systems to coordinate all the business processes associated with the activity of the organization, which deals with the service, sales, marketing and customer support, playing an important organization's intermediary role in the relationship with the client, and the information collected is centralized and directed to the client, allowing various elements of the organization to interact with that, without losing sight of its uniqueness, and achieving a more personalized service, while increasing profitability and customer retention probability.*

On the other hand, Stair and Reynolds (2008), argue the important contribution that CRM makes to the companies' relationship with customers, from the department of marketing and advertising, to the important after-sales services, highlighting how the information collected from customers, allows future work the ability to anticipate the current and potential customers needs, optimizing the way products and services are sold, increasing costumer's retention and loyalty.

3. METHODS

There are numerous studies on strategies/sales policies, and integrated marketing communications that address customer relations and the impact that they have on companies' sales. Nonetheless, very little has been researched about the power that dissatisfied customers have over potential customers and about the importance of after-sales services as a strategy for dispute resolution and customer retention.

After the sale, there are many companies that contact their customers to assess their satisfaction. In the specific case of car repair businesses there is rarely any survey of the clients′ opinions about their experience with the repair and about the service. Usually, only the larger car repair brands seek some form of clients' feedback. In this scenario the company tries to gather the customers' constructive comments or criticism when it is noticed that the clients hasn't resorted to the service for some time.

This research aims to demonstrate the significance that after-sales and CRM have in creating customer loyalty in the car repair sector. It intends to explain the way in which a structured follow-up allows an increase in loyalty and the extent to which it might directly contribute to an enhancement of results. Also, it endeavours to exemplify how the after-sales service is very important. Rather than being merely seen as a complaints department it should be regarded as a department of relational marketing, that is concerned with the complaints and needs of the clients and that understands and accepts their opinions and suggestions.

The empirical research was based on online questionnaire that was applied to 269 people who had recently used car repair services. The selected sample was constituted by 269 respondents of both sexes aged between 20 and 69 years old. The questionnaire tried to assess the importance that customers attributed to the after-sales care, if they felt motivated to reuse the service and to recommend it to other customers. The questionnaires will also be used to confirm the following hypotheses that were generated by the review of the literature:

H1: If the consumers feel motivated by the after-sale follow-up then they will adopt behaviour of repurchase [If... Then];

H2: There is a connection between the effectiveness of after-sale monitoring and organizational capacity of information management in the monitoring of customers [Non-directional];

H3: The greater the importance of monitoring for the client, the greater his/her motivation to repurchase [Directional];

H4: There is a relation between the after-sales monitoring time interval and the importance that this has for consumers. [Non Directional];

H5: The after-sale monitoring is as motivating to the customers, as the efficient management of complaints [Null];

H6: The efficient management of complaints is more motivating than the after-sales follow-up in terms of customers' repurchase [Alternative].

Since the objective of the study involves understanding the relationship and the impact of different variables, correlational study will be adopted, to verify the correlation between motivation and adoption behaviour.

4. RESULTS

The analysis of the results of the questionnaires was conducted using the method of factor analysis in principal components with varimax rotation, and it was assumed based on the analysis of the test value Keiser -Meyer- Olkin (KMO = 0.902), that the sample size was adequate to carry out the exploratory factor analysis.

Table 1. KMO and Bratlett's Test

KMO and Bartlett test		
Kaiser-Meyer-Olkin measure of sampling adequacy		.902
Bartlett´s test of Sphericity	Approx. Chi-Square	4423.878
	df	595
	Sig.	.000

The results show that the first eight factors explain about 62.05% of the variance in the total explained variance of the first factor, referred to as Customer Satisfaction that was 23.50%.

However, as found in the answers of respondents to the questionnaire distributed, the car repair companies cannot simply implement a CRM follow-up and after-sales service in their remedial workshops, it is essential to develop a set of processes that contribute to its effectiveness.

It became evident that there is a good correlation ($p = 0.632$ and $p = 0.737$) in the relation between the capacity and organization of the restorative workshop, the use of the database and CRM software to store customer information and the maximization of their relationship with them by sending often through CRM (mail, newsletter, sms) deals with information / campaigns and new services and the maintenance and updating of all customer information for future CRM (mail, phone, telephone, address, fax). However there was a very low correlation between the monitoring time interval and the relevance this has to the after service provided. When the respondents were asked about their relationship with car repair shops and if they believed that it is relevant to be contacted with questions regarding the quality and the professionalism of the service, after the repair performed 40.1% of the respondents said always. Only 13% reported that they never liked to be contacted. Notwithstanding, only 16% of respondents who liked to always be contacted, were in fact contacted by the service provider.

Around 58% of the respondents stated that the owner of the garage is the main mechanic, which leads us to conclude that most frequents small workshops, neighbourhood workshops or limit workshops clandestine, where the owner is not only the main mechanical as well as the one, which immediately shows how much the market for car repair in Portugal has to evolve, grow and segment and explains some percentages of the responses.

Although it still has much room for improvement, the car repair industry, has been following the evolution of the global market over the years. It is important to note that 68% of respondents said that the workshop that they usually resort to is often or always clean and that it is visually attractive and inspires confidence. It was certainly unthinkable to obtain such a percentage a few years ago, mainly in small workshops. Another sign of evolution that became clear in the answers of the respondents, regards to attention that the client receives. As is the case in most of the market, the majority of the respondents recognized an important commercial development in the mechanical sector, with 68.8% saying that often or always, they service providers exhibit a clear, enlightening and transparent manner throughout the repair process and the needs it generates. The participants also state that there is an increased concern for the interests and needs of the customer and not just a technical focus in the mechanical aspect of the car repair. This same perception is mirrored by the respondents. When they were asked if the main focus of the workshop is attending to their satisfaction, about 79.6% responded that this is often or always true.

With regard to the quality factor, 92.6 % of respondents said that often or always or often their level of satisfaction is decisive in their choice. In term of the price, 58% consider that it is always a factor, because we live in a time of crisis and financial difficulties and the price factor assumes most of the time a decisive role. However, given that the quality factor is equally important, it was noted that comparing the two, for more than half of respondents (55.8%) quality of service along with the monitoring and transparency of the service has a more important role than the price. Hence, it is possible to conclude that 67.3% of respondents exhaustively considered that "if I am satisfied with the quality and the monitoring of the service, I have no need to try other car repair shop, even if the price is more competitive".

In addition to the lack of quality in the technical aspects of the car repair services, an important aspect to consider and that it causes most of the customers to be displeased, is undoubtedly the distrust that they feel towards the amount that they paid. Often, the amount on the initial budget does not match the value that is displayed on the invoice and in other situations, the client suspects that he/she is paying for parts that were not put in their car. When the participants were asked about this aspect, only less than 10% reported that they have rarely or never felt that they have paid a fair value, while the majority (58.7%) states that the amounts that they have paid are fair. This shows that the prejudice that dictates that car repair shops are grossly overpriced is changing due to the fact that customers are more supported and that the employees have a stronger commercial attitude. This is another example of progress within the car repair market.

There was also a very low correlation ($p = 0.051$ and $p = 0.088$) regarding the direct relationship between sending frequent information deals/campaigns to the car repair shops' customers through CRM (email, newsletter, sms) and contacting the clients regularly (email, phone, telephone, address, fax) and the fact that they would be faithful to them whenever a problem occurs in the vehicle. It appears so that this association was not statistically significant.

There is also a low correlation ($p = 0.357$) between the level of satisfaction on the repairs made on the participants' cars and the fact that loyalty is decisive whether or not the choice of the car repair shop. Although the correlation exists, it is still remarkable that it is low. However, we had already seen earlier that, when dissatisfied with the service, 58% of respondents wished to demonstrate their discontent directly to the person who serviced. Despite being a significant value and representing the majority, this is considered a low percentage, since we are referring to the dissatisfaction of clients. This percentage becomes even lower (14%) when the respondents were asked to do so in writing and surprisingly, even lower (7.8%) when asked to immediately choose a competitor as an alternative service provider.

5. DISCUSSION AND CONCLUSION

Through this study, mainly via the literature review, it is possible to conclude that longevity and customer loyalty are becoming increasingly more significant in the relationship with customers in sustainable enterprises. Their continuity in the market depends on these, so the strategic focus in differentiating factors that can increase the competitive advantage achievement is increasingly common. Every detail of this relationship assumes a great importance, however some have been less explored in research, as is the case of CRM monitoring and after-sales service.

Several authors argue that the focus on customer satisfaction should be the constant concern of businesses when trying to acquire competitive advantages and not the traditional emphasis on competition. Also, they should invest in the creation of a long-term sustainability, in particular in the link between the different dimensions and the needs of the clients, in order to create new areas and new processes that can provide greater operational efficiency and offer customers a higher quality without representing more costs.

The loyalty strategies encompass a wide variety of complex strategic processes in the relationship with customers. They range from the concern on meeting the customers' needs, such as investment in process improvement and continuing quality of services, to attract new customers, and not just to sell or to provide a service with quality (in the view of the company). It is essential to account for a number of factors such as satisfaction, availability of simple and intuitive information, functionality and warranty, technical assistance, among other criteria that can create competitive advantage and separate a company from its competition. It has become clear that satisfied customers can bring other clients via their recommendation or just by sharing their satisfaction. On the other hand, a dissatisfied customer can prevent potential customers from using a specific service based on their anger with the service and by sharing the poor experience. Some clients do that without having claimed or demonstrated their indignation, so it is important to follow-up on the customer after the purchase has been completed. It is important to see if the customers were satisfied and if their experience with the service lived up to their expectations. The majority of the respondents (62.1%) said that they have learned about the existence of the repair shop that they use, due to a suggestion of a friend, one that was possibly so satisfied with the services that were provided that suggested them. However, only 25.2% of the respondents stated that they always recommend the car repair shop that they use to other people.

In conclusion, despite the dissatisfaction of the respondents, the existence of financial issues, the convenience, the complexity of the market, the short supply and other varied factors, people do not choose immediately to seek another alternative. This may explain why the after sales service and customer follow-up is not very strongly implemented in the sector, although it is important for these. It is expected, nonetheless, that in the near future the market will evolve, that competition will become even greater with even more options, giving customers a greater choice.

REFERENCES

Feinberg, R., & Kadam, R. (2002). E-CRM Web service attributes as determinants of customer satisfaction with retail Web sites. *International Journal of Service Industry Management, 13*(5), 432-451.

Frederick, F. R., & Sasser, W. E. (1990). Zero defections: quality comes to services. *Harvard business review, 68*(5), 105.

Gaiardelli, P., Saccani, N., & Songini, L. (2007). Performance measurement systems in after-sales service: an integrated framework. *International Journal of Business Performance Management, 9*(2), 145-171.

Kotler, P. (2000). *Marketing management: The millennium edition*: Prentice-Hall Upper Saddle River, NJ.

Kotler, P., & Armstrong, G. (2008). Principle of Marketing [M]: Pearson Prentice Hall.

Kotler, P., & Keller, K. (2006). Marketing management. *12*, 181-183.

Oliva, R., & Kallenberg, R. (2003). Managing the transition from products to services. *International Journal of Service Industry Management, 14*(2), 160-172.

ORACLE. (2012). 2011 Customer Experience Impact Report: Getting to the Heart of the Consumer and Brand Relationship.

Simon, A., & Honore Petnji Yaya, L. (2012). Improving innovation and customer satisfaction through systems integration. *Industrial Management & Data Systems, 112*(7), 1026-1043.

Stair, R., & Reynolds, G. (2008). *Principles of information systems*: Cengage Learning.

Vitasek, K. (2005). Logistics terms and glossary. *Bellevue, Washington: Supply Chain Visions. Council of Logistic Management's Website.*

THE USE OF TWITTER FOR GOVERNMENT AGENCIES IN INDONESIA

Nurhalimah Harahap[1,2] and Dr. Indra Budi[2]
[1]*Ministry of Industry, Jl. Gatot Subroto Kav.52-53 Jakarta, Indonesia 12950*
[2]*Faculty of Computer Science, Universitas Indonesia, Kampus UI Depok, Indonesia 16424*

ABSTRACT

Nowadays, e-government implementation in Indonesia does not meet the objectives of presidential regulation on "E-government Policy". Based on the report of the United Nations in 2014, Indonesia obtained 0.4487 out of 1 for e-government and 0.2941 out of 1 for e-participation. Social media is a good way to increase e-government and e-participation because it is inexpensive, easy to implement and has been implemented by several nations that have high e-government and e-participation index. Therefore, this study aimed to analyse the phenomenon of social media used by government agencies in Indonesia, particularly messages posted in Twitter. The messages are analysed based on content, tone, source, source type, forms, and response. The result showed that Corruption Eradication Commission obtains the highest index of twitter use (9.031 out of 100) among other agencies. This number indicates that the use of Twitter by government agencies in Indonesia are not optimal.

KEYWORDS

Social media, Twitter, social media metrics, e-government, content analysis, society.

1. INTRODUCTION

E-government is officially implemented as the Presidential Instruction of the Republic of Indonesia Number 3 year of 2003 on "e-government policy" enacted. However, the implementation of e-government in Indonesia is still far from its objectives which are stated in the presidential regulation. This Issue also depicted in the report of the United Nations (UN) assessment in 2014. According to the report, Indonesia's E-government Development Index (EGDI) is 0.449 out of 1 and E-participation Index (EPI) is 0.294 out of 1. As can be seen in Table 1, the growth of Indonesia's EGDI from 2003 up to 2014 is not significant, the index is about 0.4. In fact, in 2004-2005, the index was under 0.4. The Indonesia's EPI is even worse, during the same period, the highest achieved index is only 0.294 out of 1 and the EPI was almost zero in 2008. Therefore, it can be concluded that citizen participation and interaction between government agencies in Indonesia with the citizens is still low.

Table 1. Indonesia's EGDI and EPI

Index\Year	2003	2004	2005	2008	2010	2012	2014
EGDI	0.422	0.391	0.382	0.411	0.403	0.495	0.449
EPI	0.259	0.262	0.286	0.046	0.129	0.211	0.294

Source: (United Nations 2014)

There are several ways can be used to increase interaction between government and citizens, one of them is social media. Social media is a great way to use e-participation because it is easy and does not require high investments to implement (United Nations 2014), and the users also increased rapidly (eMarketer 2013). In addition, many nations whose EGDI and EPI index are high already use it, such as Korea (Kim & Park 2014), Australia (Alam & Lucas 2011), Japan (Kaigo & Okura 2015), Unites States (Mergel 2013), and Saudi Arabia (Al-Saggaf & Simmons 2015). The UN report states that in 2014, there were 118 countries that use social media for e-consultation, and 71 countries for e-government. Therefore, the use of social media by the government to build interactive communication with the citizens is promising to some extent. Hence, this study aims to analyse how government agencies in Indonesia utilize their social media, particularly Twitter, in order to increase citizens participation and communication.

2. THEORETICAL OVERVIEW

E-government is Information and Communication Technology usage to streamline and integrate workflows and processes, to manage data and information effectively, to improve public services, and to expand the communications network in order to engage and empower citizens (Fugini et al. 2014; United Nations 2014). E-government types are classified into eight categories: Government-to-Citizen (G2C), Citizen-to-Government (C2G), Government-to-Business (G2B), Business-to-Government (B2G), Government-to-Employee (G2E), Government-to-Government (G2G), Government-to-Non-profit (G2N), and Non-profit-to-Government (N2G) (Yanqing 2011). UN states there are nine channels of communication that can be used to provide public services. There are counter service, telephone service and call centre; public kiosks, intermediaries through public-private partnership, web portal, email, short message service (SMS), mobile portal & mobile app, and social media. Public services can be improved through a combination of integrated and coordinated various channels, also known as multichannel services. Web portals, mobile channels and social media will be a key driver to reach wider users and bridge the digital usage in the society (United Nations 2014). Social media is a tool designed for sharing information, communication, and social interaction among individuals, groups, communities, companies, and governments using internet (Al-Saggaf & Simmons 2015; Dawot & Ibrahim 2014; Heverin & Zach, 2010; Smith et al. 2015; Zheng & Zheng 2012). Benefits of social media for government are encourage transparency by providing information regarding government regulations and citizen rights, disseminate information about government performance, and provide information about government agency's plans, decisions, and actions (Heverin & Zach, 2010).

Social media functionalities are classified based on how people use them, as described in the honeycomb of social media. There are identity, conversations, sharing, presence, relationship, reputation, and groups. Identity is revealing person's the identity. Conversations are communication with others. Sharing is exchange content. Presence is knowing other users are accessible. Relationship is users relate to others. Reputation is grouping classes of users. Groups is creating communities and sub-communities (Kietzmann et al. 2011). Besides the entities in the honeycomb, the use of social media in public sector in government are transparency, participation, and collaboration. Transparency is providing about government activities. Participation is providing citizens opportunities to give feedback on policy formulation. Collaboration is when the citizens can evaluate and improve the level of collaboration with government and identify new opportunities for coordination (Dawot & Ibrahim 2014). Characteristics of social media are participation, openness, conversations, community, and connectedness. Participation is social media encourages contributions and feedback from any interested person. Openness is social media opens for feedback and participations. Conversations are social media is seen as a dialogue because its' two-way communication. Community is social media allows communities to be formed quickly and communicate effectively. Connectedness is the growing social media in user network (Zheng & Zheng 2012). Three social media take public attention are Facebook, Twitter, and Google (Taprial & Kanwar 2012). Twitter is a form of social media that able to post messages, called "tweets", by maximum 140 characters (F. Dianne Lux Wigand 2010; Naaman et al. 2010). Tweets displayed on the user's page and subscribers, called followers, as a stream of messages. Twitter becomes an interactive space of open communication because users can react directly to other user's tweets (Denef et al. 2013; F. Dianne Lux Wigand 2010).

Study about social media appeared since Twitter had launched in 2006. Java et al. (2007) studied about messages content posted by users in Twitter in 2007. Honeycutt and Herring (2009) and Naaman et al. (2010) conducted study in similar topic. Riemer et al. (2010) analysed messages content of social media in an enterprise environment. Furthermore, messages content analysis became more popular since studies in 2010 by analysing the content social media of government agencies (F. Dianne Lux Wigand 2010). Study conducted by Heverin and Zach (2010) was not only analysed the content of police messages, but also the content of the messages from users who posted messages to the police. Moreover, Heverin and Zach (2010) also expanded the study by analysing the messages source posted by police agencies. A similar study also conducted by Alam and Lucas (2011) in 2011, unfortunately the study only analysed messages content posted by government agencies and citizens. More complete study conducted by Zheng and Zheng (2012) in 2012. The study analysed the messages content, messages source, messages forms, and messages response posted by government agencies. The citizens messages posted to government agencies were analysed based on messages tone and messages source type (Zheng & Zheng 2012). Sobacci and Karkin (2013) studied messages content used by the mayors in Turkey in 2013. Based on the messages content, the study was expanded because it analysed not only messages content posted individually, but also messages content posted by government agencies. Unfortunately the study was not expanded like the study conducted by Zheng and Zheng (2012) in 2012 (Sobacci & Karkin 2013). Then Zheng and Zheng (2014) conducted study about messages content, forms, source, source type, and response in 2014. The study was more complete than previous studies, but unfortunately it did not analyse messages posted by citizens (Zheng & Zheng 2014). Then the study conducted by Smith et al. (2015) in 2015. The study was more complete than previous studies because it analysed messages content, tone, source, source type, forms, and response. However, the study analysed the use of social media in crisis or emergency situations (Smith et al. 2015). This study tries to perform more complete and extensive analysis than previous studies that have been described by analysing messages based on six aspects, namely content, tone, source, source type, forms, and response. The analysed messages are not only posted by government agencies, but also posted by citizens to the government agencies.

3. RESEARCH METHODS

This study is a descriptive research because it aims to capture the phenomenon of the use of social media for government agencies in Indonesia. The stages of research methods in this study can be seen in Figure 1. The initial stage is collecting preliminary data by observing the government agency's official website listed on the indonesia.go.id website (UNPACS 2015) to get social media usernames that are used by government agencies. Output of this stage is a list of government agencies Twitter username because Twitter is the most social media type that used by government agencies in Indonesia widely (58 out of 99 agencies). Messages samples were collected from September 28th to October 9th, 2015. Mapping the previous month messages posted by agencies that was conducted before determining messages samples (August 31st to September 27th, 2015). The mapping of the messages as can be seen in Table 2 shows that number of messages posted by agencies every week is quite stable. There was no significant increase in the number of messages posted. Hence, it can be concluded that the messages posted every week depicting the use of Twitter for government agencies, so it was decided to take the latest week (September 21st to September 27th, 2015) posted messages by agencies and citizens as the samples.

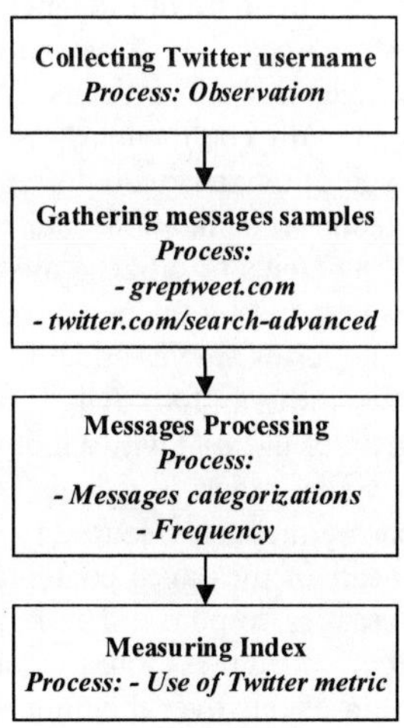

Figure 1. Research methods

Next stage is collecting samples from September 28th – October 9th, 2015. The agencies messages were collected by using greptweet.com website while citizens messages were collected by using twitter.com/search-advanced website. Afterwards, the messages were combined into datasets to be categorized based on their content, tone, source, source type, forms, and response. Messages source, forms, and response were categorized by researchers. Messages content, tone, and source type were categorized by respondents. These categorizations are believed can omit subjectivity factor. The datasets were sorted out by their frequencies. The highest frequencies were selected as the categories. Actually, there are 2.23% messages that cannot be categorized, so they are not to be counted. However, because the amount is very small it is considered will not affect the results. The final stage is formulating and calculating the index of the use Twitter by government agencies.

Table 2. Messages posted by government agencies in September 2015

Date	Total agencies messages	Averages
August 31st – September 6th, 2015	3,114	54
September 7th -13th September, 2015	4,183	72
September 14th - September 20th, 2015	3,507	60
September 21st - September 27th, 2015	3,305	57

4. RESULTS AND DISCUSSIONS

The registered government agencies on indonesia.go.id website are 99 agencies, 66 of them are central agencies while the remaining 33 are regional agencies. In fact, not all of them have social media accounts, for only 63 out of 99 agencies have official social media accounts. Twitter is the most social media type that used by agencies to share and disseminate information widely. There are 58 agencies out of 99, but unfortunately the data show that nine of them did not post any messages at all. The data also show that some agencies did not get messages from citizens, such as Nuclear Energy Controlling Board of Indonesia (Bapeten). The total messages being posted are 4,400. They are consisting 3,291 messages posted by government agencies and 1,109 messages posted by citizens to the agencies. There are 98 messages that cannot be categorized. There are 86 messages posted by government agencies and 12 messages posted by citizens, but the messages are not to be counted. Therefore the messages analysed in this study is 4,302 messages that consist of 3,205 messages posted by government agencies and 1,097 messages posted by the citizens. The messages are analysed based on six aspects, namely content, tone, source, source type, forms, and response.

Messages content are the content of messages that posted by government agencies and citizens. Messages content categories are internal information, external information, event, opinion, request information, actions, greeting, and unknown. Messages tone are the tone of the language used in the messages posted by agencies and citizens. Messages tone categories are neutral, positive, and negative. Messages source are the source of messages that posted by government agencies and citizens. Messages source categories are self-initiated, retweet without comments, and retweet with comments. Messages source type are type of accounts who retweet by government agencies and type of citizens who posted messages to agencies. Messages source type categories are government, news media, organization, individual, and unknown. Messages forms are elements contained in the government agencies or citizens messages. Messages forms categories are video, audio, image, link, and text. Messages response is the response from government agencies or citizens to the messages posted. Messages response categories are yes and no.

Government agencies use of Twitter index is formulated based on the messages posted by government agencies and citizens. Government agencies use of Twitter index is mean of agencies and citizens index. The range of the index is 0-100. The agencies index is calculated by mean of messages quantity, messages content, messages tone, messages source, messages source type, messages forms, and messages response. The citizens index is calculated by mean of messages content, messages tone, messages source, messages source type, messages forms, and messages response. The range of agencies and citizens index is 0-100. Messages quantities, messages content, messages source, messages source type, messages forms, and messages response are calculated by sum of one over the number of messages categories multiplied the total number of all messages posted the number of government agencies or citizens messages divided by total messages of agencies or citizens multiplied 100 in each category. "unknown" category is not counted in this study because it considered does not have any meaning. So does "no" category in messages response. Mathematical equations to calculate the messages quantities, messages content, messages source, messages source type, messages forms, and messages response can be seen in Figure 2. The range is 0-100. Messages tone are calculated by number of positive tone messages divided by total number of positive tone messages minus number of negative tone messages divided by total number of negative tone messages multiplied 100. The range of messages tone value is -100-100.

$$messages\ aspects = \sum_{i-1}^{n} {}^{1}/_{n} \times {}^{Pi}/_{Ti} \times 100$$

Figure 2. Messages quantities, content, source, source type, forms, and response formula

Notes :

n : Number of categories except "unknown" in messages content and messages source type, and "no" category in messages response.

Pi : Number of messages posted by agencies or citizens at the category of the i-th

Ti : The total number of all messages posted by agencies/citizens at the category of the i-th

Table 3 shows that Corruption Eradication Commission of Indonesia (KPK) is the central agency with the most optimal uses of its Twitter. KPK index value is not optimal in agencies index, but gain the highest index among other government agencies in citizens' index. Agencies messages tone gained by KPK is 29.961 out of -100-100. The same with messages source type posted by citizens, value range index is 12.266 out of 100. Many positive messages obtained by KPK indicates KPK has a good image in the society (Kietzmann et al. 2011). Citizens retweeted messages from other people and then posted to the KPK, so that open space communication between KPK and citizens created (Denef et al. 2013; F. Dianne Lux Wigand 2010; Taprial & Kanwar 2012). There are five central government agencies that are not optimal in using their Twitter. They are Coordinating Minister for Political, Legal and Security Affairs of Indonesia (Kemenkopolhukam), Ministry of Cooperatives and Small and Medium Enterprises of Indonesia (KemenKUKM), Ministry of Environment and Forestry of Indonesia (KemenLHK), Ministry of Youth and Sports of Indonesia (Kemenpora), and Judicial Commission of Indonesia (KY). They obtained zero index value because they did not post any message and did not get any message from citizens.

Table 3. Central government agencies use of Twitter index (Top 5)

Ranks	Agencies	Agencies Index	Citizens Index	Average Index
1	Corruption Eradication Commission (KPK)	3.852	**14.210**	**9.031**
2	Indonesian House of Representatives (DPR)	**12.301**	3.296	7.798
3	Local Councils of Indonesia (DPD)	11.040	0.624	5.832
4	National Police (Polri)	6.737	4.095	5.416
5	Ministry of Transportation (Kemenhub)	7.299	2.357	4.828

Table 4 shows the use of Twitter by regional agencies. It shows only 7 out of 33 regional agencies that have Twitter accounts. DKI Jakarta Province is the regional agencies with the most optimal use of its Twitter from both agencies and citizens. DKI Jakarta Province gains the highest value at messages source type aspect that posted by citizens, which is 14.914 out of 100. It indicates DKI Jakarta Province is the most interactive at the communication. The type of communications created are C2G, B2G, G2G, and N2G (Yanqing 2011). There are two regional government agencies that is worse using their Twitter. There are Nangroe Aceh Darussalam Province and South Kalimantan Province. They obtained zero because they did not post any message and did not get any message from citizens.

Table 4. Local government agencies use of Twitter index (Top 5)

Ranks	Agencies	Agencies Index	Citizens Index	Average Index
1	DKI Jakarta Province	**5.895**	**5.347**	**5.621**
2	Central Java Province	1.830	0.675	1.253
3	Riau Province	1.605	0.000	0.803
4	West Java Province	0.499	0.000	0.250
5	Banten Province	0.021	0.341	0.181

DPR gains the highest at messages quantities posted by agencies, 14.372 out of 100, messages content posted by agencies 19.851 out of 100, messages source posted by agencies 15.265 out of 100, messages forms posted by agencies 12.965 out of 100, and messages response posted by agencies 16.598 out of 100. It indicates DPR is the most active, transparent because of the diversity of the messages content (Dawot & Ibrahim 2014), attractive (Zheng & Zheng 2014), interactive (Denef et al. 2013; F. Dianne Lux Wigand

2010; Taprial & Kanwar 2012), and the most interest and enthusiastic citizens to comment so that communication can be created (Kietzmann et al. 2011; Zheng & Zheng 2014). Indonesian National Police (Polri) gains the highest at messages tone posted by agencies, 33.333 out of 100, and message forms posted by citizens 13.591 out of 100. It indicates Polri is the most interact positively agency with public like encouraging to do an action (Denef et al. 2013; F. Dianne Lux Wigand 2010) and citizens tend to post attractive messages to Polri (Zheng & Zheng, 2014). DPD is the most optimal at messages source type posted by agencies, 29.912 out of 100. It indicates DPD is the most communicative agency with citizens. The type communication built are G2C, G2B, G2G, and G2N (Yanqing 2011). Ministry of Transportation of Indonesia (Kemenhub) is the most optimum at messages response posted by agencies, 34.783 out of 100. It indicates Kemenhub is the most responsive and interactive agency to communicate with citizens (Kietzmann et al. 2011; Zheng & Zheng, 2014). Statistics Indonesia (BPS) gains the highest at messages content posted by citizens, 9.497 out of 100. It indicates that the most people expect transparency, participation, and collaboration to BPS (Dawot & Ibrahim 2014). Overall KPK is the agency with the most optimal use its Twitter among 58 government agencies, which is 9.031 out of 100. The top 10 government agencies use of Twitter index can be seen in Table 5. Therefore it can be concluded that the use of Twitter by government agencies in Indonesia have not been optimized and the interaction between government agencies and citizens has not been built. This is evidenced by the low index obtained, which is 9.031 out of 100. It is also consistent with EPI 2014 that Indonesia obtained 0.2941 out of 1 (United Nations 2014).

Table 5. Indonesia government agencies use of Twitter index (top 10)

Ranks	Agencies	Agencies Index	Citizens Index	Mean Index
1	Corruption Eradication Commission (KPK)	3.852	**14.210**	**9.031**
2	House of Representatives (DPR)	**12.301**	3.296	7.798
3	Regional Representatives Council (DPD)	11.040	0.624	5.832
4	DKI Jakarta Province	5.895	5.347	5.621
5	National Police (Polri)	6.737	4.095	5.416
6	Ministry of Transportation (Kemenhub)	7.299	2.357	4.828
7	Ministry of Finance (Kemenkeu)	5.529	2.618	4.074
8	Ministry of Public Works and Public Housing (KemenPUPR)	4.157	2.969	3.563
9	Ministry of Health (Kemenkes)	4.506	2.089	3.298
10	Ministry of Rural, Underdeveloped Regions and Transmigration (KemendesaPDT)	2.773	3.697	3.235

4.1 Government Agencies use of Twitter Index towards PeGI

PeGI is Indonesia e-government index issued by Ministry of Communications and Information Technology of Indonesia (Kemkominfo). Pegi is used to measure e-government implementation by government agencies in Indonesia. PeGI index is between 1-4 (Ministry of Communications and Information Technology of Indonesia 2015). PeGI is followed by 74 government agencies in 2014. There are 66 agencies that are aligned with this study. There are 22 central government agencies and 11 regional government agencies in this study that did not participate in PeGI. The top 10 comparison government agencies use of Twitter index in this study towards PeGI index can be seen in Table 6. According to the table, it shows that there are three agencies are in the top 10 both in Twitter index and PeGI index. They are DKI Jakarta Province, Ministry of Finance of Indonesia (Kemenkeu), and Ministry of Public Works and Public Housing of Indonesia (KemenPUPR). Based on the mapping on Table 6, it shows besides the three agencies that are in the top 10, other agencies are outside the top 20, except Ministry of Foreign Affairs of Indonesia (Kemenlu) that is ranked 13. It can be concluded the implementation e-government is inversely related to the implementation of social media. Furthermore, although e-government is considered good based on PeGI, but the interaction between government agencies and the citizens has not been built.

Table 6. Comparison of PeGI index towards the use of Twitter index

Pegi Ranks	Agencies	PeGI Index	Twitter Ranks	Twitter Index
1	**Ministry of Finance (Kemenkeu)**	**3.57**	**7**	**4.074**
2	Ministry of Education and Culture (Kemendikbud)	3.43	24	1.132
3	Ministry of Foreign Affairs (Kemenlu)	3.31	13	3.152
4	Ministry of National Development Planning (KemenPPN)	3.26	31	0.559
5	Statistics Indonesia (BPS)	3.16	22	1.214
6	**Ministry of Public Works and Public Housing (KemenPUPR)**	**3.16**	**8**	**3.563**
7	The Agency For The Assessment And Application of Technology (BPPT)	3.11	41	0.246
8	Ministry of Marine Affairs and Fisheries (KemenKP)	3.09	37	0.391
9	National Library of Indonesia (PNRI)	3.08	49	0.030
10	**DKI Jakarta Province**	**3.08**	**4**	**5.621**

Source: http://pegi.layanan.go.id/tabel-hasil-pegi-4/

Based on the results obtained, recommendations are compiled to be references matter to the agencies to optimize their use of Twitter. The recommendations are:

- Government agencies should post messages everyday regardless of the day off. It has not been known yet the ideal number of messages posted in a day, so that researchers suggest agencies should post at least 10 messages everyday. Follow back the citizens that followed or posted messages to agencies. It indicates they have interest about the agencies and messages. Follow citizens account will stimulate open and interactive communication between government and citizens.
- Messages content should include all categories. They are internal information, external information, actions, events, interactions, opinions, information requests, and greetings. Varies messages contents will stimulate public interest to comment or retweet the agencies messages. Make messages become attractive by adding videos, sounds, pictures, or links. These elements should be followed by adding appropriate texts. Because the maximum number of characters are 140, shorten link tools such as bit.ly can be used in order to create messages more optimal. Use positive tone in the messages posted, especially for the content of events, request information, and greetings. Balance between the messages initiated with retweeted. Retweet citizens messages will stimulate people to give response so communication can be built between government and Citizen.
- Respond the messages posted by citizens to create an interactive communication between agencies and citizens. The public will also more enthusiastic to comment agencies messages because of the response from agencies. Giving response to citizens also stimulate positive image to citizens, so that agencies reputation will increase in the public.

5. CONCLUSION

The highest index of government agencies use of Twitter obtained is very low because it is below 10 percentage (9.031 out of 100). Therefore it can be concluded that the use of Twitter of government agencies in Indonesia is not optimal. Government agencies can increase their use of Twitter by posting messages everyday regardless of the day off, posting attractive and various messages content, and responding messages posted by citizens.

This study analysed the text in the messages because the data retrieval tools have not been able to retrieve messages in a video or image format. Therefore, further study can analyse images or videos in the messages. Government agencies use of Twitter index in this study is in-elaborate and not yet validated the suitability. Accordingly, further study can design a model to measure use of Twitter that suitable for government agencies. This study did not analyse correlation between government agencies use of Twitter with the public relation function in the government agencies. Therefore, further study can analyse the correlation between public relations function in government agencies with agencies use of Twitter.

REFERENCES

Alam, L., & Lucas, R., 2011. Tweeting government: a case of Australian government use of Twitter. *Proceedings of the IEEE Ninth International Conference on Dependable, Autonomic and Secure Computing.* Sydney, Australia, pp. 995-1001.

Al-Saggaf, Y., & Simmons, P., 2015. Social media in Saudi Arabia: Exploring its use during two natural disasters. *In Technological Forecasting & Social Change*, Vol. 95, No. 1, pp 3-15.

Dawot, N. I., & Ibrahim, R, 2014. A review of features and functional building blocks of social media. *Proceedings of the 8th Malaysian Software Engineering Conference (MySEC).* Langkawi, Malaysia, pp. 177-182.

Denef, S., Bayerl, P. S., & Kaptein, N., 2013. Social media and the police-Tweeting practices of British police forces during the August 2011 riots. *Proceedings of the SIGCHI Conference on Human Factors in Computing Systems.* Paris, France, pp. 3471-3480.

eMarketer, 2013. *Social networking reaches nearly one in four around the world.* Available from: http://www.emarketer.com/Article/Social-Networking-Reaches-Nearly-One-Four-Around-World/1009976. [18 September 2015].

F. Dianne Lux Wigand, P., 2010. Twitter takes wing in government: Diffusion, roles, and management. *Proceedings of the 11th Annual International Conference on Digital Government Research.* Puebla, Mexico, pp. 66-71.

Fugini, M. G., Maggiolini, P., & Valles, R. S., 2014. *E-government and employment services: a case study in effectiveness.* Springer, New York, USA.

Heverin, T., & Zach, L., 2010. Twitter for city police department information sharing. *Proceedings of the American Society for Information Science and technology.* Pittsburgh, USA, pp. 1-7.

Honeycutt, C., & Herring, S. C., 2009. Beyond microblogging: Conversation and collaboration via Twitter. *Proceedings of the 42nd Hawaii International Conference on System Sciences.* Big Island, USA, pp. 1-10.

Java, A. et al, 2007. Why we Twitter: Understanding microblogging. *Proceedings of the* 9th *WebKDD and* 1st *SNA-KDD 2007 workshop on Web mining and social network analysis.* San Jose, USA, pp. 56-65.

Kaigo, M., & Okura, S., 2015. Exploring Fluctuations in Citizen Engagement on a Local Government Facebook Page in Japan. *In Telematics and Informatics*, Vol. 33, No. 2, pp 20-32.

Kietzmann, J. et al, 2011. Social media? Get serious! Understanding the functional building blocks of social media. *In Business Horizons*, Vol. 54, No. 3, pp 241–251.

Kim, J. H., & Park, H. W., 2014. Food policy in cyberspace: A webometric analysis of national food clusters in South Korea. *In Government Information Quarterly*, Vol. 31, No. 3, pp 443-453.

Mergel, I., 2013. *Social media in the public sector : A guide to participation, collaboration, and transarency in the networked world.* Jossey-Bass, San Francisco, USA.

Ministry of Communications and Information Technology of Indonesia, 2015. *About PeGI.* Available from: http://pegi.layanan.go.id/tentang-pegi/. [15 December 2015].

Naaman, M. et al, 2010. Is it really about me? Message content in social awareness streams. *Proceedings of the 2010 ACM Conference on ComputerSsupported Cooperative Work.* Savannah, USA, pp. 189-192.

President of Indonesia., 2003. *Presidential Instruction No. 3 of 2003 on national policy and strategy development of e-government.* Deputy Secretary of Cabinet Law and Legislation, Jakarta, Indonesia.

Riemer, K. et al, 2010. Enterprise Microblogging: Procrastination or productive use?. *Proceedings of the Sixteenth Americas Conference on Information Systems.* Lima, Peru, pp. 4199-4207.

Smith, B. G. et al, 2015. Tweeting taksim communication power and social media advocacy in the taksim square protest. *In Computers in Human Behavior*, Vol. 50, No. C, pp 499-507.

Sobacci, M. Z., & Karkin, N., 2013. The use of Twitter by mayors in Turkey: tweets for better public services?. *In Government Information Quarterly*, Vol. 30, No. 4, pp 417-425.

Taprial, V., & Kanwar, P., 2012. *Understanding social media.* BookBoon,

United Nations, 2014. *United nations e-government survey 2014 : E-government for the future we want.* United Nations, New York, USA.

UNPACS., 2015. *Country URLs.* Available from: http://unpan3.un.org/egovkb/en-us/Resources/Country-URLs. [15 September 2015].

Yanqing, G., 2011. The potential opportunities and challenges of e-government. *Proceedings of Management and Service Science (MASS).* Wuhan, China, pp. 1-4.

Zheng, L., & Zheng, T., 2014. Innovation through social media in the public sector: information and interactions. *In Government Information Quarterly*, Vol. 31, No. 1, pp S106-S117.

Zheng, T., & Zheng, L., 2012. Studying Chinese government microblogs: content and interactions. *Proceedings of the 6th International Conference on Theory and Practice of Electronic Governance.* Albany, USA, pp. 393-401.

INTEGRATION OF E-SERVICE QUALITY, CUSTOMER SATISFACTION AND TECHNOLOGY ACCEPTANCE

André van Friderici, Pascal Ravesteyn and Benny M.E. De Waal
HU University of Applied Sciences, P.O. Box 85029, 3508 AA Utrecht, the Netherlands

ABSTRACT

This paper examines the factors that determine the acceptance and satisfaction for Web self-service for IT-problems. A case study has been conducted to gain more insights in the acceptance and customer satisfaction of Web self-service within a financial organization in the Netherlands. In the stream of automation innovations Web self-service plays an important role. Web-based self-service technologies are expected to facilitate an improvement in customer satisfaction for the organization and at the same time reducing operating costs. However, despite the benefits of web self-service for the organization, users do not have to perceive self-service technologies as favorable for themselves. For organizations it is not clear what the factors are that contribute to a successful acceptance of Web self-service for the purpose of improving customer satisfaction. This study integrates e-service quality aspects, (SERVQUAL) customer satisfaction and the Technology Acceptance Model into a new conceptual model. The relevant hypotheses are tested by survey data collected from 149 respondents of the financial organization. The results indicate that Web self-service satisfaction is the intermediate construct through which the e-service quality aspects affects both perceived usefulness and perceived ease of use. The proposed model explained 29.9% of the variance in behavioral intention to use Web self-service.

KEYWORDS

e-service, user satisfaction, technology acceptance model, Web self-service.

1. INTRODUCTION

More and more service providers adopt self-service technologies and encourage customers to use these services (Dabholkar and Bagozzi, 2002). The core of the Web self-service concept is that the customer is not being assisted by a service desk employee, but performs certain tasks themselves using web-based technologies. Web-based self-service technologies are expected to facilitate an improvement in customer satisfaction for the organization while reducing operating costs (Sadiq and Shanmugam, 2003). However, despite the benefits of Web self-service for the organization, users do not have to perceive Web self-service technologies as favorable for themselves. Also forcing customers to use self-service technology might lead to a decrease in positive perception (Lin and Hsieh, 2006) which leads to negative attitudes toward using the self-service technology (Reinders et al., 2008). It is vital for organizations to identify the factors that determine the acceptance of a Web self-service system. Based on these observations the following research question is formulated: Which factors determine the acceptance and satisfaction of a Web self-service system for solving IT problems in an organization?

In the next section, the theoretical foundation of this research is presented. Different views will be presented next to each other and are judged on their usefulness to this research. Thereafter the research methodology is presented, followed by the description and analysis of the results. In the final section the conclusion and a discussion of the recommendations and limitations will be presented.

2. A CONCEPTUAL MODEL OF E-SERVICE QUALITY, CUSTOMER SATISFACTION AND TECHNOLOGY ACCEPTANCE

2.1 Behavior Models

The Theory of Reasoned Action (TRA) is a generally applicable behavior model developed by the psychologists Fishbein and Ajzen (1975). The model assumes that our attitudes and social norms determine our behavioral intention. If people have a positive attitude towards certain behavior and if they think others want to exhibit that behavior (subjective norm) then there is a greater intention to actually perform a specific behavior. Further investigation has shown that at times when people have the intention to show the new behavior, the actual behavior is countered. This is caused by a lack of confidence, skills and control over the behavior (Miller, 2005, p. 127). These findings have led to the development of the Theory of Planned Behavior (TPB) in which the behavior intention of a person is affected by our attitudes, the subjective norm and behavior control (Ajzen, 1991).

Davis (1989) has developed a behavior model on the basis of the TRA model, called Technology Acceptance Model (TAM), which states that the success of a system can be determined by the acceptance of the system. The TAM is designed to determine the factors that influence the acceptance and (future) use of new technology. It was initially developed with a focus on the individual acceptance of information systems in office environments. The main factor for the acceptance of the technology is also the behavioral intention. The TAM model indicates that the property of a technology (external variables) has a direct influence on the usefulness and ease of use as they are perceived by the user (Figure 1).

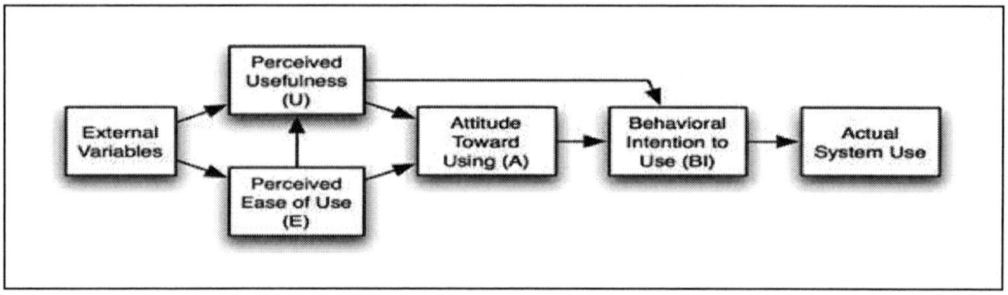

Figure 1. The Technology Acceptance Model (Davis, 1989)

According to several studies the determinants perceived usefulness and the perceived ease of use are convincingly significant user acceptance criteria (Davis, 1989; Hill et al., 1987; Venkatesh and Davis, 2000). On this basis, the attitude and behavioral intention towards the technology is determined and consequently affects the implementation of the system (Davis, 1989; Davis et al., 1989).

Perceived usefulness is one and a half times more important than perceived ease of use in influencing use (Davis, 1989). This means that designers of information systems cannot solve the problem of user acceptance by building better and more user-friendly interfaces.

Both, the TAM as TPB could be used to explain and predict the intention to use the Web self-service system. The TAM model assumes that perceived usefulness and perceived ease of use are always decisive in decisions of users. The TPB model is based on beliefs that are specific for each situation. This makes the use of the TPB-model difficult in regards to different user contexts in comparison to the TAM-model. The TAM-model can be used for quick and inexpensive analysis of acceptance or possible resistance. Also the TAM is a well-established model for measuring the acceptance and use of information systems. In several studies it explains the intention to use various electronic products in different organizational environments. In particular, it has collected empirical evidence, showing that the TAM serves as a valid model for predicting the use of Internet and intranet systems (Horton et al., 2001). Secondly, the core of the model is provided with TAM validated constructs, so that follow-up research is possible. Thirdly, numerous studies have now been published, making the acceptance of TAM proven and guaranteed (Pijpers et al, 2002). Based on the above arguments the TAM will form the basis for this research. However, the variable "attitude" will not be used in this research. Subsequent studies have confirmed that because of the direct effects of both "perceived usefulness" as "perceived ease of use" on "behavioral intention" the TAM is better able to predict user acceptance (Venkatesh, 2000). This can be explained by the assumption that individuals may find a system useful, despite the fact that they have a negative attitude towards the use of a system (Sun and Zhang, 2006).

2.2 Customer Satisfaction

The SERVQUAL model of Parasuraman et al. (1985) is one of the most discussed and applied models in the field of service quality. The quality of service is defined by five quality dimensions, namely: "tangibles", "reliability", "responsiveness", "security" and "empathy" and is measured by 22 items. The difference between the observed and expected quality, the "Gap" (also called disconfirmation judgment) forms the basis for the determination of the service quality as judged by the customer.

A situation of satisfaction arises when expectations and perceptions are equal or the perception exceeds the expectations (Parasuraman et al., 1985; Lovelock and Wirtz, 2011). The SERVQUAL model identifies five gaps. Gap 5 is seen as the difference between expected and experienced service. This difference relates to the shortcomings of the service, as it is experienced by the customer. The remaining gaps 1 to 4 relate to the internal quality weaknesses within the service organization. SERVQUAL is a framework for understanding the quality of service and allows insight in the different gaps by both the company's and the customer's side. Cronin and Taylor (1992) developed the SERVPERF-model which has the same items as SERVQUAL, but only records the performance ratings and not the expected ratings. According to Jain and Gupta (2004) the measure of only the performance evaluations shows a more reliable approach to service quality. Carrillat et al. (2007) shows that SERVQUAL and SERVPERF are equally valid predictors of overall service quality. Adapting the SERVQUAL scale to the measurement context improves its predictive validity; conversely, the predictive validity of SERVPERF is not improved by context adjustments. This implies that SERVQUAL scales require to be adapted to the study context more so than SERVPERF.

2.3 E-service Quality Dimensions

SERVQUAL was developed based on a customer - employee interaction and does not embrace the interactions of online services (Cai and Jun, 2003). Lociacono et al. (2000) by means of an empirical study developed a measuring scale, called WEBQUAL, consisting of 12 dimensions which measure the quality of a website. However, according to Zeithaml, et al. (2002) the WEBQUAL measurement scale lacks some important dimensions as "customer service" and "fulfilment." Zeithaml, et al. (2002, 2005) therefore developed the e-SERVQUAL model covering all phases of customer interaction with a website. e-SERVQUAL is defined as the degree to which a website supports efficient and effective shopping, purchasing and delivery (Zeithaml et al., 2000). The focus is on online shopping by consumers.

The quality model of Ojasalo (2010) is based on eight quality dimensions combined from literature from different studies including the e-SERVQUAL of Zeithaml, et al. (2005). According to Ojasalo (2010) the following eight aspects of quality are proposed as very relevant in the context of e-services: ease of use, website design and appearance, personalization, information, responsiveness, communication, security, and reliability. (E-) Service quality takes place before, and has been found to be an important input to customer satisfaction (Caruana and Malta, 2002).

2.4 An Integrated Model of e-Service Quality, Customer Satisfaction and TAM

Customer satisfaction and technology acceptance are research domains that evolved in parallel. According to Wixom and Todd (2005), these two streams of research must be integrated because both contribute to the information system success. Customer satisfaction of the use of a particular information system results in more usage and is preferable for a measurement of the success of information systems (Baroudi et al. 1986). On the other hand, the technology acceptance theory provides explanations for why users accept or reject new information systems. The relationship between user satisfaction and usage can be explained as follows: For a belief or attitude to be directly predictive of behavior, it needs to be consistent in time, target, and context with the behavior. User satisfaction therefor needs to be recognized as an object-based attitude (Ajzen and Fishbein, 1980) whereby it serves as an external variable with influences on intention and behavior that are fully mediated by behavioral beliefs and attitudes (Ajzen and Fishbein 1980; Eagly and Chaiken, 1993). For example, one's satisfaction with the customization and personalization of a system does not directly impact whether one will use the system.

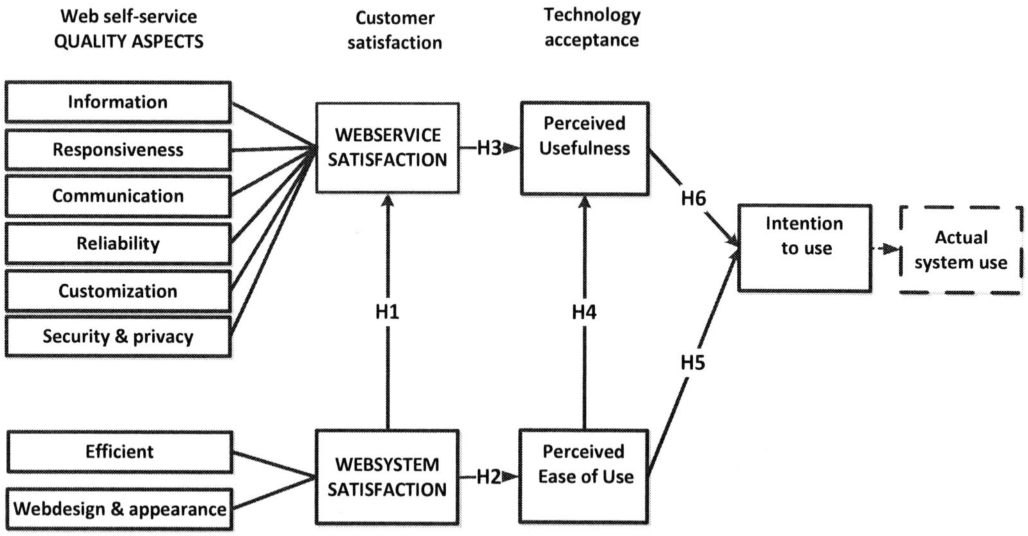

Figure 2. Conceptual model of e-Service Quality, Customer Satisfaction and Technology Acceptance

Based on the previous theoretical considerations a conceptual model based on e-Service Quality, Customer Satisfaction and Technology Acceptance has been developed (see Figure 2). The model is constructed to be able to answer our research question. Based on the relations in our conceptual model, the following hypotheses were formulated:

Hypothesis 1: The satisfaction of the customers with the quality of the Web (self-service) system has a significant positive relation on the satisfaction with the Web (self-service) services.
Hypothesis 2: The satisfaction of the customers with the quality of the Web (self-service) system has a significant positive relation on the perceived ease of use.
Hypothesis 3: The satisfaction of the customers with the quality of the Web (self-service) services has a significant positive relation on the perceived usefulness.
Hypothesis 4: The perception of ease of use has a significant positive relation on the perception of usefulness.
Hypothesis 5: The perception of ease of use has a significant positive relation on the intention to use.
Hypothesis 6: The perception of usefulness has a significant positive relation on the intention to use.

3. RESEARCH METHODOLOGY

3.1 Data Collection

The customers of the Web self-service system were the employees of the organization. In total 1674 employees were approached by email with the request to fill in the online survey, which consisted of open and closed questions. The survey was distributed on January, 2015. Twelve days later 199 surveys had been received (12%), of which 149 (75%) were finished completely. The other surveys have proven to be unusable as too much questions were left unanswered. While this response rate can be considered low, it is not uncommon. Shih and Fan (2009) found in their meta-analysis of 35 e-mail and paper surveys similar or lower rates of response to a questionnaire than in our study. Of the respondents, 65% were male and 35% were female. 15.5% of the respondents had an age of less than 40 years, 33.1% between 40 and 50 years, and 51.4% more than and 50 years.

3.2 Instrument Validation

Below the measurement of the five variables of the conceptual model are described. Furthermore the results of construct validity and reliability testing are presented.

Web service satisfaction and Web system satisfaction were measured with scales developed by Loiacono et al. (2002), and Swaid and Wigand (2009). Factor analysis was performed to analyze the construct validity of 8 items. Principal component analysis (PCA) with varimax rotation resulted in a two-factor solution with own values of 3.09 and 2.20, accounting for 38.6% and 27.4% of the explained variance. The factor loadings were between 0.925 and 0.598, which can be considered as being significant (Hair et al., 1998). The reliability of the two scales – a six-item Web service satisfaction scale and a two-item Web system satisfaction scale – was confirmed by Cronbach's alpha value of 0.816 and 0.846 respectively. Since the components have a Conbrach's alpha coefficient higher than 0.7 score, the results of the scale variables can be regarded as trustworthy (Nunnally and Bernstien, 1994).

Perceived usefulness (Davis, 1989), Perceived ease of use (Davis, 1989; Venkatesh and Davis, 2000), and Intention to use (Davis, 1989; Eizema, 2010) were measured by one item.

In the survey a 5-point Likert scale has been used. This was done because the employees at the financial organization were already familiar with this scale as this was also used for weekly customer satisfaction surveys. A pre-test of the survey questions has been performed with four employees and based on their feedback the questionnaire was slightly modified.

4. RESULTS

Before presenting the subsequent results of the correlation and regression analyses, we checked that both the dependent variables and the independent variables were not skewed in their distribution. The correlations between the variables are shown in Table 1. The correlation between all the variables in the conceptual model are significant with a p <0.05 or p<0.01 and have a positive direction.

Table 1. Correlations between variables (* = p<.05; ** = p<.01)

	Perceived usefulness	*Web system satisfaction*	*Perceived ease of use*	*Intentionto use*	*Web service satisfaction*
Perceived usefulness	1	,314**	,365**	,544**	,437**
Web system satisfaction	,314**	1	,542**	,209*	,545**
Perceived ease of use	,365**	,542**	1	,393**	,421**
Intention to use	,544**	,209*	,393**	1	,329**
Web service satisfaction	,437**	,545**	,421**	,329**	1

The way the hypotheses were tested is shown in Figure 3. The one-way-directed arrows in the figure represent the significant (standardized) regression (beta) coefficients. For the four OLS regression models applied, the potential problem of multicollinearity was investigated by computing VIF factors for each predictor in the regression model. Although in some cases correlations between independent variables were relatively high, VIF factors in none of the three models exceeded 3, which is below the commonly applied threshold of 5 (Hair et al., 1998; Rogerson, 2001).

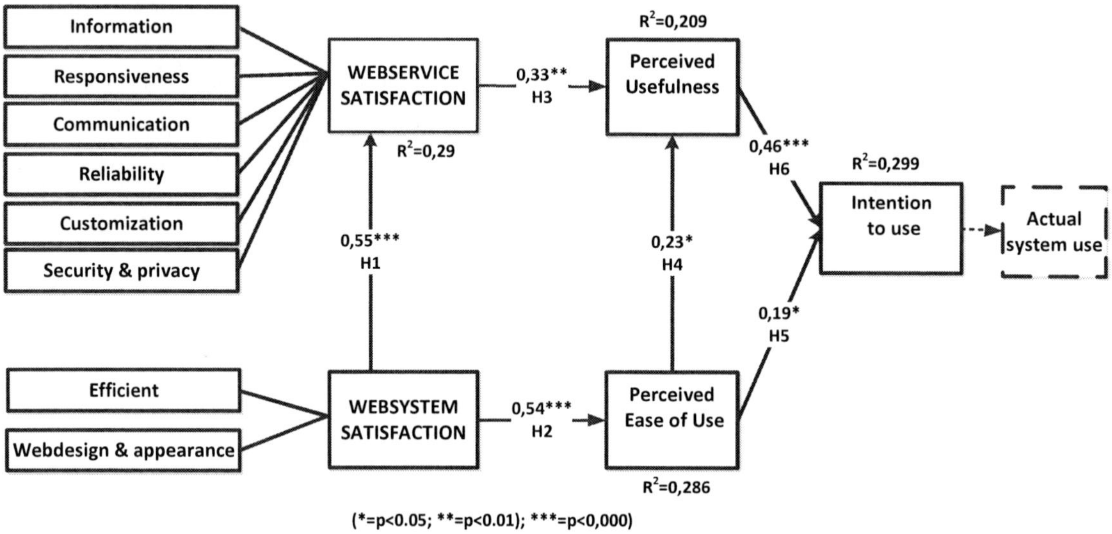

Figure 3. The conceptual model and hypothesis tested: significant standardized regression coefficients (one-way arrows between the boxes)

The results from the four regression models show that:

- Web system satisfaction holds a significant relation with Web service satisfaction, which confirms hypothesis 1. The explained variance of the regression model (adjusted R^2) is 29.0% (F=39.781, df=95, p=.000) for Web service satisfaction as a dependent variable.
- Web system satisfaction holds a significant relation with Perceived ease of use, which conform hypothesis 2. The explained variance of the regression model (adjusted R^2) is 28.6% (F=14.023, df=94, p=.000) for Perceived ease of use as a dependent variable.
- Web service satisfaction and Perceived ease of use hold a significant relation with Perceived usefulness, which confirms hypothesis 3 and 4. The explained variance of the regression model (adjusted R^2) is 20.9% (F=13.275, df=93, p=.000) for Perceived usefulness as a dependent variable.
- Perceived usefulness and Perceived ease of use hold a significant relation with Intention to use, which confirms hypothesis 5 and 6. The explained variance of the regression models (adjusted R^2) is 29.9% (F=20.212, df=90, p=.000) for Intention to use as a dependent variable.

5. CONCLUSION, LIMITATIONS AND FURTHER RESEARCH

This research has provided insight into the variables that influence the acceptance and satisfaction of Web self-service within a financial institution in the Netherlands. Different behavioral models and concepts from IS research and customer satisfaction were brought together to develop a conceptual model. Data was collected from a survey among 149 respondents from the case study organization. This resulted in the construction of valid and reliable measurements and constructs as defined in the conceptual model. Correlation and regression analysis showed that significant relations were found and that all hypotheses were confirmed. It was shown that (1) Web system satisfaction is a key determinant for Perceived Ease of Use and Web service satisfaction, (2) Web service satisfaction and Perceived Ease of Use are main drivers for Perceived Usefulness and (3) Perceived Usefulness and Perceived Ease of Use are main determinants of Intention to use.

From these results we can argue that customer's first choice for a Web self-service system is usefulness and secondly perceived ease of use. Both variables are influenced by the satisfaction with the web system and –service. Therefore we can conclude that the relationship is as follows: the higher the satisfaction of the customer with regard to a Web self-service system, the more the perceived usefulness is enhanced. If one is dissatisfied with a Web self-service system, then the strength of the perceived usefulness and / or perceived ease of use will be less.

Although the research was designed carefully, there are some limitations. The research has focused only on the client side of Web self-service system and - services and was limited to one financial organization in the Netherlands. Furthermore, it should be noted that the financial institution limited the number of items for questioning the employees. This has resulted in a minimum number of questions per variable. Nevertheless, the results obtained in the study provide a good view on the consistency of the acceptance and satisfaction factors. The results are largely in line with the results of earlier conducted research (Wixom and Todd, 2005). For financial institutions, the results can be used as a diagnostic tool in order to develop interventions to improve customer satisfaction and the acceptance of Web self-service systems and services. The relationships in the conceptual model have been tested on the basis of factor analysis, correlation analysis and (multiple) regression analysis. The model can be input for further research in the combined customer satisfaction and Technology acceptance research domains. A possibility to validate our findings further is to estimate the complete model using Structural Equation Modeling (SEM).

In follow-up research it would be good to broaden the conceptual model with one or more variables. For example, not only examining the cognitive variables but also view the more hedonistic variables. Hedonic variables focus on the sensory pleasure. There is for example the variable perception of entertainment. In an on-line shop environment it has been found that this has a significant relationship with the intention to use (Wixom and Todd, 2005).

ACKNOWLEDGEMENT

The authors like to thank the respondents and management of the case study organization. Without their corporation and support this research would not have been possibly.

REFERENCES

Ajzen, I. 1991. The theory of planned behavior. *Organizational Behavior and Human Decision Processes,* Vol. 50, No. 2, pp. 179-211.

Ajzen, I. and Fishbein, M. 1980. *Understanding attitudes and predicting social behaviour.* Prentice-Hall, Englewood Cliffs, NJ.

Baroudi, J.J., Olson, M.H. and Ives, B. 1986. An Empirical Study of the Impact of User Involvement on System Usage and Information Satisfaction. *Communications of the ACM,* Vol. 29, pp. 232-238.

Cai, S. and Jun, M. 2003. Internet users' perceptions of online service quality: a comparison of online buyers and information searchers. *Managing Service Quality,* Vol. 13, pp. 504-519.

Carrillat, F.A., Jaramillo, F. and Mulki, J.P. 2007. The validity of the SERVQUAL and SERVPERF scales. *International Journal of Service Industry Management*, Vol. 18, No. 5, pp. 472-490.

Caruana, A. and Malta, M. 2002. Service loyalty: The effects of service quality and the mediating role of customer satisfaction. *European Journal of Marketing*, Vol. 36, No. 7/8, pp. 811-828

Cronin, J.J. and Taylor, S.A. 1992. Measuring service quality: A reexamination and extension. *Journal of Marketing,* Vol. 56, pp. 55-68.

Dabholkar, P.A. and Bagozzi, R.P. 2002. An attitudinal model of technology-based self-service: Moderating effects of consumer traits and situational factors. *Journal of the Academy of Marketing Science,* Vol. 30, No. 3, pp. 184–201.

Davis, F.D. 1989. Perceived usefulness, perceived ease of use, and user acceptance of information technology. *MIS Quarterly,* Vol. 13, No. 3, pp. 319-340.

Davis, F. D., Bagozzi, R. P., and Warshaw, P. R. 1989. User Acceptance of Computer Technology: A comparison of two theoretical models. *Management Science,* Vol. 35, No. 8, pp. 982-1003.

Eagly, A.H. and Chaiken, S. 1993. *The psychology of attitudes*. Harcourt Brace Jovanovich, FortWorth, TX.

Eizema, J. 2010. Welke factoren beïnvloeden de intentie tot acceptatie van klanten van Rabobank Sneek-ZwF ten opzichte van het Multichannel Groeipad? Master Theses (essays/60460). University of Twente, Netherlands.

Fishbein, M and Ajzen, I. 1975. *Belief, Attitude, Intention, and Behavior: An Introduction to Theory and Research.* Addison-Wesley, Reading, Massachusetts.

Hair, J., Anderson. R., Tatham, R. and Black, W. 1998. *Multivariate Data Analysis (*5th edition). Prentice – Hall, Englewood Cliffs.

Hill, T., Smith, N. D., and Mann, M. F. 1987. Role of Efficacy Expectations in Predicting the decision to Use Advanced Technologies: The Case of Computers. *Journal of Applied Psychology,* Vol. 72, pp. 302–313.

Horton, R.P., Buck, R., Waterson, P.E., and Clegg, C.W., 2001. Explaining intranet use with the technology acceptance model. *Journal of Information Technology,* Vol. 16, No. 4, pp. 237–249.

Jain, S.K. and Gupta, G. 2004. Measuring service quality, SERVQUAL vs. SERVPERF scales. *Vikalpa,* Vol. 29, No. 2, pp. 25-37.

Lin, J.S.C. and Hsieh, P.L. 2006. The role of technology readiness in customers' perception and adoption of self-service technologies. *International Journal of Service Industry Management,* Vol. 17, No. 5, pp. 497–517.

Lociacono, E., Watson, R., and Goodhue, D. 2000. *WebQual™: A Web Site Quality Instrument*. Working Paper. Worcester Polytechnic Institute.

Lociacono, E., Watson, R., and Goodhue, D. 2002. WEBQUAL: A measure of website quality. *Marketing educators' conference*: *Marketing theory* and *applications.*London Conference, Academic Press, Vol. 13, pp. 432–437.

Lovelock, C. and Wirtz, J. 2011. *Services Marketing: People, Technology, Strategy* (7th international edition). Pearson Prentice Hall, Upper Saddle River.

Miller, K. 2005. *Communications theories: Perspectives, processes, and contexts*. McGraw-Hill, New York.

Nunnally, J.C. and Bernstien, I.H. 1994. *Psychometric Theory*. McGraw-Hill, New York.

Ojasalo, J. 2010. E-service quality: A conceptual model. *International Journal of Arts and Sciences,* Vol. 3, No. 7, pp. 127-143.

Parasuraman, A., Zeithaml, V.A., and Berry, L.L. 1985. A conceptual model of service quality and its implications for future research. *Journal of Marketing,* Vol. 49, pp. 41-50.

Pijpers, A.G.M., van Montfoort, K., and Heemstra, F.J. 2002. Acceptatie van ICT: theorie en een veldonderzoek onder topmanagers. *Bedrijfskunde,* Vol. 74, No. 4, pp. 76-84.

Reinders, M.J., Dabholkar, P.A., and Framback, R.T. 2008. Consequences of forcing consumers to use technology-based self-service. *Journal of Service Research,* Vol. 11, No. 2, pp. 107–123.

Rogerson, P.A. 2001. *Statistical methods for geography*. Sage, London.

Sadiq, S.M. and Shanmugam, B. 2003. E-banking and customer preferences in Malaysia: An empirical investigation. *Information Sciences,* Vol. 150, No. 3-4, pp. 207–217.

Shih, T.H. and Fan, X. 2009. Comparing response rates in e-mail and paper surveys: a meta-analysis. *Educational Research Review,* Vol. 4, No. 1, pp. 26-40.

Sun, H. and Zhang, P. 2006. The Role of Moderating Factors in User Technology Acceptance. *International Journal of Human-Computer Studies,* Vol. 64, No. 2, pp. 53-78.

Swaid, S.I. and Wigand, R.T. 2009. Measuring the quality of e-service: Scale development and initial validation. *Journal of Electronic Commerce Research,* Vol. 10, No. 1, pp. 13-28.

Venkatesh, V. 2000. Determinants of Perceived Ease of Use: Integrating Perceived Behavioral Control, Computer Anxiety and Enjoyment into the Technology Acceptance Model. *Information Systems Research,* Vol. 11, No. 4, pp. 342-365.

Venkatesh, V. and Davis, F.D. 2000. A Theoretical Extension of the Technology Acceptance Model: Four Longitudinal Field Studies. *Management Science,* Vol. 46, No. 2, pp. 186–204.

Wixom, B.H. and Todd, P.A. 2005. A Theoretical Integration of User Satisfaction and Technology Acceptance. *Information Systems Research,* Vol. 16, No. 1, pp. 85-102.

Zeithaml, V.A., Parasuraman, A., and Malhotra, A. 2000. *A Conceptual Framework for understanding e-service quality: Implications for future research and managerial practice.* Working Paper Series, Marketing Science Institute, Report No. 00-115.

Zeithaml, V.A., Parasuraman, A., and Malhotra, A. 2002. Service quality delivery through web sites: A critical review of extant knowledge. *Journal of the Academy of Marketing Science,* Vol. 30, No. 4, pp. 362–410.

Zeithaml, V.A., Parasuraman, A., and Malhotra, A. 2005. E-S-QUAL: A Multiple-Item Scale for Assessing Electronic Service Quality. *Journal of Service Research,* Vol. 7, No. 10, pp. 1-21.

STEADYSERV BEER: IOT-ENABLED PRODUCT MONITORING USING RFID

Rebecca Angeles
University of New Brunswick Fredericton, New Brunswick, CANADA
Faculty of Business Administration, Singer Hall, 7 Macauley Lane, Fredericton NB E3B 5A3

ABSTRACT

This case study features the award-winning SteadyServ keg solution with Internet-of-Things (IOT)-enabled features for beer and tap inventory management. Using the case study method and content analysis, this research project investigates the application of the structurational model of technology theory introduced by Orlikowski in order to interpret the firm's entry and participation in the IOT-impelled marketplace.

KEYWORDS

Internet of Things; radio frequency identification; supply chain management; business intelligence; product monitoring

1. INTRODUCTION

This research features a case study of SteadyServ Technologies, a firm that developed an award-winning Internet of Things (IOT)-enabled solution for beer and tap inventory management system designed to serve retailers, distributors, and beer brewers. "Internet of Things" or IOT is defined as "...a worldwide information infrastructure for the information society in which physical and virtual 'things' were uniquely identified and connected over the wired or wireless internet. These physical and virtual things could include an object or smart device, such as clothes, a watch, a camera, a washer, a building, a bridge, a car, a suite, an animal or even a person...." (Yen, 2015, pp. 2-3). In a global survey of 795 firms, Tata Consultancy Services found that four out of the five firms have already deployed IOT initiatives (Tata Consultancy Services, 2015). The four major areas for IOT application are: (1) product monitoring: tracking products by embedding sensors, software, and other technologies in physical products; (2) premises monitoring: installing sensors, digital cameras, and other devices in firms' business operations sites; (3) customer monitoring: tracking wireless mobile devices carried by customers; (4) supply chain monitoring: installing sensors, digital devices, and cameras in the production and distribution facilities (Tata Consultancy Services, 2015). The theoretical framework called the structurational model of technology introduced by Orlikowski (Orlikowski, 1992; Orlikowski and Robey, 1991) is used as the analytical lens through which SteadyServ Technologies' implementation experience is investigated and interpreted.

2. LITERATURE REVIEW

2.1 SteadyServ Technologies Background

Founded in 2012 in Carmel, Indiana, USA, SteadyServ Technologies developed the SteadyServ iKey system --- a software as a service (SaaS) based mobile software solution for inventory and order management for the beer industry (Identiv, 2014). This is a breakthrough product/service in that it provides real-time intelligence for beer retail establishments, distributors, and brewers through the use of a smartphone app that runs on IOS or Android devices and also through the use of a web-enabled SaaS portal. This solution also enables synchronization with a beer distributor's order management system to assure beer retailer customers that their inventory can always fill customer demand at any point in time.

2.2 Orlikowski's Structurational Model of Technology

This study applies Orlikowski's "Structurational Model of Technology," (Orlikowski, 1992; Orlikowski and Robey, 1991) to understand how information technology(IT) interacts with organizations. This model draws on Giddens' theory of structuration (Giddens, 1984, 1979, 1976), which proposed the concept of the "duality of structure," "...which refers to the notion that the structure or institutional properties of social systems are created by human action, and then serve to shape future human action...." (Orlikowski and Robey, 1991, p. 147). "...In Giddens' theory, structure is understood to be an abstract property of social systems. Structure is not something concrete, situated in time and space, and it lacks material characteristics. Structure cannot exist apart from the human actors who enact and interpret its dimensions. Structure has only virtual existence. Interestingly, people readily allow their actions to be constrained by these shared abstractions as social structure....The ability of organizational structures to elicit compliance and conformity in the absence of material constraints attests to the power of those socially constructed abstractions....Social structure conditions these social practices by providing the contextual rules and resources that allow human actors to make sense of their own acts and those of other people." (Orlikowski and Robey, 1991, p. 147). Furthermore, Giddens specifies that human interactions are an amalgamation of structures of meaning, power, and moral frameworks enacted in what he calls the "modalities" of these interactions: interpretive schemes, resources, and norms.

"Interpretive schemes...form the core of mutual knowledge whereby an accountable universe of meaning is sustained through and in processes of interaction (Giddens, 1979, p. 83]. Orlikowski and Robey (1991) translate Giddens' concept of "interpretive scheme" within the realm of IT and explain that IT represents reality through a set of concepts of symbols embedded in it by which end users understand their world. Thus, IT is not only a medium for the construction of social reality, but also a means of institutionalizing certain "interpretive schemes" or stocks of knowledge within the organization by standardizing, sharing, and taking them for granted.

Resources are the media through which power is exercised by human actors because it is through these resources that humans can accomplish their objectives and thus, gain "domination" (Orlikowski and Robey, 1991). Therefore, the deployment of IT institutes a certain order of authority, dictating the way work will be performed, and also, resulting in the differential distribution of power in the organization.

Norms are understood as organizational rules that shape "legitimate" behavior. IT is a medium for installing such norms in order to control human behavior in an organization (Orlikowski and Robey, 1991).

Orlikowski incorporates the following components in her framework: first, the human agents, consisting of technology designers, end users, and decision makers; second, the material artifacts that constitute IT itself, and third, the institutional properties of organizations --- structural arrangements, business strategies, ideology, culture, control mechanisms, standard operating procedures, division of labor, expertise, communication patterns, and environmental pressures ((Orlikowski, 1992; Orlikowski and Robey, 1991

The structurational model of technology discusses four critical issues (Orlikowski and Robey, 1991). First, IT is the product of human action, which is responsible for the creation, use, and maintenance of different forms of IT. It is only through the human appropriation of IT that it is able to influence human activity. Second, technology is the medium of human action. Since different forms of IT are used by organizational workers, they mediate organizational work either by facilitating it and in some ways, also constraining it. Third, organizational contexts shape human action within organizations. Human agents are influenced by the institutional properties of their setting which provide the resources, norms, and knowledge they need to work. Furthermore, IT is created and used within certain social and historical circumstances which influence the form and features of this technology. Fourth, human agents either reinforce or transform the institutional properties of an organization when using IT. Weick (1979) characterized technology as "enacted environment" whose construction is determined by an organization's structures of signification, domination, and legitimation. Any change in these three structures indicate the "appropriation" and use of technology.

"Structure of signification" refers to the way the concepts and procedures intrinsic to the knowledge embedded in IT directs the manner in which problems are interpreted and work is conducted in the organization (Orlikowski, 1992). "Structure of domination" refers to IT's ability to control the work of organizational members once it is deployed. "Structure of legitimation" refers to the ability of IT to sanction a particular mode of conducting the work and thus, propagate a set of norms about what is considered legitimate business practice. Orlikowski also incorporates the three modalities of structuration --- interpretive schemes, resources, and norms --- in her application of the structures of signification, domination, and legitimation in the deployment of IT in an organization.

3. RESEARCH METHOD

This study uses the case study approach in aligning the concepts prescribed by Orlikowski's framework to SteadyServ's RFID system. The case study is an appropriate methodology in testing the application of a conceptual framework to a real firm. The primary data used was based on the transcription of the conference presentation of RFID Journal Live! Conference on April 16-17, 2015, San Diego, California, USA. In addition, secondary data sources from academic and trade articles were content analyzed using key concepts in the model. The following are accepted definitions of the content analysis method:

> "Content analysis is any research technique for making inferences by systematically and objectively identifying specified characteristics within text." (Stone and Dunphy, 1966, p. 5).
>
> "Content analysis is a research technique for making replicable and valid inferences from data to their context." (Krippendorff, 1980, p. 21).
>
> "Content analysis is a research method that uses a set of procedures to make valid inferences from text." (Weber, 1990), p. 1).

In this study, the concepts used for content analysis were derived from the structurational model of technology. This framework forms the "context" of the content analysis method as applied to Airbus' RFID system:

> "A context is always someone's construction, the conceptual environment of a text, the situation in which it plays a role. In a content analysis, the context explains what the analyst does with the texts; it could be considered the analyst's best hypothesis for how the texts came to be, what they mean, what they can tell or do. In the course of a content analysis, the context embraces all the knowledge that the analyst applies to given texts, whether in the form of scientific theories, plausibly argued propositions, empirical evidence, grounded intuitions, or knowledge of reading habits.... The context specifies the world in which texts can be related to the analyst's research questions." (Krippendorff, 2004, p. 33).

The secondary data was analyzed within the context provided by the Orlikowski framework, which is considered the "prior theory." "Analytical constructs operationalize what the content analyst knows about the context, specifically the network of correlations that are assumed to explain how available text are connected to the possible answers to the analyst's questions and the conditions under which these correlations could change....analytical constructs ensure that an analysis of given texts models the texts' context of use..." (Krippendorff, 2004, p. 34).

The following key conceptual elements of the content analysis method as stipulated by Krippendorff (2004) were used in this study: (1) body of text selected for the analysis; (2) research question that needed to be addressed; (3) a context of analysis within which interpretations will be made; (4) analytical constructs that operationalize what the analyst knows about the context; and (5) inferences that will be arrived at to address the research question.

4. FINDINGS

The following are the findings of this study concerning the implementation of the SteadyServ keg solution.

4.1 Structure of Signification

The SteadyServ iKeg system consists of the following IT infrastructural elements (SteadyServ, 2012; Swedberg, 2013)

(1) Identiv high frequency (HF) 13.56 MHz passive RFID inlay made with NXP semiconductors chip and integrated into a label made by RR Donnelley; this tag is attached to the keg's handle;

(2) SteadyServ's Sensor ring with a built-in RFID reader and weight sensor --- which is used as a platform on which the beer keg sits;
(3) Mobile app enabling end users to manage beer inventory levels from a smartphone; the app is available for both IOS or Android devices;
(4) SteadyServ's gateway installed in every retail outlet like a restaurant, bar, etc. (Swedberg, 2013).

The Uplink/Gateway is a plastic box that contains radio receivers, computer hardware, computer software, and radio transmitters, which is mounted on the wall outside the beer cooler of the retailer's (i.e., bar or restaurant) establishment. Each Uplink/Gateway box has a unique serial number embedded in its Uplink/Gateway software. The Uplink/Gateway boxes have two major functionalities: the Zigbee hardware radio receiver and software stack receives data transmissions from keg sensor/transmitters within range. This Zigbee hardware radio receiver accepts this data, organizes it, and tags the data with information unique to the Uplink/Gateway, including the unit's unique serial number and version number. Keg sensor/transmitter data that has been organized is, then, forwarded to the code division multiple access (CDMA) cell phone gateway.

The CDMA Uplink/Gateway, on the other hand, also is a transmitter/receiver in a box containing radio hardware and software. This box could be designed by a wireless carrier partner such as Verizon Communications (in the U.S.). "This CDMA Uplink/Gateway will then join the wireless carrier's data service by connecting the closest cellphone tower to the on-premise retailer where the Uplink/Gateway has been placed....The Uplink/Gateway relays the data from the Keg Sensor/Transmitter(s) that has been collected by the Zigbee receiver. The CDMA Uplink/Gateway will communicate with the carrier's network to determine the longitude and latitude of the Gateway and will transmit that data, its software version number, and the data collected by the Zigbee receiver to the SaaS Software." (SteadyServ, 2012).

The beer distributor warehouse receives a number of keg sensor/transmitters, which are installed on the kegs. For instance, the sensor could be mounted at the bottom of the keg. Workers in the distributor warehouse have to make sure that the keg upon which the sensor/transmitter has been attached matches the items listed on the Order Pick List. The Order Pick List could be stored in an SaaS using an electronic data interchange (EDI) connection to the beer distributor's inventory system.

The distributor's warehouse usually uses a paper keg collar, clipped at the keg's top valve, which identifies the contents of the keg. Let's say that for one keg, the warehouse worker sees the label, "Coors Light." The keg sensor/transmitted for this particular keg will, then, transmit its serial number as KS1234 through the uplink Gateway. The computer monitor that shows data coming from the SaaS application will show that the keg sensor is associated to the stockkeeping unit (SKU) for "Coors Light," and confirms that the correct sensor has been attached to the right keg of beer. The Order Pick List will also be shown on the monitor from the SaaS software and this information can help the warehouse worker confirm that the beer keg leaving the distributor warehouse is the right one.

Kegs delivered from SteadyServ to the different retail establishment/customers have sensors/transmitters attached to them. These customers, then, store the kegs in coolers which puts the kegs within radio range of a mesh network that includes the keg sensors/transmitters and the uplink/gateway. Once inside the coolers, the sensors/transmitters of the kegs send data such as the weight parameter (0-20), the sensor/transmitter serial number, the software's version number, among other things. The uplink/gateway, which has its own serial number (e.g., #UG5678) and location longitude and latitude coordinates, collects the data from the sensors/transmitters. The carrier's CDMA cell phone data network, then, transmits this keg data collected by the uplink/gateway (which includes data from the gateway itself) to the SaaS software.

The SaaS software collects this data, which, it then stores in databases in a number of ways. The database supporting the SaaS software has been programmed to correlate the serial number of the sensor/transmitter and the stock keeping unit (SKU) that identifies a beer type and brand. An example can illustrate the way this works. Let us say serial numbers AB0000 to AB5678 are assigned the SKU 998877665544, which points to the product "Heineken" --- a particular beer type and brand. So, "Heineken" is written on the database by the SaaS software when data from sensor/transmitter serial number AB5676 is received, for instance. The same SaaS software has also been programmed to convert weight parameter into a percentage volume of the keg. So, say, using a weight scale of 0-20, a weight measurement of 10 from a specific keg would be converted by the SaaS software into 50% volume.

The location of the kegs in the different retail outlets is also collected by the uplink/gateway and the corresponding coordinates are also determined and recorded. So, for example, let's take the data from keg sensor/transmitter AB5676 with a weight parameter of 10 sent to the SaaS software by uplink/gateway

UG1234. The SaaS software converts the data received from the keg of "Heinken" at 4 pm today and indicates that this keg is housed in "Rhum Corner," bar is 30 percent full.

Software with embedded intelligence manage the keg sensors/transmitters and controls the frequency of transmitting data from the sensors/transmitters to the uplink/gateway. This software could be programmed so that, for instance, data will be transmitted only if the weight of the keg changes. Work is underway so that data about the ambient temperature in the cooler and the sensor/transmitter's remaining battery life could be relayed as well. Once the basic keg volume, date time, and location data is beamed from the Keg Sensor/Transmitter through the Uplink/Gateway into the SaaS software database, a number of actions will now take place that involve acting upon the data gathered.

Institutional customers of SteadyServ can set up their organizational accounts to enable their firm representatives to access their account information. The setup process requires each individual's smartphone number, among other data. All authorized individuals in that firm are allowed to access their account information which should give them insight into the status of their beer inventory and enable them to activate alerts when it is time to replenish the beer. Alerts can be sent using a number of ways: an alert sent as simple SMS text message sent to mobile phones; pop-up push alerts sent to iPhones and Android phones; email messages; recorded voice alerts sent to smartphones, etc. The alerting system uses the individual's smartphone's location based service. Workers get alerts only when they are in an area within the designated longitude and latitude boundaries associated with their workplace as defined in the SaaS database. Workers can choose to receive alerts whether or not they are working during official working hours.

A retail representative can design alerts based on the relative importance of a beer brand and type. So, for instance, if "Molson Canadian" beer is more popular than "Heineken," then, the retail representative can set up the SaaS software in such a way that he/she receives an alert when the system reports a 35 percent remaining volume for "Molson Canadian" beer and 10 percent remaining volume for "Heineken" beer.

Retailers have a number of options for reordering beer once after an alert has been received. First, using an SMS text message, they can contact their beer distributor rep directly. Second, they can send an SMS text message to an SMS gateway designed to transmit electronic data interchange (EDI) transactions to the beer distributor's ordering system. A third party system vendor usually controls this process. Third, they can use the user interface of the software to voice call to the beer distributor's sales rep. Fourth, they can use a reorder app on an iPhone or Android phone that communicates via EDI with the beer distributor's ordering system. Finally, retailers can set their accounts in such a way that automatic reorder messages tailored to the specific demand for a beer type and brand are sent to the beer distributor. So, for example, a rule can be specified in the SaaS software so that "Molson Canada" beer is automatically replenished if the volume falls below the 40 percent level only on Fridays, Saturdays, and Sundays. Developers of application programming interfaces (APIs) will also have opportunities to write software programs for applications that can access the captured data for a variety of real-time software applications.

4.2 Structure of Domination

The different elements of the RFID system used for the keg solution represents the "structure of domination" in the way work was conducted because the built-in assumptions, features, and standardized procedures embedded in business processes involved controlled the way inventory was managed in the retailer, distributor, and beer brewer establishments that used the SteadyServ keg solution. RFID system deployment involves complexities related to the physical elements of the working environment. Hershberger articulated the challenges of using RFID technology for the keg solution (Hershberger, 2015): "So it turns out using an IOT device, including RFID, in the coolers is [a] pretty hostile environment. It's pretty hard. So [it] must operate in 32-38 degree temperatures 24 by 7. It must be self-powered by lithium battery, which does not like cold. It must last three years. It must have built materials underneath $100. A full keg actually weighs 170 pounds, which gets dropped off [of] the back of a semi which is 54 inches tall. [A sensor needs to be placed underneath] and the keg could be [stacked too high]. It's a smash force of 2,000 pounds --- so you need to have an IOT device that can withstand 2,000 pounds of smash force. [You also] need to be able to measure [the beer liquid] down to a single pint of beer, which is about eight ounces out of a keg that holds 180 pints. And you need to know exactly when it's going to run out. Meaning I need to know in the next 15 seconds that that keg over there is going to be empty. You need to be able to designate up to 10 different keg sizes and 20 various options....You [also] need to be able to recognize up to 40,000 different types of beers that are commercially available globally. You must be able to use [an] RFID tag to isolate alphanumerically every single keg and never ever have the same number [used] twice. You need to remove the human process with a semi-automated intelligence process. And you need to be able to house the RFID reader and ZigBee transmitter in that device that sits in that horribly complex environment that does not like anything like temperature, power consumption, the whole nine yards…" (Hershberger, 2015).

4.3 Structure of Legitimation

Standards that govern IOT represent "the structure of legitimation" because they sanction the configuration of the specific elements of the IOT solution used and propagate a set of "norms" about what constitutes a workable IOT solution within different corporate contexts/environments. Observance of IOT standards is important because: (1) standards specify tried and tested solutions which could greatly help a firm deploy IOT solutions under real world conditions; (2) standards require specific IOT solution components provided by vendors and integrators off-the-shelf, thus, helping firms avoid unnecessary development efforts and vendor lock in; and (3) standards enable solutions that are compatible with related business applications. At this time, there is no central body of standards that can be applied to all possible IOT applications. The use of industrial IOT standards would be relevant specifically for SteadyServ's product monitoring initiative. The efforts of three bodies would have the most impact on SteadyServ.

The first organization is that of the Open Interconnect Consortium (OIC), which is supported by Intel, Samsung Electronics, Hewlett Packard, Lenovo, Dell, among a total of 50 vendor firms. These firms are working to back up open-source standards covering device discovery, communication, data exchange, among other functions. The OIC has developed the source code embodying the consortium's specifications for certified IOT products and released it to developers in 2015 (Lawson, December 24, 2014).

The second organization focusing on enterprise IOT is the Industrial Internet Consortium (IIC) consisting of about 100 members including Microsoft, Samsung, Huawei Technologies, General Electric, Cisco Systems, IBM, and Intel (Lawson, December 24, 2014). Its approach is different in that rather than developing IOT standards, it intends to work with different standards bodies to coordinate efforts of industries where IOT and older machine-to-machine technologies have been deployed. In so doing, the IIC will define requirements for standards, design reference structures, and create testbeds for these standards.

The third organization is the IEEE (The Institute of Electrical and Electronics Engineers) P2413, which has a working group devoted to organizing the variety of IOT specifications developed by different industry consortia (Lawson, December 24, 2014). It will do so by converting information from different IOT platforms into a commonly understood body of data objects.

With the variety of standards bodies emerging, a good predictor of who might prevail is the size, reputation, and momentum of the firms behind them. These are consortia that will more likely gain greater traction and immediate market recognition.

4.4 Social Consequences

4.4.1 Social Structure and Social Consequences of IT

The focus here is on how IT is implemented, assimilated, and adopted by end users and the resulting outcomes within the social structures that defined the social context of deployment. IT is the medium of human action. Using the structuration perspective, the concept of interpretive schemes, resources, and norms are used to understand how the end users's behavior in the organization is mediated by IT which either facilitates certain outcomes or constrains others. The potential of IOT to provide competitive advantage in the marketplace at this stage has been articulated by Iansiti and Lakhani (2014) and Burkitt (2014). At this stage of the game, perhaps the most significant change emerging as a result of IOT technological possibilities is the attention given to it at the "C suite" level of the firm. A major part of crafting an IOT strategy is determining a new business model for offering IOT-enabled products and services. In SteadyServ, Hershberger, CEO of SteadyServ articulated their business model, which was to deliver business intelligence-enhanced services to retailers, distributors, and beer brewers (Hershberger, 2015). SteadyServ created a technological solution enabled by IOT to solve supply chain problems associated with beer and tap management. In fact, apps for iPhone and Android smartphones have been developed to facilitate the deployment experience of retailers, distributors, and beer brewers. Without the SteadyServ beer keg solution, there was no instrumentation in place to assist in inventory management in different retail establishments serving beer. Orders and beer replenishment were based on sheer guesses. With increasing competitive pressures in the marketplace, the beer industry had to figure out how to "demand match" beer products with significant micro-trends determined by local tastes, economics, social dynamics, and product seasonality (Hershberger, 2015).

4.4.2 Action and Social Consequences of IT

Retailers using the SteadyServ's iKeg system benefit from the significant improvements in corporate decision making as a result of fine-grained tracking information that give real-time updates on the state of the firm's inventory system. Carl Bruggemeier, CEO of CZH Hospitality, a firm overseeing restaurant and hospitality projects across the US shared this:

"For me, it's all about having near real-time information about all of my draft beer products at my fingertips," Bruggemeier says (Dudley, 2015). "I can get a variety of reports and information on my handheld device. The system allows me to understand my customer's purchasing trends, look at my inventory and compare the information from SteadyServ with the reports I get from my point of sale systems, so that I can verify that I'm getting all the money I should. It has become an invaluable management tool for all the young people that work for me." "The most important thing it has done for us is that we don't run out of the beers our customers wish to purchase," Bruggemeier says. "This makes the customer very happy because previously we might have run out of a very popular and great selling product. There are two outcomes from that – you have an angry customer and you miss out on potential revenue." "We can look at a trend and say 'our customers are telling us they like pale ales' for example," Bruggemeier explains. "We may only have one or two available, but with this information we can go and find others to complement what we already sell. This helps increase customer satisfaction to thereby increase our revenues." "For many years the hospitality industry lagged behind others in the appropriate use of technology, and I think we suffered because of it," he concludes. "I think systems like SteadyServ and the explosion of this kind of technological improvement and availability of data is going to make those that adopt it eminently more powerful in their marketplace and completely responsive to their customers' needs." (Dudley, 2015).

Another significant action SteadyServ undertook was collaborating with Intel Corporation and with the world's best brewers including Heineken, Boston Beer, New Belgium Brewing, Constellation Brands, Molson Coors, and more, in developing the keg IOT-based solution (Hershberger, 2015).

4.4.3 Measures of Success

Hershberger articulated the different metrics SteadyServ recognized in measuring the success of the keg IOT-based solution (Hershberger, 2015): brewers increased the efficiencies of their marketing campaigns; in-field sales staff increased sales, revenues, and the firm's market share; distributors increased the acquisition and retention of high performing taps and high value retailers; distributors gained a better understanding of the optimum beer mix for each retailer/customer, which, in turn, enabled them to focus on high value customers; retailers increased their draft beer revenue margins and reduce waste; and SteadyServ's return on investment had gone beyond a tenfold increase annually.

5. CONCLUSIONS

In terms of structure of signification, the SteadyServ iKeg solution is expected to take off in the beer industry as word about its benefits spread especially among "on-premise" establishments such as bars, restaurants, taverns, pubs, sporting and entertainment venues, and the hospitality industry in general. It is this specific market segment that is "in the dark" when it comes to knowing consumer beer consumption accurately "on premise." In terms of its potential use in other industries, the concept behind the iKeg solution could be applicable to the wine, softdrinks, agri-chemicals, certain types of pharmaceuticals, etc. In terms of the action and the social consequences of the iKeg solution, managers of beer joints have now been empowered with a complete solution giving them more business intelligence in making beer inventory decisions.

REFERENCES

Burkitt, F. 2014. Six Ways To Define Your Internet of Things Strategy. December 5. Forbes Magazine. Available from: http://www.forbes.com/sites/strategyand/2014/12/05/six-ways-to-define-your-internet-of-things-strategy/#3462a0132eac

Dudley, S., 2015. Keeping track of supplies with SteadyServ iKeg powered by Intel. June 9. Available from: http://www.onwindows.com/Article/rss/240/sean-dudley

Giddens, A., 1984. The Constitution of Society: Outline of the Theory of Structure. University of California Press, Berkeley, California, USA.

Giddens, A., 1979. Central Problems in Social Theory: Action, Structure, and Contradiction in Social Analysis. University of California Press, San Francisco, California, USA.

Giddens, A., 1976. New Rules of Sociological Method. Basic Books, New York, New York, USA.

Hershberger, S., 2015. Awards Finalist for the Best Internet of Things Deployment: SteadyServ. *RFID Journal Live! April 16-17, 2015, San Diego, California, USA.*Transcript of the Conference Session.

Iansiti, M. and Lakhani, K.R., 2014. Digital Ubiquity: How Connections, Sensors, and Data Are Revolutionizing Business. *Harvard Business Review*, Vol. 92, No. 11, November, pp. 91-99.

Identiv, 2014. SteadyServ Technologies: iKeg NFC Tag Ensures Trust in Everyday Items. Available from: http://l.identiv.com/steadyserv/

Krippendorff, K., 2004. *Content Analysis: An Introduction to Its Methodology.* Sage Publications, Thousand Oaks, California, USA.

Krippendorff, K., 1980. *Content Analysis: An Introduction to Its Methodology.* Sage Publications, Beverly Hills, California, USA.

Lahiri, S., 2006. *RFID Sourcebook.* IBM Press, New York, New York, USA.

Lawson, S., 2014. Why Internet of Things 'standards' got more confusing in 2014. December 24. *IDG News Service.* Available from:

http://www.pcworld.com/article/2863572/iot-groups-are-like-an-orchestra-tuning-up-the-music-starts-in-2016.html

Orlikowski, W.J., 1992. The Duality of Technology: Rethinking The Concept of Technology in Organizations. *In Organization Science*, Vol. 3 No. 3, August, pp 398-427.

Orlikowski, W.J. and Robey, D.,1991. Information Technology and the Structuring of Organizations. *In Information Systems Research,* Vol. 2, No. 2, pp 143-169.

SteadyServ, 2012. U.S. Trademark Application No. 85693526 --- Intelligent Keg --- N/A, United States Patent and Trademark Office. Available from: https://tsdrapi.uspto.gov/ts/cd/casedocs/bundle.pdf?sn=85693526&type=EXA&fromdate=2012-11-30&todate=2012-11-30

Stone, P.J., Dunphy, D.C., Smith, M.S., and Ogilvie, D.M., 1966. *The General Inquirer: A Computer Approach to Content Analysis.* MIT Press, Cambridge, Massachusetts, USA. *Semistructured Data and XML.* Morgan Kaufmann Publishers, San Francisco, USA.

Swedberg, C., 1994. SteadyServ Launching RFID Solution That Keeps Beer Flowing, *RFID Journal, 22 November. Available from:* http://www.rfidjournal.com/articles/pdf?11208

Tata Consultancy Services, 2015. *Internet of Things: The Complete Reimaginative Force: TCS Global Trend Study --- July 2015.* Available from: http://www.tcs.com/SiteCollectionDocuments/White%20Papers/Internet-of-Things-The-Complete-Reimaginative-Force.pdf

Weber, R.P., 1990. *Basic Content Analysis, second edition.* Sage Publications, Newbury Park, California, USA.

Weick, K., 1979. *The Social Psychology of Organizing.* Addison-Wesley, Reading, Massachusetts, USA.

Yen, B., 2015. The Internet of Things (IOT): Shaping the Future of E-Commerce. *Case Number HK1063.* Asia Case Research Centre, The University of Hong Kong.

INTERSECTION-BASED ROUTING ON TOP OF A VIRTUALIZATION LAYER TO SUPPORT VEHICULAR CLOUD APPLICATIONS IN A SMART CITY

José Víctor Saiáns-Vázquez[1], Martín López-Nores[1], Manuel Ramos-Cabrer[1],
Jack Fernando Bravo-Torres[2] and Esteban Fernando Ordóñez-Morales[2]
[1]*AtlantTIC Research Center for Information and Communication Technologies*
Departamento de Enxeñaría Telemática, Universidade de Vigo
EE Telecomunicación, Campus Universitario s/n, 36310 Vigo, Spain
[2]*Área de Ciencias Exacta, Universidad Politécnica Salesiana, Calle Vieja 12-30 y Elia Liut, Cuenca, Ecuador*

ABSTRACT

The development of the smart cities is strongly linked to the Internet of Things (IoTs), where a lot of quotidian objects with connection capabilities interact in many applications over the network. One of the more relevant branches of the IoTs is the Internet of Vehicles (IoV), the next step in the Vehicular Ad hoc Networks (VANETS) as the number of vehicles connected to the IoTs increases. The main purpose of IoV is to combine the resources of many vehicles, things and networks to provide a robust communication capability. In this context the Vehicular Cloud applications take a great importance harnessing the wealthy resources contributed by groups of vehicles to enable innovative information services on the road. In this paper we present the architecture and the main procedures of a Vehicular Cloud Computing model on top of a virtualization layer and evaluate the adequacy to some Vehicular Cloud applications of special interest in smart cities of three different flavors of a new algorithm called VNIBR (*Intersection-Based Routing on Virtual Nodes*): reactive, proactive and encounter-based.

KEYWORDS

Internet of Vehicles, Vehicular Cloud, Virtualization, Intersection-based Routing, Vehicular Social Networks

1. INTRODUCTION

In the near future, every vehicle will be equipped with communication, computing, and sensory devices, enabling the exchange of packets with surrounding cars and with the road-side infrastructure. These new capabilities of the cars together with the increase of the wireless accessibility to the Internet from vehicles have propelled research in the area of the *Intelligent Transportation Systems* (ITS), with plenty of different approach for vehicles to exchange data in ad hoc networks (*vehicle-to-vehicle*, V2V) and with servers on the Internet through WiFi communications with roadside access points or cellular networks (*vehicle-to- infrastructure*, V2I) [1].

Taking advantage of the underutilized resources available in the vehicles many applications can be developed based on the Vehicular Cloud infrastructure. For instance, the idea of creating a datacenter using the idle resources of the cars in a parking of an airport, a company, a shopping mall or even in the streets is very coherent taking into account the fact that the vehicles spend the most of the time in the day parked in any of this sites [12]. So that, the users who decided to cede the resources of their vehicles while they are idle could be incentivized in any way (lower prices in private parkings, lower taxes for the vehicles which contribute to this service in the street, incentives for the workers of the company, etc.).

Another interesting application in this ambit and something that can really improve the quality of life in a smart city is the Virtual Traffic Lights (VTL), where the vehicles passing an intersection create and coordinate the traffic light signals by themselves improving significantly the fluency of the traffic [15]. But the VSNs also provide another kind of applications more socializing-oriented like voice chats [17] where users can join VSNs and communicate between them by mean of voice messages.

As can be noted there exist a great variety of vehicular cloud-based applications, and each of them have very different communication needs and patterns. In response to this fact, here, we present three variants of a new algorithm called VNIBR (*Intersection-Based Routing on Virtual Nodes*) that leverage the idea of intersection-based routing in different ways to ensure greater performance for different VSNs cloud-based applications. These algorithms are called VNIBR-R (reactive), VNIBR-P (proactive) and VNIBR-E (encounter-based).

In this paper, we have applied the idea exposed in [18] that Virtual Cloud Networking (VCN) can be naturally and reliably supported over the virtualization layer. As shown in Figure 1, we put the virtualization procedures into a separate layer in the stack of communication protocols, called the VaNetLayer, which manages concepts that can be readily used by the VCN logic. The exchange of messages among vehicles is achieved by the different versions of VNIBR and TCP at the transport layer. At the bottom of the stack, the MAC and physical layers are provided by IEEE 802.11p.

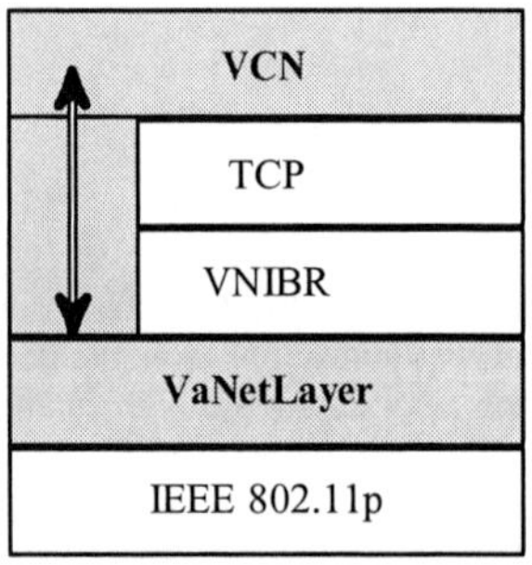

Figure 1. The stack of protocols of our proposal

Next, in Section II and III, we describe the main procedures of the VaNetLayer and the core ideas of each VNIBR flavor. In the Section IV, we describe the main procedures to support VCN over the VaNetLayer. We give a little overview of the results obtain for three preliminary experiments carried out to test the adequacy of the designed model in three different VCN applications in the section V. Finally, Section VI contains a summary of conclusions and ongoing work.

2. BACKGROUND ON THE VANETLAYER

The VaNetLayer is an evolution of the Virtual Node Layer (VNLayer), a cluster-based approach presented in [4] to handle communications in MANETs. Sitting between the link layer and the Internet layer, the VNLayer put forward procedures to engage the mobile physical nodes (PNs) in collaboration to emulate virtual nodes (VNs) that can be addressed as static server devices, thus masking out the uncertainty that arises from the MANETs' varying topology.

As shown in Figure 2, the VaNetLayer divides the geographical area of the ad-hoc network into quadrilateral regions according an intersection-based layout in such a way that every PN can send/receive data from/to every other PN in its current region and neighboring ones. One PN in each region is chosen as *leader* and takes charge of packet reception, buffering and forwarding in the communication with other VNs. Meanwhile, a subset of non-leaders works as *backups* to maintain replicas of the state information from the upper layers as well as helping the leader in its labors in case of packet losses or overload. Thus, the VNs can maintain persistent state and be fault-tolerant even when individual PNs fail or leave the region, as long as there remains at least one PN (We assume that all the PNs are equipped with an accurate localization system, and that they all have copies of the same digital map. Thus, the PNs can separately come up with the same distribution of regions in the virtual network, locate themselves and identify the VNs they have to support).

The interface between the VaNetLayer and the network layer exposes the notion of regions, the role played by a PN at the moment, and functions to send/receive messages and to get/set/check state information. This makes it is possible to adapt existing routing algorithms to lean on the VNs as stable routing entities or even as destinations for geocasting. The author of [23], for example, devised virtualized versions of AODV and RIP [5] (called VNAODV and VNRIP, respectively) and proved that the VNs helped to attain significant performance improvements in MANET settings.

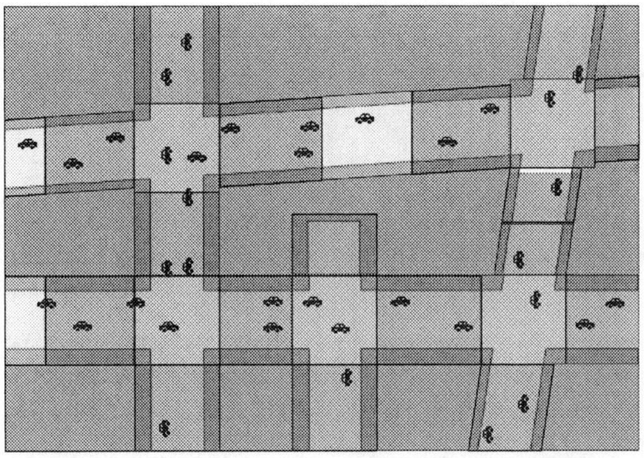

Figure 2. Static virtual nodes defined by the VaNetLayer

With this improved virtualization layer, we proved in [6] that the VNAODV algorithm of [23] could provide a valid alternative for content distribution in VANETs, considering the references of CarTorrent [20] and CodeTorrent [21]. The same algorithm failed to work on top of the original VNLayer. Later on, in [7], we showed that VNAODV performed better than the RBVT algorithms and the geographical, cluster-based approach of Passcar [8].

3. INTERSECTION-BASED ROUTING ON VIRTUAL NODES

The new layout of the virtual nodes with the VaNetLayer provides convenient grounds to develop our new combination of topological and geographical routing, with road-based paths connecting successive intersections that lead from sources to destinations. In the three proposed variants of VNIBR, we differentiate three types of routing entities:

- The level 1 entities (L1VNs) are the VNs placed at the intersections. This is where the routing decisions are made (differently in the three variants of VNIBR, as explained in the following subsections). Routing tables and tables of encounters are transparently kept by the VaNetLayer as persistent state information.
- The level 2 entities (L2VNs) are VNs neighboring an intersection. Firstly, these VNs forward packets along a road segment as mandated by the neighboring L1VN, irrespective of whichever PN actually does the transmission. This is done without any other processing than setting a *delivery bit* in the packets' header to 1 if the destination is within the current region. For example, if the vehicle PN1 of Figure 3 (a) is communicating with PN2 through the route drawn with a red solid line, the packets it sends reaches the next L1VN past vn43, which is VN4, with the delivery bit set to 1. Additionally, using a snapshots mechanism of the VaNetLayer, L2VNs can act as backing entities, trying to continue relaying packets onto other road segments during downtimes of the neighboring L1VNs. For example, the leader PN of vn44 in Figure 3 (a) can help avoid a breakage in the route depicted with a discontinuous line when there are no vehicles in the region covered by VN4.
- Finally, the VNs in intermediate positions of road segments are level 3 entities (L3VNs), which simply relay packets from one side to the other, again irrespective of specific PNs and setting the delivery bit to 1 as above.

L1VNs that are one road segment away from one another steadily exchange HELLO packets to keep track of the connectivity conditions between them. These messages are transmitted hop-by-hop across the L2VNs and L3VNs in between, each one adding the average number of physical nodes in its virtual region, calculated using an *exponentially-weighted moving average* (EWMA). When an L1VN receives a HELLO packet, it assigns a QoS value to that link, pondering the L1VN-to-L1VN transmission delay (again, filtered by EWMA), the average number of PNs in the intermediate L2VNs and L3VNs, and the amount of data traffic going through that road segment.

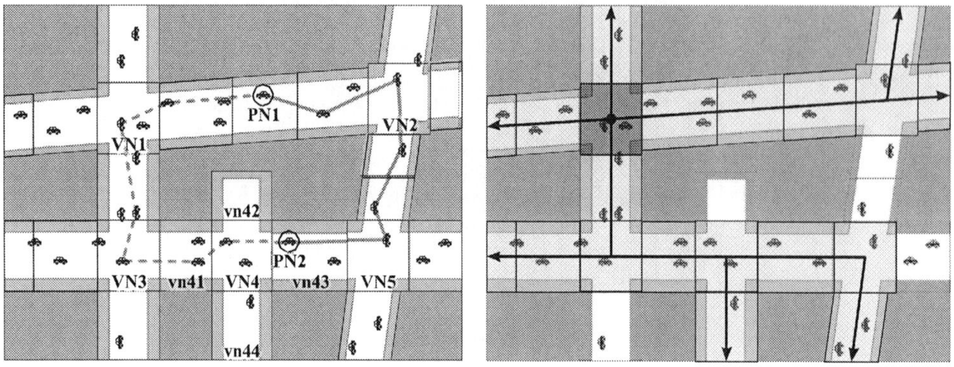

(a) (b)

Figure 3. Sample PNs, VNs and routes in VNIBR (left); and the spanning tree with the paths from one L1VN to the others in the proactive version (right)

A. *VNIBR-R: reactive VNIBR*

In the proposed reactive version of VNIBR, communication routes are created only when a source PN needs to send a packet but it does not know a route to the intended destination PN. In that case, the source PN buffers the packet and starts a flooding process by sending a *Route Request* packet (RREQ) to the L1VNs that delimit its road segment. Each one of those L1VNs puts its ID as the first element of a L1VN list in the RREQ packet header and sends a copy to other L1VNs that are one road segment away (If one road segment does not provide connectivity to the other end, as determined by the exchange of HELLO messages, it is skipped). A broadcast ID is included in the RREQ packet to prevent any L1VN to transmit the same packet more than once. A route is established (i) when the RREQ packet reaches an L1VN that knows a valid route to the destination PN, (ii) when an L1VN receives the RREQ packet with the delivery bit set to 1, meaning that the destination PN is in the road segment just traversed, or (iii) when an L1VN receives the RREQ packet with the *delivery bit* set to 0 but the destination PN is in the current intersection. Then, a *Route Reply* packet (RREP) is created that travels along the backpath, allowing the L1VNs on the way to set up a route to the destination PN in their routing tables. It is worth noting that the flooding of RREQ packets implies very little overhead because it involves only the leaders (and occasionally backups) of the traversed VNs.

Once a route between source and destination has been established, as explained in Section II, the data packets are sent VN by VN via unicast transmissions between leader nodes. When the transmitting PN detects a failure, it can either report it upstream by sending a *Route Error* packet (RERR) to the so-called *precursors* (i.e. the neighboring nodes to which an RREP packet was generated or forwarded) or try a *local repair* by broadcasting an RREQ packet and waiting for an RREP to restore the link. Thanks to the QoS sensing through HELLO messages, the L1VNs can search alternative routes when the connectivity along a segment with active connections worsens significantly.

Also regarding route maintenance tasks, VNIBR implements a correction procedure to follow the PNs' movements without incurring in local repairs that would take a long time to resolve. For example, if vehicle PN1 in Fig. 3 (a) gets to the intersection of VN1 and turns left onto the road segment between VN1 and VN3, a RREQ packet with TTL=1 and no explicit destination is sent backwards to VN1, which serves to extend the former route VN5→VN2 to become VN5→VN2→VN1, whereas another special RREQ packet with a list of the destination PNs with which it has ongoing communication sessions is sent forward to VN3, that can help discover a better route through the intersections of VN3 and VN4.

B. *VNIBR-P: proactive VNIBR*

Following the philosophy of the intersection-based routing protocol IRQV [9], the proactive version of VNIBR implements a steady exchange of messages to pre-compute a stable backbone of routes among a reduced number of *terminal nodes*, which serve as proxies to the other nodes. In our case, the terminal nodes are the L1VNs, and every PN selects a neighboring L1VN as its terminal node depending on distance and direction of movement.

Using additional fields in the HELLO packets, neighboring L1VNs exchange lists of the PNs found between them. Each list entry in the HELLO packets contains the IP address of the corresponding PN and a *terminal bit*, which is set to 1 if the PN is moving towards the destination L1VN (The terminal bit is straightforward to set thanks to state information available to the virtualization layer). That information is propagated throughout the network of L1VNs in *Topology Control* (TC) messages, which are sent whenever an L1VN detects relevant changes in topology and/or QoS values.

Thanks to the exchange of HELLO and TC messages, the L1VNs end up not only with QoS estimations for the road segments they join, but also with a global view of which PNs are served by each L1VN. With this information, they can compute a minimum spanning tree by Dijkstra's algorithm, indicating the paths to follow to reach any other L1VN in the network (see Fig. 3 (b)). The routing tables, as well as the locations and terminal nodes of the PNs, are kept in the L1VNs as persistent state. When a PN needs to send a packet to another, it only has to send it directly to its terminal L1VN and this will already know the best path to reach the terminal L1VN of the destination.

There are several important points to note regarding the amount of overhead incurred by the steady exchange of messages. First, the exchange of HELLO packets takes place between pairs of neighboring L1VNs, which are not numerous compared to PNs. Likewise, the dissemination of TC packets follows the paths determined by the spanning trees, thus implying almost the minimum number of messages. Besides, the messages do not carry information about all the PNs, but rather only of the ones that changed their terminal nodes since the last update. Therefore, there are many topology changes that do not require any action (e.g. a PN can change from one virtual node region to another, and even from one road segment to another, without changing its terminal node). The fact that the packets always make it to the end of any road segment (remember the delivery bit mechanism explained in Section III) leaves much time to react to a change of terminal node, thus allowing to reduce the frequency of the updates.

C. VNIBR-E: encounter-based VNIBR

The reactive and proactive versions of VNIBR achieve good results in small and medium urban scenarios; however, when the number and complexity of the intersections increase, the overhead due to the long route discoveries in VNIBR-R and to the increase of the TC packets dissemination in VNIBR-P hamper their scalability. To tackle this point, we propose an encounter-based version, called VNIBR-E, that provides a very simple and scalable solution applying the philosophy of FRESH (*FResher Encounter SearcH*) [10], a recursive searching algorithm that steers the search of a route to a certain node based on encounters registered at intermediate points, taking advantage of space-time correlation.

In VNIBR-E, the L1VNs store tables recording the last PN encounters in the corresponding intersections. Each entry consists of the PN's IP address, the timestamp of the last packet heard from that node and the road segment by which the node left the intersection. When a PN needs to send a packet to another, it sends the packet to its terminal L1VN. If the L1VN does not know a route to the destination, it sends an RREQ packet to its neighboring L1VNs, including a TTL value and the timestamp of the L1VN's last encounter with the PN to be found. An L1VN answers to an RREQ packet with a NAREQ (*Next Anchor Request*) if its last encounter with that PN is fresher than the one sent in the RREQ. Otherwise, the L1VN decreases the TTL value in the packet and, if it is not zero, adds its ID to the list of L1VNs traversed during the search and forwards it to other neighboring L1VNs —the RREQ packet includes a broadcast ID and a list of the L1VNs traversed, so that the forwarding process does not fall into unnecessary retransmissions. The L1VN that started the route search will wait for a certain time, and then it will answer with a NAREP (*Next Anchor Reply*) to the NAREQ with the lowest encounter time (if it has not received any NAREQ during that time, it proceeds to send a new RREQ with a greater TTL value). When an L1VN receives a NAREP, it continues with the route searching from that point, sending a RREQ packet with the TTL counter reset to its neighbor L1VNs (preserving the list of L1VNs traversed), but this time with its encounter time. In this way, the route search goes on steered to the destination helped by time-space correlation. When the destination PN is finally reached, the establishment of the route is completed as in VNIBR-R (Section III-A).

4. VEHICULAR CLOUD NETWORKING OVER THE VANETLAYER

Our proposal creates a virtual platform to structure and organize the work of the vehicles that are within a certain region so that they collaborate to perform tasks, share resources, and maintain the virtual structure. On this platform of virtual nodes, different coordination processes are performed in order to structure a cloud of virtual nodes. In this structure, the tasks are assigned per virtual node rather than individual vehicles. According to the operations proposal in [3], the process developed works as follow:

A. Cloud Resource Discovery and Cloud Formation

The vehicle running the application (application node) sends a resource discovery message (*MRDiscovery*). This message is forwarded to the neighboring L1VNs. During its trip, the message collects the information of resource and the availability of the VNs to form the cloud. The structure of the VaNetLayer and the mechanism present in it (see, Section II) allow the leaders of each VN to know the resources and processing capabilities of the devices in their regions. When the *MRDiscovery* message reaches the L1VNs, they sent back to the application node an *MRReply* message with the information collected. Once the *MRReply* message is received, the application node selects the VNs to form the cloud. An additional message (*MRAck*) is sent to the chosen VNs to reserve resources for the application.

B. Task Assignment and Result Collection

With the cloud formed, the application node proceeds to split the application into different parts which are distributed among the members of the cloud in terms of the resources available to each. Meanwhile, the leader node of each VN subdivided the tasks among idle PNs in the region. Two tables are managed in this process: one maintained by both the application node and by the leader of the VN cloud, which contains the cloud member's IDs and their tasks assigned. And a second table maintained by the leaders of each virtual node in the cloud, it contains the cloud PNs IDs and the tasks assigned.

The results are sent back to the application node for its processing. Thus, a first process of collecting and aggregation of the results is developed. The results obtained by each PN are sent to its leader who puts them in order. Finally, the leader nodes send the results back to the application node. The leader nodes sent back to the application node a complete task message (*MCTask*).

C. Content Publishing and Sharing

In the structure proposal, the results are sharing with the entire network. Depending of the application, the results can be advertised by the same application node broadcasting an ad, which is limited to the street stretch between the intersections. In this way, all VNs in the street will have known of the available applications. On the other hand, if a vehicle needs some content that has not been announced, it broadcasts a content request message (*MCRequest*), which is replicated, by one of the members of the cloud with access to content. Located the content, the vehicle begins the process to access it.

D. Cloud Maintenance and Release

Thanks to the process developed by the VaNetLayer, the structure of the virtual nodes (leader node, backups and non-leaders) is supported transparently for the applications. So when a leader node leaves the region, the new leader assumes the tasks left by its predecessor. Similarly, if the region is by going to be empty, the VN neighbors will support the VN fallen until it is restored. Nevertheless if a virtual node can not stay within the cloud, it communicates —through a *MCWithdrawal* message — this fact to the application node to select another VN to assume its tasks.

5. EVALUATION OF THE EXPERIMENTS

The routing schemes developed endow the infrastructure proposed with the flexibility that allows it to deal with almost every vehicular cloud application. For this paper three of these applications have been evaluated: Virtual Traffic Lights (VTL), a Vehicular Datacenter and a multimedia chat. The Virtual Traffic Lights (VTL) coordinates the vehicular traffic in an intersection, and therefore in a close future when most vehicles belong to the IoVs, the conventional traffic lights could be replaced by this efficient system. The system chosen was the VTL presented in [15] in which a vehicle is chosen cooperatively as the VTL leader of an intersection, and from that moment it is the responsible of the VTL signal construction and dissemination according to pre-defined rules. This mechanism strongly matches with the concept applied in the L1VN; where a leader is elected to control the data traffic through the intersection, so that this leader can be provided with the capability of generate VTLs in its intersection. As a result, the fluency of the vehicular traffic was significantly improved, specially in cases of low and medium vehicular traffic, although the results suggest that the improvement of the fluency in the intersection can reduce the stability of the virtual node in scenarios with low levels of vehicular traffic, as the average time of a vehicles in an intersection significantly decreases, and this fact could lessen the quality of the communications in the VANET.

Another application tested was a data center formed by the vehicles along a street. Both the parked and the traveling vehicles could belong to the cloud and therefore sharing their idle resources. These resources were used to create a cloud where storage some data uploaded by a subset of vehicles in the network and later downloaded by another subset of vehicles. The cloud proved to be really stable, especially due to the participating parked cars, which notably improved the stability of the virtual network and therefore guaranteed the persistence of the data in the cloud. Regarding the routing scheme, VNIBR-P achieved the best uploading and downloading times followed closely by VNIBR-R as the cloud formed did not involve a great number of intersections, and therefore the encounter-based flavor could no show its advantages.

The last application evaluated has been a multimedia chat, where the vehicles can subscribe to the VSN and start to chat by mean of voice messages. In the simulations, the cloud was maintained by the most of the cars in the VANET, while some of them sent large messages to another vehicles in the VSN causing a reply from those vehicles, simulating a voice chat. The infrastructure proved to meet the requirements of this kind of application when a minimum level of vehicular traffic is guaranteed. In scenarios with a very low traffic density the routes generated over the virtual network become unstable and many packets got lost making difficult to maintain a fluently conversation in the application. The best routing scheme seems to be VNIBR-E, which is able to efficiently create routes between vehicles separated by a big number of intersections, making possible an intelligible conversation between vehicles across a big smart city generating the lowest network congestion. The reactive and proactive versions are highly recommended for applications with higher QoS requirements, but in this case the most efficient solution is the encounter-based flavor.

6. CONCLUSIONS AND ONGOING WORK

We have presented the main procedures of a virtualization layer that can be used as the cornerstone to support the emerging paradigm of Vehicular Cloud Networking. This approach extends the classic notion of virtualization to enable the view of a reliable network of stationary virtual nodes, resulting from the collaboration of vehicles on a smart city. The inherent clustering and the differentiation of leader and backup roles among the vehicles are very convenient grounds to build up the concepts of VCN, and our experiments show that our solution can effectively aggregate the connections of several vehicles, achieving competitive results in many applications of great interest for the smart cities. Likewise, the three flavors of intersection-based routing consistently ensure meeting the communication requirements of almost every VCN application. Nowadays, we are working to develop new services in the vehicular cloud, in which the virtual nodes can be made responsible for computing, sensing, storage and communication tasks, taking advantage of the resources of the vehicles passing by their regions at any time.

As part of our ongoing work, we are extending VNIBR to support multicasting and to manage end-to-end QoS conditions (not just segment-wise connectivity). Furthermore, we are interested in developing more flavors for VNIBR, involving constructs of swarm intelligence [11] and mobility-assisted information diffusion [22].

ACKNOWLEDGEMENTS

The authors from the University of Vigo have been supported by the Ministerio de Educación y Ciencia (Gobierno de España) research project TIN2013-42774-R (partly financed with FEDER funds.

REFERENCES

[1] Y. Yang and R. Bagrodia, "Evaluation of VANET-based advanced intelligent transportation systems", in *Proceedings of the 6th ACM Intl. Workshop on Vehicular Ad Hoc Networks (VANET)*, Beijing, China, Sep. 2009.

[2] S. Olariu and M. Weigle, "*Vehicular networks: From theory to practice*", Taylor & Francis, 2009.

[3] E. Lee, E.K. Lee, S.Y. Oh, and M. Gerla, "Vehicular cloud networking: Architecture and design principles", *Communications Magazine*, vol. 52, pp. 148–155, 2014.

[4] M. Brown, S. Gilbert, N. Lynch, C. Newport, T. Nolte, and M. Spindel, "The Virtual Node Layer: a programming abstraction for wireless sensor networks", *ACM SIGBED Review*, vol. 4, no. 3, pp. 121–140, 2007.

[5] G. S. Malkin, "*RIP: An Intra-Domain Routing Protocol*", Addison-Wesley Longman, 2000.

[6] J.F. Bravo-Torres, M. López-Nores, Y. Blanco-Fernández, J.J. Pazos-Arias, and E. Ordóñez-Morales, "VaNetLayer: A virtualization layer supporting access to web contents from within vehicular networks", *Journal of Computational Science*, vol. 11, pp. 185-195, Nov. 2015.

[7] J.F. Bravo-Torres, M. López-Nores, Y. Blanco-Fernández, J.J. Pazos-Arias, M. Ramos-Cabrer, and A. Gil-Solla, "Optimising reactive routing over virtual nodes in VANETs", *IEEE Transactions on Vehicular Technology*, vol. 65, no. 4, pp. 2274 – 2294, Apr. 2015.

[8] S.S. Wang and Y.S. Lin, "Passcar: A passive clustering aided routing protocol for vehicular ad hoc networks", *Computer Communications*, vol. 36, pp. 170–179, 2013.

[9] G. Li, L. Boukhatem, and S. Martin, "An intersection-based QoS routing in vehicular ad hoc networks", *Mobile Networks and Applications*, vol. 20, no. 2, pp. 268–284, 2015.

[10] H. Dubois-Ferriere, M. Grossglauser, and M. Vetterli, "Age matters: efficient route discovery in mobile ad hoc networks using encounter ages", in *Proceedings of the 4th ACM international symposium on Mobile ad hoc networking & computing*. ACM, 2003, pp. 257–266.

[11] S. Rajagopalan and C.C. Shen, "ANSI: A swarm intelligence-based unicast routing protocol for hybrid ad hoc networks," *Journal of Systems Architecture*, vol. 52, no. 8, pp. 485–504, Aug. 2006.

[12] S. Arif, S. Olariu, J. Wang, G. Yan, W. Yang, and I. Khalil, "Datacenter at the airport: reasoning about time-dependent parking lot occupancy," *IEEE Transactions on Parallel and Distributed Systems*, vol. 23, pp. 2067–2080, 2012.

[13] R. Lu, X. Lin, H. Zhu, and X.S. Shen, "SPARK: a new VANET-based smart parking scheme for large parking lots", in *Proceedings of the 28th IEEE Conference on Computer Communications.* IEEE, 2009, pp. 1413-1421.

[14] J. Zhu, Y. Feng, and B. Liu, "PASS: parking-lot-assisted carpool over vehicular ad hoc networks", *International Journal of Distributed Sensor Networks, 2013.*

[15] M. Ferreira, R. Fernandes, H. Conceição, W. Viriyasitavat, and O.K. Tonguz, "Self-organized traffic control", in *Proceedings of the 7th ACM international workshop on VehiculAr InterNETworking*. ACM, 2010, pp. 85-90.

[16] W. Munst, C. Dannheim, M. Mader, N. Gay, B. Malnar, M. Al-Mamun, and C. Icking, "Virtual traffic lights: Managing intersections in the cloud", in *Proceedings of the 7th International Workshop* on *Reliable Networks Design and Modeling.* IEEE, 2015, pp. 329-334.

[17] S. Smaldone, L. Han, P. Shankar, and L. Iftode, "RoadSpeak: enabling voice chat on roadways using vehicular social networks", in *Proceedings of the 1st Workshop on Social Network Systems.* ACM, 2008, pp. 43-48.

[18] J.F. Bravo-Torres, M. López-Nores, Y. Blanco-Fernández, J.J. Pazos-Arias, A. Gil-Solla, and M. Ramos-Cabrer, "Connection sharing on top of a virtualization layer to support Vehicular Cloud Computing", in *Proceedings of the 3rd annual International Conference on Connected Vehicles and Expo.* IEEE, 2014, pp. 1004-1009.

[19] J. Nzouonta, N. Rajgure, G. Wang, and C. Borcea, "VANET routing on city roads using real-time vehicular traffic information," *IEEE Transactions on Vehicular Technology*, vol. 58, no. 7, pp. 3609–3626, Sep. 2009.

[20] K. Lee, S.H. Lee, R. Cheung, U. Lee, and M. Gerla, "First experience with CarTorrent in a real vehicular ad hoc network testbed", in *Proceedings on Mobile Networking for Vehicular Environments*. IEEE, 2007, pp. 109-114.

[21] U. Lee, J.S. Park, J. Yeh, G. Pau, and M. Gerla, "Code torrent: Content distribution using network coding in VANET," in *Proceedings of the 1st Intl. Workshop on Decentralized Resource Sharing in Mobile Computing and Networking.* ACM, 2006, pp. 1-5.

[22] F. Bai and A. Helmy, "Impact of mobility on mobility-assisted information diffusion (MAID) protocols," Department of Computer Science – University of Southern California, Tech. Rep., 2005. un. 2012.

[23] J. Wu, "A simulation study on using the virtual node layer to implement efficient and reliable MANET protocols," Ph.D. Thesis, The City University of New York, 2011.

ASSESSING COMMUNALITY IN WEB-BASED COMMUNITIES. THE CASE OF SPAGHETTI OPEN DATA

Federico Cabitza, Angela Locoro and Andrea Maurino
Dipartimento di Informatica, Sistemistica e Comunicazione
Università degli Studi di Milano-Bicocca
Viale Sarca 336, 20126, Milano, Italy

ABSTRACT

In this paper, we conducted a questionnaire-based user study in the Web-based community of Spaghetti Open Data in order to assess its *communality*, or sense of being and contributing in building a community. This concept is addressed both in terms of degree and type with two subscales we designed for and validated in our study. We propose this tool and the related concept to analyse Web-based communities, to assess which are the most important values for them, and to which extent the communication technology adopted by their members influences the community activities and cohesion, as well as its evolution. We present the results coming from this study and discuss its generalizability and tailorability in the context of other Web-based communities.

KEYWORDS

Degree of communality; community types; questionnaires for Web-based communities; Spaghetti Open Data.

1. BACKGROUND AND MOTIVATIONS

This paper focuses on *communality* in Web-based communities. The common notion of communality defines it as "the sense of belonging or being related to a community as a whole"[1]. In sociological thinking, *communality* is usually expressed in terms of either communication, that is speaking-together (cf. Luhmann); or as "common practice", that is doing-things-together (cf. Bourdieu). In this paper, we focus on communities of people that use the Web to communicate and exchange messages to see whether, and to what extent, these communities also develop characterizing (and characteristic) practices besides those of mediated interaction and communication: in other words, we are interested to operationalize the concept of communality, which others call *sense of community*, by defining it in terms of both *type* and *degree*.

In particular, we focus on those Web-based communities that gather together *virtually* around a Google Group. A Google Group is a discussion group (Skog, 2005) that integrates the functionalities of a Web-based forum with a mailing-list service, so that posts in topic-related threads of messages are also dispatched to the group subscribers as emails in some aggregated form (i.e., typically by showing all of the posts exchanged within a specific period of time); and, the other way round, emails are extracted and attached to the right thread on the forum according to their subject line. This functional integration allows for a richer communication among the members in virtue of the promotion of a conversation-oriented interaction, and also for a stronger participation because messages are distributed among the members, thus relieving them from the need to log in the Web-based platform. Our focus on this platform is also justified by the fact that a Google Group also provides a Web-based gateway to Usenet newsgroups: since it does not require a newsreader to read postings like Usenet newsgroups do and it offers powerful functions for the search and retrieval of posts from multiple devices, Google Groups has become one of the best resources for both communicating with peers and researching topics of interest, and already ten years ago there were more than 20,000 active Google Groups on the Web (Biersdorfer, 2006).

In regard to this particular yet broad application domain, we address the two related research questions: 1) how to assess the degree of communality of the members of these groups (Chin and Chignell, 2007); 2) how

[1] Collins English Dictionary.

to determine what kind of communality they engage in. This latter question is akin to addressing what kind of community people constitute or, also, what community *type* is more suitable to describe that community (Preece, Abras, and Maloney-Krichmar, 2004).

To assess the degree of communality, we conducted a user study to build a simple model of what elements or aspects can affect the feeling of belonging to the same social structure. To this aim, we conceived a set of items (questions) after a review of the specialist literature regarding validated scales to measure community values and attributes like the sense of community, sense of belonging, trust, well being, and so on. We selected items from these scales and conceived new ones to be included in our model, in order to identify a short set of questions that can be asked to the members of a community to gauge their feelings about these values. The aggregation of these items in higher-level constructs was validated by the user study.

Similarly, determining the kind of communality required a way to map a given social group to one (or more) of the community types that are usually considered and studied in the specialist literature. These types are: *communities of place*, whose members live or attend the same physical places (and that for this reason are also denoted as "geographically defined communities" (Manzo, 2006); *communities of interest* or *concern*, "gathering people assembled around a topic of common interest" (Henri and Pudelko, 2003); *communities of purpose*, where people are bound together by the will to achieve some common goal (Agresti, 2003); *communities of language*, where members use a specific language (a "community jargon") or apply recurring and characteristic discoursive patterns (Borg, 2003); and *communities of practice*, which are often considered in scholarly analysis and regard groups of people that share a "repertoire" of communal resources that include specific practices, the tools and techniques to perform these practices as well as the main ways to learn them, and assess the quality of their execution (Wenger, 1998).

An intuitive notion assumes that every and each type of community has some main characteristic that distinguishes itself from the others, and that real communities will hardly be associated with only a specific type, as it is more likely that each of them will present ideal traits in different ways and grade. For instance, an association of citizens can be both a community of place and a community of concern: its members join the association and partake in common initiatives because they share an interest in the welfare of the common city area where they live. Similarly, it is likely the case that a community of practice subsumes also other types of community, like a community of language, because people engaged in the same practice can end up by adopting the same linguistic conventions and technical language; and a community of interest, as the common interest can motivate people in engaging in the same practices.

Addressing the two research questions mentioned above, that is being able to detect which main community type is the closest to a given real community (at a certain time of its development), as well as to gauge its internal sense of community over time, can enable cross-sectional (that is inter-community) comparisons, also as a way to indirectly understand the role of socio-technical interventions, like promoting the use of a specific social media, or the adoption of some innovative feature in the evolution and transformation of the community itself.

In both cases, we did not rely on social network analysis, but on a reliable, short and psychometric questionnaire by which to ask the members of a community how they perceive themselves as a community, on a consensus basis. Since it is not granted that the members of a community would converge on recognizing themselves as members of a single type of community, nor can be excluded that different "souls" and motives could coexist in the same community, our approach focused on the detection of any "emergent" collective opinion and the selection of the most representative community type(s).

We validated our questionnaire by administering it to the members of the Spaghetti Open Data (SOD) community. In what follows we describe this community and then in Section 3 we will describe the method applied to conceive and set up the case study in this Web-based community, and in Section 4, we will report the results of the survey.

The community of Spaghetti Open Data (SOD) is an Italian online community founded in 2010 that gathers more than a thousand subscribers of the homonymous Google Group regarding the wide topic of the Open Data[2]. Despite this unifying interest, the SOD members differ for their geographical distribution (although they are all from Italy), and in regard to professional and cultural background: in the community there are civic hackers, software developers, civic servants, data journalists, Web designers, IT managers, academic scholars, lawyers, etc. The main ideals binding the SOD members together is the promotion of projects and initiatives by which data produced and possessed by the Italian institutions become freely

[2] https://groups.google.com/forum/#!forum/spaghettiopendata. Last accessed on the 4th of March 2016.

available and easily reusable; this also encompasses the improvement of the e-literacy of citizens, managers and policy makers, and raising the awareness of the importance of the freedom of information acts, transparency and spirit of cooperation among data users. In its 5 years of activity SOD members have launched and supported various initiatives: the set up and testing of portals of several Italian municipalities; contests for the best open data app; projects for data mapping and georeferencing; data journalism inquiries for transparency; civic campaigns for the preservation, the sharing and publication of cultural heritage information, and so on. To solicit and coordinate action and promote feedback, the community has its own Web site[3], integrating the Google Group, and a GitHub repository for the code developed by the members of the community. Furthermore, since 2013 a face-to-face event is organized yearly in order to let the members meet personally, share their best practices, organize technical learning sessions for non-technical experts, and partake civic hackathons from which to let creative innovations emerge and support the dissemination of open data initiatives.

From all these elements, it is clear that the technical element of SOD is relevant, but also coexisting with ideals not immediately related to IT, and that the community heterogeneity within a specific national context makes it a challenging testbed for our model of *communality*. As to February 2016 the subscribers of SOD were 1196, the active members[4] 386, the top contributors[5] 11, and the total amount of threads over 3,000.

2. RELATED WORK

To our knowledge no study has so far been aimed at defining a questionnaire by which to assess both the type and the extent of communality peculiar to a given community. However, in the specialist literature there are several studies focusing on related concepts and proposing questionnaires to operationalize them. The closest concept to communality is the concept of sense of community (SOC): this was defined by McMillan and Chavis (1986) as the "feeling that members have of belonging, a feeling that members matter to one another and to the group, and a shared faith that members' needs will be met through their commitment to be together". To define SOC these authors consider four related dimensions: *membership*, that is "the feeling of belonging or of sharing a sense of personal relatedness" with the other members; *influence*, i.e., "a sense of mattering, of making a difference to a group and of the group mattering to its members"; *reinforcement*, i.e., feeling support to and from the community; *shared emotional connection*, "the commitment and belief that members have shared and will share" things and experiences together. The Sense of Community Index (SCI) by Perkins et al. (1990) is a 12-items validated questionnaire, which has been widely used in different contexts to measure the sense of community of local, domain, and work communities. A brief version of SCI, the Brief Sense of Community index (BSCI) has been produced by Long and Perkins (2003) by shortening the original SCI questionnaire and focusing on three specific factors: social connections, mutual concerns, and community values. An adapted version of BSCI has been applied in (Chin and Chignell, 2007) to detect virtual communities in blogs.

A Sense of Virtual Community (SOVC) has been developed by Blanchard (2007), by taking 10 items (out of 18) from the above SOC scale and adding 8 new items to consider the differences between face-to-face communities and Web-based ones. These latter items refer to the assessment of the support given within the community by means of e-mails and Web posts. A second study to measure the SOVC was more recently undertaken by Abfalte, Zahlia, and Mueller (2012) grounded on the offline equivalent sense of community (SOC) and aimed at describing the "spirit of belonging together".

The questionnaire reported in (Preece et al., 2004) can be considered a more general and complete evaluation tool for virtual communities: in this work, sociability is defined in terms of heuristics, similarly to usability, for health online communities, to assess "key issues of importance to online community users". For the sociability heuristics these issues are grouped according to dimensions such as: purpose, policies, and procedures; administration; social presence, trust, and empathy development.

A definition, analysis and operationalization of Wenger's constructs for community of practices is available in Murillo (2008), where this construct was applied to assess to which extent a virtual community maintains its identity as a community of practice. Notably to our aims, the study investigated communities

[3] http://www.spaghettiopendata.org/.
[4] Active members are those who have written at least one post since the foundation in 2010.
[5] Top contributors are those who have written at least 10 posts since the foundation in 2010.

gathered around the Usenet network, to measure their capacity to develop as online communities of practices. Some key dimensions considered in this research are: mutual engagement (for collective problem solving and discussion within the community); learning or identity acquisition (to measure the level of influence and knowledge acquisition within the community); shared repertoire (to assess the level of knowledge and practices shared within the community); sense of community and joint enterprise (to analyse the sense of belonging and the reciprocal knowledge among the community members).

Table 1. Items of the Community Type subscale (adapted to the SOD case study)

On a scale ranging from 1 (totally disagree) to 6 (totally agree) how much do you believe that [SOD] members are more bounded together by:
Community of Place 1. their common nationality.
Community of Language 2. the fact that they speak all the same jargon and can understand each other more easily than non specialists.
Community of Concern 3. their common concerns about [open data].
Community of Practice 4. their common practices regarding [open data].
Community of Purpose 5. their common interests in [open data]; 6. their common will to acquire knowledge and expertise on [open data]; 7. their common intent to collect and diffuse the best practices concerning [open data]; 8. their common purpose to diffuse a culture of [open data].

3. METHOD

In the light of the literature review mentioned in Section 2, we developed a questionnaire encompassing 27 items divided in two subscales: the *community type* subscale (8 items, see Table 1) and the degree of communality (19 items, see Table 2). All items were defined on 6-value ordinal scales, that is scales where the respondents were asked to choose one category among those of an ordered set (indicating, e.g. the level of agreement). Subscale constructs are not determined in terms of average, but rather with an original procedure that takes into full account the ordinal nature of the items.

The community type subscale is used to determine the type (if any) that is perceived as the most characterizing one by the community members themselves. This can be done in various ways: by detecting the item (if any) with the highest central tendency parameters (i.e., median and mode); the item (if any) with the highest proportion of positive answers (e.g., 5 and 6); or, better yet, by applying a ranking procedure (Cabitza and Locoro, 2016) that considers the number of absolute rankings at case level (i.e., for each respondent). More precisely, this latter procedure derives a relative ranking from absolute evaluations, and then generates two collective item rankings according to all of the individual respondents' rankings. The first item ranking is intended to be of easy comprehensibility and great conciseness (see the column "rank" in Table 3); however, its precision is sensitive to sampling error, i.e., different samples taken from the reference population could yield slightly different rankings. The second ranking conversely defines a mapping between each item and what we call a value level (out of three levels) on the basis of a test on the null hypothesis that all items are at the same level (see column "value level" in Table 3). The three levels are: a higher value level with statistical significance (which we denote as "higher" in Table 3); a lower level with statistical significance (denoted as "lower" in Table 3); and, finally, a buffer level that contains those items for which the test has not reached statistical significance (denoted as "uncertain" in Table 3).

The *degree of communality* subscale encompasses 4 constructs, roughly corresponding to the 4 dimensions proposed by McMillan and Chavis (1986): *reinforcement*, *influence*, *membership* and *connection*. Each of these constructs results from the composition of a number of single items of the subscale: 6 items for the *connection* construct, 4 items for *membership* and *reinforcement*, 5 for *influence* (the list of the 19 items is reported in Table 2). In particular the connection construct results from the composition of further three subscales, encompassing 2 items each: *personal acquaintance*, *relation assiduity* and *bonding*. This last dimension refers to the homonymous concept defined in the Internet Social Capital Scale (ISCS) by Williams (2006), who considered online and offline contexts to measure the social capital of a community. The total score of the *degree of communality* can be defined by combining the items in a final score and then considering the central tendency parameters.

In the analysis of the study results, we will consider three null hypotheses, denoted as H_{01}, H_{02}, H_{03} respectively, and we will look for significant evidence in the responses to reject them in terms of p-values (i.e., the probability to collect the responses assuming the null hypotheses as true) that are lower than a conventional value (in our case, .05) with a confidence level of 95%.

The three null hypotheses are:

1) H01: the respondent sample will not express clearly polarized indications with respect to the value attached to the list of items reported in Table 1 and 2.

2) H02: there are no significant correlations between the item reported in Table 1 and 2.

3) H03: responses do not show significant differences between strata (e.g. people grouped by age, profession and gender) of respondents with respect to the value they assign to each item.

Table 2. The items of the Degree of communality subscale (adapted for the SOD case study)

Degree of Communality
Membership
1. I feel a sense of belonging to [SOD].
2. I feel a sense of proximity and harmony for [SOD].
3. I have a positive feeling for [SOD].
4. I feel proud to belong to [SOD].
Influence
5. My involvement in [SOD] improved my knowledge on certain topics.
6. sharing my knowledge in [SOD] is useful for the good practice of [SOD].
7. sharing my knowledge in [SOD] helps [SOD] in continuing its activity.
8. sharing my knowledge in [SOD] helps [SOD] to capitalize precious knowledge.
9. sharing my knowledge in [SOD] helps [SOD] to grow.
Reinforcement
10. sharing my knowledge in [SOD] helps me to build a reputation.
11. sharing my knowledge in [SOD] lets me strengthen my relationships with the more influential [SOD] members.
12. [SOD] members would help me so I would help any of them in case of need.
13. [SOD] members would help me if I needed it.
Connection
Personal Acquaintance
14. I have close relationships in [SOD].
15. I know some [SOD] members personally.
Relational Assiduity
16. I spend much time interacting with some [SOD] members.
17. I have frequent conversations with some [SOD] members.
Bonding
18. Sharing my knowledge in [SOD] helped me a lot to make new friends.
19. Sharing my knowledge in [SOD] strengthened my relationships with other [SOD] members.

4. THE SOD CASE STUDY, RESULTS AND ANALYSIS

As said in Section 3, in our model the construct *community of purpose* includes 4 items. Their composition is validated by the SOD case study for the detected coefficient of reliability (Cronbach's Alpha, .72). Similarly, also the *degree of communality* includes several composed constructs. In the SOD case study their composition is justified by their high alpha (reported between brackets): membership (0.91); influence (0.83); reinforcement (0.72); and connection (0.78). In its turn, the latter dimension results from the composition of further three 2-item subscales: *personal acquaintance* (0.86), *relation assiduity* (0.90) and *bonding* (0.85).

The link to the online questionnaire was advertised through the SOD Google group in a post that outlined the aim of the research and asked for the support of the SOD members; participation was then left anonymous, voluntary and with no incentives. After one month since the invitation post, the questionnaire was closed and the responses analysed. 72 people had begun the survey, but only 56 (78%) completed it[6], in an average time of 11.2 minutes (SD=6.3 min)[7].

[6] This means that all the considered items are associated with a least 56 responses,but many with more, up to 72.

[7] The readers should notice that the questionnaire contained also other items that we have not considered in this paper, so that the average completion time for the scales herein considered can be considered approximately 3 minutes.

Table 3. Ranking of the items for the type of community and degree of communality scales in the SOD community

Items ranking	Item Rank	Value Level	Median (IQR)	Mode	Positive Responses[8]	Tendencies, significance, (p-value)
Type of Community						
Purpose	1	higher	5 (2)	5	68%	Positive *** (.000)
Concern	2	higher	5 (2)	5	53%	Positive ** (.001)
Practice	3	higher	5 (2)	5	51%	Positive NS (.053)
Language	4	uncertain	3 (2)	2	11%	Negative * (.013)
Place	5	uncertain	2 (3)	1	11%	Negative * (.013)
Degree of Communality						
Influence	1	higher	6 (2,5)	6	76%	Positive *** (.000)
Membership	2	higher	5.5 (3)	6	60%	Positive * (.018)
Reinforcement	3	higher	5 (3)	6	55%	Positive * (.036)
Connection	4	higher	5 (4)	6	55%	Positive NS(.126)
Total Score	na	na	5 (3)	6	58%	Positive ** (.001)

Since it is likely that especially the active members (see above) filled in the questionnaire, we can conjecture that approximately one expert of the SOD community out of five has participated in this research. More in particular: 57% of the those who participated were male; 88% were older than 31; one respondent out of three declared to have a post-degree qualification (while only 13% did not have any master degree). The IT sector was the most represented work domain (31%) followed by the public sector (26%) and academia (22%). The 4% of the respondent sample declared to be data journalists. Half of the sample declared to be "expert" in open data. Nine respondents out of ten said to have been members of SOD for more than one year, and one fourth of these to have been members since the foundation of the community. In regard to participation, 72% declared to access the community at least weekly (28% daily) and the same proportion of respondents declared to be mainly a passive consumer of content; one third of the sample believed to be mainly either an active contributor or even an initiator of threads of discussions, while the 11% admitted to be substantially an inactive user. Since this user study was not intended to be a census of the SOD community, the detected participation is sufficient to give the results a reasonable representativity at least with respect to whom can be considered to know what SOD is and what its main aspects are, and to share the main ideals of the community: in particular 58% of the sample defined themselves an "open data enthusiast".

To analyse the responses and address the above tests, we applied non-parametric techniques with IBM SPSS (v. 21). In particular, for hypothesis H_{01} we report the statistically significant tendencies in Table 3 (rightmost column). Respondents exhibited clear positive tendencies for all of the *communality* components with the exclusion of the *connection* one. Clear positive tendencies were also detected for the feeling to be part of either a *community of purpose* (.17 vs. .83, $p = .000$) or a *community of concern* (.26 vs .74, $p = .001$); conversely, the dimensions *community of place* (.68 vs. .32, $p = .013$) and *community of language* (.68 vs. .32, $p = .013$) collected a significant proportion of negative responses. In regard to *community of practice* the sample did not exhibit a clear tendency. This result is confirmed by the ranking reported in Table 3 and shows that the SOD members consider their community to be more a *community of purpose* and, alternatively a *community of concern* or *practice*, rather than a *community of language* or a community of place. The heterogeneity of the members is probably reflected in a lack of a specific tech-oriented jargon; moreover, their distribution in the country undermines the feeling to belong to a place-specific group, although SOD from the name itself (cf. Spaghetti) is strongly connoted as an Italian community. The feeling to belong to a *community of practice* is already strong among the SOD members (see the column value level in Table 3). That notwithstanding, with reference to the general research question mentioned in Section 1, an interesting follow-up of this assessment would be aimed at seeing if the item *community of practice* rises over time, to see if the members recognize any common practice as playing a more important role in characterizing their membership.

In regard to the total score of the *degree of communality*, this was found to be high among the SOD respondents (see last row in Table 3), and the *influence* component to be the most relevant dimension (see the first row in Table 3). This finding can be interpreted as a sign that the SOD community takes knowledge

[8] For positive responses, we intend the proportion of 5 and 6 (on a 6-value scale) with respect to the total responses.

sharing in great consideration and is the most important factor binding its members together and giving them a feeling of *communality*. In Figure 1, we represent how the respondents perceived SOD in terms of main community type, according to the perceived degree of *communality* within the community. Also qualitatively speaking, it is evident that a high (perceived) *communality* is associated with practice-oriented community types like the communities of purpose and practice (i.e., types that are associated with intentional action, common projects , joint activities), while lower levels of communality are associated with the community of language, that is with a model of "communality as communication" (see Section 1).

In regard to the hypothesis H_{02} (regarding the analysis of correlations) we found a statistically significant and positive correlation between the degree of communality and the *community of practice* type (r=.513, p= .000). This may suggest that the stronger the perceived sense of community, the stronger the belief that also peculiar practices, not only communication, bind the SOD members together. In particular, if we look at the correlations among the components of the degree of communality and the types of community, *reinforcement* and *membership* resulted to be moderately correlated with the perception of SOD as a community of practice (r=.44, p= .001 and r=.50, p= .000, respectively), as well as with the *community of purpose* (r=.54, p= .000, r=.44, p= .001, respectively). The results also show a moderate correlation between the propensities to define SOD as either a *community of concern* or a *community of purpose* (r=.29 p=.036).

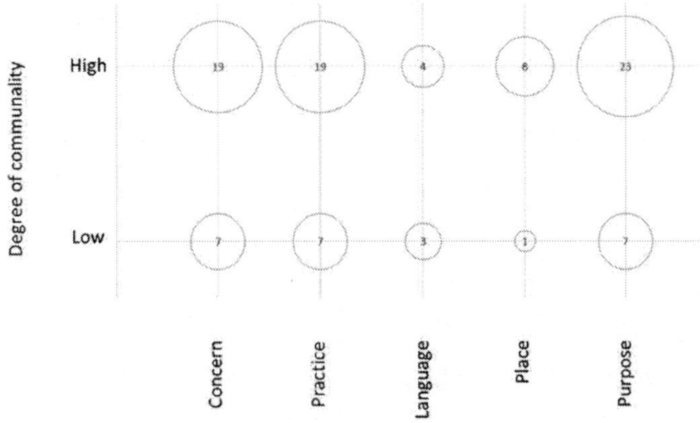

Figure 1. The degree of communality for each type of community (the number of respondents is in the bubbles)

Regarding the correlations among the single dimensions composing the degree of communality, *membership* is strongly correlated with *reinforcement* (r=.57, p= .000), whereas *reinforcement* and *connection* are moderately correlated (r=.47, p= .001, respectively). We also found a moderately positive correlation between *influence* and *membership*, *membership* and *connection* and *influence* and *connection* (r=.37, p= .007, r=.50, p= .000 and r=.50, p= .001, respectively). A moderate correlation also exists between *community of purpose* and *connection* (r=.318, p=.023), while a strong correlation was detected between this kind of community and the feeling of *membership* (r=.51, p=.000). This suggests that whenever the respondents have a propensity to define SOD as a *community of purpose*, they also consider *membership* a relevant dimension, and this is confirmed by the fact that this dimension is also an important factor in the perceived *communality* (see Table 3).

Lastly, in regard to H_{03} some significant differences were detected among groups of respondents. On average men attached a significantly greater value to the *influence* component of communality than women (U(49)= 27, p =.036). Then, on average academic people were characterized by a greater degree of communality than non-academic people (U(51)= 33, p = .011), mainly for the greater value assigned to *influence* (U(53)= 34, p =.012) and *connection* (U(53)= 35, p = .012). Likewise, academic people also believe significantly more that SOD is a *community of purpose* than non academic people (U(53)= 34, p = .017), probably because this type of community was associated with the values inherent in the dissemination of best practices and knowledge sharing. On average, people accessing SOD at least weekly believe significantly *less* that SOD is a *community of language* than people with a lower attendance (U(53)= 34, p =.042). The technical jargon used in the threads within the SOD group could be then one of the reason why some people get less involved than others in these discussions; or, alternatively, those who spend *less* time in SOD attach *more* importance to language (a communication-oriented element of communality as said in Section 1) than other aspects that are more practice-oriented (likely because they are less involved in those activities).

5. CONCLUSIONS

In this paper we have presented a lightweight tool to assess both the degree and dominant type of *communality* in an online community. The tool consists of an agile questionnaire of 27 ordinal items that can be filled in less of 5 minutes and can be tailored in order to closely reflect the main topics and explicit aims of an online community. The tool can be both used to enable inter-community comparisons (to address questions like "what is the community with the highest communality" or "what is the community where the feeling to be involved in some common practice is stronger"?); or in longitudinal studies, to assess the impact of a community building initiative, or of an improvement in the mediating technologies. In so doing, researchers could address questions like "has the new feature improved the sense of belonging to the community" (cf. the *membership* component of the communality construct) or "has organizing this initiative transformed the community into a more mature community of practice". The tool was validated within a country-specific Web-based community counting more than one thousand subscribers in the open data domain, where communality was found high and its type shifted towards the practice-oriented side of the communality spectrum.

REFERENCES

Abfalter, D., Zaglia, M. E., and Mueller, J. (2012). Sense of virtual community: A follow up on its measurement. Computers in Human Behavior, 28 (2), 400–404.

Agresti, W. W. (2003). Tailoring IT support to communities of practice. IT Professional, 5(6), 24–28.

Biersdorfer, J. D. (2006). Google: The Missing Manual. O'Reilly.

Blanchard, A. L. (2007). Developing a sense of virtual community measure. Cyberpsychol Behav, 10(6), 827-830.

Borg, E. (2003). Discourse community. ELT Journal, 57(4), 398–400.

Cabitza, F. and Locoro, A. (2016). Questionnaires in the design and evaluation of community-oriented technologies, IJWBC, Vol. 13(1).

Chin, A., and Chignell, M. (2007). Identifying communities in blogs: roles for social network analysis and survey instruments. IJWBC, 3(3), 345–363.

Henri, F., and Pudelko, B. (2003). Understanding and analysing activity and learning in virtual communities. Journal of Computer Assisted Learning, 19(4), 474–487.

Long, D. A., and Perkins, D. D. 2003. Confirmatory factor analysis of the sense of community index and development of a brief SCI. Journal of Community Psychology, 31 (3), 279–296.

Manzo, L. C. (2006). Finding Common Ground: The Importance of Place Attachment to Community Participation and Planning. Journal of Planning Literature, 20(4), 335–350.

McMillan, D.W., and Chavis, D. M. 1986. Sense of community: A definition and theory. AJCP, 14 (1), 6–23.

Murillo, E. (2008). Searching Usenet for virtual communities of practice: using mixed methods to identify the constructs of Wenger's theory. Information Research, 13(4).

Perkins, D. D., Florin, P., Rich, R. C., Wandersman, A., and Chavis, D. M. 1990. Participation and the social and physical environment of residential blocks: Crime and community context. Am J Community Psychol, 8 (1), 83–115.

Preece, J., Abras, C., and Maloney-Krichmar, D. (2004). Designing and evaluating online communities: research speaks to emerging practice. IJWBC, 1(1), 2–18.

Skog, D. (2005). Social interaction in virtual communities: The significance of technology. IJWBC, 1(4), 464–474.

Wenger, E. (1998). Communities of Practice: Learning, Meaning, and Identity. Cambridge, U.K.

Williams, D. (2006). On and off the'Net: Scales for social capital in an online era. JCMC 11(2), 593-628.

A TWO-PHASE STRATEGY FOR DETECTING COMMUNITIES

Kamal Hassan Taha
Department of Electrical & Computer Engineering, Khalifa University, UAE

ABSTRACT

One of the key objectives for representing real-world problems using networks is for detecting community structures. This is because detecting community structure is crucial for identifying the link between structure and function in complex networks, which is the key for solving many practical applications in various disciplines. The detection of "good" communities has proven to be a challenging task. This is due, mainly, to the fact that most current methods detect communities in independents. As a result, most of them do not work well on highly sparse networks. We propose in this paper a system called TPSDC that detects disjoint communities and works well on highly sparse networks. It does so by adopting the following procedure: (1) assigning a score to each vertex to reflect its relative importance to the whole network, (2) assigning a score to each link connecting two neighboring vertices to represent the degree of association between them, (3) employing a two-phase strategy for detecting disjoint communities, and (4) enhancing the density of community using a post-processing technique. We evaluated the quality of TPSDC by comparing it experimentally with nine methods. Results showed marked improvement.

KEYWORDS

Networks, community structure, community detection

1. INTRODUCTION

Most challenging scientific problems can be represented using networks in order to be empirically studied. Networks have been proven to successfully represent diverse topics related to Internet and the world wide web [22], biological systems [21], information systems [11, 26], ecosystems [13], metabolism [12, 29, 30], and scientific citations [16]. One of the important objectives for representing real-world problems and systems using networks is for detecting community structures, which are groups of densely connected vertices that are only sparsely connected with the rest of the network. There are many reasons for the identification of such communities. For example, society is organized into social groups, families, colleagues, villages, and collaborators [3]. On the World Wide Web, Webpages concerning topics that are related are densely linked among themselves [11]. In metabolic networks, densely linked groups of vertices are related to functional units (e.g., pathways) [21, 25, 29, 30]. In digital forensic investigation, detecting densely linked vertices in a criminal network may lead to the identification of criminal sub-communities and their influential leaders [31]. After a community is detected, usually the next step is to determine its common properties and functions with external factors, around which the community was constructed [28].

To detect communities from a given network, one usually selects a scoring function that either identifies high scoring vertices or quantifies the degree of association between vertices. Then one applies a procedure to identify densely connected vertices based either on their scoring or association functions. One of these procedures called modularity, which states that a good partition has a larger than expected number of internal edges and a smaller than expected number of inter-partition edges when compared to a random network with similar characteristics [9, 18]. The detection of "good" communities has proven to be a challenging task. This is due, mainly, to the fact that most current methods detect communities in independents with sparse connections among them. As a result, most of these methods do not work well on highly sparse networks.

We propose a system called TPSDC (A Two-Phase Strategy for Detecting Communities) that detects disjoint communities and overcomes the limitations of most current methods outlined above. It does so by adopting the following procedure: (1) assigning a score to each vertex to reflect its relative importance to the whole network, (2) assigning a score to each link connecting two neighboring vertices to represent the degree of association between them, and (3) employing a two-phase strategy to detect communities, as follows:

a) Finding initial communities from vertices with maximal strengths *(i.e., maximal importance scores).*
b) Expanding the partial communities by adding vertices that are tight with these communities.
c) We enhance the density of these communities by removing subset communities from the raw outputs of phases *a* and *b,* if they do not have strong associations with the rest of communities.

2. COMPUTING EDGE BETWEENNESS CENTRALITY

During past years, vertex betweenness has been measured as an indicator of the vertex's centrality and influence in a network [31]. The betweenness of a vertex v_i is defined as the number of shortest paths from all vertices to all other vertices that pass through v_i. A vertex with high betweenness centrality has a large influence on the flow of information among the vertices of the network. Girvan–Newman [27] extended the definition of betweenness centrality beyond vertex centrality by introducing the concept of Edge Betweenness (EB). The edge betweenness centrality is defined as the number of shortest paths that go through an edge in a network [27]. Let $N = (V, E)$ be a network. Let v_i and v_j be two vertices in N. Let $\sigma_{v_i v_j}$ be the number of shortest paths between vertices v_i and v_j. Let $\sigma_{v_i v_j}(e)$ be the number of shortest paths between v_i and v_j that pass through $e \in E$. The betweenness centrality of an edge $e \in V$, denoted by EB(e), is defined as: $EB(e) = \sum_{v_i \in V} \sum_{v_j \in V} \frac{\sigma_{v_i v_j}(e)}{\sigma_{v_i v_j}}$

For each vertex u, TPSDC calculates the betweenness centrality of each edge incoming to u and the betweenness centrality of each edge outgoing from u. It does so to measure the influence of each edge over the flow of information in the network.

We use the network in Figure 1-a as a running example throughout the paper. The network represents a social network, where a vertex denotes a person and an edge denotes communication attempts between two persons (e.g., phone calls). The network consists of 45 vertices and the edges connecting them.

Example 1: Consider our running network shown in Figure 1-a. Figure 1-b shows the edge betweenness centralities of all edges in the network. For each vertex u, Figure 1-b shows the betweenness centrality of each edge incoming to u and the betweenness centrality of each outgoing edge from u.

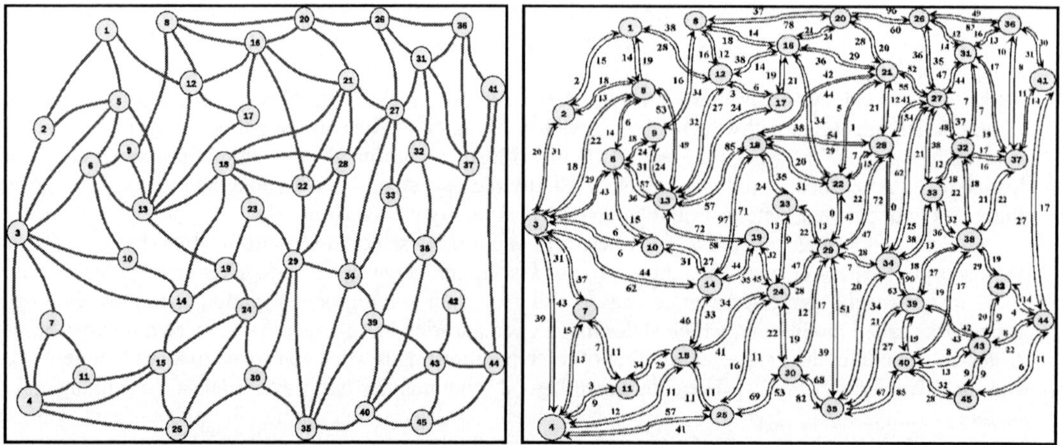

(a) (b)

Figure 1. (a) A social network with 45 vertices. A vertex denotes a person and an edge denotes the communication attempts between two persons. (b) The edge betweenness centralities of all edges in the network shown in Figure 1-a.

3. COMPUTING A SCORE FOR EACH VERTEX THAT REFLECTS ITS RELATIVE IMPORTANCE

In this section, we describe how TPSDC determines the relative importance/influence of each vertex with regards to the whole network. TPSDC employs the concept of *centrality* for determining the relative importance of vertices. The concept of *centrality* in network analysis is used to describe the relative importance of vertices or edges with regard to the whole structure of the network. In the framework of TPSDC, we determine the relative importance of a vertex based on the betweenness centralities of the edges connected to the vertex. In the framework of TPSDC, we consider the hyper-relationships of betweenness and degree centralities as an indicator of the relative importance of a vertex. However, the effectiveness of some of the methods that employ the hyper-relationships of betweenness and degree centralities to accurately capture the relative importance of a vertex is sometimes limited. This is because these methods do not take into account the global properties of a network. To overcome this, the eigenvector centrality metric assigns relative scores to all vertices in the network based on the following observation: connections to vertices with high centrality contribute more to the scores of the vertices than connections to low scoring vertices.

We use the characteristics of logarithm to capture and enhance the eigenvector observation outlined above. By using logarithm, vertices with lower number of edges are penalized and vertices with larger number of edges are rewarded according to their degrees exponentially. This helps in accounting for the discrimination between the following two range of variations: (1) the range of variations in large number of edges, and (2) the range of variations in small number of edges. For example, a change from 1 to 2 is less significant than a change from 99 to 100. We assign a score *S(u)* for each vertex *u* to reflect its global relative importance in the network. $S(u)$ is defined in Equation 1.

$$S(u) = \ln\left(\left(p_{in} \sum_{v \in adj[u]} EB(v,u)\right) \times \left(p_{out} \sum_{v \in adj[u]} EB(u,v)\right)\right) \tag{1}$$

- $EB(v,u)$, $EB(u,v)$: Betweenness centrality of an incoming and an outgoing edge from *u*, respectively.
- $Adj[u]$: The set of vertices adjacent to vertex *u*.
- p_{in} and p_{out}: Parameters that characterize the impact of the incoming edges to *u* and the outgoing edges from *u* respectively. The two parameters are determined heuristically.

Example 2: Let us compute the relative importance score for each vertex in our running network. Using Equation 1, we compute a score $S(u)$ for each vertex *u* to reflect its global importance in the network. We use the edge betweenness centralities computed in Example 1 (Figure 1-b). The results are shown in Figure 2.

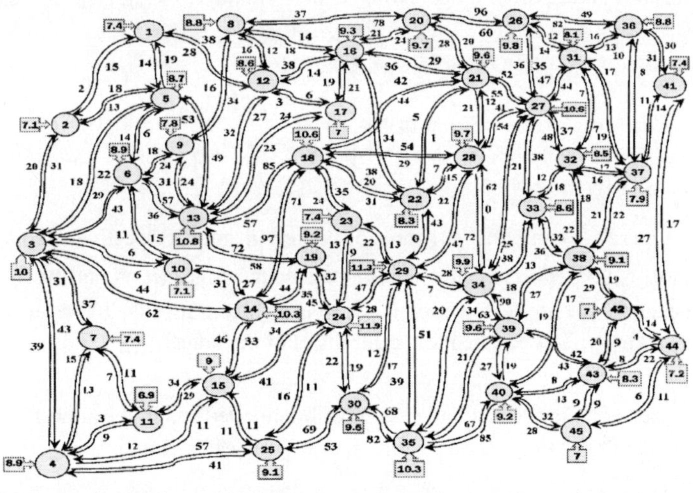

Figure 2. The relative importance score $S(u)$ for each vertex *u* in our running example computed using Equation 1. The score reflects the global importance of *u* in the network. They are determined based on the edge betweenness centralities shown in Figure 1-b.

4. COMPUTING THE DEGREE OF ASSOCIATION BETWEEN EACH TWO NEIGHBORING VERTICES

The edge-probability in each community is usually greater than the average probability of a random edge between two vertices [7, 20]. Taking this property under consideration, a number of techniques have been proposed for discovering communities. These techniques aim at identifying natural divisions in networks using various metrics that compute the strength of vertices' associations. They fall into divisive and agglomerative classes [15, 24, 27]. In the framework of TPSDC, we adopt an agglomerative-like method to discover natural divisions of a network that represent communities. Our method is an enhancement of the Girvan & Newman [27] and White and Smith [24] methods. Intuitively, the degree of relationships between vertices can be determined by the characteristics of the edges connecting them. This is because an edge (u, v) signifies a certain degree of interaction between vertices u and v. However, the edge (u, v) alone cannot identify the degree of interaction between vertices u and v. Therefore, we need a mechanism that quantifies the degree of interaction between vertices in order to identify communities.

We quantify the degree of interaction between vertices by computing vertices' association scores, which reflect their degree of relationships. That is, for each vertex u, we compute its association score S_u^v with each neighboring vertex v, where u and v are connected by an edge. Thus, the association score S_u^v reflects the degree of relationship between vertices u and v. We aim at constructing a formula that computes S_u^v and takes into consideration the following: (1) the relative importance scores of vertices u and v (*which were computed using Equation 1)*, (2) the betweenness centralities of the edges (u, v) and (v, u), (3) the betweenness centralities of the edges connecting u with all other vertices, (4) the betweenness centralities of the edges connecting v with all other vertices, and (5) the degrees of vertices u and v. We structured the formula in such a way that S_u^v increases as each of the following is satisfied:

- The relative importance scores of vertices u and v are high.
- The betweenness centrality of the edge (u, v) is high relative to the betweenness centralities of the edges connecting u with other vertices.
- The betweenness centrality of the edge (v, u) is high relative to the betweenness centralities of the edges connecting v with other vertices.
- v has fewer links with other vertices. This is because S_u^v is likely to be small, if v has many links with other varices, especially if the betweenness centralities of the edges are greater than that of edge (v, u).

Based on the above discussion, we constructed the formula shown in Equation 2, which computes S_u^v:

$$S_u^v = \ln\left(\left(S(u)\times\frac{EB(u,v)}{\sum EB(u,u')}\right)^{\frac{1}{n}} \times \left(S(v)\times\frac{EB(v,u)}{\sum EB(v,v')}\right)^{\frac{1}{m}}\right) \qquad (2)$$

- $S(u), S(v)$: The relative importance scores of vertices u and v, respectively, computed using Equation 1.
- $EB(u,v), EB(v,u)$: The betweenness centralities of the edges (u, v) and (v, u), respectively. (u, v) is an outgoing edge from vertex u to vertex v. (v, u) is an incoming edge to vertex u from vertex v.
- $EB(u,u')$, $EB(v,v')$: The betweenness centralities of the edges (u,u') and (v,v'), respectively. $(u' \neq v)$ and $(v' \neq u)$.
- n: The number of links connecting vertex u with other vertices in the network.
- m: The number of links connecting vertex v with other vertices in the network.

Example 3: Let us determine the association score of each two neighboring vertices in our running network, using Equation 2 and the techniques described above. For each vertex u, Table 1 shows its association score S_u^v with each neighboring vertex v, where u and v are connected by an edge.

Table 1. For each Vertex u in our Running Network, the Table Shows its Association Score S_u^v with each Neighboring Vertex v, where u and v are Connected by an Edge. S_u^v is Computed using Equation 2.

u	v	S_u^v	u	v	S_u^v	u	v	S_u^v	u	v	S_u^v	u	v	S_u^v
18	21	0.194	34	28	0.192	21	20	0.216	43	42	0.284	38	37	0.212
	28	0.125		27	0.227		27	0.262		44	0.263		42	0.413
	22	0.165		33	0.289		28	-0.079		45	0.051		40	-0.050
	23	0.391		39	0.579		22	-0.638		40	-0.107		39	-0.280
	14	0.375		35	0.506		16	0.221		39	0.436		33	0.389
3	2	0.477	27	26	0.323	16	20	0.148	24	30	0.096	29	23	0.317
	5	0.065		31	0.163		21	0.221		25	-0.040		22	0.138
	6	0.232		32	0.291		22	0.475		15	0.362		28	0.163
	10	-0.182		33	0.171		17	0.454		19	0.459		34	-0.081
	14	0.294		28	0.185		12	0.224		23	0.052		35	0.250
	7	0.542		34	0.227		8	0.155		29	0.323		30	-0.059
	4	0.307		21	0.262					30	0.096		23	0.317
1	2	-0.204	8	20	0.557	26	20	0.688	40	39	-0.161	6	5	-0.110
	5	-0.392		12	-0.051		31	-0.013		45	0.581		9	0.452
	12	0.619		9	0.422		36	0.723		35	0.205		10	0.261
36	31	0.195	15	14	0.296	4	7	0.210	30	25	0.686	32	31	-0.215
	37	-0.085		25	0.108		11	-0.199		35	0.614		37	0.176
	41	0.643		11	0.497		25	0.543					38	0.151
41	37	0.125	14	10	0.515	44	42	0.052	13	19	0.574			
	44	0.446		19	0.385		45	0.210		6	0.932			
5	2	0.306	31	37	0.199	17	12	-0.456	22	28	-0.082	7	11	0.142

5. DETECTING DISJOINT COMMUNITIES

We focus on identifying disjoint communities. If a vertex v belongs to more than one community, we assign it to only one of them. We assign v to the community that it has the most relationship with. We determine this community using a belonging formula. We constructed a belonging formula that takes into consideration the betweenness centralities of all edges connecting vertex v with other vertices in the network. For a community c and a vertex v, the belonging degree $B(v, c)$ between v and c is defined as shown in Equation 3:

$$B(v,c)=\frac{\sum_{u\in c}\left(EB(v,u)+EB(u,v)\right)}{\sum\left(EB(v,v')+EB(v',v)\right)} \tag{3}$$

- $EB\ (v,u)$ and $EB\ (u,v)$: The betweenness centralities of the edges (v, u) and (u, v), respectively, where u is a vertex that belongs to community c and connects with vertex v by an edge.
- $EB\ (v,v')$ and $EB\ (v',v)$: The betweenness centralities of the edges (v, v') and (v', v), respectively, where v' is a vertex connected with vertex v by an edge and it can be belonging to community c and/or any other community in the network.

Finally, we identify communities using the following steps: (i) finding an initial community c, (ii) expanding community c, and (iii) repeating steps i and ii until all vertices have been assigned to communities. We mark the vertices that were processed. Initially, all vertices are marked with the label ``$F$ ". We mark the vertices in the found communities with the label ``T ", denoted by V_T. We only consider the vertices in V_F while finding initial communities. We consider the vertices in V while expanding the initial communities. The following are the sequential steps taken by TPSDC for identifying disjoint communities:

(a) *Finding an initial community c:*

i. Select a vertex u with the largest relative importance score (i.e., the largest $S(u)$) from the set V_F.

ii. Find the neighbors of u with label ``$F$ ". For each vertex $v$ with label ``F " neighboring u, if its association score with u is greater than a heuristically determined threshold β, then assign v to the initial community c and label it with "T". That is, vertex v belongs to the initial community c, if $S_u^v > \beta$. These vertices along with u compose the initial community c. In our experiments, we hieratically determined that the optimal value of β is 0.24.

iii. For each vertex v' in community c, if its belonging score to community c is less than a threshold δ, remove it from c and label it with ``F ". That is, we remove v' from c, if $S(v',c) < \delta$. In our experiments, we hieratically determined that the optimal value of δ is 0.43.

iv. Repeat step (iii) until $\forall v' \in c$, $S(v',c) > \delta$ to obtain the initial partial community, also denoted by c.

(b) *Expanding community c:*

i. Find all neighbors N_c of community c with label "F".

ii. For each vertex $u' \in N_c$, calculate its association score with each neighboring vertex v'' (i.e., $S_{u'}^{v''}$).

iii. Find each vertex v'' whose $S_{u'}^{v''}$ is greater than β, add it into community c directly, and label it with "T". That is, we identify the following vertices: $\exists v'' \in N_c$ and $S_{u'}^{v''} > \beta$. We denote the set of these vertices by: $N_{v''} = \{v'' \mid S_{u'}^{v''} > \beta\}$. Then, we add all the vertices of $N_{v'}$ into community c and obtain a larger partial community, also denoted by c.

iv. For each vertex v'' in community c, if its belonging score to community c is less than δ, remove it from c and label it with "F". That is, we remove v'' from c, if $S(v'', c) < \delta$.

v. If $|N_{V'}| = 0$, stop expanding community c and mine it. Otherwise, repeat steps i-v.

(c) *Finding another community:*

We keep repeating steps (a) and (b) until all vertices in set V_F have been assigned to communities.

Example 4: Let us detect the disjoint communities in our running network using the same techniques described above. Figure 3 shows the detected communities based on the information shown in Figures 1-b and 2 and Table 1. We considered the thresholds β and δ as 0.24 and 0.43 respectively.

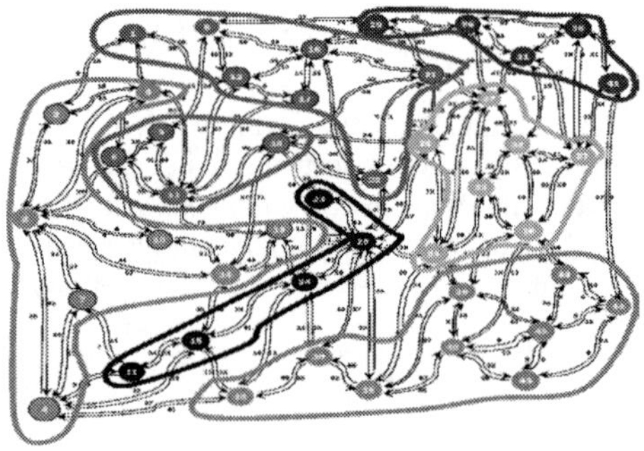

Figure 3. The disjoint communities in our running network detected using the techniques described in section 5.

6. EXPERIMENTAL RESULTS

We implemented TPSDC in Java, run on Intel(R) Core(TM) i5-4200U processor, with a CPU of 1.60 GHz and 4 GB of RAM, under Windows 8.1. We evaluated the quality and strength of communities detected by TPSDC by comparing it experimentally with the following methods: CNM (Clauset et al., 2004 [6]), Cfinder (Palla et al., 2005 [21]), Sim. Ann.(Guimera et al., 2005 [10]), EM (Newman et al., 2007 [19]), Blondel et al. (Blondel et al., 2008 [4]), SLPA (Xie et al., 2012 [14]), EIMF (Guo-Jun et al., 2012 [9]), and Hadoop (Michael et al., 2013 [17]). We used for the evaluation publicly available set of ground-truth communities compiled by Stanford Network Analysis Project (SNAP) [23]. Table 2 lists the three ground-truth network datasets used in the evaluations as well as their descriptions.

Table 2. Description of the Publicly Available Set of Ground-Truth Communities used in our Evaluation.

Name	*Nodes*	*Edges*	*Communities*
com-LiveJournal	3,997,962	34,681,189	287,512
com-Friendster	65,608,366	1,806,067,135	957,154
com-Orkut	3,072,441	117,185,083	6,288,363

We evaluated 10 methods in terms of their *Recalls* and *Precisions*. Let S be the set of vertices within one of the ground-truth communities presented in Table 2. Each of the methods will be fed a subset $S' \subset S$ and will be asked to detect the subset $\{S - S'\}$. Each method will then return a set R of vertices that it considers to be belonging to the subset $\{S - S'\}$. We measured the Recall and Prediction of each method using the standard metrics of Recall and Precision as follows: Recall $= |R \cap S| / |S - S'|$ and Precision $= |R \cap S| / |R|$. From each of the three datasets in Table 2, we randomly selected four subsets as S', where $|S'|$ equals 25%, 50%, 75%, and 90% of $|S|$ respectively. For each community and for each of the four sizes we selected S' randomly. For each of the four sizes and fractions revealed, we averaged the Recall and Precision of each method over each of the three ground-truth networks. Figures 4-6 show the results based on each fraction of vertices revealed for each of the ground-truth networks.

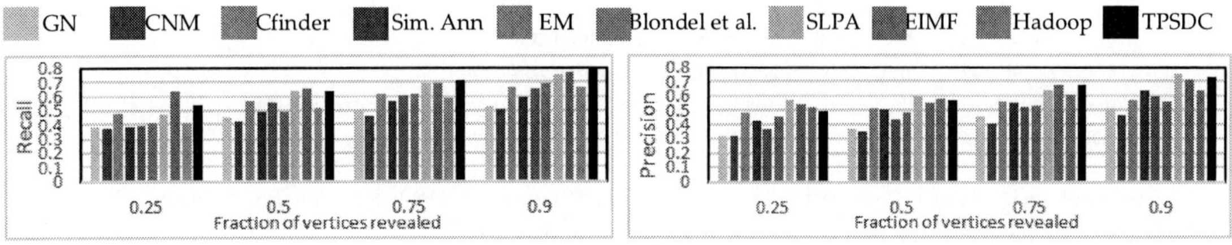

Figure 4. Average recall and precision of single community detection for com-LiveJournal network dataset

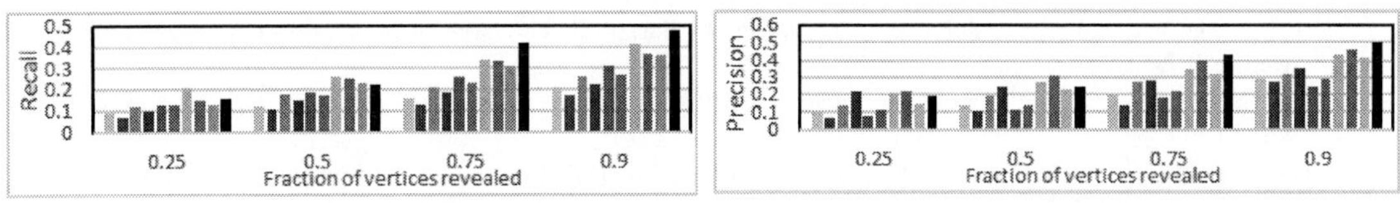

Figure 5. Average recall and precision of single community detection for com-Friendster network dataset

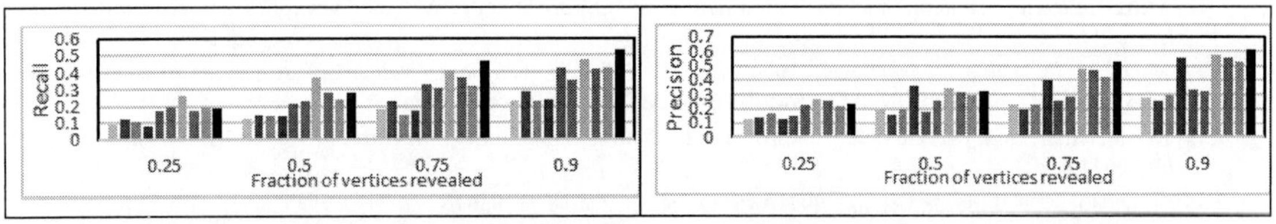

Figure 6. Average recall and precision of single community detection for com-Orkut network dataset

As Figures 4-6 show: (1) TPSDC outperformed some of the methods when the fraction of revealed vertices is small, and (2) TPSDC outperformed almost all the methods when the fraction of revealed vertices is high. The results showed that TPSDC's community detection accuracy improves constantly as the size of revealed vertices increases. This is due, in part, to the fact that TPSDC considers the relative importance of each vertex *v* with regards to the whole network and that every time a new set of vertices is revealed the relative importance of *v* is recomputed accordingly. Every time a new set *S* of vertices is revealed, TPSDC optimizes the current relative importance score of each vertex *v* based on the betweenness centralities of the incoming edges to *v* from *S* and the outgoing edges from *v* to *S*. The results showed that the accumulation of revealed vertices has no noticeable impact on the detection accuracy of some of the other nine methods. TPSDC tends to outperform all the other nine methods when the percentage of revealed vertices is over 70%. It may not accurately identify all the members of a community, whose fraction of revealed vertices is very small (e.g., communities with less than 25% of its members is revealed). This is advantageous to TPSDC, since the size of revealed vertices of a community in real-world gets larger over time.

We observed from the results that TPSDC did not detect the members of the communities of com-LiveJournal as good as it did with the other four networking datasets. This is attributed to the fact that: (1) LiveJournal classifies groups into the following categories: entertainment, culture, life/style, expression, gaming, fandom, sports, student life, and technology, (2) a large number of LiveJournal's members joins more than one grouping category, and (3) TPSDC is designed to detect only disjoint communities, while some of the other methods is designed to detect also overlapping communities.

REFERENCES

[1] A. Clauset, M. Mewman, and C. Moore. Finding community structure in very large networks. *Physical Review,* E 70, 066111, 2004.

[2] A. Clauset, C. Moore, M. E. J. Newman. Hierarchical structure and the prediction of missing links in networks. Nature, 453:98–101, 2008.

[3] BREIGER, R. L. 2004. The analysis of social networks. In *Handbook of Data Analysis*, M. A. Hardy and A. Bryman, Eds. Sage Publications, London, U.K. 505–526.

[4] Blondel, V. D., J.-L. Guillaume, R. Lambiotte, and E. Lefebvre,2008, J. Stat. Mech. P10008.

[5] B. McClosky and I. V. Hicks. Detecting cohesive groups. http://www.caam.rice.edu/ivhicks/CokplexAlgorithmPaper.pdf, 2009

[6] A. Clauset, M. Mewman, C. Moore, 2004, *Phys. Rev. E 70(6), 066111*

[7] Watts, D. and Strogatz, S. Collective dynamics of "smallworld" networks. *Nature*, 393(6684):440–442, 1998.

[8] Danon, J. Duch, A. Diaz-Guilera, and A. Arenas. Comparing community structure identification. J. of Stat. Mech.,2005.

[9] Guo-Jun Qi1, Charu C. Aggarwal, Thomas Huang1, "Community Detection with Edge Content in Social Media Networks", ICDE, 2012

[10] Guimera, R., and L. A. N. Amaral, 2005, Nature 433, 895

[11] G. W. Flake, S. Lawrence, and C. L. Giles. Efficient identification of web communities. In *6th ACM SIGKDD,* NY, USA, 2000.

[12] H. Jeong, B. Tombor, R. Albert, Z. N. Oltvai, A.-L. Barab´asi, The large-scale organization of metabolic networks. Nature 407, (2000).

[13] J. Camacho, R. Guimer`a, and L. A. N. Amaral, Robust patterns in food web structure. *Phys. Rev. Lett.* 88,228102 (2002).

[14] J. Xie and B. K. Szymanski, "Towards linear time overlapping community detection in social networks," in *Advances in Knowledge Discovery and Data Mining*, pp. 25–36, Springer, Germany, 2012.

[15] J. Scott, *Social Network Analysis: A Handbook.* Sage Publications, London, 2nd edition (2000).

[16] M. E. J. Newman, Scientific collaboration networks: II.Shortest paths, weighted networks, and centrality. Phys.Rev. E 64, 016132 (2001).

[17] Michael Ovelgonne, "*Distributed Community Detection in Web-Scale Networks*", Advances in Social Networks Analysis and Mining (ASONAM), 2013 IEEE/ACM International Conference.

[18] M. Newman and M. Girvan. Finding and evaluating community structure in networks. *Physical Review E*, 69:026113, 2004.

[19] Newman, M. E. J., E. A. Leicht, 2007, *Natl. Acad. Sci. USA 104, 9564.*

[20] Paul W. Holland and Samuel Leinhardt. Transitivity in structural models of small groups. *Comp. Group Stud.*, 1971.

[21] PALLA, G., DERENYI, I., FARKAS, I., AND VICSEK, T. 2005. Uncovering the overlapping community structure of complex networks in nature and society. *Nature 435*, 814–818.

[22] R. Albert, H. Jeong, and A.-L. Barab´asi, Diameter of the world-wide web. *Nature* 401, 130–131 (1999).

[23] Stanford Large Network Dataset Collection (online). Available at: http://snap.stanford.edu/data/

[24] Scott White and Padhraic Smyth. Algorithms for estimating relative importance in networks. In 9th *ACM SIGKDD,* USA, 2003.

[25] Taha, K. and Elmasri, R. "SPGProfile: Speak Group Profile." *Information Systems (IS)*, 2010, Elsevier, Vol. 35, No. 7, pp. 774-790).

[26] Taha, K. and Elmasri, R. "BusSEngine: A Business Search Engine. "*Knowledge and Information Systems: An International Journal (KAIS)*, 2010, LNCS, Springer, Vol. 23, No. 2, pp. 153-197.

[27] Taha, K. "Automatic Academic Advisor". *8th IEEE International Conference on Collaborative Computing: Networking, Applications and Worksharing (IEEE CollaborateCom). Pittsburgh, USA, October 2012.*

[28] Taha, K. and Elmasri, R. "CXLEngine: A Comprehensive XML Loosely Structured Search Engine." In *Database technologies for handling XML information on the web (DataX'08), France, March 2008.*

[29] Taha, K., Homouz, D., Al Muhairi, H., and Al Mahmoud, Z. "GRank: A Middleware Search Engine for Ranking Genes by [502] Relevance to Given Genes". *BMC Bioinformatics* 2013, 14:251.

[30] Taha, K. "Determining Semantically Related Significant Genes". *IEEE/ACM Transactions on Computational Biology and Bioinformatics*, 2014, Vol. 11, issue 6, pp. 1119 - 1130..

[31] Taha, K. and Yoo, P. SIIMCO: A Forensic Investigation Tool for Identifying the Influential Members of a Criminal Organization. IEEE Transactions on Information Forensics & Security, 2015, Vol. 11, issue 4.

WSN BASED SENSING MODEL FOR SMART CROWD MOVEMENT WITH IDENTIFICATION: A CONCEPTUAL MODEL

Naeem A. Nawaz[1], Ahmad Waqas[2], Zulkefli Muhammed Yusof[3] and Asadullah Shah[4]
Department of Computer Science, KICT, International Islamic University Malaysia[1,3,4]
Department of Computer Science, Ummal Qura University, Kingdom of Saudi Arabia[1]
Department of Computer Science, Sukkur Institute of Business Administration, Pakistan[2]

ABSTRACT

With the advancement of IT and increase in world population rate, Crowd Management (CM) has become a subject undergoing intense study among researchers. Technology provides fast and easily available means of transport and, up-to-date information access to the people that causes crowd at public places. This imposes a big challenge for crowd safety and security at public places such as airports, railway stations and check points. For example, the crowd of pilgrims during Hajj and Ummrah while crossing the borders of Makkah, Kingdom of Saudi Arabia. To minimize the risk of such crowd safety and security identification and verification of people is necessary which causes unwanted increment in processing time. It is observed that managing crowd during specific time period (Hajj and Ummrah) with identification and verification is a challenge. At present, many advanced technologies such as Internet of Things (IoT) are being used to solve the crowed management problem with minimal processing time. In this paper, we have presented a Wireless Sensor Network (WSN) based conceptual model for smart crowd movement with minimal processing time for people identification. This handles the crowd by forming groups and provides proactive support to handle them in organized manner. As a result, crowd can be managed to move safely from one place to another with group identification. The group identification minimizes the processing time and move the crowd in smart way.

KEYWORDS

WSN, Crowd Management, Smart Movement, IoT, Sensing-as-a-Service

1. INTRODUCTION

Safety and security are concern issues at crowded areas which could be controlled and minimized if crowd moves from one place to other with identification. As a matter of fact, individual identification consumes processing time that increases risk of crowd safety. The identification time of crowd may be minimized if the identification is automatically performed in form of groups. During the event of Hajj more than 2 million pilgrims gather in Makkah to perform the Hajj and More than 6 million Muslims perform Ummrah during a calendar year (Gazette 2016). The crowd of pilgrims moves to different places such as hotels, Al-Haram, Mina, Arfaat, Mudaulfah and Jamraat. Also from different airports to the Holy cities of Makkah and Madinah. At present, data of pilgrims is recorded at arriving airport and is verified at different check points such as boarders of Makkah, Minna and Arfaat. It is observed that individuals have to wait for long while their data is captured at different places such as airports, railway stations and check points at Makkah boarders etc. We have presented a Wireless Sensor Network (WSN) based smart crowd movement model that automatically identifies individuals in form of groups to address the problem of long waiting time. The proposed model consists of different operational phases and grouping technique to collect, disseminate and process crowd data for identification.

The concept of cloud computing is to provide the services to the large number of consumers globally via internet in efficient way which are located at many different locations while the resources (Hardware and Software) are located at few physical locations (Waqas et al. 2013; Patidar et al. 2012; Waqas et al. 2014; Waqas, Yusof, et al. 2014).

By definition, Internet of Things (IoT) allows people/anybody and things/devices to be connected anytime, anyplace/anywhere, with anything and anyone, ideally using any path/network and any service (Nesse 2013). It is one of the possible solution for the peoples (Pilgrims or Hajjaj) and Hajj or Ummrah management to use IoT to get updated information to control and mange different factors. Information received by IoT can be used by the controlling/management body such as traffic police, police stations, ministry of interior, food supplying companies for different purpose for instance finding hotel or camp location in Mina and Arafat, traffic control, temperature, humidity, overcrowded area, food and other supplies. The identification of eight critical factors of smart city initiatives are management and organization, technology, governance, policy context, people and communities, economy, built infrastructure, and natural environment (Chourabi 2012). These factors form the basis of an integrative framework that can be used to examine how local governments are envisioning smart city initiatives. The framework suggests directions and agendas for smart city research and outlines practical implications for government professionals (Perera 2014).

The clustering phenomenon plays an important role manage and affect the performance of the WSNs. There are several key limitations in WSNs, the grouping schemes must consider. For Example: limited energy, network lifetime, limited abilities, application (Bandyopadhyay 2003).

As during the Hajj and Ummrah, the city of Makkah is crowded and it is needs of the day to manage the crowd in smart way. Smart way means crowd move from one place to another place with safety, security, identification and in short time. This goal can be achieved by processing the crowd in group form with the help of WSNs model and operational phases.

1.1 Sensing as a Service Model

The main idea of sensing as service model for smart cities with support of Internet of Things is to provide benefit to the data owner as well as to the data consumers (Perera 2014). The data are sensed by sensors embedded inside the refrigerator. The sensor publisher will collect data from the refrigerator and sold to the data consumers with the permission of data owner. The data consumer can access data by requesting to the data publisher or extended service provider and pay for it to data owner. The model is composed of four layers that are sensor and sensor owner, sensor publishers, extended service provider and data consumers as given in Figure 1.

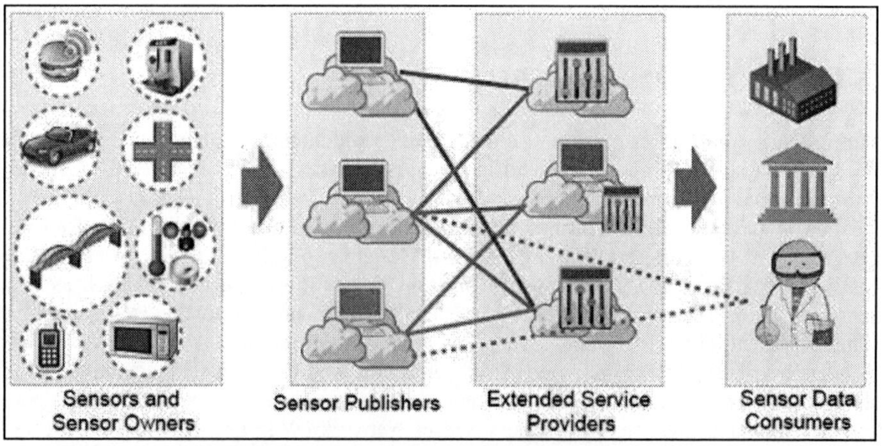

Figure 1. Sensing as a Service Model (Perera 2014)

- **Sensors and Sensor Owners Layer:** This layer consists of sensors and sensor owners. A sensor is a device that detects, measures or sense a physical phenomenon such as humidity, temperature, etc. Sensors are embedded in variety of devices and are owned by sensor owners (Akyildiz 2002).
- **Sensor Publishers Layer:** This layer consists of sensor publishers (SP). The main responsibility of a sensor publisher is to detect available sensors, communicate with the sensor owners, and get permission to publish the sensors in the cloud. Sensor publishers are separate business entities.

When a sensor owner registers a specific sensor, SP collects information about the sensor availability, owner preferences and restriction, and expected return, etc.

- **Extended Service Providers Layer:** This layer consists of extended service providers (ESP). This layer can be considered as the most intelligent among all the four layers which embed the intelligence to the entire service model. The services provided by ESPs can be varied widely from one provider to another. However, there are some fundamental characteristics of ESPs, they have to provide value added services such as location tracing, supply-demand and crowd counting (Nesse 2013) to the sensor data consumers.
- **Sensor Data Consumers Layer:** This layer consists of sensor data consumers. All the sensor data consumers need to register themselves and obtain a valid digital certificate from an authority in order to consume sensor data. Some of the major sensor data consumers would be governments, business organizations, academic institutions, and scientific research communities.

2. RELATED WORK

The concept of sensing as a service is explored and investigated by Perera et al (Perera 2014). The objective is to investigate the concept of sensing as a service model in technological, economical, and social perspectives and identify the major open challenges and issues. The billions of devices that can sense, communicate, compute and potentially actuate are investigated by Arkady et al. (Zaslavsky 2013). Data streams coming from these devices will challenge the traditional approaches to data management and contribute to the emerging paradigm of big data. A Centralized Dynamic Clustering approach in WSNs proposed by Fuad et al (Cabral 2013). In CDC approach adaptive clustering protocol organizes where the cluster head is responsible for collecting the data from all the cluster members, aggregating the data, transmitting fused information to the base station and selecting new cluster head for next round. A distributed data collection algorithm proposed by Aly et al (Aly 2011) for the storage problem. The clustering storage algorithm runs in different phases. Assume that the sensor network has 80% sensing nodes, and 20% storage nodes. All clusters in the network are established using clustering algorithms (Banerjee 2011; Prasad 2011). A networked Distributed Storage Algorithm for WSNs and study its encoding and decoding operations presented by Aly et al (Aly 2012). Other previous algorithms assume that k source nodes disseminate their sensed data throughout a network with n storage nodes using the means of Fountain codes and random walks. However, in this work they generalize this scenario where a set of n sources disseminate their data to a set of n storage nodes. Also, in this proposed algorithm they used properties of WSNs such as broadcasting and flooding.

3. PROPOSED MODEL FOR SMART MOVEMENT

A WSN based smart crowd movement model along with its operational phases is illustrated in Figure 2. The figure provides the understanding and flow of the data, and functions of each components in the proposed model. Moreover, it illustrates the flow of each phase that is involved to collect, store, disseminate and Identify the crowd in smart way. The sensor device is not only a data collector and data transmitter; it can be used for multiple purpose such as:

i. Forming the groups of sensor devices and group of sensor devices manage by the master or group device.
ii. Identification of the group members
iii. Verify the data in the form of groups

The main idea of the model in Figure 2 is taken from the sensing as a service model for smart cities. In the existing model four layered architecture is used that are sensor and sensor owner, sensor publishers, extended service provide and data consumers. The data is sensed by sensors with the permission of owner and stored by the sensor publishers. The data consumer can access data by requesting to the data publisher or extended service provider. The proposed model in Figure 2 is different than the previous model and work by clustering or grouping sensors and different operational phases.

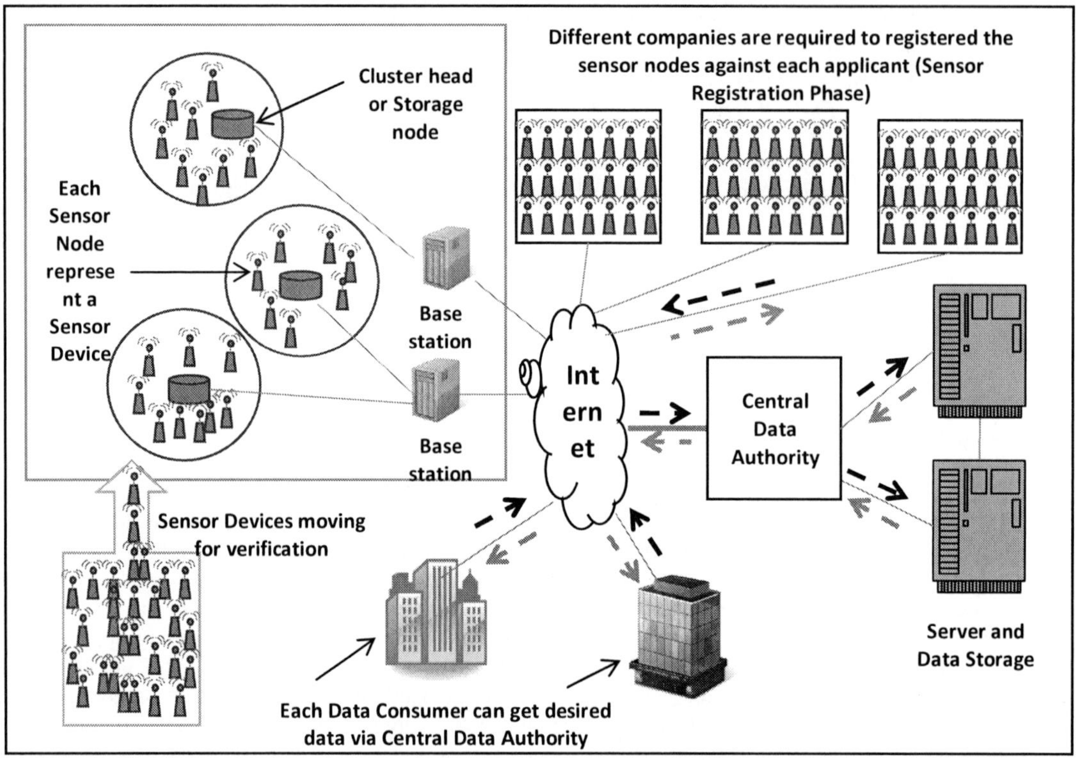

Figure 2. Proposed Model for Smart Movement

In Figure 2, proposed wireless sensor network and clustering or grouping model has different components as given below:

- **Cluster or groups:** The dense nature of crowd requires to be organized into clusters or groups in order to simplify tasks such a processing (Mishra 2013).
- **Cluster or group heads:** Cluster or group head is the organizer or leader of a cluster or group (Mishra 2013). They often are required to organize activities in the cluster or group.
- **Base Station:** The base station is at the upper level of the hierarchical WSN. It provides the communication link between the sensor network and the end-user.
- **End User:** The data in a sensor network can be used for a wide-range of applications. Therefore, a particular application may make use of the network data over the internet, using a mobile, PDA, iPad or even a desktop computer.
- **Sensors and Sensor Owners Company:** This includes the sensors devices (Sensor nodes, smart device) and sensor owners' companies responsible for the specific group of peoples. A sensor is a device which read the information about humidity, number of peoples, number of vehicles, temperature, and wind speed by measuring or sensing (Prasad 2011).
- **Central Data Authority:** Central Data Authority will play a vital role for privacy and security of the data. The people, the companies, government, business, institute or research authorities can access the data if they are registered member of Central Data Authority. This authority also check which kind of data is accessible by the different members. This authority may offer the different package about data access.
- **Sensor Data Consumers:** All the sensor data consumers need to get registered and obtain a valid digital certificate from a central data authority in order to access sensor data. Some of the major sensor data consumers are Traffic Control, Ministry of interior affairs, Police stations, Traffic wardens, hospitals, business organizations, academic institutions, and scientific research communities. Data consumers can access the data according to the privileged packages.

At present, most of the available wireless sensor devices have considerable limitations in terms of computational power, memory, efficiency and communication capabilities due to economic and technology reasons. The development of low-cost, low-power, a multifunctional sensor has gained attention from various industries for different applications. One such research problem is to create an organizational structure amongst these nodes (Akyildiz 2002).

By clustering or grouping the sensor nodes the processing power can be increased which subsequently decrease the time for processing high density data at public or overcrowded areas such as airports, railway stations, check points especially during Hajj and Ummrah, crossing of Makkah boarders etc.

The combination of the WSN with telecommunication, internet and other network devices will play vital role to collect, disseminate and process high density data globally. By the deployment of billions of sensor devices big amount of data can be sensed, stored and required to process and to get results for different applications (Perera 2014).

3.1 Operational Phases

To manage the crowd in smart way the proposed WSN model considers the operational phases (Can be further sub divided) given as:

- Sensor Registration phase
- Sensor Dispatching Phase
- Sensor clustering or grouping Phase
- Cluster or group Sensing Phase
- Cluster or group Verification Phase

Sensor Registration Phase: In this phase, sensors need to be registered. As an example of Hajj and Ummrah, as the application is approved, each company will provide approved applicant documents to the Central Data Authority. The Central Data Authority will verify the documents and register the applicant on web and also register a sensor device against each applicant. Each registered sensor device will have applicant personal information, visa number, passport number, their specific route, booking of rooms, Camp (Tent) in Mina or in Arfaat according to day and date.

Sensor Dispatching Phase: In this phase, the registered sensor devices are handed over to the company that has submitted the documents for registration of the applicants. There are different options to dispatch registered sensor devices to the applicants.

- Dispatching registered sensor devices to the ministry of concern country and the applicants get their devices from ministry after verification.
- Each company dispatch registered sensor devices to their sub offices in each country and applicants get the registered sensor device from sub offices after verification.
- Applicants verified by company at airport and provide registered sensor device to the concern applicant.

Sensor clustering or grouping Phase: In the dispatching phase, the registered sensor device is given to applicants after verification. The data for a cluster or group of registered devices will stored in a main device that is called the cluster or group head. The cluster or group devices data will be matched by the cluster or group head device. If the data is matched, then cluster or group members will present in front of immigration in a specific zone or area.

Cluster or group Sensing Phase: In the sensing phase, the Group or cluster head device will be sensed by the immigration system for data collection instead of individual sensing of each device.

Cluster or group Verification Phase: As all the sensor devices are registered and data is stored on servers, the sensed data will be verified and the applicant's status will be updated by the name of entry point (Airport name). For each verification point applicant's status will be updated by the name of entry point. For Example; Jeddah airport, Makkah boarder, Minna, Arfaat. In this way a route will also define for the applicant which he is going on. For organized movement, a specific route for different groups can be defined according to date and time so that one path does not get overcrowd.

3.2 Use-case for Smart Crowd Movement

The Company inviting the people for Hajj, Ummrah or visit is responsible to complete the process of visa or permit. As the process of visa will be completed the company will define information about route of their travel and booking plan at different locations (City, Hotel). Company will register the sensor device for individuals to Central Data Authority. The company will provide the documents having personal information of the people coming for Hajj, Ummrah or visit under their supervision to the authority.

In the first phase sensors are registered for the specific applicant by the company. These sensing devices can be provided to the people at their arrival at airport, in ministry of their country or sub office of the company in their country after manual verification. The data will be collected by the cluster or group head and verified at once by the immigration system in the form of cluster or group. When the people are managed to get into the bus (vehicles) the passenger verification will be performed automatically before entering into the bus and seat number will be allocated according to memory location in cluster or group head device. Passengers can be verified by the vehicle responsible authority or company. Bus status can be automatically verified at checkpoint.

When bus reaches to the checkpoint the data will automatically be collected from the cluster or group head device via access point. If all passengers are verified successfully (Matching of data in the cluster or group head and on web server), then no need to stop the bus. If there is some problem with verification of any passenger (device failure) the cluster or group head device will mention the seat number (memory location) so that verification for that specific passenger can be performed. Communication between cluster or group head device and checkpoint terminal can be done via WiFi, Bluetooth or 4G link. The cluster or group head device has the option to connect with terminal via wired in worst wireless scenario. At each checkpoint, whole bus passengers will be verified by using the data stored by the cluster or group head. When bus enters into the city the route of hotel for concern group will be mentioned by the cluster or group head device.

4. COMPARISON WITH EXISTING MODEL

Preliminary analysis between proposed WSN model and existing sensing as a service model for smart cities is given in Table 1.

Table 1. Preliminary Analysis between Proposed and Existing Model

S.No.	Proposed Model	Existing Model
i.	Smart sensor device is used	Individual sensors are used
ii.	Data is collected in cluster or group form	Data is collected from individual sensors.
iii.	Data verification is done by the central data authority (Government)	Data verification is done by the person (owner)
iv.	Data verification is done at multiple points (at each checkpoint)	Data verification is done only one time
v.	Pre-registration for sensor device and data	Post-registration for sensor device and data
vi.	Sensor devices are moving	Sensors are static
vii.	Every time central data authority give access of data to the data consumer	Once the person permits the data access, sensor publishers are free for data consumption.
viii.	Data is sensitive because it has personal information	Data is not so sensitive because it provides number of items left for the products
ix.	Operational phases approach	Layered approach

5. CONCLUSION AND FUTURE WORK

This paper provides an overview of the WSN based conceptual model and its application towards smart crowd movement in the Internet of Things (IoT) paradigm. We discussed the model from perspective of processing time. We examined how the conceptual model minimize the processing time by using clustering and different operational phases. Explanation is done by use-case of the smart crowd movement. We also compared the sensing as a service model and WSN based Sensing Model for Smart Crowd Movement with Identification.

If WSN based Smart Crowd Movement (Conceptual Model) is commercially implemented and deployed, it provides many application scenarios, such as:

1. To generate route planning of the crowd on the move.
2. To generate alerts for deploying remote resources such as ambulances, water etc. in context of emergency situation of the crowd.
3. To generate the shortest path to the incident location.
4. Path finding in case of getting lost in mostly unknown territory.
5. Lost contact with cluster.
6. Re-gathering plans with cluster.
7. Generating the SOS calls in cases of real emergency situations. For examples: Sensing the level of the oxygen, if level is too low then generates the alert and give the direction where the level is better. In worst condition generate alert to medical emergency with current location (Sensor storage number). Sense the blood pressure and count heartbeat, if level is too low or high then generates the alert to the medical emergency with location.

REFERENCES

Akyildiz, I.F., Su, W., Sankarasubramaniam, Y. and Cayirci, E., 2002. A survey on sensor networks. *Communications magazine, IEEE, 40*(8), pp.102-114.

Aly, S.A., Ali-Eldin, A. and Poor, H.V., 2011, February. A distributed data collection algorithm for wireless sensor networks with persistent storage nodes. In *New Technologies, Mobility and Security (NTMS), 2011 4th IFIP International Conference on* (pp. 1-5). IEEE.

Aly, S.A., 2012. Distributed data collection and storage algorithms for collaborative learning vision sensor devices with applications to pilgrimage. *International Journal of Sensor Networks*, *12*(3), pp.137-148.

Banerjee, P., Friedrich, R., Bash, C., Goldsack, P., Huberman, B., Manley, J., Patel, C., Ranganathan, P. and Veitch, A., 2011. Everything as a service: Powering the new information economy. *Computer*, (3), pp.36-43.

Bandyopadhyay, S. and Coyle, E.J., 2003, April. An energy efficient hierarchical clustering algorithm for wireless sensor networks. In *INFOCOM 2003. Twenty-Second Annual Joint Conference of the IEEE Computer and Communications. IEEE Societies* (Vol. 3, pp. 1713-1723). IEEE.

Cabral Pinto, F., Chainho, P., Pássaro, N., Santiago, F., Corujo, D. and Gomes, D., 2013. The business of things architecture. *Transactions on emerging telecommunications technologies*, *24*(4), pp.441-452.

Chourabi, H., Nam, T., Walker, S., Gil-Garcia, J.R., Mellouli, S., Nahon, K., Pardo, T.A. and Scholl, H.J., 2012, January. Understanding smart cities: An integrative framework. In *System Science (HICSS), 2012 45th Hawaii International Conference on* (pp. 2289-2297). IEEE.

Gazette, S. (2016). Kingdom to focus on Haj and Umrah for revenue. Retrieved March 27, 2016, from http://saudigazette.com.sa/saudi-arabia/kingdom-focus-haj-umrah-revenue/

Mishra, N.K., Jain, V. and Sahu, S., 2013. Survey on recent clustering algorithms in wireless sensor networks. *International Journal of Scientific and Research Publications*, *3*(4), p.1.

Nesse, P.J., Svaet, S.W., Strasunskas, D. and Gaivoronski, A.A., 2013. Assessment and optimisation of business opportunities for telecom operators in the cloud value network. *Transactions on Emerging Telecommunications Technologies*, *24*(5), pp.503-516.

Perera, C., Zaslavsky, A., Christen, P. and Georgakopoulos, D., 2014. Sensing as a service model for smart cities supported by internet of things.*Transactions on Emerging Telecommunications Technologies*, *25*(1), pp.81-93.

Perera, C., Zaslavsky, A., Christen, P. and Georgakopoulos, D., 2014. Context aware computing for the internet of things: A survey.*Communications Surveys & Tutorials, IEEE*, *16*(1), pp.414-454.

Patidar, S., Rane, D. and Jain, P., 2012, January. A survey paper on cloud computing. In *Advanced Computing & Communication Technologies (ACCT), 2012 Second International Conference on* (pp. 394-398). IEEE.

Rimal, B.P., Jukan, A., Katsaros, D. and Goeleven, Y., 2011. Architectural requirements for cloud computing systems: an enterprise cloud approach. *Journal of Grid Computing*, *9*(1), pp.3-26.

Waqas, A., Yusof, Z.M., Shah, A. and Khan, M.A., 2014, June. ReSA: Architecture for resources sharing between clouds. In *Information Assurance and Cyber Security (CIACS), 2014 Conference on* (pp. 23-28). IEEE.

Waqas, A., Yusof, Z.M. and Shah, A., 2013, December. A security-based survey and classification of Cloud Architectures, State of Art and Future Directions. In *Advanced Computer Science Applications and Technologies (ACSAT), 2013 International Conference on* (pp. 284-289). IEEE.

Waqas, A., Muhammed Yusof, Z., Shah, A. and Mahmood, N., 2014, September. Sharing of attacks information across clouds for improving security: A conceptual framework. In *Computer, Communications, and Control Technology (I4CT), 2014 International Conference on* (pp. 255-260). IEEE.

Zaslavsky, A., Perera, C. and Georgakopoulos, D., 2013. Sensing as a service and big data. *arXiv preprint arXiv:1301.0159.*

DESIGN OF AN ONTOLOGY FOR THE USE OF SOCIAL MEDIA IN EMERGENCY MANAGEMENT

Matthias Moi and Nikolai Rodehutskors
University of Paderborn
33095 Paderborn, Germany

ABSTRACT

As social media services are on the rise, people increasingly share information about emergencies on social media. Sometimes information about disasters even finds its way faster to social media websites than it reaches regular news companies and emergency services. Yet emergency services still have not found a way to put this potential to an effective use. Within our project "EmerGent", we are developing a system for emergency services to process and analyse information from social media. The aim is to transform the high volume of noisy data into a low volume of rich content that is useful to emergency personnel. To achieve this goal, it is important to understand both, the nature of social media, and emergency services as the target domain. Hence, we decided to design an ontology that covers the fields of social media and emergency management (SMEM). In this paper, we explain the steps we took during the development process of the ontology and the structure of the ontology itself.

KEYWORDS

Ontology; Semantic Data Model; Emergency Services; Social Media; Social Networks; Crisis Management

1. INTRODUCTION AND PROBLEM DEFINITION

Social media services grow exponentially each year. Twitter for instance had more than 100 million active users in 2011, posting 230 million tweets a day. One year later, the number of active users and the number of tweets per day had doubled (Etherington 2012). This means, that the general usage of social media is getting more and more important to share information. Hence, to handle the vast amount of data, information from social media streams has to be transformed into a low volume but rich information model. Because of the huge amount of potentially useful data created on a variety of social networks, direct usage of social media is impracticable to extract useful information. Hence, advanced filter techniques are required (Pirolli 2009). This need is amplified by the fact that even the main social network providers are using different concepts for communication, information sharing and the establishment of relationships. The concept of relations between users in social networks is also implemented in different ways. Beside 'friendship' relations, users are able to come together in groups, follow other users and institutes, or can share information publically for everyone to see.

With requirements on data processing and information querying continuously growing, several approaches have emerged to represent machine-readable information. When file-based approaches reached their limits in structuring data, relational databases became popular (Martinez-Cruz et al. 2012); however, these are not well suited to the challenges of semantic processing. With the emergence of the Semantic Web, the role of semantic technologies became increasingly important. The Semantic Web is often discussed as the predecessor of novel concepts like the "Internet Of Things" and "Ubiquitous Computing". It extends the network of hyperlinked human-readable web applications by machine-readable metadata about applications and how they are related to each other (World Wide Web Consortium (W3C) 2009). It standardises the way to build semantically enriched applications and can be used to build them on the top of vocabularies, taxonomies and ontologies. (World Wide Web Consortium (W3C) 2009) Ontologies provide a very effective way to structure and categorise knowledge. In emergency response, ontologies can also unify and normalise data from different resources, e.g. social media, syntactically and semantically and associate it with emergency domain knowledge. Furthermore, on-going research has shown that the need for a common understanding of concepts within and across domains is important to avoid misunderstandings (Galton & Worboys 2011; Grolinger et al. 2011). They help to create meaningful relationships between information resources and to allow machines to process, infer, or combine the information from different sources automatically into a consistent body of knowledge.

These ontology features are needed for our project, as social media offers many information sources to enhance social media awareness. People in the affected area are able to report about the situation and emergency services can use social media information for decision support. Social media may also help in understanding the overall situation (Yin et al. 2012). Social media communication can also allow emergency services to get in direct contact with citizens and forward important information. While many emergency and healthcare services already try to use social media for information gathering and authority to citizen communication (Thackeray et al. 2012; Reuter et al. 2016), the full potential of these networks is still not used. Emergency services fight to keep up with the huge and daily growing load of unfiltered social media messages and try to gather valuable information, while forwarding important information to citizens.

Often ontologies are built from scratch, which does not tap the existing potential of relevant, domain-related knowledge bases. Thus ontologies are often implicitly tailored to a specific need (Bontas et al. 2005). To facilitate information exchange with external systems, projects or domains it is necessary that new developments build upon existing standards. Therefore information models like FOAF (Brickley & Miller 2010), SIOC (Bojars & Breslin 2009) or MOAC (Limbu 2012) must be considered in order to build an ontology that associates information from SM with domain knowledge.

So far, there is no ontology in existence that unifies information from social media with the emergency domain and enhances it with additional information and emergency domain knowledge adequately. This forces us to design an ontology that serves exactly this purpose by extending existing ontologies. This paper describes a subset of the requirements placed in the ontology we developed, the evaluation process of existing ontologies in this area, as well as the development and structure of the ontology. This ontology handles social media in emergency management (SMEM) and is therefore abbreviated SMEM ontology.

1.1 Methodological Approach

Our SMEM ontology has to be understood as an ontology that connects the information generated by citizens on social media platforms and emergency services on an information level. It is part of an IT system that is developed in the European Union's Seventh Framework Programme funded project "Emergency Management in social media Generation", short "EmerGent", and that offers a complete solution for emergency services to handle social media, combine social media information with emergency domain knowledge. This solution allows for the gathering and processing of emergency relevant social media information for use in emergency management, as well as two-way communication between citizens and authorities (Moi et al. 2015). Several ontologies describe either social media or emergencies. A unified ontology that covers both domains adequately does not exist and is direly needed to effectively put information from social media to use in emergency management and help the responders during an operation. Therefore, the emergency and the social media domains have to be considered simultaneously. Before developing the ontology, the main stakeholders for this topic were identified, then the development of the ontology took place in three steps.

First, in cooperation with the main stakeholders, the emergency services and the citizens, we developed a set of requirements and use-cases, which needed to be regarded during the development of the ontology. Secondly, we used these requirements to evaluate existing ontologies that describe social media and emergencies and that could be usefully combined in our final SMEM ontology. Finally, after the evaluation of these ontologies, we built a mapping between domain-related information and information from social media and designed a first draft of the SMEM ontology.

2. REQUIREMENTS AND EXISTING ONTOLOGIES

As we started the development process, we realized that both, the emergency and the social media domain were already well researched and thoroughly described with ontologies and standards. In the emergency domain, ontologies, like the Management of a Crisis vocabulary (MOAC) (Limbu 2012), and the standard HXL, the Humanitarian Exchange Language (Kessler & Hendrix 2015), already describe many different aspects of emergencies and emergency management. In the domain of social media, commonly ontologies used to describe social networks are the Friend-of-a-friend vocabulary (FOAF) (Brickley & Miller 2010) and SIOC, the vocabulary for Semantically-Interlinked Online Communities (Bojars & Breslin 2009).

Besides these well-known and common ontologies, many other ontologies exist in the emergency service and social media domain, and many more can be used to describe other aspects of these domains, e.g. the BasicGeo ontology, which describes the World Geodetic System in its 1984 revision (Brickley 2003). To evaluate all these already existing ontologies and to assist in the decision, whether the ontologies could or should be used in our SMEM ontology, we needed to regard and potential use-cases for our ontology and define requirements for the ontology and the ontologies that should be used in it.

2.1 Requirements, Use-Cases And Future Potential

As emergency services are the most relevant stakeholders of the IT system, they had an active part in the definition of requirements. For this purpose, we selected a group of 19 experts from ten European countries. This group of experts is called the End-user Advisory Board (EAB) and serves as a platform by which the experts in the domain of social media and emergency management can share their vision, expertise and domain knowledge. They can give feedback and their advice is captured. Citizens were also regarded as the requirements were defined. Citizens are not the end-users of the IT system, but are seen as stakeholders of this project and therefore their opinion is important for the design of the SMEM ontology.

The final IT system is supposed to show emergency services alert related posts, which can be seen in the following mock up (Figure 1). The ontology has to help in classifying and categorizing the gathered data in order to make it properly usable for this system.

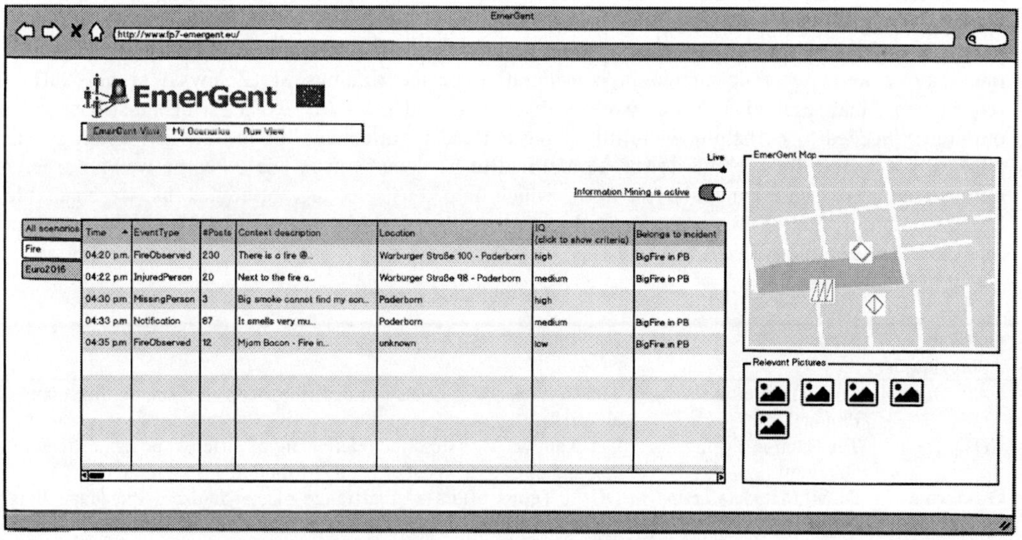

Figure 1. Mockup of the IT system's frontend

The result of workshops held with the EAB and citizens was a set of two main use-cases for the ontology and a list of requirements that were placed in the SMEM ontology. For the ontology, two main use cases were identified. The first use case regards the communication from citizens to authorities (C2A). During emergencies, considering this use case, citizens can share information within social media as done in the past but with the possibility and with the awareness that their contribution may help emergency services during emergency handling. The second use case describes authorities to citizens (A2C) communication. Here the authorities can speak to the citizens directly and can share information about incidents or guidelines.

The two most important requirements that became known were the possibility to add multimedia files to created alarms and to evaluate the information quality of social media information. The addition of multimedia files, like photographs, videos and audio files represents a huge advantage that results from the connection of social media and emergency services. Citizens get the ability to share information with the emergency services, and emergency services can gain the ability to gain an impression of an incident, even before the situation has been reconnoitred. At the same time, the consideration of information quality, especially the trustworthiness of an author and a post in social media is regarded as important. The information about the quality of a post gives the emergency services the ability to assess, whether a post depicts the truth about a situation and if a post should be taken seriously (Akerkar et al. 2016). Figure 2 depicts the exemplary logical structure of a post and appended information, such as media files, connected alerts and information quality.

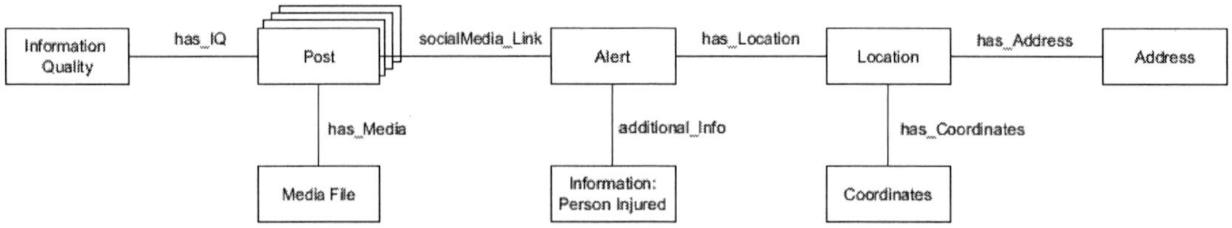

Figure 2. Connection of social media information with an exemplary alert

2.2 Evaluation of Existing Ontologies

According to the proposals for ontology evaluation published by Zelewski et al., additionally to the mentioned requirements and use-cases, we also regarded several other indicators (Zelewski et al. 2001). For the evaluation of the ontologies, that have already been designed for the domains social media and emergency services, we used an adaption of the MoSCoW prioritization method developed by Clegg and Barker (Clegg & Barker 2004). This prioritization technique usually categorizes the requirements into must-have, should-have, could-have and won't-have. Following this approach, a set of should-have and must-have criteria were developed in consideration of the findings of (Zelewski et al. 2001) and the requirements that resulted from our work with citizens and the EAB. To pass the must-have criteria, the ontologies needed to be helpful in fulfilling the defined requirements for the SMEM ontology, had to be publically available for use and download and had to be documented. The outcome was an ordered list of ontologies that passed the must-have criteria, which helped us selecting ontologies that were suitable for the SMEM ontology. Out of 40 evaluated ontologies, the following 15 ontologies and standards were integrated into the SMEM ontology listed in Table 1.

Table 1. List of included ontologies

Ontology Abbreviation	Name	Description
CAP	Common Alerting Protocol	The CAP standard is used to describe alerts in a standardized way (Jones et al. 2010).
CiTO	The Citation Typing Ontology	CiTO allows us to describe referencing of different posts in social media, e.g. one author cites the post of another (Shotton & Peroni 2015).
DC-Terms	DCMI Metadata Terms	DCMI Terms offers a great range of standardized metadata. It is used to describe metadata of posts and media files (DCMI Usage Board 2012).
EM-DAT	Emergency Events Database	EM-DAT is an online database of disasters, reaching back into the 20th century. It has a very precise categorization of events, which we used to describe incidents (Université Catholique de Louvain 2009).
FOAF	Friend of a Friend	FOAF describes relations between persons, such as which people know each other. In combination with SIOC it is used to describe social media networks (Brickley & Miller 2010).
BasicGeo	W3C Basic Geo	Basic Geo describes the most fundamental information about locations, coordinates (Brickley 2003).

HXL	Humanitarian Exchange Language	HXL describes additional information for disasters, e.g. number of people affected or injured (Kessler & Hendrix 2015).
iContact	International Contact Ontology	iContact offers many different classes to describe international addresses. It is used in the description of locations (Fox 2015).
LODE	Linking Open Descriptions of Events	LODE allows us to link information to events (Shaw et al. 2010).
MA-Ont	Ontology for Media Resources	MA-Ont provides a set of descriptive properties for media files and a mapping of different metadata formats (Michel 2012).
RDFG	Named RDF Graphs	RDFG is used to describe graph structures in ontologies. We used it to describe a graph for information quality (Carroll et al. 2005).
SCOT	Social Semantic Cloud of Tags	SCOT describes tagging in the Semantic Web (Scerri et al. 2012).
SEM	Simple Event Model Ontology	SEM defines the context of events and describes involved actors and other properties (van Hage & Ceolin 2011).
SIOC	Semantically-Interlinked Online Communities	SIOC describes the structure of social networks and is used in combination with FOAF to describe social networks and social media (Bojars & Breslin 2009).
SKOS	Simple Knowledge Organization System	SKOS defines a data model to describe knowledge organization systems and is used to describe our ontology (Miles & Bechhofer 2009).

3. SMEM ONTOLOGY STRUCTURE

Based on the evaluation results and the requirements placed in the ontology as described before, we designed our SMEM ontology. It unifies several different and already existing ontologies and extends them to perfectly fulfil its objective, as described in section 2.1. The ontology is designed to be easily extendable, which will be useful for possible functionality extensions in the future. An exemplary use of these relations can be found in Figure 2. It does not contain all used information and is only supposed to describe the general concept of our design.

Here a set of posts that was gathered from a social network, containing media files, e.g. images, gets enhanced with additional information about the quality of the posts. These posts are linked to a specific emergency alert that contains information about an operation to save an injured person. The alert also contains emergency related information, like the location, or the type of an event. With the usage of media files, like pictures, the emergency responders gain insight into the situation, before even arriving on site. This saves valuable moments that can be used to save the injured person's life.

The SMEM ontology consists of six main parts, describing alerts, incidents and events, social media, information quality, agents and metadata, like locations and time (Table 2). To describe the relations between these parts, we use semantic relations and properties. These connections and relations enable us to link information with a lot of other information and to draw conclusions from these relations.

Table 2. Parts of the SMEM ontology

Ontology Part	Description
Alerts	The alert part defines the usage of the Common Alert Protocol (CAP) alert and an enhanced alert. Both containing crucial information about a certain emergency, e.g. location, time, source. The enhanced alert also contains references to social media sources and media files.
Events	The event part further describes and defines different event and incident types. It allows a classification according to the specifications of the International Disaster Database (EM-DAT), therefore making our results widely compatible and able to handle a huge variety of different incident types. Later, this ontology will be expanded to contain further information for specific types of incidents, e.g. special emergency responses.
Information quality	The information quality part defines a RDF Graph used to evaluate information quality (IQ Graph). Here, different criteria, like trustworthiness, are used to calculate a value that represents the information quality. Using this value, it is possible to assess each information and each informant.
Social media & tl web	The web part describes social media platforms, online information and user interaction on the web. Here external ontologies like SIOC and FOAF are used to describe social networks.
Agents	The agent part describes agents and their respective roles on the web. Persons, organizations, online accounts, software, etc. can be agents.
Metadata	The metadata part describes standardized metadata that is used to define events. This part includes but is not limited to the usage and reference of DCMI-terms and HXL.

To ensure interoperability of the IT system, for which the SMEM ontology was created, with existing command and control software, and to simplify data exchange it was important to regard existing exchange formats for alert information that can be used in real emergencies. The Common Alerting Protocol (CAP) standard is a format for exchanging all hazard emergency alerts and public warnings over all kinds of networks and is already successfully implemented in several countries (Jones et al. 2010). We defined a CAP alert, which is derived from the CAP standard and contains all information demanded by the standard, to ensure compatibility with real world incidents and to allow for standardized emergency communication.

Realizing that the CAP standard alone cannot contain much of the information, that we gathered from social media, we decided to extend it. We called this extended alert the "EmerGent Alert" and it allows us to additionally transmit information about social media information and posts that reference the incident at hand. Also this alert allows us to transmit information that is demanded in other emergency related data exchange formats, such as EDXL (Raymond et al. 2006).

Additionally to the EmerGent Alerts, we defined a graph that allows us to represent the quality of gathered information. Such assessment of information quality for the information gathered in social networks was one of the major concerns of the EAB. The graph serves as a general representation of the information quality of a posting and the trustworthiness of a content creator. Information quality refers to the content of the information received, capturing a wide range of variables, which are divided into indicators and criteria. Criteria summarize all of its corresponding indicators. The value of each criterion consists of the value of its sub-criteria and indicators. The user can decide the weighting of each criteria and indicator individually.

The following graph (Figure 3) depicts the main classes used in the SMEM ontology. Many classes have several subclasses, e.g. "Incident" has 80 subclasses, describing different types of incidents. To allow for better comprehensibility we decided to not depict all classes and relations in the following figure, but to only show a high-level view of our ontology, which only contains the main classes and relations. These classes just depict a very abstract view of the ontology, which is far larger and more complex.

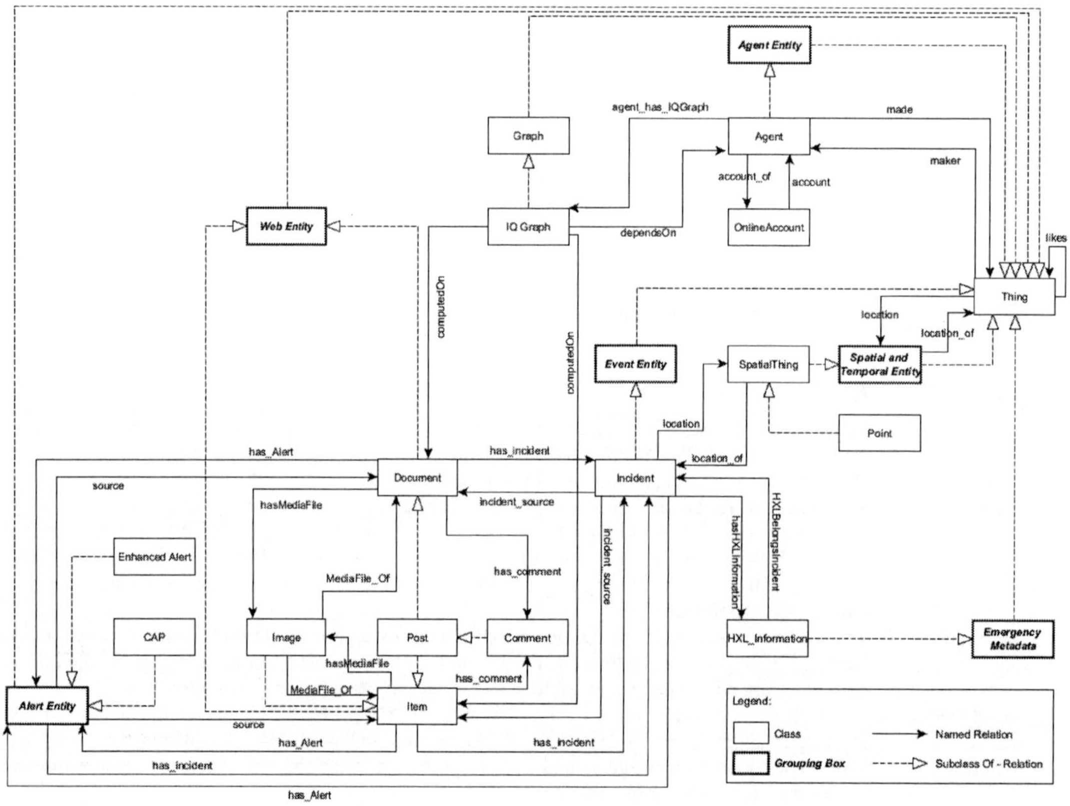

Figure 3. Main classes and relations of the SMEM ontology

In the context of the overall IT system, which is being developed in EmerGent, the ontology is used to structure the gathered data in a condensed way, which can be used effectively by the IT system and emergency services. The structuring according to alerts or situations makes it possible to link mined social media posts, to already existing information and domain knowledge, thus reducing the overall noise generated during situations and making relevant information easily displayable. The mock up presented in Figure 1 shows the IT system's frontend, which displays the gathered, mined and stored data in our final system. Emergency services can use this simple interface to view posts from social media and their corresponding alerts.

4. CONCLUSION & FUTURE WORK

Ontologies, as a way to categorize and structure information, provide a good basis to build an IT system for emergency services to for linking social media data with emergency related information. This paper described the development process of our SMEM ontology, which will, as part of an IT system, help emergency services to achieve this goal. We intended to assist emergency services with the efficient use of social media. By designing this ontology for social media in emergency management (SMEM ontology), we developed the means to categorize data from social media, associate it with emergency domain knowledge and interlink it with other information to allow effective semantic querying using SPARQL. To increase interoperability, we evaluated existing ontologies in the social media area and the emergency domain. Following this evaluation, we built our SMEM ontology, which provides the grounds to categorise and link the data and information from social media with specific emergency domain knowledge and the additional information that is needed to properly describe an incident and aid the emergency services before, during and after emergencies.

Further research is planned include additional standards, to regard research conducted on this topic in the US and to extend the ontology in order to include emergency response and more specific information for different kinds of incidents. This breakdown with event specific information would enable us to store information about how to react to certain incidents, which might be a useful extension in the future. Furthermore, it would be helpful for planning an appropriate or even automated response.

As our IT system needs to handle high volume data sets in near-real time, we already started with the technical analysis of RDF storage solutions in terms of scalability. It is commonly known that dealing with high volume data sets in RDF storage solutions may cause scalability issues in terms of storage and processing time (Khadilkar et al. 2012). We need to tackle this issue to ensure good overall performance for our IT system.

ACKNOWLEDGEMENT

This research has received funding from the European Union's Seventh Framework Programme for research, technological development and demonstration under grant agreement no 608352.

REFERENCES

Akerkar, R., Friberg, T. & Amelunxen, C., 2016. *Deliverable 3.5: User Requirements, Version 2*, Paderborn.

Bojars, U. & Breslin, J.G., 2009. SIOC Core Ontology Specification. Namespace document, DERI, NUI Galway.

Bontas, E.P., Mochol, M. & Tolksdorf, R., 2005. Case Studies on Ontology Reuse. In *Proceedings of I-KNOW'05*. pp. 345–353.

Brickley, D., 2003. Basic Geo (WGS84 lat/long) Vocabulary. *W3C Semantic Web Interest Group*.

Brickley, D. & Miller, L., 2010. FOAF Vocabulary Specification. *Namespace Document*, 3, p.http://xmlns.com/foaf/spec/.

Carroll, J.J. et al., 2005. Named graphs, provenance and trust. In *Proceedings of the 14th international conference on World Wide Web*. pp. 613–622.

Clegg, D. & Barker, R., 2004. *Case Method Fast-Track: A Rad Approach*, Addison-Wesley.

DCMI Usage Board, 2012. DCMI Metadata Terms.

Etherington, D., 2012. Twitter Passes 200M Monthly Active Users, A 42% Increase Over 9 Months. *TechCrunch*.

Fox, M.S., 2015. International Contact Ontology: Addresses, phone numbers and emails.

Galton, A. & Worboys, M., 2011. An Ontology of Information for Emergency Management. *International Conference for Crisis Response and Management (ISCRAM)*, 8(May), pp.1–10.

Grolinger, K., Brown, K. & Capretz, M., 2011. From Glossaries to Ontologies: Disaster Management Domain.

van Hage, W.R. & Ceolin, D., 2011. The Simple Event Model. *Web Semantics: Science, Services and Agents on the World Wide Web*, 9(2), pp.128–136.

Jones, E., Systems, W. & Westfall, J., 2010. Common Alerting Protocol Version 1.2. , (July), pp.1–47.

Kessler, C. & Hendrix, C., 2015. The Humanitarian eXchange Language: Coordinating disaster response with semantic web technologies. *Semantic Web*, 6, pp.5–21.

Khadilkar, V. et al., 2012. Jena-HBase: A distributed, scalable and efficient RDF triple store. *CEUR Workshop Proceedings*, 914(ii), pp.85–88.

Limbu, M., 2012. Management of a Crisis (MOAC) Vocabulary Specification. *Online at http://observedchange.com/moac/ns.*

Martinez-Cruz, C., Blanco, I.J. & Vila, M.A., 2012. Ontologies versus relational databases: Are they so different? A comparison. *Artificial Intelligence Review*, 38(4), pp.271–290.

Michel, T., 2012. Ontology for Media Resources 1.0 Namespace Document.

Miles, A. & Bechhofer, S., 2009. SKOS simple knowledge organization system reference. *W3C recommendation*, 18, p.W3C.

Moi, M. et al., 2015. Strategy for Processing and Analyzing Social Media Data Streams in Emergencies. In *Proceedings of the International Conference on Information and Communication Technologies for Disaster Management (ICT-DM)*. Brest, France.

Pirolli, P., 2009. Powers of 10: Modeling Complex Information-Seeking Systems at Multiple Scales. *Computer*, 42(3), pp.33–40.

Raymond, M., Webb, S. & Aymond, P.I., 2006. Emergency data exchange language (edxl) distribution element, v. 1.0. *OASIS Standard EDXL-DE v1. 0*, 1, p.354.

Reuter, C. et al., 2016. Emergency services' attitudes towards social media: A quantitative and qualitative survey across Europe. *International Journal of Human-Computer Studies*, p.-.

Scerri, S. et al., 2012. SCOT Ontology Specification.

Shaw, R., Troncy, R. & Hardman, L., 2010. LODE: An ontology for Linking Open Descriptions of Events.

Shotton, D. & Peroni, S., 2015. CiTO, the Citation Typing Ontology.

Thackeray, R. et al., 2012. Adoption and use of social media among public health departments. *BMC Public Health*, 12(1), pp.1–6.

Université Catholique de Louvain, 2009. EM-DAT: The OFDA/CRED International Disaster Database.

World Wide Web Consortium (W3C), 2009. W3C EIIF Incubator Group Report. *W3C*.

Yin, J. et al., 2012. Using Social Media to Enhance Emergency Situation Awareness. *IEEE Intelligent Systems*, 27(6), pp.52–59.

Zelewski, S., Schütte, R. & Siedentopf, J., 2001. Ontologien zur Repräsentation von Domänen. In *Wissen in Unternehmen. Konzepte, Massnahmen, Methoden*. pp. 183–221.

IMPACT OF SOCIAL COMPUTING ON BUSINESS OUTCOMES

Marie D Fernando, Athula Ginige and Ana Hol
Western Sydney University, Australia.

ABSTRACT

A new computing paradigm termed Social Computing has gained rapid growth during recent past. Social Computing has introduced a myriad of web and mobile based applications. These applications are enhancing the traditional brick and mortar businesses as well have caused emergence of new web and mobile based business models known as sharing economy, peer economy, market economy, crowd companies, or collaborative consumption. These new business models possess advanced business processes built entirely upon Social Computing applications. To define Social Computing and understand the dynamic behaviour of Social Computing characteristics a generic model for Social Computing was developed and in this paper we extend that model to investigate the impact of Social Computing on business outcomes. We applied qualitative inductive content analysis coupled with causal chains to current and well researched business scenarios published in established business magazines. This approach has helped root out reliable inferences about the causes of the phenomenon and extract an emerging multistage causal model. This multistage causality will give a deeper meaning of the causal inference between Social Computing and these beneficial business outcomes. This understanding will help businesses to take a more methodical approach to effectively implement social computing.

KEYWORDS

Social Computing, business outcomes, content analysis, open coding, causal chains, multistage causality.

1. INTRODUCTION

Recent technological developments have brought forth broadband mobile and WiFi connectivity, back end cloud computing and front end mobile devices with sensors such as tablets and most specifically smartphones. This has caused a rapid mobile penetration measuring up to a 51% of global population (Kemp 2015) within the last decade generating a ubiquitously connected society. This universal connectivity has enabled the rapid growth of this new computing paradigm termed Social Computing that involves many applications. The most popularly used social application is the social networking site, Facebook, which was launched in 2004. Today it has reached 1.59 billion monthly active users, almost one fifth of the global population (Statista 2016). The second most popularly used is the content sharing application YouTube which was launched in 2005 and now has 1.0 billion monthly active users (Statista 2016). Similarly there are many such social applications freely available for usage. These applications can be categorised depending on specific tasks they perform such as blogs like Blogger, micro blogs like Twitter, wikis like Wikipedia, social collaboration sites such as Yammer, content sharing sites which share images such as Instagram, communication sites such as Messenger, and gaming applications such as Candy Crush. Recently we saw some business applications emerged and gained rapid growth. Airbnb, a web and mobile based accommodation sharing application founded in 2008, gained the fastest growth and has the highest user number. Today it has surpassed all the reputed hotel chains and has reached a guest number of 60 million with their presence in more than 190 countries in 34,000 cities with over 2,000,000 properties listed with them (Airbnb 2016). There are many other applications for sharing accommodation such as Couchsurfing, Roomorama, HouseExchange, Knock, FlipKey and HomeAway to name a few. Just a year later than Airbnb was established Uber a ride sharing application that connects drivers and ride seekers more efficiently than ever before as the location aware smartphone app enables users to pick the car located nearest to them. This application has grown to 8 million users today being present in 375 cities around the globe (Uber 2016). RelayRides, BlaBlaCar, Lyft, Zipcar, FlightCar are a fraction to name from the large amount of car sharing applications. These peer to peer access driven business models are transforming established business processes whether borrowing goods, renting homes, taxi services or serving up micro-skills in exchange for access or for money. They are not without deployment issues as any disruptively innovative scheme when introduced first. There are questions whether some of these business models are within industry-specific regulations when it comes to insurance and legal liabilities. But the socio economic and environmental benefits these business enhancements bring about have caused countries, states and cities to consider revising their legal policies to accommodate these Social Computing advancements today. While these new businesses built efficient business models upon Social Computing applications, some existing traditional businesses transformed their processes to more efficient processes by implementing Social Computing applications. One example is Australia's almost two centuries old iconic department store David Jones Ltd. which embraced Social Computing in 2013 by launching their catalogue on a custom built business application and also becoming present in existing social applications such as Facebook, Twitter, Instagram, Pinterest and YouTube coupled with digital mirrors within their landmark stores which automatically posted photos to customers' social profiles. They claimed in their ASX report that by doing so they gained 711% sales increase within the very first quarter (Reilly 2013). There are similar success stories of existing large companies such as KLM introducing Meet&Seat application integrated with LinkedIn which increased their customer base, Ford used Twitter to enhance their PR process, IBM used blogging to enhance communication, leadership and corporate identity, a few to name. The new businesses relied on ratings and reviews to build trust among their users. Staying in a stranger's apartment or riding in a stranger's car in an unknown city seemed less daunting when one can read testimonials from previous users. In addition, peer-to-peer businesses integrate with Facebook to let users check to see whether they have friends or friends of friends in common (Economist 2013). Even though some of these social applications and business applications are adopted by masses causing significant business enhancements, some applications such as StartupSQUARE, Pingjam, Cusoy, Everpix, failed (Oppong 2015) and how those successful applications caused significant benefits to businesses remains unclear. This mystery motivated us to explore the causation between these applications and business enhancements. To uncover the deep seated causal relationship between the two domains, Social Computing and business outcomes one suitable way is to deconstruct the two domains into their elements. Only when in a deconstructed form we could observe various patterns or mappings amongst the two domains. From the perspective of this study business outcomes held already an elemental state as our main interest is in business outcomes. However Social Computing held a more abstract state which needed deconstruction for a deeper understanding.

Thus to investigate this causality, in section 2 we reviewed Social Computing and it's characteristics, in section 3 we discussed the methodology we adopted, in section 4 we present the analysis of data. In final and 5th section we present our conclusions - a multistage causal model for Social Computing impacts on business outcomes, which would enable effective implementation of Social Computing.

2. REVIEW OF SOCIAL COMPUTING AND ITS CHARACTERISTICS

The phenomenon of interest of this paper is the causality between business outcomes and this new computing paradigm Social Computing. As Social Computing being an abstract concept we sought for literature that reported it in a deconstructed form such that our search for relationships would be more discernable. Our initial finding was several scholarly definitions of Social Computing as listed in *Table 1* below.

Table 1. Scholarly Definitions of Social Computing

Source	Definition
(Liu et al. 2010)	Social computing concerns the study of social behaviour and context based on computational systems.
(Parameswaran and Whinston 2007b)	Social computing is a set of applications and services that facilitate collective action and social interaction online with rich exchange of multimedia information and evolution of aggregate knowledge.
(Fu et al. 2009)	Social computing is the natural evolution of collaboration: a shift from a focus on content to focus on people.
(Wang et al. 2007)	Social computing is a computational facilitation of social studies and human social dynamics as well as the design and use of ICT technologies that consider social context.
(Schuler 1994)	Social computing is described as any type of computing application in which software serves as an intermediary or a focus for social relation.
(Hassan 2008)	Social computing is the interplay between persons' social behaviour and their interactions with computing devices.

These definitions indicated that there is a relationship between Social Computing and human behavior, not necessarily business outcomes. Thus we further reviewed for literature that related elemental properties of Social Computing. We found a very explanative deconstruct, listings of Social Computing characteristics as in *Table 2* below.

Table 2. General Characteristics of Social Computing

Source	General Characteristics
Hassan (2008)	Available for others, Bottom-up, Collaboration, Collective action, Communication, Communities, Community interactions, Decentralized, Democratic approach, Disseminate social information, Dynamic content, Dynamic information spaces, Easy to deploy and use, Flexible structure, Focus on social relations, Free content, Free-form structure, Gather social information, Grassroots, Hyperlinks and cross- references, Informal, Information sharing, Interactive, Large scope of interaction, Lightweight, Mash-up, No governance structure, Online, Online collaboration, Output to the network, Ownership by creators and users, Portable, Process social information, Relationships, Represent social information, Rich content, Scalable, Sharing, Social interactions, Social networks, Transparent, User diversity, User-generated content, Users control creation and configuration
Huijboom et al. (2009)	Empowerment, Transparency of users, Instant hype wave, (online communities are more) Inclusive, Community sense, In perpetual beta, Efficient allocation of resources, Long tail effect
Parameswaran and Whinston (2007a)	Mostly decentralized, Highly dynamic, Highly transient, Minimal loosely defined structure, Fluid boundaries - overlaps with other stake holders like customers scope, Rich content, enhanced by dissemination structures and peer influence mechanisms, Highly mobile, Very high scalability

These characteristic lists contained duplication, they also comprised of Web2.0 as well as Web1.0 characteristics all mixed together. Though they are Social Computing characteristics some of them indicated an analogical relation to business concept as well. Thus we carried out a systematic reorganization of these characteristics (Ginige and Fernando 2015) that gave rise to two sets of characteristics – Application Characteristics (ACH) that arise due to functionality of the application and Emergent Characteristics (ECH) that arose within the user due to usage of the application. In that publication we presented a generic model for Social Computing with a formal definition of Social Computing and application and emergent characteristics of Social Computing as visualised in *Figure 1* below.

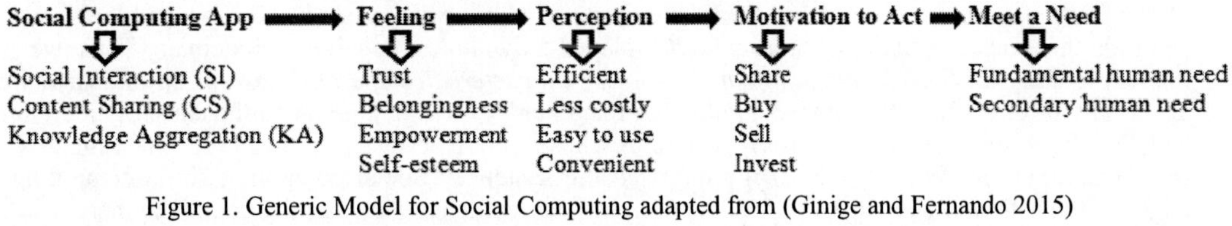

Figure 1. Generic Model for Social Computing adapted from (Ginige and Fernando 2015)

This model defines Social Computing as a set of applications facilitated by front end (mostly) mobile devices, broadband mobile or WiFi connectivity, backend cloud computing and Web2.0 technologies. The basic application functions are organised in such a way to achieve 3 essential application characteristics - Social Interaction (SI), Content Sharing (CS) and Knowledge Aggregation (KA). Users interact with the application using Rich Multimedia and Access Control which enable users to share their information in a controlled manner creating notion of groups. Content Personalisation provides the users with context specific content and aggregated knowledge that is relevant to the user at the time. When in use these application characteristics give rise to emergent characteristics which are either feelings within the user or perceptions that user attributes to the system that motivate repeated user action to fulfil a fundamental or secondary human need (Ginige and Fernando 2015).

3. METHODOLOGICAL APPROACH BASED ON AVAILABLE DATA

With this understanding of what Social Computing is and its dynamic characteristics in previous section we now seek an optimal methodology to uncover the phenomenon of interest: the causality between Social Computing and business outcomes. Our data set is well researched business scenarios published between 2010 and now in established business magazines such as "Economist". These scenarios reported how different social and business applications impacted varied business outcomes. This broadened the scope of this study to many business outcomes due to many different applications so as to determine a common pattern. We analysed many scenarios and for the purpose of this paper we selected six scenarios. Four popularly used business applications which are also known as 'sharing economy' namely accommodation sharing application Airbnb, ride sharing application Uber, skills sharing application Skillshare and crowd sourcing application Fundrise. We also analysed most popularly used social interaction application Facebook and content sharing application YouTube.

We sought for a methodology to analyze this vast secondary textual data set and extract the causality between Social Computing and business outcomes. When considering available methods we noticed primary gain of content analysis method is reducing the enormous textual information to a controllable amount. We comprehended that the key methods of reducing the amount of data are condensation and categorisation. Condensation is done by manually or automatically coding the transcripts, newspaper articles, audio and video data and categorisation is done by further grouping these codes (Blumberg et al. 2011; Quinlan 2011).Content analysis can take either a qualitative or a quantitative approach. In quantitative content analysis textual information is transformed into numerical data such as how often a certain word or relationship occurred in the text and then further analysed statistically. A more advanced form is qualitative content analysis which will examine in which context that certain word or relationship appeared within the data set. Also content analysis can be used inductively for theory building and deductively for evaluation of previously existed theory (Blumberg et al. 2011; Quinlan 2011). Thus to investigate in which context this causality between Social Computing and business outcomes exists, and to extract same as a new theory, we selected qualitative inductive approach of content analysis as the optimal methodology.

3.1 Open Coding

The purpose of coding is to reduce the large amounts of textual data to a manageable and contextually rich smaller amount of data such that we can observe emerging patterns. Scholarly literature produced supporting evidence of the presence of causality between Social Computing and business outcomes. Our key interest was *business outcomes* caused by *Social Computing*. Our previous study (Ginige and Fernando 2015) signified that *Social Computing characteristics* played a dynamic role within the domain. Thus, we scanned the text looking for *Social Computing applications , characteristics and business outcomes*. When we came across any of these three themes we highlighted that chunk of text and assigned the causality therein a short code in the format of "A caused B" where A=cause and B=effect. For example one scholarly article (Parameswaran and Whinston 2007b) comprised the sentence "Social computing shifts computing to the edges of the network, and empower individual users", we extracted the causality contained therein as "Social Computing caused empowerment". Within this code "Social Computing" is the cause while "empowerment" is the effect. We list below in *Table 3* a brief sample from 35 open codes we gleaned from scholarly literature.

Table 3. Examples for Causality found in Literature

Original Text (Parameswaran and Whinston 2007a; Parameswaran and Whinston 2007b)	**Causality (Code)**	**Cause**	**Effect**
It is due to the wide availability of broadband connectivity and more powerful personal computers that social computing has started growing phenomenally	Broadband connectivity enabled SC	Broadband connectivity	SC
	Powerful computers enabled SC	Powerful computers	SC
Collectively, social computing represents the next step in the evolution of the Web, with great potential for social and business impact	SC caused business impact	SC	Business Impact
Popular blogs attract groups of users that engage in discussions using easy interfaces, and blogs often link to posts in similar or complementary blogs,	Blogs caused engagement	Blogs	Engagement
Wikis are popularly used as knowledge sharing tools	Wikis caused content sharing	Wikis	Content Sharing (CS)
Social computing networks find moderate use in placement and recruiting activities mainly by virtue of recommendations from peers.	SCN caused recommendations	SCN	Knowledge Aggregation (KA)
	Recommendations caused recruiting	Recommendations (KA)	Recruiting
loyal readers leads to various means of leveraging that influence with significant economic impact: placing advertisements (*blogads*, for example)	Blogs caused economic impact	Blogs	Economic impact

Since above codes were extracted from generic scholarly literature some terms took a more generic form such as Social Computing (SC) but when analysing data of a specific scenario more specific terms such as 'Social Computing Application', or 'Airbnb App' is extracted. To make the code as brief as possible we used common abbreviations such as SCN for 'Social Computing networks', similarly a phrase such as 'knowledge sharing' we substituted with 'content sharing'=CS. These abbreviations and substitutions were listed and systematic steps for open coding were documented in an "Open Coding Procedure" such that this study can be replicated.

3.2 Cause, Effect Grouping

Open coding has reduced the textual data into a manageable set of individual codes. As the next step in content analysis to further reduce the amount of data such that we can observe emerging patterns we categorized the causes and effects. We perceive that some of these causes and effects belong to a higher, collective and more generic group while others belonged to a more specific group. For an example the cause in 3rd code within the *Table 3* above was Social Computing (SC) a generic term while the cause in 4th code is Blogs a more specific term, similarly effect in 3rd code is business impact a more generic term while effect in 4th code is engagement a specific characteristic. Hence we grouped the generics as "Super Class" and specifics as "Sub Class" and arrived at 6 groups as in *Table 4* below. How we arrived at these 6 super classes is: *Social Computing* and *business outcomes* were the key interest of this study. *Technology* is the immediate antecedent or cause for Social Computing. *Application/Emergent Characteristics* and *User Actions* were propositioned by the generic model and further supported by the literature.

Table 4. Cause, Effect Grouping using text from Literature

Super Class	**Sub Class**
Technologies	Broadband connectivity, powerful computers
Social Computing (Applications)	Blogs, Wikis
Application Characteristics	Content Sharing (CS), Knowledge Aggregation (KA)
Emergent Characteristics	Engagement
User Action	Recruiting
Business Outcome	Economic impact

Causal Chains

The very first code in *Table 3* above reads as "Broadband connectivity enabled SC". 3rd code reads as "SC caused business impact". We can explain this as a certain cause gives rise to a certain effect, and that effect becomes a cause to an even higher effect. If we placed them in a row as below:

Broadband connectivity ———→ SC

SC ———→ Business impact

Now we can combine these 2 causal links into one causal chain as below:

Broadband connectivity ———→ SC ———→ Business impact.

Always singular causal links are extracted from text. A closer inspection of these singular causal links will display matching patterns that can help develop meaningful multistage causal chains as we did above. In the context of this paper the primal cause is "technologies" and ultimate effect is "business outcome". We do not know how many causal links there will be in between the two, but creating the longest causal chain will increase the reliability of this study such that this method can be applied to any other domain. A significant way to determine the correct order for a chain is to organise the links in the sequence of occurrence of causation using inductive reasoning. Causal links from literature will act as the code directory of reference for this paper when developing new open codes from data. For example if Airbnb had 3 sources of data namely A, B and C, each source will give rise to different number of causal links (codes) but a combination of these links may give rise to a more complete chain. The scope of the data analysis is developing longest possible causal chains for each of the six scenarios we are analysing within this paper.

3.3 Aligning Causal Chains

Under section *3.2 Cause and Effect Grouping* exercise above we have identified 6 Super Classes that all these causes and effects can be categorized into. These are (1) Technologies, (2) Social Computing Applications, (3) Application Characteristics, (4) Emergent Characteristics, (5) User Actions and (6) Business Outcomes. As the final step in this methodology we would horizontally arrange these six Super Classes in sequence and underneath will place the extracted causal chains in rows aligning specific cause or effect under relevant Super Class. This would help an abductive inference of a common pattern amongst the six scenarios we are analyzing within the next section.

4. DATA ANALYSIS

With 3 themes (1) *applications, (2) characteristics* and (3) *business outcomes* as the guide to look for when scanning the text we open coded all six scenarios and extracted these nodes or causal relationships as displayed in the *Figure 2* below. Each node represented a singular causal link such as "A caused B".

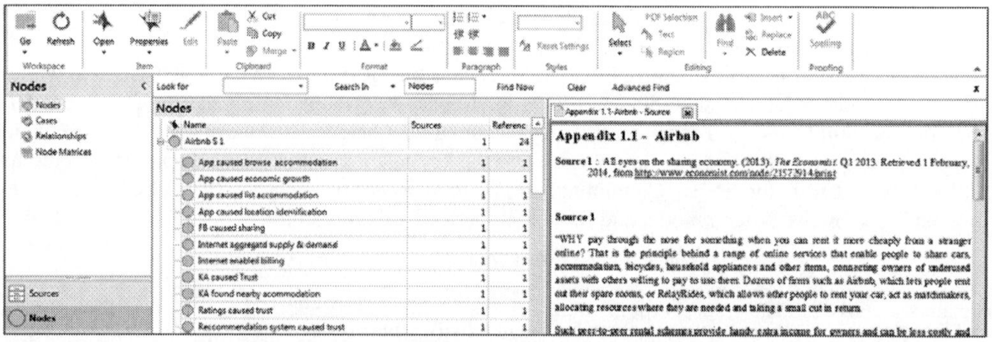

Figure 2. Nodes (Open Codes) extracted from text using NVivo

Content analysis has enabled us condense the vast amount of textual data into a manageable and contextually rich amount of nodes as shown above. Each scenario consisted of average 27 nodes. We extracted these nodes into a Node Matrix such that any emerging patterns can be observed. We indexed each individual node for identification purpose and probable future extension of this analysis. We assigned a threefold number as the code ID with first two digits representing scenario number, next two digits source number and final two digits individual node number. For the six scenarios we are analyzing for this paper we have extracted a total of 166 codes of which only a sample is displayed in *Table 5* below.

Table 5. Individual Code Matrix

Scenario & Source #	Code ID	Code	Scenario & Source #	Code ID	Code
Airbnb 1	3.01.01	App caused browse accommodation	Airbnb 2	3.02.01	App caused belongingness
	3.01.02	App caused economic growth		3.02.02	App caused connection
	3.01.03	App caused list accommodation		3.02.03	App caused unique experience
	3.01.04	App caused location identification		3.02.04	App cut cost
	3.01.05	FB caused sharing		3.02.05	App filled empty spaces
	3.01.06	Internet aggregatd supply & demand		3.02.06	App generated income
	3.01.07	Internet enabled billing		3.02.07	App is scalable
	3.01.08	KA caused Trust		3.02.08	App is user friendly
	3.01.09	KA found nearby acommodation		3.02.09	Sharing enabled meet demand
	3.01.10	Ratings caused trust	Airbnb 3	3.03.01	Trust enabled sharing
	3.01.11	Reccommendation system caused trust	Uber 1	4.01.01	App caused less mileage
	3.01.12	Reviews caused trust		4.01.02	App enabled feedback(KA)
	3.01.13	Reviews increased demand		4.01.03	App enabled ordering
	3.01.14	Sharing caused efficiency		4.01.04	App enabled paying
	3.01.15	Sharing caused environmental bebefits		4.01.05	App enabled rating(KA)
	3.01.16	Sharing caused income		4.01.06	App is flexible
	3.01.17	Sharing is cheap		4.01.07	App located closest car
	3.01.18	Sharing is convenient		4.01.08	Feedback(KA) caused growth
	3.01.19	Sharing is less costly		4.01.09	Flexibility lowered overheads
	3.01.20	Smartphne enabled KA		4.01.10	Less mileage reduced pollution
	3.01.21	SN caused KA		4.01.11	Rating(KA) caused better drivers
	3.01.22	SN caused trust		4.01.12	Rating(KA) caused right price
	3.01.23	Technology caused SM	Uber 2	4.02.01	App caused expansion

App=specific application, SN=social networks, SM=social media, FB=Facebook, KA=knowledge aggregation,

Executing the grouping method in *Section 3.2* of our methodology we grouped the causal links extracted from data as in the *Table 6* below.

Table 6. Cause, Effect Grouping using Data

	Super Class	Sub Class
1	Technology	Internet, Smartphone
2	Social Computing Application	Social Networks(SN), Social Media (SM), Facebook(FB), Blogs, Wikis, YouTube, LinkedIn, Airbnb
3	Application Characteristics	Knowledge Aggregation(KA), Content Sharing(CS), Social Interaction(SI), Ratings, Recommendations, Reviews
4	Emergent Characteristics	Community, Empowerment, Collaboration, Easy to use, Dynamic, Trust, Goodwill, Belonging, User friendly
5	User Actions	Marketing, Recruiting, Content Creating, Sharing, Browsing, Listing, Billing
6	Business Outcomes	Promotion, Business Impact, Innovation, Scalability, Rapid Growth, Brand Visibility, Bargaining Power, Extra Income, Nearby Accommodation, Economic Growth, Demand, Efficiency, Cheap, Environment Benefits, Convenience, Less Cost, Fast Growth, Unique Experience, Cot Cost, Filled Empty Spaces, Income, Scalability, Meet Demand

We tabulated these Super Classes in sequence of occurrence based purely on inductive reasoning as technology had been the antecedent or cause to give rise to Social Computing applications. Social Computing applications with their different functionalities give rise to application characteristics. Application characteristics induced different emergent characteristics in the users: a feeling or a perception. These feelings and perceptions made users act in such ways and these user actions caused business outcomes.

Table 5 above consists of individual causal links which are the basic codes we extracted from the text that took the format "A caused B". But a closer look at this code matrix exposed that these singular causal links within a scenario even if they came from different sources S1, S2 or S3 can be linked to each other. For example code ID 3.01.05: "FB caused sharing" can be linked with code ID 3.01.14: "Sharing caused efficiency". By linking such matching causal links together we can develop causal chains. A singular causal link for example code ID 3.01.02: "App caused economic growth" adds value by highlighting that application has caused economic growth. But it is not explanative enough for someone to use this same App and obtain economic growth or use another app or even develop a similar app and gain economic growth in another domain. Thus we propose if we gathered as many possible related causal links within this scenario using *Table 5* and constructed longest possible causal chain that takes us from "App" to "economic growth" as in *Figure 3* below.

Facebook
Technology ➔ FB ➔ Instant Articles (CS) ➔ Convenient to read ➔ Advertising ➔ Revenue

YouTube
Mobile devices ➔ YouTube ➔ Content Sharing (CS) ➔ Community ➔ Advertising ➔Revenue

Airbnb
Technology ➔ Airbnb App ➔ Knowledge Aggregation (KA) ➔ Trust ➔ Sharing ➔ Extra Income

Uber
Smartphone ➔ Uber App ➔ Reviews ➔ Trust ➔ Transacting ➔ Income

Skillshare
Skillshare App ➔ Content Sharing (CS) ➔ Empowerment ➔ Teaching ➔ Revenue

Fundrise
Fundrise App ➔ Crowdfunding ➔ Community ➔ Investing ➔ Economic Development

Figure 3. Longest Causal Chains of Six Scenarios

Our aim was to construct the causal chain that undertook the longest possible path such that it would represent a more explanative and reliable causal inference. Above are the longest causal chains we derived from six scenarios but we could not make any inferences by inspecting them as they are. However *Table 6* above has categorized these causations into a set of 6 Super Classes. Thus following suit we tabulated the 6 Super Classes horizontally and aligned the causal chains of (1) Facebook, (2) YouTube, (3) Airbnb, (4) Uber (5) Skillshare and (6) Fundrise, underneath these Super Classes in rows as in the *Table 7* below.

Table 7. Aligning Causal Chains

Technology	Code ID	SC App	Code ID	ACH	Code ID	ECH	Code ID	UA	Code ID	BO
Technology	1.02.07 →	FB	1.01.03 →	Instant Articles (CS)	1.01.12 →	Convenient to read	1.02.01 →	Advertising	1.01.01 →	Revenue
Smartphone	1.02.11 →	FB	1.02.08 →		→	Engagement				
Mobile Devices	2.01.03 →	YouTube	2.01.04 →	CS	2.02.16 →	Community	2.02.13 →	Advertising	2.03.01 →	Revenue
		YouTube	2.02. 01 →	CS	2.02.06 →				→	Scalability
Technology	3.01.25 →	Airbnb App	3.01.23 →	Reviews (KA)	3.01.10 →	Trust	3.03.09 →	Sharing	3.01.18 →	Extra Income
				Testi-monies (KA)	3.02.01 →		→	Sharing	3.02.6 →	Cut Cost
Smartphone	4.03.13 →	Uber App	4.03.08 →	Reviews (KA)	4. 03.12 →	Trust	4.03.04 →	Transacting	4.03.15 →	Income
		Uber App	4.02.02 →	Ratings (KA)	4.02.09 →	Trust				
		Skillshare App	5.01.04 →	CS	5.01.08 →	Empowerment	5.01.12 →	Teaching	5.01.13 →	Revenue
		Skillshare App	5.02.10 →	CS	5.02.08 →				→	Skill Expansion
		Fundrise App	6.01.04 →	Crowd funding	6.02.02 →	Community	6.01.12 →	Investing	6.01.10 →	Economic Development
		Fundrise App	6.02.01 →		→	Community	6.03.03 →		→	Neighborhood Development

App=Application, ACH=Application Characteristic, ECH=Emergent Characteristic, UA=User Actions, BO=Business Outcome, FB=Facebook, CS=Content Sharing, KA=Knowledge Aggregation

When these causal chains were aligned under the "Super Classes" we began to observe a pattern of sequential causal advance like: cause ➔ effect ➔ cause ➔ effect, such that an effect of one cause becoming a cause to a higher effect. Nor all scenarios achieved the same causal inference neither they consisted of same number of causal links.

For example 1st scenario Facebook comprised a complete causal chain beginning from first Super Class – Technology. Technology has enabled the social application Facebook. Facebook has enabled 'Instant Articles' by allowing third party newspaper companies such as New York Times to host their content on Facebook (Economist 2015) such that users can read the newspaper from their newsfeed without having to leave Facebook and being directed to a newspaper website via a weblink. This application characteristic *Content Sharing (CS)* has caused an *Emergent Characteristic*: a perception in the user such that it is 'convenient to read'. Because of this convenience more and more of 1.59 billion Facebook users have started reading the newspapers via Facebook. This has caused newspapers the ability to sell the advertising that appears next to their stories or let Facebook sell that advertising space on their behalf. This causes the ultimate business outcome – revenue from advertising, to both parties, Facebook and third party newspaper companies.

If we considered the second causal chain of the same scenario the outcome is different. This too begins with a Sub Class of the very first Super Class – Technology, 'Smartphone'. The mobile device Smartphone has enabled Facebook. The next causal link skips 3rd Super Class and aligns under the 4th Super Class Emergent Characteristic: causing 'engagement' and the causal chain ends therein. Of course 'engagement' is an important characteristic towards business outcomes though not a final outcome, also how did engagement occur simply using Facebook, which application characteristic gave rise to the same, and what would be the effect of 'engagement' are all questions unanswered within this short causal chain. Hence is the importance of developing the longest possible causal chains which would explain the causal inferences step by step enabling a profound understanding of the entire causal process such that it becomes applicable elsewhere.

Similarly within the business scenario Airbnb: *Technology* has enabled *Airbnb app*. App has enabled users to peer *review*: guest reviewed about the host and accommodation property while host reviewed the behavior of the guest causing *knowledge aggregation (KA)*. This aggregation of knowledge built a *trust* within the peers. This human trust enabled users *share* their properties with strangers they've only known online. This *user action* of sharing brought forth the ultimate *business outcome*: Extra Income.

Such were the causal patterns identified within other scenarios YouTube, Uber, Skillshare and Fundrise each of which gave rise to scenario specific step by step causal inferences. This aligning made it possible to perceive though causal inferences were scenario specific they followed a generic to all sequential causal path.

5. DISCUSSION AND CONCLUSION

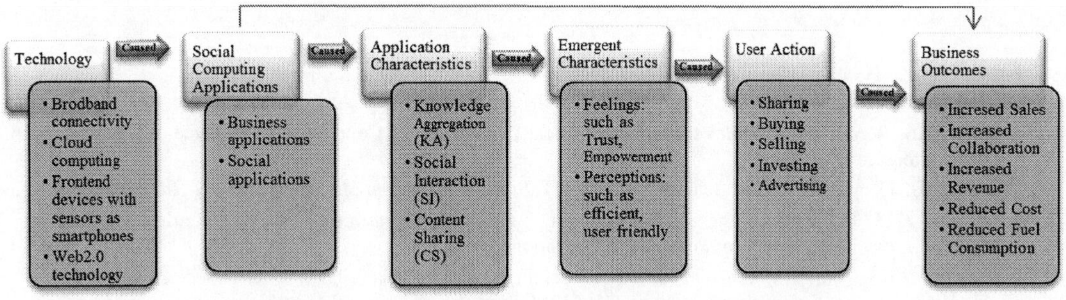

Figure 4. Multistage Causal Model for Social Computing and Business Outcomes

By consolidating the individual causal chains we have derived this generic model in *Figure 4* above which highlights that the underlying causality between Social Computing and all these positive business outcomes take a multistage causal inference. Some causal extractions within data illustrated singular causal relation from technology unto final business outcome such as "Smartphone caused economic growth" which is also correct but is not explanative enough. In contrast this model presents more comprehensive multistage causal path of inference. Our analysis has helped categorise these multiple causal stages which we call super classes that sequentially advance until ultimate business outcome is met. Primary super class is the latest technologies that cause Social Computing applications. Next these applications cause several application characteristics. These application characteristics cause emergent characteristics within the user. These emergent characteristics cause users to act in such a way that causes these positive business outcomes such as cost reduction, revenue growth and sustainability. It is through knowing these causal steps and their dynamics that one can make use of these benefits using Social Computing.

Each of these causal super classes comprised of several sub classes that played a significant role in this sequential causal inference. 1st subclass comprised of enabling technologies such as powerful personal computers or mobile devices with sensors such as GPS or cameras, broadband connectivity, cloud servers and web 2.0 technologies to name some. In the past there were applications which were web based though today most applications are mobile based, and some applications used location identification functionality while others didn't depending on their business requirements. 2nd subclass comprised of social applications such as Facebook, YouTube or specific business applications such as Airbnb, Uber. 3rd subclass included application characteristics: *Social Interaction (SI), Content Sharing (CS)* and *Knowledge Aggregation (KA)* that gave rise to 4th sub class emergent characteristic which is a feeling within the user or a perception user assigned to the application. *Social Interaction* such as friending, creating groups, chatting caused *engagement, community building* or *belongingness* and users also perceived that the application is *easy to use*, *economical* or *efficient. Content Sharing* in the form of text, images, audio or video caused product/service *knowledge*, *empowerment*, or *self-esteem. Knowledge Aggregation* such as location identification systems caused finding nearest taxi or accommodation, one significant *Knowledge Aggregation* was peer reviews, rankings, ratings, feedback, testimonials and system developed recommendations that caused *trust* within the users: for the first time in history trust building took place online amongst total strangers causing users to act in such ways like buying, investing, sharing properties such as one's own home, apartments, rooms, vehicles and even rides. Since these user actions took place online user access was large in number, social applications had millions or billions of users as we discussed in *Section 1*, also as all business applications were integrated with social applications such as Facebook, Twitter or LinkedIn this caused rapid business diffusion thus causing scalability and rapid growth.

Hence this multistage causal model imparts a deeper understanding of these chronological causal dynamics amongst Social Computing and business outcomes. This understanding can now help businesses in two ways. If the business has already implemented Social Computing they can further increase the efficiency by maneuvering the causes to effect the dynamic business requirements by referring to the corresponding specific causal chain. On the other hand if a business intends to newly implement Social Computing having a specific business requirement they can refer to the corresponding specific causal chain for specific causal inferences that leads to required business impact and use the generic model as the ultimate guideline in implementing Social Computing effectively. Thus based on this model businesses can now take a more methodical approach towards effective implementation of social computing.

REFERENCES

Airbnb. 2016. "Rent Unique Places to Stay from Local Hosts in 190+ Countries." Retrieved 17 January, 2016, from www.airbnb.com

Blumberg, B., Cooper, D. R., and Schindler, P. S. 2011. *Business Research Methods*. McGraw-Hill Higher Education.

Economist. 2013. "All Eyes on the Sharing Economy." *Technology Quarterly* Q1 2013. Retrieved 1 February, 2014, from http://www.economist.com/node/21572914/print

Economist. 2015. "News Companies and Facebook:Friends with Benefits?" Retrieved 1 October, 2015, from http://www.economist.com/news/business/21651264-facebook-and-several-news-firms-have-entered-uneasy-partnership-friends-benefits?zid=291&ah=906e69ad01d2ee51960100b7fa502595

Fu, A., Finn, C., Rasmus, D., and Salkowitz, R. 2009. "Social Computing in the Enterprise. Microsoft Vision for Business Leaders," *Microsoft White Paper*).

Ginige, A., and Fernando, M. D. 2015. "Towards Generic Model for Social Computing and Emergent Characteristics," in: *Asia Pacific World Congress on Computer Science & Engineering*. Fiji.

Hassan, H. A. 2008. "Corporate Social Computing Taxonomy Development," *Positive Desidn*).

Huijboom, N., van den Broek, T., Frissen, V., Kool, L., Kotterink, B., Meyerhoff Nielsen, M., and Millard, J. 2009. "Key Areas in the Public Sector Impact of Social Computing," *European Communities*).

Kemp, S. 2015. "We Are Social." *We are Social's Compendium of Global Digital Statistics* Retrieved 1 October, 2015, from http://www.slideshare.net/wearesocialsg/digital-social-mobile-in-2015

Liu, H., Salerno, J., and Young, M. J. 2010. *Social Computing, Behavioural Modelling and Prediction.* Springer.

Oppong, T. 2015. "Over 50 Startup Founders Reveal Why Their Startups Failed ".

Parameswaran, M., and Whinston, A. B. 2007a. "Research Issues in Social Computing," *Journal of the Association for Information Systems* (8:6), p. 22.

Parameswaran, M., and Whinston, A. B. 2007b. "Social Computing: An Overview," *Communications of the Association for Information Systems* (19:1), p. 37.

Quinlan, C. 2011. *Business Research Methods.* South-Western Cengage Learning Andover.

Reilly, C. 2013. "David Jones' Strategy Targets Omnichannel, Staffing and Store Renewal." Retrieved 1 February, 2014, from http://www.retailbiz.com.au/2013/09/25/article/David-Jones-strategy-targets-omnichannel-staffing-and-store-renewal/GLUNCVUIBN

Schuler, D. 1994. "Social Computing," *Communications of the ACM* (37:1), pp. 28-29.

Statista. 2016. "The Statistics Portal." Retrieved 15 February 2016, from http://www.statista.com/

Uber. 2016. "Your Ride, on Demand." Retrieved 15 February, 2016, from https://www.uber.com/

Wang, F.-Y., Carley, K. M., Zeng, D., and Mao, W. 2007. "Social Computing: From Social Informatics to Social Intelligence," *Intelligent Systems, IEEE* (22:2), pp. 79-83.

PROFIT-BASED LOGISTIC REGRESSION TRAINED BY MIGRATING BIRDS OPTIMIZATION: A CASE STUDY IN CREDIT CARD FRAUD DETECTION

Azamat Kibekbaev* and Ekrem Duman
Department of Industrial engineering, Özyeğin University, Istanbul, Turkey
**Corresponding author*

ABSTRACT

The amount of online transactions are increasing considerably with the development of modern technology in the finance industry, government, corporate sectors, and for ordinary consumers. Thus, forcing financial institutions to continuously improve their fraud detection systems is inevitable to minimize their losses. In recent years, there has been research done on many machine learning and data mining techniques for credit card fraud prevention and detection. However, most studies used some sort of misclassification measure to evaluate different solutions in terms of probability, and do not take into account the profitability or costliness of detecting a fraudulent transaction. The key contribution in our study is to focus on the profit maximization in the model building step. Proposed logistic regression algorithm in this study works based on profit maximization instead of minimizing the error of prediction. In addition, literature studies have shown that the maximum likelihood estimator which works as a gradient based algorithm, usually gets trapped in local optima and swarm-based (metaheuristic) algorithms are more successful in this respect. In this study, we train our profit maximization LR using the Migrating Birds Optimization, Particle Swarm Optimization, Genetic Algorithm and Artificial Bee Colony.

KEYWORDS

Fraud detection, Logistic regression, MBO, PSO, GA, ABC

1. INTRODUCTION

There are lots of studies in the field of statistical learning for credit card fraud detection. They utilized supervised learning techniques including Decision Trees (ID3, C4.5, and C&RT), Logistic Regression (LR), or more complex models like Artificial Neural Networks (ANN) and Support Vector Machines (SVM) (Leonard 1993; Chan et al. 1998; Chan et al. 1999; Chen et al. 2004; Chen et al. 2005; Sahin et al. 2011). Generally, these studies maximize the number of correct classified observations (accuracy). However, some of them investigated effect of cost-sensitive classification on performance of the algorithms. These studies implemented class-dependent costs of misclassification for observations. Moreover, they did not consider profit for correct classification which is targeted in this study.

Due to aforementioned reasons, in most of business problems, we have to develop a profit/cost-wise prediction models. From this point of view, equal costs of misclassification are assigned for observations in different classes in credit card fraud detection studies. As first step of developing cost-sensitive approach, researchers proposed a cost-matrix representing the costs for different types of misclassification in credit card fraud detection problem. "Misclassified fraudulent observations (false negative) charge significantly more cost than the mislabeled legitimate ones (false alarms)", this is why such approach is necessary in credit card fraud detection (Langford 2006; Zhou et al. 2006). However, the individual cost of misclassification should be considered while developing classification model for real-life credit card fraud detection problem. Because each credit card has its individual risk based on usable limit available on the card. So, the available usable limit on the card is taken into account in order to define example-dependent profit and cost of classification. This issue has been studied in some fraud detection problems (Duman et al. 2011; Duman et al. 2013; Kibekbaev et al. 2015). In the original version, LR trained by maximum likelihood estimator (MLE) and all of the misclassifications have same costs, which is not a realistic assumption in most of the real-world problems. For instance, in patient diagnosis problems, misclassification of an unhealthy as healthy is more risky and costly than misclassification of a healthy person as unhealthy. This issue motivated most of researchers to investigate the effect of different misclassification costs on classification models. For this reason, most of the works are related to cost-sensitive LR.

In statistics, the LR model has a wide range usage in many areas which is generally used to create models for the classification of the factors that might determine whether or not an outcome happens. Mihelis (2001) developed a method to determine customer satisfaction using an ordinal regression based approach. Another model for assessing the value of customer satisfaction was developed by Rust and Zahorik (1993). They used logistic regression to link satisfaction with attributes of customer retention. They claim that the logistic function can be interpreted as providing the retention probability. Kim and Yoon (2004) used a binomial logit model to determine subscriber churn in the telecommunications industry, based on discrete choice theory. Discrete choice theory is the study of behavior in situations where decision makers must select from a finite set of alternatives. Hwang (2004) discovered that logistic regression performed best for predicting customer churn when compared with neural networks and decision tree. It should be noted that Hwang were investigating a prediction of the customer lifetime value (CLV), with the intent of including customer churn; they suggest that logistic regression was the best model for their purpose.

Evolutionary algorithms with the ability to broaden the search space in the attempt to avoid local minima have been developed over the past decades. Metaheuristics deal with complex problems despite they are unable to reach a globally optimum solution. There is a huge number of problems for which finding an exact solution, any guaranteed bound, or optimal solution is very dificult. Meta-heuristics can be applied to find satisfactory near-to-optimal solutions for such problems (Boussa et al. 2013). Metaheuristics provide a more robust and efficient approach for solving complex real-world problems and are often able to offer a better trade-off between solution quality and computing time. Since they are heuristic and stochastic, they are less likely to get stuck in local minimum, and they are based on populations made up of individuals with a specified behavior similar to biological phenomenon. These common characteristics led to the development of evolutionary algorithms as an increasing important field. The search strategies of different metaheuristics are highly dependent on the philosophy of the metaheuristic itself. For this reason, benchmarking the results of metaheuristic algorithms and MBO-based algorithms are our aim in this paper. The reason for selecting MBO among other metaheuristics are twofold: first, it is rather new and thus not much elaborated; second, it performed very good in individual profit-based CC fraud detection. So, we tried to improve the results in fraud detection, or at least to filter out the ones that are promising in LR training for fraud applications. But one must acknowledge that the attention should be paid to possible pitfalls when proposing the novel metaheuristic methods or using the already known ones to solve different novel tasks (Weise et al. 2013). Also, not all new metaheuristics turn out successful and useful for the practical problems (Črepinšek et al. 2013), trying different methods and comparing the results will be the best way to give strong decisions.

The rest of the paper is as following: section 2 is about details of LR, MBO algorithm and its modified version. Section 3 presents the methodology part of our study. Section 4 introduces experimental results obtained and comparison of the performances of benchmarked algorithms in terms of statistical and profit-based measures, and the paper is concluded in section 5.

2. METHODOLOGY

LR is often used when the dependent variable takes only two values and the independent variables are continuous, categorical, or both. The goal in LR is to find the best fitting, and most parsimonious model, to describe the relationship between a response or outcome variable, and a set of explanatory or predictor variables. LR model predicts the probability of occurrences, so if the odds of occurrences are higher than fifty percent or other preset threshold, then the prediction will be assigned to class denoted by binary variable "1", if less it is class "0". The distinctive feature of the Logit is that, the outcome variable is binary or dichotomous. Generally fraudelent data is being used to develop a proper logistic regression model by identifying the important attributes in the data, which are important in predicting the given outcome. As a result the created model can be used to classify a newly provided fraudelent data through placing in LR model to calculate the probability P of a given outcome. The equation for the dichotomous logistic regression is given below as follows:

$$Y_i = \sum_{i=1}^{k} \beta_i x_i + \varepsilon_i$$

where

$$\ln\left(\frac{p}{1-p}\right) = Y_i$$

and

$$P(Y_i) = \frac{1}{1+e^{-Y_i}}$$

From the equations above the P is the probability of a customer to be predicted as fraudelent or not, β_0 which is a constant or intercept and β_1 ... β_k are the models parameters which play the role of constants for each attribute. Equations above are summarized in the Figure 1.

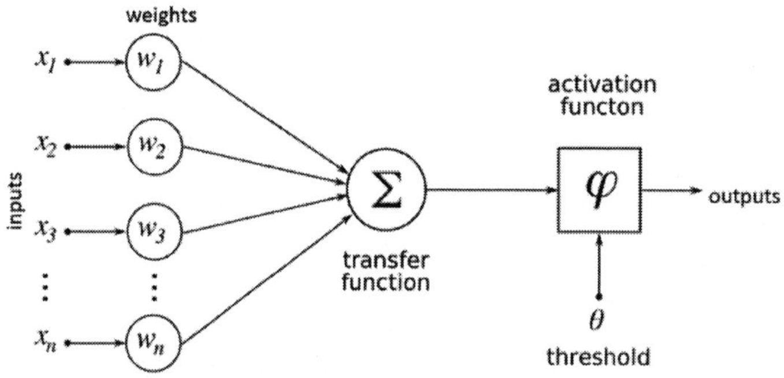

Figure 1. Logistic Regression [19]

2.1 Migrating Birds Optimization

Duman, Uysal, & Alkaya (2012) explained the story of birds migration and interpret the MBO algorithm for solving large scale problems. Here, just the algorithm will be explained. The Migrating Birds Optimization (MBO) starts with initial solutions corresponding to the birds which are sorted out in a V formation. Solving process starts with the first solution and moves on toward the tails where each solution tries to be improved by its neighbor solutions. Wherever an improvement is done to a solution by its neighbors, it is replaced with that one. Another particular property of MBO is benefit mechanism which is defined as sharing the best unused neighbors to the following solution. By this mechanism, each solution is improved using not only its own generated solutions but also unused neighbor solutions of others. When all solutions are improved and leader position is changed by predetermined number of tours, another loop starts. Finally, the algorithm stops after finite number of iterations.

Below, one may see the pseudo-code of MBO (adopted from (Duman et al. 2012)):

```
Generate n initial solutions in a random manner and place them on an hypothetical V formation
arbitrarily
    i = 0
while (i < K)
        for (j = 0, j < m, j + +)
            Try to improve the leading solution by generating and evaluating k neighbors of it
            i = i + k
            for each solution s_r in the flock (except leader)
                Try to improve s_r by evaluating (k − x) neighbors of it and x unused best
                neighbors from the solution in the front
                i = i + (k − x)
            endfor
        endfor
        Replace one of the second solutions with leader solution and move it to bottom of the tail
endwhile
Return the best solution in the flock
```

2.2 LR and MBO-Based Learning for Profit Maximization

In this study, we have used LR model with MBO algorithm to find the appropriate weights by which, the profit function is maximized. The profit function is defined using individual profits of instances which is the usable limit of each customer. If the model detects the fraudelent customer it will save the corresponding usable limit. The total net profit (NP) which can be gained by implementing the classification method is calculated with the following equation:

$$NP = \sum_{i=1}^{N_{TP}} (UL_i - c) + \sum_{k=1}^{N_{FP}} (-c)$$

Here, ULi represents the lifetime value of the ith customer and c is the cost of action offer which is selected for this customer. N_{TP} and N_{FP} indicate the number of true positives and false positives, respectively. The original LR is working with error function based on gradient descent method. However, the proposed LR uses metaheuristic algorithms to maximize the profit function.

In this study, objective function is the total savings that can be obtained from the test set. Where, it is calculated by summing overall ULs of corresponding fraudelent customers detected by the model. Formula is given below:

$$saving = \sum_{k=1}^{p} UL_k \ , \quad k \in \{x_i \mid \hat{y}_i = 1 \ \& \ y_i = 1\}$$

Here, UL_k is the amount of usable limit for customer k which is a correctly detected positive instance where there are total N_{TP} actual positive instances in the test set. $\hat{y}_i$ and y_i are the ith instance output and target value, respectively.

For example, Metaheuristics based LR is shown below and equation is as following:

$$h_\theta(x) = \theta_0 + \theta_1 x_1 + \theta_2 x_2$$

This equation represents the all inputs are multiplied by their corresponding weights and a bias is added to the result.

$$o_{1j} = g(\theta^T x) = \frac{1}{1 + e^{-\theta^T x}}$$

This equation gets the weighted average of inputs and applies the sigmoid function to calculate the output.

$$u = \sigma_1 + \sum_{j=1}^{10} \vartheta_j o_{1j}$$

Then as shown by equation above, the outputs are multiplied by their corresponding weights and then summed up to determine the output value (u) of the output result.

$$y = \frac{1}{1 + e^{-u}}$$

Finally sigmoid function is applied to determine the outputs. By this equation we ensure that the output of the LR will be a value between zero and one which corresponds to the probability of being positive (fraudulent) for each transaction. In statistical learning this output is called as score of the instance which is popular in most of the data science studies.

3. RESULTS AND DISCUSSION

The fraud data in this study has been gathered from a well-known Turkish bank and after pre- processing it contains 9243 customers information with 12 different attributes one of which is usable limit. This attribute shows profitability of them and this attribute has been used to reach the aim of maximizing total net profit by detecting the fraudelent truly. The dataset is divided into training and test sets with proportion of 70% and 30%. Therefore, there are 313 fraudulent instances and 2817 legitimate ones in the test set. Moreover, we have benchmarked three other well-known metaheuristic algorithms, Particle Swarm Optimization (PSO), Artificial Bee Colony (ABC) and Genetic Algorithm (GA) to train the LR with the same objective function which MBO uses and compare the proposed model performance with both of them in terms of statistical and profit-based performance. We made statistical tests (F-test and T-test) to find the significance of the results.

Table 1. True Positive Rate and Total Net Profit

	True Positive Rate (%)			Total Net Profit %		
	Min	Average	Max	Min	Average	Max
LR-ABC	80	81.73	82.29	86.67	89.83	96.15
LR-GA	72.35	79.73	86.97	83.14	87.98	91.55
LR-PSO	72.35	80.43	86.03	81.14	86.38	89.26
LR-MBO	79.65	82.11	83.5	86.8	**90.18**	92.96
Org. LR	81.51	**82.83**	83.61	76.66	82.11	85.47

Table 2. P-values

	P-Values				
	LR-ABC	LR-GA	LR-PSO	LR-MBO	Org. LR
LR-ABC	0	-	-	-	-
LR-GA	0.049	0	-	-	-
LR-PSO	0.009	0.0302	0	-	-
LR-MBO	0.484	0.0438	0.0089	0	-
Original LR	0.017	0.002	0.0047	0.021	0

Table 1 and 2 shows the results of all mentioned models in terms of well-known statistical measures in binary classification problems. In all algorithms we used total saving as the objective function for metaheuristic algorithms instead of MLE function and the algorithms will try to maximize the total profit instead of minimizing the prediction error. According to results in Table 1, in terms of true positive rate, the original LR have better performance. This is because; these models try to minimize the number of misclassifications. In terms of net profit, the proposed MBO-based LR have better performances as they try to maximize the total profit and give priority to the customers with higher usable limit.

Among all results, the LR model which uses MBO algorithm to maximize the total maximum net profit, has significantly superior performance to other models in terms of total maximum net profit. Also, maximum and minimum performances of the LR version confirms that the MBO-based LR is more stable than the others (it has tighter range in all of the results). This may be influenced by particular property of MBO benefit mechanism which is defined as sharing the best unused neighbors to the following solution. Finally in Table 2, according to statistical results p-values between results are less than α=0.05 except LR-MBO and LR-ABC, which means all algorithm results are different from each other. As the p-value amount between LR-MBO and LR-ABC is higher than $\alpha = 0.05$, there are no significant difference between this two model results.

4. CONCLUSION AND FUTURE WORK

In this study, a novel MBO-based LR classifier is proposed where it works based on profit maximization instead of prediction error minimization. MBO, the new nature-inspired metaheuristic algorithm used in this study to maximize the profit function, is a swarm intelligence optimization approach which tries to skip the local optima and find a better maybe global optimum for its objective function. In the experimental section of the study, MBO-based LR competed with the original LR and also three other profit-based scenarios each of which uses well-known metaheuristic methods to find the optimum point (PSO, ABC and GA). Results represent that, in terms of net profit, the MBO-based LR which uses a profit function and maximizes it result in a significantly better performance than the other three scenarios but it is less successful in terms of statistical measures such as accuracy, TP rate and TN rate in comparison with original LR.

ACKNOWLEDGEMENT

With a deep sense of gratitude the authors would like to thank The Scientific and Technological Research Council of Turkey (TÜBİTAK) under Project No: 113M063.

REFERENCES

Boussa, J. et al, 2013. A survey on optimization metaheuristics, *Information Sciences*, vol. 237, pp. 82-117.

Chan P. K. et al, 1998. Toward scalable learning with non-uniform class and cost distributions: A case study in credit card fraud detection., *in KDD*, vol. 1998, pp. 164-168.

Chan P. K. et al, 1999. Distributed data mining in credit card fraud detection, *Intelligent Systems and their Applications, IEEE*, vol. 14, no. 6, pp. 67-74.

Chen, R.C. et al, 2004. Detecting credit card fraud by using questionnaire-responded transaction model based on support vector machines, *in Intelligent Data Engineering and Automated Learning IDEAL*, pp. 800-806.

Chen, R.C. et al, 2005. Personalized approach based on svm and ann for detecting credit card fraud, *in Neural Networks and Brain, 2005. ICNN&B'05*. International Conference on, vol. 2, pp. 810-815.

Črepinšek, M., Liu, S-H. and Mernik, M. (2013). 'Exploration and exploitation in evolutionary algorithms: a survey', ACM Computing Surveys, Vol. 45, No. 3, pp.35:l–35:33.

Duman E. et al, 2011. Detecting credit card fraud by genetic algorithm and scatter search, *Expert Systems with Applications*, vol. 38, no. 10, pp. 13057-13063.

Duman E. et al, 2013. Solving credit card fraud detection problem by the new metaheuristics migrating birds optimization, in *Advances in Computational Intelligence*, pp. 62-71, Springer.

Duman, E. et al, 2012. Migrating Birds Optimization: A new metaheuristic approach and its performance on quadratic assignment problem, *Inf. Sci. (Ny).*, vol. 217, pp. 6577.

Hwang H., et al, 2004. An LTV model and customer segmentation based on customer value: a case study on the wireless telecommunication industry. *Expert Systems with Applications* 26, pp. 181-188.

Kibekbaev, A., et al, 2015. Profit-based Logistic Regression: A Case Study in Credit Card Fraud Detection, *The Fourth International Conference on Data Analytics*, Nice-France.

Kim H. S. et al, (2004). Determinants of subscriber churn and customer loyalty in the Korean mobile telephony market. Telecomm. *Policy*, 28(6): 751-765.

Langford J., 2006. Sensitive error correcting output codes, *in Learning Theory*, pp. 158-172, Springer.

Leonard, K. J., 1993. Detecting credit card fraud using expert systems, *Computers & industrial engineering*, vol. 25, no. 1, pp. 103-106.

Mihelis G., et al, 2001. Customer satisfaction measurement in the private bank sector, *European Journal of Operational Research*, (130), 2, 347-360.

Montgomery, D. C. et al, 2009. *Engineering Statistics*, John Wiley & Sons.

Rust, R., et al, 1993. Customer Satisfaction, Customer Retention, and *Market Share. Journal of Retailing*, 69(2), 193–215.

Sahin Y. et al, 2011. Detecting credit card fraud by ann and logistic regression, *in Innovations in Intelligent Systems and Applications (INISTA)*, 2011 International Symposium on IEEE, pp. 315-319.

Weise, T. et al, 2012. 'Evolving distributed algorithms with genetic programming', Vol. 16, No. 2.

Zhou Z.-H. et al, 2006. Training cost-sensitive neural networks with methods addressing the class imbalance problem, *Knowledge and Data Engineering*, IEEE Transactions on, vol. 18, pp. 63-77.

TWITTER TEMPORAL EVOLUTION ANALYSIS: COMPARING EVENT AND TOPIC DRIVEN RETWEET GRAPHS

Giambattista Amati[1], Simone Angelini[1], Francesca Capri[2], Giorgio Gambosi[2], Gianluca Rossi[2] and Paola Vocca[3]
[1]*Fondazione Ugo Bordoni, Rome, Italy*
[2]*Univ. of Rome Tor Vergata, Rome, Italy*
[3]*Univ. of Tuscia. Viterbo, Italy*

ABSTRACT

We study the retweet graphs evolution over time. We compare two different retweet graphs: the event driven retweet graph, filtered by topics about specific events (i.e. the Black Friday 2015 and the World Series 2015) and the sampling retweet graph, filtered by language (i.e. Italian) from the whole Twitter stream. To obtain the Italian Twitter sample we use a list of the most used Italian stop words and the Twitter native selection function for languages. We analyze the evolution of these retweet graphs over a period of two months, and compare the main structural measures that are generally used to characterize the nature of graphs: average distance, clustering coefficient, max in-out degree, max in-degree and out-degree, the size of the largest component, number of connected components.

Results show a significant difference between these two type of graphs, both in the way they grow, and in the way the above measures evolve. In particular, the sampling retweet graphs dimensions (edges and vertices sizes) and the considered measures grow almost linearly in the observation period, while the event driven graphs show a skewed distribution and reach a predictably saturation point at end of the event. The measures for the sampling retweet graph are more similar to a social network, such as Facebook, than to an information network, whilst the event driven retweet graphs is the opposite.

The study of the temporal evolution and the classification of different Twitter graphs is a preliminary work in order to better understand the nature of Twitter, how trends evolve over time, to detect both authoritative and spamming accounts, and to derive a suitable mathematical evolutionary model of Twitter communities.

KEYWORDS

Graph analysis, social media, Twitter graph, retweet graph, graph dynamics.

1. INTRODUCTION

Twitter is a widespread micro-blogging platform which allows for different user activities, each producing an interaction between users and thus a different kind of network [Amati et al. 2015].

The most studied, but relatively static type of interaction, is the following/follower graph, obtained by a directed edge if one follows or is followed by the other. These are the most natural and intuitive network representation of the Twitterverse and has been widely studied for quantitatively gauge the Twitter network [Kwak et al. 2010]; to compare Twitter with respect a pure social network [Myers et al 2015]; to identify authoritative accounts [Java et al. 2007, Weng et al. 2010]. Unfortunately the following/follower graph datasets are prohibitive to crawl on a massive scale due to the very restrictive policy of Twitter.

Another important kind of relationship we can use is the *retweet* link. In Twitter an account can either post a message (a *tweet*) of a maximum of 140 characters or forward a tweet of another account. These messages are called retweets. A retweet is sometimes accompanied by comments of the retweeters. A retweet network is defined thus as a directed graph where nodes are accounts and edges between accounts A and B is when A retweets a tweet of B. Surprisingly, this kind of network was studied only to detect spammers [Bild 2015]. Retweet graphs may be also relevant to study information propagation, because they better encode topic interests and trust relationships among accounts than the follower graphs, modelling thus more precisely the information network underlying the Twitterverse.

Moreover the, due to limitations of the API of Twitter the followers graph is difficult to construct, and only partial networks can be physically derived[1].

We study different kind of retweet graphs and analyze their temporal evolution. More precisely, we analyze two classes of retweet graphs: the (1*) event driven retweet graphs* derived by monitoring specific and limited in time events; and (2) *sampling retweet graphs* which contain the tweeting-retweeting activity of the Twitter network over a period of time, possibly limited by language, geographical area, and/or keywords.

The event driven retweet graphs are built filtering tweets and following the corresponding retweets based on keywords (hashtags, relevant accounts, etc) that describe the event, while in the sampling retweet graph, the filters are set on a list of stop words (common words of a specific language, or a set of accounts, etc) which allows to limit the size of the network. In our case, for the event driven retweet graphs, we studied the Black Friday 2015 and the World Series 2015 and, for what concern the network sampling, we filtered the tweets using a list of stop-words that allows to isolate the Italian tweeting-retweeting activity.

In order to study the temporal evolution we have constructed a sequence of graphs, derivable by the snapshots of the retweet graph taken every 4 hours. On these graphs we performed a set of structural measures (average distance, largest connected component, number of components, etc) and study their evolution. These measures allows to evaluate the topological properties of these graphs and are of fundamental importance to evaluate the structure and to predict the evolution of the Twitter network both from the social and from the information point of view. Additionally, understanding these graphs is important to improve current systems and to design new applications of online social networks.

The experiments reveal a substantial difference between the two classes of graphs both comparing the final states and their evolution. We conjecture that two are the possible interpretations of this phenomenon. On one hand, the difference may show the dual nature of Twitter network: social and information network. In fact, the Italian sampling is more similar to a social network showing a smaller shortest path, a larger clustering coefficient, larger connected component compared with the two event driven graphs. On the other hand, we conjecture that the evolution of the sampling general network can be derived as the convex hull of the events happened in the observation period. Our approach allows not only to evaluate the growth of the Twitter network but also to find out the evolution discontinuities due to events duration and, hence, the kind of collection considered.

Finally, we performed a correlation analysis which show a strict dependence between the different measures. Once again the dependency is different for the two kinds of retweet graphs.

2. RELATED WORK

There is a large literature on Twitter social network evolution. Some papers [Kwak et al. 2010, Myers et al 2015] compare Twitter with other social networks with a widely analyzed behavior; other papers, study the temporal evolution to model topic trends [Bhattacharya et al. 2012, Zhou et al 2010] or to asses authoritative users [Bhattacharya et al. 2012, Zhou et al 2010, Thij et al 2015,Thij et. Al 2016, Zubiaga et al 2015]. [Kwak et al. 2010] and in [Myers et al 2015] try to assess the social nature of Twitter, whether it is a social network or a social media. In particular, the analysis is not conclusive since both behaviors can be explained [Myers et al 2015]. On the other side, the temporal evolution of Twitter is mainly studied for trends analysis. The diffusion of news in Twitter and in several popular news media accounts and find that follow a star-like phenomenon of the information flows [Bhattacharya et al. 2012]. Similar results are derived for the diffusion of information on Twitter during the Iranian election on 2009 [Zhou et al 2010]. The results showed that the flows tend to be wide, not too deep and their size follow a power law-distribution. In [Bhamidi et al 2012], the authors proposed and validated on the superstar random graph model to represent the condensation phenomenon represented by the largest component of the retweet graph. Based on this approach, [Thij et al 2015] and successively [Thij et. Al 2016] define a mathematical model that describes the evolution of a

[1] Due to limitations of the Twitter Api, it is possible to make at most 30 follower queries every 15 minutes. https://dev.twitter.com/rest/reference/get/followers/list

retweet graph on some basic characteristics, such as the density of edges and the size and density of the largest connected component. In [Zubiaga et al 2015], the authors explore the types of triggers that spark trends on Twitter, through a categorization that allows to quickly identify types of trend.

3. EXPERIMENTATION COLLECTIONS

3.1 Dataset Description

We perform network analysis of the evolution of the retweet graphs using three different Twitter collections that were built by monitoring the activities in three different context. Two of the them are *event driven retweet graphs* derived by observing the Black Friday 2015 and the World Series 2015, while the third is a *sampling retweet graph*, denoted by *Italian sampling*. These streams are obtained as follows:

1. **Italian sampling.** The tweets extraction is based on the set of stop words typical of the Italian language: articles, prepositions, conjunctions, adverbs etc. The tweets are also filtered by Italian language.
2. **World Series.** The keywords used to extract the pertinent tweets are: #worldseries, world series, #Royals, #Mets, @Mets, #Royals, @Royals, @KCRoyals. The tweets are also filtered by English language. The event started 10-27-2015 and ended the 11-1-2015. From Table 1, we can see that the observation period started after the beginning of the event.
3. **Black Friday 2015.** The keywords used to extract the pertinent tweets are: blackfriday, black friday, @blackfriday_fm. The event was on the 11-27-2015, and it falls within the observation period.

Table 1. Collection description summarizes the principal features of the collections.

Table 1. Collection description

	Start	End	# tweets
Italian Sampling	10-26-2015 11:27:12AM	12-12-2015 05:50:45AM	74,749,330
World series	10-30-2015 2:07:07PM	11-27-2015 11:06:06AM	1,932,330
Black Friday	11-13-2015 2:38:16PM	12-18-2015 1:32:17PM	9,891,400

3.2 Graphs Construction

The graphs are constructed as follows: The node set represents the accounts and there is a directed edge from an account A towards an account B, if A retweets a tweet of B. Each edge (A,B) is labeled with the timestamp of the first time A retweets B. We use the timestamps to construct the temporal sequences of graphs. Every four hours, we build the graphs up to that instant of time. Note that the graphs never decrease since only new vertices (accounts) and edges (retweets) are added and no deletion occurs.Table 2 shows the sizes of the final graph obtained. Comparing the number of total tweets observed (see Table 1), the retweetting rate with respect to accounts, is lower in sampling graph than in the event driven graphs.

Table 2. Dimensions of the Final graphs

	Italian Sampling	Black Friday	World series
Vertices	2,541739e+06	2,7e+06	4,74e+05
Edges	1,3708317e+07	3,8e+06	8,40e+05
Tweets/edges	5,45	2,603	2,3
Tweets/vertices	29,4	3,66	4

In Figure 1, we show the evolution of the dimensions of three datasets over the period of observation. It is interesting to note that while, in the sapling graph the growth is almost linear in the period of observation, unsurprisingly, for the event driven graphs both the dimensions reach a saturation point after the end of the events (ca. 100 hours for the World Series, ca 400 hours for the Black Friday).

Figure 1. Number of vertices and number of edges of: italian sampling (green), world series (blue), and black friday (black) as functions of hours. blue and black vertical lines show the ends of the corresponding events

4. MEASURES DESCRIPTION AND TREND

In the following paragraphs we describe the results obtained by performing structural measures on the three graphs

4.1 Average Distance

The charts in Figure 2 show the different distribution of the average distance in the three datasets as a function of hours, number of vertices and number of vertices. The average distance $Avg(G)$ defined as follows:

$$Avg(G) = \frac{\sum_{d \geq 1} d \cdot \text{number of pairs of vertices at distance } d}{\text{number of connected pairs of vertices}}$$

The large dimensions of the data sets made computationally infeasible the exact calculation of the shortest path lengths. For this reason, we used a sample of a square root of the total vertices of the graphs obtaining an high statistical confidence (an estimated 1% error). It is important to underscore the convergence to 6 of the Italian sampling showing the more social behavior of this network with respect the event driven graphs which attain a convergence to more than 8 for the World Series and more than 16 for the Black Friday. It is important to underline that, in spite of the linear growth of the sampling graph, both in terms of the edges and vertices, the average distance in almost constant during all of observation after a first initial adjustment period. The convergence to a constant factor for the event driven graphs is not surprising since after the end of the events, the graphs do not change.

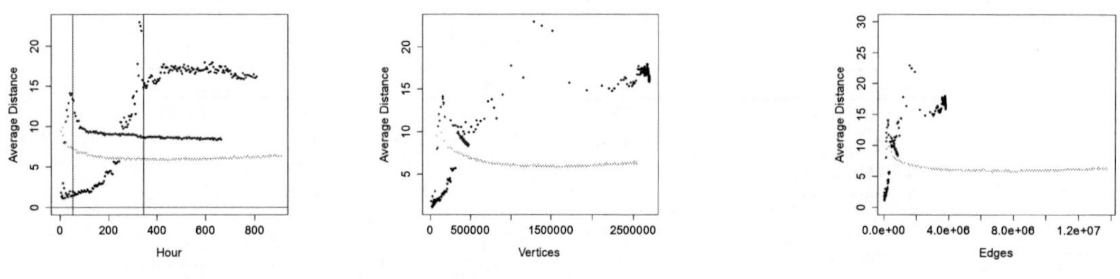

Figure 2. Average distance of the italian sampling (green), world series (blue), and black Friday (black) as function of hours, vertices and edges. Blue and black vertical lines show when the two events end

4.2 Clustering Coefficient

As a second feature we considered the evolution of the global clustering coefficient as widely used in social science and introduced by Barrat and Weigt [Barrat 2000] in the mathematical and physical literature. The global clustering coefficient quantifies the probability that if a vertex A is connected to vertex B and vertex B is connected to vertex C then the vertex A will also be connected to vertex C. In other word, the probability that the friend of your friend is likely also to be your friend. Thus, the clustering coefficient be quantified as follows:

$$C = \frac{3 \times number\ of\ triangles\ in\ the\ network}{number\ of\ paths\ of\ length\ 2}$$

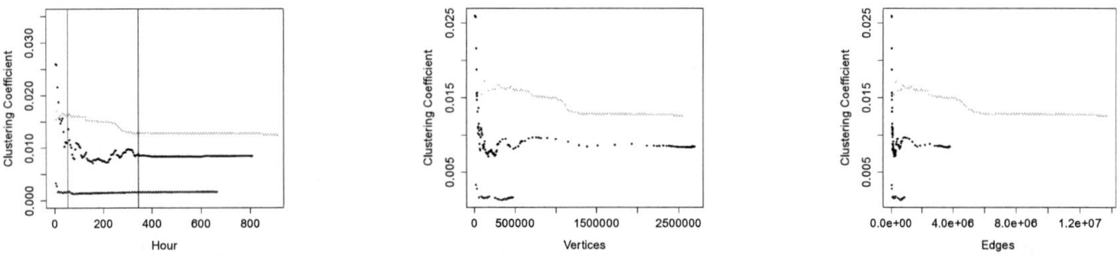

Figure 3. Clustering coefficient of the italian sampling (green), world series (blue), and black Friday (black) as function of hours, vertices and edges. Blue and black vertical lines show when the two events end

In Figure 3, we show the clustering coefficient evolution in the three datasets. A high clustering coefficient is another property commonly attributed to social networks. In [Myers et al 2015] the authors considered the local clustering coefficient as introduced by Watts and Strogatz [Watts et al. 1998]. The results derived are as follows: 0.23 average clustering coefficient for the Twitter mutual follower graph for degree =5 while for Facebook is 0.4 (under the same assumption for the degree); for degree = 20, Facebook is 0.3 and the mutual graph is 0.19. Again, in our collections the evolution of the clustering coefficients testifies the difference between the event driven retweet graphs and the sampling graph. The clustering coefficient in the sampling graphs is of one order of magnitude greater that the ones in the World Series and the Black Friday, showing a more social behavior of the sampling graph. Also in this case, even if both the dimensions of the sampling graph increase almost linearly, the clustering coefficient, after an initial period of decrease, remains nearly constant.

4.3 Max in- and out-degree

In Figure 4 we show the max in- and out degree of the three datasets. In all the three graphs both the max-out and the max-in degree grow linearly over the time with different steepness.

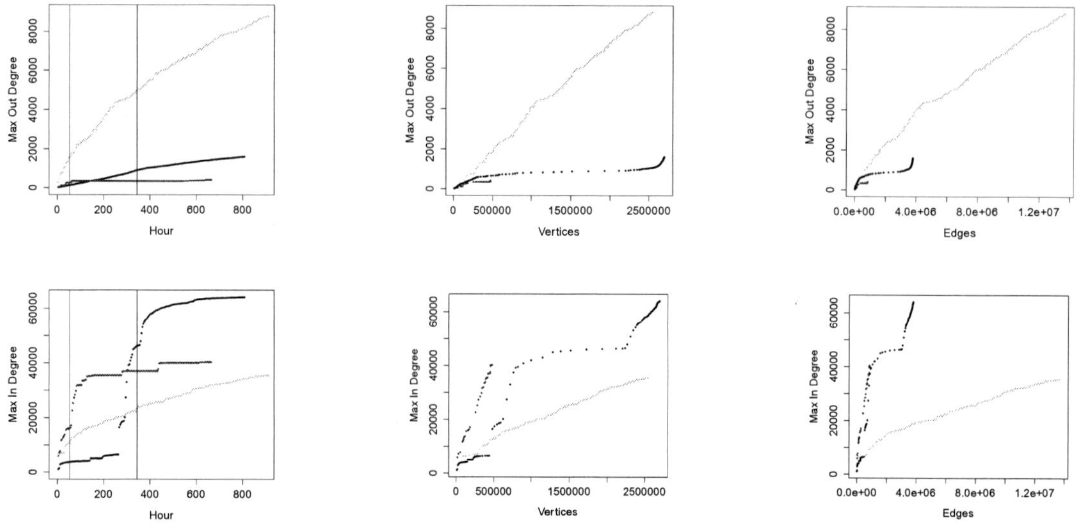

Figure 4. Max-out-degree and Max-in-degree of the italian sampling (green), world series (blue), and black Friday (black) as function of hours, vertices and edges. Blue and black vertical lines show when the two events end

4.4 Number of Connected Components

Figure 5 shows the evolution of the number of strongly connected components that grows linearly with respect to number of nodes. This is probably because the graphs are sparse and the there is a large number of small components.

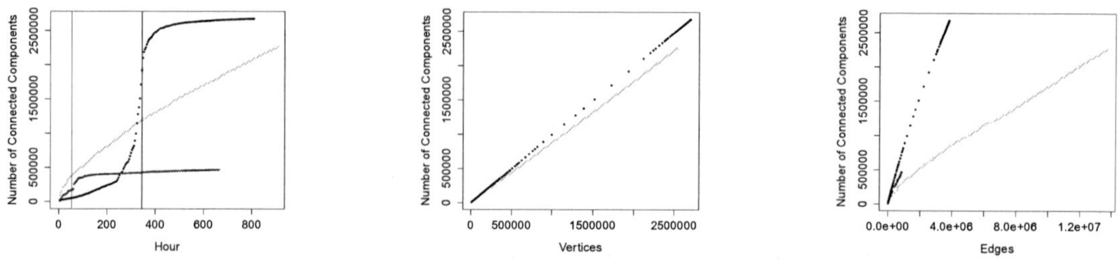

Figure 5. Number of connected components of the italian sampling (green), world series (blue), and black Friday (black) as function of hours, vertices and edges. Blue and black vertical lines show when the two events end

4.5 Size of the Largest Components

Figure 6 shows that, opposite to the result in [Myers et al 2014] where the authors showed that the size of the largest weakly connected components contains 92,9% of all active accounts, in our retweet graphs the largest connected component is only the 11% of the number of nodes in the sampling retweet graph and around the 1% for the event driven graph. This does not contradict the result in [Thijet al. 2015], since they consider the weak largest component while in our analysis we consider the strong connected components.

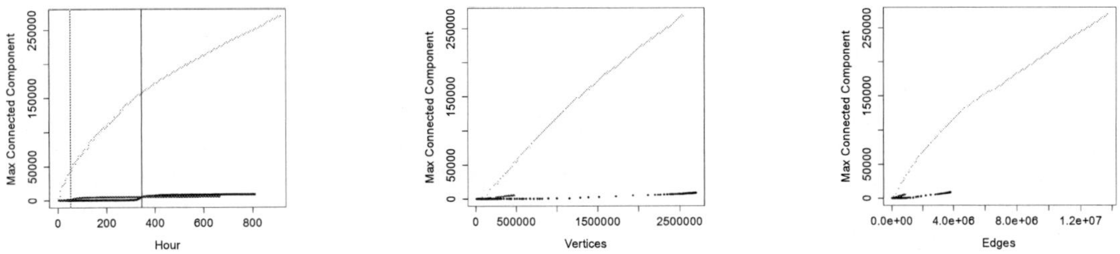

Figure 6. Size of the largest strongly connected component of the italian sampling (green), world series (blue), and black Friday (black) as function of hours, vertices and edges. Blue and black vertical lines show when the two events end

5. ANALYSIS

The performed analysis can be summarized as follows (see Figure 1):

1) All measures are not perturbed in the Retweet graph evolution over time with a significant sample of the stream. Average Distance and Clustering Coefficient are the only measures that converge.
2) Clustering Coefficient of the Retweet graphs of events do also converge over time but to a limit much below the limit of the Clustering Coefficient of the Streaming Sample.
3) The Average Distance of event-driven Retweet graphs do also converge over time but to a limit that is much above that of the Average Distance of the Streaming Sample.
4) Ignoring perturbations, all the other measures (Max-In-Degree, Max-Out-Degree, Number of Connected Components, Max size of a Connected Component) grow almost linearly with respect to graph size (either in terms of vertices or edges).
5) Max-In-Degree and Max-Out-Degree have a steep growth just after the end of the observed event. These two measures are much larger than the corresponding values of the Sampling Retweet Graph. The reason is that after the end of an event there are a few number of hubs and authorities that Retweet or are Retweeted respectively.
6) Linear regression models over time show that Clustering Coefficient and Average Distance can be strongly characterized in all Retweet graphs.
    i) In particular, we have observed that the Average Distance can be characterized by a positive correlation with the Max-Out-Degree and inversely correlated to the size of the retweet graph in terms of the number of edges and the Maximum Connected Component.
    ii) More significantly the Clustering Coefficient has a positive correlation with the Max-Out and Max-in Degrees, the number of connected components and negative correlation with the size of the graph both in terms of the number of vertices and edges.

Figure 7. Linear Regression Models for the Cluster Coefficient and Average Distance. Cluster Coefficient depends on three significant measures, number of Vertices, Max Connected Component and Max-Out-Degree. Average Distance depends on the number of Edges, Vertices and Connected Components, and Max-In-Degree and Max-Out-Degree. Residuals accumulate to zero at increasing time. Outliers are at the beginning of Retweet graph constructions

6. CONCLUSIONS

Thanks to the Big Data technology, we have performed an extensive analysis of the evolution of retweet graphs relative to three Twitter streams for different periods of time. This is one of the first papers that systematically studies the temporal growth of graphs generated by a social network. We conducted the analysis on two types of graphs: the event-driven graphs and the graph constructed by sampling. The measures considered have strongly discriminated against the two types of graphs. From this preliminary analysis we can derive abstract models for classification and evolution. One open problem remains in to rigorously define a mathematical model that describes the evolution of Twitter graphs according to topic, communities and type of events.

ACKNOWLEDGEMENTS

This work was conducted in the Laboratory of Big Data of ISCOM-MISE (Institute of communication of the Italian Ministry for Economic Development).

REFERENCES

Amati G., Angelini S., Bianchi M., Fusco G., Gambosi G., Gaudino G., Marcone G., Rossi G. and Vocca P. 2015. Moving Beyond the Twitter Follow Graph. *In proceeding of DART 2015,* DOI: 10.5220/0005616906120619.

Barrat, A. and Weigt, M., (2000). On the properties of smallworld networks, Eur. Phys. J. B 13, 547–560.

S. Bhamidi, J. M. Steele, and T. Zaman. (2012) Twitter event networks and the superstar model. *arXiv preprint arXiv:1211.3090.*

Bhattacharya D., Ram S. (2012) "Sharing News Articles Using 140 Characters: A Diffusion Analysis on Twitter", *In Advances in Social Networks Analysis and Mining (ASONAM), 2012 IEEE/ACM International Conference on*, pages 966-971. IEEE.

Bild D.R., Liu Y., Dick R. P., Z. Morley Mao, and Dan S. Wallach. 2015. Aggregate characterization of account behavior in Twitter and analysis of the retweet graph. *ACM Trans. Internet Technol.*, 15(1):4:1–4:24, March 2015

Kwak H., Lee C., Park H., and Moon S. (2010). What is twitter, a social network or a news media? *In Proceedings of the 19th International Conference on World Wide Web, WWW '10*, pages 591–600, New York, NY, USA, 2010. ACM.

Myers S.A:, Sharma A., Gupta P., and Lin J. (2014). Information network or social network?: The structure of the twitter follow graph. *In Proceedings of the Companion Publication of the 23rd International Conference on World Wide Web Companion, WWW Companion '14*, pages 493–498, Republic and Canton of Geneva, Switzerland, 2014. International World Wide Web Conferences Steering Committee.

Java A., Song X., Finin T., and Tseng B. (2007) Why we twitter: Understanding microblogging usage and communities. *In Proceedings of the 9th WebKDD and 1st SNAKDD 2007 Workshop on Web Mining and Social Network Analysis, WebKDD/SNA-KDD '07*, pages 56–65, New York, NY, USA, 2007. ACM.

Thij M, Ouboter T, Worm D, Litvak N., Hans van den Berg, Sandjai Bhulai, (2015). Modelling of Trends in Twitter Using Retweet Graph Dynamics. *Algorithms and Models for the Web Graph, Lecture Notes in Computer Science*, Vol. 8882, pp 132-147.

Thij M. and Bhulai S. (2016) Modelling Trend Progression Through an Extension of the Polya Urn Process. *Proceedings of Advances in Network Science: 12th International Conference and School*, NetSci-X 2016, Wroclaw, Poland, January 11-13, 2016, Springer International Publishing, pp.57-67.

Watts D. J. and Strogatz S. H. (1998). Collective dynamics of'small-world' networks. *Nature*, 1998.

Zhou Z., Bandari R., Kong J., Qian H., and Roychowdhury V.. (2010) Information resonance on Twitter: watching Iran. *In Proceedings of the First Workshop on Social Media Analytics,* pages 123-131. ACM.

Zubiaga A., Spina D., Martínez R., Fresno V.. (2015) Real-time classification of Twitter trends. *Journal of the Association for Information Science and Technology,* Vol. 66, 3, pp. 462.

THE ROLE OF DATA ASSETS IN THE ORGANIZATIONAL SUCCESS

Stanislav Mamonov[1] and Tamilla Mavlanova[2]

[1]*Assistant Professor, Department of Information Management and Business Analytics, Feliciano School of Business Montclair State University, Montclair, NJ 07030*

[2]*Assistant Professor in Residence, Department of Operations and Information Management, School of Business, University of Connecticut, Storrs, CT 06268*

ABSTRACT

In this paper we examine the role of data resources in the organizational success. We contrast the resource-based view and the relational view theories to examine how data resources can help organizations create and capture value. We use two case studies from two different industries to understand how different types of data resources can contribute to the organizational success. We conclude that while data often serve as a required resource for entry into new markets, strategic partnerships play a critical role in capturing value created through exploitation of data resources.

KEYWORDS

Big Data, data resource, relational view, resource-based view

1. INTRODUCTION

Data resources are generally viewed as an important organizational IT resource [13], however there has been relatively little work examining how data resources contribute to value creation and capture across different industries. Data resources often require a significant investment in IT infrastructure and management costs. Understanding how data resources can contribute to the organizational success would help in the organizational strategy formulation and investment decisions. This is particularly true in the world of Big Data that is characterized by the increasing data availability [5].

Extant research on how IT creates value for a firm has been done from either the internal or the external perspectives. Internally focused view emphasizes the role of unique organizational processes and resources in establishing a competitive advantage in a given market. Externally focused view emphasizes the role of inter-organizational partnerships in value co-creation. To understand how data resources are used and how they contribute to the organizational success, we compare two theories widely used in the studies on IT value. The resource-based view (RBV) of the firm supports the internal view, and it posits that certain organizational resources, if maintained and used wisely, can provide a sustainable competitive advantage [1,2]. The relational view (RV) of the firm [10,11] supports the external view, and it posits that partnerships and cooperation among the firms as well as sharing resources are the keys to successful inter-organizational competitive advantage.

To address the value of data, we are going to contrast the resource-based view and relational view of the firm using two case studies. The case studies examine two different emergent industries and different types of data resources. This comparison is valuable because it contributes to the theoretical basis for our understanding how data can contribute to value creation and how firms capture this value.

The paper is organized as follows. The next section introduces the resource-based view. It also discusses data resources and the attributes that differentiate data from other types of IS resources. Then a relational view of the firm is introduced. This is followed by a presentation of two case studies. The last section summarizes our findings and contributions as well as study limitations and opportunities for further research.

2. THE RESOURCE-BASED VIEW OF THE FIRM

The resource-based view of a firm emphasizes the role of organizational resources in providing a competitive advantage [1,2,3]. RBV suggests that firms possess two subsets of resources. The first subset empowers the firms to achieve a competitive advantage, and the second subset leads to a greater long-term performance [2,23]. For the organizational resources to be valuable, they have to be rare and appropriable to provide a firm with a competitive advantage. The advantage can be sustained for longer periods of time if the firm manages to protect the resources against imitation, transfer and substitution [23].

Wade and Hulland (2004) grouped resources into either assets, tangible and intangible resources that can be used in producing goods and services, or capabilities, actions used to create goods and services. In Information Systems, assets may include hardware, software, networks, and infrastructure; whereas capabilities can include managerial skills and processes, such as systems development and integration [23]. Tangible IS assets are considered the easiest resources to copy, and therefore they are least likely to provide a firm with a source of sustainable competitive advantage. Meanwhile, capabilities and intangible assets are harder to imitate [20] and they can drive the firm's performance [22].

Data resources are different from other IS resources used in resource-based research such as hardware, software, networks, and IT infrastructure [23]. Levitin and Redman (1998) analyzed data as a resource and found that data have unique characteristics [16]. Unlike other resources, data are shareable, and they can be utilized by many users at the same time, while producing different information products. Data are copyable and transportable, and considering the speed of transferring digital files, data can be transported efficiently. Data are nonfungible, meaning that although we can substitute one dataset with a similar dataset, we cannot substitute one data item with another data item because data items are unique. Data are versatile and can be used for many different purposes. Data are also characterized by depreciability. However, unlike other resources, data depreciates not from inevitable wear and tear, but from time. Newer data can have more relevance than old data, although data mining techniques can reveal interesting patterns in historical data. In addition, unlike many other resources, data are renewable and new data can be collected and analyzed all the time [16].

3. THE RELATIONAL VIEW OF THE FIRM

In contrast to the resource-based view, that suggests that the source of competitive advantage is contained within the firm, the relational view argues that a firm's critical resources may extend beyond firm boundaries. In other words, firms that combine their resources in certain ways may realize an advantage over competing firms that are unable or unwilling to create partnerships [10].

According to Dyer and Singh (1998), the competitive advantage of partnerships is based on four components. First, firms need to invest in relation-specific assets. Second, they should establish knowledge exchange and joint learning. Third, firms should combine their complementary resources and capabilities, especially if they are scarce, to create new products and services. Fourth, firms should promote effective governance mechanisms.

Grover and Kohli (2012) expanded the relational view by applying it to the IT context in a form of four layers. The asset layer involves specific IT skills or assets that enhance the relationship between firms. The knowledge layer is powered by common knowledge sharing platforms and analytics. The capabilities layer involves unique IT skills, and the governance layer provides effective management of the other three layers.

Data resources can be classified as a shareable asset. Data can easily be shared with partners, however similar to other relationship-specific assets, data have to be safeguarded to avoid opportunism, as suggested by Dyer and Singh (1998). Data are a useful resource to establish input for knowledge exchange and learning, and can be used for the development of new products, services and processes. Data can interact with complementary resources, such as additional datasets and analytics, and become a source of value that a partner could not capture individually. The governance focuses on promoting value creating initiatives such as investing in relation-specific assets, sharing knowledge or merging complementary resources [10]. Thus, the effective governance mechanisms may allow partners to make greater investments in relation-specific data resources; credibly assure partners that knowledge produced based on data resources will not be easily shared with others, and complementary resources will not be copied or duplicated.

The resource-based view and the relational view perspectives offer distinct recommendations on how firms should leverage data assets to create and capture value. On the one hand, the RBV perspective suggests that firms are best served by exclusively exploiting their data resources and safeguarding wherever possible from potential imitation and substitution. The relational perspective suggests that firms need to leverage existing resources to establish partnerships with other market participants that would help the firms to create and capture value. To ascertain the validity of the predictions of the two competing perspectives, we conducted two case studies focusing on two emergent data-intensive industries.

4. RESEARCH DESIGN

The question of how data resources affect organizational success requires the assessment of a broad set of contextual and organizational factors. Case study methodology is a recommended approach for the study of complex phenomena in real-world contexts [12,24]. The two case studies presented here focus on Small & Medium Business Financing and Online Display Advertising industries respectively.

The results and analysis presented here is a part of an on-going research program that began in 2012. The data presented here cover the period between November 2012 and July 2015. In order to maximize the internal validity of the case studies, we triangulated across multiple sources of information. We interviewed the company executives, and reviewed published annual reports and other materials shared by the companies. For the Online Display Advertising case study we also interviewed the executives from competing companies to further expand our understanding of the key industry practices.

Table 1. Data sources

Case study	Data sources
SMB Financing	Primary data sources: Several rounds of interviews with senior executives in November 2013, March 2014, March 2015, June 2015. Secondary data sources: OnDeck Capital S1 Statement, OnDeck Capital Annual Report 2014, OnDeck Capital Investor Presentation, Q1, 2015.
Online Display Advertising	Primary data sources: Interviews with executives in display advertising industry, December 2013, April 2014, April 2015. Secondary data sources: Criteo Annual Report 2014, Criteo Investor presentation Q1, 2015.

Below we present a brief overview of the emergent market structures in the respective industries. In each case, we focus on the role of data resources in providing the initial and the sustainable competitive advantages for the leading companies in the respective industries. Following the recommendations for "best practices" in case study research [24], we conclude with a comparative discussion on the role of data resources and IT-enabled partnerships as the critical sources of the initial and the sustainable competitive advantage in each industry.

5. CASES

5.1 Case 1. Alternative SMB Financing Industry

The 28 million small and medium size businesses (SMBs) provide nearly half of all jobs in the private sector in the United States and contribute about 48% of the gross domestic product [21]. Oliver Wyman, a management consulting firm, estimates the unmet demand in the SMB financing industry at $80-$120 billion [4]. This presents a tremendous business opportunity. The evolution of the Internet as a business-to-business (B2B) service channel offers a novel conduit for acquiring and servicing SMB loans by non-traditional lenders. However, the challenge of assessing SMB creditworthiness requires the development of a novel approach to credit scoring. OnDeck Capital is among the leading companies in this space. The company was founded in 2007 to specifically focus on SMB lending [18]. The company built a proprietary credit-scoring model leveraging transactional business bank account data as the key source of information about SMB creditworthiness. Intuitively, this approach makes perfect sense. SMB ability to repay a loan is directly dependent on the free cash flow generated by the business. The bank accounts provide a reliable third-party source of this information.

OnDeck partnered with Yodlee, a company that provides real-time access to transactional data in business bank accounts, and built a proprietary credit scoring model based on the financial transactional data captured in the bank accounts. Instead of focusing on the personal SMB owners' credit scores, OnDeck assesses the financial health of the applicant SMBs reflected in the transactional business bank account data [18].

OnDeck faced a significant cold start problem in assessing SMB loan credit risk. To assess the creditworthiness of a new SMB loan application, the company needed to have past loan performance data that could be used to predict loan repayment. To gather the data necessary to build the credit-scoring model, OnDeck collected industry, financial and geographic data about the businesses that applied for loans. To determine the outcome of individual lending decisions, the company needed to risk its own capital and issue loans to the SMBs applying for credit. According to the company, the average value of a loan issued by the company is $35,000 [18]. This means that the company risked $70 million in capital to collect just 2000 records to build the initial credit-scoring model.

OnDeck went public in December 2014 and the company shared its operating performance results with the investors in the pre-IPO disclosures. OnDeck announced that in the period between 2007 and 2014, the company had issued over 27,000 SMB loans with the combined value over $1.2 billion [18]. The collected data presents an invaluable data resource underpinning OnDeck operations. Our discussions with the company senior management revealed that the first version of the credit-scoring model built by OnDeck in 2008 could not evaluate creditworthiness of more than 35% of loan applications – the company simply did not have enough historical data to assess the risk. OnDeck Capital reports that the fifth version of its credit-scoring model can evaluate 99% of the applications that the company receives [19].

Being the first mover in the alternative SMB lending space afforded OnDeck the opportunity to gain the initial advantage over the later entrants into the market by building the key intangible data asset (past SMB loan performance data) that underpins the company ability to reliably assess SMB credit risk. Given the initial advantage developed by OnDeck, one would expect that the company place in the SMB lending space would be secure. However, the company IPO filing also had unintended consequences.

OnDeck pre-IPO disclosures [18], that were released in the third quarter of 2014, revealed the attractiveness of the alternative SMB lending business to other potential market participants. Shortly following the disclosures, a new set of players entered the SMB lending market. Many of these players came from the personal loan industry that rebranded themselves as SMB loan providers [17]. Without the benefit of historical loan-performance data and driven by the voracious appetite for new revenue, the new players in the SMB lending space often offer terms to potential clients that are not supported by any financial business performance records provided by the applicants. The new competition is undermining OnDeck margins. OnDeck 2014 Annual Report states that "the fourth quarter of 2014 marked our eighth consecutive quarter of price reductions as we continue to pass savings along to our customers", reflecting the growing competition in the SMB lending space [19].

In the ongoing competition, the main objective of both well-informed and poorly-informed market participants is to gain as much market share as possible. In this environment, partnerships with companies that can offer access to the SMB owners is very important for the long term success. Recognizing the importance of such partnerships, OnDeck developed a platform that allows small business consultants to offer SMB loans to their clients in exchange for a fee. OnDeck has also signed an agreement with Intuit, the maker of popular QuickBooks accounting software used by many SMB owners. The strategic partnerships supported through IT platforms will allow OnDeck to reach their target audience and they will likely prove to be the critical strategic asset in defining long-term company success. Figure 1 summarizes the key data resources and industry participants in SMB lending.

5.2 Case 2. Online Display Advertising Industry

Online marketing is rapidly gaining its share of the overall marketing budgets (Ad Council 2015). Online display advertising is expected to reach $63.2 billion globally in 2015 (Lunden 2014). The sophistication of online consumer targeting has evolved rapidly in the past several years. Online Ad Exchanges, that sell available advertising inventory in near real-time as the consumers load the web pages, now handle more than half of all available online display advertising inventory (BI Intelligence 2015). The Ad Exchanges bring together Publishers, operators of content web sites that make money by selling advertising, and Advertisers, entities interested in displaying ads to specific consumers. Potential ad impressions are offered on Ad Exchanges as the consumers visit specific web pages and Advertisers have about 100 milliseconds to place bids for the available inventory (BI Intelligence 2015). The second best bid auction format stimulates the bidders to reveal their reservation prices and the bid floor levels offer the same for the Publishers. Floor prices reflect the minimum bids that would be accepted by a Publisher on a specific advertisement spot. The floor levels are typically known only to the exchanges and they are hidden from the Advertisers.

Consumer data plays a critical role in online advertising optimization. Behavioral tracking facilitated by placing cookies typically follows consumers across a panel of about 15,000 web sites that serve as proxies for consumer interests and current purchase considerations. For example, a visit to the ESPN web site would signal a general interest in sports, while a visit to cars.com would serve as a signal of possible consumer interest in purchasing a car. Estimates suggest that companies engaged in online consumer tracking collect information on roughly 190 million consumers in the United States and about 500 million consumers globally [8]. Collecting data on such scale generates petabytes of data on a weekly basis and requires sophisticated technical infrastructure to support data collection and analysis. To understand the role of different IT assets in providing the initial and the sustained competitive advantage in the online display advertising industry we will focus on Criteo, a leader in the online advertising optimization industry.

Criteo was founded in Paris, France in 2005 and the company went public in 2013 [8]. The company initially focused on developing recommendation engine solutions for e-retail clients and Publisher web sites, but it quickly emerged as a leader in online marketing. In its latest annual report for 2014, Criteo reported revenues of €745 million (approximately $846 million) with 83.7% of the revenues coming from outside of France [8]. The company is unique in the online advertising space in that it offers solutions to both Publishers and Advertisers. It counts over 10,000 Publishers and 7,000 Advertisers as clients. Criteo effectively performs SSP and a DSP functions for their Publisher and Advertiser clients respectively. The company reports having delivered over 1.7 trillion targeted ads in 2014 and generating over $16.5 billion in sales from targeted ads for their Advertisers [8]. Criteo infrastructure includes several globally distributed data centers hosting over 11,000 servers with the combined storage capacity over 38 petabytes.

What is truly remarkable is that Criteo established this position with seemingly little in the way of technical innovation. The company reports that it has only a single patent issued in France, and only three patents issued in the United States, while six patent applications are pending [8]. The very limited technical intellectual property portfolio suggests that Criteo is primarily relying on commodity hardware and common algorithmic solutions to perform advertising optimization for their clients. Our interviews with the executives revealed that the minimum technical infrastructure required to capture petabytes of data and to build predictive models is quite expensive, with the minimum required investment of $50-60 million for the infrastructure. While it is a significant barrier for industry entry, there is little that differentiates the competing offerings in terms of the underlying technology.

The time sensitivity of the underlying data undermines the value of data resources possessed by Criteo. The most recent consumer behavior data offers the best clues to the specific consumer interests and the data beyond the most recent few weeks generally have little predictive value [6]. Petabytes of historical data have little value beyond just a few weeks from the moment of collection.

Although the company executives are hesitant to publicly discuss company strategy, it is clear that Criteo management recognized these industry constraints early on and instead of developing intellectual property to protect its market position, the company instead invested heavily in developing partnerships with its Publisher clients. Criteo has built one of the largest advertising networks in the industry that includes over 10,000 Publishers. While the advertising network relies on commodity technology, its value stems from the access that it offers to advertisers. Larger advertisers prefer to work with advertising networks that can reach a wide audience. Since Criteo offers a one-stop solution for accessing and optimizing advertisements across a broad network, it has attracted a loyal patronage from top-tier advertisers. This creates a virtuous cycle of partner relationships supported through IT infrastructure. The company offers access to a large audience, which attracts advertisers. Criteo's ability to monetize the publisher web sites through advertising attracts new high quality publishers to join the advertising network. Criteo annual report states that the company revenue from established accounts grew 146% from 2013 to 2014 [8]. The most recent filings from the company suggest that this trend continues [9].

6. DISCUSSION

6.1 Case Analysis

Applying the resource-based view of the firm perspective to the case studies, we find a significant variation in the type of data resources that are critical to the two industries. Loan performance datasets are relatively small, however they are very costly to obtain. The data asset utilization profile in the online display advertising industry operates with Big Data of petabyte size. These data require a substantial investment in technical infrastructure for capture and analysis. The industry also faces a rapid depreciation of the data value. Table 2 summarizes the key dimensions of data resources according the RBV perspective.

Table 2. RBV dimensions of data resources in the SMB Lending and Digital Advertising industries

	SMB Lending Industry. Data resource: past loan performance data.	**Digital Advertising Industry.** Data resource: consumer behavior data
Size	Relatively small dataset, however the feature set is growing.	Big Data, petabytes of data covering 500+ million consumers across 15,000+ web sites.
Appropriability	Past loan performance data is required for risk assessment of new business loan applications.	Recent online consumer behavior data is essential for digital advertising optimization.
Assessment of rarity	The data resource is rare, requires a significant investment of capital and time to obtain.	The data resources are potentially available from multiple third parties.
Vulnerability to imitation, transfer and substitution.	The early entrant in the industry is facing "naked" imitation from competitors that do not possess the data asset.	The data resource is highly time sensitive, information loses value quickly.

The following insights emerge from the cross-industry analysis of the data resource utilization. First, while Big Data dominates the media, relatively small data resources can be extremely valuable. The SMB lending industry illustrates the value of relatively small datasets.

The second insight from the cross-industry analysis is that Big Data resources may have a very limited useful lifespan. The data resources commonly used in the Digital Advertising Industry require a significant investment in infrastructure to collect, however the value of information depreciates rapidly. The relative lack of differentiation among the data providers in online display advertising has contributed to the perception of Big Data assets being a commodity in this industry diminishing the perceived value of these assets.

The third insight that emerges from the cross-industry analysis is that, in some cases, the companies that made the strategic investment in data resources, may face competition from "naked" imitators. Thus, the data resources in themselves do not afford a source of sustainable competitive advantage to the first movers that make the investment in the requisite data resources. The example of the SMB lending industry reveals that it is possible to imitate data resources by effectively decoupling analytical capabilities tied to data resources (business loan credit risk assessment) from business function (loan offer). Imitators in the SMB space make loan offers to prospective borrowers contingent on the successful procurement of a loan offer from the company possessing the required credit default risk evaluation expertise thus bypassing the need to collect the data required for credit risk assessment themselves.

The relational view emphasizes the importance of partnerships for creating and capturing business value. Applying the relational perspective to the SMB lending and online display advertising industries, we find that both industries reveal the importance of strategic partnerships in converting the first mover advantage into a sustainable leadership position. In the case of SMB lending industry, OnDeck developed a strategic relationship with a key vendor in the SMB service space (Intuit) thus gaining access to the millions of small businesses that already use the Quickbooks accounting platform. OnDeck also developed an IT-enabled platform that offers partnerships to SMB consultants and advisors. Recognizing that data resources for digital marketing are highly time sensitive and historical data offers little value, Criteo, a leading company in the online display advertising industry, invested heavily into building partnerships with Publishers. This focus reflected the importance of the audience reach as the key factor in advertising budget allocation – the larger advertisers need global reach. It also reflects the complementarity of capabilities and resources between the traditional publishers and the technology companies in this industry. The Publishers specialize in content development that attracts an audience to online resources. The technology providers create value by optimizing monetization of the user traffic by personalizing the digital advertisements shown to each visitor.

Applying the four level framework proposed by Grover and Kohli (2012), we find that in both industries, the SMB lending and the online display advertising, there is little in the way of asset, knowledge or capability sharing. In both industries, the companies that made an investment in developing data assets have tightly integrated those assets within the core IT-enabled services that they offer, however the data assets are not shared with any partners and neither is there sharing of knowledge nor capabilities. Further, the two case studies do not support the Relational View proposition (Dyer and Singh 1998) that trust provides an effective governance structure in supporting value co-creation. Both OnDeck and Criteo rely on legal contracts to precisely structure their relationships with the key partners. Table 3 summarizes the observed asset, knowledge, and capability sharing arrangements as well as the governance structures within each industry.

Table 3. Value co-creation layers in the SMB lending an online display advertising industries

	SMB Lending Industry. Key partners: SMB service providers, e.g. Intuit, business advisors.	**Digital Advertising Industry.** Key partners: Publishers, Advertisers.
Assets	Assets are not shared with partners. Assets are converted to services. Loan performance data powers the risk assessment within an integrated SMB loan service.	Assets are not shared with partners. Consumer behavior data is embedded in SSP/DSP service.
Knowledge	Proprietary knowledge (SMB credit scoring expertise) is not shared with the partners.	Knowledge is not shared with the partners.
Capabilities	No joint capabilities development. IT-enabled systems enable partner revenue growth.	No joint capabilities development. IT-enabled systems enable partner revenue growth.
Governance	Contractual relationship.	Contractual relationships.

6.2 Contributions

Our study contributes to both theory and practice. We contrasted two industries and two different types of data resources, and evaluated how data resources along with strategic partnerships bring value to the firms.

From the theoretical perspective, our results suggest that the RBV and RV theories can be successfully used in studying the combined effect of valuable resources and strategic partnerships. We also find that data as a resource have to be evaluated differently as opposed to other resources due to the dynamic complexity surrounding this resource. For example, we find that while the data resources played a key role in the creation of novel business models in the SMB lending and online display advertising industries, as is suggested by the RBV perspective, we also find that over the longer term, unique data assets fail to offer a sustainable competitive advantage due to strategies employed by later industry entrants. Consistent with the relational view, we find that business partnerships do become an important source of competitive advantage, but instead of an investment in shared assets, knowledge and capabilities through partnerships, contractual relationships leveraged unique capabilities of each partner.

Our key contribution to practice emerges from the analysis of the commonalities of strategies employed by both OnDeck and Criteo in the respective industries. While the two industries share little in common in terms of the structure or the core data resources, the emergent strategies employed by the early entrants that are successfully managing the transition to more mature industry structures are strikingly similar. In both cases, the companies have used the initial advantage gained through novel applications of data sources and information technology to develop standardized IT-enabled service offerings and immediately focused on the development of standard, contractually governed partnerships that accelerated the adoption of IT-enabled services by a large network of customers and partners. This approach affords the protection of proprietary data resources, because they are encapsulated in IT systems and prevent any partner from misappropriating the data. At the same time, encapsulation of data resources and analytical capabilities in standardized IT-enabled service offerings maximized the efficiencies in marketing the services to potential clients.

Lastly, we would like to note that no research is without limitations. Our analysis employs the case study methodology that affords the study of complex phenomena in natural contexts, but it is nonetheless limited by the selection of the specific case studies. Consequently, the results may not generalize to other contexts. Further research would be required to evaluate the generalizability of the results presented here.

REFERENCES

[1] Barney, J. Firm resources and sustained competitive advantage. *Journal of Management 17*, 1 (1991), 99–120.

[2] Barney, J. Information Technology and Sustained Competitive Advantage: A Analysis IT and Competitive Advantage. *MIS Quarterly 19*, 4 (1995), 487–505.

[3] Barney, J.B. Strategic Factor Markets: Expectations, Luck, and Business Strategy. *Management Science 32*, 10 (1986), 1231–1241.

[4] Carroll, P. and Hoffman, B. *Financing Small Businesses.* 2014.

[5] Chen, H., Chiang, R., and Storey, V. Business Intelligence and Analytics: From Big Data to Big Impact. *MIS Quarterly 36*, 4 (2012), 1165–1188.

[6] Chen, J. and Stallaert, J. An economic analysis of online advertising using behavioral targeting. *Mis Quarterly 38*, 2 (2014), 429–449.

[7] Council, C. *Big Shift to Digital and Data Marketing Is Shaking up Client Relationships with Ad/Media Agency Partners.* 2015.

[8] Criteo. *Criteo Annual Report 2014.* 2015.

[9] Criteo. Criteo Reports Record Results For The Third Quarter 2015 And Reiterates Its Full-Year 2015 Outlook Despite Negative Foreign Exchange Impacts. *Criteo Investor Relations*, 2015.

[10] Dyer, J.H. and Singh, H. The relational view: Cooperative strategy and sources of interorganizational competitive advantage. *Academy of Management Review 23*, 4 (1998), 660–679.

[11] Dyer, J.H. *Collaborative advantage: Winning through extended enterprise supplier networks.* Oxford University Press, 2000.

[12] Eisenhardt, K.M. Building Theories from Case Study Research. *Academy of Management Review 14*, 4 (1989), 532–550.

[13] Fisher, T. *The data asset: How smart companies govern their data for business success.* John Wiley & Sons, 2009.

[14] Grover, V. and Kohli, R. Cocreating IT Value: New Capabilities and Metrics for Multifirm Environments. *MIS Quarterly 36*, 1 (2012), 225–232.

[15] Intelligence, B. The Programmatic Advertising Report: Mobile, video, and real-time bidding drive growth in programmatic. *Business Insider*, 2015. http://www.businessinsider.com/buyers-and-sellers-have-overwhelmingly-adopted-programmatic-with-mobile-leading-growth-2015-3.

[16] Levitin, A. V. and Redman, T.C. Data as a resource: properties, implications, and prescriptions. *Sloan Management Review 40*, 1 (1998), 89–101.

[17] Lunden, I. Disgraced Payday Lender Wonga Sells SMB Business To Orange Money, Cuts 325 Jobs. *Techcrunch*, 2015. http://techcrunch.com/2015/02/24/wonga-everline-job-cuts-klein/.

[18] OnDeck. *OnDeck S1 Registration.* 2014.

[19] OnDeck. *OnDeck Annual Report 2014.* 2015.

[20] Reed, R. and DeFillippi, R.J. Causal Ambiguity, Barriers to Imitation, and Sustainable Competitive Advantage. *Academy of Management Review 15*, 1 (1990), 88–102.

[21] SBA. Small Business GDP: Update 2002-2010. 2012. https://www.sba.gov/content/small-business-gdp-update-2002-2010.

[22] Teece, D.J., Pisano, G., and Shuen, A. Dynamic capabilities and strategic management. *Strategic Management Journal 18*, 7 (1997), 509–533.

[23] Wade, M. and Hulland, J. Review: The resource-based view and information systems research: Review, extension, and suggestions for future research. *MIS Quarterly 28*, 1 (2004), 107–142.

[24] Yin, R. Case study research: Design and methods . Beverly Hills. 1994.

BIG DATA ANALYTICS IN THE PUBLIC SECTOR: A CASE STUDY OF NEET ANALYSIS FOR THE LONDON BOROUGHS

Daqing Chen[1], Babatunde Asaolu[1] and Chao Qin[2]
[1]Division of Computer Science and Informatics, School of Engineering, London South Bank University
103 Borough Road, London SE1 0AA, UK
[2]School of Electronics and Information, Northwestern Polytechnical University
127 West Youyi Road, Xi'an 710072, China

ABSTRACT

For decades, the issue of young people who are aged 16 -18 and not in employment, education, or training (NEET) has been a major concern for governments and local authorities. In this paper, a big data perspective is taken to examine the NEET issue in order to highlight factors that are correlated with NEET, the negative consequences and causes of NEET, and potential solutions to NEET. The NEET dataset about the 33 London Boroughs has been considered along with other seven datasets relating to population, crime offences, benefits claimants, median property price, active businesses, immigrants, and conception under 18. All the datasets are public-accessible and comprise a data collection of the same period of time from 2009 to 2013. Each of them represents a particular measure. Hierarchical variable clustering, *k*-means clustering, and correlation analysis have been conducted using SAS Enterprise Miner and Tableau in this work. These tools enable us to analyse the problem in a multi-dimensional, hierarchical, integrated, and longitudinal way. The research has demonstrated that a) The NEET issue is much more severe in outer London than in inner London; b) The main factors correlated with NEET vary from inner London to outer London; c) Each of the measures considered has a certain correlation strength with the NEET rate, and amongst them, median property price is a simple and seemingly accurate indicator of areas likely to suffer from NEET and thus to take appropriate precautions in order to reduce the likelihood of further increases in NEET; and d) The London Boroughs can be grouped based on similarities in terms of a set of given measures, and the memberships of the groups remain stable.

KEYWORDS

Big data analytics, NEET analysis, *k*-means clustering, Hierarchical clustering, SAS Enterprise Miner, Tableau.

1. INTRODUCTION

For decades, the issue of young people who are aged 16 -18 and not in employment, education, or training (NEET) has been a major concern for governments and local authorities (Stoten 2014, Woolford 2012). In London particularly, NEET remains a problem within the London Boroughs although many courses of action have been taken and met with varying degrees of success (GLA 2007).

It has been evident that the costs of young people who are NEET can be high, with long-term consequences, not only to the individual, but also to the entire society and the economy as a whole. Therefore, various qualitative and quantitative approaches and techniques have been employed in the attempt to better understand the NEET phenomenon, analyse and identify the main factors that are attributed to NEET, and develop measures to address NEET accordingly (Bymer and Parsons 2002, Stoten 2014, Woolford 2012, Britton, Gregg, MacMillan and Mitchell 2011, Egan M., Daly M., Delaney L 2015). Due to the social and economic complexity of the NEET problem, it becomes essential that multiple factors should be taken into account in the research to reflect the nature of the problem, that is, how various factors are correlated with, and potentially have collectively affected, the existence of the NEET problem.

In this paper, a big data perspective is taken to examine the NEET issue in order to highlight factors that are correlated with NEET, the negative consequences and causes of NEET, and potential solutions to NEET. The NEET dataset about the 33 London Boroughs has been considered along with other seven datasets relating to population, crime offences, benefits claimants, median property price, active businesses, immigrants, and conception under 18. All the datasets are public-accessible and comprise a data collection of the same period of time from 2009 to 2013. Each of them represents a particular measure. Hierarchical variable clustering, *k*-means clustering, and correlation analysis have been conducted using SAS Enterprise Miner and Tableau in this work. These tools enable us to analyse the problem in a multi-dimensional, hierarchical, integrated, and longitudinal way.

The reminder of this paper is organized as follows. In Section II a brief discussion on the relevant work on NEET is given, and the approach adopted to the problem in this research is highlighted. In Section III, the datasets to be considered in this research are described in detail. Further the relevant activities for data pre-processing are discussed in order to deal with data quality issues and to get the data fit for the required analysis. Detailed analysis is given in Section IV, upon which, the main findings from the analysis are discussed in Section V. Finally, the concluding remarks and suggestions for future work are provided in Section VI.

2. RELATED WORK

The issue of NEET has been a concern for governments and local authorities since it was first identified as a problem (Stoten 2014). Various studies have been carried out to identify the characteristics and the causes of NEET. The Youth Cohort Study (Wolford 2012) identified several factors relating to NEET:

- Having no formal qualification;
- Being excluded from school in years 10 or 11;
- Having a disability or health problem;
- Constant truancy in year 11;
- Parent are not in full-time employment;
- Living separately from parents; and
- Looking after own children.

In addition, the study has proposed a more creative approach, known as LIFT, to tackle the issue, including attendance, motivation, behavior, and post-16 participation.

Stoten (2014) explored the problem of NEET in the Cleveland area by looking at what features define NEETs, what would be the best responses in tackling NEET across the region. Stoten designed two plans to address the issue. The first one was a reduction strategy plan, which brought together a consortium of organizations that worked closely together in tackling the issue. It was found that the reduction strategy plan actually had some success and reduced the local NEET rate from 12.8% to 10.2%. The second plan was to raise the school leaving age, and the key to this plan was to minimize young people dropping out post 16.

The Greater London Authority (GLA) performed a study on what were the best practices that stopped young people from being NEET in London, and further recommended various ways to help reduce and prevent NEET in London (GLA 2007).

In the research undertaken by Bymer and Parsons (2002), there were two fundamental questions that the research was concerned and intended to find answers to: 1) Are NEETs simply a group who have failed to do well in school or are there other factors which set them on a route with little or no opportunity; and 2) Is being NEET just a temporary stage in life due to disadvantages and failures or does being NEET itself constitute as a condition that makes it hard to adjust to adult life. A longitudinal dataset from the British birth cohort study in the 1970s was used and a logistic regression model was employed in the research. The dataset was collected from a variety of sources, including interviews with teachers, parents, self-completed questionnaires and tests. Young males and females were assessed separately as variables for predicting who can be classified as NEET. Bymer and Parsons concluded that, there is little doubt that poor educational qualifications have an impact on being branded as NEET. Lack of parental interest in children's education, labour market, and teen-age pregnancy are also important factors to consider.

All these insightful studies have identified several key factors that could help explain the NEET phenomenon and address the NEET problem in their social environment; however, due to the social and economic complexity of the NEET problem, there are other possible factors, such as crime offences and benefits claimants, that should be explored in order to provide a complete account of the problem. This research intends to further expand on some of the issues raised in these studies, and use big data approach to examine various factors that are correlated with and possibly attributed to NEET.

3. DATA CONSIDERATION

3.1 The Datasets

Various open datasets from the public sector are available. These datasets are usually spatially and temporally related, comprehensive, and are accumulated year on year. As an enriched data repository for analytics, these open datasets provide different measures on various aspects of our society.

In this study a number of open datasets are selected. In addition to the NEET dataset itself, the following seven datasets about the 33 London Boroughs have been chosen. These datasets are considered correlated with NEET in some implicit or explicit ways by their nature:

- Number of crime offences;
- Population of male and female aged 16 - 18;
- Number of immigrants;
- Number of people claiming benefits;
- Number of active businesses;
- Median house price; and
- Number of conceptions under 18.

The data sources and the relevant URLs are shown Table 1. The 33 London Boroughs are listed in Table 2 along with the Local Authority District (LAD) codes. These Boroughs can be grouped as inner and outer London groups. Note that only the Borough level's data is considered in this paper, although other geographical levels' data is available, for instance, LSOA and Ward levels. All the datasets comprise a data collection of the same period of time from 2009 to 2013.

3.2 Data Pre-processing

No quality data, no quality analysis outcomes. Data pre-processing is essential in any data analytics project. Typical data pre-processing tasks include dealing with data quality issues (such as missing values, outliers, and noisy data), and normalizing and transforming the original data to make it fit the required analysis and modelling. In this research, the main activity performed for data pre-processing involves, for each of the eight datasets, transforming all the absolute values (numbers) into the corresponding percentages per Borough. This ensures that meaningful comparison can be made across all the London Boroughs based on a given measure. For example, transforming the number of NEETs of each Borough into a corresponding percentage out of the total number of NEETs in all London Boroughs allows us to compare each Borough's performance with the others based on the measure of the NEET rate. In the following Sections, we use the NEET rate and the number of NEETs interchangeable, and similarly to all the other 7 factors (measures).

All the transformed datasets were further integrated into a fact table which contains the following 12 fields (measures): Borough, Year, Male_Population, Female_Population, Crime_Offences, Active_Businesses, Benefits_Claimants, Immigrants, Conception, NEET, Inner/Outer_London, and Median_House_Price. The fact table was then uploaded into Tableau and SAS Enterprise Miner for analysis.

Table 1. Data Collection

Dataset name	Website name and URL
Number of NEETs	The Greater London Authority data store http://data.london.gov.uk/dataset/young-people-not-employment-education-or-training-borough
Number of crime offences	The Metropolitans Police http://maps.met.police.uk/tables.htm
Population of male and female aged 16 - 18	The Greater London Authority data store http://data.london.gov.uk/dataset/office-national-statistics-ons-population-estimates-borough
Number of immigrants	The Greater London Authority data store (collected by The Office of National statistics (ONS)) http://data.london.gov.uk/dataset/national-insurance-number-registrations-overseas-nationals-borough

Number of people claiming benefits	The government website GOV.uk https://www.gov.uk/government/statistics/census-output-area-data-on-workless-benefit-claimants-YEAR*-london * To be substituted with the year required, e. g., 2009.
Number of active businesses	The Greater London Authority data store http://data.london.gov.uk/dataset/business-demographics-and-survival-rates-borough
Median house price	The Greater London Authority data store http://data.london.gov.uk/dataset/average-house-prices-borough
Number of conceptions under 18	The Greater London Authority data store http://data.london.gov.uk/dataset/teenage-conceptions-borough

Table 2. List of the London Boroughs

LAD Code	LAD Name	Inner/Outer London	LAD Code	LAD Name	Inner/Outer London
E09000001	City of London	Inner	E09000018	Hounslow	Outer
E09000002	Barking and Dagenham	Outer	E09000019	Islington	Inner
E09000003	Barnet	Outer	E09000020	Kensington and Chelsea	Inner
E09000004	Bexley	Outer	E09000021	Kingston upon Thames	Outer
E09000005	Brent	Outer	E09000022	Lambeth	Inner
E09000006	Bromley	Outer	E09000023	Lewisham	Inner
E09000007	Camden	Inner	E09000024	Merton	Outer
E09000008	Croydon	Outer	E09000025	Newham	Inner
E09000009	Ealing	Outer	E09000026	Redbridge	Outer
E09000010	Enfield	Outer	E09000027	Richmond upon Thames	Outer
E09000011	Greenwich	Outer	E09000028	Southwark	Inner
E09000012	Hackney	Inner	E09000029	Sutton	Outer
E09000013	Hammersmith and Fulham	Inner	E09000030	Tower Hamlets	Inner
E09000014	Haringey	Inner	E09000031	Waltham Forest	Outer
E09000015	Harrow	Outer	E09000032	Wandsworth	Inner
E09000016	Havering	Outer	E09000033	Westminster	Inner
E09000017	Hillingdon	Outer			

4. ANALYSIS AND DISCUSSION

4.1 Correlation

Although NEET is correlated with multiple factors and some of them may be considered influential (attributing) factors, each factor involved may have a different degree of correlation strength with NEET. Determining the degree of correlation strength of each factor is important in NEET analysis as it helps identify potential influential factors and highlight factors that have similar degree of potential influence. It is particularly useful if a very high number of factors to be considered in the analysis.

In order to investigate the degree of correlation strength, a hierarchical clustering of the variables and their correlation with the NEET rate were conducted in SAS Enterprise Miner (Cerrito 2006, Aggarwal and Kosian 2011) (using the Variable Clustering node and the StatExplore node). The results are shown in Figure 1 and Figure 2.

As illustrated in Figure 1, the factors under consideration can be grouped into three clusters, labelled as CLUS1, CLUS2, and CLUS3, respectively, in a hierarchical way. CLUS1 includes 5 variables: NEET, Male_Population, Female_Population, Conception, and Median_House_Price. The variables in this cluster are correlated with the NEET rate closely. CLUS2 has 3 variables: Immigrants, Benefits_Claimants, and Crime_Offences, and these variables have relatively weak correlation with the NEET rate. CLUS3 only has one variable Active_Businesses, and it has the weakest correlation with the NEET rate.

Figure 2 provides consistent results that the correlation strength of each variable with the NEET rate can be shown in a descending order as Male_Population, Female_Population, Conception, Crime_Offences, Benefits_Claimants, Immigrants, Active_Businesses, and Median_House_Price. Among them, Male_Population, Female_Population, and Conception are the most positively correlated variables, and Median_House_Price is the most negatively correlated variable.

The correlation strength was further examined by inner and outer London groups, and it has been found that the correlation strength of each variable with the NEET rate varies with Boroughs in inner and outer London. For the inner London group, Median_House_Price, Immigrants, and Active_Businesses are more significantly correlated with the NEET rate than in the outer London group. In addition, the outer London group has a much higher NEET rate (43% higher) than the inner London group.

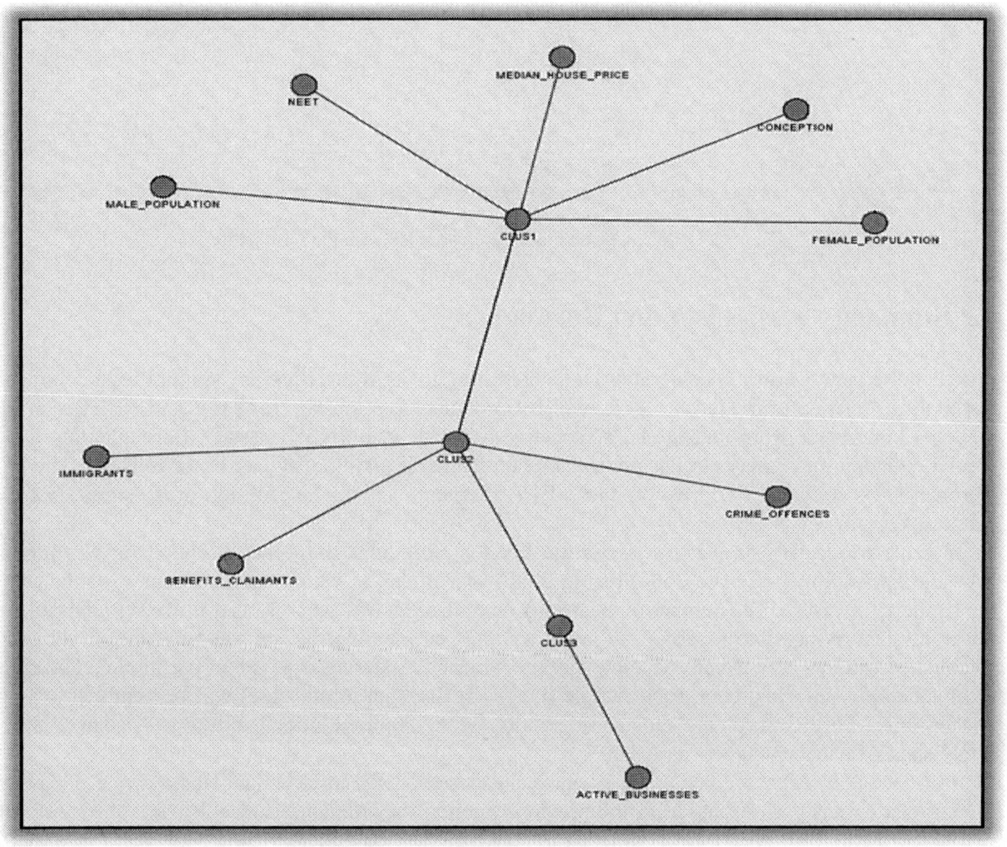

Figure 1. Hierarchical clustering of the variables

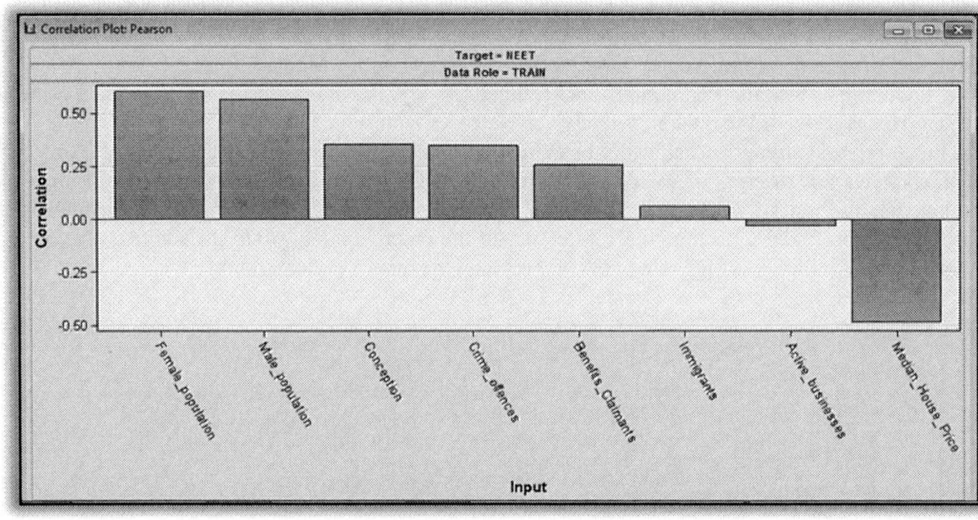

Figure 2. Correlation of the variables with the NEET rate

4.2 Similarity across London Boroughs

Based on the factors under consideration, it is interesting to see if there are any similarities across the London Boroughs in relation to the factors, e. g., which Boroughs have similar crime rate and NEET rate. This is of practical importance from managerial perspective in tackling the NEET issue - Boroughs that are under a similar situation may apply similar policies and strategies if a similarity can be established. Therefore, one Borough's experience in addressing the NEET problem can be helpful for other similar Boroughs to generalize.

In order to identify similarities across the London Boroughs, the *k*-means clustering was performed in SAS Enterprise Miner (Cerrito 2006) (using the Cluster node), in which the Euclidean distance was used as the similarity measure. The number of clusters (i.e., centroids) was set to 3, as it is always advisable to use as fewer clusters as possible to group as many samples as possible, as long as meaningful clusters can be established within a certain context. Note that the *k*-means clustering is a type of partitional clustering, which means that after the clustering, each sample (i.e., each Borough in our case) will be assigned to a particular cluster only. Furthermore, the clustering results were imported into Tableau to visualize the clusters established with their members associated.

Two factors were considered in the *k*-means clustering: NEET and Median_House_Price. This is based on the correlation analysis discussed in the previous Section that Median_House_Price is the most negatively correlated factor with NEET. In addition, the clustering was conducted using four years data 2010, 2011, 2012, and 2013 separately in order to identify if the similarity and cluster memberships have changed over time. The results are shown in Fig. 3. It becomes evident from the *k*-means clustering results that there are indeed some clear similarities across the London Boroughs. For instance, these 7 Boroughs: Camden, Harrow, Kingston upon Thames, Hammersmith and Fulham, Richmond upon Thames, and Wansworth, and Westminster usually had similar NEET rate and Median_House_Price rate, i.e., low NEET rate and high Median_House_Price rate. In comparison, Boroughs like Barking and Dagenham, Bromley, Croydon, and Enfield usually had a high NEET rate with a low Median_House_Price rate. The memberships of the clusters in general remain stable over the 4 years although there are some variances.

4.3 Discussion

From the analysis results illustrated in the previous Sections, we have the following remarks:

a) Each factor under consideration has a certain degree of correlation strength with the NEET rate across all the London Boroughs. The degree of correlation strength varies with different factors and with the inner and outer London groups as well.
b) Amongst all the 8 factors, Median_Property_Price rate was the most negatively correlated factor with the NEET rate. In other words, this factor may be used as an indicator of areas that are likely to suffer from NEET and thus to take appropriate precautions in order to reduce the likelihood of further increases in NEET. Note that, though, this doesn't mean the NEET problem has been caused by low property prices in an area.
c) Boroughs across London do have similarities based on a given set of factors. As such, the London Boroughs can be segmented into several meaningful groups, each containing a number of Boroughs that have similar situation and issues. In addition, this segmentation remains stable over the period of time considered. This finding could be beneficial to Boroughs in the same segment in that they can work together sharing experiences and adopting similar strategies in tackling the NEET issue.
d) The similarity analysis can be further conducted at other geographical levels, such as Ward and LSOA levels. Usually from the local authority's perspective, analysis at LSOA level is of more practical importance. Note that the amount of data to be handled is big if data at all those levels is used, since there are roughly 649 Wards and 4642 LSOA codes across the London Boroughs.

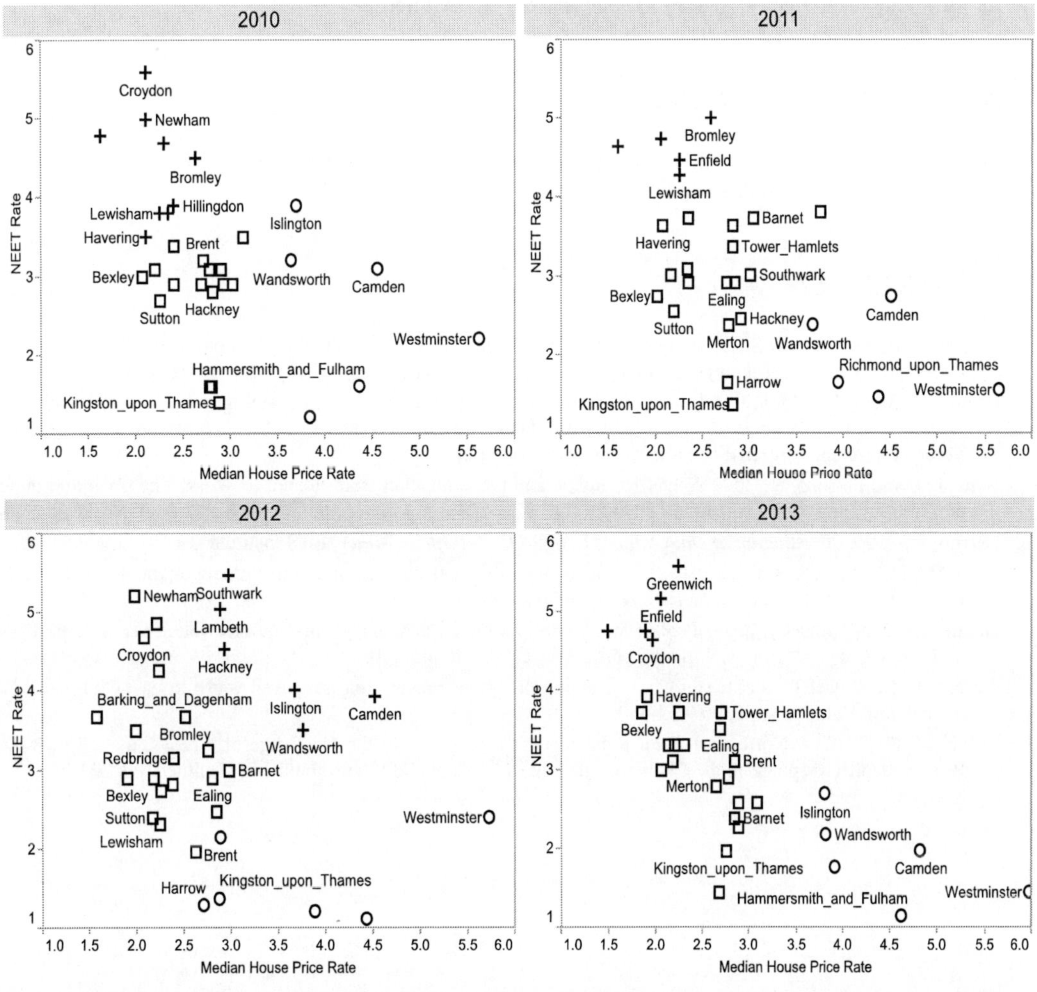

Figure 3. Similarity identified across the London Boroughs by using *k*-means cluster analysis based on two factors (variables). Data of 4 years was used separately. 3 clusters were considered, labelled by the signs plus, square, and circle, respectively

5. CONCLUSION AND FUTURE WORK

The NEET issue is complex and involves many factors to be considered. In this paper, a big data approach has been adopted to analyse the problem by taking into account as many factors as possible that are implicitly or explicitly relevant. The main advantage to use this approach is that it potentially can reveal valuable insight which may not be uncovered if only considering some of the factors. It is an integrated, holistic approach. It has been demonstrated that: a) The NEET issue is much more severe in outer London than in inner London; b) The main factors correlated or potentially attributing to NEET vary from inner London to outer London; c) Each of the measures considered has a certain correlation strength with the NEET rate, and amongst them, median property price is a simple and seemingly accurate indicator of areas likely to suffer from NEET and thus to take appropriate precautions in order to reduce the likelihood of further increases in NEET; and d) the London Boroughs can be grouped based on similarities in terms of a set of given measures, and the memberships of the groups remain stable.

We intend to include more factors in the future and to work jointly with the local authorities in London. Also, other geographical levels' data will be considered including Ward and LSOA levels. In the longer term, a data platform should be developed in order to accommodate more data in a dynamical and substantial way, and scalable clustering algorithms need to be explored. In addition, appropriate APIs should be implemented for retrieving data effectively from various sources on the Internet.

ACKNOWLEDGEMENT

The authors would like to thank the seven anonymous reviewers for their valuable comments and suggestions to improve the quality of this paper.

REFERENCES

Aggarwal V., and Kosian S., 2011. Feature Selection and Dimension Reduction Techniques in SAS®, Northeast SAS Users Group 2011 Proceedings. Available at: http://www.lexjansen.com/nesug/nesug11/sa/sa08.pdf.

Britton J., Gregg P., MacMillan L. and Mitchell S., 2011. The early bird...preventing young people from becoming a NEET statistic. Available at: http://www.bristol.ac.uk/media-library/sites/cmpo/migrated/documents/earlybirdcmpo.pdf

Bynner, J. and Parsons, S., 2002. Social Exclusion and the Transition from School to Work: The Case of Young People Not in Education, Employment, or Training (NEET). *Journal of Vocational Behavior*, Vol. 60, No. 2, pp. 289-309.

Cerrito, P., 2006, *Introduction to Data Mining Using SAS Enterprise Miner*. SAS Institute.

Egan M., Daly M., Delaney L. 2015. Childhood psychological distress and youth unemployment: Evidence from two British cohort studies. *Social Science & Medicine*, Vol. 124, pp. 11-17.

Greater London Authority, 2007. Toolkit for London Extended Schools – working with young people NEET, Available at: http://legacy.london.gov.uk/mayor/children/docs/neet-toolkit.pdf

Stoten, D., 2014. NEETs: a case study in addressing the issues relating to disengaged youth in East Cleveland, *Education + Training*, Vol. 56, No. 5, pp. 467-480.

Woolford, C., 2012. A North East Pupil Referral Unit's Response to the Challenge of NEETs, in: A North East Pupil Referral Unit's Response to the Challenge of NEETs, in: Emerald Group Publishing Limited, pp. 223-236.

FACTORING THE HABITS: COMPARING METHODS FOR DISCOVERING BEHAVIOR PATTERNS FROM LARGE SCALE ACTIVITY DATASETS

Onur Yürüten and Pearl Pu
Human-Computer Interaction Group
School of Computer and Communication System Sciences, Ecole Polytechnique Federale de Lausanne

ABSTRACT

The abundance of wearable sensors leads to massive growth of datasets of Activities of Daily Living (ADLs). Many ADL-based applications will thus need to incorporate scalable and efficient methods to organize this data. This requires an in-depth understanding of the empirical properties of alternative clustering methods. In this spirit, we present a comparative analysis of two powerful candidates based on matrix factorization. While the first approach stems from computer vision applications (Low Rank and Sparse Decomposition - LRSD), the second approach is a collaborative filtering method used in recommender systems to model temporal trends (Time-SVD++).

We describe the necessary modifications to adapt these approaches to ADL datasets, and then compare and contrast them in two major aspects: scalability and clustering quality. We quantify our comparisons with run-time complexity analysis and clustering quality measurements on two different datasets (one ADL dataset and one ratings dataset) with statistical significance. Our results not only confirm these methods' superiority over basic clustering approaches, but also demonstrate notable differences between ADL datasets and customer ratings datasets. We conclude that in contrast to traditional recommender systems approaches, ADL clustering methods should specifically handle the density and noise in ADL datasets.

KEYWORDS

Time series analysis; activities of daily living; behavior profiling

1. INTRODUCTION

The abundance of wearable sensors helps people track their Activities of Daily Living (ADLs), and promises substantial opportunities in pervasive healthcare. For instance, existing medical studies depend on self-reported survey data (Ogden et al., 2012; Reyes et al., 2012), but they could be complemented with sensor-based measurement. Additionally, there is an ongoing effort to develop personalized lifestyle recommendations based on people's daily habits (Farrel et al. 2012).

Such ambitious objectives require a reliable means to organize (e.g. clustering) massive, sensory ADL data into categories of temporal patterns followed by people. Each of these patterns would characterize the temporal dynamics of a general behavior trend - for instance, an increase of daily number of steps by 5000 steps over 30 days. People's data would be associated to these trends with additional temporal dynamics such as possible deviations (e.g. two exceptional days of inactiveness) and warps (achieving the same goal over 34 days instead of 30). Until recently, this need was tried to be addressed with activity recognition methods with data labeling and probabilistic modeling. They would be subsequently evaluated by their recognition accuracy. However, this requires expert knowledge and content-dependent modifications over standard modeling techniques - which are costly, and unlikely generalizable over different, ever enlarging datasets (Yin et al., 2015 and Yürüten et al., 2014). An alternative approach is to use matrix factorization, which requires minimal external supervision. However, given the myriad of such methods (Adomavicius and Tuzhilin, 2005), there is a need to assess their applicability to ADLs.

The purpose of this study is, therefore, a critical assessment of matrix factorization approaches on analyzing ADL datasets. More concretely, we perform a comparative evaluation of two state-of-the-art approaches (Low Rank and Sparse Decomposition – LRSD and Time-SVD++). Neither of these two state-of-the-art approaches were originally designed with ADLs in mind: LRSD (Lin et al., 2010) is used to reduce the dimensionality in a possibly corrupted image data so as to capture regular and symmetric structures. However, this design could also permit it to characterize ADL data in terms of common trends and minor deviations, and identify the temporal patterns that people follow. Likewise, TimeSVD++ (Koren, 2009) can model the changes of user product preferences over time very successfully - especially considering the fact that such datasets are notably sparse, i.e., they have many missing points to be fixed. This suggests that TimeSVD++ may, in a similar manner, model the changes in people's ADLs over time, so that distinct temporal patterns can be easily identified by a subsequent clustering method.

We evaluate these approaches through two criteria: scalability and clustering quality. In measuring clustering quality, we also assess how well these methods perform with the varying levels of missing data points (i.e., sparsity or data density). With our results we first confirm that these methods' superiority over basic clustering approaches, and also demonstrate notable differences between ADL datasets and customer ratings datasets.

2. RELATED WORK

2.1 Probabilistic Modeling

Activity recognition approaches (Cook and Krishnan, 2014; Cook, 2012) typically propose probabilistic approaches like Bayes classifiers, Conditional Random Field Models and Hidden Markov Models, driven by the motivation to recognize and understand people's ADLs using wearable and environmental sensors. These approaches typically designate a set of probabilistic transitioning rules between some states (either of well-being or of distinct activity patterns), and try to validate these rules on a dataset. Topic modeling, a technique adapted from document-word analysis for mining semantic data, is another alternative for probabilistic modeling of behaviors (Castanedo et al., 2013; Farrahi and Perez, 2013).

One issue in the probabilistic modeling approach for activity recognition is that there is no standard probabilistic model that is scalable for every kind of dataset. Thus each study proposes a special modification (especially Hidden Markov Model variants), so that the model can handle the properties of some specific dataset. Consequently, where some methods employ simple clustering procedures for preprocessing (Scott et al., 2005), other studies resort to more complex variations such as Hidden Semi-Markov Model (Duong et al., 2005), Markov Logic Network (Gayathri et al., 2014), or voting Multi-HMM model constructed with frequent pattern mining (Rashidi et al., 2011). These variations imply the requirement of an immense amount of expert knowledge and additional computational complexity for each separate case. As a result, their solutions often lack generalizability.

2.2 Matrix Factorization

Matrix factorization is a well-known approach to reduce dimensionality in large datasets. Recommender systems (Adomavicius and Tuzhilin, 2005) typically use this to obtain item and user profiles for many applications including product, music, and movie recommendations. Further applications for matrix factorization include adaptive web searches based on user profiles (Sugiyama et al., 2004), and image and video processing (Wang and Yeung, 2013).

In addition to its extensions to accommodate temporal relations (Ding and Li, 2005; Koren, 2009), contextual information (Verbert et al., 2012) and probabilistic relations (Popescul et al., 2001; Wang and Yeung, 2013), collaborative filtering requires minimal (if any) effort from users in constructing user preference profiles, making it a suitable approach for behavior profiling. Some studies empirically demonstrate this usefulness on sparse mobile phone data (Zheng et al., 2013).

Another prominent example is Principal Component Analysis. Eagle and Pentland (2009) employ Principal Component Analysis to decompose behavioral patterns from mobile phone data into eigenvectors, which they name as "eigenbehaviors". With this strategy, each user can be modeled as a weighted combination of eigenbehaviors, allowing further analysis to predict the missing patterns during a single day. On the other hand, Principal Component Analysis is known to be very sensitive to noise, and this study does address this problem. A more recent study (Yürüten et al., 2014) employ a noise-tolerant variant of PCA, called Linearized Alternating Direction Method (Lin et al., 2010) on wearable accelerometer data. However, this PCA variant has a cubic computational complexity, rendering this proof-of-concept approach impractical to apply on large datasets.

2.3 Summary

Many probabilistic methods suffer from one or more of the following shortcomings: dependence on supervised labels or expert knowledge, or high computational complexity. As such, thus they are not scalable and efficient enough for large and unlabeled datasets for ADLs. Matrix Factorization approaches are however an exception, therefore they are more practical for our task. We now proceed to describe and compare two major alternatives in more detail.

3. METHODS

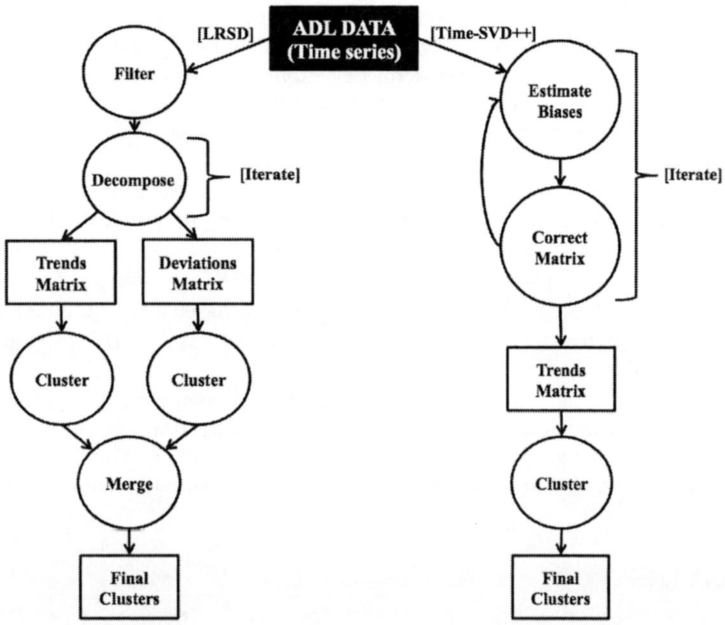

Figure 1. The flow of data processing in LRSD- and TimeSVD++-based clustering. LRSD, decomposes the data into two components (trends and deviations), while TimeSVD++ discards the deviations altogether

3.1 Low Rank and Sparse Decomposition

The studies of computer vision place great effort on algorithms to treat abnormalities in the image data, which gave rise to the notion of Low Rank and Sparse Decomposition (LRSD). LRSD variants aim to emphasize regular and symmetric structures in a data matrix (Liang et al., 2012). The deviations from such structures might be treated as errors, or could still be treated as useful information – such as objects on a plain background (Kyrillidis and Cevher, 2012). LRSD variants are widely applied in the field of computer vision. However, some studies suggest its applicability on other problems (such as topic modeling) as well (Min et al., 2010). Given a matrix M, the decomposition is achieved by solving:

$$min \ \|A\|_* + \lambda\|E\|_1 \text{ such that } M = A+E$$

here, $\|.\|_*$ denotes the nuclear norm of a matrix (a good approximation of the rank of the matrix), and $\|.\|_1$ is the number of non-zero entries in a matrix. λ is a positive parameter, and theoretical studies suggest to set this to $1/\sqrt{\max(n_1, n_2)}$, where (n_1, n_2) are the number of rows and columns of M. We follow this suggestion in our experiments.

The most common method to solve the equation above has a time complexity of $O(N^3)$(Lin et al., 2010), which would render this variant and the methods that employ it (e.g., (Yürüten et al., 2014)) prohibitively costly for large datasets. For an optimized performance, we instead use Robust Grassmann Averages. This approach models the dimensionality reduction problem as the averages of subspaces spanned by the data. This modification helps the method discern the local deviations to a great extent (Hauberg et al., 2014).

Given the input data $y_{1:N}$, each iteration in Robust Grassman Average is as follows:

$$\omega_n \leftarrow sign(u_n^T q_{i-1})\|y_n\|, q_i \leftarrow \frac{\mu_{rob}(\omega_{1:N}, u_{1:N})}{\|\mu_{rob}(\omega_{1:N}, u_{1:N})\|}$$

where $\omega_{1:N}$ would denote weights, q_i is the weighted average computed at iteration i, $u_n = {}^{y_n}/_{\|y_n\|}$, and μ_{rob} denotes a robust average. In this study, we specify μ_{rob} as the trimmed mean.

Adoption Approach: We use LRSD in a flow of time series processing that captures common trends and deviations, followed by clustering based on Dynamic Time Warping (see Figure 1). We pre-process the ADL time series data with a simple moving average filter, and apply the decomposition to obtain two separate matrices for long-term patterns and short-term deviations. We separately cluster these two matrices, using Dynamic Time Warping (DTW) (Berndt and Clifford, 1994) with Keogh's lower bounding (Keogh, 2005) as the distance metric. We then perform a cross product of the two separate cluster sets to find the final memberships for each time series object.

The DTW distance compensates nonlinear misalignments between similar time series objects (for instance, having lunch break 10 minutes longer and commuting back to home 40 minutes later than usual). DTW between the time series data Y and Z can be calculated as:

$$DTW(Y,Z) = \ min_w\ [\textstyle\sum_{k=1}^{K} d(w_k)\ ]\mathrm{DTW}(Y,Z) = \min_w\ [\textstyle\sum_{k=1}^{K} d(w_k)],$$

where $d(w_k) = (y_i - z_j)^2$ such that $(y_i,\ z_j)$ is on the warping path w (Fu, 2011). Studies on various time series datasets (e.g. kitchen tool usage (Pham et al., 2010)) validate DTW's superiority over Euclidean distance in classification tasks.

In this naïve form, the dynamic time warping costs $O(D^2)$ for comparing a single pair of time series objects. Various alternatives reduce this complexity (Sakoe and Chiba, 1987; Keogh and Pazzani, 1999). For an optimized performance, we use Keogh's lower-bounded Dynamic Time Warping as the distance metric in the clustering phase (Keogh, 2005). Furthermore, we employ the simple moving average filter to circumvent DTW's sensitivity to noise.

3.2 TimeSVD++

TimeSVD++ (Koren, 2009) is a variant of Collaborative Filtering that models temporal changes in customer preferences, i.e., *concept drift*. TimeSVD++ extends the existing factor model SVD++ and incorporates the temporal dynamics under three bias components (user bias $b_u(t)$, item bias $b_i(t)$, and global bias μ) at a given time t. TimeSVD++ uses these components, along with the user u's preference $p_u(t)$, item i's characteristics c_i, factor vector f, and the set of items already rated by user ($R(u)$) to predict the rating of user u for item i with the following prediction rule (Koren, 2009):

$$\hat{r}_{ui}(t) = \mu + b_i(t) + b_u(t) + c_i^T(p_u(t) + |R(u)|^{-\frac{1}{2}} \sum_{j\in R(u)} f_j)$$

Without disregarding its original function as a recommender system routine, we can also interpret TimeSVD++ as a procedure to reconstruct a time series dataset with missing values. The design of TimeSVD++ intends to capture long-term trends of temporal data, while avoiding the short-term patterns that would not have a predictive influence on future trends. Furthermore, as demonstrated in Netflix dataset, its predictive capabilities outperform existing state-of-the-art factor models (SVD, SVD++) while running very fast in rating datasets (Koren, 2009).

Adoption Approach: We adopt TimeSVD++ as follows (Figure 1): we run the algorithm on the dataset with initializing the bias components based on the dataset's properties. This initialization maps the global bias μ to the global average of ADL levels (e.g. calorie expenditure) per unit of time (day, hour or minute), the user bias $b_u(t)$ to the average ADL level of the user up to time t, and the item bias $b_i(t)$ to the average ADL level of all users up to time t. $p_u(t)$ naturally maps to the current ADL level of u at time t, and f maps to other users' ADL level. With this setup, the algorithm corrects the matrix at time t based on past data and updates the bias parameters for future data. Thus, the warps and deviations are discarded. We then cluster the corrected matrix.

4. COMPARISON RESULTS

4.1 Scalability: Computational Complexity Evaluation

We denote U as the set of users, $|U| = N$, and D as the maximum possible number of observations (total number of businesses recorded in rating datasets and the length of sensor utilization in ADL datasets).

4.1.1 LRSD

The complexity of LRSD depends on the total complexity of filtering, decomposition and clustering phases (see Figure 1).

Filtering Phase: The simple moving average transforms a given time series object $X = (x_1, x_2, \dots, x_D)$ to a rolling average $Y = (y_1, y_2, \dots, y_D)$ by the following formula:

$$y_k = y_{k-1} + \frac{x_k - x_{k-w}}{l}$$

where l is the length of the sliding window. This takes takes $O(1)$ operations to complete for each observation in the time series object, amounting the complexity for a single entry to be processed in $O(D)$ and the entire dataset to be processed in $O(ND)$.

Decomposition Phase: A single iteration in The Robust Grassmann Averages (TGA) has a computational complexity of $O(KND)$, where the parameter K denotes the number of components to be found in the dataset (Hauberg et al., 2014). It always holds that $K \leq D$, so the worst-case performance of TGA is bounded by $O(DND) = O(ND^2)$, raising the overall complexity of LRSD to $O(ND) + O(ND^2) = O(ND^2)$.

4.1.2 Time-SVD++ Based Clustering

A single iteration to train a model based on TimeSVD++ is determined as $O(\sum_{u\ in\ U} |R(u)|^2)$, where $R(u)$ denotes the set of items rated by the user u (Koren, 2009). This makes TimeSVD++ is designed to work in highly sparse item rating datasets where $|R(u)| \ll D$. In datasets such as *HealthyWalkers*, however, the dataset is dense: $R(u)$ naturally converges to D, raising the complexity to $O(ND^2)$.

In summary, with the same number of iterations, matrix factorization steps in LRSD and TimeSVD++ have the asymptotically equivalent runtimes. Furthermore, since Euclidean distance and DTW with Keogh's lower bounding is the same, i.e., $O(D)$, both algorithms also have the same runtime for clustering.

4.2 Clustering Quality

4.2.1 Datasets

We evaluate the capabilities of the methods through two activity datasets that contain temporal patterns followed by people. The principal difference between these datasets is the level of sparsity, i.e., the amount of missing data points. Thus we can measure how well the algorithms scale with the level of data density.

The YELP Dataset. YELP dataset contains approximately 2.3 million ratings from 70,000 users for 15,000 businesses. In this study, we analyse the 2014 version of this ever-growing dataset, which includes the ratings within the time period from 01-02-2005 to 28-01-2014. Similar to other rating datasets, the YELP dataset is very sparse: there are 402 out of 3284 days with no records of ratings or reviews. On average, each user has 33.69 ratings (minimum 1, maximum 3286). We process this dataset as a matrix where each row represents a business, and each data point is the cumulative rating of the business for a single day. In this manner, each cluster represents a distinct rating pattern for businesses.

HealthyTogether. In a previous study (Chen and Pu, 2014), we have conducted a user study to investigate the effects of self-monitoring and social intervention on the overall activeness of users. The end product of this study is the *HealthyTogether* dataset, which contains the calorie expenditure data of 83 users wearing Fitbit (a wearable accelerometer) between September 2013 and September 2014. Users participated to this study for 12 to 235 days (μ = 48.36, σ = 54.85). Contrary to YELP dataset, this dataset do not have any missing values. We process the data in a matrix where each row represents a day, and each data point represents one minute. With this representation, there are a total of 4014 rows, each of which has 1440 data points, and users' data are processed altogether. In this manner, the clusters can be used to identify common daily routines adopted by the wearable sensor users. Such a segmentation of activity routines could help us develop specialized interventions to improve each of the daily routines.

4.2.2 Results

We use Average Silhouette Width (ASW) in comparing the clustering quality of the three approaches. Kaufman and Rousseauw (2009) proposed this metric to measure in-cluster consistency and inter-cluster distinctiveness. ASW scores are bounded in the interval [-1, 1]. When comparing two methods, the one with a higher ASW score is said to be producing clusters with higher quality. Furthermore, ASW has suggested values for validation: any score below 0.25 would indicate a bad quality of clustering (comparable to random partitioning), scores within [0.25, 0.5] would indicate an acceptable level of quality, and scores above 0.5 would indicate a high quality of clustering.

Table 1 summarizes the clustering qualities of three alternative approaches: first approach is Hierarchical Agglomerative Clustering without any of the matrix factorization steps, and the other two are LRSD-based and Time-SVD++-based approaches. Wilcoxon signed-rank test on silhouette scores indicate statistically significant differences between their performances. ($p < 0.05$). Both TimeSVD++ and LRSD improve the clustering quality as opposed to baseline method.

While all methods perform well in YELP dataset, the data density in *HealthyTogether* dataset takes its toll on their performances. The clustering qualities of baseline metod and TimeSVD++ suffer particularly more (-43% and -32%, respectively) than LRSD (-12%). While both TimeSVD++ and LRSD can produce clusters with highly reliability in YELP dataset, only LRSD can do so in *HealthyTogether* dataset.

Table 1. The ASW scores for clustering algorithms on HealthyTogether and YELP datasets. Higher scores imply better clustering quality. (*) indicates an acceptable level, while (**) indicates a good level. The differences in the scores are statistically significant (Wilcoxon signed-rank test: $p < 0.05$)

Method	HealthyTogether	YELP
HAC without Factorization	0.26	0.46 (*)
LRSD	0.69 (**)	0.79 (**)
TimeSVD++	0.40 (*)	0.59 (**)

5. CONCLUSION

Future applications on Activities of Daily Living require a good level of understanding of ADL data clustering. In this paper, we presented our efforts to improve this understanding via a comparative study of alternative methods. We first briefly reviewed why methods based on matrix factorization are more suitable than other approaches for this task. Then, we described two particular matrix factorization techniques used in different fields (computer vision and recommender systems, respectively). Following the discussion of their respective design strategies, we elaborated the modifications necessary to adapt these techniques for clustering ADL data. Then we presented their similarities and differences through theoretical and experimental analysis, with a particular emphasis on runtime complexity analysis and measuring the clustering qualities through experiments on a physical activity dataset and a ratings dataset, who have different levels of data sparsity.

From a conceptual point of view, our study enhances our understanding of the properties of ADL datasets: they resemble to image datasets, in the sense that they can be dense and arbitrarily noisy. This became evident in the course of our comparisons as Time-SVD++, which is engineered for and works great in sparse ratings datasets, produces suboptimal results in clustering ADL datasets. We therefore validated the suggestion of Farrell et al. (2012) that behavior-profiling methods should not be sensitive to the level of sparsity in the datasets, and we add that such methods must also explicitly deal with noise and temporal dynamics (i.e., warps and deviations).

The clustering task we study is also closely related with the well-known collaborative filtering scheme in recommender systems. As such, from a practical point of view, our study can help enhance the engineering process of lifestyle recommender systems (Farrel et al., 2012), where the system would suggest healthy lifestyle changes relevant to the users' "behavior profile" (i.e., the ADL clusters). This could potentially add a further dimension to compare matrix factorization strategies: while one may result in a similarity-based recommender system, another one may result in a difference-based recommender system.

ACKNOWLEDGEMENT

We thank Yelp (https://www.yelp.com/dataset_challenge) for sharing the academic dataset with us. We thank Fitbit (http://www.fitbit.com) for providing us with the access to data of the users of HealthyTogether. We like to thank the Swiss Research Program on Engineering Multi-Scale Systems for Health, Security, Energy and Environment for funding our research under the grand title "Tera-Health: Strategic Action on Pervasive Health".

REFERENCES

Adomavicius, G., & Tuzhilin, A. (2005). Toward the next generation of recommender systems: A survey of the state-of-the-art and possible extensions. Knowledge and Data Engineering, IEEE Transactions on, 17(6), 734-749.

Berndt, D. J.; and Clifford, J. (1994, July). Using Dynamic Time Warping to Find Patterns in Time Series. In *KDD workshop* (Vol. 10, No. 16, pp. 359-370).

Castanedo et al. (2014). Learning routines over long-term sensor data using topic models. Expert Systems, 31(4), 365-377.

Chen, Y., & Pu, P. (2014, April). HealthyTogether: exploring social incentives for mobile fitness applications. In *Proceedings of the Second International Symposium of Chinese CHI* (pp. 25-34). ACM.

Cook, D. J. (2010). Learning setting-generalized activity models for smart spaces. IEEE intelligent systems, 2010(99), 1.

Cook, Diane J., and Narayanan Krishnan (2014). "Mining the home environment." Journal of intelligent information systems 43.3 (2014): 503-519.

Ding, Y., & Li, X. (2005, October). Time weight collaborative filtering. In Proceedings of the 14th ACM international conference on Information and knowledge management (pp. 485-492). ACM.

Duong et al. (2005, June). Activity recognition and abnormality detection with the switching hidden semi-markov model. In Computer Vision and Pattern Recognition, 2005. CVPR 2005. IEEE Computer Society Conference on (Vol. 1, pp. 838-845). IEEE.

Eagle, Nathan, and Alex Sandy Pentland (2009). "Eigenbehaviors: Identifying structure in routine." Behavioral Ecology and Sociobiology 63.7 (2009): 1057-1066.

Farrahi, K., & Gatica-Perez, D. (2014). A probabilistic approach to mining mobile phone data sequences. Personal and ubiquitous computing, 18(1), 223-238.

Farrell et al. (2012, September). Intrapersonal retrospective recommendation: lifestyle change recommendations using stable patterns of personal behavior. In *Proceedings of the First International Workshop on Recommendation Technologies for Lifestyle Change (LIFESTYLE 2012), Dublin, Ireland* (p. 24).

Fu, T. C. (2011). A review on time series data mining. Engineering Applications of Artificial Intelligence, 24(1), 164-181.

Gayathri et al. (2015) "Hierarchical activity recognition for dementia care using markov logic network." Personal and Ubiquitous Computing 19.2 (2015): 271-285.

Hauberg et al. (2014, June). Grassmann averages for scalable robust PCA. In *Computer Vision and Pattern Recognition (CVPR), 2014 IEEE Conference on* (pp. 3810-3817). IEEE.

Kaufman, L.; and Rousseeuw, P. J. (2009). *Finding groups in data: an introduction to cluster analysis* (Vol. 344). Wiley. com.

Keogh, E. J.; and Pazzani, M. J. (1999). Scaling up dynamic time warping to massive datasets. Principles of Data Mining and Knowledge Discovery, 1-11.

Keogh, E., & Ratanamahatana, C. A. (2005). Exact indexing of dynamic time warping. *Knowledge and information systems*, *7*(3), 358-386.

Koren, Y. (2009). Collaborative filtering with temporal dynamics. *In Proceedings of the 15th ACM SIGKDD International Conference on Knowledge Discovery and Data Mining, 447-456.*

Kyrillidis, A.; and Cevher, V. (2012, August). Matrix alps: Accelerated low rank and sparse matrix reconstruction. In Statistical Signal Processing Workshop (SSP), 2012 IEEE (pp. 185-188). IEEE.

Liang et al. (2012). Repairing sparse low-rank texture. In *Computer Vision – ECCV 2012* (pp. 482-495). Springer Berlin Heidelberg.

Lin et al. (2010). The augmented lagrange multiplier method for exact recovery of corrupted low-rank matrices. UIUC Technical Report UILU-ENG-09-2215.

Min et al. (2010, October). Decomposing background topics from keywords by principal component pursuit. In *Proceedings of the 19th ACM international conference on Information and knowledge management* (pp. 269-278). ACM.

Ogden et al (2012). Cluster analysis of the national weight control registry to identify distinct subgroups maintaining successful weight loss. Obesity, 20(10), 2039-2047.

Olguın et al. (2009) "Capturing individual and group behavior with wearable sensors." Proceedings of the 2009 aaai spring symposium on human behavior modeling, SSS. Vol. 9. 2009.

Pham et al. (2010). A dynamic time warping approach to real-time activity recognition for food preparation. *Ambient Intelligence*, LNCS 6439, 21-30.

Popescul et al. (2001, August). Probabilistic models for unified collaborative and content-based recommendation in sparse-data environments. In Proceedings of the Seventeenth conference on Uncertainty in artificial intelligence (pp. 437-444). Morgan Kaufmann Publishers Inc..

Rashidi et al. (2011). Discovering activities to recognize and track in a smart environment. Knowledge and Data Engineering, IEEE Transactions on, 23(4), 527-539.

Reyes et al. (2012). Similarities and differences between weight loss maintainers and regainers: a qualitative analysis. Journal of the Academy of Nutrition and Dietetics, 112(4), 499-505.

Sakoe, H.; and Chiba, S. (1978). Dynamic programming algorithm optimization for spoken word recognition. *Acoustics, Speech and Signal Processing, IEEE Transactions on*, *26*(1), 43-49.

Scott, et al. (2005). "Hidden Markov models for longitudinal comparisons." Journal of the American Statistical Association 100.470.

Sugiyama et al. (2004, May). Adaptive web search based on user profile constructed without any effort from users. In Proceedings of the 13th international conference on World Wide Web (pp. 675-684). ACM.

Verbert et al. (2012). Context-aware recommender systems for learning: a survey and future challenges. Learning Technologies, IEEE Transactions on, 5(4), 318-335.

Wang, Naiyan, and Dit-Yan Yeung. (2013) "Bayesian robust matrix factorization for image and video processing." Computer Vision (ICCV), 2013 IEEE International Conference on. IEEE, 2013.

Yang et al. (2013). Bayesian-inference-based recommendation in online social networks. *Parallel and Distributed Systems, IEEE Transactions on*, *24*(4), 642-651.

Yin et al. (2015, August). Unsupervised daily routine and activity discovery in smart homes. In *Engineering in Medicine and Biology Society (EMBC), 2015 37th Annual International Conference of the IEEE* (pp. 5497-5500). IEEE.

Yürüten et al. (2014, June). Decomposing Activities of Daily Living to Discover Routine Clusters. In *Twenty-Eighth AAAI Conference on Artificial Intelligence.*

Zheng et al. (2013, March). Effective routine behavior pattern discovery from sparse mobile phone data via collaborative filtering. In Pervasive Computing and Communications (PerCom), 2013 IEEE International Conference on (pp. 29-37). IEEE.

PREDICTING MORTGAGE DEFAULT: LESSONS FROM DATA MINING FANNIE MAE MORTGAGE PORTFOLIO

Stanislav Mamonov[1] and Raquel Benbunan-Fich[2]
[1]*Montclair State University, 1 Normal Ave, Montclair, NJ USA*
[2]*Baruch College, CUNY, 1 Bernard Baruch Way, New York, NY USA*

ABSTRACT

Recent advances in information technology have made possible the analysis of vast amounts of data. One promising area for the application of the new analytical methods is finance. We perform data mining on the Fannie Mae mortgage portfolio from the fourth quarter of 2007 that includes 341,348 mortgages with the total principal value of more than $70 billion. This portfolio had the highest delinquency rate in the agency's history – 19.4% versus the historical average of 1.7%. We find that although a number of information variables that were available at the time of mortgage acquisition in Q4, 2007 are correlated with the subsequent delinquencies, application of data mining techniques fails to accurately capture the mortgage delinquency patterns in the historical data. These results are consistent with an exogenous shock explanation and reveal a fundamental challenge that can arise in data mining large datasets.

KEYWORDS

Data mining, mortgage default, government sponsored enterprises, delinquency, credit score, loan-to-value, debt-to-income

1. INTRODUCTION

Recent advances in IT have made possible the analysis of vast amounts of data with the use of sophisticated techniques. One promising area for the application of this technique is finance where substantial amounts of data are routinely collected and are thus available for subsequent analysis (Anandarajan et al. 2012).

The financial crisis of 2007-2008 is considered to have been the worst financial crisis since the Great Depression of the 1930s (Financial Crisis Inquiry Commission 2011). The crisis was precipitated by rapid declines in the housing prices in the United States that triggered a complex web of events leading to insolvency of a number of financial institutions and consequent freezing in the credit markets that had broad effects across the economy (Financial Crisis Inquiry Commission 2011). The United States GDP contracted 0.3% in 2008 and another 3.1% in 2009 (Young 2013). The financial crisis affected many people. Nearly $11 trillion in household wealth had vanished. 4 million families lost their homes to foreclosure (Young 2013). Unemployment reached 10% in the fall of 2009 (Statistics 2015) and the effects of the crisis persist seven years later (Andriotis 2015).

Approximately 70% of real estate purchases in the United States are financed (Financial Crisis Inquiry Commission 2011), meaning that the buyers borrow at least a part of the home value to facilitate the purchase. Government-sponsored enterprises (GSEs), Fannie Mae and Freddie Mac, were established in 1938 and 1970 respectively, to make it easier for individual homebuyers to afford a home (Peterson 2008). The agencies buy mortgages from banks and financial intermediaries, offering liquidity in the mortgage markets and making it easier for individual homebuyers to find financing. The GSEs back nearly 60% of all individual real-estate mortgages in the United States (Kan & Robotti 2007). The agencies securitize mortgages for sale to investors and they also hold a substantial portfolio of mortgages on their balance sheets. Fannie Mae is the larger of the two agencies. In 2007, the Fannie Mae mortgage portfolio was valued at $403 billion, while the Freddie Mac portfolio was valued at $75 billion (Mae 2008; Mac 2008). Both agencies were highly leveraged and the decline in the real estate values associated with the financial crisis effectively bankrupted both agencies, leading the Federal Housing Finance Agency to place both in conservatorship in 2008 (Financial Crisis Inquiry Commission 2011).

The GSEs have been frequently criticized for loose underwriting standards in the period preceding the crisis (Wallison & Calomiris 2009). However, to the best of our knowledge, no systematic analysis of the agencies' mortgage portfolios has been published to substantiate the criticism, and, even more importantly, to extract lessons for the future. We take the first steps in this task here. We review the Fannie Mae prime mortgage portfolio delinquencies in the period 2000-2014 and we identify Q4, 2007 as the mortgage portfolio with the highest rate of severe delinquencies. We perform extensive data mining on this portfolio to understand the extent to which data mining techniques can be used to build predictive models based on the identification of systematic patterns and salient predictors. The answers to these questions promise to shed light on the underlying causes of mortgage defaults during the financial crisis and inform practice and policy decisions going forward in order to prevent a similar crisis from occurring in the future. In the sections that follow, we provide an overview of previous studies on mortgage delinquencies associated with the financial crisis of 2007-2008 as well as a brief summary of prior work on applying data mining techniques to predict credit defaults. We describe the dataset in our study and present the data mining results. We conclude with the discussion of our findings and their implications for practice and policy.

2. BACKGROUND

2.1 Data Mining Studies of Credit Defaults

Data mining, also often called "knowledge discovery in databases" (KDD) refers to algorithmic discovery of patterns in data (Fayyad et al. 1996). Published data mining studies of mortgage defaults have been primarily done using datasets originating from outside the United States. A seminal study which evaluated the efficacy of different modeling techniques using eight credit scoring datasets from UK and Benelux suggested that support vector machines and artificial neural network algorithms could deliver the best results (B. Baesens, T. Van Gestel, S. Viaene, M. Stepanova, J. Suykens 2003). A study or mortgage defaults in Israel found that the decision tree algorithm offered the best accuracy in predicting defaults (Feldman & Gross 2005), and a study of a synthetic German credit dataset based on real-world data showed that random forest algorithm outperforms other techniques in predicting the loan defaults (Ghatasheh 2014). In other words, data mining studies with international credit data sets did not produce conclusive findings regarding the best way to model credit defaults. This has been confirmed in recent work that showed that different algorithms offer better performance across different international credit-related datasets (Zurada et al. 2014).

2.2 Research on the Mortgage Defaults Associated with the Financial Crisis of 2007-2008

Government estimates show that there are approximately $13.4 trillion in outstanding mortgage obligations in the United States (BGFRS 2015). Mortgage lending in an important area of practice, however after a surge of academic research through the early 1990s (Quercia & Stegman 1992), there has been relatively little academic work published on mortgage default modeling recently (B. Baesens, T. Van Gestel, S. Viaene, M. Stepanova, J. Suykens 2003). This is likely due to the sensitive nature of the mortgage loan data that can potentially expose private information about the borrowers and the lenders. The published studies on mortgage defaults have been largely descriptive. For example, a study of loan delinquencies showed that loans originated in 2006 and 2007 had the highest historical delinquency rates (Jiang et al. 2014).

Mortgage underwriters typically collect certain information about the borrowers at the time of mortgage origination to ascertain the applicants' creditworthiness. Individual credit score is one of the key parameters used in mortgage underwriting (Avery et al. 1996). Credit agencies aggregate consumer credit information and correlate it with public records producing a summary credit score that reflects individual default risk (Corporation 2015). A study of a dataset involving 270,000 borrowers in Florida during the financial crisis of 2007-2008 shows that increasing FICO score (a credit score developed by Fair Isaac Corporation) is associated with refinancing activity whereas decreasing FICO is associated with increasing likelihood of default (Smith 2011).

There are several studies that examined the relationship between mortgage origination data and subsequent defaults (Chan et al. 2013; Elul et al. 2010). For example, a study of a regional mortgage sample revealed that loan amount, loan-to-value ratio, first time ownership, owner occupancy of the property, single borrower, borrower's income, cash reserves, credit score are significant predictors of loan defaults (Jiang et al. 2014). A life event study had shown that sudden unemployment (38.9%), illness (16.25%), and marital difficulties (9.45%) are trigger events that are significantly correlated with mortgage defaults (Hayre et al. 2006).

In the wake of the financial crisis, there have been investigations into the factors that affect mortgage default decisions that revealed some unexpected findings. Initial studies suggested that the decline in housing prices produced negative equity (outstanding mortgage balance being higher than the value of a home) for many borrowers. The negative equity was proposed as the motive underlying the rising rate of defaults (Bajari et al. 2008; Foote et al. 2008). A later study of mortgage defaults in 2008 showed that negative equity was not an immediate trigger for a mortgage default as may be expected from a completely rational real estate investor, but rather most home owners with negative equity did not default until the negative equity reached 40% of the value of the home (Campbell & Cocco 2011). Subsequent studies showed that there is an interplay between liquidity shocks (loss of income) and negative equity which better describes the mortgage default patterns (Elul et al. 2010). To add a further dimension to the complexity of the decisions underlying mortgage defaults, a recent survey of mortgage borrowers showed that individual numerical ability is negatively correlated with mortgage defaults after controlling for general cognitive ability as well as demographic and financial variables (Kristopher Gerardi, Lorenz Goette 2010).

3. METHOD

3.1 Data Source

We obtained the Fannie Mae mortgage origination and mortgage performance data covering the period between the first quarter of 2000 and the first quarter of 2014 directly from the agency. The mortgage origination dataset contains information that was available to the agency at the time of mortgage acquisition. These data include individual borrower characteristics, e.g. personal credit score, as well as information about the property (number of units) and the financial details of the transaction, e.g. loan-to-value ratio. The complete data dictionary is provided in the Appendix. The full dataset includes 21.7 million mortgages with the combined principal value of $4.186 trillion acquired by Fannie Mae between January, 2000 and March 2014.

The mortgage performance dataset contains information about how the specific loans performed over time after acquisition by Fannie Mae on a monthly basis. The dataset contains over 917 million records pertaining to 21.7 million individual mortgages. Each record in the mortgage performance dataset contains the Loan Identifier field that is related to the Loan Identifiers specified in the mortgage origination dataset. This correspondence allowed us to relate the mortgage origination data with the mortgage performance data.

Industry practice shows that mortgage payers who fall behind by 3 months nearly invariantly end up in default on the mortgage obligation (Sun 2013). The delinquency for a period of 3 months is often referred to as "technical default" in the banking industry (Quercia & Stegman 1992). However, to avoid confusion with the actual mortgage default which requires the transfer of legal rights to the property and is often delayed in relation to the technical default, we will refer to the delinquency for 3 months as a "*severe delinquency*" in our study.

To develop the dataset for our analysis we combined the information containing the predictor variables from the mortgage origination dataset with the subsequent delinquency status of the individual mortgages from the mortgage performance dataset. We created a binary dependent variable – Severe Delinquency, which we assigned the value of 1 if a loan became delinquent for 3 or more months and 0 otherwise.

3.2 Exploratory Analysis

In the first step of our analysis, we examined the historical delinquency rates for mortgages acquired by Fannie Mae over the period from Q1, 2000 to Q1, 2014. The delinquency rate rose through the end of 2007.

The portfolio of mortgages acquired by Fannie Mae in Q4 of 2007 had the highest default rate over the history of the agency – 19.4%. The historical mortgage default rates in the Fannie Mae portfolio averaged 1.7% (Peterson 2009). The Fannie Mae Q4, 2007 prime mortgage portfolio includes 341,348 mortgages with the total principal value of more than $70 billion.

In the next step, we examined the historical variability of the key factors known to affect mortgage defaults: borrower credit scores, debt-to-income and loan-to-value ratios. The analysis did not reveal any drastic changes in the borrower characteristics (credit scores) or the loan characteristics (debt-to-income, loan-to-value) over the period preceding Q4, 2007. There was a significant rise in the average borrower credit score following the financial crisis, reflecting credit tightening that occurred in the aftermath of the financial crisis (Shenn 2012), but no obvious deterioration in the borrower credit scores, financial leverage (debt-to-income ratio) or increasing amount of borrowing vis-a-via the value of the properties (loan-to-value) are evident in the period prior to Q4, 2007.

The exploratory analysis did not produce any obvious insights into the potential causes of the significant rise in the delinquency rates in the Fannie Mae portfolio of mortgages in 2007-2008. This raises the question of whether there are systematic patterns of delinquencies in the Fannie Mae portfolio which can shed light on the underlying causes of delinquencies and help prevent similar events in the future. To address this question, we performed data mining on the dataset of mortgages acquired by Fannie Mae in Q4, 2007, seeking to build predictive models able to capture patterns in the mortgage delinquencies that occurred. In the next section, we discuss the data mining algorithms that we employed in our analysis.

3.3 Prediction Models

Loan delinquency prediction is a binary classification problem. Prior research has shown that different data mining algorithms perform better on different loan datasets (Zurada et al. 2014). We evaluated six data mining algorithms in their ability to predict loan delinquencies in our sample: logistic regression (Hosmer Jr & Lemeshow 2004), decision tree (Safavian & Landgrebe 1991), random forest (Breiman 2001), boosted trees (Bauer & Kohavi 1999), support-vector machines (Amari & Wu 1999) and artificial neural networks (Yegnanarayana 2009). The space constraints preclude us from discussing the details of the individual techniques. Instead we refer the reader to the references provided for each model in the list above.

3.4 Model Performance Evaluation

The performance of binary classification algorithms is commonly assessed by splitting the data, using a part of the data (training set) to build the models and then assessing the model performance on the remaining data (test set) using the classification matrix and the derived metrics. In this study, we relied on three model performance measures: sensitivity, specificity and accuracy.

$$\text{Sensitivity} = TP / (TP + FN)$$
$$\text{Specificity} = TN / (TN + FP)$$
$$\text{Accuracy} = (TP + TN) / (TP + TN + FP + FN)$$

Where: TP – true positives, TN – true negatives, FP – false positives, FN – false negatives.

It is important to note, that sensitivity of the individual models is a critical measure of the model performance for predicting loan delinquencies. A false negative, a mortgage delinquency which is not predicted accurately at origination, exposes the underwriter to the potential loss of the principal. The average value of a loan in the Q4, 2007 portfolio was $211,000. In other words, every false negative puts $211,000 of capital at risk.

We followed the recommended practice of k-fold cross-validation (Breiman et al. 1984) for the evaluation of the individual algorithm performance. Research suggests that 10-fold cross-validation is generally sufficient to establish model performance estimate (Breiman et al. 1984; Kohavi 1995).

We used R (64-bit, version 3.1.3) software to build and evaluate the data mining models in this study (Anon 2015). R includes an implementation of the general linear models (glm) in the default distribution. We used this implementation for the logistic model in our analysis. We made use of the following packages to build the respective models: rpart (decision tree), randomForest, ada (boosted trees), kernlab (SVM), nnet (neural networks).

4. RESULTS

All models had difficulty with the accurate prediction of mortgage delinquencies. Artificial neural network algorithm showed the best results, accurately predicting 18.7% of delinquencies on average. The SVM model performed the worst, accurately predicting just 1.2% of delinquencies in the dataset. The results of 10-fold cross-validation for each of the modeling techniques are summarized in Table 1.

Table 1. Model performance summary

	Sensitivity	Specificity	Accuracy
Logistic regression	16.9% ± 1.7%	96.6% ± 0.4%	81.3% ± 0.2%
Decision tree	12.8% ± 2.7%	96.8% ± 0.7%	80.6% ± 0.2%
Random forest	15.3% ± 1.3%	96.6% ± 0.3%	81.0% ± 0.1%
Boosted trees	14.3% ± 1.4%	97.2% ± 0.3%	81.2% ± 0.2%
SVM	1.2% ± 0.9%	99.9% ± 0.1%	80.9% ± 0.1%
Neural network	18.7% ± 2.3%	95.6% ± 0.5%	80.9% + 0.2%

The logistic regression algorithm was the second best performer based on the sensitivity metric. The logistic regression model on average accurately predicted 16.9% of delinquent mortgages. To gain insights into which factors are important in the prediction of mortgage delinquencies, we examined the results of the logistic model in detail. The following predictors were statistically significantly associated with the probability of a mortgage delinquency:

- The borrower credit score is negatively correlated with the probability of mortgage delinquency. Borrowers with higher credit scores were less likely to default.
- Loan-to-value ratio – the proportion of the purchase price that the homebuyer was borrowing to finance the home purchase is positively correlated with the probability of mortgage delinquency.
- Debt-to-income – the monthly debt payments as a proportion of the monthly income is positively correlated to the probability of mortgage delinquency.
- Purpose of the loan – loans used to purchase a home were less likely to become delinquent compared to loans used for refinancing.
- Occupancy – mortgages used to buy homes that served as the primary residence were less likely to become delinquent compared to mortgages used to buy a second home.
- The interest rate associated with the mortgage was positively correlated with the probability of delinquency.
- The original unpaid balance at mortgage origination was positively correlated with the probability of mortgage delinquency.

We had also examined the importance of individual predictors in the random forest model which performed similarly to the logistic regression model in terms of model sensitivity. The random forest modeling technique provides two methods for estimating individual variable importance. First, the algorithm estimates the impact of withholding each of the variables on the overall model accuracy using the "out-of-bag" subsample. The results revealed that the borrower credit score, cumulative loan to value ratio as well as the LTV and the purpose of the loan were the key predictors of mortgage defaults.

5. DISCUSSION

In this study we sought to understand the extent to which data mining techniques can be used to build predictive models based on the identification of systematic patterns and salient predictors. The list of factors identified as significant predictors of mortgage delinquencies in our models suggests that mortgage underwriters, including Fannie Mae, are collecting information that can be useful in predicting future delinquencies. We found that certain thresholds are associated with significantly higher delinquency rates in the Fannie Mae portfolio from Q4, 2007. Borrower credit score below 724 was a strong predictor of serious delinquency. Nearly 30% of borrowers with credit scores below 724 were in technical default on their mortgages in our dataset, compared with less than 9% of borrowers with credit scores above 724. The size of the mortgage in relation to the property value (LTV) was also a significant predictor. Borrowers putting down payments of less than 20% were much more likely to become severely delinquent on their obligations. Overleveraged borrowers, for whom the combined monthly debt obligations exceeded 40% of their gross monthly incomes (DTI) were also much more likely to fall behind on their mortgage payments. Spotty prior credit history, limited personal financial investment in the property and excessive borrowing against income make perfect sense as predictors of mortgage delinquency. Following the crisis, Fannie Mae had announced tightening in the credit requirements for the qualified mortgages (Reuters 2008; Shenn 2012). The agency raised the minimum required credit score to 640. The minimum required credit score was just 580 prior to the crisis. The agency also raised the minimum required down payment to 20%.

The surprising finding from our analysis was that we largely failed to build an accurate prediction model for mortgage delinquencies using the data from the Fannie Mae portfolio. Our best model predicted only 18.7% of mortgage delinquencies. This means that in a portfolio where 194 out of 1000 mortgages became delinquent we could only correctly identify 36 delinquencies based on the information that was available at the time of mortgage acquisition. This level of accuracy would have helped to reduce the delinquency rate from 19.4% to 15.8%. However, this would not have saved Fannie Mae from bankruptcy.

This brings up the next question, how can we build a better model to predict mortgage delinquency. One possible reason for the challenges that we encountered in building the models could be information insufficiency. We may be missing key information that could help us build better models. Collection of additional information at the time of mortgage origination would offer a possible solution. Prior research offers some support for this proposal. Credit default analysis on a dataset from Israel, for example, identified the level of education and the type of professional employment as the key predictors of credit defaults (Feldman & Gross 2005). Therefore, collection of additional information at the time of mortgage origination, including the education level and professional employment, may help improve the quality of the models.

Another possible explanation for the challenges that we encountered in building an accurate prediction model using the Fannie Mae mortgage portfolio dataset is that there may had been an exogenous cause of mortgage defaults. In this scenario, the information that was available at the time of mortgage origination simply would not be helpful in accurately predicting the consequences of a crisis for the portfolio. The exogenous cause explanation would imply that there was an external shock to the system that affected the base rate of mortgage delinquencies as well as the nature of the deterministic and probabilistic relationships among the data available at origination. Exogenous causes are often discussed in macro-economic models, e.g. models of unemployment (Zivot & Andrews 2002). The Great Depression and the oil crisis of the 1980s are classic examples of exogenous events that caused disruptions of linkages among macro-economic factors and make it difficult to build accurate econometric models spanning these periods of history. The financial crisis of 2007-2008 may have had a similar effect on mortgage delinquencies.

The financial crisis of 2007-2008 had a number of causes. The issuance of 5/1, 3/1 and 2/1 adjustable-rate mortgages (ARMs) and their securitization were among them (Financial Crisis Inquiry Commission 2011). Adjustable rate mortgages that carry a low introductory interest rate, which resets after the initial 2, 3 or 5-year period, gained in popularity in 2005-2006. Many of the ARMs were issued to subprime borrowers. As the interest rates on these mortgages began to reset in 2007, the mortgage payments for the borrowers grew drastically, triggering defaults (Mayer et al. 2009). Although ARMs constituted a relatively small part of the overall mortgage market in 2007, the defaults on these mortgages produced a domino effect (Sherlund 2010). As the properties bought with ARMs went into foreclosure they triggered rapid general declines in property values as well as a series of events that affected all sectors of the economy, including prime mortgage borrowers. The economic downturn led to many people losing their jobs and the loss of steady income triggered many delinquencies on the traditional fixed-rate mortgages that were a part of the Fannie Mae portfolio.

The exogenous cause explanation for the failure of data mining techniques to accurately capture the patterns of defaults in the dataset imply that economic shocks will drastically increase mortgage default rates even among well-qualified borrowers. We examined the default rates among the best-qualified borrowers, those with credit scores above 760 for whom the historical delinquency rate is less than 2% (Corporation

2015). We find that the delinquency rate for this group varied between 5.5-6.4% for the mortgages acquired by Fannie Mae in 2007. This evidence supports the role of the financial crisis as an exogenous shock.

The practical implication of the financial crisis being an exogenous shock is that even if Fannie Mae restricted mortgage purchases to the most qualified borrowers, the agency would have still faced bankruptcy. In this scenario, a significant reduction in the financial leverage of the agency would be necessary for the agency to weather the next financial crisis. The crisis of 2007-2008 brought the Dodd-Frank reform to the banking sector, effectively reducing financial average among the largest banks from 30:1 before the crisis to less than 10:1 after the reform (Acharya et al. 2012). A similar reform would be required to safeguard GSEs from bankruptcy going forward.

6. CONCLUSION

In the present study we examined the predictive value of several data mining techniques using the Fannie Mae mortgage dataset from the fourth quarter of 2007, which had the highest delinquency rate in the agency history. Our data mining efforts on this dataset revealed that the borrower credit score, loan-to-value and debt-to-income ratios were the most important predictors of mortgage delinquencies. The artificial neural network was the best performing model in our analysis. However, the ANN model still had very low sensitivity, failing to correctly predict the majority of delinquencies. The most likely reason for the predictive model shortcomings is that the economic crisis served as an exogenous shock, the effects of which cannot be accurately modeled using the data available at mortgage acquisition. This result suggests that Fannie Mae's current efforts to reduce future delinquencies by tightening mortgage qualification requirements may prove insufficient and without a significant reduction in the financial leverage the agency would likely once again find itself in bankruptcy during the next economic downturn. Our results also illustrate a fundamental challenge in data mining – exogenous shocks can reshape the nature of the relationships in the data and make it difficult to build accurate models even with large and complete datasets.

REFERENCES

Acharya, V., Engle, R. & Richardson, M., 2012. Capital shortfall: A new approach to ranking and regulating systemic risks. *The American Economic Review*, pp.59–64.

Amari, S. & Wu, S., 1999. Improving support vector machine classifiers by modifying kernel functions. *Neural Networks*, 12(6), pp.783–789.

Anandarajan, M., Anandarajan, A. & Srinivasan, C.A., 2012. *Business intelligence techniques: a perspective from accounting and finance*, Springer Science & Business Media.

Andriotis, A., 2015. Home-Equity Lines of Credit See Jump in Delinquencies. *Wall Street Journal*.

Anon, 2015. The R Project for Statistical Computing. Available at: http://www.r-project.org/.

Avery, R.B. et al., 1996. Credit risk, credit scoring, and the performance of home mortgages. *Fed. Res. Bull.*, 82, p.621.

B. Baesens, T. Van Gestel, S. Viaene, M. Stepanova, J. Suykens, J.V., 2003. Benchmarking State-of-the-Art Classification Algorithms for Credit Scoring. *The Journal of the Operational Research Society*, 54(6), pp.627–635.

Bajari, P., Chu, C.S. & Park, M., 2008. *An empirical model of subprime mortgage default from 2000 to 2007*, National Bureau of Economic Research.

Bauer, E. & Kohavi, R., 1999. An empirical comparison of voting classification algorithms: Bagging, boosting, and variants. *Machine learning*, 36(1-2), pp.105–139.

BGFRS, 2015. *Mortgage Debt Outstanding*, Available at: http://www.federalreserve.gov/econresdata/releases/mortoutstand/current.htm.

Breiman, L. et al., 1984. *Classification and regression trees*, CRC press.

Breiman, L., 2001. Random forests. *Machine learning*, 45(1), pp.5–32.

Campbell, J.Y. & Cocco, J.F., 2011. *A model of mortgage default*, National Bureau of Economic Research.

Chan, S. et al., 2013. The role of neighborhood characteristics in mortgage default risk: Evidence from New York City. *Journal of Housing Economics*, 22(2), pp.100–118. Available at: http://dx.doi.org/10.1016/j.jhe.2013.03.003.

Corporation, F.I., 2015. How my FICO Scores are calculated. *myFico.com*. Available at: http://www.myfico.com/crediteducation/whatsinyourscore.aspx.

Elul, R. et al., 2010. What "Triggers" Mortgage Default. *SSRN Electronic Journal.*

Fayyad, U., Piatetsky-Shapiro, G. & Smyth, P., 1996. From data mining to knowledge discovery in databases. *AI magazine*, 17(3), p.37.

Feldman, D. & Gross, S., 2005. Mortgage default: Classification trees analysis. *Journal of Real Estate Finance and Economics*, 30(4), pp.369–396.

Financial Crisis Inquiry Commission, 2011. The financial crisis inquiry report. *US Government Printing Offi ce.*

Foote, C.L., Gerardi, K. & Willen, P.S., 2008. Negative equity and foreclosure: Theory and evidence. *Journal of Urban Economics*, 64(2), pp.234–245.

Ghatasheh, N., 2014. Business Analytics using Random Forest Trees for Credit Risk Prediction : A Comparison Study. *International Journal of Advanced Science and Technology*, 72, pp.19–30.

Hayre, L. et al., 2006. Modeling of Mortgage Prepayments and Defaults. *Citibank.*

Hosmer Jr, D.W. & Lemeshow, S., 2004. *Applied logistic regression*, John Wiley & Sons.

Jiang, W., Nelson, A.A. & Vytlacil, E., 2014. Liar's loan? Effects of origination channel and information falsification on mortgage delinquency. *The Review of Economics and Statistics*, 96(I), pp.1–18.

Kan, R. & Robotti, C., 2007. The 2008 federal intervention to stabilize Fannie Mae and Freddie Mac.

Kohavi, R., 1995. A study of cross-validation and bootstrap for accuracy estimation and model selection. In *IJCAI*. pp. 1137–1145.

Kristopher Gerardi, Lorenz Goette, and S.M., 2010. Financial Literacy and Subprime Mortgage Delinquency: Evidence from a Survey Matched to Administrative Data. *Federal Reserve Bank of Atlanta Working Papers*, (September).

Mac, F., 2008. *Freddie Mac Annual Report 2007*, Available at: http://www.freddiemac.com/investors/ar/pdf/2007annualrpt.pdf.

Mae, F., 2008. *Fannie Mae Annual Report 2007*, Available at: http://www.fanniemae.com/resources/file/ir/pdf/proxy-statements/2007_annual_report.pdf.

Mayer, C., Pence, K. & Sherlund, S.M., 2009. The rise in mortgage defaults. *The Journal of Economic Perspectives*, 23(1), pp.27–50.

Peterson, C.L., 2008. Fannie Mae, Freddie Mac, and the home mortgage foreclosure crisis. *Loyola University New Orleans Journal of Public Interest Law*, pp.149–170.

Peterson, C.L., 2009. Fannie Mae, Freddie Mac, and the home mortgage foreclosure crisis. *Loyola University New Orleans Journal of Public Interest Law*, 10, pp.149–170.

Quercia, R.G. & Stegman, M. a, 1992. Residential Mortgage Default : A Review of the Literature *. *Journal of Housing Research*, 3(2), pp.341–380.

Reuters, 2008. Fannie Mae Tightens Loan Standard to Protect Itself. *The New York Times*. Available at: http://www.nytimes.com/2008/04/02/business/rtlend-web.html.

Safavian, S.R. & Landgrebe, D., 1991. A survey of decision tree classifier methodology. *IEEE transactions on systems, man, and cybernetics*, 21(3), pp.660–674.

Shenn, J., 2012. Fannie Mae Tightens Mortgage Standards for Some Home Buyers. *BloombergBusiness*.

Sherlund, S.M., 2010. *Mortgage Defaults*,

Smith, B.C., 2011. Stability in consumer credit scores: Level and direction of FICO score drift as a precursor to mortgage default and prepayment. *Journal of Housing Economics*, 20(4), pp.285–298. Available at: http://dx.doi.org/10.1016/j.jhe.2011.09.001.

Statistics, B. of L., 2015. Labor Force Statistics from the Current Population Survey. *Databases, Tables & Calculations*. Available at: http://data.bls.gov/timeseries/LNS14000000.

Sun, Z., 2013. *Classification System for Mortgage Arrear Management*. University of Groningen.

Wallison, P.J. & Calomiris, C.W., 2009. The Last Trillion-Dollar Commitment: The Destruction of Fannie Mae and Freddie Mac. *The Journal of Structured Finance*, 15(1), pp.71–80.

Yegnanarayana, B., 2009. *Artificial neural networks*, PHI Learning Pvt. Ltd.

Young, J.T., 2013. The Worst Four Years Of GDP Growth In History: Yes, We Should Be Worried. *Forbes*.

Zivot, E. & Andrews, D.W.K., 2002. Further evidence on the great crash, the oil-price shock, and the unit-root hypothesis. *Journal of Business & Economic Statistics*, 20(1), pp.25–44.

Zurada, J., Kunene, N. & Guan, J., 2014. The Classification Performance of Multiple Methods and Datasets : Cases from the Loan Credit Scoring Domain. *Journal of International Technology and Information Management*, 23(1), pp.57–82.

MUTUAL AUTHENTICATION PROTOCOL FOR SECURE NFC BASED MOBILE HEALTHCARD

Divyashikha Sethia[1], Daya Gupta[1], Huzur Saran[2], Rishabh Agrawal[1] and Amogh Gaur[1]
[1]*Delhi Technological University, New Delhi, India*
[2]*Indian Institute of Technology, New Delhi, India*

ABSTRACT

Near Field Communication (NFC) enabled smart phones, have various applications in a variety of areas such as payment, ticketing and healthcare. Security is a major concern in these applications. Our main emphasis in this paper is on the application of NFC in healthcare systems. Electronic storage of patient information on health cards requires high security to ensure patient confidentiality and privacy as suggested in our previous work related to healthcards on NFC based devices and smartcard technology on tamper resistant Secure Element (SE) for storing credentials and secure data. We extend this work with proposal of mutual authentication protocol for secure interaction and Host Card Emulation (HCE) for valid patient and valid medical professional devices to directly interact through a simple tap without requiring any external reader. Secure Element based mutual authentication ensures right timely treatment is provided to a patient. We propose an architecture design, implementation and testing for Mutual Authentication (MA) using SE for NFC based healthcards over HCE which can be extended later to ubiquitous interfaces. The protocol ensures protection against a variety of attacks such as relay attacks, masquerading etc. Testing results indicate that although time is slow due to overheads of access of SE on java cards such as microSD card, it can be further improved by using higher version java cards or other tamper resistant solutions.

KEYWORDS

Host Card Emulation; Near Field communication; secure element; mutual authentication; e-health card; patient health record;

1. INTRODUCTION

Near field communication (NFC) is a wireless communication technology that works in a short range, of about 10 cm. The data transmission frequency used between the devices is 13.56 MHz. It supports communication speed up to 424 kbps (Finkenzeller 2010). Host Card Emulation (HCE) (S.C.A. Mobile and N.F.C. Council, 2014) enables NFC equipped devices to "emulate" contact-less smart cards to perform transactions.

NFC has a major application in the field of health care such as storage of health records on mobile device as suggested in our previous work (Sethia et al, 2014). Electronic Health Records (EHR) can be retained in the form of a healthcard on mobile device of a patient, with credentials in a hardware tamper resistant storage on Secure Element (SE). It can provide fast and readily available access to health records which can assist in treatment specially in case of an emergency.

Security is of prime importance in this scenario. The nature of the data here is very confidential and sensitive. Tampering with the prescription records of the patient can harm his health and risk his life. Measures must be taken for not only to verify the validity of the patients but also to verify the validity of the medical professionals who will be accessing and updating the patients' records. This is necessary to ensure that patient data stays private and in safe hands. Hence mutual authentication is necessary in this scenario. We would like to clarify that although a complete security framework must include authentication, authorization and access control, our work just emphasizes on the authentication aspect of the security framework. There are a number of stakeholders which are termed as medical professionals such as doctor, nurse, pharmacist, lab technician, insurance who must be authenticated before accessing the healthcard of a patient.

Figure 1. Relay attack Fraud Doctor Scenario

Figure 2. Relay attack Fraud Patient Scenario

The objective of this work is to develop an authentication system with high security and usability. The cryptographic computations and signature verifications are performed on smart cards used as secure elements so that the information remains safe even if the operating system is compromised. Our authentication scheme depends on public key infrastructure and is known as *HCE with Asymmetric Mutual Authentication (HAMA)*, which can be extended for mutual authentication over ubiquitous interfaces such as Bluetooth and remote access. It is capable of preventing a number of threats such as man in the middle attack, masquerading etc. It is especially designed to countermeasure relay attacks. Consider two cases for possibility of a relay attack in the usage scenario of mobile based health cards:

Case 1: A patient interacts with a fraud doctor as shown in figure 1, who can relay information to a valid doctor, who might be forced by an accomplice of the fraud doctor to give wrong medication to the patient to harm him.

Case 2: A fraud patient can relay information from a valid patient as shown in figure 2 in order to obtain medications from a valid doctor, to sell them illegally or to seek a costly medical treatment which his insurance does not cover. Moreover, if insurance details are also incorporated in the healthcard, where financial interactions are involved, relay attack can lead to financial fraud (Drimer and Murdoch 2007).

Our scheme uses location based measures to prevent such remote malicious health interactions between patient and medical professionals so that the patient is not harmed and only the right patient gets the right treatment. Stronger relay attack countermeasures with fraud entities in the same location can be handled by using multi factor authentication such as PIN and biometrics.

The rest of the paper is organized as follows. In Section 2, we provide literature on the major technologies used by us. This is followed by Section 3 which explores the related work in this field and compares it with our work. Section 4 further explains the system architecture and the sequence flow of the protocol. In Section 5, we present the proof of concept implementation, followed by a security analysis of our protocol in Section 6. In section 7, we conclude the paper.

2. LITERATURE REVIEW

2.1 e-Health Cards

With a number of industries utilizing the benefits of smart card technology, health care industry too has adopted this technology in order to provide trustworthy health information systems. E-Health Cards are smart cards issued to patients and health care professionals. Typical health cards include administrative, clinical, emergency and prescription data which can be accessed only by a valid health professional card. Moreover, these cards can be configured to reveal different data to different stakeholders. For example, it can reveal different data to a psychiatrist than it would to a paramedic, general practitioner or obstetrician. Plastic smart card based systems have been deployed in various countries including Germany (Hoerbst et al, 2010)(Sunyaev et al, 2009), Austria (Dorda et al, 2008) and Taiwan (Liu et al, 2006). A mobile based e-healthcard system is proposed in our previous work in (Sethia et al, 2014) using NFC for access and hardware tamper resistant secure element based on microSD cards for storing credentials.

2.2 Near Field Communication

The NFC technology is a radio based technology which uses electromagnetic radiation of a specific frequency (13.56 MHz) to transfer signals through free space. NFC complies with ISO/IEC 14443 and ISO/IEC 18092 standards and MIFARE and FeliCa specifications. NFC is capable of achieving transfer speed up to 424 Kbit/s. Connection is established by holding two NFC enabled devices close together (about

10cm). There are three communication modes (S.C.A. Mobile and N.F.C. Council, 2014) defined for a NFC device:

1. Read/Write, where the device is in active state.
2. Card Emulation, where the device is in passive state.
3. P2P, where the device can be either in active or in passive state.

Devices in active state have their own power while passive devices use magnetic induction to receive power from an active device. When two active devices communicate, only the sender generates a RF signal while the receiver is 'quiet'. The role of sender and receiver can swap during the communication process.

2.3 Host Card Emulation

HCE is a technology which enables an NFC device to emulate a contactless smart card. Users can tap the device to initiate transactions with an application without the requirement of a secure element (SE) in the device. This emulated card can be read by any NFC device which is working in Read/Write mode. This emulated card can be used to make payments, display tickets and vouchers and present ID. Research In Motion (RIM), on the Blackberry platform (Roland 2012), were the first to incorporate this functionality in their phones. Subsequently Cyanogenmod integrated some patches (Yeager) to the Android OS which permitted NFC enabled mobile phones to perform card emulation from the host. However, HCE attracted most attention when Google incorporated it within Android 4.4 (KitKat).

Prior to HCE, SE was used for card emulation. The data in the form of Application Processing Data Units (APDUs) was directly routed to the SE by the NFC controller without any role of the operating system. In HCE, this data is sent to the operating system of the device which subsequently routes this data to an app or SE (Google API guides).

This change comes, however, at a price. Roland mentions that absence of a secure environment leaves the system vulnerable which can be easily exploited by a malware residing in the device's main memory to obtain critical data (2012). Moreover, interference by other applications is possible. Generally HCE based solutions use cloud systems for storing and retrieving credentials. Storing sensitive data in a secure remote location offers some protection against this vulnerability. However, to ensure complete protection, a secure environment on the device is necessary.

3. RELATED WORK

A complete NFC based secure mobile healthcare system was proposed in our previous work (Sethia et al, 2014), which utilized NFC and Smart Card technology for retaining security credentials and EHR. In this work we extend the concept using HCE which requires patient mobile device with portable health records and it can be accessed with a simple tap by mobile device of a medical professional. Our work incorporates design, implementation and testing of Mutual Authentication phase in the security framework for mobile based healthcard.

There are several solutions to secure HCE. Practical solutions (S.C.A. Mobile and N.F.C. Council, 2014) use tokens to reduce the impact of eventual exposure. A token is a value which replaces an actual credential (like PAN in the payment service ecosystem). Tokens have limited validity and scope depending on the business rules by the issuer. A customer's device is provisioned with these tokens beforehand in order to avoid latency. For transactions, these tokens are presented to the merchant's Point of Sale (POS) who forwards these tokens to the issuer. The issuer (or an entity acting as the token vault on behalf of the issuer) authorizes the transaction after verifying the token and identifying the associated credentials. Although tokenization reduces the impact of credential exposure, it can't eliminate the risk. One should also keep in mind that accessibility and availability of cloud services can be limited or compromised by Denial of Service (DoS) attacks. In the health card scenario, we propose the usage of hardware tamper resistant secure element for storing credentials in order to secure communication over HCE.

Relay attacks are one of the biggest threats in the contactless domain including HCE (Francis, Hancke, Mayes and Markantonakis 2010), causing illegal usage of a card. In this type of attack, the attacker masquerades itself as a valid reader by relaying the information received from the card to an actual reader and by relaying back the response as shown in figure 1 and 2. There are counter measures such as Distance

Bounding Protocols (Drimer and Murdoch 2007) which allow a verifier to establish an upper bound on the distance of the claimant. Typical protocols measure the round trip delay time of some challenge bits and then compute the upper bound from the information. The distance bound computed by a RF distance bounding protocol is very sensitive to even the slightest processing delay. Hence these protocols are not suitable for HCE based mutual authentication as HCE is known to have time variations (Umar et al, 2015). In order to use Distance Bound protocols, they would require additional time sensitive hardware. We propose a mutual authentication which provides countermeasure to relay attack, by generating session key based on security handshake to secure communication over HCE and further exchanging location information to ensure that patient and medical professional are valid and in allowed to interact in the same location.

4. SYSTEM ARCHITECTURE

This section illustrates the design of the proposed scheme.

4.1 Overview

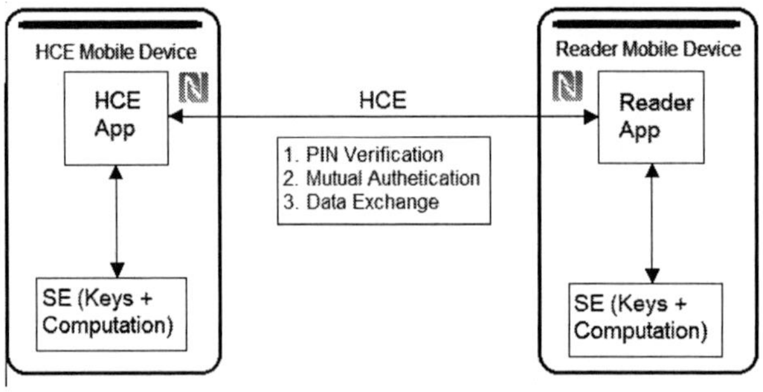

Figure 3. System Architecture

Figure 3 shows the architecture of the system. It consists of two NFC enabled mobile devices. Since device is working in Read/Write mode while the other works in Card Emulation mode, two different applications are required to handle the different modes. The applications are responsible for establishing an HCE connection and transferring data. Also, each application has an access to a local secure element. Credentials such as keys, IDs and PIN are stored on these SEs during an initial one time setup phase securely. They also provide the necessary environment for performing computations such as encryption, decryption and sign verification. To start the applications, both users have to enter a PIN on their devices. Once an application receives the correct PIN, it is ready to perform the mutual authentication sequence. Only after this security handshake the data transfer is allowed.

4.2 Protocol Design for Mutual Authentication

Table 1. Terminologies

Term	Description
RAND_C & RAND_R	The random numbers generated by the card SE and the reader SE respectively
ID_C & ID_R	Identification numbers of card and reader respectively
KPbc & KPbr	The public keys of the card and reader respectively
KPrc & KPrr	The private keys of the card and reader respectively
KPbs & KPrs	The public and private keys of the certifying authority
Sigc & Sigr	The signatures of the card and reader respectively
Ks	The session key created
Loc_C & Loc_R	Location information of card and the reader respectively

The terminologies used in HAMA protocol are given in Table 1. It is based on the idea of storing asymmetric keys and certificates on secure element which is embedded in a microSD card.

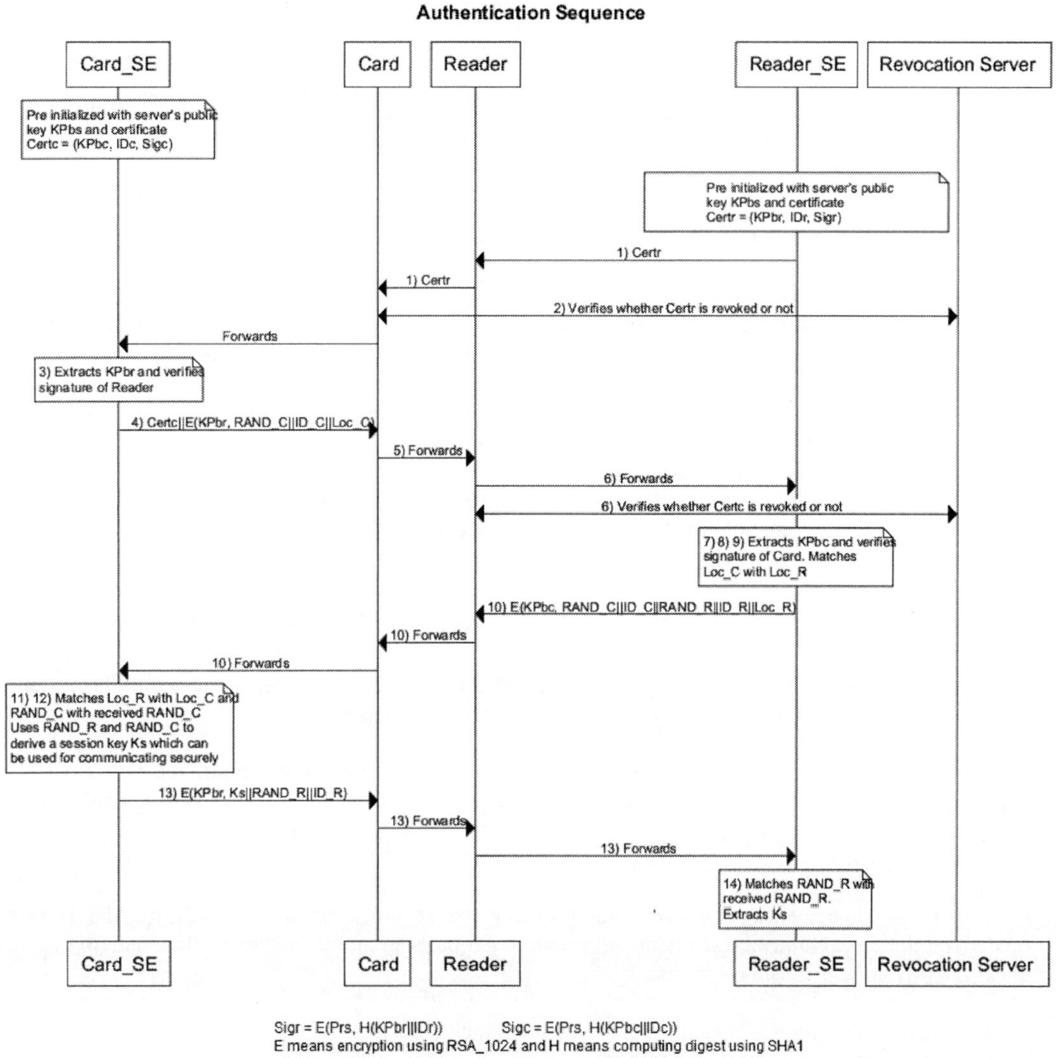

Figure 4. HAMA (HCE with Asymmetric Mutual Authentication)

Figure 4 shows the sequence diagram for HAMA. It uses asymmetric cryptography based authentication scheme to authenticate reader and card to each other. They have been personalized beforehand with the public key of the certifying authority (CA) and their certificates signed by the CA in a personalization phase. Both parties exchange their certificates and verify them using the public key of the CA as shown in steps 3 and 7. The certificates are also cross checked with a revocation server in order to verify their validity. The certificates contain the public key and the identification of their corresponding parties. The protocol is a challenge response scheme. Both parties generate a random number, encrypt it using the public key of the other party and send it across. The other party proves its authenticity by decrypting the nonce using its private key. Also location information Loc_C and Loc_R are exchanged for prevention of relay attacks. This location information is passed along with the respective random nonces and upon receiving this information both parties check their location with their location. If they don't match, then a relay attack is detected and the authentication sequence is aborted. All of this processing takes place on the two applets which reside on the secure elements of the card and the reader. They perform the cryptographic operations to authenticate the certificates, validate the nonces and cross check the locations. Here, we assume that both the parties have a secure and a reliable method to obtain their locations. The applets are only accessible by special mobile applications which are compiled with card service provider libraries to ensure secure access. The mobile applications interact with the secure elements internally for all cryptographic operations to be done on secure elements and communicate it further on the HCE interface to the remote mobile device application. Hence it is a mutual authentication which is end to end between two secure elements interfacing over HCE. In this way, the private key stays secure. The protocol is designed in such a way, that at all exchanges are in encrypted form and hence a snooper cannot gain any valuable information.

5. IMPLEMENTATION AND RESULTS

We implemented the proposed protocol using two Xperia M2 mobile devices running Android 5.0 (Lollipop), as reader and card, which supports HCE with NFC support and GOTrust MicroSD Javacards (GO-Trust microSD JAVA) as secure elements. Java Card is one of the most widely used multi-application smart card platform (Mayes and Markantonakis 2007). It is at least partly responsible for the success of smart cards as the "write-once-run-everywhere" concept brought smart card application developers more flexibility and platform independence.

Testing showed that HAMA protocol using GO Trust Java cards take about 3551 milliseconds to complete the authentication process. The bottleneck of the process was found to be the access time for the java cards. This implementation was tested for security vulnerabilities, stability and performance.

6. SECURITY ANALYSIS FOR MUTUAL AUTHENTICATION

This security analysis is only for mutual authentication. There are other issues with healthcard like authorization, revocation etc. which are beyond the scope of this paper.

Threat model: To analyze the security of our system, we first have to determine the *threat model* (Web application threat model), including the *security objectives*, the *trust boundaries* as well as possible *threats*.

Security objectives

The primary objective of our authentication scheme is to ensure secure mutual authentication between the reader and the card. No invalid entity must be able to get past the mutual authentication, and no information about the private keys must be exposed.

The security objectives of an authentication system include:

- Private credentials must stay secure.
- Attackers should not be able to get themselves authenticated.
- Further actions after mutual authentication must also take place securely.

Trust Boundary

The java card environment is assumed to be secure. This is a valid assumption as it resides on a tamper proof and restricted access card, which can only be accessed using command APDUs. The personalization phase of the cards, during which it is loaded with the key of the certifying authority is assumed to be held in a secure environment. This is generally true for a real world application.

- **Malware attack-** HCE is based on the involvement of the mobile OS. A compromised OS is a major threat to its security. A malware on the device can access unauthorized information, initiate or terminate a transaction. Our proposal is secure against such threat as the critical computations are taking place on the tamper proof, restricted access secure element.
- **DDOS attack on cloud-** In regular HCE, a cloud is usually used to provide backend authentication. But a Distributed Denial of Service (DDOS) attack on such a server can hinder our authentication

process. In the proposed scheme, this role is played by the SE, which resides on the device, and protected against such attacks.

- **Masquerading-** The most important function of the authentication process, is to prevent unauthorized access. A card masquerading itself as an valid card must not be able to get past the authentication process. The digital certificate in our protocol would prevent this from happening.
- **Replay attack-** Another form of attack which can be used to compromise the system is a replay attack. It is a man-in-the-middle attack, where the attacker can record the data exchanges between the card and the reader and use this information, to attack later. Our proposal uses nonces, which are arbitrary numbers used only once in a cryptographic communication. As different numbers are generated for each transaction, a replay attack is computationally infeasible and practically impossible.
- **Relay attack-** Relay Attack is a type of attack where an adversary initiates communication with both parties and then relays messages between the two parties. As a result, both parties think that they are communicating directly to each other, which is not the case. The adversary talks to one party by posing as the other party in between. In this way relay attacks are related to man in the middle attacks. However unlike MITM attacks, the adversary does not need to know a shared secret in order to launch a relay attack.

In HAMA protocol, we countermeasure relay attack using the concept of proximity and location information which is used to verify the location of a device and reader (Francis et al, 2010), hence preventing them to interact in case they are not in the same proximity. There are many methods to acquire this information. Some of these are as follows-

1. **Ambience Sensing Protocols**: Halevi et. al. (2012) have developed a technique to securely detect proximity of devices by collecting contextual information from environment such as sound and light. Since many NFC enabled phones are also equipped with a variety of sensors which can measure light, sound, orientation and proximity to a physical object, this technique can be easily implemented with these phones. In order to achieve greater security, the contextual information should be based a large number of factors (Akram et al, 2015)
2. **Location Matching Protocols**: As suggested by Drimer and Murdoch (2007), GPS data can be used to determine the location of both devices and verify that the devices are in close proximity. However, this approach has its drawbacks. Firstly, this approach relies on additional infrastructure. Secondly, GPS doesn't work properly in an indoor environment. Lastly, this approach raises location privacy concerns.

We limit the relay attack by verifying the location of the entities to be in the same proximity. In case attacker is in the proximity then countermeasures such as multi factor authentication, small sized location, "chain of trust" mechanism (Francis et al, 2010) can be used.

7. CONCLUSION AND FUTURE WORK

In this paper, we have a proposed a mutual authentication protocol to be used in an NFC based secure mobile health card for HCE. Secure identification is the backbone of an e-healthcard system as it prevents invalid access. Our mutual authentication protocol plays a crucial role in this regard by providing mutual authentication between patient cards and medical readers by using the concept of trusted cryptographic processing on secure elements and communication over HCE interface. It would also play a significant role in preventing medical frauds in developing countries such as India, where medical funds are already limited. We have implemented this protocol over two Android 5.0 devices with GO Trust Java cards as secure elements. We tested the system to obtain security and performance information. We demonstrated that the system is secure against various threats and attacks. HAMA takes about 3551 milliseconds to authenticate the reader and card to each other. Hence we found out that these results are acceptable. The time is slow as the bottleneck is the access time for java cards. In our future works, we may use Trusted Execution Environment (TEE) trustzone ARM as the secure element which would lead to an improvement in performance. Work also needs to be done for access control, auditing and key management of healthcard with modern cryptographic techniques such as Attribute Based Encryption and Identity Based Encryption.

REFERENCES

[1] Akram, R.N. et al, 2015. We Were Wrong: Ambient Sensors Do Not Provide Proximity Evidence for NFC Transactions.

[2] Dorda, W. et al, 2008. Austria's path toward nationwide electronic health records. *Methods of information in medicine*, *47*(2), pp.117-123.

[3] Drimer, S. and Murdoch, S.J., 2007, August. Keep Your Enemies Close: Distance Bounding Against Smartcard Relay Attacks. In *USENIX Security* (Vol. 2007).

[4] Finkenzeller, K., 2010. *RFID handbook: Fundamentals and applications in contactless smart cards, radio frequency identification and near-field communication. 3rd ed.* A John Wiley and Sons, Ltd. Publication, Chichester, United Kingdom.

[5] Francis, L. et al, 2010, November. A location based security framework for authenticating mobile phones. In *Proceedings of the 2nd International Workshop on Middleware for Pervasive Mobile and Embedded Computing* (p. 5). ACM.

[6] Francis, L., Hancke, G., Mayes, K. and Markantonakis, K., 2010. Practical NFC peer-to-peer relay attack using mobile phones. In *Radio Frequency Identification: Security and Privacy Issues* (pp. 35-49). Springer Berlin Heidelberg.

[7] Google API guides. Host-based Card Emulation. http://developer.android.com/guide/topics/connectivity/nfc/hce.html, [Online; accessed on 15-Dec-2015].

[8] GO-Trust microSD JAVA, http://www.go-trust.com/products/microsd-java/ [Online; accessed on May 26, 2016]

[9] Halevi, T. et al, 2012. Secure proximity detection for NFC devices based on ambient sensor data. In *Computer Security–ESORICS 2012* (pp. 379-396). Springer Berlin Heidelberg.

[10] Hoerbst, A. et al, 2010. Attitudes and behaviors related to the introduction of electronic health records among Austrian and German citizens. *International journal of medical informatics*, *79*(2), pp.81-89.

[11] Liu, C.T., et al, 2006. The impacts of smart cards on hospital information systems—An investigation of the first phase of the national health insurance smart card project in Taiwan. *International Journal of Medical Informatics*, *75*(2), pp.173-181.

[12] Mayes, K. and Markantonakis, K., 2007. *Smart Cards, Tokens, Security and Applications*. Springer Science+Business Media., Berlin, Germany.

[13] Roland, M., 2012. Software card emulation in nfc-enabled mobile phones:great advantage or security nightmare? *In Fourth International Workshop on Security and Privacy in Spontaneous Interaction and Mobile Phone Use (IWSSI/SPMU).*

[14] S.C.A. Mobile and N.F.C. Council, 2014. Host Card Emulation (HCE) 101. *Smart Card Alliance, Tech. Rep., August.*

[15] Sethia, D. et al, 2014, January. NFC based secure mobile healthcare system. In *Communication Systems and Networks (COMSNETS), 2014 Sixth International Conference on* (pp. 1-6). IEEE.

[16] Sunyaev, A. et al, 2009. Analysis of the Applications of the Electronic Health Card in Germany. In *Wirtschaftsinformatik (2)* (pp. 749-760).

[17] Umar, A. et al, 2015, Performance variation in host-based card emulation compared to a hardware security element. *IEEEC, 2015.*

[18] Web application threat model. http://msdn.microsoft.com/enus/library/ms978531.aspx. [Online; accessed on 15-Dec-2015]

[19] Yeager, D., Added nfc reader support for two new tag types: Iso pcd type a and iso pcd type b. https://github.com/CyanogenMod/android packages apps Nfc/commit/d41edfd794d4d0fedd91d561114308f0d5f83878. [Online; accessed on 15-Dec-2015]

IBGP SOLUTION BY COMBINING ROUTE REFLECTION AND SHARED TREE BASED MULTICAST

Toshihiko Kato, Yao Koffi Hubert Wilfried, Celimuge Wu and Satoshi Ohzahata
University of Electro-Communications, 1-5-1, Chofugaoka, Chofu, Tokyo 182-8585, Japan

ABSTRACT

There are many researches focusing on the scalability problem in the external route information dissemination by the *internal Border Gateway Protocol* (iBGP). The traditional one is a scheme to use the route reflectors, which redistribute the external route to their clients. Although this scheme is used in an actual network management, they still have some problems such that they suffer from wrong paths in case of network failures and that there may occur transient loops at the external route update. In order to resolve those problems, *LOUP* (Link-Ordered Update Protocol) proposes a multicast based route information dissemination scheme. It constructs a shortest path multicast tree per a border router and delivers UPDATE messages over the tree. LOUP can resolve the above problems but its concept is close to the full mesh structure in iBGP, and so it has another problem that the number of UPDATE messages becomes large. In this paper, we propose a new external route information dissemination scheme which combines the route reflection and the shared tree based multicast. Our scheme named *RESTERM* (Reflection Enabled Shared Tree External Route Multicast) charges the route reflectors with behaving as the root of trees, and builds shared trees necessary for establishing the best routes for all *RESTERM* routers. This paper also describes the results of performance evaluation focusing on the number of hops in delivering UPDATA messages and shows that *RESTERM* provides better performance than the traditional route reflection scheme and LOUP.

KEYWORDS

iBGP, Route Reflector, Multicast, Shared Tree, PIM-SM

1. INTRODUCTION

The *Border Gateway Protocol* (*BGP*) [Rekhter, Y., et al., Ed. 2006] is a routing protocol designed for exchanging the information on routes among *autonomous systems* (*ASes*), which is called *external routes*. According to the growth of the Internet, the role of BGP becomes more and more important. At the end of 2015, the number of ASes reaches 52,700 and they correspond to roughly 580,000 blocks of IP addresses [Huston, G. 2016], which are exchanged by BGP.

BGP is in fact categorized into two protocols: *external BGP* (*eBGP*) and *internal BGP* (*iBGP*). An AS is connected with other ASes through border routers, which are BGP speaking routers (*BGP speakers*) communicating with the border routers in other ASes. eBGP is used for exchanging route information between them. iBGP is used to exchange external route information between a border and an internal BGP speaker and among internal BGP speakers. These two are based on the same protocol specification, but adopt slightly different rules. Especially, when a BGP speaker receives an UPDATE message from an *internal peer*, it shall not re-distribute the routing information contained in that message to other internal peers. This limitation is adopted for avoiding routing loops, but it introduces a situation that all BGP speakers within one AS must be fully meshed. This represents a serious scalability problem that has been well documented with several alternatives being proposed.

In order to resolve the scalability problem, IETF introduces the *route reflection* approach and the *confederation* approach [Park, J. H., et al., 2012], among which the former is widely adopted in the current Internet. This approach allows a BGP speaker (known as a "*route reflector*") to advertise iBGP learned routes to its clients [Bates, T., et al., 2006]. More specifically, the iBGP peers in the route reflection approach are divided into two groups: client peers and non-client peers. When a route reflector receives a route from iBGP peer, it selects the best route, and then it will do the following depending on the type of the peer from which it is receiving the best path route: A route from a non-client iBGP peer is reflected to all the clients, and a route from a client peer is reflected to all the non-client peers as well as to the client peers.

Although the route reflection decreases the number of iBGP sessions, it introduces another problem that some BGP speakers do not obtain their best route within the AS. This is because the route reflectors only advertise their own best routes to the clients. In order to resolve this non-optimal routing, several approaches for the route reflection are proposed [Buob, M. O., et al., 2007], [Buob, M. O., et al., 2008], [Vutukuru, M., et al., 2005], [Balon, S. and Leduc, G., 2009], [Ballani, H., et al., 2008].

There are new proposals which introduce a new routing protocol among iBGP speakers. One trend is to separate routing from routers, such as Routing Control Platform (RCP) [Feamster, N., et al., 2004] and oBGP [Oprescu, I., et al., 2011]. Another trend is to exploit multicast trees among iBGP speakers. LOUP (Link-Ordered Update Protocol) is an example [Gvozdiev, N., et al., 2013].

This paper focuses on the multicast approach because of its stable routing information dissemination. LOUP uses a shortest path tree based multicast. Here, separate trees are constructed for disseminating UPDATE messages, each of which has a border router as its root node. So, it has a feature that the UPDATE messages are delivered properly to each iBGP speaker. In LOUP, however, the multicast trees are constructed as many as the number of border routers. Therefore, there might be a case that the number of messages becomes larger than the route reflection approach. In this paper, we propose a new multicast based external routing information dissemination scheme, which uses a shard tree as that used in the Protocol Independent Multicast – Sparse Mode (PIM-SM) multicast routing [Fenner, B., et al., 2006], where route reflectors work as its root node. We call our scheme *RESTERM* (Reflection Enabled Shared Tree External Route Multicast). At the joining to the shared tree, *RESTERM* routers inform the route reflector of their nearest border router, and only the required routing information is delivered through the tree. *RESTERM* provides the proper and minimal delivery of UPDATA messages.

The rest of paper consists of the following section. Section 2 shows related works on iBGP routing information dissemination. Section 3 proposes the design of *RESTERM.* Section 4 gives the results of performance evaluation. In the end, section 5 gives the conclusions of this paper.

2. RELATED WORKS

[Buob, M. O., et al., 2007] introduced a concept of *fm-optimality* (full mesh optimality), which is a sufficient condition to ensure that the selected route to every border router is the best route which should be chosen by a full mesh configuration. It proposed a formal method to check the optimality of the route choice in a route reflection graph. [Buob, M. O., et al., 2008] built an algorithm which chooses the minimal number of iBGP sessions satisfying the fm-optimality for a given route reflector configuration.

In contrast with the above works starting from the given route reflectors, [Vutukuru, M., et al., 2005] proposed a heuristic algorithm to locate route reflectors within a given Interior Gateway Protocol (IGP) topology. The proposed algorithm called *BGPsep* is based on the construction of a graph separator [Spielman, D. and Teng, S., 1996] for an IGP topology. The algorithm works in the following way.

- For an IGP graph *G*, it chooses a graph separator *S*. Nodes in *S* are the router reflectors. Between each pair in *S*, a non-client iBGP session is maintained.
- For each subgraph *Gs* consisting of the nodes in *G* excluding those in *S*, the followings are applied.
  - Between each node in *Gs* and each node in *S*, a client iBGP session is maintained.
  - The algorithm is applied recursively to *Gs* and the resultant sessions are added.
- If the number of nodes in *G* (or *Gs*) is 1, then algorithm stops. If the number of nodes in *G* (or *Gs*) is 2, then a non-client iBGP session is maintained between them and the algorithm stops.

[Gutierrez, E., et al., 2014] published a software tool based on this algorithm.

There are other approaches to improve the route reflection function. [Balon, S. and Leduc, G., 2009] focused on the link weight used in the IGP routing, trying to optimize the link utilization. For a precise optimization, it is required to estimate accurately all link utilizations resulting from the application of the optimized weights in the AS. It proposes the IGP link weight optimizer considering the iBGP routing taking account of route reflectors. It can forbid solutions leading to non-optimal route selection.

Another approach is to shrink the routing table size on routers. [Ballani, H., et al., 2009] proposed a technique named *ViAggre* (Virtual Aggregation) which allows an AS to modify its internal routing such that individual routers in the AS network only maintain a part of the global routing table. The paper proposes the design how *ViAggre* can be applied to route reflectors. However, *ViAggre* has a negative aspect that some traffic is not transferred through the best path.

In spite of those efforts for the route reflection approach, it still has some problems. One example is that the large size of routing table for external route information is hard to manage in BGP speakers which process the packet forwarding together. Another example is that the best route cannot be maintained in the case of the IGP network failures such as link disconnects and node downs. Therefore, there are some proposals on the new routing architecture.

For the purpose of releasing the burden of external route processing, the separation of routing from routers is discussed. As described above, [Feamster, N., et al., 2004] presented a design of RCP that aims to offer separate selection of routes on behalf of routers. RCP introduces three modules: the IGP Viewer to collect topology information, the BGP engine which learns the BGP routes, performs the BGP decision process and informs of the routers of the best paths, and the Route Control Server which processes messages received from the other two modules and maintains the preference of the border routers of external routes for each BGP speaker. [Oprescu, I., et al., 2011] extended this works by using a distributed overlay of routing software. In this work named *oBGP*, the prefix table is split, making possible parallel computation of routes while in the RCP solution, all the BGP information is concentrated in one point.

As an example of new routing architecture coping for the IGP network failures, [Gvozdiev, N., et al., 2013] proposed a multicast based routing architecture named LOUP, as described above. In order to provide the best route for every iBGP speaker and avoid transient forwarding loops during route updates, LOUP adopts two dissemination techniques: *reverse forwarding tree* and *backward activation*. The reverse forwarding tree is a technique used in an IP multicast tree construction [Savola, P., 2008]. A tree to leaves in terms of a specific root node is constructed by reversing a path from an individual leaf to the root and combining those paths. LOUP uses one tree per a border router intending to disseminate external route information. This mechanism corresponds to a *shortest path tree* used by IP multicast routing such as PIM-DM (Protocol Independent Multicast – Dense Mode) [Adams, A., et al., 2005]. The backward activation is a technique such that, when a border router withdraws a route (or worsen a route), the change is applied first by routers furthest from the border router. It is for avoiding transient loops in a withdrawal case. LOUP does not use IP multicast but uses a multicast mechanism over the TCP level. It establish a TCP connection between peering routers and LOUP messages traverse these TCP connections with an IP TTL (Time To Live) parameter set to 1. Since the shortest path trees are constructed for individual border routers, the number of trees increases as the number of border routers increases, similarly with full mesh iBGP sessions, although, thanks to the multicasting, the number of UPDATE messages is smaller than that of full mesh iBGP.

The scheme we propose in this paper adopts the shared tree paradigm instead of the shortest path tree paradigm. A shared tree used in PIM-SM is constructed for one IP multicast group address. The root node of the tree is called a *rendezvous point*, and all senders in the group send an IP multicast datagram to the rendezvous point by tunneling it in a Register message, which then delivers them along the shared tree. Our scheme uses the route reflectors as rendezvous points. The BGP speakers know their corresponding route reflector and the nearest border router, and when joining to the shared tree, they inform the nearest border router of the route reflector. Based on this information, the necessary external route information for the best routes in individual BGP speakers will be delivered.

3. DESIGN OF *RESTERM*

3.1 Design Principles

We have adopted the following design principles for *RESTERM*.

- In *RESTERM*, an AS is constructed by *RESTERM* routers working in conformance with our design. Some of *RESTERM* routers work as route reflectors, and some as border routers. The others are internal *RESTERM* routers. One router may have the responsibility of both router reflector and border router. In case that non *RESTERM* router (IGP router) exists, we assume that some of *RESTERM* routers are connected via the tunneling mechanism to keep the neighboring condition.

- We use multi-level route reflectors as described in [Bates, T., et al., 2006]. Different from the conventional route reflection scheme, we use the shared tree multicast paradigm to deliver external route information. A shared tree is constructed among a route reflector and its clients, and the route reflector works as the rendezvous point in the tree.
- Trees are constructed recursively, i.e. a router reflector works as a client for the upper level route reflector. Each shared tree is identified by the IP address of its rendezvous point.
- Among the top level route reflectors, a shortest path multicast tree is constructed with each top level route reflector being its root. The shortest path tree is identified by the IP address of rendezvous point with character string "top" in the rest of paper.
- Similarly with LOUP, the multicast data transfer is done over the TCP connections established among neighbor *RESTERM* routers.
- We assume the followings for the tree construction.
  - All the *RESTERM* routers in an AS know the IP addresses of the associated next level route reflector and the associated top level route reflector.
  - All the *RESTERM* routers in an AS know the IP address of the nearest border router.
- Our scheme consists of three sub-protocols: the *neighbor discovery protocol*, the *tree construction protocol* and the *route information dissemination protocol.*
- The neighbor discovery is for establishing a TCP connection between neighbor *RESTERM* routers. Using the IGP routing table, each *RESTERM* router obtains the IP address of the neighbor *RESTERM* routers, and tries to establish a TCP connection for the multicast operation. It also supports the keep alive mechanism over the TCP connections.
- The tree construction protocol defines the procedure for establishing the shared multicast trees from the route reflectors. *RESTERM* routers know the associated router reflectors and send *JOIN messages* up to the reflectors. A JOIN message includes the IP address of the route reflector, the IP address of the nearest border routers of the sender and indicated by the downstream routers. While transferring JOIN messages, the routers create the *multicast forwarding table* including the name of tree, the IP addresses of indicated border routers, and the downstream interfaces to which UPDATE messages should be forwarded.
- The route information dissemination protocol defines the procedure for transferring *UPDATE messages*. When a border router obtains an external route from its eBGP peer, it sends an UPDATE message to the associated top level router reflector. This is done over a TCP connection directly established between the border router and the top level route reflector. If the route information from this border router is requested over the multicast tree, the route reflector disseminates the UPDATE message containing the information to its clients (and to the other top level route reflectors). The dissemination is done over the TCP based multicast tree constructed beforehand. If some clients are next level route reflectors, the same procedure is invoked recursively.

3.2 Detailed Design

In this subsection, we describe the detailed design of *RESTERM* using a network configuration depicted in Figure 1. The circles in the figure represent *RESTERM* routers, among which routers 1 and 2 are border routers and RR1 is a route reflector. The number attached to edges are IGP costs assigned to the links. We assume that border routers 1 and 2 have the same degree of preference for external address "D."

3.2.1 Neighbor Discovery and Tree Construction

As described above, each *RESTERM* router establishes a TCP connection with neighbor router. Figure 2 (a) shows this procedure. After the TCP connections are established, the tree construction is done as depicted in Figure 2 (b). The *RESTERM* routers except RR1 send JOIN messages to RR1. A JOIN message contains the name of multicast tree, "RR1" in this case, and the nearest border router address.

For example, router 3 sends a JOIN message specifying RR1, and router 2 as the nearest border router. This message is sent from router 3 to RR1 directly following the IGP routing table in router 3. After RR1 receives JOIN messages from routers 2 and 3, it creates the multicast forwarding table containing two entries as shown in the figure; (interface to link to router2, router 2 as the nearest border router) and (interface to link to router 3, router 2 as the nearest border router).

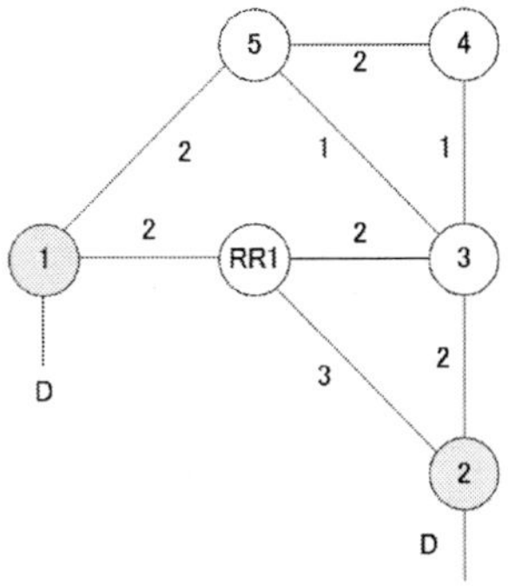

Figure 1. A network configuration

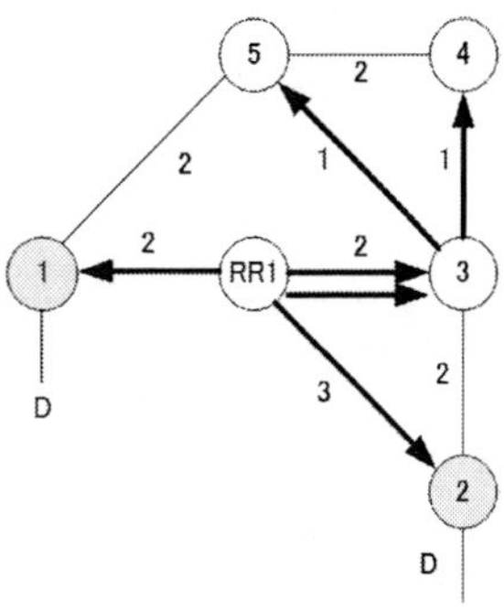

Figure 3. Shared tree configuration

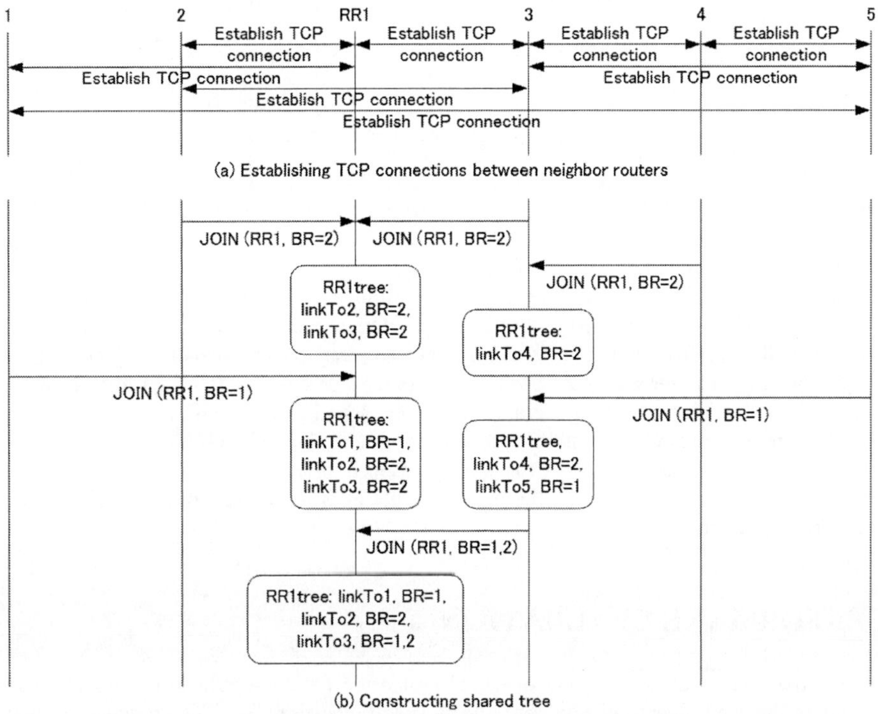

Figure 2. Neighbor discovery and shared tree construction

Routers 4 and 5 send JOIN messages containing router 2 or 1 as the nearest border outer, respectively. Those messages are sent to router 3 as it is the next router to RR1. After receiving those two messages, router 3 creates the multicast forwarding table with two entries as shown in the figure. Then router 3 send a new JOIN message because border router 1 is now added in the forwarding table. In the end, RR1 has the multicast forwarding table for RR1 tree with three entries. It should be noted that the multicast forwarding tables are maintained only at the routers which have some child routers in the shared tree. In the example here, only RR1 and router 3 have them. Figure 3 shows the configuration of the shared tree constructed in this communication. The two arrows from RR1 to router 3 indicate the branches for border routers 1 and 2.

3.2.2 Route Information Dissemination

Then border routers invoke the dissemination of external route information. Figure 4 shows an example of this procedure. Here, an UPDATE message similar with that defined in BGP is used. The border router address which generated the message is added as a new parameter.

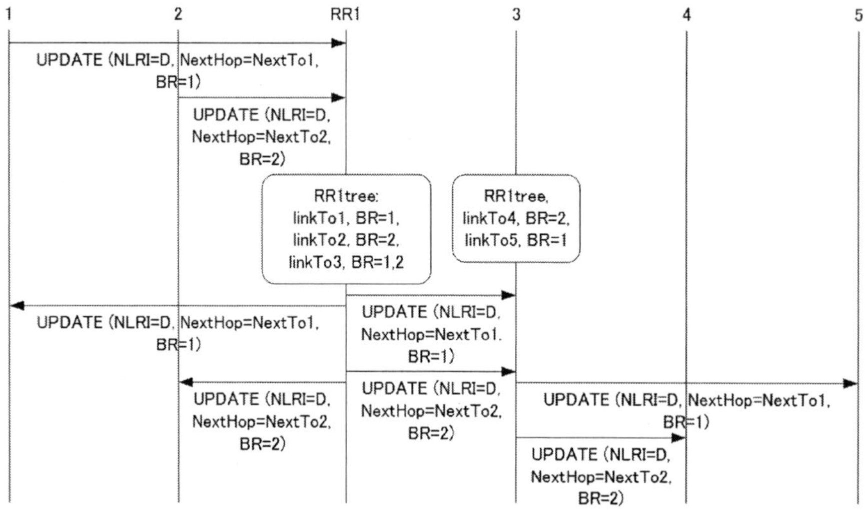

Figure 4. Route information dissemination

In the beginning, border routers 1 and 2 send UPDATE messages for external destination D to their associated router reflector, RR1. In this case, the root reflection is only one level and so RR1 becomes the top level reflector. In this message, parameters NLRI (Network layer reachability information) and NextHop are those defined in BGP, and BR is introduced here.

RR1 sends UPDATE messages according to the multicast forwarding table for RR1 tree. It should be noted that the trees are characterized by the border routers associated to the branches in the tree. Only the UPDATE messages related with the border routers are transferred through the corresponding link. For example, Only UPDATE message generated border router 1 or 2 is sent to router 1 or 2, respectively. On the other hand, the UPDATE messages generated by routers 1 and 2 are transferred to router 3 according to the multicast forwarding table. When router 3 receives them, it sends the UPDATE message from border router 2 to router 4, and that from border router 1 to router 5, respectively.

Following these procedure, the only the external route information required to build the best routes for all the *RESTERM* routers in an AS.

4. PERFORMANE EVALUATION

This section describes the results of performance evaluation for the overhead of dissemination of UPDATE messages with the same degree of preference for a specific destination. We compare the hops of UPDATE message traversal for the full mesh iBGP, the route reflectors allocated in accordance with the scheme in [Vutukuru, M., et al., 2005], LOUP and our proposal *RESTERM*.

Figure 5 shows the schematic procedure of each scheme. Here, the network configuration used in [Vutukuru, M., et al., 2005] is adopted for the evaluation. It has ten routers, routers *a* through *h*, all of which handle the external route information. Some of them are border routers and the other are internal routers. In Figure 5, the situation where routers *a* and *b* are working as border routers. In the evaluation, the number of border routers increases from 1 to 10, in the alphabetic order. The IGP costs of all links are assumed to be the same, and the IGP route is selected according to the rule that the router with lower alphabet order is selected if more than one paths has the same cost. The UPDATE message hop count is shown in the figure.

Figure 5 (a) shows the full mesh iBGP configuration. Black lines with arrow are sessions from border router *a*, and grey lines are from router *b*. Nine sessions are established from routers *a* and *b*, respectively. The UPDATE message hop count is 45 in this case. This figure shows only the case of two border routers, but it can be imagined that there are large number of sessions in the case that the number of border routers is large.

Figure 5 (b) shows the route reflector configuration according to [Vutukuru, M., et al., 2005]. According to the BGPsep algorithm, routers *i* and *j* are selected as route reflectors at first. Then, routers *a*, *f* and *h* are

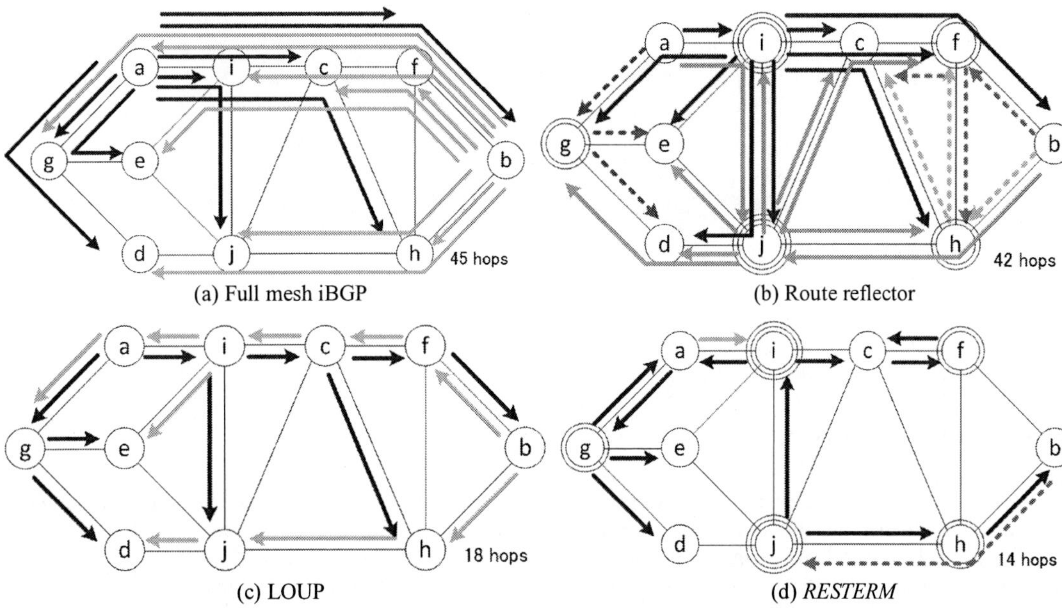

(a) Full mesh iBGP (b) Route reflector

(c) LOUP (d) *RESTERM*

Figure 5. Comparison of message hops when routers *a* and *b* are border routers

selected as router reflectors from the remaining subgraphs. The black solid lines are the sessions between the top level reflector, router *i*, and its clients. The grey solid lines are the sessions for reflector *j*. The sessions for route reflectors *g*, *f* and *h* are depicted in dashed lines with arrows. In this figure, routers *a* and *b* are border routers, and so, the arrows from them are upstream direction from a client to the reflector. The other arrows are downstream direction from the reflector to a client. In this scheme, the number of sessions is expected not to increase largely even if the number of border routers

Figure 5 (c) shows the LOUP reverse forwarding tree for UPDATE messages in the case of routers *a* and *b* being border routers. The black lines with arrow are for router *a*, and the grey lines are for router *b*. UPDATE messages are delivered to all routers other than the border router, and this dissemination is similar with the full mesh iBGP case, although the UPDATE message hop counts are limited by multicasting. But it is expected that the hop counts will increase along with the increase of border routers.

Finally, Figure 5 (d) shows the shared tree configuration in *RESTERM* when routers *a* and *b* are border routers. The route reflectors used here are the same as those in Figure 5 (b). The association between the route reflectors and the clients are assumed to be as follows in this evaluation.

- Router *g* selects reflector *i*. Router *f* selects reflector *i*. Router *h* selects reflector *j*.
- Router *b* selects reflector *h*. Router *c* selects reflector *f*.
- Border router *a* selects top level reflector *i*. Border router *b* selects top level reflector *j*.

Black lines with arrow are the shared tree for UPDATE messages. In this figure, routers *a* and *b* are border routers, and routers *d*, *e*, *g*, *i* and *j* use router *a* as the border router and routers *c*, *f*, and *j* use router *b* as their border router. Routers *c* and *j* have the same IGP cost to two border routers but the alphabetic order is used to select IGP routes. Gray line from *a* to *i* and dashed line from *b* to *j* indicate upstream UPDATE messages from border routers to the associated top level route reflectors. When the number of border routers increases, the upstream UPDATE message transfers and the multicast tree branches required by new border routers are added, but their number seems to be limited.

Figure 6 shows the results of evaluation when the routers come to work as border routers in the alphabetic order in the four schemes. As this figure shows, our proposal, *RESTERM*, has the best performance. Although the number of border routers increases, the UPDATE message hop counts do not increase so much. The hop count for LOUP is low while the number of border routers is low, but the hop count increases linearly according to the number of border routers. The route reflector scheme according to [Vutukuru, M., et al., 2005] has a low increase rate but the hop count value itself is high compared with our proposal. The results show that our proposal *RESTERM* establishes low overhead for the external route information dissemination.

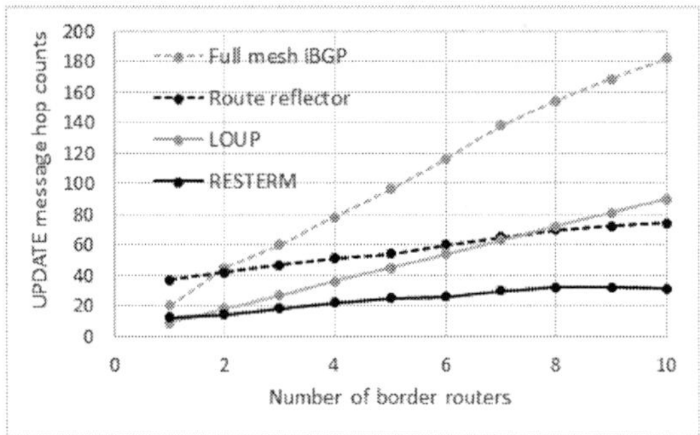

Figure 6. Result of UPDATE message hop counts

5. CONCLUSIONS

In this paper, we presented a new external route dissemination scheme, *RESTERM*, combining the route reflection scheme and the shared tree based multicasting paradigm. *RESTERM* charges the route reflectors with the role of rendezvous points in the shared trees. *RESTERM* routes join the trees by specifying their nearest border routers, and this mechanism assure to route information dissemination necessary for establishing the best routes for all routers. This results of performance evaluation focusing on the UDPATE message hop counts show that *RESTERM* provides better performance than the full mesh iBGP, the traditional route reflection scheme, and LOUP that is a scheme based on the shortest tree based multicasting.

REFERENCES

Rekhter, Y., et al., Ed. 2006. *A Border Gateway Protocol 4 (BGP-4)*. IETF RFC: 4271.

Huston, G. 2016. *BGP in 2015.* https://blog.apnic.net/2016/02/01/bgp-in-2015/, accessed at Mar. 2016.

Park, J. H., et al., 2012. BGP Route Reflection Revisited. *IEEE Communications Magazine*, pp.70-75.

Bates, T., et al., 2006. *BGP Route Reflection: An Alternative to Full Mesh Internal BGP (IBGP)*. IETF RFC: 4456.

Buob, M. O., et al., 2007. Checking for optimal egress points in iBGP routing. *Proc. IEEE International Workshop on the Design of Reliable Communication Networks (DRCN 2007)*, pp. 1-8.

Buob, M. O., et al., 2008. Designing Optimal iBGP Route-Reflection Topologies. *Proc. Networking 2008, LNCS 4982*, pp. 542-553.

Vutukuru, M., et al., 2005. How to Construct a Correct and Scalable iBGP Configuration. *Proc. IEEE INFOCOM 2006*, pp. 1-12.

Balon, S. and Leduc, G., 2009. BGP-aware IGP Link Weight Optimization in Presence of Route Reflectors. *Proc. IEEE INFOCOM 2009*, pp. 316-324.

Ballani, H., et al., 2009. Making Routers Last Longer with ViAggre. *Proc. 6th USENIX Symposium on Networked Systems Design and Implementation (NSDI '09)*, pp. 435-466.

Feamster, N., et al., 2004. The case for separating routing from routers. *Proc. ACM SIGCOMM workshop on Future directions in network architecture*, pp. 5-12.

Oprescu, I., et al., 2011. oBGP: an Overlay for a Scalale iBGP Control Plane. *Proc. Networking 2011, LNCS 6640*, pp. 420-431.

Gvozdiev, N., et al., 2013. LOUP: The Principles and Practice of Intra-Domain Route Dissemination. *Proc. USENIX Symposium on Networked Systems Design and Implementation (NSDI '13)*, pp. 413-426.

Fenner, B., et al., 2006. *Protocol Independent Multicast – Sparse Mode (PIM-SM): Protocol Specification (Revised)*. IETF RFC: 4601.

Spielman, D. and Teng, S., 1996. Spectral partitioning works: Planar graphs and finite element meshes. *Proc. IEEE Symposium on Foundations of Computer Science*, pp. 96-105.

Gutierrez, E., et al., 2014. RRLOC: a tool for iBGP Route Reflector topology planning and experimentation. *Proc. IEEE Network Operations and Management Symposium (NOMS) 2014*, pp. 1-4.

Savola, P., 2008. *Overview of Internet Multicast Routing Architecture*. IETF RFC: 5110.

Adams, A., et al., 2005. *Protocol Independent Multicast – Dense Mode (PIM-DM): Protocol Specification (Revised)*. IETF RFC: 3973.

AN ADAPTIVE HYBRID GENETIC ALGORITHM FOR PAVEMENT MANAGEMENT

João Santos[1], Adelino Ferreira[1] and Gerardo Flintsch[2]

[1]Road Pavements Laboratory, Research Center for Territory, Transports and Environment, Department of Civil Engineering, University of Coimbra, Rua Luís Reis Santos, 3030-788, Coimbra, Portugal

[2]Center for Sustainable Transportation Infrastructure, Virginia Tech Transportation Institute, Department of Civil and Environmental Engineering, Virginia Polytechnic Institute and State University Transportation Research Plaza, Blacksburg, VA 24061, USA

ABSTRACT

Throughout the years, Genetic Algorithms (GA) have been successfully applied to tackle the computational complexity of many real-world global optimization problems, such as those faced in determining the optimal long-term maintenance and rehabilitation (M&R) strategies of road pavement sections. However, it is increasingly recognized that pure GA may not be suitable to fine-tune searches in complex combinatorial spaces due to their limited ability to combine, in an optimal way, the exploration of the search space for promising solutions and the exploitation of the best solutions found during the running time of the algorithm. In order to address this drawback, Local Search (LS) techniques have been incorporated into GA to improve the overall efficiency of the search, either by accelerating the discovery of good solutions, for which evolution alone would take too long to find, or by reaching solutions that would otherwise be unreachable by evolution or a local method alone. In this paper, a novel Adaptive Hybrid Genetic Algorithm (AHGA) is proposed which contains two dynamic learning mechanisms to adaptively guide and combine the exploration and exploitation search processes. The first learning mechanism aims to reactively assess the worthiness of conducting an LS, and to efficiently control the computational resources allocated to the application of this search technique. The second learning mechanism uses instantaneously learned probabilities to select, from a set of pre-defined LS operators which compete against each other for selection, which one is the most appropriate for a particular stage of the search to take over from the evolutionary-based search process. The new AHGA is compared to a non-hybridized version of the GA by applying the algorithms to several case studies with the objective of determining the best pavement M&R strategy that minimizes the present value of the total M&R costs. The results show that the proposed AHGA statistically outperforms the traditional GA in terms of efficiency and effectiveness.

KEYWORDS

Genetic algorithms; adaptive local search; hybridization; pavement management; pavement maintenance and rehabilitation costs.

1. INTRODUCTION

In the current economic paradigm, the need to maintain and preserve existing highway infrastructure assets has been at the forefront of the transportation infrastructure decision-makers' concerns. This is reflected by highway agency budgets shifting funding from new construction and/or reconstruction to maintenance. This shift in priorities is not likely to change over the coming decades, underlining the importance of establishing consistent procedures and developing innovative and optimization-based engineering management systems to achieve effectiveness in: (1) managing huge investments in maintenance and rehabilitation (M&R) of pavement systems; (2) identifying and implementing proven maintenance, rehabilitation and preservation practices and techniques; and (3) ensuring proper timing and intensity of application of those treatments.

Optimization is a broad concept that can be applied at different levels of evaluation and for different categories of infrastructure assets. Pavement M&R is one of the most critical and costly forms of infrastructure asset management that has benefited from the potentialities of the optimization techniques. However, the growing complexity of large-scale problems required to be solved optimally, such as those that the PMS have to deal with, has imposed great obstacles to the efficiency and effectiveness of the traditional optimization techniques. For instance, the problem of identifying adequate M&R activities for individual pavement segments is usually formulated using integer variables to represent M&R activities selected for individual pavement segments. This problem is a combinatorial one which, due to a huge solution space, is very difficult to solve optimally using the traditional optimization techniques.

Evolutionary algorithms (EA), which is a subfield of artificial intelligence, have demonstrated their effectiveness over the last few decades as powerful optimizers for difficult, nonlinear, multimodal optimization problems (Eiben and Smith, 2010). Genetic algorithms (GA) are a popular type of EA and have been object of considerable attention in the field of infrastructure management (Ferreira *et al.*, 2002; Mathew and Isaac, 2014).

Notwithstanding the advantages recognized due to the stochastic search mechanisms behind the GA and the remaining bio-inspired and space-based EA, there may also be drawbacks with algorithms as follows: (1) long computing time; (2) premature convergence; and (3) limited capacity to fine-tune solutions. Several research studies have found that a skilled combination of EA with local search (LS) heuristics, named "memetic algorithms" (MA) (Moscato, 1989), can improve the performance of EA in terms of efficiency (i.e. requiring orders of magnitude fewer evaluations to find optimal solutions) and effectiveness (i.e. identifying higher quality solutions), especially when dealing with real-world and large scale problems. In the past few years several GA-based MA have been developed in various engineering fields. However, to the best of our knowledge no study exists in the literature that has applied this concept to the pavement management sector.

In this paper, a new adaptive hybrid GA (AHGA) combing GA with an LS mechanism is presented for solving the pavement M&R strategy selection problem. The AHGA framework is provided with a pool of LS operators and an Adaptive Local Search Operator Selection (ALSOS) method to decide dynamically and on-the-fly on the relevance of conducting an LS according to a given search strategy. Online learning probabilities are then used to select both the LS operator from the pool and the LS intensity that leads to the best gains of search efficiency and effectiveness.

2. ADAPTIVE HYBRID GENETIC ALGORITHM FRAMEWORK

The framework of the proposed AHGA is illustrated in simple terms in Figure 1. It features the following main components: (1) the encoding of solutions; (2) the initial population generation; (3) the solutions' fitness evaluation; (4) the parents selection; (5) the reproduction process; (6) the population replacement process; (7) the stagnation prevention methodology; (8) the iterations stopping criteria; and (9) the adaptive LS mechanism.

In the developed AHGA an integer coding is adopted to represent the M&R alternatives. Each individual represents a potential solution (M&R strategy) and consists of a sequence of $S\times T$ genes, where S is the number of pavement sections considered for analysis, T represents the project analysis period (PAP) defined by the decision-maker, and the allele values for each of these genes represent a possible M&R activity. Posteriorly, an initial population with size N is randomly generated, and the best $N\times Elite\_rate$ individuals are copied and stored in an archive pool according to a user-defined rate (*Elite_rate*). This scheme prevents solutions of the highest relative fitness from being excluded from the next generation through the nondeterministic selection process.

Once the population has been created at each generation, the individual's fitness has to be evaluated according to the objective function and constraints corresponding to the features of the problem being tackled. For cost minimization problems, the fitter individual is the one with lower present value of the total M&R costs. Given that GA do not have any explicit constraint-handling mechanism, the application of the traditional genetic search operators, which are ''blind'' with respect to constraints, may produce infeasible solutions. In this research work, a dynamic and parameter-free penalty approach based on the concept of superiority of feasible solutions was developed and incorporated into the AHGS. In order to determine which solutions of the population will be used by the reproduction operators to generate new solutions, called offsprings, a Ranking-based Selection (RS) method (Chuang *et al.*, 2015) was implemented. It was selected after preliminary experiments revealed the superiority of this method over the traditional tournament selection method.

The reproduction process is carried out through two operators: crossover and mutation. Crossover is the process by which one or more new individuals are created through the combination of genetic material selected from two or more parents of the source population, to form the members (offspring chromosomes) of a successor population. In the proposed AHGA, a Direction-based Crossover (DBX) operator was implemented (Chuang *et al.*, 2015). In turn, the mutation operator aims to introduce new genetic material into an existing individual, ensuring that the full range of allele is accessible for each gene. Thereby, it allows the exploration of different areas of the search space by potentially generating solutions that have never been analyzed while it prevents the search from being trapped in a local optima. In the proposed AHGA each pair of parents which do not meet the crossover criterion will automatically undergo mutation according to the Dynamic Random Mutation (DRM) operator (Chuang *et al.*, 2015)

Once the reproduction has been performed, parents, offspring and elite members (if applicable) are subject to a replacement process to determine which solutions are selected to compose the successor population. In the developed AHGA a *replacement-with-elitism* methodology was adopted. By this process, each offspring chromosome is directly compared with its parent and the better (fitter) chromosome moves to the next generation. The survivor chromosomes are posteriorly joined by the elite chromosomes initially preserved. In this way, the performance of the algorithm is enhanced by ensuring that the good individuals survive to the next generation

Due to the evolutionary nature of the GA, it may happen that at some given time the population achieves a low diversity level such that the search process stalls around a local optimum. To avoid this situation, a stagnation prevention methodology was implemented in the proposed AHGA. It consists of refreshing all chromosomes of the population, excepting the current best one, whenever a stagnation index (*SI*), expressed by the standard deviation of the population's fitness, falls below a pre-defined convergence threshold value (τ). Once the stagnation prevention methodology is triggered, the population is regenerated according to two mechanisms, a random regeneration and a biased regeneration, aiming to strike a balance between the exploration of the search space and the exploitation of the best solution. In the random regeneration, 25% of N individuals are randomly generated in order to introduce some diversity into the genetic material available for generating new offspring chromosomes in the upcoming recombination processes. With respect to the biased regeneration, the best individual is used to construct the remaining individuals by using two especially designed operators.

The implementation of an efficient stopping criterion is an important aspect for any iterative method. If properly designed it may lead to substantial savings in computational times. The proposed AHGA incorporates the following termination criteria: (1) the number of generations attains the user-specified maximum number (*Max_gen*); and (2) the number of continuous generations without improvement of the best solution attains the user-specified maximum number (*Max_gen_NoImprov*). A generation is considered to be a no improvement with regard to its predecessor if the difference of the fitness values of their best individuals is inferior to 0.01%.

In the proposed algorithm, a GA with a classic framework without any kind of LS is hybridized with an adaptive LS mechanism that aims to either accelerate the discovery of good solutions, for which evolution alone would take too long to discover, or to reach solutions that would otherwise be unreachable by evolution or a local method alone (Krasnogor *et al.*, 2006). Specifically, the LS is carried out on the current best solutions of a generation based on a best first improvement strategy. That means that the LS stops when the first better neighbor solution is found, up to a user-specified maximum number of attempts (*MaxNumLS_iter*). If the LS succeeds, the improved solution replaces the starting solution. In turn, if no better solution has been found by the time the LS process is halted, the solution that underwent LS is kept in the archive of best solutions.

To avoid a waste of algorithm resources due to an improper use of eventually expensive LS, the AHGA incorporate a dynamic approach that controls both the LS frequency, i.e. the number of continuous uninterrupted generations that a GA performs before applying LS (El-Mihoub *et al.*, 2006) and the LS intensity, or, in other words, the maximum number of LS iterations allowed for the LS algorithm to get a successful move (*MaxNumLS_iter*).

The LS frequency is initially set to 1, but after a given number of unsuccessful LS executions, the decision on whether or not to perform LS is made probabilistically according to a user-defined probability (*p_minLS*). For that purpose, a sliding time window with a user-defined size *W_LS* is adopted to record the performance of the last *W_LS* LS operations. When none of the last *W_LS* LS operations were successful, the execution of the LS at a given time point t is triggered probabilistically.

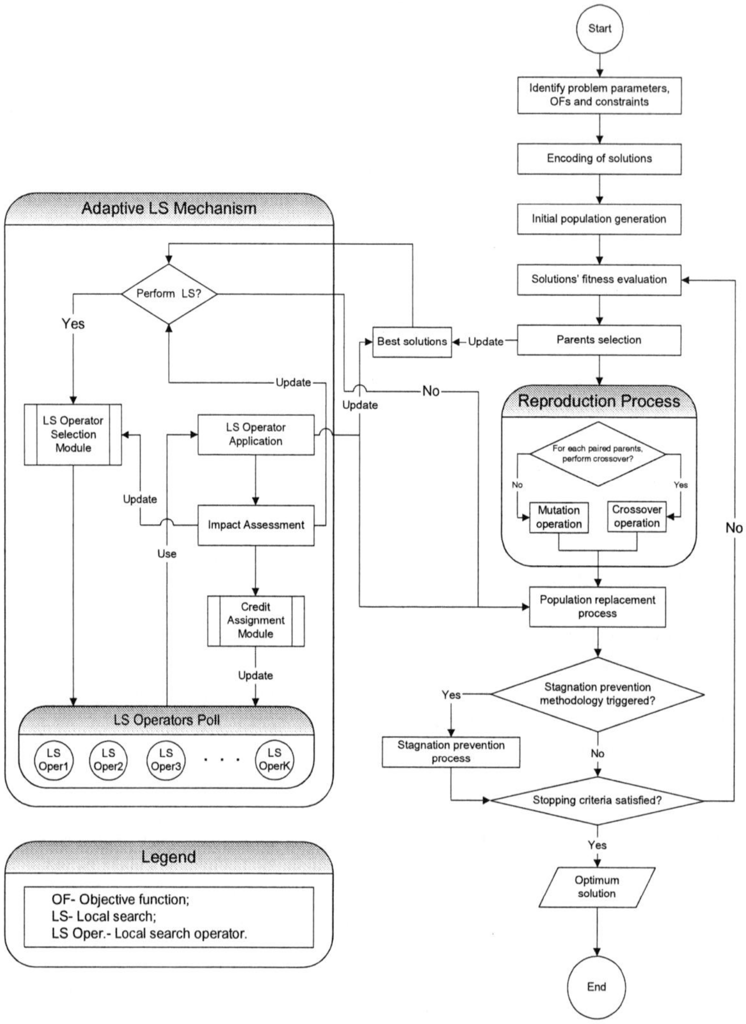

Figure 1. AHGA framework

With respect to the LS intensity, the value of *MaxNumLS_iter* at time point *t* is initially set to *MaxNumLS_itermax* and will be linearly reduced according to the consecutive number of unsuccessful LS operations (*UnsucLS_iter*) up to a user-defined limit value (*MaxNumLS_itermin*) (Equation 1). The *MaxNumLS_iter* is restored to the initial value whenever a LS operation is successful.

$$MaxNumLS\_iter = MaxNumLS\_iter_{max} - \frac{MaxNumLS\_iter_{max} - MaxNumLS\_iter_{min}}{W\_LS} \times UnsucLS\_iter \qquad (1)$$

Given the underlying idea in the previous paragraph, a sensible LS design approach would not be based on a priori choice of one single LS operator that may prove to be unproductive for the problem at hand. Rather, a more efficient design would consider the incorporation of multiple LS operators and the decision of which LS operator to apply on a given search moment would be more rational if made dynamically. This system of adaptive LS process promotes both cooperation and competition among various problem-specific LS operators and favors neighborhood structures containing high quality solutions that may be arrived at by low computational efforts (Ong *et al.*, 2006). To this aim, the AHGA framework is provided with a pool of LS operators and an Adaptive Local Search Operator Selection (ALSOS) method in order to decide dynamically and on-the-fly, based on their recent performances, if it is worthy to perform an LS, and if so, to select the LS operator, from the several available options, that leads to the best gains in search efficiency. The ALSOS method is divided into two main modules: (1) a credit assignment module, which assigns a reward to each LS operator based on their impacts on the progress of the search; and (2) an operator selection module, which selects the operator to apply to the next LS step, based on the credits previously assigned. In the credit assignment module the assessment of the performance of each LS operator, based on the impact of its application on the progress of the search, is carried out by applying the fitness improvement rate (FIR) method (Equation 2):

$$FIR_{i,t} = \frac{f(X^{Neighbor}) - f(X^{Initial})}{f(X^{Initial})} \tag{2}$$

where $f(\vec{X}^{Neighbor})$ is the fitness value of the neighbor solution and $f(\vec{X}^{Initial})$ is the fitness value of the initial solution.

Once the performance is assessed, the reward of each operator is determined according to the *Extreme Value* approach (Fialho *et al.*, 2008). For that purpose, a sliding window with fixed size *W_CredAssig* was adopted for each LS operator to store the FIR values resulting from the last *W_CredAssig* applications of the LS operators. The sliding windows work as a first-in, first-out (FIFO) queue, to the extent that the most recent FIR values are added at the tail of the sliding window, while the oldest ones are removed to preserve the window size. The reward of each LS operator at the point time *t* is then calculated as the greatest FIR value among the current values stored in the sliding window (Equation 3).

$$rew_k(t) = max\{FIR_{k,1}, FIR_{k,2}, ..., FIR_{k,W\_CredAssig}\} \tag{3}$$

where *t* is the current time point; $FIR_k(t)$ is the fitness improvement rate observed at search time *t*; and $rew_k(t)$ is the expected reward for LS operator *k* at search time *t*.

As far as the LS operator selection is concerned, it is performed by implementing the Adaptive Pursuit (AP) method (Thierens, 2005). The AP method, originally proposed for learning automata, adopts a winner-takes-all strategy to increase the chance of selecting the best LS operator k^* up to p_{max} while the remaining probabilities are decreased to p_{min}.

In the proposed AHGA, a set of LS operators were considered to generate several neighbors' structures, and consequently neighborhood solutions for the problem being tackled. It should be mentioned that the choice of LS operators for the pool is to some extent subjective, as there is no conventional procedure in the literature for guiding the selection of the best set of LS operators for a given problem. Thus, the choice of the LS operators presented in the list below was based on the authors' knowledge of the problem and on empirical evidence, and resulted from narrowing down an initial extended list. The LS operators are the following: (1) swap mutation (SWM); (2) forward shift mutation (FSM); (3) backward shift mutation (BSM); (4) Cauchy distribution-based mutation (CaDM); (5) chaotic dynamic-based mutation (ChDM); and (6) delete mutation (DM).

3. PARAMETERS SETTING FOR THE PROPOSED AHGA

Before measuring and comparing the performances of the AHGA and traditional GA when applied to different case studies, a parameter tuning campaign based on the Taguchi approach (Roy, 2010) was undertaken to determine the set of parameter values that yields the best algorithm performance. Extensively used for engineering process optimization, Taguchi designs experiments using orthogonal arrays (OAs) to systematically vary and test the different levels of the control factors (i.e. parameter settings). The appropriate levels for those factors are those that make the system more "robust", or in other words, less sensitive to variations in uncontrollable (noise) factors. To conclude on the robustness of a given process or system, a criterion entitled Signal-to-Noise (S/N) ratio (η_{dB}) is adopted, where factor levels that maximize the appropriate S/N ratio are optimal. Once all of the S/N ratios have been computed for each run of an experiment, the Taguchi method suggests a graphical approach to analyze the data. According to this approach, the S/N ratios and average responses are plotted for each factor against each of its levels. The graphs are then examined to determine the optimal factor level, i.e. to select the factor level which (1) best maximizes the mean of the S/N rations and (2) minimizes the mean of the average responses.

To concretize the parameter tuning process, the AHGA was applied to a case study consisting of determining the best M&R strategy that minimizes the total discounted M&R costs of a one-way road pavement section of an Interstate highway in Virginia, USA. The parameters (control factors) that were calibrated through the Taguchi method are the following: (1) maximum number of LS iterations (*MaxNumLS_itermax*); (2) minimum number of LS iterations (*MaxNumLS_itermin*); (3) probability of performing LS (*p_minLS*); (4) size of the sliding time window used to store the status of the LS operations (*W_LS*); (5) size of the sliding time window used to store the performance of the LS operators, expressed in terms of FIR (*W_CredAssig*); (6) adaptation rate (α) considered by the credit assignment module of the ALSOS method; (7) minimum probability of selecting a given operator (p_{min}) considered by the AP method; and (8) learning rate (β) also considered by the AP method. Overall, for each parameter three alternative values (levels) were considered based on preliminary tests (Table 1). According to the Taguchi method, for a calibration process with such features, i.e. eight parameters with three alternative values, the L18 OA is recommended for the matrix experiment. The optimal parameter values were then identified by applying the Taguchi's parameter design approach, according to which the optimal parameter values are the ones that best maximize the mean of S/N rations and minimize the mean of the average responses, expressed in terms of computational running time (seconds). Table 1 summarizes the three alternative levels considered and the optimal level of the parameters. These parameter values will be used by the AHGA when comparing its performance against that of the non-hybridized version of the GA.

Table 1. Parameters levels initially considered in the calibration procedure and optimal level obtained after applying Taguchi's parameter design approach

ID	Name	L1	L2	L3	Optimal level
1	$MaxNumLS\_iter_{max}$	50	150	-	L2
2	$MaxNumLS\_iter_{min}$	5	25	45	L3
3	*p_minLS*	5%	20%	50%	L3
4	*W_LS*	5	15	25	L3
5	*W_CredAssig*	10	50	100	L3
6	α	0.1	0.5	0.9	L1
7	p_{min}	5%	10%	15%	L3
8	β	0.2	0.5	0.8	L2

4. COMPARISON OF THE ALGORITHMS PERFORMANCE

The AHGA is compared with the non-hybrid version of the GA with respect to: (1) its ability to consistently reach the fittest solution achieved by employing the two algorithms; and (2) the convergence behavior during the search process. The fittest solution obtained from the usage of both algorithms is considered the point of comparison of the effectiveness of the algorithms because the problem size (i.e. number of M&R considered and PAP length), the complexity of the pavement performance prediction models (PPPM) and the way they relate to each other make it difficult or even impossible for the analytical or exhaustive optimization approaches to reach the global optimum solution within the span of a human lifetime.

Both algorithms were applied to several case studies with the objective of determining the best pavement M&R strategy that minimizes the total discounted M&R costs of a one-way road pavement section of an Interstate highway in Virginia, USA. With respect to pavement conditions, 16 different scenarios were considered, and for each scenario ten independent computational runs were performed. They differ from each other in the following features: PAP length; initial pavement age; initial pavement critical condition index (CCI); and CCI warning level. To provide a fair basis for the comparison of the performance of both algorithms, they were run considering the same values for the parameters common to both algorithm. In turn, the parameter setting displayed in Table 1 was adopted when specifically applying the AHGA.

In order to examine the statistical difference between the algorithms, two non-parametric tests were carried out: the Wilcoxon signed-rank test (Hollander *et al.*, 2014); and Page's trend test (Page, 1963). Specifically, the non-parametric Wilcoxon signed-rank test was conducted to compare the algorithms' final results with the significance level (α) of 5%. In turn, the Page's trend test was adopted to assess the algorithms' convergence performance, considering intermediate results instead of just the final results in each case study. This test is applied under the assumption that an algorithm with a good convergence performance will advance towards the optimum faster than another algorithm with a worse performance (Derrac *et al.*, 2014).

Regarding the performance of each algorithm with respect to their ability to consistently reach the fittest solution obtained by employing the two algorithms, the AHGA was always able to reach the best known solution regardless of the case study considered, whereas the GA did not present this general capacity by failing to converge to the best solution in one of the case studies. With respect to the ability of the algorithms to more consistently achieve the best know solutions, the AHGA was found to almost always converge to the best known solution in 10 out of the 10 computational runs, with the exception of two case studies. By contrast, GA was only able to converge to the best known solution in all of the ten computational runs when it was applied to 6 out of the 16 case studies. In terms of the Wilcoxon signed-rank test results, it was observed that the AGHA does not present an overwhelming superiority over the GA with respect to its capacity to consistently achieve fitter solutions. Indeed, the null hypothesis was rejected in only 4 of the 10 case studies in which differences were observed in the fitness of the best solutions obtained by the algorithms in at least 1 of the 10 computational runs. Therefore, the overall conclusion that can be extracted from the Wilcoxon signed-rank test results, if only the fitness of the best solutions produced by the algorithms were to be analyzed, would be that the two algorithms exhibit a similar behavior. However, this conclusion should not be overemphasized since it strongly depends on the stopping criterion adopted. In fact, if enough time is given to the GA (it seems to be what happened in the case studies analyzed) it will reach a comparable solution to the AHGA, but the point of using the AHGA is not only to obtain high-quality solutions but also to do it in a shorter time. In the next section, the issue of how quick the algorithms are in achieving the best know solutions will be addressed.

In order to assess the statistical significance of the difference of the algorithm's convergence performance throughout the search process, Page's trend test was conducted. Table 2 displays the cut-point rankings (*rj*) computed for the absolute difference in the objective function value of the best solutions produced by the two algorithms and the summation of all *rj* per cut-point (*Rj*). From the results presented in this table, a Page's L statistic value of 3182 was computed, which corresponds to a *p*-value inferior to 0.0001 at a significance level of α=0.05. Thus, given the low *p*-value the hull hypothesis can be strongly rejected. This fact allows us to conclude that the increasing trends in the rankings observed in the last row of the Table 2 are backed up statistically, or, in other words, that the AHGA converges faster than the GA. Therefore, the overall conclusion that can be extracted from the Page's trend test results is that if the computational running time is a limiting factor, the AHGA may achieve better results in less time through the definition of stopping criteria that terminates the optimization process either when a determined amount of improvement is not achieved after a given number of iterations or when a predefined number of iterations is reached.

Table 2. Computation of ranks for Page's trend test

Case study ID	Cutting-point ID (generation ID)							
	1 (12)	2 (24)	3 (36)	4 (48)	5 (60)	6 (72)	7 (84)	8 (96)
1	1	2	3	4	5	6	7	8
2	1	2	3	4	5	6	7	8
3	1	5	3	2	4	6	7	8
4	1	2	3	4	5	6	7	8
5	1	2	3	4	5	6	7	8
6	1	2	3	4	5	6	7	8
7	1	2	3	5	8	7	6	4
8	1	2	3	4	6	5	7	8
9	1	2	3	4	5	6	7	8
10	8	7	2	1	3.5	3.5	5.5	5.5
11	1	2	3	4	5	6	7	8
12	1	2	3	4	5	6	7	8
13	1	2	3	4	5	6	7	8
14	1	2	3	4	5	6	7	8
15	1	2	3	4	5	6	7	8
16	1	2	4	7	3	6	5	8
R_j	23	40	48	63	79.5	93.5	107.5	121.5
j	1	2	3	4	5	6	7	8
$R_j \times j$	23	80	144	252	397.5	561	752.5	972

5. CONCLUSION

This paper presents the development of an AHGA intended to help decision makers in the field of pavement management tackle the optimization problem consisting in minimizing the life cycle M&R costs of a given pavement section throughout its PAP, while keeping the pavement condition above a predefined threshold value, meeting technical constraints and considering deterministic and non-linear PPPM. The proposed algorithm maintains the exploring ability of a traditional GA and improves its exploiting aptitude through the execution of LS operations. Its main novelty lies on the inclusion of a pool of LS operators and the use of an adaptive LS operator selection approach within the framework of a traditional GA. Specifically, a dynamic-based learning mechanism was developed to decide on the worthiness of performing an LS and to automatically select which LS operator should be applied at each instant of the search, while solving the problem, according to how well each of the LS operators included in the pool have recently performed in the same optimization process. After the algorithm parameters had been calibrated using the Taguchi method, its efficiency and effectiveness were compared with those of a traditional GA through its application to several case studies designed to replicate Virginia Department of Transportation's real-pavement management problems for a pavement section. The outcomes of the comparative experiments undertaken and accordingly supported by statistical tests proved the superiority of the proposed algorithm in consistently converging to the optimum solution while requiring a lower computational running time.

ACKNOWLEDGEMENT

João Santos wishes to thank the Portuguese Foundation of Science and Technology for a personal research grant (SFRH/BD/79982/2011). The authors also thank the ACIV for the financial support for the presentation of this research work in the 5th International Conference on Theory and Practice in Modern Computing.

REFERENCES

Chuang Y.-C. et al, 2015. A Real-Coded Genetic Algorithm with a Direction-Based Crossover Operator. *In Information Sciences*, Vol. 305, pp. 320-348.

Derrac J. et al, 2011. A Practical Tutorial on the Use of Nonparametric Statistical Tests as a Methodology for Comparing Evolutionary and Swarm Intelligence Algorithms. *In Swarm and Evolutionary Computation*, Vol. 1, pp. 3-18.

Eiben, A. and Smith, J., 2003. *Introduction to evolutionary computing*. Springer-Verlag Berlin Heidelberg, NY, USA.

El- Mihoub T. et al, 2006. Hybrid Genetic Algorithms: a Review. *In Engineering Letters*, Vol. 13, No. 2, pp. 1-14.

Ferreira A. et al, 2002b. A Segment-Linked Optimization Model for Deterministic Pavement Management Systems. *In International Journal of Pavement Engineering*, Vol. 3, No. 2, pp. 95-105.

Fialho A. et al, 2008. Extreme Value Based Adaptive Operator Selection. *10th International Conference on Parallel Problem Solving From Nature (PPSN X)*, Sep 2008, Dortmund, Germany. 5199/2008, pp.175-184, 2008, Lecture Notes in Computer Science; Parallel Problem Solving from Nature- PPSN X.

Hollander M. et al, 2014. *Nonparametric Statistical Methods*. 3rd Edition, John Wiley & Sons, Inc., Hoboken, NJ, USA.

Krasnogor N. et al, 2006. *Memetic algorithms*. In Metaheuristics in Neural Networks Learning, volume 35 of Operations Research/Computer Science Interfaces Series, Alba, E. and Martí, R. Eds. Springer US, pp. 225-247.

Mathew, B. and Isaac, K., 2014. Optimisation of Maintenance Strategy for Rural Road Network Using Genetic Algorithm. *In International Journal of Pavement Engineering*, Vol.15, No. 4, pp. 352-360.

Moscato, P., 1989. *On Evolution, Search, Optimization, Genetic Algorithms and Martial Arts: Towards Memetic Algorithms*. Tech. Rep. C3P 826, California Institute of Technology, Pasadena, CA.

Ong Y.-S. et al, 2006. Classification of Adaptive Memetic Algorithms: a Comparative Study. *In IEEE Transactions on Systems, Man, and Cybernetics- Part B: Cybernetics*, Vol. 36, No. 1, pp. 141-152.

Page, E., 1963. Ordered Hypotheses for Multiple Treatments: a Significance Test for Linear Ranks. *In Journal American Statistics Association*, Vol. 58, No. 301, pp. 216-230.

Roy, R., 2010. *A Primer on the Taguchi Method*. Society of Manufacturing Engineers, Michigan, USA.

Thierens, D., 2005. An Adaptive Pursuit Strategy for Allocating Operator Probabilities. In Beyer, H.G., ed.: *Proc. GECCO'05*, ACM Press (2005), pp.1539-1546.

Short Papers

THE INFLUENCE OF THE KAZAKH LANGUAGE SEMANTIC PECULIARITIES ON COMPUTER SIGN LANGUAGE

Saule Kudubayeva[1], Dmitriy Ryumin[1] and Marat Kalghanov[2]
[1]Department of Informatics, Kostanay State University named after A. Baytursynov, Kostanay, Kazakhstan
[2]Kostanay State Pedagogical Institute, Kostanay, Kazakhstan

ABSTRACT

The article deals with topical issues of designing information technologies for the Kazakh language sign language visualization. Important peculiarities of the Kazakh spoken language and its translation into Sign language are considered. The analysis of semantic links in the Kazakh spoken language in order to solve the problems for automated identification of the elements of sign language for deaf people is carried out. A computer synthesis model and architecture of multi–module human–computer interaction database are suggested.

KEYWORDS

Signs, gestures, dactyl, dactylology, vocabulary, semantics.

1. INTRODUCTION

The main means of inter-human communication among deaf people is the national sign language (SL) in which every semantic concept (or a group of synonymous concepts) has a certain unique sign equivalent. SL is not universal worldwide, as it appears and develops naturally in different local communities and changes in time with the appearance of new vocabulary items. SL consists of different sign systems, combining the language of deaf people and signs generally used in the society. Numerous issues connected with the use of dactyl and sign languages are not studied thoroughly enough yet. Thus, the aim of the article is to describe a sign language computer synthesis model based on the Kazakh language semantic peculiarities analyzer.

2. VARIETIES OF SIGN LANGUAGE

Sing language of deaf people is not a universal system. Extensive linguistic studies currently carried out in numerous European and US research centers have revealed that sign languages of the deaf of different countries are characterized by unique vocabularies and grammatical structures. Besides national sign systems there is an international sign language called “Gestuno”. It is a so-called Sign Esperanto (though, unlike Esperanto Gestuno does not possess special grammar). Creators of Gestuno faced the problem of facilitating the communication between the deaf while conducting the events initiated by the World Federation of the Deaf.

Though recently much attention is paid to the improvement of living conditions of people with hearing impairments, it is difficult for them to adjust to constantly developing information society.

Sing language was introduced on TV channels with sign translation of the news reports to enhance messages’ informational contents and improve spoken language level of the deaf.

The necessity of visualization of information at schools for the deaf will considerably facilitate acquisition of the data by the deaf, since it is a well-known fact that they grasp the material much better if various means of information transfer are combined into a single set including visually represented objects: models, pictures, etc. On the other hand, the problem of students’ spoken language improvement, being one of the most important problems of deaf education, must be solved while using sign translation as well. Thus, it is also necessary to work on the vocabulary. It is clear enough that while carrying out sign translation of lectures, excursions, etc. the meaning of unfamiliar words is hardly possible to explain. However, it is vital to define a number of key words (chosen with the lecturer). They may be written down on posters, blackboards, projectors, overhead projector films, etc.

Gestural speech is represented by a system of manual signs based on concrete images and indicates or renders directly objects, actions, features, properties and even situations on the whole [2]. Unlike this, in dactyl speech definite positions of fingers denote letters that compose words or sentences. According to speech pathologist F. Rau, dactyl speech is a variation of written verbal speech. Fleury V. defined dactyl speech as a replica of written speech, which is very slow in reproduction [8]. Dactylology is an aid in reproduction and perception of oral speech in the process of acquisition of letter and phonetic word composition, while the introduction of unfamiliar words into speech. Reproduction of dactyl speech presupposes compliance with the following necessary parameters:

- Hand position;
- Accuracy of dactylemes' reproduction;
- Fluency and unity of dactyling;
- Clarity and expressiveness of data transfer;
- Synchronicity of pronunciation;
- Observing of spelling norms in oral speech as well as the spelling principle in dactyling;
- Observing the rules of dactyling while reproducing compound shortenings, words with double consonants and capital letters;
- Similarity of configuration of some dactylemes.

As a rule proper names, local names, shortened words, endings in some words or unfamiliar words are pronounced with the help of dactyl. Thus, dactyl speech is a certain kinetic form of verbal speech, of verbal communication. The dactyl speech functions are amplitudinous enough: dactylology is used in the communication of people without hearing problems (teachers, parents, etc.) and the deaf, as well as interpersonal communication of the deaf carried out mainly with the help of gestural speech [1]. The system of sign communication of the deaf Kazakhs has a complicated structure, including two variations of gestural speech: spoken and replicating. Kazakh spoken gestural speech (KGS) is a form of communication via the means of Kazakh sign language of the original linguistic system possessing distinctive vocabulary, grammar, etc. Replicating gestural speech (RGS) replicates the linguistic structure of a verbal language. Replicating gestural speech is a secondary sign system, which is acquired on the base and in the process of learning verbal speech skills by a deaf child. Signs or gestures here are equivalents of words, and the word order is the same as in a conventional sentence.

3. SOME PECULIARITIES OF THE KAZAKH SIGN LANGUAGE

Morphological meanings are transferred in RGS in different ways: via dactylemes, pronouncing words with lips and so on. The most important peculiarity of the RGL morphology is the possibility of changing the way of producing a sign and forming paradigms representing an indissoluble set, in which motor-spatial features of gestures and their consituational meanings are interconnected and mutually conditioned.

Another peculiarity of morphology is that verb forms, on which phrases of sound language are based in GL are substituted with nouns. E.g., "shangy tebu" ("to go skiing") by "shangy" ("skies"). Different types of morphological changes of words: plurality - to the gesture of the initial form is added the gesture of "kop" (many) or "arturly" (various). Thus, phrases "ui kop" ("house many"), "agash arturly" ("tree different"), "oin kop" ("game many") mean: "uiler", "agashtar", "oindar" ("houses", "trees", "games").

"Sabi", "nareste", "bala", "bope", "bobek", "baldyrgan" (meaning "baby, child") will be transferred by one and the same gesture as synonyms.

To indicate different time reference of actions additional gestures are used: "was/were", "is", and "will be". E.g., to say "worked" we should use two gestures: "work+was" or to add word-gesture: "yesterday", "ago".

This way semantics of the Kazakh language functions. In gestural speech semantic contents is transferred via synonyms of gestures-nominatives (gestures in the initial form).

To transfer words in imperative mood "imperative" facial gestures and pantomime are resorted to (bring!, take!). In case we need to express "desirability" or "conventionality" we add "e+g+e+r" ("i-f") by dactyl.

In the sound Kazakh language with free word order morphological changes of lexemes reflect their positional distribution and the verb, as a rule, is put in the end of the sentence. In the sign language subject–object characteristics are defined by certain rules of the gestures' order. Typical sentence structure looks the following way: Subject-Object-Verb.

- To indicate verbs in the Past/Future the following two patterns are used:
  1. Words "bolady/boldy" ("was/were") go straight after the Infinitive. E.g., "Men sut satyp aldym" ("I bought milk") - "Men+sut+boldy+satu" ("I+milk+was+to buy"), the phrase "satyp aldym" ("bought") is substituted by the infinitive SATU (TO BUY) + gesture of the Past time reference "BOLDY" ("WAS"). The same is true concerning the Russian Sign language [4].
  2. In the beginning of the sentence the tense should be indicated, and then the Infinitive of the verb may be used. E.g., "was once/yesterday/next weekend+. . .+verb".
- All negations follow the word they make negative.
- Gestures denoting the object's attributes (e.g., color, size, etc.) may either precede or follow the object.
- Question words (Why?, How?, When? and others) in interrogative sentences are accompanied by facial expressions.

A girl's name "Kymbat" and the word "kymbat" ("dear"), - property, feature, - sounding identically, are shown by different gestures: the first one - by dactyl, the second one - by a special gesture. This is only an incomplete list of the language peculiarities, which are impossible to consider within the frames of just one article.

4. MODEL AND ARCHITECTURE OF THE KAZAKH SIGN LANGUAGE COMPUTER SYNTHESIS

Solving the problem of conversion of the Natural Kazak Language (KL) into Kazakh Sign Language (KSL) will allow to actualize intellectual systems aimed at maintaining effective human-computer interaction [5]. Current intellectual systems are unable to independently process input data and convert it into a visual pattern, for example, that of the data flow in the form of gestures of the deaf. Thereby it is necessary to have models and architectures capable of analyzing input data using grammatical, morphological, syntactic and semantic peculiarities of the Kazakh language. Having studied the peculiarities and properties of the natural Kazakh language and comparing it to the Kazak Sign language, a computer synthesis model (CSM) has been designed. It is represented on Fig. 1 and includes text analysis, gestures' synthesis and visualization. The model also contains the Database Architecture (DA).

The input parameter of the CSM is a text in the KL, which undergoes graphemic, morphological, syntactic and semantic analyses [3]. Then the division of the analyzed text into semantic units of the KSL is due. The final stage includes synthesis and visualization of the KSL. So, let us consider each stage in more detail.

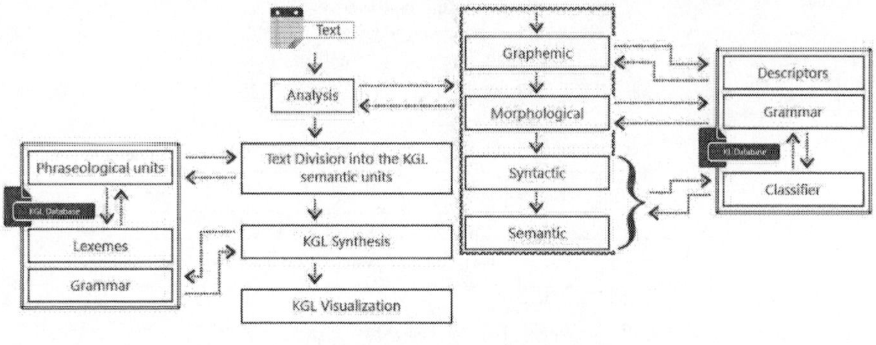

Figure 1. Computer Synthesis Model

Graphemic analysis (GA) - initial analysis of the KL. As a result of the analysis the division of the input parameter (text) into lexemes with detailed characteristics in the form of mandatory descriptors, described in Table 1, occurs.

Table 1. Mandatory graphemic descriptors of the KL

Symbol	Description	Examples
KL	Kazakh lexeme, is attributed to sequences consisting of the Kazakh language alphabet	Men (I)
DL	Divider	", *, ', «, », “, ”
PN	Punctuation mark	., comma, !, ?, :, ;
NM	Sequences consisting of digits	123456
UD	Sequences without the mentioned above properties	
OP	Opening (Closing) parenthesis	{, [, (, },],)
HP	Hyphen	–
SP	Space	
az	Sequences consisting of the lower case symbols	ana
Az	Sequences consisting of the first symbol of the upper case	Ana
AZ	Sequences consisting of the upper case symbols	ANA
NM?	Lexeme, maybe, a part of a proper name	

The GA result must be represented by the line:

$$word_1(d_1\$d_2\$...\$d_n)|word_2(d_1\$d_2\$...\$d_n)|..|word_m(d_1\$d_2\$...\$d_n)\# \quad (1)$$

where

- is the divider of sentences;

$word_1, word_m$ - sequence number of a lexeme in a sentence;

| - lexemes divider;

$d_1, d_2, ..., d_n$ - lexemes descriptors;

$ - descriptors divider.

There are many strictly observed grammatical rules in the KL. Lexemes are changed by means of adding a word-forming suffix to the root, then word changing affixes are added, this is shown on Figure 2.

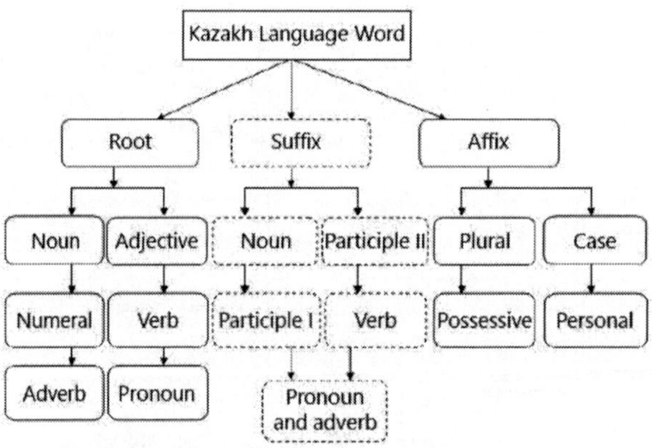

Figure 2. Morphological structure of the KL lexemes

Morphological analysis (IA) takes the GA line as an input parameter with subsequent division of the taken line's lexemes into the initial form, suffix and affixes. The MA result must be represented by the line:

$$!word_1\{s\}[a_1,a_2,...,a_k](d_1\$d_2\$...\$d_n)$$
$$|\,!word_2\{s\}[a_1,a_2,...,a_k](d_1\$d_2\$...\$d_n)$$
$$|...|\,!word_m\{s\}[a_1,a_2,...,a_k](d_1\$d_2\$...\$d_n)\# \quad (2)$$

where

! - the lexeme's initial form;

s - word-forming suffix;

$a_1, a_2,..., a_k$ - word-changing affixes.

Syntactic analysis (SynA) is the process of correlation of the KL lexemes' sequence with its grammar. The aim of SynA lies in the composing syntactic trees of the sentences based on the identification of lexemes' syntactic roles in the sentence (S) (Subject (S), predicate (P), attribute (A), object (O), adverbial modifier (AM)) and identification of the nature of syntactic links between the lexemes [6], e.g. of which is given on Figure 3.

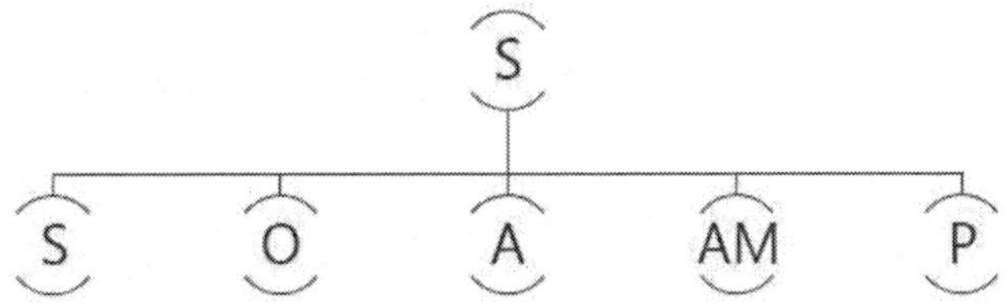

Figure 3. KL Syntactic tree

Depending on the syntactic link between lexemes formula 2, will correspond to formula 3:

$$!word_s\{s\}[a_1,a_2,...,a_k](d_1\$d_2\$...\$d_n)$$
$$|\,!word_o\{s\}[a_1,a_2,...,a_k](d_1\$d_2\$...\$d_n)$$
$$|...|\,!word_p\{s\}[u_1,a_2,...,a_k](d_1\$d_2\$...\$d_n)\# \quad (3)$$

where

$word_s, word_o, word_p$ - are the subject, object, predicate respectively.

Semantic analysis (SemA) is aimed at defining each lexeme's correlation with the definite class. The architecture of classes is built up on general features [7]. E.g., Class $12321 #> Nouns #> Settlements #> Buildings #> Dwelling #> House or Class $12378 #> Nouns #> Living #> Human #> SNP #> Name.

The received correlations will allow substituting the input lexeme with the lexeme of similar characteristics:

$$!word_{s(i_1>i_2>..>i_l)}\{s\}[a_1,a_2,...,a_k](d_1\$d_2\$...\$d_n)$$
$$|\,!word_{o(i_1>i_2>..>i_l)}\{s\}[a_1,a_2,...,a_k](d_1\$d_2\$...\$d_n)$$
$$|...|\,!word_{p(i_1>i_2>..>i_l)}\{s\}[a_1,a_2,...,a_k](d_1\$d_2\$...\$d_n)\# \quad (4)$$

where

$(i_1 > i_2 > ... > i_l)$ - the chain of the lexeme's belonging to definite classes.

As the KSL has numerous phraseological units, the stage of division of the text into the KSL semantic units is necessary for the conversion of the analyzed text into the text corresponding to the requirements of the KSL with subsequent synthesis and visualization of the KSL.

5. CONCLUSION

The issue of people with impaired hearing information resources access is still topical. Information resources in the form of the computer synthesis model and database are necessary for teaching any modern system of automated conversion of the text into gestures.

Further studies will be directed at combining the proposed model with Kinect sensor rangefinder for designing the KSL identification system. The combination mentioned above will allow us to receive three–dimensional video stream of information in the form of a depth map or three-dimensional dot cloud, visible by a space sensor, with subsequent processing by means of the proposed model.

REFERENCES

1. Bazoev, V. and Paleny V., 2002. *A Human from the World of Silence.* I.: Academkniga.
2. Dimskis, L., 2002. *Learning Sign Language: Manual for students of defectology dep. higher ed. institutions.* I.: Academy. p. 128.
3. Farkhadov, M. and Kudubayeva S., 2013. Acoustic Simulator for the Hearing Impaired People. *American International Journal of Contemporary Research,* Vol. 3 No. 11, pp. 122-125.
4. Karpov, A. and Kagirov, I., 2011. Lexicon Formalization for a Computer System of Sign Language Synthesis. *Works of SPRIRAS*, No. 1, pp. 123–140.
5. Kudubayeva, S. and Yermagambetova, G., 2014. Parametric Representation of the Kazakh Gestural Speech. *16th International Conference, SPECOM.* Novi Sad, Serbia, pp. 337-344.
6. Manueva, Yu. and Grif, A. and Kozlov, A., 2014. Design of the Russian Language Computer Sign Translation System. *Works of SPRIRAS*, No. 6, p. 176.
7. Tuzov, V., 2003. *Computer Semantics of the Russian Language: Manual.* SPb: SPbSU. p. 391.
8. Zaitseva, G., 2004. *Gestural Speech. Dactylology: Manual*. I.: VLADOS. p. 192.

OUR FUTURE – WITH THE GOOD, THE BAD OR THE UGLY ESERVICES?

Maija Korhonen
Mikkeli University of Applied Sciences, Patteristonkatu 2, FI-50100 Mikkeli - Finland

ABSTRACT

We live in an ever changing world. Despite that many new and excellent reforms are achieved, this period of time is also very confusing when many things which were regarded as concrete are becoming virtual. In spite of all this incompleteness, our common goal should be a good information society and the purpose of this paper is to find out some factors which reveal the steps toward it. What comes to economic growth, it seems that eServices are a response to the growth objectives in the future. The question we ask in this paper is how to find a balance between these two things from the human point of view - a good life and eServices. The key findings pointed to issues in the needs of structural changes in the society, while at the same time we need to acquire special skills in order to be able to read and comprehend digital information. Another challenge that can be observed and which will be in the most essential role in the future, is the ownership and control over My Data.

KEYWORDS

eService, good information society, My Data, business, economic growth, structural change in society

1. INTRODUCTION

The world is in a great structural change and it seems that the economic growth will be more and more based on services in the future. (European Comission, 2015; Jungner, 2015; Koch et al., 2015) ICT has had a significant role for decades and that trend still seems to continue, however, in a changing world, the role of ICT has also had to change from a technical role to a more user-oriented role (Digitalization, 2016; Koch et al., 2015; Jungner, 2015). At the same time when we will encounter so many economic challenges, our common objective should still be the steps towards a good life and good information society (Liideri, 2015). But what does good life mean to us? Very different matters, of course, depending on your perspective. The Finnish government has a vision that by the year 2030 Finland is a good place to live a meaningful and dignified life for everyone. The starting point is an individual's dignity and right to live a good and dignified life. Firstly the aim is to take each of us as an individual personality and secondly to emphasize self-determination, while, on the other hand, carrying responsibility for ourselves as well. (Korhonen, 2016).

Today, knowledge is the raw material and one of the factors of production. Thinking about business life, it can be said that companies are implementing good life by doing profitable business with knowledge. In practice this means that good eServices are established to people, other companies and society. When a good life is figuring a point of view of the society, the main purpose of eServices is to help and motivate people to take care of themselves as well as possible (Korhonen, 2016). To some, it means health and wellbeing services, some others are motivated by hobbies, entertainment or gaming, while for many contacts with the family, neighbors and friends is the most important. Digital services also allow new forms of work, as well as different combinations of work and life.

The eServices and related matters are reviewed and considered in this paper. In the beginning digitalization is discussed in general and eServices are introduced via three Finnish application examples widely adopted by users: Firstbeat, OnniBus.com, and 112 Suomi. Generally stated, unfortunately, all eServices are not good ones. It can be said that there are way too many bad eServices, even ugly ones and that is why we will consider features of eServices. Users should demand more and better applications and one key to promote this is try to create awareness of possibilities of applications and add understanding and knowledge of the users. Personal data and My Data are closely linked to eServices. Therefore the possibilities of these topics are also discussed. Who owns and controls personal data in the future? The service providers or the person her/himself? What will be the roles of the service provider and the user?

The purpose of this paper is to find out some factors which reveal the steps toward the good information society. It seems that, after all, digital services are the most important building blocks of a good life in the future. However, there are also several significant challenges.

2. ESERVICES – THE BUILDING BLOCKS OF GOOD LIFE

2.1 eServices in General

As mentioned earlier, the world is really changing now: we had transferred via industrial revolution to the information revolution and are now rushing fast toward the digital world, where the information is the raw material. (Porter, 2001; Liideri, 2015; Korhonen, 2015) In summary it can be said that in the 19th century gold and other metals were mined, whereas in the 20th century enormous amounts of products were produced in factories to the "market" and now in the 21st century it will be data mining which brings revenue to most companies and the economic growth will be based on eServices. Hofacker et al. (2007) defined eService as "an act or performance that creates value and provides benefits for customers through a process that is stored as an algorithm and typically implemented by networked software." Entirely new opportunities exist already to the use of the existing information and archives for the creation of innovative digital services by enriching, reformulating and combining digitally stored information and therefore it seems that eServices will have a lot to give us as the building blocks for a good life.

In the Finnish government´s vision our country is described as a good place to live a meaningful and dignified life for everyone. The starting point is the individual's dignity and right to live a good and dignified life. On the other hand an aim is to take each of us as a unique personality and also to emphasize self-determination. The community is written into this vision too - everyone can be her/himself and is accepted by the society. The above mentioned description applies also directly to the characterization of a good digital service. The starting point is the customer need, customer experience data is gathered and analyzed and finally the user-friendly service is personalized based on that data. A service is also available as needed, independent of time and place, in the form and in a channel as desired by the user. The aim and purpose of an eService is to make users' life easier and better. Communication with the near-ones and interaction with the known and unknown persons is made possible. Furthermore, the eServices are also entertaining and promote sense of community. In summary, all of these are essential elements of a good quality of life. (Korhonen, 2016) The next three applications are some examples of how to make ones´s everyday life easier. These examples are demonstrated the needs for structural change in society, too.

The first example describes a person´s own activities to promote her/his own health. A company called Firstbeat Technologies Ltd has developed a heart rate analysis and their mission is to bring the actual measurement data as the basis for the decisions relating to the personal wellbeing and performance. The application transforms heartbeat data into personalized insights on stress, exercise and sleep. It can be said that invisible things become visible and because of that you really become aware of your own situation and can choose the optimal level of nutrition, exercise and rest to improve your health and wellbeing. Subsequently in the future we will increasingly measure and monitor our own health ourselves by the means of new applications and eServices. Consequently this development calls for reform of the society, especially of those public organizations that provide health and social services. (Firstbeat Technologies, 2016)

The second example is related to travel and mobility. OnniBus.com is an innovative inter-city express bus service which is based on a new customer-oriented business model. Tickets are priced dynamically starting from one Euros, so that the earlier you purchase your ticket the cheaper it becomes, which underlies OnniBus.com´s philosophy "An empty seat is the most expensive seat". The company operates modern, fuel efficient coaches which are equipped with air condition, toilets, free Wi-Fi and limited mobility access. With excellent service, new routes and flexible pricing it has proved to be a new alternative to air, train and car travel in Finland. The company started in 2014 and just after one year of operation significant changes could be seen throughout to whole travel business segment. The state railways monopoly, as well as other bus companies, had to react on the altered behavior and demands of the customers. This resulted in more customer-oriented operation, more friendly service, lower prices and better routes in the whole country. (OnniBus.com, 2016)

The third example, 112 Suomi, is a public smartphone application which makes it easier and more secure to get aid and help in case of emergency. Surprising many, the citizens immediately adopted the service. The application enables the automatic delivery of the caller's location information to the emergency service dispatcher (in Finland). The service is especially valuable in places where the determination of the exact location is difficult, such as on streets with the same names in cities or on a traffic accident scene on a highway. The application uses phone's data network connection to transmit the location information. However, the application shows the GPS location information on the phone screen and by reading them the user can forward her/his location to the emergency service dispatcher even without phone's data network connection. 112 Suomi application is a positive example of that we are heading for a good information society. (112 Suomi, 2016).

2.2 Good, Bad or Ugly?

In the previous paragraph an eService was defined from the use and customer perspective. Today, the customer must be in the center of action. A successful service is personalized, easy to use and affordable (Lakaniemi, 2014). Unfortunately, in addition to good digital services, there are a lot of not-so-good-services too and when the goal is a good information society and further a good life, it is important to recognize a good eService, which is not always an easy task. Our research is based on user-orientation and we have considered how to help and encourage users to identify differences in eServices. In general, there is a lot of discussion on digitalization, its benefits and threats, but it seems that the debate often takes place on a too abstract level, and we have also found out that many users are tired of the continuous grinding on the subject, which does not get a grip. One useful way has proven to be to illustrate the difference between a bad and an ugly eService. As an example words good, bad and ugly are described below simply using a dictionary (Table 1.). It is amazing how well the meaning of words also correlates with the features of an eService, including the importance of visuality and ownership of your personal data. Again, the world has changed: in the industrial era literacy was an essential skill, the transition to a knowledge society gave birth to a need for media literacy, so do we need digital information literacy today, i.e. special skills to be able to read digital information, because it is no longer possible to get by with the means of traditional?

Table 1. Explanations of words good, bad and ugly and correlation with features of eService (Cambridge dictionary, 2016)

Term/word	good	bad	ugly
Explanation and correlation with features of eService	- morally excellent; virtuous; righteous; pious: - satisfactory in quality, quantity, or degree - of high quality; excellent - right, proper, fit, well-behaved - kind, beneficent, or friendly: to do a good deed - honorable or worthy; in good standing - profit or advantage; worth; benefit: What good will that do? - excellence or merit; kindness: to do good - moral righteousness; virtue: to be a power for good - having admirable, pleasing, superior, or positive qualities; not negative, bad or mediocre - suitable or efficient for a purpose - pleasant, enjoyable, interesting - healthy - successful - positive, suitable, satisfaction	- not good in any manner or degree - having a wicked or evil character; morally reprehensible - of poor or inferior quality; defective; deficient - inadequate or below standard; not satisfactory for use - inaccurate, incorrect, or faulty - invalid, unsound, or false: a bad insurance claim; bad judgment - causing or liable to cause sickness or ill health; injurious or harmful - a bad condition, character or quality - not good; of poor quality; inadequate; inferior: bad workmanship, bad soil, bad light for reading - (often foll by at) lacking skill or talent; incompetent: a bad painter, bad at sports (often foll by for) harmful: bad air, smoking is bad for you	- very unattractive or unpleasant to look at; offensive to the sense of beauty; displeasing in appearance. - disagreeable; unpleasant; objectionable: ugly tricks; ugly discords. - morally revolting: ugly crime. - threatening trouble or danger: ugly symptoms - mean; hostile; quarrelsome: an ugly mood; an ugly frame of mind. - (especially of natural phenomena) unpleasant or dangerous - ill-favored - hard-featured - unsightly - unlovely - heinous, vile, monstrous - corrupt - disadvantageous - ominous - spiteful, stormy, tempestuous

3. CHALLENGES

3.1 Personal Data and My Data

The term My Data can be described as a human-centric approach to the management and processing of personal data, in which people are given permission and access to the data gathered on them while they have been using digital service channels. Therefore My Data includes one´s shopping history, phone logs, traffic data, health records and other data accumulated into the records of different internet service providers. Subsequently, it can be concluded that, what becomes essential over time, is the ability and possibility for the users of these services to transfer this data either to her/himself or into some other authorized service in a more reusable form. (Poikola et al., 2014).

However, with the ever expanding and wider use of the personal data, more and more uncertainty and doubt is arising among people regarding the possible loss of privacy (Asp 2014). It is a common perception among private persons that companies and governments already know too much of them, which in turn makes them feel uncomfortable. On the other hand, people do not understand the various ways and methods in which personal data is used in promoting goods and services in the social media and in the general directed and personalized marketing in the web. Furthermore, they have no idea of what kind of personal data and how much of it each individual service provider possesses of them. Related to this, we can again talk about the bad and ugly eServices, because it is important for the users of the services to be able to distinguish and understand whether their personal data is used for executing business, crime or other illegal activity or if the method of data collection is just clumsy and the collected data will eventually turn into benefit of the user or, in some cases, for the common good in the form of statistical data or via general research.

Related to this, Poikola et al. (2014) point out that the traditional perspective to the protection of privacy is such that the less personal data is collected, the better. This point of view, however, neglects the value of accumulated data to the person her/himself and is in contradiction with the megatrend of increasing amount and usage of personal data. The goal should be enabling the collection and usage of personal data in such a way that the benefits are maximized and the threat of the exposure of personal data is minimized. The key to reach this is to enforce individual's role, rights and practical means in the management of the data related to them.

Big data and open data are concepts often discussed in conjunction with digitalization and they are naturally and closely related to eServices. When interviewing companies and public authorities it was revealed that as the most important factors in the usage of big data were regarded the usability of the data, abundance and real-time nature of the collection points, enhanced forecasting potential created by the accumulated amount of data and, finally, utilization of combination of dissimilar datatypes and user experience. On the other hand, as obstacles for the utilization of this data were seen, for example, the vast quantity of data, questions related to the cost i.e. free vs. chargeable access to data, issues with ownership of and access to data, risks involving abuse and loss of data and, last but not least, vague status of the rights of the parties handing over their data. (Valtioneuvosto, 2016)

When considering open data and My Data, common characteristics can be observed. Both call for an agreement on common principles, wise regulation and machine-readable interfaces, standards and services for a managed transfer of data, storage, processing and analysis. According to the definition of open data, anyone is technically and juridically free to use, reuse and share it. Correspondingly, My Data could be defined as data owner of which is technically and juridically free to use, reuse and share it. (Poikola et al., 2014)

Furthermore, almost any mass data can contain aspects of My Data i.e. "my-own-data" and, therefore, it plays a critical role in the development of the mass data ecosystem. As an example, a growing group services are related to personal health that combine data from several separate sources together. In order to solve the issues related to My Data it is obvious that we need new practices in which the emphasis shifts from jurisdiction to the tools for managing the data. It is estimated that one of the most promising possibilities for the creation of tools for managing My Data are so called blockchain technologies which are well suited to distributed data backup, processing and security and, further, to sharing of a value or resources. (Valtioneuvosto, 2016).

3.2 The Structural Changes of Society

Already twenty years ago, in 1995, Tapscott (2016) painted a picture where people are beginning to ask, "Will the smaller world our children inherit be a better one?" The question is very essential at the moment: changes have touched all of us and transformations can be seen in governments, organizations and companies as well as in relationships between people. Digitalization has changed and is changing our everyday lives. Tapscott also pointed out signs by which a new economy has not led to a better life, but on the contrary, for example our privacy is vanishing.

Existing laws and norms, structures and practices do not work in the new situation. Our information society is built on the foundation of administration and, therefore, the change takes place very slowly. Although we are well aware that major reforms in the structures are needed, all parties want to hold on to the benefits achieved, and therefore all substitutes for the laws, norms and practices are difficult to execute. In addition, this rapidly changing world does not accept preparation times that last years or months. Governments are not adequately equipped to meet the new public expectations, as was also thought by the Governance Committee (2013). According to the survey many governments are following a logic of simply and directly converting existing processes and products into their online versions. Some improvements can be observed, but mostly the governments spent their time and resources digitalizing existing models and practices instead of rethinking the whole system by the requirements of the digital age (Tapscott, 2016).

Also the Finnish society is currently undergoing a big structural reform. Several studies show that the digital skills of Finns are on a high level and, therefore, the prerequisites for the utilization of digitalization are excellent, when, paradoxically, at the same time we are unable to turn this knowledge into practice. (Digile, 2015; Korhonen, 2015) However, important background work has been done in several projects: National Service Architecture Programme 2014-2017, eServices and eDemocracy Acceleration Programme 2009-2015 and The Finnish Open Data Programme 2013-2015 (Valtioneuvosto, 2016).

4. CONCLUSIONS

We live in an ever changing world. Although many new and excellent reforms are achieved, this period of time is also very confusing when many things which were regarded as concrete are becoming virtual. In spite of all this incompleteness, our common goal should be the good information society. As for the economic growth, it seems that eServices are a response to the growth objectives in the future. The question we ask in this paper is how to find a balance between a good life and eServices.

As a conclusion, it seems that digital services will be the most important building blocks of good life in the future. The main purpose of eServices is to help and motivate people to take care of themselves as well as possible. To some, it means health and wellbeing services, some others are motivated by hobbies, entertainment or gaming, while for many contacts with the family, neighbors and friends is the most important. Digital services also allow new forms of work, as well as different combinations of work and life. However, also challenges have been identified. The major issue seems to be the need for a structural chance in the society. From the human point of view, we need special skills to be able to read and comprehend digital information, since it is no longer possible to get by with the means of traditional literacy: it certainly can be said that, at the moment, we cannot see the forest from the trees.

There is a lot of discussion of digitalization and eServices in general, its benefits and threats, but it seems that the debate often takes place on a too abstract level, and we have found that many users are tired of the continuous grinding on the subject. A useful way has proven to be to illustrate practically the difference between a good, a bad and an ugly eService. Another challenge that can be observed and which will be in the most essential role in the future, is the ownership and control over My Data. (Poikola et al., 2014).

Summa summarum, we must have courage and determination to demand better and improved eServices. Successful companies take into account the customer experience and continuously develop their businesses based on this information. Tapscott (2016) says that, when you look last twenty years back i.e. the period between 1995 and 2015, it can be detected that technology alone does not create prosperity, good democracy or justice, but it requires the involvement of the humans too. So, when we set our sight twenty years into the future, it is only the very choices of each of us that can make a good life possible.

REFERENCES

Asp, E. 2014. In Poikola et al. 2014. My Data – johdatus ihmiskeskeiseen henkilötiedon hyödyntämiseen. Markprint. Lahti.

Cambridge dictionary.2016. Define words good, bad, ugly. Retrieved from http://dictionary.cambridge.org/dictionary/english/good ; http://dictionary.cambridge.org/dictionary/english/bad ; http://dictionary.cambridge.org/dictionary/english/ugly

DIGILE, Liikenne- ja viestintäministeriö, Tekes, Teknologiateollisuus ja Verkkoteollisuus. 2015. Digibarometri 2015. Helsinki: Taloustieto Oy.

Digitalization. 2016.Valtionvarainministeriö. Retrieved from: http://vm.fi/digitalisaatio?p_p_id=56_INSTANCE_SSKDNE5ODInk&p_p_lifecycle=0&p_p_state=normal&p_p_mode=view&p_p_col_id=column-2&p_p_col_count=1&_56_INSTANCE_SSKDNE5ODInk_languageId=fi_FI

European Commission. 2015. A Digital Single Market for Europe: Commission sets out 16 initiatives to make it happen. Press release 6 May 2015. Retrieved from http://europa.eu/rapid/press-release_IP-15-4919_en.htm

Firstbeat Technologies. 2016. Company information. Retrieved from www.firstbeat.com

Governance Committee OECD. 2013. Public Governance and Territorial Development Directorate Public Committee OECD. E-Government Project Draft OECD Principles on Digital Government Strategies: Bringing Governments Closer to Citizens and Businesses.

Hofacker, C. et al. 2007. E-services: A Synthesis and Research Agenda. Retrieved from: http://myweb.fsu.edu/chofacker/pubs/Hofacker_Goldsmith_Bridges_Swilley_2007.pdf

Jungner, M. 2015. Otetaan digiloikka – Suomi digikehityksen kärkeen. Elinkeinoelämän keskusliitto. Helsinki.

Koch, V. et al. 2015. Industry 4.0 - Opportunities and challenges of the industrial internet. Retrieved from: http://www.strategyand.pwc.com/media/file/Industry-4-0.pdf

Korhonen, M. 2015. Hidden Opportunities - Ecommerce in Finland. MCCSIS E-commerce and Digital Marketing. Spain.

Korhonen, M. 2016. Sujuvampaa arkea digitaalisuudella. ReAD verkkolehti huhtikuu 2016. Mikkelin amk. Mikkeli.

Lakaniemi, I. 2014. Taitojen puute yritysten suurin haaste digitalisaatiossa. The Finnish Chamber Commerce. Retrieved from http://kauppakamari.fi/wp-content/uploads/2014/09/kauppakamarin-yritysjohtajakysely-digitalisaatiosta.pdf

Liideri – Business, Productivity and Joy at Work Programme 2012-2018. Tekes – the Finnish Funding Agency for Technology and Innovation.

Onnibus.com. 2016. Company information. Retrieved from http://www.onnibus.com/fi/tietoa-yrityksesta.htm

Poikola, A et al. 2014. My Data – johdatus ihmiskeskeiseen henkilötiedon hyödyntämiseen. Markprint. Lahti.

Porter, M. E. 2001. Strategy and the Internet. Harward Business Review. March 2001.

Tapscott, D. 2016. After 20 years its harder to ignore the digital economys dark side. Harward Business Revied March 11th 2016. Retrieved from https://hbr.org/2016/03/after-20-years-its-harder-to-ignore-the-digital-economys-dark-side

Valtioneuvosto. 2016. Massadatan tehokkaampi käyttö vaatii ymmärrystä sen potentiaalista ja panostusta osaamiseen. Valtioneuvoston selvitys- ja tutkimustoiminnan julkaisusarja 16/2016.

FACEBOOK AND WHATSAPP AT SCHOOL, PRESENT SITUATION AND PROSPECTS IN ITALY

Marco Lazzari[1], Letizia Caso[1] and Alessandra De Fiori[2]
[1]*University of Bergamo, Department of Human and Social Sciences, Piazzale Sant'Agostino 2 – I-24124 Bergamo ITALY*
[2]*Istituto Comprensivo Giovanni XXIII, Via San Luigi 4 – I-24060 Borgo di Terzo (BG) ITALY*

ABSTRACT

In the last few years, social media have become one of the main communication vehicles among young generations. Gradually, they are also entering the school. Starting from data collected through a questionnaire administered to approximately 2000 secondary school students and those gathered from a questionnaire and interviews with about 300 teachers of schools of the same order, we try to take stock of the spread of social networks such as Facebook and WhatsApp as a means of communication between teachers and students for educational purposes, with a main focus on the reasons for the choice for or against using social networks at school.

KEYWORDS

Social networks, secondary school, Facebook, WhatsApp, friendship between teachers and students.

1. INTRODUCTION

The widespread dissemination of electronic communication services and the great success met by social networks have led researchers to wonder about their potential in formal learning environments.

With a series of investigations into the world of adolescents' communication (Lazzari & Jacono Quarantino, 2010, 2013, 2015) we followed the evolution of Facebook and WhatsApp outside and inside Italian schools, and with ongoing research, we are trying to figure out whether, how and why secondary school teachers are ready to accept them as tools to support learning processes.

As for the students, about 8000 high school students were given a questionnaire over the course of three surveys, the latest of which, in the spring of 2015, involved about 2000 students of secondary schools in the city of Bergamo and its province. With regard to the teachers, we have begun to administer a questionnaire, which has already reached over 200 teachers of secondary schools, for now in the Bergamo province, in northern Italy, in future in the rest of Lombardy. We also carried out interviews with approximately 50 teachers and school principals.

2. STATE OF THE ART

Martin (2009), in one of the first studies on the impact of social networks on student achievement, showed that there was no correlation between the time spent online in social services and the grades of a sample of more than 1000 students at a North American university. Later, Roblyer et al (2010) found that students are more keen than teachers on using social networks in educational settings, and that the latter believe that Facebook is more suitable for personal and social use rather than for educational purposes. In a more recent study, Lim and Richardson (2016) reveal that the intensity of using social networks has a significant correlation with students' perceptions of using social networks for educational purposes, and that the advances in social networking capabilities increase the possibility for educational social networks to act as a means to overcome issues such as students' isolation or lack of community. And Lambić (2016) shows that while the generic use of Facebook does not affect academic performance, its use for educational purposes influences it.

Even Mehmood and Taswir (2013), in a survey of 100 undergraduates, show that whereas some students perceive social networks in the learning environments mainly as a source of distraction, a majority considers them their favorite tools for information retrieval, to participate in educational networks, to orient themselves to look for career opportunities, and eventually to build a sense of belonging to the academic community (p. 122).

Some scholars believe that social networks encourage the participation and development of new social and communicative skills, which prepare students for the roles that they will undertake as citizens and workers (Jenkins, 2010). Legaree (2014) claims that Facebook is an ideal vehicle to provide information and educational materials to students, since they do not need to be encouraged to attend the platform, which they already visit in their leisure time. Moreover, the students' habit to exploit the communicative mechanisms of Facebook, such as comments, leads them to be actors of the communication processes and not just passive recipients.

Mazer et al. (2007), in a seminal work on teacher-student interactions on Facebook, state that high school teachers' self-disclosure may lead students to higher levels of motivation and affective learning, and fosters a positive classroom climate. On the other hand, more recently, Camus et al. (2016) suggest that while Facebook may be better for encouraging social processes among students, learning management environments may be more effective for educational purposes. Dyson et al. (2015) suggest that the successful integration of social media into the classroom is hard to predict, because it results from complex interactions of several environmental and individual factors, related to the learners' perspective on the use of social media for educational aims.

To date, the number of reflections on the interaction of students and teachers on social networking sites is growing, often confined to the dilemmatic question of whether teachers should accept students' friendship requests within Web 2.0. With our research, we are trying to get a picture of the existing situation in Italy, to see if and how Facebook and WhatsApp can become support tools in teaching and learning processes in our secondary schools.

3. EMPIRICAL EVIDENCE AND DISCUSSION

The overwhelming success of WhatsApp is the largest evidence certified by our survey of 2015 on media consumption of adolescents; among them, the multimedia communication app has even become the first tool of communication with families, replacing the traditional phone call.

By examining in a diachronic perspective the data collected through our three student surveys, we may follow the trend of Facebook spread, from autumn 2008, in a first pilot administration, when still only 30% of secondary school students claimed to have used it a few times, through spring 2009, when percentage rose to 66%, to spring 2012, when it arrived at 90%; eventually, in the spring of 2015 it stood at 81.4%. The decline is not so clear, although the percentage of daily users decreased (from 65% in 2012 to the current 49.3) in favor of other services such as WhatsApp and Instagram. In summary, the data point out that Facebook is intended as an elective tool for information, WhatsApp for direct communication, Instagram for the dissemination of images.

The percentage of Facebook daily users progressively grows from 10.4% for the second year of middle school, to 32% of the first year of high school, reaching 63.1% for the pupils in their final year. Note that from the sample we excluded, for several reasons, the first year of the middle school, that is 12-year-old pupils; on the other hand, Facebook might not be used before the age of 13 and WhatsApp before 16. The data may be interpreted in various ways: the phenomenon can be regarded as a sign of progressive disaffection over Facebook by the new cohorts, or rather as a sign that Facebook is a more appropriate tool for more "mature communications".

In the meantime, Facebook has entered Italian schools, with a trend characterized by rapid growth and an equally quick descent: from an almost alien tool in 2008, to a service frequently used by more than half of high school students in 2012 (closed groups), then falling in 2015 to just over 30% in high schools and around 20% in middle schools, crushed by the emergence of WhatsApp, which is used frequently by 74.5% of middle school students and by 84.6% of high school students.

Despite this high rate of use of social media by students, these platforms are still struggling to be adopted in schools, mainly because of a lack of involvement by teachers. Namely, while they are rather keen on exploiting sharing tools, such as, first of all, Dropbox (teachers participate in more than 90% of the uses of Dropbox), Facebook groups and WhatsApp do not meet with the favor of teachers (13.7 and 8.4% respectively).

The attitude against WhatsApp is quite understandable, probably due to their desire not to share their phone number. As for Facebook, the choice is due to remarks about the opportunity of befriending students (even if joining groups does not require being friends).

To examine the problem we have set a new research agenda, based on a questionnaire administered to secondary school teachers (N = 215 up to now) and on interviews with teachers (41) and school administrators (10). The survey is not easy to complete, because of difficulties in building the sample. For the interviews, initially we contacted teachers directly known by the research team, then we applied a snowball strategy; for the online questionnaire, contacts are reached through the trade union organizations, which forward our web address to their mailing lists; their mediation guarantees a rather uniformly distributed sample. In any case, the survey is slowly advancing, with a main focus on the reasons for the choice for or against the use of social networks in class, looking for any correlations with:

1. Teachers' digital skills: eight questions, such as:
    a. *Do you find using computers difficult? Would you be able to generate a table of contents using Word?*
    b. *Would you be able to write an Excel formula such that the content of a cell is OK if the content of the adjacent cell is greater than 5 and XX else?*
2. Their perception of personal self-efficacy: 11 questions, such as:
    a. *Are you able to engage even the most reluctant and difficult pupils?*
    b. *Are you able to gain the trust and esteem of your colleagues?*
    c. *Do you know how to deal with the problems related to the inclusion of pupils with special educational needs?*
3. Their perception of collective self-efficacy, that is of the school in which they operate: seven questions, such as:
    a. *Does your school convey a positive image?*
    b. *Does your school know how to adapt teaching to the opportunities provided by educational technology?*

The whole questionnaire includes about 70 questions; the answers will receive careful consideration when the sample is more robust, but from a first glance at the data gathered until now, some evidence begins to emerge, which is in keeping with the updates of the questionnaire administrations.

First of all, about half of the respondents have a Facebook account, which is used quite briskly: 75% left a Like in the last 72 hours.

About 76% are against friendship in Facebook between teachers and students, less than 9% agree, and the others are in a neutral position. On the other hand, less than 44% agree with those school principals who have banned teachers from befriending students on Facebook. This share is more or less equivalent to that coming from interviews with school principals: 4 out of 10 agree with those colleagues who banned friendships on Facebook, 3 disagree and 3 are neutral; 6 out of them are against friendship on Facebook between teachers and students, 3 are favorable, 1 is neutral.

Among Facebook users, only 18% say that they use it to exchange teaching materials with students, either directly or indirectly (through a student who acts as a bridge). According to the interviews, reasons for non-use are explained in reference to two types of concerns:

1. Privacy:
    a. *I believe that the personal life of a teacher should remain private in the eyes of their students and families.*
    b. *I'd feel uncomfortable, knowing that they use the network daily, and therefore frequently would have access to my pictures or information.*
2. Fear of compromising the teacher student relationship:
    a. *It fosters a too confidential rapport, which puts a strain on the relationship between teachers and their own pupils.*
    b. *I think it is absolutely detrimental to accept a friend request from your own students. They bring the relationship to an inadequate level.*

c. *The teacher's role is also to judge. A friend, even if Facebook friendships are rather different from the real ones, does not judge you, so there's just the risk of confusing the two planes and compromising the educational relationship.*

Regarding the fear of privacy invasions, it is interesting to note, however, that only 2 out of 41 interviewees report that they publish personal contents, and in any case both of them have students among their friends. The lack of appropriate specific digital skills is rejected as a significant reason not to use Facebook at school.

4. FUTURE DEVELOPMENTS

The research presented here for the first sharing with the scientific community, in order to stimulate reflection and gather valuable information, continues with the administration of the questionnaire to teachers and the coding and interpretation of the interviews, which have so far generated about seventy pages of typewritten text.

As soon as the statistical sample is more consistent, a statistical model will bc applied to spot the correlations among data. Our main hypotheses aim at verifying whether the resistance of teachers to using Facebook at school is influenced by low levels of digital competencies and a feeling of personal or collective self-efficacy, as well as their age, number of years teaching, or educational background.

REFERENCES

Camus, M. et al., 2016. Facebook as an Online Teaching Tool: Effects on student Participation, Learning, and Overall Course Performance. *College Teaching*, Vol. 64, No. 2, pp.84-94.

Dyson, B. et al., 2015. Evaluating the Use of Facebook to Increase Student Engagement and Understanding in Lecture-based Classes. *Higher Education*, Vol. 69, No. 2, pp. 303-313.

Jenkins, H., 2009. *Confronting the Challenges of Participatory Culture*. MIT Press, Cambridge, MA.

Lambić, D., 2016. Correlation between Facebook Use for Educational Purposes and Academic Performance of Students. *Computers in Human Behavior*, Vol. 61, pp. 313-320.

Lazzari, M. and Jacono Quarantino, M. (Eds.) 2010. *Adolescenti tra piazze reali e piazze virtuali*. Bergamo University Press, Bergamo, Italy.

Lazzari, M. and Jacono Quarantino, M. (Eds.) 2013. *Identità, fragilità e aspettative nelle reti sociali degli adolescenti*. Bergamo University Press, Bergamo, Italy.

Lazzari, M. and Jacono Quarantino, M. (Eds.) 2015. *Virtuale e/è reale. Adolescenti e reti sociali nell'era del* mobile. Bergamo University Press, Bergamo, Italy.

Legaree, B.A., 2014. Using Facebook to Engage Microbiology Students outside of Class Time. *Journal of Microbiology & Biology Education*, Vol. 15, No. 2, pp. 301-303.

Lim, J. and Richardson J.C., 2016. Exploring the Effects of Students' Social Networking Experience on Social Presence and Perceptions of Using SNSs for Educational Purposes, *The Internet and Higher Education*, Vol. 29, pp. 31-39.

Martin, C., 2009. *Social Networking Usage and Grades among College Students*. UNH Whittemore School of Business, Durham, NH.

Mazer, J.P. et al., 2007. I'll See You on "Facebook": The Effects of Computer-mediated Teacher Self-disclosure on Student Motivation, Affective Learning, and Classroom Climate. *Communication Education*, Vol. 56, No. 1, pp. 1-17.

Mehmood, S. and Taswir, T., 2013. The Effects of Social Networking Sites on the Academic Performance of Students in College of Applied Sciences, Nizwa, Oman. *International Journal of Arts and Commerce*, Vol. 2, No. 1, pp. 111-125.

Roblyer, M.D. et al., 2010. Findings on Facebook in Higher Education: A Comparison of College Faculty and Student Uses and Perceptions of Social Networking Sites. *The Internet and Higher Education*, Vol. 13, No. 3, pp. 134-140.

BRINGING HEALTHCARE ANALYTICS TO WHERE BIG DATA RESIDES USING A DISTRIBUTED QUERY SYSTEM

Shawn Murphy MD, Ph.D[1], Alyssa Goodson MS[2], Michael Mendis[2], Marykate Murphy RN[1], Lori Phillips MS[2], Yanbing Wang MS[2] and Christopher Herrick MBA[2]
[1]*Massachusetts General Hospital, Boston, MA, USA*
[2]*Partners Healthcare System, Boston, MA, USA*

ABSTRACT

It is generally difficult to move Big Data and put it into a central location. Ordinarily this would prevent one from querying several repositories of patient-oriented Big Data as a unified whole. However, we have been developing a distributed query system where the Big Data is indexed in the location where it typically lies, and surrounding each index we have created software based upon the Informatics for Integrating Biology and the Bedside (i2b2) project to access the index used to organize the Big Data. We have applied this to allow us to query Genomics, Imaging, and Textual data to be queried along with traditional coded Healthcare data. We have developed an Application Programming Interface (API) that allows patient-centric queries to be formulated across these Big Data resources in our Healthcare system with the goal of performing research on the Healthcare Data, incorporating novel approaches to sharing common ontologies that represent the Big Data and novel approaches to linking the patients across the participating Big Data sites.

KEYWORDS

Healthcare, Genomics, Imaging, i2b2, Distributed, Query

1. INTRODUCTION

One of the primary missions that an Information Systems department needs to fulfill at a research-oriented Academic Medical Center is to allow the Medical Center's healthcare data to be used to perform clinical research. There is tremendous value in using the data 1) for finding patients that could qualify for clinical trials, 2) for investigating possible hidden associations of drugs to adverse events or diseases with biomarkers, and 3) for understanding better the course of a disease or what helps predict a particular outcome for a disease (Masys, 2012).

We based the formulation of our Big Data distributed query system around Integrating Biology & the Bedside (i2b2), which contains a simple data model and user interface for querying clinical data, typically derived from electronic health records sufficiently flexible to enable current users to include clinical trials, imaging, and genomic data (Murphy, 2010). The data is stored in a relational database using a star schema, which includes a single "observation-fact" table containing all clinical observations, such as patients' diagnoses, laboratory test results, and medications. This can serve an index to hold many of the features from a set of Big Data. A hierarchical ontology describes the types of data contained within an i2b2 instance and allows users to start with very broad medical concepts and drill down to find more specific attributes about the patients they would like to study. To add new types of data, institutions modify the ontology, but they do not need to create new database tables or change the software code. The simplicity of i2b2 has facilitated its adoption, and it is now used at many institutions worldwide (see http://healthmap.org/i2b2/). The software is fully open source and available at https://www.i2b2.org) and built in a highly adaptable architecture that has allowed it to be extended in many ways by a vibrant i2b2 community (Kohane, 2011).

2. DESCRIPTION

The value of the data cannot be utilized by medical researchers if it remains locked in data silos. Therefore, we created a distributed Big Data network that presents medical researchers with a consolidated view of the data and allows them to query across phenotypic, genomic, and imaging-focused data repositories that reside in separate locations across the enterprise.

Researchers are able to formulate queries from a central metadata repository and distribute them to relevant nodes of the Enterprise Big Data network. At the nodes of the Big Data Network, data remains in the laboratories and repositories, governed by patient consents and data use agreements, and yet common patients in the data can be found and relevant features of the data can be extracted from the individual data repositories at the nodes. Thus a scientist interested in how a novel genomic variant correlates with hippocampal volumetric analyses in high resolution functional brain MRI imaging can operate this query which will be satisfied in the data that resides in the two distinct datasets.

1. The Big Data Network operates with a central node surrounded by distributed nodes in a hub-and-spoke network model (see figure 1). The central node manages the query infrastructure and may host its own repository of data. Messages between nodes contain structured query elements, previously resolved patient lists, computational instructions for nodes, and patient linkage probabilities.
2. The nodes are able to exchange messages through an Application Programming Interface which are implemented in a RESTful fashion such that they consist of stateless messages with a Query in the URL and an XML payload. The message is generally in the form of a query that contains attribute of patients that are of interest, and the result is generally a set of patient coded identifiers. Each attribute that a patient could have includes such items as a type of disease, use of a medication, a genomic variant, or a feature on a radiology scan These API messages flow from the central node (labeled "Clinical" in figure 1) where the query is received from the researcher, to the remote nodes (three of which exist in figure 1), and back to the central node which does some presentation and/or analysis of the patient data that is returned from the remote nodes (illustrated is the creation of a simple table).

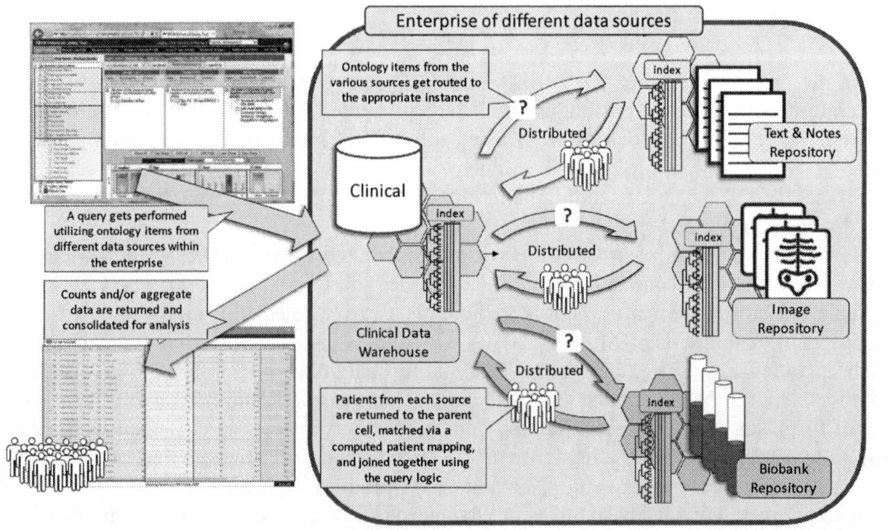

Figure 1

3. A query into the network is initiated with a client application as shown in figure 2. The client is available in a web browser and a demonstration of the client software can be seen at https://www.i2b2.org/webclient. Queries are formulated to find a set of patients. The patients are completed de-identified and only aggregate numbers are returned. The query consists of selecting patient attributes from a standard set of ontologies available in tree structures on the left and dragging them to

the upper right where there are 3 panels that act like the circles of a Venn diagram. As seen in figure 2, the attribute “cerebrovascular disease” in the first panel is being intersected with “Asian” in the second panel and a specific Single Nucleotide Polymorphism variant in a Gene represented by an RS Identifier. The search results in the identification of a single common patient in the Enterprise Big Data Network.

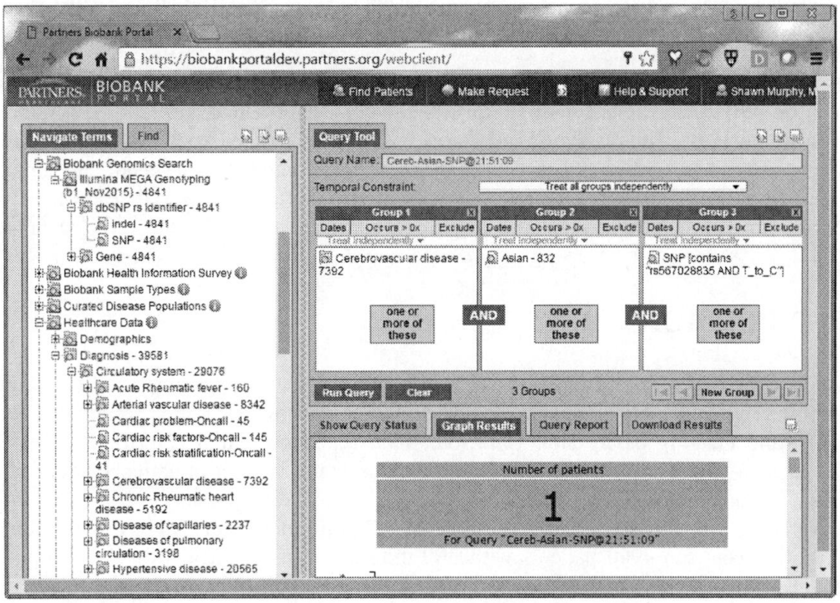

Figure 2

4. The central node manages research projects and user permissions segmenting the data into projects that protect patient privacy. Institutional Review Board policies and patient preferences expressed in consents and opt-in/opt-out authorizations are linked to identifiers in the central node. Within the system, patients are represented as coded data, for efficiency and confidentiality.
5. As seen in figure 2, each node itself has an indexed data repository implemented as a star schema. The patient table of the index is associated with patient linkage information in the central node. The metadata registry is used only by the Central Node for its role in query formulation and coordinating data computation at the remote nodes.

The distribution of sub-queries to different remote nodes from the central node is navigated through the ontologies. The terminologies were published from all the remote nodes to the centralized node and reconciled so that the terms can be used in a query. A term is associated with each feature defined at each location and placed in a hierarchically organized terminology. By looking up the terms, the query can be directed to the appropriate node where the database index holds the list of patients who have that attribute. The patients ate looked up based on that term/attribute and the list of patients is returned from the remote nodes to the central node.

Patients were de-duplicated using rules established by the Enterprise Patient Matching Index (EMPI) to uniquely identify an individual patient within the system. Once the above was implemented, queries could now be formulated at the central site and distributed to the nodes which run the query against the index at each node and return the set of patients who have the featured terms. Boolean logic can then intersect and combine the sets of patients that result from the sub-queries according to the query logic. The table of matched patient identifiers is used to normalize the patient sets into a single set of identifiers prior to the application of the Boolean logic.

The specialized nodes were created independently at locations where the Big Data resided. The indexes are maintained through different processes using different update methodologies. As an example, the Image Repository was developed using the Medical Imaging Informatics Bench to Bedside (mi2b2) open source platform. Medical images are queried, selected, and then downloaded from the clinical Picture Archive

Communication System (PACS) using the m2ib2 software. Once downloaded, the DICOM headers of these images can be extracted, transformed, and loaded into an i2b2 based "index" within the Imaging Repository; this allows the node to participate with the broader Big Data network. An ontology of these DICOM based terms was created and then uploaded to our centralized parent node. Medical researchers who then wish to find cohorts of patients based on the imaging information can drag over these terms, as well as other terms from our phenotypic, genomic, and notes repositories, to build complex queries that uniquely identify patients relevant to their studies.

It is important to note that this process can be done in parallel; multiple queries for individual ontology items can be sent out simultaneously to optimize query performance and take advantage of the distributed nature of the network. The results of each term based query run on each "child" node is a list of patients. These patients are sent back to the centralized node and combined together using the constraint logic defined by the initial query. An aggregate count is presented back to the medical researcher indicating the total number of unique patients found with the specified constraints across the entire Big Data network.

3. CONCLUSION

The distributed query architecture shows the power of a distributed query API to find counts of persons from the combined results of very different database architectures, including those optimized for storing genomic, text based, and imaging based data. The four main repositories that contribute to the Big Data network continue to grow over time and offer accelerating value as the number of patients that span multiple instances increases. To date, the Big Data network includes a clinical data repository made of 6.7 million patients with 2.4 billon facts, a text based notes repository of 4.3 million patients with 130 million notes, a genomic repository that contains 4900 patients with 300 thousand Single Nucleotide Polymorphism variants and a total count of 1.7 billion facts, and an imaging repository with close to 20,000 patients and the extracted DICOM data from close to 5TB of medical images.

ACKNOWLEDGEMENT

This work was conducted with support from National Institutes of Health Centers of Excellence for Big Data Computing in the Biomedical Sciences (U54), Grant Number 1U54HG007963-01 and National Institute of Biomedical Imaging and Bioengineering (RO1), Grant Number R01EB014947.

REFERENCES

Masys DR, et. al. Designing a Public Square for Research Computing. Science Translational Medicine. Aug 29 2012;4(149):149fs132-149fs132.

Murphy SN, et al. Serving the enterprise and beyond with informatics for integrating biology and the bedside (i2b2). J Am Med Inform Assoc. Mar 1 2010;17(2):124-130.

Kohane IS, et al. A translational engine at the national scale: informatics for integrating biology and the bedside. Journal of the American Medical Informatics Association : JAMIA. Nov 10 2011.

TECHNICAL FUNCTION DISCOVERY IN PATENT DATABASES FOR GENERATING INNOVATIVE SOLUTIONS

Dmitriy M. Korobkin, Sergey A. Fomenkov, Sergey G. Kolesnikov
and Alexander B. Golovanchikov
Volgograd State Technical University
Russia, Volgograd, Lenin av. 28

ABSTRACT

Patents contain a large quantity of technical information that can be useful for new technical solutions design. The purpose of the research is to detect and extract information about the technical functions from text of several patents brought together in patent databases. Method is designed for informational support of solving creative problem of new technical decision synthesis. For technical functions extraction the natural language processing is performed. Ways of technical function implementations are represented by "object-condition-action" model. The extraneous syntactic parser is used for assigning of syntactic category to words from patent claims section. The context-sensitive grammar was developed for achieving compliance of parsed text words to "object-condition-action" model components.

KEYWORDS

Patent, context-sensitive grammar, parsing, link grammar, international patent classification, verb class.

1. INTRODUCTION

New technical opportunities search has always been an important task in domain of technique development. Nowadays due to heightened competition for markets of goods and services topicality of this task is only increasing. Often new invention may be obtained by replacing one element in famous system or changing of used physic-technical effect [1] that results in new properties of this element, and it becomes the separate invention. Sometimes there is a necessity of improving the properties of well-known object that may be achieved by a small change in its structure. People ubiquitously began to take an increasing interest in computational creativity issues lately, they resort to innovative ways of inventions obtaining. New technical decision synthesis requires knowledge about the state of affairs in corresponding subject domain. All the newest achievements in scientific fields are represented in patents therefore we can get information about existing ways of technical function implementations by patent data analyzing. This paper describes method of patent databases analysis for the fundamental idea search for new technical solution synthesis.

Analysis of systems using the technical function' implementations: TechOptimizer, Goldfire, Ko-Brain, Knowleadgist, IdeaFinder+, Innovation WorkBench, etc., and knowledge extraction from Natural Language texts: AeroText, TextAnalyst, GATE, Natural Language Toolkit, RapidMiner, etc., showed that none of them does not allow to automate the extracting process of the technical functions descriptions from natural language text.

2. SUMMARY OF THE METHOD

The proposed method aims to extract data from patents for support of solving creative problem of synthesis. For this, the patent data analysis is performed. Patent database is contained in xml format file. Source of file is the USPTO bulk downloads, where patents published by USPTO weekly are placed. This file size exceeds 500 MB, the file contains an average of 6 thousand patents that were issued by USPTO last week. Text of every patent contained in xml file is structured by tags according to standard [2]. In the most succinct and sufficient volume the invention essence is represented in patent part called claims, <claims> tag. In turn, patent claims can consist of several points, and the first point is the most common, the rest points are the modifications of the first point, i.e. they limit invention from all sides. According to proposed method we must analyze only the first point of patent claims where the ways of technical function implementations protected by patent are contained. The method is based on technical function representation as four sets in the following form:

$$F = < D, X, H, {}_{f}P >, \quad (1)$$

where D - a set of actions leading to desirable result; X - a set of objects (action operands) that actions are directed to; H - a set of specific conditions and limitations of executed actions; ${}_{f}P$ - a set of functional features that allow to concretize and hierarchically structure function description [3]. Thus it is proposed to extract a number of tuples in accordance with the model (1) from the first point of patent claims. For tuple obtaining it was decided to perform syntactic analysis of sentence during which parts of speech and relations between words are defined. Basing on the relations, the word takes part in, we can determine the syntactic category of word and assign the appropriate component of model (1) to it. It is supposed to construct the generalized morphological table from obtained tuples. The tuples must be entered in it as variants of technical function implementations, and generalized functions themselves must be formed basing on the English verb classes collection.

3. STAGES OF PROCESSING

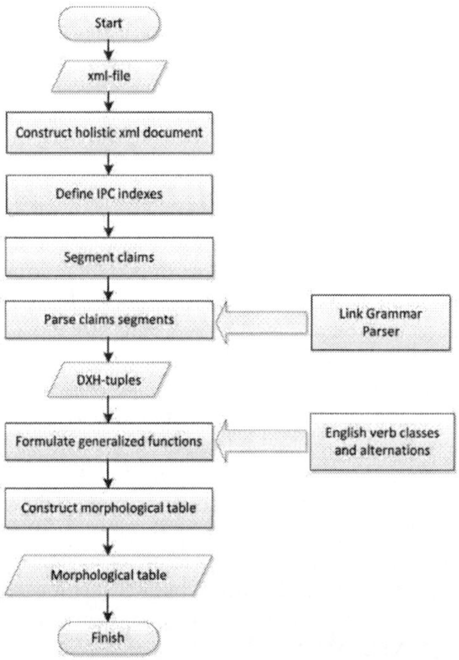

Figure 1. Flowchart illustrating the proposed method of patent data processing

3.1 Holistic Xml-Document Construction

On the first stage xml-file that was downloaded from USPTO bulk downloads is started to process. This file is an exactly patent database, because it contains lots of standard xml-documents listed sequentially. On the first stage of processing this file is reduced to the form applicable for parsing by xml reader: header of each separated document is deleted, except first, the contents of root elements <us-patent-grant> remain unchanged and tag <patent-database> is added after the first header and is closed in the last string of file, i.e. it becomes the new root element.

3.2 IPC Indexes Recognition

In the second step the constituted xml-document is viewed to detect International Patent Classification (IPC) indexes of patents. It is calculated how many patents were categorized by every detected index. Selected level of the index detail: section and class. The user is allowed to choose IPC classes that patents belong to must be analyzed for the technical functions detecting. In the next step the selected classes' patent claims are extracted.

During the xml-document parsing we obtain just classification codes. But when the user works with our system he needs to know index titles, i.e. codes decryption, for more information. Since IPC classes are provided by World Intellectual Property Organization (WIPO) only in text documents and aren't contained in databases, separate application was written for this problem decision. It analyzes once text document that contains IPC titles and fills specially created database. In further the database is used in automated system realizing the proposed method. Thus, when IPC indexes are found in compiled xml-document, their informative headers are taken from the database.

3.3 Segmentation

Patent claims' sentences are constructed on the same template that differs from usual sentence structure. Most often, the patent claims represent the one or several complex sentences containing a few subordinate clauses, each of which complements properties of the object that is spoken about in main clause.

Syntactic parsing of such a long sentence will be very time-consuming and resource intensive procedure. To reduce the error count in the parsing results and economize the computer resources, the sentence of patent claims' the first point is divided into several parts. Then every part of the source sentence is parsed separately. Sentence segmentation is held on the following punctuation marks: comma, semicolon. In the work [4,5] algorithm of complex sentences partition into simple ones was developed for solving the segmentation problem.

3.4 Claims Parsing

To parse sentence fragment the extraneous software was used. It was syntactic parser of the natural language English text - Link Grammar Parser based on link grammar. Given a sentence, the system assigns to it a syntactic structure, which consists of a set of labeled links connecting pairs of words [6]. Link is formed when two connectors connect, interconnection rules are prescribed in dictionary for each word. Parsing of a set of sentences showed that patent claims' sentences have the same syntactic structure. This observation allowed creating context-sensitive grammar for extraction of model (1) components from patent claims' sentences by link analysis:

$$G = (T, N, < S >, R) \qquad (2)$$

where T - a set of terminals {action, object, condition}; N - a set of non-terminals {<S>, <MV>, <O>, <J>, <I>, <A>, <M>}; <S> - start non-terminal; R - production rules.

Derivation of sentence using grammar (2) means that word staying in any terminal position is respectively either action, or object, or condition depending on terminal type. Automatic detection of separate functional features in accordance with model (1) is a very difficult linguistic task, so by default all technical function characteristics will be defined as conditions of action implementation. Non-terminal symbols except <S> represent the links of Link Grammar Parser. Grammar (2) uses only links that directly relate to action, object or condition, i.e. sentence derivation starts with either MV- link, or O- link. Left operand of MV- link (verb) is always an action in the model (1), right operand of MV- and other links of this operand are the action characteristics, i.e. conditions of model (1). O- link is a connection of action and its object.

3.5 Generalized Functions Formulation

According to the results of the parsing of patent claims' the first point we obtain a few descriptions of technical functions represented as (1). Number of obtained tuples varies depending on size and structure of claims. These tuples DXH are used in constructing a morphological table (the 6th processing stage) as alternatives of generalized technical function implementations [7]. Alternatives are arranged in rows of the morphological table. Generalized technical functions are arranged in columns of the morphological table. They are formulated in the 5th stage of the method using “English Verb Classes and Alternations: A Preliminary Investigation” collection created by Levin [8]. Class is defined for every verb meaning action in the DXH model. In further these classes become titles of the output morphological table columns. All detected verb classes are reviewed and the verbs, having the same class, are written in the same column of morphological table with its model (1) components, i.e. its object and conditions. Thus we obtain lots of generalized technical functions that are represented by verb classes, and ways of technical function implementations that are represented by DXH tuples. In the work [9] new idea is also represented as a text phrase but it is received after tokenization and term filtering of unstructured problem solving text; afterwards term vectors are built representing these text phrases and a specific idea mining measure evaluates new ideas for novelty and usefulness by comparing vectors that represent a problem to vectors that represent a problem solution idea. In work [10] it was proposed to extract information not only about the functions, but the physical behaviors and the states of the system directly from the text of a patent in an automatic way.

It should be noted that the verb can have more than one class according to Levin’s classification. In this case we take the first determined class. The verb can’t be represented in this classification either. All the verbs, for which classes weren’t found, are written in the separate table column with their object and condition.

4. RESULTS

For example we consider the sentence taken from the patent US8973213: “a container formed in an empty cylindrical shape and filled with water to a predetermined height above a lower wall”. Since this sentence doesn’t contain punctuation signs “colon”, “semicolon”, it is not required segmenting. The diagram of parsing of this sentence by Link Grammar Parser is shown in Figure 2.

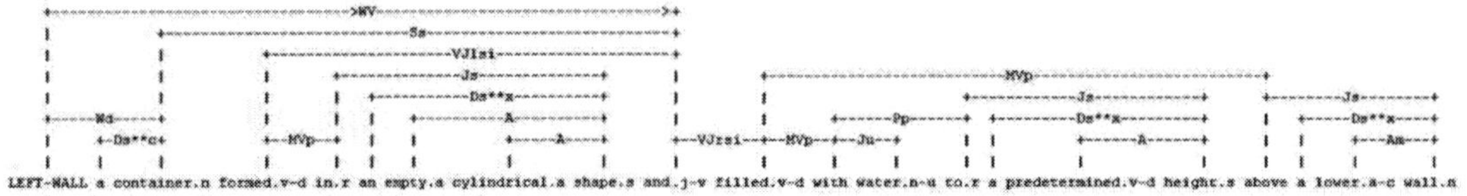

Figure 2. Links found by Link Grammar Parser in the test sentence

Technical functions contained in this sentence, will be represented by the next components of model (1) that were derived in accordance with grammar (2):

D_1 = formed; X_1 = Empty; H_1 = in empty cylindrical shape.

D_2 = filled; X_2 = Empty; H_2 = with water above lower wall

As we can see, these tuples do not contain object of action. Thus the grammar (2) was composed in such way that object is not a compulsory element as well as condition. But there are conditions of action in the most of sentences.

Using English verb classes collection we can determine that class of the verb “form” is “Reflexive of Appearance Alternation”, and class of the verb “fill” is “Spray/Load Alternation”. So we obtain:

- the first generalized function is “Reflexive of Appearance Alternation” and way of its implementation is “form in empty cylindrical shape”;

- the second generalized function is “Spray/Load Alternation” and way of its implementation is “fill with water above lower wall”.

At the moment we parsed just one sentence and received 2 generalized functions for each of which we have one alternative of its implementation. This sentence is only the fragment of patent claims. When we parse at least whole claims or a few patent claims, we will obtain several alternatives of these or other generalized functions. Then morphological table will contain quite a lot of useful information.

During testing of the proposed method it was suggested that it was necessary to analyze patent description for more informativeness and the action to look more detailed. But patent description contains mathematical formulas, references to figures and other points and the description itself is very detailed. According to the method verbs must be extracted, and in the description section not all the verbs mean actions. Thus it is not needed to analyze patent descriptions instead of claims.

5. CONCLUSION

The morphological table expands the degree of freedom of creative thinking and enhances human creative potential. It shows various variants of some technical function implementation that are concentrated in one place. Overview of all possible ways of technical function implementations can prompt user either the idea of existing structure improving or new technical solution creating. However it is necessary to remember that idea novelty itself doesn't guarantee its price.

In addition to building a morphological table from technical functions of analyzed patents, information obtained can be also used for constructing an image of each individual patent. Representation in the form of technical functions is representation of main function performed by invention object and described by several actions. A few technical functions that were found in patent claims characterize certain patent unambiguously. It means that this representation is alternative for existing representation in the form of keyword vector, where words don't bind to each other. Representation in the form of technical functions set can be used as image of patent in tasks of patents analogues search and search of analogues of patent application among patent grants, method of automated classification, method for detection of patent trends. If you use automatic translation module, you can search for patent applications in one language among patents in another language. Extraction of key actions according to model (1) allows producing annotation, referencing scientific articles and patents.

ACKNOWLEDGEMENT

This research was supported by the Russian Fund of Basic Research (grants 15-07-09142 A, 16-07-00534 A).

REFERENCES

1. Korobkin, D., Fomenkov, S., Kolesnikov, S., Lobeyko, V., Golovanchikov, A., 2015. Modification of physical effect model for the synthesis of the physical operation principles of technical system. Proceeding of CIT&DS 2015, pp. 368-378.
2. "U.S. Patent Grant Data/XML v4.3, Documentation identifying the use of XML Tags and Content" www.uspto.gov/sites/default/files/products/Patent_Grant_XML_v4.3.pdf, 4 Dec. 2012.
3. Bagaev, D., 2007. Development of a system model of a technical object. In Systems engineering, No. 5 (in Russian).
4. Korobkin, D., Fomenkov, S., Kravets, A., Kolesnikov, S., Dykov, M., 2015. Three-Steps Methodology for Patents Prior-Art Retrieval and Structured Physical Knowledge Extracting. Proceeding of CIT&DS 2015, pp. 124-136.
5. Fomenkov, S., Korobkin, D., Kolesnikov, S., Kamaev, V., Kravets, A., 2015. The automated methods of search of Physical Effects. In International Journal of Soft Computing, Vol. 10, No. 3, pp. 234-238.
6. Temperley, B. "An Introduction to the Link Grammar Parser" www.link.cs.cmu.edu/link/dict/introduction.html, 22 Mar. 1999.
7. Polovinkin, A.I., 1988. Fundamentals of engineering creativity. Mashinostroenie Publ., Moscow (in Russian).
8. Levin, B., 1993. English Verb Classes and Alternations: A Preliminary Investigation. University of Chicago Press, Chicago, USA.
9. Thorleuchter, D., Den Poel, D.V., Prinzie, A., 2010. Mining Ideas from Textual Information. In Expert Systems with Applications, No.37, pp. 7182-7288.
10. Fantoni, G., Apreda, R., Dell'Orletta, F., Monge, M., 2013. Automatic extraction of function behaviour-state information from patents. In Advanced Engineering Informatics, No. 27, pp. 317-334.

DESIGN OF A SMART BUILDING THERMAL COMFORT DEVICE

Lúcia Satiko Nomiso, Eduardo Hideki Tanaka and Daniel Augusto Guerra da Costa
Eldorado Research Institute, Brazil

ABSTRACT

This paper presents the design of a low cost device capable of monitor temperature and humidity in indoor environments and estimate the thermal sensation of the environment. Moreover, as thermal comfort may have many other variables to consider, the proposed device also allows people to vote about their subjective thermal comfort. Therefore, combining and analyzing both the data collected by sensors and the votes of the subjective thermal comfort, Air Conditioning Systems technicians can tune it up in order to achieve a reasonable thermal comfort as well as energy efficiency.

KEYWORDS

Thermal comfort, smart buildings, interaction design, low cost

1. INTRODUCTION

Traditionally, when setting up an Air Conditioning System (ACS) for a building, only the installation costs and the energy consumption are taking into account. However, too hot or too cold offices may cause discomfort to workers so that they may lose attention and have a lower performance in their day-to-day tasks (Jensen, Toftum, and Friis-Hansen, 2009; UK Health and Safety Executive, 2016). In other words, thermal comfort should be added to the equation when setting up or managing an ACS (Seppänen, Fisk and Lei, 2006).

Models to estimate the indoor thermal comfort level usually adopt traditional parameters such as air temperature, ventilating and humidity. For example, ISO 7730 (ISO, 2005) proposes a seven-point scale, from "hot" to "cold", to predict the level of thermal comfort/discomfort in indoor environments, taking into account these traditional parameters as well as clothing and metabolic rate. Table 1 illustrates this scale.

Table 1. Thermal sensation scale proposed by ISO 7730

Value	Description
+3	Hot
+2	Warm
+1	Slightly warm
0	Neutral
-1	Slightly cool
-2	Cool
-3	Cold

In addition to the parameters used by ISO 7730 to predict thermal comfort/discomfort, several other factors may influence people's thermal sensation. Li et al. (2010) highlight that cultural and climate differences among countries and people's habits, age, height and weight may be related to thermal sensation. However, adding these variables to a model to estimate thermal sensation would increase the complexity of the model, making it too difficult to apply.

Alternatively, a simpler approach would be ask people's opinion about the thermal comfort in an indoor environment. This is exactly the objective of ISO 10551 (ISO, 2011): "Assessment of the influence of the thermal environment using subjective judgement scales". With these "judgement scales", people can express their personal feelings and preferences about indoor thermal comfort as well as the acceptance and the tolerance of the environment (Parsons, 2014). Table 2 presents the preference scale of ISO 10551.

Table 2. Preference scale proposed by ISO 10551 (*I would prefer to be*)

Value	Description
+3	Much warmer
+2	Warmer
+1	A little warmer
0	Neither warmer or colder
-1	Slightly cooler
-2	Cooler
-3	Much cooler

However, in a large building, with dozens of offices and hundreds of workers, it would not be an easy task to apply all the judgement scales proposed by ISO 10551 and then set up the ACS to enhance thermal comfort of a room. Therefore, this project proposes a simple, low cost device that automatically collects the temperature and the humidity values of the room as well as allow people to vote how they feel about the thermal sensation. Then, all data gathered by the device (temperature, humidity and votes) are sent to a server and used to plot graphs on a Web portal, presenting both historical data and real time measures of temperature and humidity.

The next sections will present more details about the proposed device to assess thermal comfort in indoor environments. Section 2 will present some similar devices used in other contexts. Section 3 will describe a little bit more about the design and development of the proposed device and the faced challenges. Finally, concluding remarks and future work will be in section 4.

2. RELATED WORK

Nowadays, there are some devices in the market that are simple, inexpensive, and easy to learn, that allow users to vote, give their opinions or even order selected items in an online store. These devices will be briefly described in the next sub-sections.

2.1 Clickers and Audience Response Systems

Clickers and audience response systems are broadly used when a poll or survey is requested to be applied to a given target audience. In general, the devices have no need for configurations and are easy to learn and to use. The simplest ones are wireless, have just a few buttons to allow people select an option in a poll or a numeric pad (0-9 digits) similar to a TV remote control. A LED or a small LCD display is present in the devices to give a feedback when selecting an option. A server or a desktop computer collects the responses from all devices and can present them in charts or tables. Depending on the technology, it is possible to automatically plot charts and show tables in a presentation software such as Microsoft PowerPoint. Television shows with theater audience, conferences, training and education programs are some of the areas that typically utilize clickers and audience response systems. Figure 1 shows some examples of clickers typically used in education.

(a) (b)

Figure 1. Example of clickers: (a) IML Click (IML, 2016) and (b) iClicker + (iClicker, 2016)

More recently, physical clicker devices have been replaced by mobile applications that do practically the same job. In one hand, as pros, no special hardware is required and it is straightforward to add more clickers to a poll or a survey. On the other hand, there are some cons: users must have a smartphone, install a specific application and have Internet access to participate of the poll or survey.

2.2 Amazon Dash Button

Recently, another simple device that emerged from the market was Amazon Dash Button (Amazon, 2016). The device proposes to solve a simple problem: never running out a favorite product at home. As its name suggests, there is only a single button in the device. Pressing this button will place an order in Amazon.com with a pre-selected item (currently, just a restricted list of products from specific brands have a Dash Button, so that users may need to have a Dash Button for laundry soap, another one for alkaline batteries, another one for diapers, etc.). A green LED in the device indicates that the order was placed and the user receives a message in his/her phone with the order confirmation.

Despite the simple design proposed by Amazon, reviews from the media were not all positive. The ultimate objective of increase consumption (and, consequently, the increase of trash produced) and the lack of an effective error prevention mechanism were some of the blames (Roberts, 2015; Crouch, 2015; Resnick, 2015).

2.3 O'Reilly Data Sensing Lab

O'Reilly Data Sensing Lab has created and experimented many devices to continuously monitor environments and people, without need for manual intervention (O'Reilly, 2016). Among the sensors present in their devices, there are temperature, humidity and pressure sensors, which could be useful to estimate indoor thermal comfort. However, as the key objective of the devices is to monitor only the data that are collectable through sensors, without any direct user interaction, the proposed devices could not get people's subjective thermal sensation, as their hardware doesn't really have a user interface (at least at the time this paper was written).

3. PROPOSED DESIGN AND DEVELOPMENT

The whole design and development process of the device occurred during a few cycles of prototyping and informal review with engineering and design teams. Both teams worked together to understand the hardware requirements and provide the best user experience as possible. Also, the teams had in mind the need for a low cost device, as one of the requirements was to be able to install dozens or maybe hundreds of devices to track thermal comfort in different office rooms of a company.

Then, and considering all related work previously presented, a first prototype of the device was designed as static images. The idea was to add to the device temperature and humidity sensors as well as let users to express their opinions about the thermal comfort of a room. To make it as simple as possible and based on the judgment scales of ISO 10551 (ISO, 2011), three voting buttons were proposed to allow users to vote about the current thermal sensation: "hot", "nice" and "cold". Additionally, there was a QR code in the prototype to redirect users to the Web portal containing real time and historical data about thermal comfort of the rooms. This first prototype can be seen in Figure 2 (a). It is interesting to notice that the photo of the black box in the prototype was actually the whole hardware (i.e., microcontroller and sensors) required to collect data and communicate with the server and the size of the photo was exactly the same as the black box.

Other interesting aspect of this first prototype was that the voting buttons were red to represent thermal discomfort ("hot" or "cold") and black to represent an adequate level of thermal comfort. Although design team complained that it would be confusing to the users, especially to associate a red button to "cold", this decision was based on a finding from the engineering team when analyzing the required hardware components: red and black buttons would cost much lesser than other colors.

A second prototype was designed in order to reduce the overall size of the device, which, consequently, would reduce costs too. To achieve this, the voting buttons were vertically aligned. In addition, and to try to give to the users a better understanding of the thermal comfort scale, a thermometer image was included in the background of the voting buttons. In terms of ergonomics, changing the orientation of the voting buttons favored the usage of the device as well, as it became easier to hold and press a voting button with only one hand. Figure 2 (b) shows this second prototype. Another issue was identified, though: there was too much text in the proposed prototype.

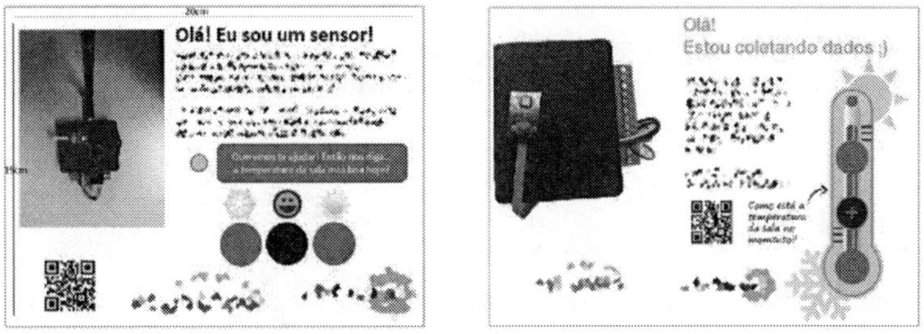

(a) (b)

Figure 2. Prototype versions: (a) First Prototype (b) Second Prototype

In the third prototype, another change in the device was proposed in order to reduce even more the size (and the costs) of it: the microcontroller and the sensors were moved to the back side of the device. Also, some rewording was done to reduce a little bit of the text. As a result, the front side became cleaner, as viewed in Figure 3. Other minor adjustments were done too, such as color changes in the background image of the scale (the thermometer) and added smiles and labels close to the voting buttons to clarify them.

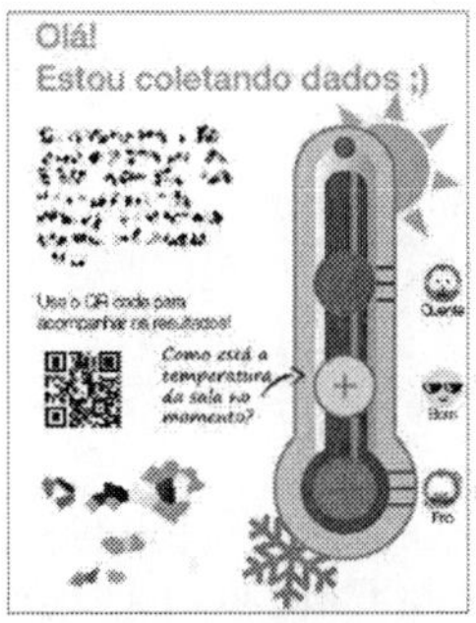

Figure 3. Third prototype, Illustrator version (color of the real buttons was not represented)

Based on this third, static image prototype, an enclosure of the device was produced. With this enclosure, it was noticed that the microcontroller box would fit between the front and back sides of the supporting plates of the device, so that just the sensors would need to be kept in the back side.

After this assessment of the enclosure, the final version of the device was then ready to be produced and can be seen in Figure 4. Also, as engineering team was able to find a green button that would not cost too much than other colors, it was decided to make a minor change in the voting scale: red button for “hot”, green button for “nice” and black button for “cold”. A LED was also added to the device to indicate when a voting button was pressed. The color of the LED is the same as the voting button scale (red, green or blue).

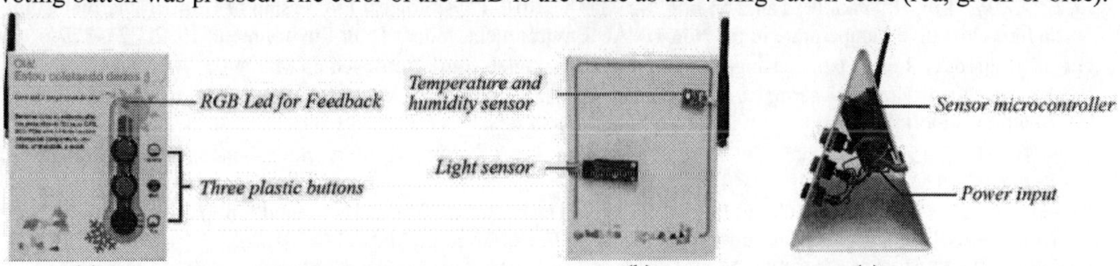

(a) (b) (c)

Figure 4. Final prototype version: (a) Front view (b) back view and (c) side view

By the time of this paper was written, 80 devices had been manually assembled. To test the effectiveness of the proposed solution, 47 devices were distributed and installed in rooms of 3 different buildings of the same company. The devices have been tracking thermal comfort for at least 3 months and all collected data (temperature, humidity and votes) have been stored in a database and utilized to plot graphs in a Web portal. Given the results so far, it is possible to say that the device is robust, as few hardware issues were found, and users learned fast the meaning of the buttons and how to use them. In addition, a usability survey was applied, but, at the time this paper was written, the number of responses was not enough to identify usability issues, although the overall feedback was positive and highlighted the relevance of thermal comfort for workers.

4. CONCLUSION

Monitoring indoor thermal comfort has become a need for many companies, as workers' performance may be negatively impacted. However, the current models to estimate thermal comfort require a large number of parameters, making their practical application a complex task. The proposed device collects two key parameters for any thermal comfort model, temperature and humidity, as well as allows workers to give their opinions about their personal and subjective thermal comfort perception. Thus, using these data, ACS technicians would be able to make predictions to balance both thermal comfort and energy consumption in all rooms from a large building. Costs to install the device in a large number of rooms should not be a serious issue, as it is easy to install and not expensive. As future works, the authors plan to finish the usability survey, conduct user tests and fix the critical usability issues that will be eventually found.

ACKNOWLEDGEMENTS

The authors would like to thank all team members that contributed with in this project.

REFERENCES

Amazon. 2016. Get to Know Your Dash Button. http://www.amazon.com/gp/help/customer/display.html?nodeId=201746300. Retrieved on Feb. 12, 2016.

Crouch, I. 2015. The Horror of Amazon's New Dash Button. http://www.newyorker.com/culture/culture-desk/the-horror-of-amazons-new-dash-button. Retrieved on March 06, 2016.

iClicker. 2016. iClicker +. https://www1.iclicker.com/products/iclicker-plus/. Retrieved on March 06, 2016.

IML. 2016. IML Click. http://lumiinsight.com/products/iml-click/. Retrieved on March 06, 2016.

ISO. 2005. ISO 7730:2005 Ergonomics of the thermal environment -- Analytical determination and interpretation of thermal comfort using calculation of the PMV and PPD indices and local thermal com-fort criteria.

ISO. 2011. ISO 10551:2011 Ergonomics of the thermal environment -- Assessment of the influence of the thermal environment using subjective judgement scales.

Jensen, K. L.; Toftum, J.; Friis-Hansen, P. 2009. A Bayesian network approach to the evaluation of building design and its consequences for employee performance and operational costs, Building and Environment, 44, 456-462.

Kalz, D.; Pfafferott, J. 2014. Thermal Comfort and Energy-Efficient Cooling of Nonresidential Buildings. Springer.

Li, B.; Li, W.; Liu, H.; Yao, R.; Tan, M.; Jing, S.; Ma, X. 2010. Physiological Expression of Human Thermal Comfort to Indoor Operative Temperature in the Non-HVAC Environment, Indoor Built Environment, 19, 2: 221–229.

O'Reilly. 2016. O'Reilly Data Sensing Lab. http://datasensinglab.com/. Retrieved on March 06, 2016.

Parsons, K. 2014. Human Thermal Environments: The Effects of Hot, Moderate, and Cold Environments on Human Health, Comfort, and Performance. Third edition, CRC Press.

Resnick, M. 2015. Ergonomics in Design: Amazon Dash. http://ergonomicsindesign.com/2015/04/amazon-dash/. Retrieved on March 06, 2016.

Roberts, P. 2015. Will Technology Like Amazon's Dash Button Make Us Stupid? http://time.com/3770127/will-technology-like-amazons-dash-button-make-us-stupid/. Retrieved on March 06, 2016.

Seppänen, O.; Fisk, W. J.; Lei, QH. 2006. Effect of Temperature on Task Performance in Office Environment. Ernest Orlando Lawrence Berkeley National Laboratory, Berkeley, CA.

UK Health and Safety Executive. Thermal comfort. http://www.hse.gov.uk/temperature/thermal/. Retrieved on Feb. 12, 2016.

RESPONSE TO SECURITY THREATS: APPRAISAL OF PROTECTION AND AVOIDANCE ACTIONS

Noushin Ashrafi, Jean-Pierre Kuilboer and One-Ki (Daniel) Lee
University of Massachusetts Boston
100 Morrissey Blvd., Boston MA 02125 - USA

ABSTRACT

At the age of Big Data, security and privacy issues are magnified and dealt differently from traditional tactics. However, the traditional security threats have become a source of constant fear and costly to individuals and organizations. Security experts have explored the intertwined role of technology and human behavior concerning security protection actions. This research offers an integrated model building on existing theories such as Protection Motivation Theory (PMT), Health Behavior Model (HBM), and Extended Parallel Processing Model (EPPM). We address the impact of the users' awareness of security threats on their protective actions while taking into consideration the mediation influence of fear. We also examine moderation effects of intrinsic as well as extrinsic factors such as users' perception of self-efficacy and the benefits and barriers of protective actions respectively. Structure Equation Modeling (SEM) is used to measure the proposed mediation and moderation effects. Our integrated theoretical model evolves around the assumption that security protection actions are formed by complex human behavior, rather than mere deployment of protective technology. The proposed model will be tested on data gathered from the US and Europe targeted population. This context-specific dimension will allow examination of cultural differences between US and Europe. Our results may shed light on the problem that despite advances in security protection technology, the deployment of such technologies is governed by human behavior and influenced by cultural background of the individuals.

KEYWORDS

Security Threat, SEM, PMT, HBM, EPPM

1. INTRODUCTION

Since the privatization of the Internet for e-commerce in the 1990s, which lead to an exponential growth of the flow of information, information security has become a source of trepidation. Information security is the protection of personal data against unauthorized access or modification while ensuring its availability to legitimate users, confidentiality, and integrity. There is no question that the Internet has become a ubiquitous platform for social and business activities. Although the public, at large, is aware of its cost/benefit tradeoffs, a potential downside such as breach of security is often talked about, but hardly reflected on end-users' behavior. What is telling is that with the increasing outcry by the public as well as the advancement of security related technology, there is no notable reduction in number of breaches (Barker, 2014) and they are becoming costlier. Researchers contribute the continuing occurrence of security breaches to end users' negligence to adopt security protection measures (Williams et al. 2014; Herath and Rao 2009). The ambiguity persists as end-users and businesses jointly spend billions of dollars on products and upgrades to address new threat categories and set of exploits, yet, there is little evidence that protective solutions are actually used as safeguards to battle increasingly incoming threats. This paradox has drawn researchers' attention leading to a number of studies addressing the end-users' mental status such as their fears, attitudes, and motivations, and the end-users' specific behaviors such as their security actions and avoidance.

Each study has its own interpretation of security protection orthodoxy, but mostly they have relied on two well-known theories from health care and psychology, Health Belief Model (HBM) and Protection Motivation Theory (PMT) respectively. PMT was originally proposed by Rogers (1975) suggesting fear as an effective mental condition protecting one against threat and consequently leading the individual away from threat. The assumption is that protection motivation arises from fear appraisal that an event will occur. The extent of fear, however, is influenced by the belief regarding the effectiveness of a recommended coping response. A revision of PMT (Rogers, 1983; Maddux and Rogers, 1983) has provided support for the importance of sources of information initiating the coping process and added self-efficacy as an intrinsic factor. Self-efficacy theory suggests that psychological change is processed through an individual's expectancies of personal mastery or efficacy. The revised PMT incorporates self-efficacy as a cognitive mediating process. The seminal work of Bandura et al. (1980) and Condiotte and Lichtenstein (1981) have established that changes in behavior and changes in self-efficacy expectancy are positively correlated.

Leventhal (1970) proposed a parallel response model that stressed the importance of differentiating emotional responses from cognitive responses (fear control versus danger control). Witte (1994) further developed an Extended Parallel Processing Model (EPPM) by adopting the original PMT's explanation of "danger control processes that lead to message acceptance (one side of the parallel process model), and defines and expands the fear control processes which lead to message rejection (the other side of the parallel process model)" (Witte 1994, p.337). EPPM explains the possible responses people may have to a fear appeal message and places them into three broad categories: non-responses, danger control responses, and fear control responses. The theory makes predictions about which of these three response types individuals will demonstrate depending upon the interaction between their perceptions of the threat and their perceptions of efficacy to avert the threat.

Another relevant model used in information systems (IS) literature to study user' behavior regarding computer security protection is Health Belief Model (HBM). The theory was developed in the 1950's by a social psychologist Hochbaum (1956) and was adopted by Rosenstock (1966) to explain the failure of people participating in programs to prevent and detect disease. Since then, HBM has been evolved and applied to a broad range of population behavior.

These theories were modified or combined by researchers to adapt to security threat protection phenomenon. Boss et al. (2015) constructed a complete overview of IS articles that use portions of PMT. Ng et al. (2009) successfully operationalized and extended primarily HBM to study user's computer security behavior. They focused on "understanding of user computer security behavior in the context of the organization" (p.823). Liang and Xue (2010) deployed a modified version of HBM to assess avoidance behavior of the users. They focused on Spyware as security threat and defined avoidance behavior as using and updating anti-spyware software regularly. Tu et al. (2015) and Williams et al. (2014) proposed a security belief model where they drew information from PMT as the reference theory and leveraged the HBM to examine users' cognitive behavior when confronted with security threats. Tu et al. (2015) integrated PMT with the social learning theory to assess users' coping appraisals in the specific context of mobile device loss or theft. Chen and Zahedi (2016) added a new dimension to security threat research by comparing cognitive behavior when it comes to security actions. They drew on "two complementary theoretical bases: (1) the contextualization of PMT to online security behavior and (2) a polycontextual lens for the cross-national comparison of users' security behaviors in the United States and China" (p.205).

The existing research, however, falls short of providing a clear picture of individuals' conduct driven by fear. In the context of security threat, the user's response, whether it is taking a protective action or avoiding online transactions, has consequences on solutions for security threats. This research examines the impact of the users' awareness of security threats on their protective behaviors. We draw on three theoretical models to fill the gap mentioned above and show a clear path from knowledge to fear to possible actions. The organization of the paper is the following: next section presents out integrated theoretical model followed by research method including a brief conclusion.

2. THEORETICAL MODEL

This research offers an integrated model building on existing theories such as PMT, HBM, and EPPM. Our integrated theoretical model takes into account the powerful features of PMT such as fear as the central motivation factor for taking protection actions against security threats. To emphasize the atmosphere of digital age where information about security threats could easily become a personal experience or cause tremendous fear by media exposure, we added awareness as the independent variable and fear as mediating factor. We consider the awareness of security threat as the combination of personal experience and knowledge induced by social media leading to fear and noxiousness. Our interpretation of EPPM, in the context of security threat is also different. The theoretical scope of the EPPM is limited to explaining and predicting reactions to fear appeals only. This study, however, draws on HBM and takes into consideration the interaction effects of the positive and negative outcomes. We take into consideration the intrinsic factor such as self-efficacy to manipulate the association between awareness and fear. In the context of security threat, self-efficacy, as an interaction effect, portrays an individual's confidence in her or his competency to deal with security threat. It impacts the degree of association between awareness and fear. Figure 1 depicts our research model.

The model depicts that fear of security threat is shaped by knowledge and prior experience of threats while self-efficacy moderates the intensity of the effect. Furthermore, we are postulating that the effect of fear on protection actions is moderated by perceived degree of effectiveness as well as undesirable attributes of the outcome. The assumption is that belief about potential positive and negative aspect of protective actions could intensify the level of fear, which in turn impacts the probability of taking actions or avoiding activities online. We consider two possible responses; (1) taking action to protect threat security and (2) avoiding to get engaged in sensitive transactions online.

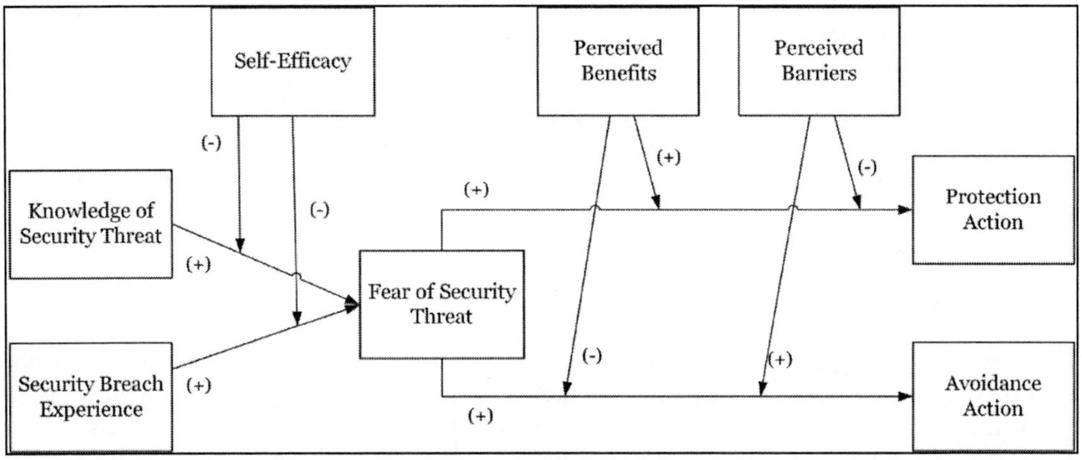

Figure 1. Moderation and mediation model

These new perspectives allude to the possibility of examining concerns such as 'why despite the availability of cyber security protection technology, does security threats remain as an unresolved problem?" Our future research will look into the impact of the types of platforms (e.g., Apple versus Windows) to assess the influence of technology type on users' perception and anxiety level of security threats. Finally, this work-in-progress will incorporate a cross-national comparison of users' security behaviors in the United States and Europe – we are in the process of data collection both in the United States and a European country.

2.1 Methods

The proposed model will be tested through a large-scale multi-national field survey by conducting the following steps: (1) measurement development, (2) pilot study, (3) survey translation (if necessary), (4) multi-national field survey, (5) model test and group comparison, and (6) implication development. First, in developing our survey measurements, every attempt will be made to use existing validated measurements that have good psychometric properties. In cases where there are no existing measurements appropriate to the context of our study, new measurements will be developed based on definitions of the variables and their relevant literature.

Second, the existing and new measurements will be validated through a pilot study. We are planning to conduct a pilot study in the United States. About 50 samples will be gathered for this pilot test. Based on the validity test results of the pilot study, some necessary changes will be made for the original measurements.

Third, to gather data from multiple countries having different cultural backgrounds and user behavior patterns, the original measurements will be translated into local languages if necessary. In particular, we will use a translation committee approach, i.e., committee of bilinguals (van de Vijver and Leung 1997).

Next, the data gathered from the multi-national field survey will be used to test proposed model. Considering the proposed multi-stage and causal relationships in our research model, we believe a structural equation modeling (SEM) approach is best fitting to our model test. In particular, the multi-national differences will be tested a sub-group analysis and other relevant techniques, such as a path comparison and a cluster analysis (Chin 2003; Sia et al. 2009). The results will also be reflected on some well-adopted cultural dimensions, such as different levels of uncertainty avoidance and long-term orientation (Hofstede and Bond 1988).

3. CONCLUSION

Upon completion of the research, based on our findings through our model test using multi-national data, both theoretical and practical implications will be developed. For academics, our findings will be used to validate and justify the proposed extension of existing theories. The practical implications will provide useful guidance regarding end-users' behavior to install necessary security measures and minimize their avoidance of the security-concerned transactions. The context-specific dimension will allow examination of cultural differences between the United States and Europe regarding individual protection behavior against security threat. Last, but not least, our overall results may shed light on the problem that despite advances in security protection technology, the deployment of such technologies is governed by human behavior and influenced by cultural background of the individuals.

REFERENCES

Bandura, A., 1982. Self-efficacy Mechanism in Human Agency. *In American Psychologist*, Vol. 37, No. 2, pp.122-147.

Barker, K. 2014. The Gap between Real and Perceived Security Risks. *In Computer Fraud & Security*, Vol. 4, pp. 5-8.

Boss, S. R. et al., 2015. What do Systems Users Have to Fear? Using Fear Appeals to Engender Threats and Fear that Motivate Protective Security Behaviors. *In MIS Quarterly*, Vol. 39, No. 4, pp. 837-864.

Chen, Y. and Zahedi, F. M., 2016. Individuals' Internet Security Perceptions and Behaviors: Polycontextual contrasts between the United States and China. *In MIS Quarterly*, Vol. 40, No. 1, pp. 205-222.

Chin, W. W., 2003. A Permutation Procedure for Multi-group Comparison of PLS Models. *Proceedings of 2003 PLS International Symposium: PLS Related Methods*, Lisbon, Portugal.

Condiotte, M. M. and Lichtenstein, E., 1981. Self-efficacy and Relapse in Smoking Cessation Programs. *In Journal of Consulting and Clinical Psychology*, Vol. 49, No. 5, pp. 648-658.

Herath, T. and Rao, H. R., 2009. Protection Motivation and Deterrence: A Framework for Security Policy Compliance in Organisations. *In European Journal of Information Systems*, Vol. 18, No. 2, pp. 106-125.

Hochbaum, G. M., 1956. Why People Seek Diagnostic x-rays. *Public Health Reports*, Vol. 71, No. 4, pp. 377-380.

Hofstede, G. and Bond, M. H., 1988. The Confucius Connection: From Cultural Roots to Economic Growth. *In Organizational Dynamics*, Vol. 16, No. 4, pp. 5-21.

Leventhal, H., 1970. Findings and Theory in the Study of Fear Communications. *In Advances in Experimental Social Psychology*, Vol. 5, pp. 119-186.

Liang, H. and Xue, Y., 2010. Understanding Security Behaviors in Personal Computer Usage: A threat Avoidance Perspective. *In Journal of the Association for Information Systems*, Vol. 11, No. 7, pp. 394-413.

Maddux, J. E., and Rogers, R. W., 1983. Protection Motivation and Self-efficacy: A Revised Theory of Fear Appeals and Attitude Change. *In Journal of Experimental Social Psychology*, Vol. 19, No. 5, pp. 469-479.

Rogers, R. W. 1975. A protection motivation theory of fear appeals and attitude change. *The journal of psychology*, *91*(1), 93-114.

APPLYING EQUIVALENCE ALGORITHMS IN SOLVING PATTERN MATCHING PROBLEMS. CASE STUDY FOR EXPERT SYSTEM DESIGN

Alina Andreica
Babes-Bolyai University, Cluj-Napoca, Romania

ABSTRACT

The paper focuses on means of applying simplification and equivalence algorithms in solving pattern matching problems. This solution is very useful in designing expert type systems, bringing important advantages in software design. We apply these principles in designing an expert system for plant therapy and we discuss general application principles, revealing their advantages in software design.

KEYWORDS

Equivalence and simplification algorithms, pattern matching, software design, expert systems.

1. INTRODUCTION AND WORKING FRAMEWORK

Software design principles apply systematic techniques in application design, usually apply abstract patterns for process modeling and implement adequate tools for problem solving. Software design often has to tackle design problems regarding expert systems (Giarratano, Riley. 2004), which are usually based on pattern matching techniques.

Within this framework, we propose means of using simplification and equivalence algorithms for solving pattern matching problems. Equivalence algorithms can be implemented in an abstract manner, based on category theory (Andreica et al. 2012).

Symbolic implementations of category theory are developed in two main directions: a constructive manner (Dragan, Watt. 2005) and in a systematic logical approach (Buchberger 2003), which enables the definition of categories, domains, operators and their properties in a manner which facilitates automatic proving.

Generic techniques are useful both for design reasons and for tackling problems using specific certain mathematical models (Andreica et al. 2012).

Within section 2 we address means of implementing simplification and equivalence algorithms on various entities, including hierarchical structures. Section 3 describes the way in which specific pattern matching problems can be solved by using equivalence algorithms. These principles are applied in implementing an expert system for plant therapy. Conclusions reveal the most important topics presented in the paper and future research and development directions.

2. EQUIVALENCE ALGORITHMS

Within this section we present means of implementing equivalence algorithms (Buchberder, Loos. 1982) on various entities, including hierarchical structures. We use the implementation framework that we have introduced in (Andreica et al. 2012).

Since the data volume that has to be processed is usually large, the most efficient way of organizing it is using a relational database, in which entities are retained in dedicated tables. Database structuring principles for processing equivalent entities are introduced in (Andreica et al. 2012).

An equivalence relation '~' verifies reflexivity, symmetry, transitivity properties (Buchberder, Loos. 1982). In this paper, we use as well tables for retaining the entities on which equivalence algorithms are applied. For example, within the plan therapy expert system we have been implementing, entities like plants, disorders, or active substances effect types are retained in dedicated tables: *Disorder* table contains the disorders, *EffectType* table contains the effect types for the active substances, *Plants* table, contains the therapeutic plants.

We process entities belonging to the dedicated tables that retain those entities:

$$\text{IsSpecificEntity(d)} := \begin{cases} true, d \in Tbl\_Entity[\text{id\_entity}] \\ false, otherwise \end{cases}$$

In particular, in the plant therapy system for example, disorders are retained in the *Disorders* table:

$$\text{IsDisorder (d)} := \begin{cases} true, d \in Tbl\_Disorders[\text{id\_disorder}] \\ false, otherwise \end{cases}$$

Hierarchical data structures are often necessary to be processed in a database; such structures may be retained in relational databases by means of ascendant / successor pointers in dedicated tables. Principles for retaining and processing hierarchical structures and a comparison of their processing techniques are presented in (Andreica et al. 2012).

We note that such a hierarchical structure can often be encountered and therefore is useful to be processed. For example, disorders are organized in a tree structure, containing disorder types of various levels, which generate hierarchies of disorders; these are retained in a dedicated table DisorderType / TipAfectiune.

```
DisorderType[Id_DisorderType,DisorderType,Id_BasicDisorderType,Id_SystemType,Obs]
   // Id_DisorderType is the id of the disorder type and DisorderType - its name
   // Id_BasicDisorderType is the id of the "basic" disorder, which is retained
   in the tree root
   // Id_SystemType is the id of the anatomical system type where the disorder
   appears
```

Disorder type entities belong therefore to the DisorderType table:

$$\text{IsDisorderType(m)} := \begin{cases} true, m \in Tbl\_DisorderTypes[\text{id\_disorder\_type}] \\ false, otherwise \end{cases}$$

In (Andreica et al. 2012) we present means of processing hierarchical structures at database level, using a dedicated table for retaining the corresponding entities and a 4 pointers retaining technique: ascendant, descendant, predecessor (same level), successor (same level).

In (Andreica et al. 2012) we detail these principles for processing modules of didactic activities. The implementation uses stored procedures parameterized with the level value, data selection operations being performed dynamically, in respect with this value. The system uses a MS SQL database (MCSD 2003) and the hierarchical structures which model curricula information are mainly processed by means of stored procedures – see (Andreica et al. 2012) for details .

Postorder type n-ary tree evaluation algorithms based on the above described tree representation are implemented in order to parse the hierarchy of entities.

Some efficiency studies we have performed on processing hierarchical structures at database level are given in (Stuparu et al. 2005).

In a general hierarchical entity structure, leaf entities are the ones retained in the basic dedicated tables.

$$\text{IsLeafEntity(m)} := \begin{cases} true, \forall d \in m : IsSpecificEntity[\text{d}] \\ false, otherwise \end{cases}$$

For example, in (Andreica et al. 2012), we process hierarchies of modules in which all non-leaf modules consist only of modules.

Let d1, d2 be two entities – for example, disorders. We use the notation '~' for describing the equivalence of two entities. In the case of disorders, d1, d2 are equivalent d1 ~ d2 in the sense that they refer to the same basic disorder and can be treated using the same treatment (therapeutically equivalent). The relation is an equivalence one since it verifies reflexivity, symmetry, transitivity properties.

The canonical representative of an entity equivalence class is important since it will be further used in pattern matching rules – see section 3.

In the case of disorders, the canonical representative is the one denoted with BasicDisorderCode (usually having the smallest identifier code).

We implemented the simplification algorithm for determining the canonical representative (Buchberger, Loos. 1982) for a given entity, which can be used in particular, for disorders and other entities that have to be processed in the plant therapy system – see section 3. Based on this algorithm, we may also test the equivalence of two entities by verifying they have the same canonical representative – in the case of disorders, the same BasicDisorderCode.

By generically denoting with '~' an equivalence relation for categories of entities (for example, disorder types), we may state that:

$$e1 \approx e2 \Leftrightarrow (\forall d1 \in e1, \exists!\, d2 \in e2 : d1 \sim d2\ ) \wedge\ (\forall d2 \in e2, \exists!\, d1 \in e1 : d1 \sim d2\ )$$

For a leaf category of entities e, we consider Canonic (e) = {Canonic(d) | d∈e} – the set of canonical representative for the contained entities (for example, disorders) . It can be shown that two leaf equivalent entities have the same sets of canonical representatives. For a category of entities we can recursively compute its canonical representative set as:

$$\text{Canonic(e)} = \begin{cases} \{\text{Canonic(d)} \mid \text{d} \in e\}, \mathit{IsLeafEntity}[e] \\ \{\text{Canonic(ed)} \mid \text{ed} \subset e\}, \mathit{otherwise} \end{cases}$$

Intuitively, the canonical set for a category of entities is obtained by "flattening" its category sub-tree and computing the union set of all canonical sets corresponding to its descendant leaf entities. Generically, we may state: Canonic (e) = {Canonic(d) | d∈e}

3. PATTERN MATCHING PRINCIPLES

We implement pattern matching rules for equivalent entities by reducing the mapping between two elements, belonging to the two equivalence classes that are to be mapped, to mapping their canonical representatives, as described below:

Let $e_i \in$ E class of equivalent entities, $em_j \in$ EM class of equivalent mapped entities, e_0 – the canonical representative of class E and em_0 – the canonical representative of class EM. Then we reduce a mapping of two entities e_i , em_j belonging respectively to the equivalence classes E, EM to the mapping between the two canonical representatives $e_0 \in$ E, $em_0 \in$ EM – see figure 1:

$$e_i \text{ -> } em_j \rightarrow e_0 \text{ -> } em_0, \text{ where } e_i \in E,\ em_j \in EM$$

We may as well use the equivalent mappings:

$$e_i \text{ -> } em_0 \text{ or } e_0 \text{ -> } em_j, \text{ where } e_i \in E,\ em_j \in EM$$

For the case of equivalence classes with hierarchical representations – see figure 2 – the canonical representatives are the roots of the corresponding trees (figure 2). Parsing algorithms for finding the canonical representatives generally use the ascendant pointer – see section 2.

We can use the above described rules in managing pattern matching problems on equivalence classes that occur in the design of expert systems. We implement these rules in solving the pattern matching problems which occur in the plant therapy system that we present as case study.

For the plant therapy expert system that we exemplify, we define pattern matching rules for:

- recommended therapies;
- effects – based on which we can propose therapies;
- inadvisable therapies / cautions – associations between disorders and active substances effects which are not allowed for those disorders.

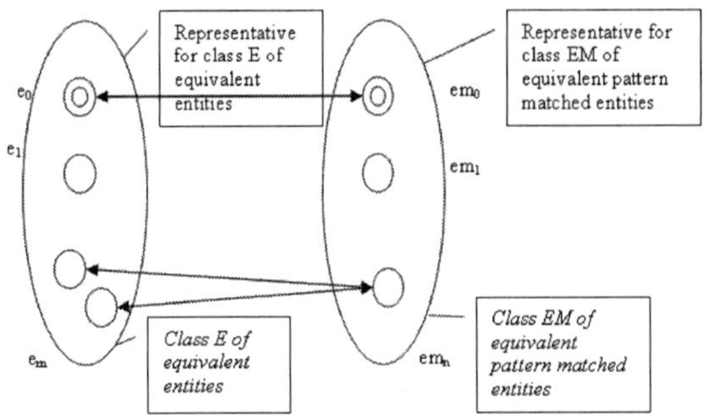

Figure 1. Pattern Matching scheme for Equivalence classes

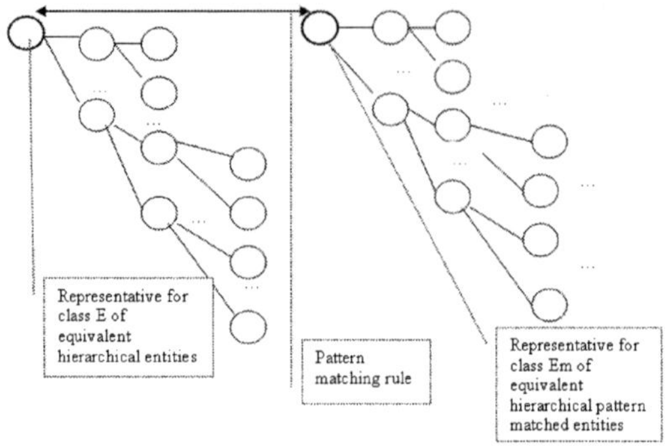

Figure 2. Pattern Matching on Hierarchical Structures of Equivalence Classes

Therefore, we have been implementing the following pattern matching capabilities:

1. *Recommended therapies*: Pattern matching rules associating disorders and plants (using the ids of their representatives) are managed by means of a user friendly interface within the phase of system learning and encoded in a dedicated table – **`Recipes (Retete)`**
   We note that actually we use, more generally, Plant mixture entities, which retain specific proportions for each plant code (retained with its representative name); in particular, a unique plant has the proportion equal to 100%.
2. *Effects* : Pattern matching rules associating:
   a. recommended effects and disorders mappings (using the ids of their representatives) are managed by means of a user friendly interface within the phase of system learning and encoded in the dedicated table:

   ```
   RecommendedEffectsForDisorders[DisorderCode, Id_EffectType]
   ```

   b. recommended effects and anatomic subsystems mappings (using the ids of their representatives) are managed by means of a user friendly interface within the phase of system learning and encoded in the dedicated table:

   ```
   RecommendedEffectsForSystems[SystemCod, Id_EffectType]
   ```

   We use a table of active substances:

   ```
   ActiveSubstances[Id_ActiveSubstance, ActiveSubstranceName,
     ASAlternateName, Id_EffectType]
   ```

   and a table of effect types, which is used in pattern matching procedures:

   ```
   EffectType[Id_EffectType, EffectTypeName, Id_BasicEffectType]
   //hierarchical representation
   ```

3. *Inadvisable associations / Cautions*: Pattern matching rules between plants and effect types that must not occur are managed by means of a user friendly interface within the phase of system learning and encoded in a dedicated table

   ```
   InadvisableAssociations[Id_EffectType, BasicDisorderCode, Characteristics,
     PriorityCode, Obs]
   ```

   We also retain certain priorities, referring to the importance / weight of the association.

We note that for the database representation it is important to improve table access speed table by indexing the tables in respect with the search id, this principle is very useful to be applied as well in managing hierarchical representations at database level, which are frequently processed in order to find the canonical representative.

4. CONCLUSIONS AND FUTURE WORK

In software design, and particularly in expert system implementation, it is important to develop means and specifications that ensure simplification and equivalence implementations, since these methods can also be used to solving specific pattern matching problems in a systematic manner, which increases software design efficiency

The paper proposes means of implementing simplification and equivalence algorithms for solving various problems, as well as using them in efficiently implementing pattern matching mechanisms. The implementation of these methods has important proficiency advantages in software and expert system design.

The method we propose addresses means of implementing simplification and equivalence algorithms on various entities, including hierarchical ones, and using them in further implementing pattern matching rules using canonical representatives. Implementations can also be performed on hierarchical data structures, which often occur in data collections.

Case studies are performed in designing and implementing an expert system for plant therapy and use database representations.

We reveal the advantages of applying the algebraic equivalence model and of applying canonical representatives' properties in solving pattern matching problems.

Future work is related to refining techniques of software design by implementing specific mathematical models and properties in order to increase software efficiency. We also intend to study additional means of processing equivalence classes and hierarchical structures, as well as complexity analysis in order to improve software design techniques.

REFERENCES

Andreica, A, Stuparu, D, Mantu, I, 2005. "Symbolic Modelling of Database Representations", *International Symposium on Symbolic and Numeric Algorithms for Scientific Computing 2005*, IEEE Press, p 59-62

Andreica, A, 2005, *Calcul simbolic şi aplicaţii,* Ed. Dacia, Cluj-Napoca

Andreica, A, 2006. "Implementing Parameterized Type Algorithm Definitions in Mathematica", Eighth International Symposium on Symbolic and Numeric Algorithms for Scientific Computing, IEEE Proceedings, p.35 - 40

Andreica, A, Stuparu, D, Miu, C, 2010. "Design Techniques in Processing Hierarchical Structures at Database Level", *Proceedings of Iadis Information Systems 2010*, Porto, 18-20 March 2010 , IADIS Press, Ed: M Nunes, P Isaias, P Powell, p. 483-488

Andreica, A, Stuparu, D, Miu, C, 2012. *Applying Mathematical Models in Software Design*, 2012 IEEE 8th International Conference on Intelligent Computer Communication and Processing, Cluj-Napoca, Romania, Proceedings of ICCP 2012, IEEE, Ed: Ioan Alfred Letia, p. 87-90

Buchberger, B, Loos, R, 1982. *Algebraic Simplification*, Computing, Suppl. 4, Springer Verlag, p.11-43

Buchberger, B, 2003. "Automatic Invention and Verification by Lazy Thinking", D. Petcu, V. Negru, D. Zaharie, T. Jebelean Eds, *Proceedings of "Symbolic and Numeric Algorithms for Scientific Computing" SYNASC 2003,* p. 2-26

L. Dragan, S. Watt, 2005. "Performance Analysis of Generics in Scientific Computing", *International Symposium on Symbolic and Numeric Algorithms for Scientific Computing SYNASC 2005,* JD Cantarella ed, IEEE Computer Society Press, p. 93-100

Gamma E, Helm R., Johnson R., Vlissides J., 2002 *Design Patterns*, Teora

Giarratano, C, Riley, G. D, 2004. *Expert Systems: Principles and Programming*, 4th Edition, Course Technology

MCAD/MCSD Training Kit: Developing XML Web Services & Server Components with MS Visual Basic .NET and MS Visual C# .NET Editor, 2003. MS Press, Redmond

Ramakrishnan, R., 2002 Database Management Systems, 3rd edition, New York: McGraw-Hill

Stuparu, D, Andreica, A, Mantu, I, 2005. "Comparing Access Techniques on Databases in Distributed Application Frameworks", *Proc. of Collaborative Support Systems in Business and Education*, BBU, Cluj-Napoca, p 1-10

3- and n-Tier Architectures http://www.corba.ch/e/3tier.html , accessed November 2015

Reflection Papers

ICT AND JAPANESE PHILOSOPHY: GAMIFICATION FOR SKILLED ANIMALS

Per Fors
Uppsala University
Lägerhyddsvägen 1, 75237, Uppsala, Sweden

ABSTRACT

In this reflection paper, I have drawn on the Imamichian notion of the skilled animal in order to better understand gamification, the use of game elements in non-game context (Imamichi 2009, Deterding et al 2011). I distinguish between meaningful and meaningless gamification. While meaningless gamification, often used for marketing purposes, does not require long-term behavioural change, meaningful gamification aims to intrinsically motivate the user to carry out real-life activities related to for example fitness, sustainability and education (Nicholson 2015, Fors and Lennerfors forthcoming, Fors and Laaksoharju forthcoming). The skilled animal, according to Imamichi (2009), is a human being in the technology-mediated environment of modern societies that do not understand or question the inner workings of technological artefacts. By using this theoretical backdrop to gamification, it can be concluded that meaningful gamification is inherently different from meaningless gamification in a number of aspects, which in turn has practical implications for the development of gamified applications. First of all, I suggest that in order to develop gamification for meaningless purposes, the user of the gamified application will not have to move beyond the skilled animal approach to technology as the only purpose of these applications is to teach the skilled animal a few more tricks. However, in order to develop gamification for meaningful purposes, the application must be designed to let the user surpass the skilled animal phase in order to find intrinsic motivation for the gamified task.

KEYWORDS

ICT, gamification, skilled animal, Imamichi, Eco-Ethica, ICT and behaviour

1. INTRODUCTION

Studies of technology, and ICT in particular, rarely pay attention to animals, not even in a metaphorical sense. Although many animals use tools, they are seldom able to operate the highly complex technological appliances of the 21th century, with some exceptions. Many service dogs are now equipped with computer vests, allowing them to contact other humans if their handler is in danger. They can also learn how to trigger SOS alarms with GPS coordinates. Some pets are also very fond of touch screen technology, and there are games for portables developed exclusively for animals. One could argue that most of these animals have no clue of what they are actually doing or why when operating this kind of technology, but then again, do humans?

The Japanese philosopher Tomonobu Imamichi has been comparing humans who use technology in an unreflective manner with skilled animals (2009). He is describing the skilled animal as follows: “When I buy a new CD player, and I ask how to use it, the shop assistant says: ‘When you push this button you can record. This button is for rewinding.’ Most people would then, like me, reply: ‘Oh, I get it.” But what does ‘getting it’ mean? … Apart from knowing how to operate it, I have no understanding of how the setup works. And nor has the sales assistant … This is exactly the same as how animals get into trouble if they don’t wait to eat when told to do so and how they start eating once given the okay, even though they have no understanding of the words at all” (p. 27). Being inspired by philosophy when studying hypermodern phenomena such as gamification might seem odd, but consistent with Poltronieri's claim that "one can see that there is a great effort on the part of academics in making [gamification] be dealt with by newer approaches, when there are already disciplines, such as philosophy, which have observed the issue of games for many centuries" (Poltronieri 2014, p. 183).

In this paper, I will discuss how gamification could be designed for humans approaching technology as skilled animals. Gamification is often used to motivate users of a particular product or service by letting them compete with other users and gather points and rewards. There are several reasons why applications are gamified, but usually it is a way of imposing a particular behaviour on the user. Most critical studies on gamification suggest that the most common form of gamification, BLAP (badges, leaderboards, achievements and points) based applications, are unsustainable and will only last for as long as new content can continuously be offered. Although most gamified applications do neither require their users to keep on playing forever nor radically change their behaviour outside the application, meaningful gamification does. By assuming that most users of technology are in the Imamichian sense merely unreflective, skilled animals with no interest in or understanding of the context of the gamified application; is meaningful gamification still viable? I suggest that while a skilled animal approach is necessary for BLAP gamification to be effective, more sophisticated solutions will be required to move beyond the skilled animal phase and motivate intrinsically.

2. GAMIFICATION

Adding elements of playfulness in all kinds of contexts such as marketing, education and fitness is now a major trend within the ICT industry. Badges, leaderboards, points and to some extent also narratives are often implemented in applications in order to promote a particular behaviour. This implementation is often referred to as gamification. Even though character progress and narratives could indeed play important roles in some gamified applications, the rewards are often what the developers regard most important (Robertsson 2010). These rewards are sometimes tangible, such as discounts or samples, but most applications exclusively offer intangible rewards. Intangible rewards include experience points, in-game items and similar types of rewards with no value outside of the gamified environment. These are all examples of extrinsic rewards, but there is also a contrasting type of reward, namely intrinsic. These are offered when a user of a particular application find the behaviour that the application is imposing on them, for example working out or eating healthy, intrinsically rewarding in that they feel stronger, happier or more healthy. When extrinsic rewards are used, the overjustification effect will often decrease the intrinsic motivation for the gamified task. For example, rewarding pupils gold stars when doing schoolwork will reduce the time they spend studying (Lepper et al. 1973). Kohn (1999) has demonstrated that people will spend less time performing a certain task, and do it more poorly, once they start receiving extrinsic rewards. Nicholson (2015) argues that (extrinsic) reward-based gamification is useful within some contexts, for example when organizations look for "immediate and short-term change … [a]s long as the organization is willing to continue supplying rewards" (p. 2). "Once you start giving someone a reward, you have to keep her in that reward loop forever" (Zichermann and Cunningham 2011, p. 27).

For long-term change, more sophisticated solutions are thus required. According to Nicholson, "the long-goal of [meaningful gamification] should be to escort a player into deeper engagement with the real-world context and then to leave him or her in the real world" (2015, p. 14). Nicholson (2015) is proposing a framework for long-term behaviour change through the means of gamification called RECIPE, which is a layer-based framework where layer after layer can be removed until the user is stuck in the real world and still can find intrinsic motivation for the previously gamified task.

3. IMAMICHI'S SKILLED ANIMAL

Tomonobu Imamichi (1922-2012) was a Japanese philosopher best known for the development of Eco-Ethica, a new ethical framework for the technology-mediated environment (TME) of today (2009). The TME is described by Imamichi as an environment consisting of technological artefacts which exists alongside our natural environment. In many respects, the TME has altered our relation to other humans and to nature. We rarely interact directly with other people, but indirectly through the internet, when playing games or using social media. This means that the physical distance between people has increased by the means of the TME. On the other hand, our friends are now easier to reach and previously unknown people have become our new neighbours: "With the technology-mediated environment people in far-flung corners of the globe become our neighbours via the telephone. [D]ialling a wrong number … means that you end up waking a complete stranger in the middle of the night, far off in some foreign country" (Imamichi 2009, p. *x*).

In order to explain how to interact with technologies such as ICTs within the TME, Imamichi coins the notion of the skilled animal. As described briefly in the introduction to this paper, the skilled animal is a metaphor describing users of technology that nor reflect upon the inner workings of technology, nor the consequences of their actions while using technology: "If we respond passively to the technology-mediated environment that has emerged today, we will be going against our track record of trying to transcend our environment, and we will lose what makes us human" (ibid, p. 29). The skilled animal is only concerned about the input and the direct output of the use process, e.g. that text is appearing on the screen when working in a word processor. If most users of ICT, thus most users of gamified applications, are skilled animals as Imamichi suggests ("we are forced to realize that at some point we have turned into animals" (p. 28)), how come practitioners and researchers alike argue that gamification could be the silver bullet for intrinsic motivation and behaviour change? Could the skilled animals become human once more by the means of gamification?

4. DISCUSSION AND CONCLUSION

Neuringer (1969) has discovered that animals such as rats and pigeons that received food from carrying out simple tasks would continue to carry these tasks without the reward. For example, rats continued to pull a lever to receive food pellets, even though free pellet were available. This suggests that even animals express intrinsic motivation for carrying out tasks that includes problem solving. My reading of Imamichi suggests that there is in fact little difference between human beings and animals when it comes to using technology. This would mean that because these users lack the ambition to reflect upon their actions and the context of the application, they do not attempt to connect the dots between the gamified environment inside an application and the reality, which is the main challenge for meaningful gamification (Nicholson 2015). However, as meaningless gamification relies on inherently different mechanisms, these applications often require the unreflective skilled animal approach, such as in the case of Neuringer's rats (1969). Surpassing this phase would mean that once the user start reflecting upon the context the game, they will quickly lose interest as BLAP based, ludo-aesthetical applications are intrinsically unrewarding (Fors and Lennerfors forthcoming, Nicholson 2012). Meaningless gamification will thus not be able to radically change the behaviour of the user; it will only be able to teach the skilled animal a few new tricks (Fors and Laaksoharju forthcoming).

Based on this assumption, gamified applications aiming towards motivating their users intrinsically will need to be designed quite differently from meaningless gamification, as noted by Fors and Lennerfors (forthcoming), Nicholson (2015), Deterding (2012). I suggest that meaningful gamification must be able to produce *reflexivity*, the ability understand and reflect upon the meaning and consequences of using the gamified application, in order to be used for meaningful purposes. Allowing the user of gamified application to produce reflexivity can be done in many ways. First of all, as noted by Ruffino (2014) and Fors and Lennerfors (forthcoming), a gripping narrative is yet to become a thing within gamified applications. As proposed by narratologists such as Murray (1997), the narrative in video games could have a truly transformative power, which could be exploited to let the user transcend the skilled animal phase. Another fruitful aspect to consider could be the palette of affects used in gamification. Today, gamification is invoking positive affects such as fun and enjoyment, but in order to promote reflexivity in gamified applications, more affects such as anxiety and frustration – native to books, video games and movies – will have be used. Moreover, a skilled animal will not have to consider the consequences of its decisions in game, while a user who has surpassed that phase will need to consider every action in order to get a rewarding experience using the application.

REFERENCES

Deterding, S. et al, 2011. Gamification: Using game-design elements in non-gaming contexts. *Proceedings of CHI'11 on Human Factors in Computing Systems*. Vancouver, Canada, pp. 2425-2428.

Deterding, S., 2012. Gamification: designing for motivation. *Interactions*, Vol. 19, No. 4, pp 14-17.

Fors, P. and Lennerfors, T.T., forthcoming. Gamification for Sustainability: Beyond the Ludo-Aesthetical Approach. In Dymek, M. and Zackariasson, P. (Eds.) *The Business of Gamification*. Routledge, New York.

Fors, P. and Laaksoharju, M., forthcoming. An intuition-based approach to sustainable ICT: Lessons from Eco-Ethica. In Lennerfors, T.T. (Eds.) *Technology and Japanese Philosophy.* Springer, Berlin, Heidelberg

Frasca, G. (2003). Simulation versus narrative: Introduction to ludology. In M. J. P. Wolf & B. Perron (Eds.) *The video game theory reader*. Routledge , New York.

Huizinga, J., 1967. *Homo ludens: A study of the play-element in culture.* Beacon Press, Boston.

Imamichi, T., 2009. *An Introduction to Eco-ethica.* University press of America, Lanham.

Kohn, A., 1999. *Punished by rewards: The trouble with gold stars, incentive plans, A's, praise, and other bribes.* Houghton Mifflin Harcourt, Boston.

Lepper, M. et al, 1973. Undermining children's intrinsic interest with extrinsic reward: A test of the "overjustification" hypothesis. *Journal of Personality and social Psychology*, Vol. 28, No. 1, pp 129-137.

Murray, J. H., 1997. *Hamlet on the holodeck: The future of narrative in cyberspace.* Simon and Schuster, New York.

Neuringer, A. J., 1969. Animals respond for food in the presence of free food. *Science*, Vol. 166, No. 1, pp. 399-401.

Nicholson, S., 2012. Strategies for meaningful gamification: Concepts behind transformative play and participatory museums. *Presented at Meaningful Play 2012*. Lansing, Michigan. Available online at http://scottnicholson.com/pubs/meaningfulstrategies.pdf

Nicholson, S., 2015. A RECIPE for meaningful gamification. In Reiners, T. and Wood, L.C. (Eds.) *Gamification in education and business.* Springer, Berlin, Heidelberg.

Poltronieri, F., 2014. Communicology, Apparatus, and Post-History: Vilém Flusser's Concepts Applied to Videogames and Gamification. In Fuchs, M. et al (Eds.) *Rethinking Gamification*. meson press.

Robertson, M., 2010. Can't play, won't play. Hide & Seek: Inventing New Kinds of Play, October 6. Accessed 19 March 2015. http://www.hideandseek.net/2010/10/06/cant-play-wont- play/.

Ruffino, P., 2014. *From Engagement to Life, or: How to Do Things with Gamification?* In Fuchs, M. et al (Eds.) *Rethinking Gamification.* meson press.

Zichermann, G., & Cunningham, C., 2011. *Gamification by design: Implementing game mechanics in web and mobile apps.* O'Reilly Media, Inc. Available online at http://books.google.de/books?id=Hw9X1miVMMwC.

ATELIER – ASSISTIVE TECHNOLOGIES FOR LEARNING, INTEGRATION AND REHABILITATION

Anabela Gomes[1, 2], César Páris[1], Jorge Barbosa[1], Álvaro Santos[1], Nuno Martins[1] and Ana Rita Teixeira[3,4,5]

[1]*Engineering Institute of Polytechnic of Coimbra, Rua Pedro Nunes, Quinta da Nora, 3030-199 Coimbra, Portugal*

[2]*Centre for Informatics and Systems – University of Coimbra, P. II - Pinhal de Marrocos, 3030-290 Coimbra, Portugal*

[3]*Coimbra Education School of Polytechnic of Coimbra, Rua D. João III Solum, 3030-329 Coimbra, Portugal*

[4]*Institute of Electronics and Informatics Engineering of Aveiro – University of Aveiro, Campus Universitário de Santiago, 3810-193 Aveiro – Portugal (FCT Ref:SFRH/BPD/101112/2014)*

ABSTRACT

A special needs individual is a broad term used to describe a person with a behavioural or emotional disorder, physical disability or learning disability. Many individuals with special needs are limited in verbal communication, or in many cases non-verbal, making communication and learning a challenging task. Additionally, new forms of communication based on technology aren´t designed for them, making them increasingly isolated in social and educational terms. In spite of this, and fortunately, new forms of interaction do exist and they enable these particular users to access knowledge and provide them with the ability to interact with others, undertaking otherwise impossible. In this project the technology used will not be an end in itself but only a way to "drop" the mouse/keyboard paradigm making use of affordable devices available in the market that could be adopted by people with special needs that are unable to apply the traditional forms of interaction, thus assisting people in their education, integration and rehabilitation activities.

KEYWORDS

Assistive Technologies, Games, Integration, Learning, Rehabilitation, Special Needs

1. INTRODUCTION

The success of individuals with special needs, in terms of learning, work and social integration, is very dependent on the continued support that society can give them. These individuals are usually denied access to a set of essential services for their social and professional integration, mainly due to the lack of equipment and solutions that enable them to overcome their needs whether in or outside the classroom. The basis of this work focuses on the fact that in the first instance people need to communicate in order to integrate into society. However, people with cerebral palsy who are nonverbal or whose speech is not clear to communicate effectively have severe problems. To overcome the communication problem augmentative communication devices have been created. They include tools and methods that help individuals to communicate more easily and effectively, such as, communication boards, symbol systems, programmable switches, electronic communication devices, speech synthesizers, recorded speech devices, communication enhancement software and voiced word processing. Our group has already developed an alternative communication platform (Santos et al., 2015), a pictographic system with the interface customization of the communication system, meeting the special needs of each user. In recent years there has also been a huge advance in the exploration of new and low cost equipment, allowing the acquisition of biometric data (neuronal, ECG, EDA, EMG,...) which open the way to new forms of interaction with the computer, facilitating their INTEGRATION into a society increasingly dominated by new technologies, simplifying their LEARNING and contributing towards their REHABILITATION. Also the appearance of different platforms as EyeToy (Sony's PlayStation2) and the later version of Move (Sony's PlayStation3), Kinect (Microsoft's Xbox 360) and Nintendo's Wii have allowed new forms of interaction with the user, without having to handle some kind of physical interface. Even though these platforms have been used primarily for gaming, on commercial terms, its use is not restricted for this purpose and can be used to address accessibility issues for users with special needs. In this sense, the people involved in this project have already developed some studies (Teixeira, Tomé and Lang, 2011) and applications with Kinect (Almeida et al., 2012). However, this research also intends to study new forms of multimodal interaction for efficiency comparative purposes. The combination of these and other suitable equipment to the needs of each individual can provide them with a better integration in our society. The technology alone is not the solution. In the context of this project we intend to develop a set of software packages that allow fostering EDUCATION, REHABILITATION, LEARNING and INTEGRATION. This is a cross-sectional project covering different knowledge areas: Special Education, Multimedia, Signal Processing, Human Computer Interaction, Games and Computer Graphics.

2. PLAN AND METHODS

This section describes the plan and methods defined to accomplish the presented research project. Some points of views and possible methodologies to adopt are shown. Also briefly described are how the project will contribute to the advance of the state of the art and also the ideas that will allow achieving these goals.

2.1 Phase 1 – Study and Characterization of Cerebral Palsy Disease

Our main public are people with Cerebral Palsy (CP) due to the fact that we have already work initiated with them, working in cooperation with some local institutions in the field of children with disabilities, in particular with APCC (a Portuguese acronym for the Association of Cerebral Palsy of Coimbra) and APPACDM (a Portuguese acronym for the Association of Parents and Friends of the Mentally Disabled Citizen). Although patients with cerebral palsy may have cognitive delays, this does not directly imply that they have a deficit of intelligence, they may only have learning difficulties for sensory reasons or lack of ability to interact with the surroundings. This phase involves the analysis and classification of CP types, based on the nature of the movement disorder and the typographical distribution. It is common to use the Surveillance for Cerebral Palsy in Europe (Cans, 2000). In addition to this classification we also want to classify the level of functional severity and activity limitation among children with CP. The basis for this study can be the Gross Motor Function Classification System (Palissano et al., 1997) widely employed, however other possibilities will be explored. Thus, the first stage of this phase will be the characterization of CP in its various aspects and types. Followed by research on existing games and applications commonly used to help people with this problem. The analyses will enable us to determine software and interaction needs. This task will also require the implementation of specific prototypes in order to test some small aspects of interaction. From this we intend to prepare a report that includes: The Characterization of the CP in terms of typologies and level of functional severity; The examination and compilation of the evidence for the application of interactive computer games and applications in the interaction of people with sensorimotor disorders; The study of different types of devices and ways of interaction usually used by individuals of various diseases as well as the study and obtaining of a list of different types of requirements.

2.2 Phase 2 – Multimodal Interfaces Analysis

Human-Computer Interaction is a fast growing topic/subject which is inflowing to a multimodal stage that goes beyond the WIMP (Windows-Icons-Menus-Pointers) paradigm. Voice, gestures, force feedback and many other existing sensors can enhance human interaction with computers and allow people with disabilities to interact with them. Combining the practice of new devices and using them in multimodal interface applications will be a common action in the near future and the challenge of this work is to study, test and develop multimodal interfaces that will allow individuals with physical or cognitive disabilities to take advantage of the applications that are available. Several interaction devices and tools can be used for this purpose. Head and eye tracking systems (from lower cost cameras, such as the common webcams, to expensive systems using infrared cameras like Nintendo), Microsoft Kinect, Brain-Computer Interfaces, Physiological sensors (EMG-electromyography, EDA-electrodermal activity, or ECG-electrocardiography), could be integrated as forms of interaction in the applications we intend to develop. Therefore, we intend to develop, implement and evaluate a personalized multimodal recognition system to improve access to assistive technology for individuals with significant speech and motor impairments as the ones with CP. It will use multiple sensors to capture vocalizations, head movements, hand and body movements filtering out involuntary gestures and sounds. These aspects will be preceded by an evaluation whether access to different interaction low-cost modalities improves the motor interaction control in the individuals, exploring and comparing the applicability of various kinematic measurements in order to propose new and feasible interaction instruments used to assess motor control activity.

2.3 Phase 3 – Integration through the Improvement of Symbolum

A person that cannot communicate often experiences great amounts of frustration, affecting his/her self-esteem, and preventing their progress in many aspects of life – learning, relationships and more. A wide variety of Augmentative and Alternative Communication (AAC) systems have been used with children who are nonverbal. In this task, we intend to improve software that we've already developed (Symbolum) allowing individuals with verbal communication problems to communicate. This application will be integrated with several different interfaces, identified in Task 2, creating a multimodal approach so that individuals can take advantage of the most effective method for a particular situation. Aiming towards the INTEGRATION of these individuals, this application should allow interaction in widely known social networks such as Facebook or Twitter. As some individuals may not have the recommended age, or may not be prepared for integration into a vast network, a private social network will also be implemented. In that network the admission will be controlled, allowing different users to share the same reality and problems while establishing contacts among themselves and their families, in a more private and controlled environment avoiding situations such as cyberbullying. Another consideration is the physical impairments that limit the use of the system by CP individuals. As portability is very important for someone who needs to use a wheelchair we considered the use of tablets as the most suitable equipment to implement in this system, due to the screen size combined with the portability advantages. This system already has a standard interface based on direct manipulation. However, several other improvements based on the above-cited explanations will be considered. In conclusion, we expect to complete an application, which will be made available in online application stores as well as the development of a private social network.

2.4 Phase 4 – Games for Posture Rehabilitation

There is clearly a need for more research regarding commercial video games in rehabilitation for people with CP. But, before we can start to plan large controlled studies we need to explore if such games are actually feasible to use in training. Computer games aren't usually thought of by health practitioners for their health benefits, but they may become a prominent part of rehabilitation programs. Using games to stimulate physical therapy for a person with cerebral palsy is our intention for this task. Therefore, we want to analyze, define and develop motion interactive games to attempt to keep the interest of the CP users and produce physical interaction enabling rehabilitation contributing to promote short-term motivation for practice and general physical training. Specific effects on motor control need to be further explored and there is also a need for reliable tests that are adequate and sensitive enough to capture changes in movement control. In the development of interactive games for rehabilitation purposes, it is a challenge to preserve the motivational and social features of games while at the same time optimizing an individualized physical training. In conclusion, we aim to achieve the following main stages: The examination and compilation of interactive applications and games for the rehabilitation of individuals with sensorimotor disorders; The creation of an application that detects if the user has bad posture (This application should be based as much as possible, in low-cost sensors (webcam, Kinect and other sensors identified in Phase2)); The creation of an interactive multimedia application on the precautions regarding posture and physical therapy exercises associated with pain zones located in the body; The creation of games where people can practice good posture while playing; The feasibility evaluation of interactive games used in physical rehabilitation in children with cerebral palsy.

2.5 Phase 5 - Games for Learning and Integration

From a popular perspective, computer games evoke fun reactions. However Gaming also has been used in educational circles since at least the 1900s. The early 2000s saw a surge in different types of educational games, especially those designed for the younger learner. More recently different types of games approaches have also been developed to engage students in the process of learning. Kazimoglu et al. (2012) discuss Computer video games and game-like environments are strategies commonly used as a motivational tool to engage students in learning programming. Nowadays there is also a great enthusiasm concerning serious games (Eagle and Barnes, 2009). However the main idea in this task is to design, implement and test a package of instructional games that can be as engaging as action games and at the same time could bring useful learning outcomes for people with disabilities. We are particularly worried with young people suffering from these disorders. However, for the development of these types of games several sets of guidelines should be followed. BBC Accessible Games Standard (Lee, 2010) and the Game Accessibility Guidelines (Elis et al., 2012) are some examples. These guidelines are the product of experts in game design and accessibility standards. We will also focus on defining guidelines for games that will train their cognitive and learning skills. As a result of this research a report is expected, laying down the foundations for the work to be undertaken. We will start developing a series of games that will allow them to train their cognitive skills, using different interfaces. These games must have a fun element, engaging people while they are interacting with the computer. Field trials will be carried out, and the games will be evaluated taking into consideration all the relevant aspects – the way children engage, their pedagogical value and their usability and ease of use. The best game will be selected for improvement, and to add a social component allowing players to interact socially with other players.

3. CONCLUSION

The major concern of this work is researching and developing tools that allow people with special needs, especially those with communication needs, to integrate into society. Our group has already developed some systems that correspond to these objectives. However, we are now looking for solutions implying low cost equipment and new forms of interaction with the least possible maneuvering of physical interfaces. Therefore, this research intends to study, integrate and develop new forms of multimodal interaction facilitating the INTEGRATION into a society, the LEARNING and contributing towards the REHABILITATION of people with special needs. This paper describes the plan and methods defined to accomplish this idea. Some points of views and possible methodologies to adopt are presented. Also briefly described are how the project will contribute to the advance of the state of the art, the ideas that will allow the team to achieve the goals and the results expected.

REFERENCES

Almeida, B. et al, 2012. Applications for people with special needs using Kinect. *Proceedings of Portuguese Conference on Pattern Recognition.* Coimbra, Portugal.

Cans, C., 2000, Surveillance of cerebral palsy in Europe: a collaboration of cerebral palsy surveys and registers. *In Developmental Medicine & Child Neurology*, Vol. 42, pp. 816-824.

Eagle, M., and Barnes, T. 2009. Experimental evaluation of an educational game for improved learning in introductory computing. *Proceedings of the 40th ACM Technical Symposium on Computer Science Education.* Chattanooga, TN, USA, pp. 321-325.

Ellis, B. et al, 2012. Game Accessibility Guidelines. Available: http://www.gameaccessibilityguidelines.com/. [Accessed: 26- Jan-2016]

Kazimoglu, C. et al, 2012. A Serious Game for Developing Computational Thinking and Learning Introductory Computer Programming. *In Procedia-Social and Behavioral Journal*, Vol. 47.

Lee, E., 2010. BBC - Future Media Standards & Guidelines - Accessible Games Standard v1.0, Available: http://www.bbc.co.uk/guidelines/futuremedia/accessibili ty/games.shtml. [Accessed: 26- Jan-2016]

Palisano, R. et al, 1997. Development and reliability of a system to classify gross motor function in children with cerebral palsy. *In Developmental Medicine & Child Neurology*, Vol. 39, No. 4, pp. 214-223.

Santos, A. et al, 2015 Symbolum –An Alternative Communication pictographic board for people with inability to communicate verbally. *Proceedings of World Congress on Special Needs Education.* Philadelphia, U.S.A.

Teixeira, A. R., Tomé, A. M. and Lang, E. W., 2011. Unsupervised feature extraction via kernel subspace techniques. *In Neurocomputing*, Vol. 74, No. 5, pp. 820-830.

ON HOW ICT CAN SUPPORT ORGANIZATIONAL CREATIVITY

Maria Mach-Król
Katowice University of Economics, Bogucicka 3, 40-226 Katowice, Poland

ABSTRACT

The paper presents selected ICT tools supporting different aspects of organizational creativity process. This is done in order to point out the main features, and functionalities that an organizational creativity support system should possess to help the creative members of organization in a complex manner. The main, and distinctive characteristics of organizational creativity are discussed, then various IT systems are shortly presented, stressing their possibilities in the context of creative process in organizations.

KEYWORDS

ICT, organizational creativity, creative process, organizational creativity support system.

1. INTRODUCTION

The main aim of the paper is to present selected IT solutions that may be used to support organizational creativity (OC). This will enable to point out main features of an IT system that would support OC in a complex manner. First of all it should be presented why OC needs computer support. This need may be seen in the definitions of organizational creativity. Shalley, et al. (2000) point out that organizational creativity results in ideas and processes, which may be treated as knowledge – and knowledge should be codified, and stored in a knowledge base; Amabile (1996) stresses the heuristic nature of organizational creativity (p. 33), so classical analytic tools cannot be used; Baer (2012) points to changeability, and dynamics of a creative organization; in e.g. (Mumford, et al., 2012) authors claim that OC is connected with problems having a badly defined structure.

Summing up, definitions of OC suggest which areas of activity in a creative organization need to be supported by IT solutions. These areas and possible IT support will be discussed in subsequent sections of the paper.

2. COOPERATION, AND GROUPWORK

Organizational creativity is a team activity that needs effective co-operation of all the members of organization. Thus, the areas that may be supported by IT technologies encompass e.g. brainstorming, categorization of ideas, alternatives analysis, knowledge sharing, organizing, and assessing, decision making, and activity planning (Hayen, et al., 2007). The IT initiatives should be therefore oriented mainly towards facilitating group discussions, as e.g. Group Support Systems (GSS) or group work systems. A creative group may need IT support also in formulating alternative business decisions, assessing them, prioritizing, and choosing the ultimate one by group members. Here, apart from GSS, the Group Decision Support Systems may be used.

Very often organizational creativity processes make use of crowdsourcing. The IT support here may encompass social networks, WWW platforms, and also GSS (Pedersen, et al., 2013).

Smith, et al. (2008) discuss factors influencing organization's innovativeness, which is strictly connected to creative processes. They point out the possibility of IT supporting in this area by group work software, and GSS. They define its role as supporting of idea generation, idea gathering, codifying, and explanation.

The heart of any creative process is generation of ideas, which very often come from interactions among people. Obviously, communication between creative employees needs some IT support. In modern organizations, members are often away from each other, and the broadly understood CMC (Computer-mediated communication) systems can be used. These systems encompass any means enabling to use the Internet as communication medium.

3. GENERATING NEW IDEAS

This process needs IT support not only for facilitating communication. More important is to assist people in generating ideas, improvements, and in communicating them to the managerial staff. Thus, what needs to be supported is: communication between employees and managerial staff, collecting, assessing, and rewarding of ideas coming from employees, formulation of suggestions, group work.

The suggestion systems can be used for the above purposes (Bianco, 2014). They are perceived as technical means aimed at promoting innovativeness among employees (Arif, et al., 2010). Suggestion systems are composed of two main elements: a set of administrative procedures, and an infrastructure, which together enable to gather, assess, and reward ideas coming from organization members. As Vijayarani and Radjamanogary (2014) point out, implementing a suggestion system in organization results in greater involvement of employees in their work, and in greater effectiveness of organization (p. 28). The team work on new ideas may be also supported in concurrent creation of ideas, simultaneous display of many ideas, flexible grouping of ideas, capturing and recording of every stage of brainstorming, etc. Such functionalities are offered e.g. by tabletop computers.

4. INNOVATIONS

Innovations constitute an important element of organizational creativity. Designing and implementing innovations is in fact similar to generating new ideas, thus also here the IT support may be utilized. It may concern e.g. (Adamczyk, et al., 2011):

- Ideas reporting, commenting, and assessing, so that authors of ideas get feedback,
- Learning by participating in different activities linked with innovativeness,
- Integrating of innovators from inside and outside of organization,
- Providing information,
- Creating a system of innovation incentives,
- Supporting and counseling,
- Recommending,
- Creating contextual support mechanism.

To support the above areas, an organization may utilize open innovation platforms (Haller, et al., 2011). The creative process of innovations can be also IT-supported in e.g. story writing, brainstorming, unconventional thinking, or criticizing (Bitter-Rijpkema, et al., 2011). Also the IT support is needed in information gathering, critical thinking, knowledge utilization, problem formulation (EDUCAUSE Learning Initiative, 2007).

5. KNOWLEDGE MANAGEMENT

Knowledge management and usage are immanently linked with OC, so ICT should assist also these activities. The domain knowledge is fundamental for OC, and for creative co-operation (Cheung, et al., 2008), moreover, knowledge enables innovations, and thus is linked with organizational creativity. The knowledge management and usage processes for OC can be decomposed into several tasks, as e.g. (Saldanha, 2012):

- Knowledge generation,
- Access to specialized knowledge,
- Converting explicit knowledge into tacit one, and vice versa,
- Searching, linking, and information tagging,
- Joint creation of content, and new ideas,
- Interacting with other participants of the creative process,
- Recombining of previously existing ideas.

Such tasks may be performed thanks to e.g. Web 2.0 technologies or social networking software (Richter, et al., 2013), as well as knowledge management systems. As research shows, using these tools is positively correlated with explicit and tacit knowledge sharing (He, et al., 2013).

A very important task in OC is knowledge visualization. The main aim of visualization is to facilitate access to knowledge, its assessing, or discussing it. Knowledge may be visualized using several techniques, as e.g. conceptual diagrams and graphs, visual metaphors, knowledge maps, knowledge cartographies or knowledgescapes (Eppler & Burkhard, 2008).

6. CREATIVITY SUPPORT

The core of organizational creativity is the creativity of organization members, which also should be supported by ICT. It seems that this support should concern the following aspects (Indurkhya, 2013):

- Enhancing user's ability to perform creative tasks,
- Assisting organization's members in acquiring the domain knowledge, in order to stimulate their creativity,
- Stimulating user's imagination,
- Creative processes modeling,
- Information collecting – by facilitating search, and visualization,
- Defining linkages between different types of information,
- Supporting creative processes by e.g. enabling free associations, testing solutions, reviewing ideas,
- Disseminating the effects of creative co-operation.

Generally speaking, the ICT tools should provide a certain virtual environment for collaboration. Thus, e.g. the Creativity Support Systems may be used (Mûller & Ulrich, 2013).

7. CONCLUSION

In the paper, several capabilities of selected IT systems for supporting OC have been presented. Obviously, each of discussed IT tools can support a part of the creative process, not the whole of it. It is then necessary to develop a concept of a new IT system, which may be called an organizational creativity support system (OCSS), aimed at assisting users on every stage of the organizational creativity process.

From the characteristics of OC, as well as from the above analysis of different IT tools in the context of the creative process, the functionalities of the OCSS can be deduced. Such a system should actively assist users in the following tasks:

- Identification of problems, and of organization's creative needs,
- Acquisition of knowledge assets,
- Generation of new ideas, and innovations,
- Assessment and selection of ideas, and innovations,
- Dissemination of selected solutions in the whole organization,
- Knowledge evolution, and organizational learning.

The design assumptions of an OCSS having the above functionalities have been presented for the first time by (Olszak & Bartuś, 2015).

The main achievements of the paper are: clear presentation of the most important features of organizational creativity, influencing the IT needs of a creative organization, selection from existing ICT solutions these possibly supporting OC, and clear formulation of functionalities for a complex and complete organizational creativity support systems.

ACKNOWLEDGEMENT

This paper has been supported by a grant: „Methodology for Computer Supported Organizational Creativity" from National Science Centre in Poland, 2013/09B/HS4/00473.

REFERENCES

Adamczyk, S., Bullinger, A. & Moeslein, K., 2011. Commenting for new ideas: insights from an open innovation platform. *International Journal of Technology Intelligence and Planning*, 7(3), p. 232-249.

Amabile, T. M., 1996. *Creativity in Context: Update to The Social Psychology of Creativity.* Boulder: Westview Press.

Arif, M., Aburas, H., Al Kuwaiti, A. & Kulonda, D., 2010. Suggestion Systems: A Usability-Based Evaluation Methodology. *Journal of King Abdulaziz University: Engineering Sciences*, 21(2), p. 61-79.

Baer, M., 2012. Putting Creativity to Work: The Implementation of Creative Ideas in Organizations. *Academy of Management Journal*, 1 October, 55(1), p. 1102-1119.

Bianco, D., 2014. *Suggestion Systems.* http://www.referenceforbusiness.com/encyclopedia/Str-The/Suggestion-Systems.html [Accessed 31 10 2014].

Bitter-Rijpkema, M. et al., 2011. A new approach to collaborative creativity support of new product designers. *International Journal of Web Based Communities*, 7(4), p. 478-492.

Cheung, P.-K., Chau, P. & Au, A., 2008. Does knowledge reuse make a creative person more creative? *Decision Support Systems*, 45(2), p. 219-227.

EDUCAUSE Learning Initiative, 2007. *7 things you should know about digital storytelling.* https://net.educause.edu/ir/library/pdf/ELI7021.pdf [Accessed 03 11 2014].

Eppler, M. & Burkhard, R., 2008. Knowledge Visualization. In: M. Jennex, ed. *Knowledge Management: Concepts, Methodologies, Tools, and Applications.* Hershey, PA: IGI Global, p. 781-793.

Haller, J., Bullinger, A. & Moeslein, K., 2011. Innovation contests - an IT-based tool for innovation management. *Business and Information Systems Engineering*, 3(2), p. 103-106.

Hayen, R., Swaby, S. & Huang, Z., 2007. Use of Group Support Systems in Today's Society. *Issues in Information Systems*, VIII(2), p. 120-126.

He, W. et al., 2013. *Linking Knowledge Sharing and Employee Creativity: Decomposing Knowledge Mode and Improving the Measure of Tacit Knowledge Sharing.* Proceedings of PACIS, Paper 219.

Indurkhya, B., 2013. On the role of computers in creativity-support systems. In: A. Skulimowski, ed. *Looking into the Future of Creativity and Decision Support Systems.* Kraków: Progress & Business Publishers, p. 233-244.

Mûller, S. D. & Ulrich, F., 2013. Creativity and Information Systems in a Hypercompetitive Environment: A Literature Review. *Communications of the Association for Information Systems (CAIS)*, 32(1), p. 175-201.

Mumford, M. D., Medeiros, K. E. & Partlow, P. J., 2012. Creative Thinking: Processes, Strategies, and Knowledge. *The Journal of Creative Behavior*, March, 46(1), p. 30-47.

Olszak, C. & Bartuś, T., 2015. Multi-Agent Approach in Designing of Organizational Creativity Support. In: J. Chen, D. Xinghua, W. Hu & R. Zhan, eds. *IS Management and IS Engineering in the Era of Big Data.* Reading: Academic Conferences and Publishing International Limited, p. 93-102.

Pedersen, J. et al., 2013. Conceptual Foundations of Crowdsourcing: A Review of IS Research. In: R. J. Sprague, ed. *Proceedings of the 46th Annual Hawaii International Conference on System Sciences.* Wailea, Maui, HI: IEEE, p. 579 - 588.

Richter, A., Stocker, A., Müller, S. & Avram, G., 2013. Knowledge management goals revisited: A cross-sectional analysis of social software adoption in corporate environments. *VINE*, 43(2), p. 132 - 148.

Saldanha, T. J. V., 2012. *Mechanisms Underlying IT-Enabled Business Innovation: Review, Theoretical Framework, and Empirical Analyses.* http://deepblue.lib.umich.edu/handle/2027.42/93844_[Accessed 25 10 2014].

Shalley, C. E., Gilson, L. L. & Blum, T. C., 2000. Matching Creativity Requirements and the Work Environment: Effects on Satisfaction and Intentions to Leave. *Academy of Management Journal*, 1 April, 43(2), p. 215-223.

Smith, M., Busi, M., Ball, P. & Van Der Meer, R., 2008. Factors influencing an organisation's ability to manage innovation: A structured literature review and conceptual model. *International Journal of Innovation Management*, 12(4), p. 655-676.

Vijayarani, S. & Radjamanogary, D., 2014. Employee Suggestion System: A Tool for Improving Employee Involvement. *International Journal of Business and Management Invention*, 3(2), p. 26-28.

Posters

AUGMENTED REALITY IN LIMITED ENVIRONMENT, ANALYSIS OF USABILITY

Maritzol Tenemaza[1], Elisa Mena-Maldonado[1], Fernando Ledesma[1], Mauricio Llumiquinga[1] and Sergio Luján-Mora[2]

[1]*Escuela Politécnica Nacional, Ladrón de Guevara E11·253 [PO·Box 17-01-2759], Quito Ecuador*
[2]*University of Alicante, Carretera San Vicente del Raspeig, s/n, 03690, Alicante, Spain*

ABSTRACT

Augmented reality (AR) is an emergent technology; the AR usability in limited environments is not experimented. The analysis of AR usability presented by other researches was conducted on applications that work on open environments, or in other experiments, objects defined by QR codes were used. When this type of programs are developed, the environment is not totally delimited, the programmers define additional routes for adjusting user`s requirements, in this situation is necessary to define useful attributes of the interface. In this paper, GeoEPN, a mobile application, is presented. GeoEPN was developed to guide people visiting our university; this application was published in Google Play Store. It is proposed to analyze AR usability compared with the common geographical maps in limited environment.

KEYWORDS

Adaptive augmented reality, augmented reality, usability, limited environments

1. INTRODUCTION

Augmented reality (AR) is a technology that displays information required by user on the real word and on real time (Mendez and Schmalstieg, 2007, Doswell and Skinner, 2014). When the information is helpful and adapted to each user's interest and context, it is called adaptive augmented reality (A^2R) (Damala et al., 2012).

Usability with the standard ISO 9241[1] is defined as "*Extent to which a product can be used by specified users to achieve specified goals with effectiveness, efficiency and satisfaction in a specified context of use*". There are several researches which analyze AR usability for education environments (Ferrer et al., 2013) and AR usability analysis in general (Martins et al., 2012).

This work presents a mobile application called GeoEPN based in AR adapted to user's interest and it work also integrates user's contextual situation (user's position is always into account). This application guides people visiting our university. The focus in our research is to know what happens with the usability with both AR and maps interfaces. The objective is to analyze the user experience while using the application: its presentation, functionality, performance and interaction. The following variables are measured: Effectivity, efficiency, error tolerance, engaging, and ease to learn (Nielsen, 1994). Problems in usability were identified to improve the application.

2. DEVELOPMENT OF APPLICATION A^2R

GeoEPN is an application designed to comply with the following objectives: A^2R guiding sighted people through our university, for each user's geographical location was considered, the reality observed by the camera was presented and the distance between the user and the place to visit was specified. A map guiding

[1] http://www.iso.org/iso/catalogue_detail.htm?csnumber=52075

sighted people through our campus to find the required place, in this interface the route to the place to visit was presented, this route changes while the user changes his position.

In the analysis of the problem domain, Google has to define only a main street in the university, for this reason, new routes between buildings and other places were necessary to be defined. The interface for displaying results uses both AR and maps. However AR has priority over maps. Only the zone required of map for reducing unnecessary information was downloaded. Orders by multimodal form e.g. voice and data typed was entered.

Two architectures were designed: The *mobile application*, the MVP (Model View Presenter) was applied because it is an architectonic patron of user interface designed for facilitating the unit test. And, the *web panel architecture* is Façade type. This type of architecture provides a unified interface for a group of system interfaces. The clients communicate with the subsystems through a request to Façade; this ensures the elimination of the complexity on inferior level. Additionally, it translates and manages the communication between systems. For web application, it was used Scala Lift, which communicates with the service constructed on Twitter Finagle on Thrift. The service interacts with Mongo DB Database; this service also updates the data in each device that uses the application through Google Cloud Messaging.

3. METHOD

Ten people participated; all of them were university students. Each participant installed the GeoEPN application in their mobile device. The purpose of each student was to arrive to their school, laboratory or investigation building, depending on what each participant chose. All individuals performed a series of basic tasks on the application, e.g. visit specific building, first with AR and next with maps. Then, each participant filled a survey presented in the Table 1.

Table 1. User's survey

Number	Question	Use
1	What do you think of the amount of time used to find a place required with Augmented Reality?	Efficient
2	What do you think of the amount of time used to find a place required with maps?	Efficient
3	Were the elements of navigation of Augmented Reality clear?	Efficient
4	Were the elements of navigation of maps clear?	Efficient
5	On the map, was the marker of his position (context) correctly positioned?	Effective
6	On Augmented Reality, was the position of the compass on the place required precise?	Effective
7	Was information presented on Augmented Reality useful?	Effective
8	On the map, Did you find the place required?	Effective
9	On the Augmented Reality, did you find the place required?	Effective
10	If your GPS was not activate, did you received a notification?	Error Tolerant (satisfying)
11	Was the application capable to detect errors when you used the voice for orders?	Error tolerance (satisfying)
12	Did you application work when you did not have Internet connection?	Error tolerant (satisfying)
13	Was Augmented Reality interface pleasant and satisfying to use?	Engaging (satisfying)
14	Was Maps interface pleasant and satisfying to use?	Engaging (satisfying)
15	Was the analysis of his context by application appropriate in relation to your requirement?	Engaging (satisfying)
16	Was the style of interaction of Augmented Reality pleasant?	Engaging (satisfying)
17	Was Augmented Reality easy to learn?	Easy to learn
18	Were Maps easy to learn?	Easy to learn
19	Was Augmented Reality intuitive to learn?	Easy to learn
20	Were Maps Augmented Reality intuitive to learn?	Easy to learn
21	Do you consider useful that the application has two interfaces?	Satisfying
22	What do you think of the augmented reality?	Satisfying
23	Will you recommend this application to friends?	

The following variables were measured: effective, efficient, error tolerant, engaging and easy to learn. The search questions are:

Q1: How long does not take to learn AR in respect to the maps?

H1: The AR is easier to learn than maps.

H2: The maps are easier to learn than AR.

Q2: What is the result of comparing the usability between AR and maps?

H1: AR is more efficient technology than maps.

H2: AR is more effective technology than maps.

H3: AR is more satisfying technology than maps.

4. RESULTS

AR technology has not been known in our country. In this research the results presented are based in the Table **1**. User's survey.

Result of Q1: How long does not take to learn AR in respect to the maps? The sample was constituted by young people, for them both AR and maps are easy to learn.

Result of Q2: What is the result of comparing the usability between AR and maps? Both AR and maps are efficient because people easily reached to the place required. The information presented at the AR interface was necessary and sufficient. All sensors are important at the moment to help user. In general, AR is more satisfying than maps because it is a new technology and it is relevant for users. A map signaling from the user's position to the searched building is clear and easy to follow, but when the user passes to the AR interface, they require understanding and separating the real view and the information presented. When the user understands the compass, AR is easier and clear.

ACKNOWLEDGEMENT

The authors gratefully acknowledge the financial support provided by the Escuela Politécnica Nacional, for the development of the project PII–DICC–008–2015: "Proposal for adaptive Augmented Reality (A^2R) based on ontologies and collaborative adaptation".

REFERENCES

Damala, A., Stojanovic, N., Schuchert, T., Moragues, J., Cabrera, A. & Gilleade, K. 2012. Adaptive augmented reality for cultural heritage: ARtSENSE project. *Progress in Cultural Heritage Preservation.* Springer.

Doswell, J. T. & Skinner, A. 2014. Augmenting Human Cognition with Adaptive Augmented Reality. *Foundations of Augmented Cognition. Advancing Human Performance and Decision-Making through Adaptive Systems.* Springer.

Ferrer, V., Perdomo, A., Rashed-Ali, H., Fies, C. & Quarles, J. How Does Usability Impact Motivation in Augmented Reality Serious Games for Education? Games and Virtual Worlds for Serious Applications (VS-GAMES), 2013 5th International Conference on, 2013. IEEE, 1-8.

Martins, V. F., Makihara, E. L., Soares, L., Pinto, R., Mattos, V. & De Paiva Guimarães, M. Usability metrics for augmented reality applications. Informatica (CLEI), 2012 XXXVIII Conferencia Latinoamericana En, 2012. IEEE, 1-10.

Mendez, E. & Schmalstieg, D. Adaptive Augmented Reality using context markup and style maps. Proceedings of the 2007 6th IEEE and ACM International Symposium on Mixed and Augmented Reality, 2007. IEEE Computer Society, 1-2.

Nielsen, J. 1994. *Usability engineering*, Elsevier.

EXPLORING THE USER – IT PROFESSIONAL RELATIONSHIP

Dr Matthew Hinton
Open University Business School
Walton Hall, Milton Keynes, MK6 3EP, United Kingdom

ABSTRACT

Drawing on theoretical developments within the innovation literature, a conceptual model has been developed that draws a distinction between the adoption and assimilation of information technology (IT). The substantive conclusions are that a number of incongruences exist between IT professionals and end-users. These cover 1) the mismatch between business needs and the technology solution 2) inability of adoption processes to address issues of a social, organizational, or user nature 3) failure to recognize the importance of the process of interaction between various parties to technology assimilation. By addressing the assimilation process, the conceptual model offers a way to reframe our understanding from a user perspective.

KEYWORDS

User satisfaction; technology assimilation; service delivery

1. INTRODUCTION

It has long been argued that a gulf exists between the investment made in information technology and organizations' ability to reap significant business benefit from it (Hinton & Kaye, 1996; Coughlan et al 2005). Iyengar et al (2015) observe that "IT has become more powerful, relatively cheaper, and has spread throughout organizations at a rapid rate". Hand in hand with the dramatic increases in the availability of the technology is the rapid diffusion of IT applications within organizations, permeating all aspects of activity and reshaping business processes. This is undertaken in the belief it will lead to strategic competitive advantage (Pavlou & El Sawy, 2006). However, the ability to develop new technology would appear to have outstripped the ability to apply it to suitable business scenarios. The adoption of IT by organizations is seen to result from the rapidity of computer industry generated change. Change is stimulated by successive waves of manufacturer and vendor promoted technologies. Accordingly, business culture has become oriented towards finding the quick technological fix (Castells, 2011). For example, the development of CRM systems has been recognized as relying on 'technology push' (Batista et al, 2012) or technical hype with respect to cloud computing (Buyyaa et al, 2009). Consequently, the technical orientation of IT professionals has been highlighted in a number of studies (*most recently* Lyytinen & Newman, 2015; Bell, 2013). By neglecting to address the needs of the technology users, organizations are failing to realize the full potential of their IT resources. The need to understand the relationship between those using the technology and those responsible for supporting and administering it becomes more intense. This relationship is central to the transformation from technological innovation to business application, especially if significant improvements in business performance are to be realized.

2. RESEARCH DESIGN

The Empirical evidence is gathered within a multinational petro-chemicals organization. The first phase utilizes responses to a questionnaire developed using service delivery concepts; most notably the SERVQUAL framework (Parasuraman et al, 1991) and service co-production (Larsson & Bowen, 1989). The purpose for conducting this survey is to understand better what issues computer users perceive to be important in the delivery and quality of the information systems and services which they use. This utilized the five dimensions identified by Parasuraman et al (1991):

Tangibles:	*Physical facilities, equipment and appearance of personnel.*
Reliability:	*Ability to perform the promised service dependably and accurately.*
Responsiveness:	*Willingness to help customers and provide prompt service.*
Assurance:	*Knowledge & courtesy of employees; their ability to inspire trust and confidence.*
Empathy:	*Caring, individualized attention the firm provides its customers.*

This questionnaire is tested on a wide range of end-users, as well as IT support and technical staff. This identified, 1) significant heterogeneity within the user group, and 2) marked differences between users and the IT professionals. From this a model is derived that draws a distinction between the process of IT adoption and the process of IT assimilation. In the second phase, a set of follow-up interviews are undertaken that explore the adoption-assimilation model. Interviewees are selected from distinctive user clusters identified in the first phase. The clusters reflect differences in levels of discretionary usage, diversity of demand and disposition to participate, as well as skill and expertise and organizational position.

3. FINDINGS

What is apparent from the results of phase one is that, when asked to rank statements, users place most emphasis on groups B, reliability and competence, and C, responsiveness and access. Furthermore, the majority of users chose to place the tangible aspects (group A) of the service as least important. However, analysis of the aggregate scores for individual questions supports the credence which users give to the service aspects of reliability and competence, but does not show a clear emphasis on responsiveness and access. Instead, users place much greater importance on the statements which correspond to group D, the human interaction skills of support staff (empathy, communication and understanding). Again, the tangible aspects are the least important attributes of service quality and delivery. What is clear is that users do not perceive IT support services in terms of a single, technology focused perspective. It is apparent that a number of other considerations are perceived as being more important than the technology alone. This conflicts with the techno-centric approach adopted by IT professionals. They respond to externally driven change, rather than internally driven change, where organizational change is predominantly framed in terms of technical change alone.

The survey highlighted a variety of different user types and characteristics. Three distinct user clusters are identified, relating to differing usage patterns. The findings suggest that the demand for each service type relates to the stage of adoption and assimilation which a particular user has reached. The user clusters reflect differences in levels of discretionary usage, diversity of demand and disposition to participate, as well as skill and expertise and organizational position. Despite the various users' characteristics, described above, the uniformity of responses suggest that perceptions of service quality show a homogeneity for all users, regardless of organizational background and IT experience.

In phase two users broadly recognize adoption and assimilation as two distinct processes, however both processes are seen as interrelated. Negative influences on the adoption process relate to 'user involvement' (imposition of changes without regard for user needs) and the 'nature of change' (perception of change as technology push). What is interesting about the negative influences of the adoption process is that they do not appear to become detrimental until the assimilation process. IT professionals tend to see themselves as technology controllers, rather than service providers, concerned only with IT adoption. This fails to recognize that both 'adoption' and 'assimilation' are *processes*, both interacting and occurring simultaneously. Three constraints to the assimilation process were identified. These were concerned with the availability of IT, the availability of time, and a lack of knowledge and understanding of the technology to allow or improve its utilization.

4. CONCLUSION

The overall conclusions suggest that there is considerable incongruence between the delivery of IT services and the receipt of IT services. Furthermore, the perspectives which IT professionals and users bring to the process of IT adoption and assimilation are substantially different.

IT professionals have a tendency to perceive themselves as technology controllers, rather than service providers. Consequently, the approach taken by IT professionals to the adoption and assimilation of IT is predominantly from a technical perspective. By contrast, users perceive the IT support services from a number of different perspectives. In addition, it is the intangible considerations, which users perceived as being more important than the technology alone. So, the overall perspective which users hold draws on the amalgamation of a variety of different perceptions.

There is a strong tendency amongst IT professionals to perceive technical change as a linear process. More specifically, the process is viewed as uni-directional, with change perceived as technology driven. New IT developments are believed to occur as the product of computing industry activity. Accordingly, it is perceived that it is an IT department's responsibility or organizational role to react to such developments and to transfer them to the users. By contrast, users perceive technical change as arising from the interaction of users and IT professionals in response to a mixture of business needs, user needs and technology developments. Technical change emerges from a multi-directional interaction between IT professionals and users in an attempt to satisfy need.

IT professionals fail to attach any relevance to the different characteristics which exist between users. However, the users themselves acknowledge that different characteristics alter the nature of IT service receipt. IT professionals approach adoption and assimilation from a predominantly technical perspective and place far greater emphasis on the process of adoption, rather than assimilation. Once such a position has been adopted, any understanding of the influence user characteristics may have becomes minimal. Consequently, IT professionals perceive users as a homogenous group. The users, on the other hand place a greater importance on IT assimilation. From this position, users recognize that they require alternative types of service. Accordingly, there is a need for a responsive IT function which changes its approach to support depending on the recipient.

REFERENCES

Batista, L; Hinton, M; Dibb, S & Meadows, M (2012). Improving organisational responsiveness through CRM – strategy, system effectiveness and staff empowerment perspectives. In: 6th European Conference on Information Management and Evaluation (ECIME 2012), 13-14 September 2012, Cork, Ireland.

Bell, S (2013) Learning with Information Systems: Learning Cycles in Information Systems Development, Routledge (London)

Buyyaa, R, Yeoa, C, Venugopala, S, Broberga J, Brandicc, I. (2009) Cloud computing and emerging IT platforms: Vision, hype, and reality for delivering computing as the 5th utility, Future Generation Computer Systems, Vol 25, No. 6, pp 599–616

Castells, M (2011) The Rise of the Network Society, Wiley-Blackwell (London), 2nd edition.

Coughlan J., et al. 2005. *Understanding the business–IT relationship*, International J of Information Management, Vol.25, No. 4, pp 303–319

Hinton, M. and Kaye, R. 1996. *The hidden investment in information technology: the role of organizational context and system dependency*. International J of Information Management, Vol 16, No. 6, pp. 413–427.

Iyengar K, et al. 2015. *Information technology use as a learning mechanism: the impact of IT use on knowledge transfer effectiveness, absorptive capacity, and franchisee performance*. MIS Quarterly, Vol 39, No. 3, pp 615–641

Larsson R. & Bowen, D. 1989. *Organization and Customer: Managing Design and Coordination of Services*, Academy of Management Review, Vol 14, No. 2, 213-233

Lyytinen K. & Newman, M. (2015) A tale of two coalitions – marginalising the users while successfully implementing an enterprise resource planning system, Information Systems Journal, Vol 25, No. 2, pp 71–101,

Parasuraman, A. et al. 1991. *Refinement and Reassessment of the SERVQUAL: Scale*, Journal of Retailing, Vol 67, No. 4, pp 420-450

Pavlou, P. & El Sawy, O. 2006 *From IT Leveraging Competence to Competitive Advantage in Turbulent Environments: The Case of New Product Development*, Information Systems Research, Vol 7, No. 13, pp198 - 227

ACCURATE INDOOR POSITIONING UTILIZING INTERPERSONAL RELATIONSHIP

Hiroki Saito and Yuya Ueda
Department of Frontier Media Science,
School of Interdisciplinary Mathematical Sciences,
Meiji University
Nakano 4-21-1, Nakano-ku, Tokyo, 164-8525, Japan

ABSTRACT

Mobile applications such as pedestrian navigation, geo-fencing, geo-social service, etc. require accurate location information of mobile devices. The localization technology is important in both technical and commercial aspects. In this paper, we propose a novel indoor localization method that provides mobile phone users in a pedestrian crowd with their own position information. We assume that some of users can reveal interpersonal information such as loving couple, family, friend or acquaintance, etc, and they can enter its information to the system. The system estimates distance of mobile devices based on person-to-person proximity information obtained by pre-defined interpersonal relationship, and estimate position of users accurately by combined with physical signal measurement and interpersonal distance. Through our simulation experiments, we show that our system can estimate users position accurately.

KEYWORDS

Indoor localization, Interpersonal relationship, Proxemics, Mobile devices

1. INTRODUCTION

Spreading popularity of location dependent mobile applications, the importance of localization technology is getting higher in both technical and commercial aspects. Today's mobile applications such as pedestrian navigation, geo-fencing, geo-social service, etc. require accurate location information of mobile devices. GPS technology is serving for such location dependent applications. However, GPS does not work well in indoor environments where radio signals emitted from satellites are often blocked out, and it is the limitation of availability of such location dependent applications in indoor environments. In order to overcome the problem, many research efforts have been done in indoor localization. One of approach is to deploy anchor devices at known location, and then mobile devices measure the distance from those anchors using RF [Bahl, P., et al., 2000] , ultra-sound [Addlesee, M., el al., 2001] [Harter A., el al., 1997] [Priyantha, N., el al., 2000] or ultra-wideband radio [Gezici, S., el al., 2005] [Fontana, R., J., el al., 2003] . However, transmission range of the measurement signals is limited. For example, communication range of ultrasound signals is about 10m or 20m. Therefore, large amount of anchor devices need to be deployed. Moreover, due to diffraction and reflection of signal, positioning error can be increased where the environment that walls and ceiling exist and not open.

In this paper, we propose a novel indoor localization method that provides mobile phone users in a pedestrian crowd with their own position information. We assume that some of users can be defined interpersonal information such as loving couple, family, friend or acquaintance, etc, and some of users can enter its information to the system. The system estimates distance of mobile devices based on pre-defined interpersonal distance, and estimate position of users accurately by combined with physical signal measurement and interpersonal distance. Through our simulation experiments, we show that our system can estimate users position accurately.

2. INDOOR POSITIONING BY USING INTERPERSONAL RELATIONSHIP

This study aims to estimate position of mobile devices with users in a pedestrian crowd by utilizing human spatial characteristics. We explain the study of human spatial characteristics that effects human behavior, communication, and social interaction. In the works of social sciences [Hall, T., E., 1963][Hall, T., E., 1966], the proxemics behavior (the use of space) on interpersonal communication has been shown. They concluded that there is a direct correlation between social standings and physical distances between people. It means when someone consider other person to be in his/her 'friend's zone', he/she literally prefer in a certain distance, and stay away from his/her intimate space, but close enough to be a friend. The personal distance is divided into four main zones. These zones serve as reaction circle when someone enters a specific zone, he/she automatically activate certain psychological and physical reactions in that person:

- **Intimate distance** for embracing, touching or whispering (15cm-46cm):
  Within this distance, we rely on our senses of smell and touch. The intimate activities are usually restricted to private encounters which can be performed comfortably at intimate distances. We tend not to get this close to person who are not intimate with, and usually try to escape.

- **Personal distance** for interactions among good friends or family (48-122cm):
  At this distance, haptic feeling is minimal, and vision and hearing become important. We use the distance to interact with friends. Within this range, normal conversations are easy. We allow strangers into the outer limits, and we reserve the inner limits for friends.

- **Social distance** for interactions among acquaintances (1.2m-3.7m):
  This distance includes the space requirement for more formal social interactions. Hearing and vision are the primary sensing. The social distance is often utilized in business meeting.

- **Public distance** used for public speaking (3.7m or above):
  At this distance, interpersonal interaction is no longer possible. There is little detail involved in communication. A public speaker (such as acting or public speech) communicates only one way to audience.

Our system performs location estimation as the following procedure:

1. Some of people (not all people) in pedestrian crowd reveal their interpersonal relationship, and they enter the relationship into the application on their mobile devices.
2. Mobile devices exchange the information of relationship via short-range wireless communication such as Bluetooth.
3. The system improves precision of measured position information physically using the distance between the mobile devices based on interpersonal relationship. If physical measurement infrastructure is temporarily unavailable due to diffraction and reflection of signal, the system performs trilateration by using the location of surrounding mobile devices.

3. EVALUATION

As the first step of this work, to evaluate performance of the proposed system, we conducted simulations using a Java-based human mobility simulator. In the experiments, we assume a free space of 1000m x 1000m, pedestrians walk around the field based on the following random mobility model: Each person randomly selects a destination from the field and then moves to it at constant speed (1m/sec). After arriving at the destination, the pedestrian selects the next destination. In the simulation field is installed physical localization infrastructure by using anchor signal devices, and its availability is limited. For proximity estimation, we assume that interpersonal relationship is defined the following three categories: (1) Intimate relationship (such as loving couple), (2) Personal relationship (such as friend), and (3) Social relationship (such as acquaintance). With the assumptions above, we executed simulations 1000sec and evaluated error in the estimated position that is mainly caused by limitation of physical measurement infrastructure.

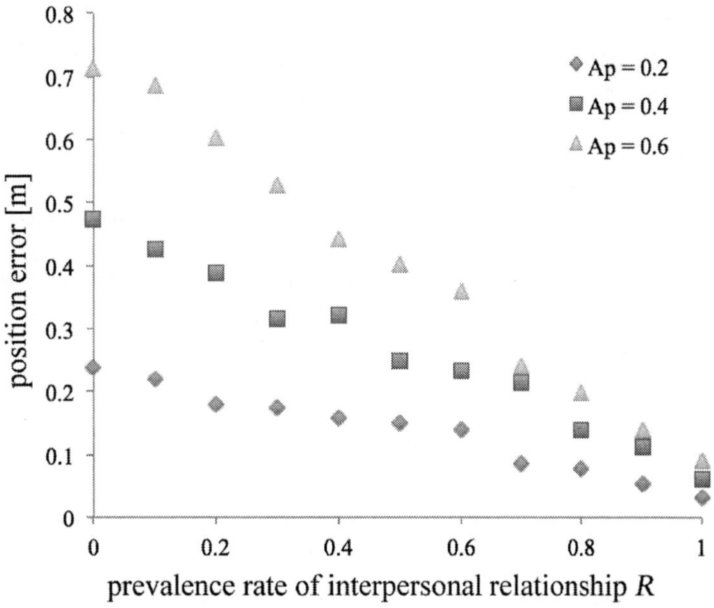

Figure 1. Position Error and Prevalence Rate of Interpersonal Relationship

Figure 1 shows the average position error where the prevalence rate of interpersonal relationship *R* is changed from 0 to 1.0, and the availability of physical measurement infrastructure *Ap* is set to 0.2, 0.4 and 0.8. The result shows that the average position error is proportional to the prevalence rate of interpersonal relationship *R*. Compared with position error at *R*=0.0 and *R*=0.5 in *Ap*=0.2, position accuracy of our method is 37%. Therefore, assuming that some of people (not all people) in pedestrian crowd reveal their interpersonal relationship, our system enables us to estimate users location effectively.

4. CONCLUSION

This paper described a novel indoor localization method that provides mobile phone users in a pedestrian crowd with their own position information. Assuming that some of users reveal their interpersonal information, and they enter its information to the system. The system estimates distance of mobile devices based on person-to-person proximity information obtained by pre-defined interpersonal relationship, and estimate position of users accurately by combined with physical signal measurement and interpersonal distance. Through our simulation experiments, we have shown that our system can estimate users position accurately. Our approach provides to enable indoor localization systems that can offer precise position information to support location-based mobile applications.

REFERENCES

Bahl, P., etl al., 2000, RADAR: An in-building RF-based user location and tracking system, *In Proceedings of IEEE INFOCOM 2000*, pp. 775–784.

Addlesee, M., el al., 2001, Implementing a sentient computing system, *In IEEE Computer*, Vol. 34(8), pp. 50–56.

Harter A., el al., 1997, A new location technique for the active offce, *In IEEE Personal Communications*, Vol. 4, pp. 42–47.

Priyantha, N., el al., 2000, The cricket location-support system. *In Proceedings of the 6th Annual International Conference on Mobile Computing and Networking (MobiCom '00)*, pp. 32–43.

Gezici, S., el al., 2005, Localization via ultra-wideband rádios: A look at positioning aspects for future sensor networks, *IEEE Signal Processing Magazine*, Vol. 22, No. 4, pp. 70-84.

Fontana, R., J., el al., 2003, Commercialization of an ultra wideband precision asst location system, *In Proceedings of UWBST*, pp. 369-373.

Hall, T., E., 1963, A System for the Notation of Proxemic Behaviour, *American Anthropologist*, Vol. 65 (5), pp.1003–1026.

Hall, T., E., 1966, The hidden dimension, *Doubleday*, NewYork, USA.

VISUAL TREND ANALYSIS METHOD FOR ONTOLOGY BASED OPINION MINING ON MOVIE REVIEWS

Seongmin Mun*, Ginam Kim**, Gyeongcheol Choi* and Kyungwon Lee***
Life Media Interdisciplinary Program, Naver corp**, Department of Digital Media ****
Ajou University, 206, World cup-ro, Yeongtong-gu, Suwon-si, Gyeonggi-do 443-749, KOREA

ABSTRACT

The rapid development of the Web 2.0 era has generated a huge amount of online word-of-mouth information, which has influenced the society in various fields. Effects of Word of Mouth on movies, in particular, has become the new standards to evaluate a movie that affects potential audiences' decision. Therefore, this research proposes a methodology to analyze the responses of movie audiences in two ways; overall regardless of time flow and trending which reflects the changes of audience opinions over time. Review analysis was conducted through ontology followed by opinion mining, further visualized via polar chart network, clustering and timeline. Visualization designed in this process is presented in "http://54.255.190.140/index/v0".

KEYWORDS

Clustering, Data Visualization, Network, Ontology, Opinion, Polarity.

1. INTRODUCTION

As film industry is growing every year with the advance of media technology, online movie reviews are getting becoming predominant on potential audience behaviors to decide whether to be a consumer. We thus designed the ontology based upon such audience reviews in order to propose a methodology to analyze movie reviews in two ways; overall reviews regardless of time flow, and trending reviews reflecting how the opinions have changed over time. To demonstrate, we first constructed ontology to reflect the contents of individual reviews. Second, we conducted opinion mining based on the ontology. We next visualized the results and analyzed such results, presenting a scenario through the methodology of this research to analyze the changes of opinions in a movie review.

2. ONTOLOGY CONSTRUCTION

In order to construct an ontology for opinion mining, we first selected the categories of ontology and its evaluation keywords associated with each category. After extracting the index terms with high frequency in review data, we screened them as potential keywords and classified the finally selected terms. We further verified such process with topic modeling. Keywords utilized in our ontology in consequence of this progress are presented in Table 1.

Table 1. Final sets of keywords applied in our ontology

Element class	Feature words
Director	Director, Direction, Composition, Editing, DirectionSkill, Attraction
Movie	Movie, Work, Overall, Scale
Actor	Performance, Actor, Character, MainCharacter, PerformanceSkill, Lines, SupportingActor, Casting, Voice, Style, Person, Appearance, Dubbing, Actress, Performer, Role, CastMember
Vision	Vision, Sequence, Scene, Spectacle, Atmosphere, Expression, Screen, Visual, Background, Graphic, MakeUp, Visuality, ImageBeauty

Story	Story, Content, Material, Telling, Tale, Closing, Ending, Scenario, Probability, Synopsis, Setting, OriginalWork, Finish, Subject, Accident, Structure, ContentTelling, StoryLine, Reading, StoryTelling, CastMember, StoryComposition
Sound	Sound, Song, Volume, Soundtrack, Melody, Music

3. VISUALIZATION

As well as providing the positive/negative tendency of each movie review, our new visualization method enables users to compare the evaluations of different movies since it forms clusters between movies with similar reviews, by comparing most heavily evaluated elements of each movie. After positive/negative tendency information visualization was performed, we further visualized clustering data in order to form the clusters of movies with similar reviews. We also designed an interface to facilitate more various visualization analyses through interaction with users.

3.1 Individual Movie Analysis

Mining results of individual movies in this visualization are presented as one set of a pie chart and a bar graph. A pie chart, containing six directions of 12, 2, 4, 6, 8 and 10 o' clock, indicates the frequency and polarity of each evaluation element. Size of a sector would increase when the elements are considered important as evaluation elements depending on its frequency, and vice versa.

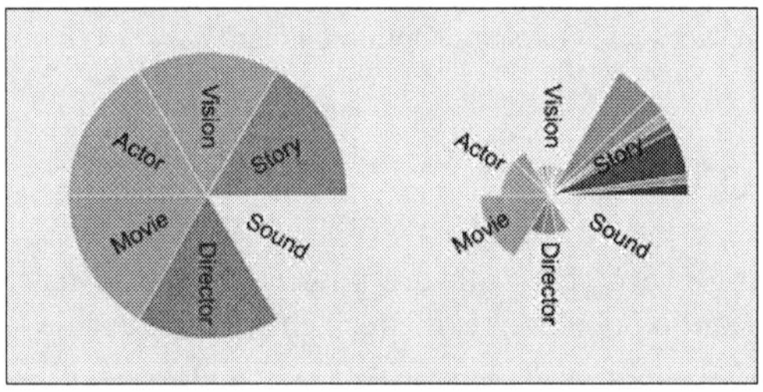

Figure 1. Opinion Mining Visualization for the each movie

3.2 Analysis on Node Position

Our finding that the location of nodes is determined according to the weight of evaluation elements when visualizing the clusters in Opinion Analyzer also implies that the location of nodes provides information on the weight of each element suggesting its importance. Figure 2 indicates the weight of evaluation elements of New World, Secretly Greatly and Tower. It is revealed that while the Actor/Actress was of similar importance, Plots have appeared more frequently suggesting its importance, as the nodes are located to the right.

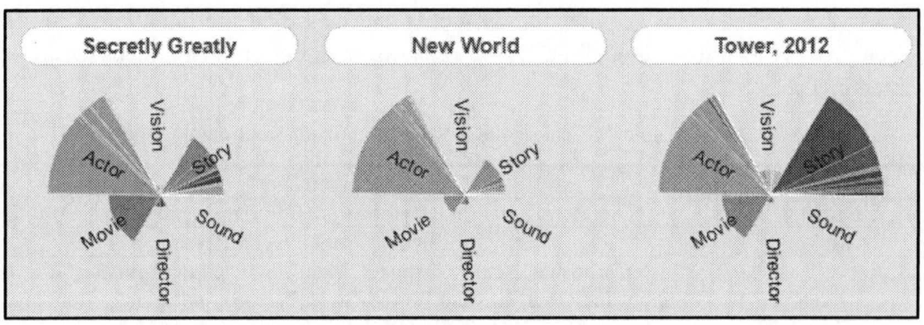

Figure 2. Evaluation elements of *Secretly Greatly, New World* and *Tower*

3.3 Analysis on Clustered Movie Groups

Since it is general to analyze the relationships between the pre-clustered data groups if the amount of data is too large, sample movies of this research were divided into three groups.

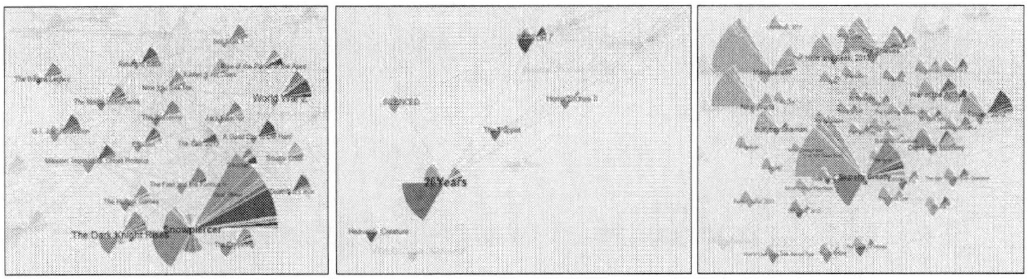

Figure 3. Overall Visualization of the 130 movies in this research, indicating three different clusters

3.4 Network Analysis between Movies

Network Analysis represents a method to signify similar nodes, determining which node shares similar data with other nodes located in different clusters. For instance, movies located at the center of cluster groups such as Meet the In-Laws in Figure 4, is linked to other movies sharing similar attributes. All the movies of which links are connected belong to different groups, suggesting that the network contributes to discovering new clusters.

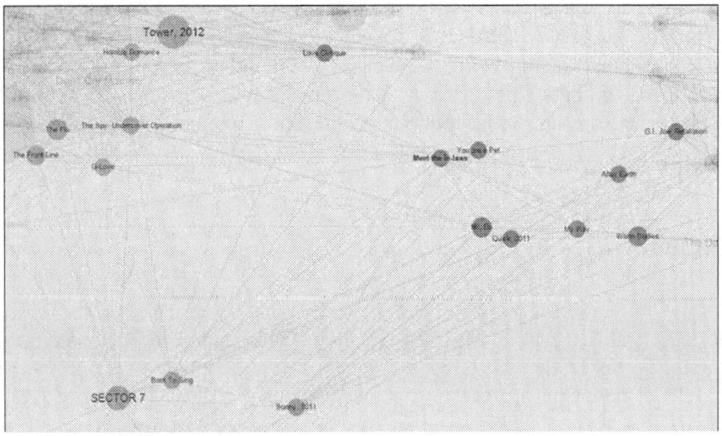

Figure 4. Network of movies relevant to *Meet the In-Laws*

4. TREND ANALYSIS FOR THE MOVIE REVIEWS

In addition to analysis and visualization of the overall reviews of a movie, this methodology can reflect the time flow as suggested in Figure 5 which is a pilot data visualization of a movie Snowpiercer. In 2013 when the movie was first released, its plot was a major evaluation element, positive and negative reviews accounting for approximately equally. However it is found that Actors/Actresses gained more popularity in the movie review as time went on, with high positivity. It is also noticed that locations of nodes thereby changed according to the importance weight of evaluation elements

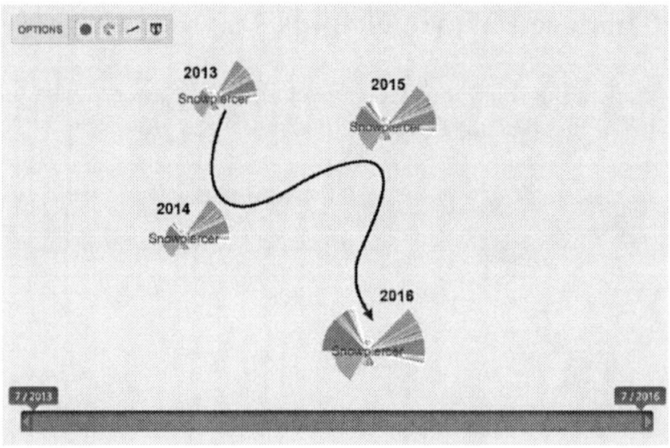

Figure 5. Changes of reviews on *Snowpiercer* over time

5. CONCLUSION

This study aimed to propose a methodology to analyze and visualize the movie reviews in two ways; overall and trending. We thus constructed an ontology of movie reviews and suggested a visualization analysis methodology in order to analyze the movie reviews. Major conclusions of this research are as follows. First, visualization analysis on each movie revealed that overall tendency of reviews of each movie differ from each other. Second, 130 films as samples in this research were clustered as three groups depending largely on the feedback from the audience. Third, it is suggested that this visualization analysis methodology can be applied to review trend analysis that reflects the changes of audiences' opinion over time.

In addition to these findings, this research also proposes a new framework of ontology on movie domain applying keyword extraction and topic modeling, and that argument structure identification was applied in opinion miming.

REFERENCES

Journal

1. Fruchterman, T. M. and Reingold, E. M, 1991. Graph drawing by force-directed placement. Software: Practice and Experience, Vol. 21, No. 11, pp. 1129-1164.
2. Gruber T. R, 1993. A translation approach to portable ontology specifications. Knowledge acquisition, Vol. 5, No. 2, pp. 199-220.
3. Jaeseok Myeong et al, 2008. A Korean Product Review Analysis System Using a Semi-Automatically Constructed Semantic Dictionary. Journal of KIISE, Vol. 35, No. 6, pp. 392-402.
4. Yunjeong Lee et al, 2009. Analysis and Visualization for Comment Messages of Internet Posts. The Journal of the Korea Contents Association, Vol. 9, No. 7, pp. 45-56.
5. Moon Yul Huh and Woon Ock Cha, 2008. Information Theory and Data Visualization Approach to Poll Analysis. The Korean journal of applied statistics, Vol. 20, No. 1, pp. 61-78.

Conference paper or contributed volume

1. Anaïs Cadilhac et al, 2010. Ontolexical resources for feature based opinion mining : a case-study, Proceedings of the 6th Workshop on Ontologies and Lexical Resources(Ontolex 2010). Beijing, China, pp. 77-86.
2. Bjørkelund, E. et al, 2012. A study of opinion mining and visualization of hotel reviews. In Proceedings of the 14th International Conference on Information Integration and Web-based Applications & Services. Bali, Indonesia, pp. 229-238.
3. Borth, D. et al, 2013. Sentibank: large-scale ontology and classifiers for detecting sentiment and emotions in visual content. Proceedings of the 21st ACM international conference on Multimedia. Barcelona, Spain, pp. 451-460.

THE INTERNET OF THINGS ARCHITECTURE AND IMPEDED SECURITY

Jean-Pierre Kuilboer and Noushin Ashrafi
University of Massachusetts Boston, 100 Morrissey Blvd., Boston MA 02125 - USA

ABSTRACT

Internet of Things (IoT) ecosystem is gaining more value as it offers the opportunity for improved life for consumers and efficient production systems for industries. The list of appliances and applications is rapidly expanding in areas such as smart home, health/fitness, infotainment, and smartphone extension. In the Industrial side, more and more companies are trying to transform both their product lines and the internal efficiency of their organizations. The increasing appeal of IoT has created excitement overlooking its potential drawbacks in terms of both physical dangers and breach of information due to security threats. It is important for the consumers and industry executives to be aware of security issues while IoT is becoming the Internet of Everything.

KEYWORDS

Internet of Things, Security, Architecture

1. INTRODUCTION

Internet of Things (IoT) ecosystem is gaining more value as it offers the opportunity for improved life for consumers and efficient production systems for industries. The Internet of Things can be briefly defined as the network of physical or virtual smart objects that contains embedded technology to communicate and sense or interact with their internal states or the external environment. Porter and Heppelman (2014, 2015) provided an interesting perspective stating that the first wave of information technology automated individual activities, the second wave and the Internet unleashed inexpensive and ubiquitous connectivity, and in the emerging third wave, IT is becoming a part of the product itself.

IoT is everywhere and advances are likely to emerge from synergistic activities conducted in different fields of knowledge (Atzori, 2010). IoT applications in industrial Internet are making significant inroads in the national infrastructure from power production and transport to transportation. Delivery on IoT promises is contingent on the integration of several technologies and communications solutions (Gubbi, 2013). In the wearable, health, and fitness space, gadgets allow us to track everything from heart rate to location. Other sectors of the economy, which are similarly affected include water management, highway traffic (Singh, 2014), and agriculture (Dlodlo, 2015).

2. ARCHITECTURE

IoT is the practice of capturing, analyzing, and acting on data generated by distributed networked objects and smart machines. The architecture of IoT contributes to its exposure to security Threats. A few examples would clarify the connectivity schema of IoT and its points of vulnerability. A simple system could be a smartphone controlling directly switching lights on and off where there is just one layer of interaction. A more complex system with two layers of interaction would be some mobile device talking to a controller/bridge and the bridge controls smart objects such as lights or door opener. The level of complexity increases when another layer is added. For example, one can dial-in to a management platform on the cloud, the management platform then connects to a Wi-Fi controller inside the home allowing the controller forward command to an end-point such as a baby-monitor, outside webcam, or connected heater/thermostat (smart HVAC). Figure 1 depicts these configurations.

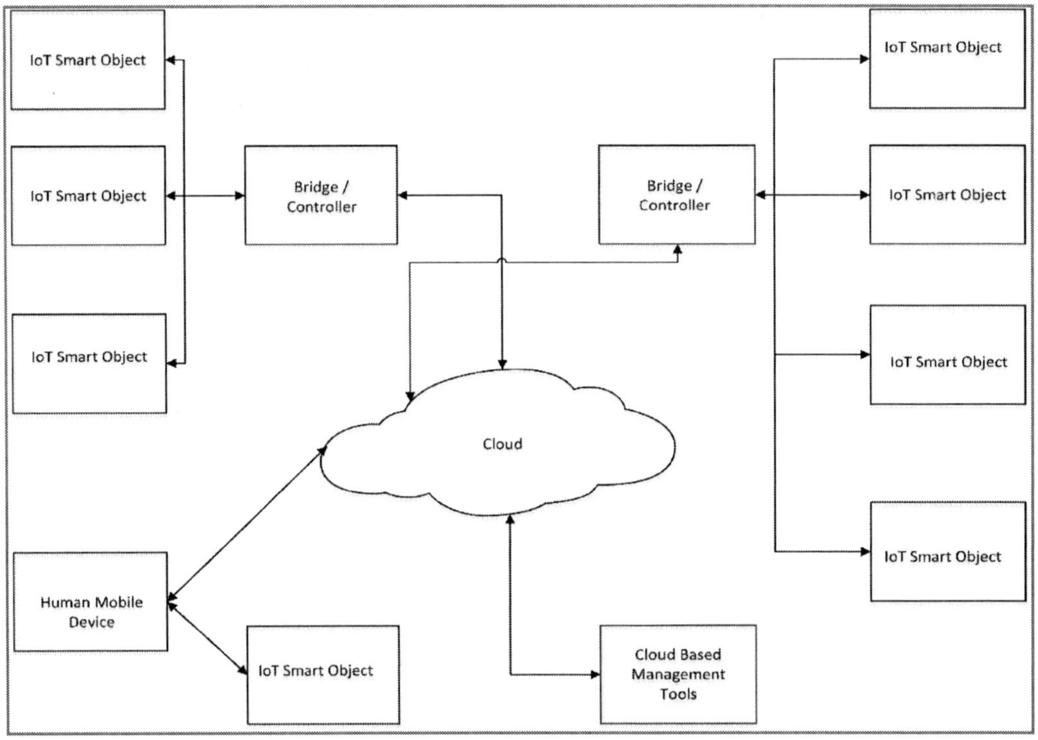

Figure 1. Generic IoT architecture

As the level of complexity increases so does the possibility of security breaches.

3. SECURITY

A close look at the design, development, and release of IoT products and solutions shows that security and privacy have consistently been relegated to the lowest priorities. The distributed nature of IoT requires a close harmony of the hardware, software, and processes while multiple attack surface could be subject to hacking or gaps in the information privacy from end-to-end. Table 1 shows some potential vulnerability of IoT infrastructure.

Table 1. IoT network stack

Layer	Security Issues
Application	Lack of encryption
Transport	Man in the middle attack; Flooding
Network	Data Dropped; Low lower lossy network
Data Link	Variety of protocols, Synchronization; Power efficiency; Collision, battery exhaustion
Physical	Data rate; Modulation, Transmission mode; Encoding; DOS

These are just examples of security threats in each level. Additional threats are to be discussed.

4. CONCLUSION

To have secure IoT environments there is a need for change of priorities from a rush to market to a more stable, upgradable, and balanced ecosystem. The future adoption of standards is for better IoT ecosystems. Several bodies including IETF, IEEE P2413, ITU-T SG20, the European IERC, OWASP IoT project, and OMG have recognized the need for standardization and interoperability and are actively working on best practices, frameworks, and standards.

REFERENCES

Atzori, L., Iera, A., & Morabito, G. 2010. The internet of things: A survey. In *Computer networks*, vol. 54, No. 15, pp. 2787-2805.

Dlodlo, N., & Kalezhi, J. 2015, May. The internet of things in agriculture for sustainable rural development. In *Emerging Trends in Networks and Computer Communications (ETNCC), 2015 International Conference on* (pp. 13-18).

Gubbi, J., Buyya, R., Marusic, S., & Palaniswami, M. 2013. Internet of Things (IoT): A vision, architectural elements, and future directions. In *Future Generation Computer Systems*, Vol. 29, No. 7, pp. 1645-1660.

Porter, M. E., & Heppelmann, J. E. 2014. How smart, connected products are transforming competition. In *Harvard Business Review*, Vol. 92, No. 11, pp. 64-88.

Porter, M. E., & Heppelmann, J. E. 2015. How Smart, Connected Products Are Transforming Companies. In *Harvard Business Review*, Vol. 93, No. 10, pp. 96-114.

Singh, D., Tripathi, G., & Jara, A. J. 2014, March. A survey of internet-of-things: future vision, architecture, challenges and services. In *Internet of Things (WF-IoT), 2014 IEEE World Forum on* (pp. 287-292).

AUTHOR INDEX